New Perspectives on European Women's Legal History

This book integrates women's history and legal studies within the broader context of modern European history in the late nineteenth and twentieth centuries. Sixteen contributions from fourteen countries explore the ways in which the law contributes to the social construction of gender. They analyze questions of family law and international law and highlight the politics of gender in the legal professions in a variety of historical, social, and national settings, including Eastern, Southern, Western, Northern, and Central Europe. Focusing on different legal cultures, they show us the similarities and differences in the ways the law has shaped the contours of women's and men's lives in powerful ways. They also reveal how women have used legal knowledge to struggle for their equal rights on the national and transnational level. The chapters address the interconnectedness of the history of feminism, legislative reforms, and women's citizenship, and build a foundation for a comparative vision of women's legal history in modern Europe.

Sara L. Kimble is a historian at DePaul University.

Marion Röwekamp is a historian and lawyer at Freie University Berlin.

Routledge Research in Gender and History

For a full list of titles in this series, please visit www.routledge.com

17 **Female Agency in the Urban Economy**
Gender in European Towns, 1640–1830
Edited by Deborah Simonton and Anne Montenach

18 **Women and the Media**
Feminism and Femininity in Britain, 1900 to the Present
Edited by Maggie Andrews and Sallie McNamara

19 **Gender in Urban Europe**
Sites of Political Activity and Citizenship, 1750–1900
Edited by Krista Cowman, Nina Javette Koefoed and Åsa Karlsson Sjögren

20 **Women and the Reinvention of the Political**
Feminism in Italy, 1968–1983
Maud Anne Bracke

21 **Women in Higher Education, 1850–1970**
International Perspectives
Edited by E. Lisa Panayotidis and Paul Stortz

22 **Gendering the Settler State**
White Women, Race, Liberalism and Empire in Rhodesia, 1950–1980
Kate Law

23 **Women in Magazines**
Research, Representation, Production and Consumption
Edited by Rachel Ritchie, Sue Hawkins, Nicola Phillips and S. Jay Kleinberg

24 **New Perspectives on European Women's Legal History**
Edited by Sara L. Kimble and Marion Röwekamp

New Perspectives on European Women's Legal History

Edited by Sara L. Kimble and Marion Röwekamp

Routledge
Taylor & Francis Group
NEW YORK AND LONDON

First published 2017
by Routledge
711 Third Avenue, New York, NY 10017

and by Routledge
2 Park Square, Milton Park, Abingdon, Oxon OX14 4RN

Routledge is an imprint of the Taylor & Francis Group, an informa business

Library of Congress Cataloging-in-Publication Data
Names: Kimble, Sara L. | Röwekamp, Marion, 1974–
Title: New perspectives on European women's legal history / edited by Sara L. Kimble and Marion Röwekamp.
Description: New York : Routledge, 2017. | Series: Routledge research in gender and history | Includes bibliographical references and index.
Identifiers: LCCN 2016013718 (print) | LCCN 2016014338 (ebook) | ISBN 9781138805545 (alk. paper) | ISBN 9781315739564 ()
Subjects: LCSH: Women—Legal status, laws, etc.—Europe—History—20th century. | Domestic relations—Europe—History—20th century. | Women lawyers—Europe—History—20th century. | Women—Europe—Social conditions—20th century. | Sociological jurisprudence—Europe.
Classification: LCC KJC1019 .N49 2017 (print) | LCC KJC1019 (ebook) | DDC 342.408/78—dc23
LC record available at http://lccn.loc.gov/2016013718

ISBN: 978-1-138-80554-5 (hbk)
ISBN: 978-1-315-73956-4 (ebk)

Typeset in Sabon
by Apex CoVantage, LLC

To Leora, Ingrid, Lars, Reeva, and Dan with love. SLK
Farewell Misia, welcome Emilio. MR

Contents

Figure

Preface

These comparative insights into the history and biographies of the first female lawyers in Europe illuminate not only the history of a profession whose all-male leadership had strenuously resisted women's attempts to achieve access, certification, and career advancement, but also open up an important new chapter in the gendering of legal history. The female pioneers, in what had traditionally been an exclusively male field of knowledge, were simultaneously spearheading equal rights for women in the law; indeed, their interest in the law itself originated in their commitment to answering the "woman question" of their time. As legal experts and allies they set out, from the beginning of the twentieth century, to play an important role within the women's movements of their respective countries. The lives and career paths of female lawyers, coupled with their activity in professional organizations and their growing international connections, are intrinsic to the comparative history of women's movements, which in the many varied political or national contexts nevertheless exhibit many parallels and similarities.

Of primary importance are the motives that drove certain women to study law. They had become aware that the legal position of women (especially that of married women) was not only unjust and outdated, but also outrageous. The first female lawyers resolved not to tolerate such injustice any longer and determined to do what they could to change the societal conditions by law. One example for this new awareness of injustice appears in the chapter by Iwona Dadej, who quotes from the memoirs of one of the first Polish female lawyers. As a young girl she found in the library of her grandmother an edition of the French Civil Code, which was applicable in parts of Poland. As she read, she realized with a shock what an unworthy, even deplorable, legal situation she would find herself in if she ever married. For many leading feminists the existential experience of injustice, particularly as it applied to women, became the catalyst for a new legal consciousness and for mobilizing a women's movement. It was not self-evident in those times that paternalism, discrimination, or even violence toward women should no longer be experienced as an individual matter—inevitable, or even normal—but could be recognized in legal categories as evidence of injustice. According to traditional societal norms, to abide and to endure was a central component of women's traditional role; actually, such customs built the foundation of a patriarchal gender order. Outrage by itself was not enough to fuel change. In addition, "knowledge and opinion about law" was required, coupled with recognition of what is "right" and no longer tolerable, taking into account changing social standards of justice. The idea of human rights and its "vindication" by and for women (see Olympe de Gouges, in France, or Mary Wollstonecraft, in England) was of enduring importance since the end of the eighteenth century and set new standards for justice. Especially in times of upheaval and fundamental social change, the concept of human rights offered women a legitimate instrument for translating their own experiences of injustice into the language of law.

In the nineteenth and twentieth century, women's movements, both in the Old World and the New, would open up opportunities for action that could translate women's experiences of injustice into claims for law and justice. First, these claims took a stand against legal barriers to women's education and employment, but also against exploitation and violence, and requested equal pay for the female worker. In a second step the law revealed its double function—not only as a hegemonic body of knowledge and as a political apparatus of coercion, but also as a tool for change, yes, the only nonviolent means available to women for contesting (male) domination and oppression. Legal issues thus turned into the decisive hinge or the "transmission belt," which women had to employ to challenge the solely male-centered jurisprudence. Actually, the first female lawyers did not only offer legal aid to distressed women, they also used the daily newspapers and the widely read women's press to convey their new knowledge of the scandalous disregard for women's rights in the law and to call for women's engagement in demanding legal reforms. Thus, as consultants of legal reform commissions and as advocates of the broader women's movements, these new female lawyers contributed their expertise to petitions and memoranda and to the submission of legal drafts, all justifying more and equal rights for women. Let me emphasize that, depending on the particular need and context, female lawyers used arguments based on equality and equal rights but also deployed arguments based in gender difference, since legal equality after all can only be realized by considering the differences among people, in this case, also the different needs, life situations, and orientations between women and men.

This present collection, undergirded by convincing documentation, edited by Sara Kimble and Marion Röwekamp, and set in a wide range of social and political circumstances, demonstrates impressively just how strong was the resistance to women's access to the legal sciences and the legal professions, and especially the resistance to women serving as judges in all countries represented. Resistance to women's egalitarian advancement was particularly evident in family law, as several chapters in this volume show, because family law was deeply embedded in cultural and religious traditions and everyday customs. Thus the gendered division of labor was fiercely defended against those who would advocate legal reform and social change. Finally it has to be reconsidered that the reform proposals prepared and drafted in the 1920s by the first female lawyers in all respective countries were only implemented with great delay in most countries as compared, say, to the granting of women's suffrage. In most cases these reforms in the laws concerning women in the family only took place after World War II and in the course of the "new" women's movement of the 1970s.

International organizations provided crucial support as well as an influential sphere of action for the circle of the first advocates of women's legal rights, who would develop their transnational connections there. While the international organizations of the women's movement, namely the International Council of Women and the International Woman Suffrage Alliance, had already offered stimulation, motivation, and a platform for the struggle for the franchise and for married women's legal rights, it seems clear that the representation of women's experiences and interests by organizations of female lawyers provided an indispensable vehicle for lobbying after World War I in the League of Nations, the International Labor Organization, and, following World War II, in the United Nations. Without any doubt, it is in this arena of transnational agitation that we find a wide open field for further research on women and the law.

A particular strength of this innovative collection of essays is precisely its international comparative perspective. It provides an important contribution that will help to further bridge the gap between conventional legal history and gender history, and in fact transform the former. These essays also contribute to the gendering of legal history.

Ute Gerhard

The essays in this volume actually do more than "bridge the gap" between legal history and women's/gender history; they engage with the "gendering" of legal history, and with the challenges of comparative history. They are a very welcome contribution to an ever-growing body of scholarship on women and the law.

The editors are certainly correct in viewing the law as Janus-faced—serving both as an instrument of repression and also as a tool for change. The law itself provides a tool for regulating human societies; it has both constraining and emancipatory aspects, and as the epitome of a social construction can be manipulated to achieve certain societal effects. Once thought to be immutable (under the auspices of organized religions and their authorities), the advent of secular law itself was a breakthrough. Law can shape and even enforce societal norms, and as authoritarian regimes weakened under the demands for liberty, equality, fraternity, and especially representation, changing the law became a matter of paramount importance. Of course, the content, substance, and interpretation of the law depends on who the legislators and judges are, and historically the legislators and judges were men, who carried around in their heads patriarchal, or at least paternalistic, notions of social structure. Well into the eighteenth century, these European legislators and judges continued to vest legal authority in male heads of households, viewing women as subordinate, unequal, even weak creatures who should be protected (but also disempowered). Changing this perspective to admit of women's potential equality and their possibility to help make and interpret law would take centuries. But it did eventually take place. By the early nineteenth century, Europeans had begun to question this male-dominated order of things and women's quest for emancipation—legal, educational, economic, social, political, and sexual—had begun. The essays in this book focus on developments after 1850.

The contributors to this volume enlighten us about the challenges to the subordinate legal situation of women, especially as wives, in a variety of European societies, and about the advent of women as lawyers and judges. Here we learn about the situation in countries that have not normally been included in surveys: Spain, Portugal, Greece, Belgium, Switzerland, and Bulgaria, even as we gain further insights into legal developments in the better-known "big three," the dominant countries of Great Britain, France, and Germany. We also learn about the effects on legal matters concerning women and legislation in the newly independent countries of the early twentieth-century, such as Finland, Czechoslovakia, Yugoslavia, and Poland, and about feminist efforts to insist (ultimately with success) that repressive national laws needed to be addressed at the international level.

This book will open the eyes and broaden the perspective of many who continue exclusively to address issues in the law, including women's admission to law schools and to the bar, at the national level. There are many commonalities, even as one can distinguish particularities in context and practice that make each case study "exceptional." May *New Perspectives on European Women's Legal History* find the success it deserves.

Karen Offen

Acknowledgments

This book was imagined by the editors who hoped to craft a volume which could address the breadth and depth of questions about women in the legal professions, gender difference in family law, and gender in international perspectives. We worked together across multiple time zones spanning our geographical distance. We are grateful to our contributors who mostly research and write in languages other than English and who persisted with us through this process.

Our thanks go especially to Karen Offen and Ute Gerhard, who inspired and encouraged our scholarship. We wish to thank also Gisela Bock, Rachel Fuchs, and Stephan Meder for their valuable help. Sara also wishes to thank DePaul University and especially Dean Marisa Alicea for her support of this project. We were fortunate to benefit from the valuable editorial assistance from many individuals at the DePaul University Center for Writing-based Learning including: Director Lauri Dietz, Jennifer Finstrom, Matthew Fledderjohann, Kate O'Brien, Melanie Knippen, Carolyn Rudinsky, and Keli Tucker. We also thank Max Novick, our editor at Routledge.

Between the time that this book was imagined and produced, we editors welcomed our own children into the world. This book is dedicated to our families whose patience, love of books, and *joie de vivre* enrich our lives immeasurably.

Sara L. Kimble (Chicago) and *Marion Röwekamp* (Berlin)

Introduction

Legal Cultures and Communities of Female Protest in Modern European History, 1860–1960s

Sara L. Kimble and Marion Röwekamp

New Perspectives on European Women's Legal History integrates women's history and legal studies within the broader context of modern European history. This collection brings gender-conscious historical analysis to bear on questions of national family law and international law, highlights the politics of gender in the legal professions, and underscores the gendered dimensions of the sociopolitical construction and application of the law in a variety of European settings. In particular, our contributors explore the ways in which the law helps to shape the social construction of gender. Law by itself has been "infused" with male bias and shaped by male dominance, as legal scholar Catharine MacKinnon has argued.[1] It is no secret that ideas about gender have permeated laws and legal practice, as laws have been made by men, interpreted by men and, until recently, exercised exclusively by men. Obviously this has had broad consequences for individuals, families, and nations. Nor is it a secret that these laws have operated in oppressive ways, and in conjunction with religion and other patriarchal social forces, have reinforced systems of power to the disadvantage of women. At the same time, women and men have also used legal systems, legal knowledge, and political structures to voice opposition to the inequalities created or reified by law. This movement for legal equality has been an important component of women's legal history and of the transnational movement for women's rights.

By examining the law in different national contexts and international intersections, the contributing authors investigate and question prescribed gender norms from the mid-nineteenth to the mid-twentieth century. Part I of the book is dedicated to an examination of gender and power in family law during the century spanning the 1860s to the 1960s. Part II focuses on women's entrance into the legal profession and the relationship of this event to the women's rights movement in a comparative perspective. The chapters in Part III engage with questions concerning international reforms initiated in response to or affecting women's legal status. Together these chapters critically analyze the law and human experience through the lens of women's and gender history to illustrate human agency and dynamic reform processes within a variety of social and historical contexts.

The chapters in this book provide insight into the current debates and developments in the field but are not intended to be comprehensive due to practical limitations. The chapters in Part I, in particular, reflect the complexity of the subject of family law where the two chapters on Czechoslovakia offer a case in point. Our collection contributes exciting scholarship to the debates and should be read as an invitation for further research regarding women's rights and family law in national and comparative perspectives.

European Legal Codes and Challenges to Women's Unequal Legal Status, 1750–1900

The research questions central to many chapters of this book concern how Europeans responded to the new restraints on women's rights that emerged as a result of the codification processes of the late eighteenth and early nineteenth century. Women's unequal legal status was reified in family law at the moment when state interests competed with those of established religions.[2] The family itself became a political site as liberal rights became associated with masculinity in ways that further disadvantaged women's opportunities.[3] The following brief overview of the history of European legal codes highlights the centrality of gender relations within these codes and thus explains why they became nexuses for reform.[4]

The relations of men and women, particularly within marriage, were a central preoccupation of modern European legal codes.[5] The recodification of the Codex Maximilianeus Bavaricus of 1756 and the Prussian Civil Law of 1794 were inspired by Enlightenment ideals and the legal equality of the sexes both in their specific ways. The Bavarian code stated: "Humans are divided in different ways by nature, primarily in the male and female sex. [. . .] In general no sex has a preference over the other one." The Prussian law stated: "The rights of both sexes are equal as long as no exceptions have been established by special laws or by legally valid declarations of intent."[6] These proclamations of the legal equality of the sexes inspired by natural law did not triumph over customs where women remained subordinate to men in the family and in society.[7] The Austrian Civil Code of 1811 did not mention the equality of the sexes because its author, Franz von Zeiller, thought it was a matter of course that men and women should be equal in private law.[8] Among these three, the Prussian Civil Law is regarded as marking progress for women's legal status because it ended the former *Geschlechtsvormundschaft* (gender guardianship, *cura sexus*) of men over women (§ 24, I 1). However, guardianship (*cura martialis*) was reintroduced for married women in subsequently codified norms.[9] In Prussian Civil Law, men were designated as legal heads of households (§ 184 II, 1), and the code established the husband's authority over his wife in intimate detail. The wife administered the household (§ 194, II, 1) and had to seek spousal authorization to work outside the home (§195 II, 1). Both spouses were obligated to "perform the conjugal duty" (§ 178, II, 1) for the purpose of procreation

(§1, II, 1). The enforceability of many of these legal requirements was doubtful, yet the laws spoke to the societal view of the reproductive mandate within marriage in a patriarchal society. Husbands gained control over married women's property (§ 205, II, 1), but women could negotiate some authority through a marriage contract (the right to *Vorbehaltsgut* or reserved property, §§ 206–209 and 221–230, II, 1). At the same time, some regulations offered married women an improvement over the previous legal situation: divorce was made possible under certain circumstances (§§ 668ff, II, 1), including the possibility of divorce based on mutual agreement (§716, II, 1). The legal situation of the unwed mother and her children was also relatively liberal. The legal situation in the German-speaking areas remained diverse despite attempts to unite and simplify the code.[10] Studies on the jurisdiction of the *Reichsgericht* (superior court), based on at least four different legal sources (French Civil Code, customary law, Prussian Civil Law, and the German Civil Code) until 1914, would prove to be useful in the attempts to limit women's legal rights in family law during codification processes.[11] In fact, the German Civil Code of 1900 tightened the Prussian Civil Law again to women's disadvantage.[12]

French jurists had been impressed with the Prussian Civil Law and used it to inform the French codes but without adopting the legal terms beneficial to women.[13] They also turned their backs on some of the legal reforms of the French Revolution concerning children. During the French Revolution, following intense legislative debates, women were prohibited from pursuing paternity claims against a seducer (1791), though a father could recognize his out-of-wedlock child (1793) as long as that child did not attempt to claim an inheritance at the expense of "legitimate" children (1794). The Revolutionaries also secularized marriage and liberalized divorce (1792).

One of the French Civil Code's instrumental formulators, Jean-Jacques Regis de Cambacérès, designed it to reflect natural law and to establish liberty; however, in practice, the laws prescribed ideals and reflected cultural and social norms. The French Civil Code (1804) and the French Penal Code (1810) unified canon law, Roman law, and customary law under Enlightenment precepts and Napoleon's own patriarchal attitudes. Napoleon likened women to possessions—even fruit-bearing trees—who were "destined to make children."[14] Indeed, Ursula Vogel argued that the Code's framers legitimized the subordination (*incapacité*) of wives and reinforced male authority (*puissance maritale*) by using modern language that naturalized the complementarity of the sexes and sentimentalized marriage such that married women's "individual property rights and legal equality could appear as singularly inappropriate."[15] Moreover, the marriage contract received a "secular sanctity" that divested it from its "individualistic and voluntarist elements," while empowering a husband's control over the person and the property of his wife.[16] In marriage, a wife owed her husband "obedience," and he was charged with her "protection" (Article 213). Concurrently, the Penal Code imposed harsh sanctions against women for adultery, including the possibility of prison sentences and/or divorce, to ensure paternity for the transmission of property within the family. A husband was considered justified if he murdered his wife and her lover in the event that he interrupted their passions in the conjugal home (Article 324). By contrast, a husband was not restricted from extramarital affairs unless he brought his lover into the home. The French Civil Code retained civil marriage from the Revolutionary period as an affirmation of state authority (religious ceremonies were henceforth not recognized as valid). When divorce was reinstated in 1884, it was restricted to three causes: criminal conviction of a spouse, spousal abuse, and adultery.

As a result of the Napoleonic wars (1803–1815), the influence of the French Code spread to Italy, the Netherlands, Luxembourg, Belgium, Spain, Portugal, Romania, Poland, parts of Germany and Greece, as well as to the French colonies, Quebec, Louisiana, and much of Latin America.[17] Critics denounced the French Civil Code for its inequalities. Among them German legal sociologist Marianne Weber (1870–1954) condemned the French Code because it "preserved the traits of medieval patriarchy in its longest and purest form."[18]

The system of "coverture" in English common law established power relations within marriage. Jurist William Blackstone remarked, "By marriage the husband and the wife are one person in law; that is, the very being or legal existence of woman is suspended during marriage."[19] From the early seventeenth century, married women in England were denied the right to contract because they were considered to have no separate legal identity or right to own property, unlike the unmarried woman or "feme sole."[20] According to Ute Gerhard, "The legal situation of wives not only contradicted the legal position of unmarried women, but also was a blatant defiance of early constitutional institutions in England—its parliamentary traditions, its separation of powers, and constitutional guarantee of property—and came under increasing pressure with growing industrialisation and commercialisation."[21]

The criticism of women's subordinate place within these national codes centered on the inequalities women suffered in marriage, especially the denial of their control over themselves and their children, their earned income, and their inherited property.[22] The legal distinction made between married and unmarried women had significant consequences for their enjoyment of rights. Gender paradigms influenced the formalization of family law codes whose provisions were disadvantageous to women's pursuit of recognition as individuals and legal persons. This collection highlights the common legal background of the European women's rights movement even as the exact timing of such challenges was contextually specific.

The critique of women's status under these European legal codes was central to the emergence of the women's rights movement of the nineteenth century. Protests against the subordinate position of married women under the French Civil Code occurred in the 1830s when the *Gazette des Femmes* petitioned the king and the deputies to reform Article 213 arguing that by virtue of the 1830 charter, French men and women were "equals before the law."[23] Women's rights advocates associated with the Saint-Simonians in France and beyond sustained a campaign of protests against the subordination of women under the law.[24] In Italy, Anna Maria Mozzoni (1837–1920), for example, launched her criticism of the new Italian Civil Code (1865), faulting it as detrimental to women's rights and their position in society.[25] She acknowledged the power of the law to place "the destiny of families in the hand of men" and its concurrent "impotence" to grant to men the skill to guide their families.[26] Mozzoni also called for the end of state-regulated prostitution. She translated John Stuart Mill's *The Subjection of Women* (1869) into Italian (1879) and created an inter-class association for women's rights (1881).[27] In Poland, Eliza Orzeszkowa (1841–1910) published a powerful novel, *Marta* (1872), featuring a young widow struggling to survive in a society that denied women their basic legal rights. She then became a leader on women's rights.[28] In the next phase of Polish activism, Paulina Kuczalska-Reinschmit (1859–1921) would urge divided reformers to make civil code reform a priority.[29] In 1878, Léon Richer (1824–1911) and Maria Deraismes (1828–1894), among other feminists, extended the criticism of the legal oppression of women and the arguments for reform at the first International Congress on Women's Rights held in Paris.[30] At a conference in 1889, Belgian feminist Marie Popelin condemned the French Civil Code because it "abased" women and relegated them to a sphere "outside of thinking humanity."[31] By 1896, French feminist Jeanne Chauvin (1862–1926) could insist that legal knowledge was essential for women's empowerment: "Today, more young women and women of the world dare to call themselves feminists and are convinced of the injustice of the [French Civil] Code."[32] On the centennial of the promulgation of the French Civil Code in 1904, a coalition of feminists including Hubertine Auclert (1848–1914), Caroline Kauffmann (1840–1926), Eliska Vincent (1841–1914), and Jeanne Oddo-Deflou (b. 1856) engaged in a series of disruptive protests. They attempted to burn a copy of the Code at the Place Vendôme in Paris, condemning its treatment of married women, who in rights were equivalent to "minors, convicts, and madmen." As such, they declared, the Code violated democratic principles because it "encourages" men to "annihilate, oppress, diminish, [and] exploit women."[33] Oddo-Deflou carried her critique to an international audience in Belgium through which such ideas were more broadly diffused.[34]

The German women's struggle against the civil code, the so-called *Frauenlandsturm*, developed into the movement's most significant reform effort.[35] Women challenged the German Civil Code in a number of petitions.[36] One of the women's movement organizations, the Bund Deutscher Frauenvereine, petitioned in 1899 against the codification and pointed out, "In other legal areas women are responsible legal personalities, only in the case of the marriage women still are under the guardianship of men." The petition stressed that since serfdom and feudalism had ended within Europe, the only legal situation that enslaved humans was the contract of marriage, which gave the husband the function of legislator, judge, and party in one person while taking away women's legal personality.[37] Poor women in troubled or violent marriages faced acute challenges to their survival and wellbeing. According to German feminist Alice Salomon (1872–1948), for working-class women, marriage was tyranny: "She lives like a prisoner, or like an old dog," and her only hope was "that she does not receive any beatings and that she isn't deceived by her husband."[38] Similar protests occurred in Austria and Switzerland.[39]

Activists also attacked women's unequal legal status under English common law. Caroline Norton (1808–1877) fought back against the abuses of her husband and would promote acts of parliament passed to benefit women through the Custody of Infants Act (1839), the Matrimonial Causes Act (1857), and the first Married Women's Property Act (1870). The second Married Women's Property Act (1882) largely abolished the laws under which wives were placed under their husbands' authority. Married women were no longer required to surrender their personal property in marriage and could own, buy, and separate their property. Their legal identity as individuals was restored. Yet the Act did not affect the personal relations of spouses in that a wife was still "bound to follow her husband's domicile, at home and abroad, and to cohabit with him if he so require;" and fathers continued to benefit from guardianship rights over their children. In the case of divorce, the court gave guardianship to the innocent party.[40] In these examples, we see women's legal activism as the catalyzing force for eventual reform.[41]

The history of the reform process in South Eastern and Eastern Europe is more complex. As countries such as Greece, Poland, Czechoslovakia, and Hungary emerged or re-emerged from the constraints of multi-national empires and other external political forces, the newly formed nation-states inherited "foreign" legal systems and contended with multi-ethnic, multi-cultural, and multi-linguistic populations that lived under different legal traditions. Internecine struggles occurred simultaneously as ethnic minorities sought representation of their collective and separate identities within the state.[42] In the effort to harmonize these different minorities, the legislators who drafted the national civil codes attempted to clarify a concept of the nation and, consequently, inscribed their notions of an appropriate gender order.

In Part I, the four contributing authors situate legal change within family law in their respective contexts of Greece, Czechoslovakia, and Spain. Evdoxios Doxiadis describes the Greek codification process in which legislators endeavored to follow principles of Western European civil codes and legal ideas that produced a debate on the nature of the family to the detriment of women's rights (chapter 1). There, national codification led to a decline in women's participation in judicial proceedings. In other places where new national codes disadvantaged women, resistance would arise, though with difficulty.

In Spain, as Gloria Nielfa illustrates (chapter 2), the revolutionary government instituted women's rights reforms against the wishes of the majority. Historically, Spanish society and law had maintained conservative gender roles, due primarily to the influential role of the Catholic Church.[43] With the establishment of the Second Republic in 1931, the parliament granted suffrage rights to women and, with relatively little opposition, passed laws to equalize power relations within family law. These gender equality reforms proved unpopular and suffered a reversal after Franco's 1936 coup d'état. Only late in the twentieth century, and following a renewed women's rights movement, did Spain reestablish women's equal rights in family law.[44]

Ethnicity and other aspects of identity complicated the solidarity among and efficacy of female reformers, as the contributions by Melissa Feinberg and Jana Osterkamp (chapters 3 and 4) demonstrate. The state of Czechoslovakia, created in 1918 out of the Habsburg monarchy, was culturally, ethnically, and linguistically divided and confronted by several different legal systems with varied consequences for women. Feinberg analyzes the Czech women's reform movements, while Osterkamp researches the German and Slovak situations from historical and legal perspectives. These two scholars locate common denominators in the failure of legal reform, yet they draw diverging conclusions. Nonetheless, their complementary chapters reinforce the findings that women's claims for changes in family law met continuing resistance despite the active involvement of the women's rights movement in legal questions. The constitutional provisions establishing equality were not implemented until 1949, when, under Communist rule, Czechoslovakia adopted a comprehensive family law reform. This reflects a larger pattern within Europe whereby fundamental changes for women did not occur simultaneously with other progressive reforms.[45] In Poland, for example, the women's rights movement refused to recognize the validity of heteronomous legal codes and could only engage in legal fights after achieving some internal cohesiveness.[46] These significant differences aside, women's legal history in Eastern Europe during the interwar years shares many similarities with that in the West, particularly at the intersection of women's history and family law.[47]

The commonalities within legal history in diverse regions of Europe diverged with the advent of Communist rule. The Bolshevik Family Code of 1918 formally ended women's subordination to men within the family, legalized divorce, and instituted protections for unwed mothers, women's paid labor, and their property.[48] While the reform potential was partly undermined under Joseph Stalin's leadership (1924–1953),[49] women's equal rights were implemented in the laws of other Eastern European countries under Communist rule during and after World War II.[50] The chapters by Gordana Stojaković on Yugoslavia (chapter 7) and Krassimira Daskalova on Bulgaria (chapter 8) illustrate the ways in which Communism created some opportunities to advance women's rights, notably through employment, but also that gender relations within the family actually changed very little in the face of persistent mentalities and culture.

A different pattern existed in Scandinavian countries.[51] By the end of the nineteenth century, a first wave of legal reforms gave unmarried women the rights to education and to work, and married women won some economic rights. In Denmark, Finland, Iceland, Norway, and Sweden, reforms in civil law and international private law altered women's position within marriage from the end of the nineteenth century through the 1920s.[52] The emancipation of women under family law was facilitated further by the diminishing influence of religion and traditional values.[53] The resulting egalitarian Nordic marriage model became a success to emulate for some women's organizations claiming equal rights in their respective countries.[54]

By the 1960s and 1970s, Western European countries finally achieved comprehensive family law reform. Some of these reforms stemmed out of decades-long efforts by women's rights advocates to use strategic arguments based in "civic maternalism" or "social housekeeping," justifying social and legal reform on the grounds that it would benefit women's maternal roles and strengthen the family.[55] Further reform efforts would be needed to address issues such as equal pay for equal work, tax laws, legislation on prostitution, and the division of labor within the family.[56]

A Comparative History of Women's Entrance into the Legal Profession and Judiciary

In all European countries, women's entrance into law schools and the legal profession was a watershed event that highlighted the gendered construction of the field of law. Moreover, their successes contributed to the destabilization of the persistent cultural claims about the inferiority of women's intellect.[57] The legal profession, with its roots in the Enlightenment, idealized the rationality, objectivity, and intellectual rigor that were traditionally associated with masculinity. In the civil law and common law systems, legal education contributed to the definition and functioning of lawyers as a cohesive social group, especially in terms of privilege, common outlook, and habitus.[58] The requirements of legal education contributed to the formation and maintenance of an all-male elite within the legal profession and the judiciary that, in turn, influenced the court system, the legislature, and academic understanding of the law.[59] Women's participation in the legal profession threatened and effectuated a change to this paradigm.

The historiography on women's history in the legal profession has tended to focus on the resistance that women encountered as they attempted to enter the profession, especially during resurgent professionalization at the end of the nineteenth century.[60] Women and their supporters contended with antifeminist arguments that denied women the capacity for rationality and objectivity. They also contended with separate arguments that women posed a competitive economic threat to an already overcrowded profession, as a number of the chapters in Parts I and II point out. Advocates of women's rights regularly argued that no legislative or regulatory text denied women the right to enter the profession, concluding that their exclusion was based on the prejudicial interpretation of statutes.[61] Some reformers also deployed the rhetoric of motherhood,[62] affirming women's responsibility for the home while arguing for their expanded role in the public sphere. Such arguments stressed that women's moral purity and nurturing capacities could serve to clean up corrupt politics, strengthen their nations, and enhance justice, as Röwekamp illustrates for Germany.[63] Another recent development has located the participation of a few men as advocates of women's right to work in the legal profession, such as Belgian feminist Louis Frank and French lawyer Georges Lhermitte.[64] Scholarly efforts to identify pioneering female lawyers have uncovered an underappreciated pattern in the employment of women as non-professionals or "lay" attorneys. During the mid-to-late nineteenth century, women found their way into legal practice in a number of ways. For example, under extraordinary circumstances, the Serbian widow Marija Milutinović-Punktatorka (1810–1875) worked in the field starting in 1847.[65] In Russia, female lay attorneys practiced until Alexander II barred women from serving as private advocates in 1876.[66] In Finland, as Mia Korpiola's research illustrates (chapter 12), women worked as lay attorneys during the 1880s and the 1890s. Similarly, in Sweden, Anna Pettersson established her own law firm in 1904 despite the fact that she had not completed the traditional academic training or exams.[67] This exceptional access continued until either governments or corporate pressures within the legal profession closed the loopholes.

The majority of the chapters in Part II consider the efforts of women who wanted to gain access to the legal professions by first securing a legal education then restricted to men. In this case, most chapters share a common emphasis on the intersection between feminism and the political efforts to open law schools and professional opportunities and also to advocate for the needs of women and children in society. "Women learn to bear the burden of the law, they don't study law," German feminist Louise Otto had remarked in 1890.[68] To teach women about their rights, many altruistic advocates created legal aid clinics or protective agencies to assist women in asserting their legal claims.[69] The daily practice of these agencies heightened feminists' awareness of the law's role in women's lives and also informed the first female lawyers, some of whom worked with disadvantaged groups. In Estonia, Vera Poska-Grünthal (1898–1986) worked in a legal aid office (Bureau of Legal Advice) where her clients were often women in need of legal advice regarding domestic disputes and divorce. Realizing that the Baltic Civil Code (1864) was outdated and contradicted the constitution of the new Republic of Estonia, Poska-Grünthal became active in the women's movement. Working with other lawyers, notably Vilma Anderson and Olinde Ilus, they proposed reforms of the family law code.[70] In the Czech Republic, Milada Horáková, a member of the Czech National Council of Women, proposed changes in family law and worked across political lines for reforms, as Feinberg points out (chapter 3).[71] In France, Germany, and Romania, women's knowledge of the law similarly intertwined with the grassroots fight for women's legal rights, including direct legal aid to women.[72] National differences aside, these activists were united by a common dedication to social justice within women's networks of solidarity.

Besides becoming aware of the need for legal reform, the rise of a feminist legal movement was also dependent on educational and professional reforms. In the late nineteenth century, expansion of primary and secondary education provided a considerable boost to the numbers of women who sought advanced study at universities. Women's admission to law schools coincided with the broader demands for women's rights that led to gradual and piecemeal admissions. Women could study for law degrees alongside men in France in the 1880s but were prohibited from doing so in Russia until 1916 and in Hungary until World War II.[73] The fact that educational opportunities and work opportunities were not coordinated led to both individual hardships and motivated advocacy among female lawyers within the women's rights movement. The Swiss lawyer Emilie Kempin-Spyri (1853–1901) graduated from the University of Zurich in 1887 and initially worked in New York teaching law and collaborating with American colleagues to provide legal services to the poor (1888–1891).[74] In Belgium, Marie Popelin (1846–1913), a graduate of the Free University of Brussels in 1888, campaigned unsuccessfully for the admission of women to the legal profession but spent her life as a teacher and political activist. She would not live to see the 1921 legislative reform admitting women to the bar, as Eva Schandevyl points out (chapter 6).[75] The Romanian Sarmisa Bilcescu (1867–1935) studied law in Paris at the Faculty of Law and then returned to Bucharest, where she gained authorization from the Bar Association in 1891 and participated in such prestigious groups as the Société de législation comparé and advocated for higher education for women.[76] Despite this earlier advance, Ella Negruzzi (1876–1949) would face resistance in 1913 in her efforts to register for the bar exam in Romania; her entrance was delayed until 1920.[77] In Prussia, female university students were denied access to exams, thus barring their admission to law schools.[78] In most countries, however, the pattern of exclusion restricted access to the profession itself—that is, to apprenticeship and bar associations—rather than to university training.[79]

The vast majority of European countries admitted women to the bar between the two world wars: Portugal (1918); Scotland and Wales (1920); Northern Ireland (1921); Belgium, Czechoslovakia, England, and Germany (1922); Poland (1925); Hungary (1928); and Austria (1929). In Denmark, women were admitted into the lower ranks of the juridical professions in 1906 but were granted access to all positions only in 1919.[80] In Sweden, only unmarried women were allowed to practice from 1918.[81] Italy was one of the first countries in which women fought for access to the legal profession in the 1880s but only in 1919 did they secure this right.[82] In Hungary, women were prohibited from studying law, and the five or six female attorneys who practiced law after 1928 had studied abroad. In 1937, however, a new law explicitly excluded women from the bar.[83] Access in Bulgaria came later, when Vera Zlatareva (1905–1977) was admitted as the first female attorney in 1944, as Krassimira Daskalova explains (chapter 8). Scholarly work to document and analyze the history of European female lawyers of the early twentieth century is ongoing.

One important disjuncture within women's legal history is the phenomenon that women's admission to bar associations did not inevitably coincide with their admission to the judiciary. In Norway, the first female judge on the local level was admitted in Hammerfest in 1913,[84] yet women's admission to the judiciary more broadly did not occur until 1921.[85] Russia authorized female judges after the revolution of 1917.[86] In Ireland, four female magistrates started work in 1920.[87] Lithuania had the first female judge in 1924 and Sweden and Germany in 1927 (see chapter 10).[88] In Poland, the first woman became a juvenile judge in 1929 (see chapter 9). In the 1930s, Finland and Czechoslovakia announced their first female judges,[89] and Denmark followed in 1933.[90] In Spain's Republican civil war zone, the first female judge was appointed in 1936 (see chapter 2). Some countries where women were granted early and pioneering access to the legal profession nonetheless denied their admission to the judiciary until the conclusion of the Second World War. England's first female judges appeared in 1945–1949,[91] France's in 1946,[92] and Austria's in 1947.[93] Other countries followed, including the Netherlands (1947), Belgium (1948), Greece (1959), Italy (1963), and Switzerland and Portugal (1974).

The chapters by Iwona Dadej (Poland), Krassimira Daskalova (Bulgaria), Sara Kimble (France), Gloria Nielfa (Spain), Marion Röwekamp (Germany), Eva Schandevyl (Belgium), and Gordana Stojaković (Yugoslavia) attest to the significant association between women's professional and political emancipation. Having women within the legal professions was a new step in the history of women's legal rights because as women became legal experts, they could—and did—challenge the system from within the profession. In some states, they did this even within the governmental system. Anne Logan's study of the history of women in the development of criminology illustrates how women's early experiences in charity and social work expanded into advocacy within criminal law in England (chapter 11). Feminists active in prison reform efforts called for legal changes to improve the treatment of prisoners. In the process, their international networking and research contributed to the creation of criminology and the reinvention of themselves as "criminologists."

Women's opportunities to unite with similarly situated women in associations strengthened their ability to critique their position within society and to articulate political, social and professional concerns. Among the women's legal reform societies operating in the interwar period was the first transnational association of female lawyers and judges: the International Federation of Women in the Legal and Juridical Careers (FIFCJ; Figure I.1).[94] This federation intended to establish connections of "amity and solidarity," to facilitate women's access to "all juridical careers," to "improve women's professional circumstances," to study laws, and to "spread the idea of world peace."[95] The Federation was created in 1928 by an alliance of female lawyers and judges from Estonia, Germany, France, Spain, Poland, and Britain. This group appears to have been the first viable and most influential international legal sorority of the era (after the short-lived U.S.-based "Woman's International Bar Association" of 1888), forging connections among women from a number of emerging republics.[96] Officially, the FIFCJ was neutral and "apolitical," but by 1929, it was recognized as a non-governmental organization with the right to approach the League of Nations.[97] The FIFCJ received delegates from national female lawyers' associations at conferences held in Paris (1929, 1930, 1937), Naples (1934), and Vienna (1936). By 1936, members claimed to represent thirty-seven countries, an indicator of the association's reach across Europe and significance as a legal sorority.[98] As participants in "internationalism," the women of the FIFCJ used legal

Figure I.1 Meeting of the International Federation of Women in the Legal and Juridical Careers (circa February 1929), including Marcelle Kraemer-Bach (first row, first from left); Agathe Dyvrande-Thévenin (first row, second from left); Margarete Berent (top row, first from right); Clara Campoamor (top row, second from right); Wanda Grabińska-Wojtowicz (second row, first from right); and Vera Poska-Grünthal (third row, first from the right). Source: Polish Digital Archives.

precedents, legal arguments, and the legal situation of women in other European states as a point of comparison in their arguments for legal reform. Their efforts highlighted women's issues as matters of international importance.[99] Initial research suggests that association leaders were keenly concerned with advocating for women's rights from the start, but the infiltration of fascist members, particularly from Italy and Germany, combined with the active discrimination against women, disrupted any semblance of unity by 1936.[100] The consequences for female lawyers under the German Reich or Nazi-occupied countries would prove to be devastating.[101]

International Feminism and Legal Questions of Women's Status, 1880s to 1930s

The themes in Part III engage the international dimensions of gender, citizenship, and women's political voices. The broader context for these research topics is the history of global networks, exchanges, and entanglements that have long shaped the national and transnational women's movements.[102] Women's rights associations had long been concerned with strategies to ameliorate women's inferior legal status.[103] Legal reform was a cornerstone to belle époque women's rights organizations' platforms. In 1878, at the first International Congress on Women's Rights held in Paris, speakers engaged with the criticism of the legal oppression of women and the arguments for reform.[104] The International Council of Women (ICW, founded in 1888 in the United States) and its national affiliates also prioritized the reform of women's position under the law with consequences for Europeans. In 1900 in Paris at the Deuxième congrès international des œuvres et institutions féminines, legally trained women, including Belgian Marie Popelin, French Jeanne Chauvin, and German Anita Augspurg, debated legal issues with leaders including ICW president May Wright Sewall.[105] The ICW inspired the formation of national women's rights associations, which would then coordinate their efforts and send delegates to its international meetings. The German Bund Deutscher Frauenvereine (BDF) was established in 1894 to answer the ICW's call. The French Conseil National des Femmes Françaises (CNFF) was established in 1901 to address legal and social issues for women, including equality between spouses in family law, equal employment opportunities, equal pay for equal work, political rights for women, and independent nationality rights for married women.[106] By 1903, ten national councils had formed. As Anne Cova's research (chapter 13) reveals, the legislation committee within the ICW-affiliated National Council of Portuguese Women (Conselho Nacional das Mulheres Portuguesas, CNMP), established in Lisbon in 1914, devoted a third of its energies to juridical questions. At the same time, the ICW drew on its members to chair specialized committees, for example, the appointment of French attorney Maria Vérone (1874–1938) to its committee on law. Following World War I, Vérone would advocate for women's rights at the League of Nations.[107]

Among the most important transnational legal issues were citizenship and married women's right to their own nationality. Regina Wecker illustrates in her history of Swiss citizenship (chapter 14) how the gendering of citizenship made the search for equality extraordinarily challenging in a place where multiple factors, including municipal affiliations and local legal customs, have complicated the process. Wecker writes poignantly of the contemporary situation, in which globalization further complicates the pursuit of individual rights as the "battle for equality continues."[108] Catherine Jacques (chapter 15) documents and examines the uphill battle faced by feminist activists who, though skilled in law and politics, struggled to make their voices heard among diplomatic circles on matters of international law. These activists prioritized the reform of married women's nationality law and family law during the interwar years when they sought access to the League of Nations.[109] These women's associations pursued international law as a "neutral vehicle for taking on the world's most complex issues and pressing problems."[110] Their members viewed the law as a moral and reasoned force, an echo of the Grotian tradition of international law.[111] As activists working within non-governmental organizations for comprehensive reforms, female lawyers played a role in the reemergence of an "international society."[112] Contributing to our understanding of international feminism in Geneva, Susan Zimmermann (chapter 16) highlights another central legal issue of women's transnational engagement: labor regulation as influenced by race and gender. Jacques's and Zimmermann's contributions underscore how women's engagement at the League of Nations and the International Labour Organization (ILO) indicates both their skill in legal arguments and their investment in these organizations as a means to secure rights for women.

As the histories in Part III of this book illustrate, comparative history can contribute to a deeper understanding of women's relationships to democratic ideals and practices in the search for belonging and equitable treatment as individuals, in families, and in societies. In their struggle for equal rights, the European women's movement leaders, and especially the female lawyers associated with them, advocated legal reform as a solution to the tension between restrictive social norms and women's desire for equality. Within the women's rights movements, comparisons of laws and legal systems constituted essential knowledge used in national contexts to pressure governments for legal change. Women's rights associations were nationally based, yet many activists saw their fights as simultaneously belonging to a larger European—if not global—struggle for liberty, equality, and sorority.

The questions of gender within the intersecting spheres of family law, labor law, political rights, and citizenship continue to resonate within our increasingly interconnected world. We hope that readers will benefit from the exciting exchange of ideas and analyses about the gendered history of European legal cultures offered in this book. Moreover, in light of the current project to craft a common European civil code, we hope that European legislators will learn from the past while envisioning our future.

Notes

1 Catharine A. MacKinnon, *Feminism Unmodified—Discourses on Life and Law* (Cambridge, MA: Harvard University Press, 1987), 32–45.
2 On women in the revolutionary era, see chapters in Christine Fauré ed., *Political and Historical Encyclopedia of Women*, trans. Richard Dubois (New York: Routledge, 2003); Sarah Hanley, "The Monarchic State in Early Modern France: Marital Regime Government and Male Right," in *Politics, Ideology and the Law in Early Modern Europe*, ed. Adrianna E. Bakos (Rochester, NY: University of Rochester Press, 1994), 107–126.
3 Joan B. Landes, *Women and the Public Sphere in the Age of the French Revolution* (Ithaca: Cornell University Press, 1988), 93–206.
4 Ute Gerhard, *Debating Women's Equality: Toward a Feminist Theory of Law: A European Perspective* (New Brunswick: Rutgers University Press, 2001); Karin Gottschalk ed., *Gender Difference in European Legal Cultures: Historical Perspectives* (Stuttgart: Franz Steiner Verlag, 2013); Grethe Jacobsen and Heide Wunder eds., *East Meets West: A Gendered View of Legal Tradition* (Kiel: Solivagus, 2015); Stephan Meder and Christoph-Eric Mecke eds., *Family Law in Early Women's Rights Debates: Western Europe and the United States in the Nineteenth and Early Twentieth Centuries* (Cologne: Böhlau, 2013); Stephan Meder and Christoph-Eric Mecke eds., *Reformforderungen zum Familienrecht International. Band 1: Westeuropa und die USA (1830–1914)* (Cologne: Böhlau, 2015); Eva Schandevyl ed., *Women in Law and Lawmaking in Nineteenth and Twentieth-Century Europe* (Farnham: Ashgate, 2014).
5 The work of jurists such as Robert Joseph Pothier (1699–1772) in France, William Blackstone (1723–1780) in England, and Christian Wolff (1679–1754) in Germany formed the basis of the era's influential legal codes. See Stephan Meder, *Familienrecht. Von der Antike bis zur Gegenwart* (Cologne: Böhlau, 2013), 105.
6 Wiguläus Xaver Aloys Freiherr von Kreittmayr, *Anmerkungen über den Codicem Maximilianeum Bavaricum Civilem. Worinn derselbe sowol mit dem Gemein- als ehemalig- Chur-Bayerischen Land-Recht genau collationirt, Sohin der Unterschied zwischen dem alt- und neueren Recht samt Urquellen, woraus letztere geschöpft worden ist, überall angezeigt, und dieses dadurch in ein helleres Licht gesetzt wird* (Munich: Vötter, 1759), I 3 par. 2 nota 1, 124; Hugo Rehbein, *Allgemeines Landrecht für die Preußischen Staaten* (Berlin: Pauli, 1794), part I, I, § 24; see: Samuel Freiherr von Cocceji, *Project des Corporis Iuris Fridericiani* (Halle: Waisenhaus, 1750), part I, L. I, Tit. IV § 16 II. See in general Meder, *Familienrecht*, 105–106.
7 Marion W. Gray, *Productive Men, Reproductive Women: The Agrarian Household and the Emergence of Separate Spheres During the German Enlightenment* (New York: Berghahn Books, 2000), 158–164.
8 Franz von Zeiller, *Commentar über das allgemeine bürgerliche Gesetzbuch für die gesamten Deutschen Erbländer der Österreichischen Monarchie*, vol. 1 (Vienna: Hof und Staatsdruckerey, 1811), I, 1, paragraph 21, 2), footnote on 116.
9 See, for example: Hermann Conrad, "Die Rechtsstellung der Ehefrau in der Privatrechtsgebung der Aufklärungszeit," in *Aus Mittelalter und Neuzeit. Gerhard Kallen zum 70. Geburtstag*, ed. Josef Engels and Hans Martin Klinkenberg (Bonn: P. Hanstein, 1957), 260; Ute Gerhard, *Verhältnisse und Verhinderungen: Frauenarbeit, Familie und Rechte der Frauen im 19. Jahrhundert: mit Dokumenten* (Frankfurt a.M.: Suhrkamp, 1978); Dietmut Majer, *Frauen - Revolution - Recht. Die grossen Europäischen Revolutionen in Frankreich, Deutschland und Österreich. 1789 bis 1918 und die Rechtsstellung der Frauen. Unter Einbezug von England, Russland, der USA und der Schweiz* (Zürich, Baden-Baden: Dike, 2008), 145–147; against: Meder, *Familienrecht*, 117; Hannelore Schröder,

Die Rechtlosigkeit der Frau im Rechtsstaat. Dargestellt am Allgemeinen Preußischen Landrecht, am Bürgerlichen Gesetzbuch und an J.G. Fichtes Grundlage des Naturrechts (Frankfurt, Main/New York: Campus, 1979); Marianne Weber, *Ehefrau und Mutter in der Rechtsentwicklung: eine Einführung* (Tübingen: J. C .B. Mohr, 1907), 331–341; Susanne Weber-Will, *Die rechtliche Stellung der Frau im Privatrecht des Preußischen Allgemeinen Landrechts von 1794* (Frankfurt, Main/New York: Lang, 1983), 281–286.

10 Ute Gerhard, "Legal Particularism and the Complexity of Women's Rights in Nineteenth Century Germany," in *Private Law and Social Inequality in the Industrial Age: Comparing Legal Cultures in Britain, France, Germany, and the United States*, ed. Willibald Steinmetz (Oxford: Oxford University Press, 2000), 137–154; Ursula Vogel, "Fictions of Community: Property Relations in Marriage in European and American Legal Systems of the Nineteenth Century," in *Private Law*, 91–122.

11 Christina Damm, "Die Stellung der Ehefrau und Mutter nach Urteilen des Reichsgerichts von 1879 bis 1914. Eine Untersuchung zum Spannungsverhältnis zwischen dem Ideal der Gleichberechtigung und der von Recht und Ideologie legitimierten sozialen Wirklichkeit," PhD diss., law, University of Marburg, 1983.

12 Ute Gerhard, *Debating Women's Equality*, part II; Stephan Meder, Arne Duncker, and Andrea Czelk eds., *Die Rechtsstellung der Frau um 1900. Eine kommentierte Quellensammlung* (Cologne: Böhlau, 2010); Stephan Meder, Arne Duncker, and Andrea Czelk eds., *Frauenrecht und Rechtsgeschichte: Die Rechtskämpfe der deutschen Frauenbewegung* (Cologne: Böhlau, 2006); Tanja-Carina Riedel, *Gleiches Recht für Mann und Frau: die bürgerliche Frauenbewegung und die Entstehung des BGB* (Cologne: Böhlau, 2008); Weber, *Ehefrau und Mutter*, 407–505.

13 *Allgemeines Landrecht* (1794) quoted in translation in Susan Groag Bell and Karen M. Offen eds., *Women, the Family and Freedom: the Debates in Documents*, vol. 1 (Stanford, CA: Stanford University Press, 1983), 38–39.

14 Quoted in Albert Damez, *Le libre salaire de la femme mariée et le mouvement féministe* (Paris: A. Rousseau, 1905), 22.

15 Vogel, "Fictions of Community," 114–115.

16 Ibid., 114–115.

17 See Suzanne Desan, *The Family on Trial in Revolutionary France* (Berkeley: University of California Press, 2004) and Rachel G. Fuchs, *Contested Paternity. Constructing Families in Modern France* (Baltimore: The Johns Hopkins University Press, 2008).

18 Weber, *Ehefrau und Mutter*, 318–319. For Weber on the code civil in general, see 318–331.

19 William Blackstone, *Commentaries on the Laws of England*, 12th edition (Oxford: Clarendon, 1973–1975. Originally 1765), 445; Weber, *Ehefrau und Mutter*, 361–371.

20 "Feme Covert," *OED Online*, Oxford University Press (March 2015), accessed June 5, 2015.

21 Ute Gerhard, "Mothers between Individualisation and Institutions: Cultural Images of Welfare Policy," in *Working Mothers in Europe. A Comparison of Policies and Practices*, ed. Ute Gerhard, Trudie Knijn, and Anja Weckwert (Cheltenham; Northampton, MA: Edward Elgar, 2005), 28–29.

22 *Women's Position on the Laws of the Nations. A Compilation of the Laws of Different Countries, prepared by the I.C.W. Standing Committee on Laws Concerning the Legal Position of Women; with intro. by Mme d'Abbadie d'Arrast* (Karlsruhe: Braunsche Hofbuchdruckerei, 1912).

23 Madeline Poutret de Mauchamps, "Petition au Rois, à Messieurs les Députés des départments, et à MM. les pairs du Royaume de France . . .," *Gazette des Femmes* I, no. 2 (August 1, 1836): 33–38 *Women the Family and Freedom,* 159–161.

24 On Saint-Simonians see Claire Goldberg Moses, *French Feminism in the Nineteenth Century* (Albany: State University of New York Press, 1984), 84–85.

25 The Italian Code differed from the French by failing to provide for divorce, a decision designed to protect state relations with the Vatican and the Catholic Church (*concordato*). The resistance of the Vatican would stall divorce reform until 1970 (law of 898). Mauro Cappelletti, John Henry Merryman, and Joseph M. Perillo, *The Italian Legal System: An Introduction* (Stanford, CA: Stanford University Press, 1967), 139–140; Elisabeth Dickmann, "The Passing of the Civil Code in Italy in 1865," in *Family Law in Early Women's Rights Debates*, 143–169.

26 Anna Maria Mozzoni, "Women and the New Civil Code in Italy (1865)," in *Lives and Voices: Sources in European Women's History*, ed. Lisa DiCaprio and Merry E. Wiesner (Boston: Houghton Mifflin, 2001), 298–301.

27 "Mozzoni, Anna Maria," in *Encyclopedia of Women Social Reformers: M–Z*, ed. Helen Rappaport and Mariam Wright Edelman, vol. 2 (Santa Barbara, CA: ABC-CLIO, 2001), 463–465; Karen Offen, *European Feminisms, 1700–1950: A Political History* (Stanford, CA: Stanford University Press, 2000), 125.

28 Laura York, "Orzeszkowa, Eliza (1841–1910)," in *Women in World History: A Biographical Encyclopedia*, ed. Anne Commire, vol. 12 (Detroit: Yorkin Publications, 2002), 164–165; *Gale Virtual Reference Library* accessed June 10, 2015.

29 Bogna Lorence-Kot and Adam Winiarz, "The Polish Women's Movement to 1914," in *Women's Emancipation Movements in the Nineteenth Century*, ed. Sylvia Paletschek and Bianka Pietrow-Ennker (Stanford, CA: Stanford University Press, 2004), 219.

30 See Offen, *European Feminisms*, 151–154.

31 *Congrès français et international au droit des femmes, Paris 1889* (Paris: Dentu, 1889), 238–245, 240.

32 Jeanne Chauvin, "La Question féministe devant les chambres françaises," *La Ligue. Organe Belge du droit des femmes* (1896): 57–65, quote 64.

33 "Le centenaire du code et les femmes," *Le XIXe siècle: journal quotidien politique et littéraire* (October 29, 1904): 2; I. [Isabelle] Gatti De Gamond, "Le Féminisme et le Centenaire du Code civil 1804–1904," *Cahiers feminists* 9, no. 12 (1904): 1–3; "Protestation des Femmes contre le Code civil," *Cahiers féministes* 9, no. 15 (1904): 2; H. Ludwig, "Zur Zentenarfeier des Code Napoléon," *Die Frau: Monatsschrift für das gesamte Frauenleben unserer Zeit* 12, no. 3 (December 1904): 151–152; Käthe Schirmacher, "Die Frauen und der Code Napoleon," *Die Frauenbewegung* 10, no. 22 (November 15, 1904): 170–171.

34 Jeanne Oddo-Deflou was leader of the Groupe français d'études féministes (French Group of Feminist Studies), founded in 1898. Christophe Verbruggen and Julie Carlier, "Laboratories of Social Thought: The Transnational Advocacy Network of the Institut International pour la Diffusion des Expériences Sociales and its Documents du Progrès (1907–1916)," in *Information Beyond Borders International Cultural and Intellectual Exchange in the Belle Époque*, ed. W. Boyd Rayward (Farnham: Ashgate, 2014), 123–142.

35 Ute Gerhard ed., *Frauen in der Geschichte des Rechts. Von der Frühen Neuzeit bis zur Gegenwart* (Munich: C.H. Beck, 1997); Sabine Klemm, *Frauenbewegung und Familienrecht 1848 bis 1933: eine Betrachtung anhand von Quellen* (Tübingen: Campus, 1999); Meder et al., *Frauenrecht und Rechtsgeschichte*; Riedel, *Gleiches Recht für Mann und Frau*; Weber, *Ehefrau und Mutter in der Rechtsentwicklung*, 407–505.

36 For more information, see Meder et al., *Frauenrecht und Rechtsgeschichte.*

37 Olga von Beschwitz, "Begleitschrift zur Massenpetition des Bundes deutscher Frauenvereine betreffend das Familienrecht des neuen B.G.B.," *Centralblatt* 5 (1899): 33–36, quote 33.

38 Alice Salomon, "Stumme Märtyrerinnen," *Die Frau* 16 (1909): 264–276, quote 272; Lynn Abrams, "Martyrs or Matriarchs? Working-Class Women's Experience of Marriage in Germany Before the First World War," *Women's History Review* 1, no. 3 (1992): 357–376; Karen Hagemann, *Frauenalltag und Männerpolitik: Alltagsleben und gesellschaftliches Handeln von Arbeiterfrauen in der Weimarer Republik* (Bonn: J.H.W. Dietz, 1990).

39 "Ist die Besserstellung der Frau im künftigen schweizerischen Familienrecht anzustreben?" *Schweizer Frauen-Zeitung* 16, no. 29 (1894): 113–114; Anna Mackenroth, *Ueber die Rechtsstellung der Frau im Vorentwurf zum schweizer. Civilgesetzbuch. Vier Vorträge* (Zurich: Schröter, 1901); Elisabeth Frysak, "Legale Kämpfe: Die petitionsrechtlichen Forderungen der österreichischen bürgerlichen Frauenbewegung zur Änderung des Ehe- und Familienrechts um die Jahrhundertwende," *L'Homme* 14, no. 1 (2003): 65–82.

40 Alexina K. Orred, Catherine M. Melliss and Rosa M. Barrett, "Report on Great Britain and Ireland," in *Women's Position in the Laws of the Nations*, 44–45; Weber, *Ehefrau und Mutter*, 361–371.

41 Women's movements within common law systems focused on opportunities for education and employment for unmarried women, while married women's rights were secondary, according to Rebecca Probert, "Family Law Reform and the Women's Movement in England and Wales," in *Family Law in Early Women's Rights Debates*, 170–193; Fiona A. Montgomery, *Women's Rights: Struggles and Feminism in Britain, 1770–1970* (Manchester: Manchester University Press, 2006).

42 See Patrizia Albanese, *Mothers of the Nation: Women, Families, and Nationalism in Twentieth-Century Europe* (Toronto: University of Toronto Press, 2006); Benedict Anderson, *Imagined Communities: Reflections on the Origin and Spread of Nationalism* (London: Verso, 1991); and Rogers Brubaker, *Citizenship and Nationhood in France and Germany* (Cambridge, MA: Harvard University Press 1992).

43 Mary Nash, "The Rise of the Women's Movement in Nineteenth Century Spain," in *Women's Emancipation Movements in the 19th Century*, 243–262.

44 Similarly, the French came close to passing meaningful reforms to emancipate married women in civil terms in 1938, encountered setbacks under the Vichy Regime (1940–1944), and only succeeded under post-Liberation governments. See Paul Smith, *Feminism and the Third Republic Women's Political and Civil Rights in France, 1918–1945* (Oxford: Clarendon Press of Oxford University Press, 1996), chapter 4.

45 A similar process is described for Hungary and Poland. Claudia Kraft, "Das Eherecht in der Zweiten Polischen Republik (1917–1939) und das gescheiterte Ideal gleichberechtigter Staatsbürgerschaft," in *Zwischen Kriegen. Nationen, Nationalismen und Geschlechterverhältnisse in Mittel- und Osteuropa 1918–1939*, eds. Johanna Gehmacher, Elizabeth Harvey, and Sophia Kemlein (Osnabrück: Fibre, 2004), 63–82; Anna Loutfi, "Legal Ambiguity and the 'European Norm.' Women's Independence and Hungarian Family Law, 1880–1913," in *Women's Movements: Networks and Debates in Post-communist Countries in the 19th and 20th Centuries*, ed. Edith Saurer, Margareth Lanzinger, and Elisabeth Frysak (Vienna: Böhlau, 2006), 507–521; Anna Loutfi, "Hungarian Family Law and The Struggle for Gender Order: 1848–1913," PhD diss., Central European University, 2006.

46 Kraft, Ibid., 63-82.

47 Claudia Kraft, "Die Geschlechtergeschichte Osteuropas als doppelte Herausforderung für die 'allgemeine' Geschichte," in H-Soz-u-Kult, June 6, 2006, http://hsozkult.geschichte.hu-berlin.de/forum/2006–06–005; Claudia Papp, *"Die Kraft der weiblichen Seele," Feminismus in Ungarn 1918–1941* (Münster: LitVerlag, 2004); Natali Stegmann, *Die Töchter der geschlagenen Helden. "Frauenfrage," Feminismus und Frauenbewegung in Polen 1863–1919* (Wiesbaden: Harrossowitz, 2000).

48 Wendy Z. Goldman, *Women, the State and Revolution: Soviet Family Policy and Social Life, 1917–1936* (Cambridge, UK and New York, USA: Cambridge University Press, 1993); Gail Warshofsky Lapidus, *Women in Soviet Society: Equality, Development, and Social Change* (Berkeley: University of California Press, 1978).

49 Goldman, *Women, the State and Revolution*, 337.

50 Barbara Einhorn, *Cinderella Goes to Market: Citizenship, Gender and Women's Movements in Eastern Central Europe* (London: Verso, 1993); Saurer, Lanzinger, and Frysak, *Women's Movements*.

51 See Christina Carlsson Wetterberg, "Gender Equality and the Welfare State. Debates on Marriage Law Reform in Sweden at the Beginning of the 20th Century," and Harry Willekens, "The Pioneer Role of the Scandinavian Countries in Family Law Reform: A Comparative Perspective," both chapters in *Family Law in Early Women's Rights Debates*, 255–280, 281–312.

52 Carlsson Wetterberg, "Gender Equality and the Welfare State," 255–280; Mel Moore, "Sweden," in *Cultural Sociology of Divorce: An Encyclopedia*, ed. Robert E. Emery (Thousand Oaks, CA: SAGE Publications, 2013), 1176–1179; Willekens, "The Pioneer Role of the Scandinavian Countries in Family Law Reform," 281–312.

53 Maarit Jänterä-Jareborg, "On the Cooperation between Religious and State Institutions in Family Matters: Nordic Experiences," in *Family, Religion and Law: Cultural Encounters in Europe*, ed. Prakash Shah, Marie-Claire Foblets and Mathias Rohe (Farnham: Ashgate, 2014), 81–82; Kari Melby, Ana Pylkkänen, Bente Rosenbeck, and Christina Carlsson Wetterberg eds., The *Nordic Model of Marriage and the Welfare State* (Copenhagen: Nord, 2000).

54 For the use of the Nordic model in Germany, see: Stephan Meder, "Das nordische Ehemodell als Vorreiter für die Reform des Ehe- und Familienrechts im Common Law und in Deutschland zur Zeit der Weimarer Republik," in *Reformforderungen zum Familienrecht international*, 669–696; Urte Nersemann, *Die schwedische Familiengesetzgebung von 1734 bis zur den Reformgesetzen von 1915 bis 1920 und deren Einfluss auf die Gesetzgebungsprojekte der Weimarer Republik* (Frankfurt/Main: Lang, 2003).

55 Seth Koven and Sonya Michel eds., *Mothers of a New World: Maternalist Politics and the Origins of Welfare States* (New York: Routledge, 1993).

56 Mary Ann Glendon, *The Transformation of Family Law. State, Law, and Family in the United States and Western Europe* (Chicago, IL: University of Chicago Press, 1997).

57 Cartesian Poullain de la Barre declared that "the mind has no sex," in *De l'égalite des deux sexes* (1673; reprint Paris: Fayard, 1984). See Erica Harth, *Cartesian Women: Versions and Subversions of Rational Discourse in the Old Regime* (Ithaca: Cornell University Press, 1992) and Londa Schiebinger, *The Mind Has No Sex?: Women in the Origins of Modern Science* (Cambridge: Harvard University Press, 1989).

58 Max Weber, *Economy and Society: An Outline of Interpretive Sociology*, 2 vol. (Berkley, CA: University of California Press, 2013); Pierre Bourdieu, "The Force

of Law: Toward a Sociology of the Juridical Field," *The Hastings Law Journal* 38 (1987): 814–853; Hannes Siegrist, *Advokat, Bürger und Staat: Sozialgeschichte der Rechtsanwälte in Deutschland, Italien und der Schweiz (18.–20. Jahrhundert)* (Frankfurt, Main: Klostermann, 1996); Zoran Pokrovac ed., *Juristenausbildung in Osteuropa bis zum Ersten Weltkrieg* (Frankfurt, Main: Klostermann, 2007).

59 Richard L. Abel and Philip Lewis, *Lawyers in Society: Comparative Theories* (Washington, DC: Beard Books, 2005), 84–85; Richard Collier, *Masculinity. Law, and the Family* (London, New York: Routledge, 1995); Michael Grossberg, "Institutionalizing Masculinity: The Law as a Masculine Profession," in *Meanings for Manhood: Constructions of Masculinities in Victorian America*, ed. Marc C. Carnes and Clyde Griffen (Chicago: University of Chicago Press, 1990), 133–151.

60 Abel and Lewis, *Lawyers in Society*; Mossman, *The First Women Lawyers:* Schandevyl ed., *Women in Law and Lawmaking*; Ulrike Schultz and Gisela Shaw eds., *Women in the World's Legal Professions* (Oxford, Portland, OR: Hart Pub., 2003); Ulrike Schultz and Gisela Shaw eds., *Gender and Judging* (Oxford, Portland, OR: Hart Pub., 2013).

61 Ernest Glasson opinion "Avocat," in *Jurisprudence générale. Cours d'appel et tribunaux. 1898, Partie 2* (Paris: Bureau de la Jurisprudence générale, 1899), 185–195.

62 As an ideology described by scholars, "maternalism" served to further women's civic involvement grounded in an exaltation of "women's capacity to mother and extended to society as a whole the values of care, nurturance, and morality." See Seth Koven and Sonya Michel, "Womanly Duties: Maternalist Politics and the Origins of Welfare States in France, Germany, Great Britain, and the United States, 1880–1920," *American Historical Review* 95, no. 4 (1990): 1076–1108, quote 1079.

63 Ann Taylor Allen, *Feminism and Motherhood in Germany, 1800–1914* (New Brunswick: Rutgers University Press, 1991); Ann Taylor Allen, *Feminism and Motherhood in Western Europe, 1890–1970: The Maternal Dilemma* (New York: Palgrave Macmillan, 2005); Marian van der Klein et al. eds., *Maternalism Reconsidered: Motherhood, Welfare and Social Policy in the Twentieth Century* (New York: Berghahn Books, 2012); Offen, *European Feminisms*; Meder and Mecke, *Family Law in Early Women's Rights Debates.*

64 Alban Jacquemart, *Les hommes dans les mouvements féministes. Socio-histoire d'un engagement improbable* (Rennes: PUR, 2015); Mossman, *First Women Lawyers*, 239–275.

65 Nena A. Vasojević, "Marija Milutinović-Punktatorka," accessed July 3, 2015, http://knjizenstvo.etf.bg.ac.rs/en/authors/marija-milutinovic.

66 Ruth Arlene Fluck Dudgeon, "Women and Higher Education in Russia, 1855–1905," PhD diss., George Washington University, 1975, 161–166; Eugene Huskey, *Russian Lawyers and the Soviet State: The Origins and Development of the Soviet Bar, 1917–1939* (Princeton, NJ: Princeton University Press, 1986), 12–26; Moisei Ostrogorski, *The Rights of Women: A Comparative Study in History and Legislation* (London: George Allen and Unwin, 1908), 155; James C. Albisetti, "Portia Ante Portas: Women and the Legal Profession in Europe, ca. 1870–1925," *Journal of Social History* 33, no. 4 (2000): 825–857, quote 833–834.

67 Ellen Kleman, "Vår kvinnliga advokatfirma," *Hertha* 8 (1919): 146–149; Gunilla Strömholm, *Elsa Eschelsson: Sveriges första kvinnliga jurist* (Uppsala: Iustus, 1997), 72. There is no entry on Pettersson in the book on pioneering women in Sweden, although she is mentioned in Elsa Andén's "Andén, Elsa," in *Svenska kvinnor, föregångare—nyskapare*, ed. Carin Österberg, Inga Lewenhaupt and Anna Greta Wahlberg (Lund: Signum, 1990), 20–21.

68 Louise Otto-Peters, *Das erste Vierteljahrhundert des Allgemeinen deutschen Frauenvereins gegründet am 18. Oktober 1865 in Leipzig* (Leipzig: Kommissionsverlag Schäfer: 1890), 64.

69 Felice Batlan, *Women and Justice for the Poor: A History of Legal Aid, 1863–1945* (New York: Cambridge University Press, 2015); Beatrix Geisel, *Klasse, Geschlecht und Recht. Vergleichende sozialhistorische Untersuchung der Rechtsberatungspraxis von Frauen- und Arbeiterbewegung (1894–1933)* (Baden-Baden: Nomos, 1997); Gisela Shaw, "Conflicting Agendas: The First Female Jurists in Germany," *International Journal of the Legal Profession* 10, no. 2 (2003): 177–191. In this volume, see: Kimble, chapter 5; Dadej, chapter 9; Röwekamp, chapter 10.

70 Vera Poska-Grünthal, *See oli Eestis, 1919–1944 (Memoirs 1919–1944)* (Stockholm: Kirjastus Välis-Eesti & EMP, 1975); Sirje Tamul, "Poska-Grünthal, Vera (Veera) (1909–1986)," in *Biographical Dictionary of Women's Movements and Feminisms in Central, Eastern, and South Eastern Europe, 19th and 20th Centuries*, ed. Francisca de Haan, Krassimira Daskalova, and Anna Loutfi (Budapest, New York: CEU Press, 2006), 450–453.

71 Dana Musilová, "Horáková, Milada (1901–1950)," in *Biographical Dictionary*, 178–180.

72 Maria Bucur, "Negruzzi, Ella," in *Biographical Dictionary*, 363–365.

73 "Russia," *International Women's News* 5, no. 10 (1916): 69; Justine Klotz, "Women Lawyers in Europe," *Women Lawyers Journal* 6 (1916–1917): 41–42 indicates that women were allowed in law schools in 1906; Albisetti, "Porta ante Portas," 833–834; Papp, *Feminismus in Ungarn*, 411–417.

74 Christiane Berneike, *Die Frauenfrage ist Rechtsfrage. Die Juristinnen der deutschen Frauenbewegung und das bürgerliche Gesetzbuch* (Baden-Baden: Nomos, 1995), 81–102; Marianne Delfosse, *Emilie Kempin-Spyri (1853–1901). Das Wirken der ersten Schweizer Juristin unter besonderer Berücksichtigung ihres Einsatzes für die Rechte der Frau im schweizerischen und deutschen Privatrecht* (Zurich: Schulthess, 1994); Verena Stadler-Labhart, "Erste Studentinnen der Rechts- und Staatswissenschaften in Zürich," in *Ebenso neu als kühn. 120 Jahre Frauenstudium ab der Universität Zürich*, ed. Verein für feministische Wissenschaft (Zurich: Verein Feministische Wissenschaft, 1988), 74–112; Mossman, *The First Women Lawyers*, 242–243; "Emilie Kempin [-Spyri]," in *Dictionnaire historique de la Suisse*, accessed February 2, 2011, http://www.hls-dhs-dss.ch/textes/f/F9342.php.

75 Julie Carlier, "Moving Beyond Boundaries. An Entangled History of Feminism in Belgium, 1890–1914," PhD diss., University Gent, 2010, 58; Linda L. Clark, *Women and Achievement in Nineteenth-Century Europe* (Cambridge: Cambridge University Press, 2008), 225; Éliane Gubin, Catherine Jacques, Valérie Piette, and Jean Puissant eds., *Dictionnaire des femmes belges: XIXe et XXe siècles* (Bruxelles: Éditions Racine, 2006), 459–462.

76 President of the Chamber of Deputies Demeter Gianni and the bar association of Ilfov (includes Bucharest) authorized (Sarmisa or Sarmiza) Bilcescu to practice the profession on June 26, 1891 according to: "La femme avocat," *L'Etranger. Revue Internationale* 2 (1898): 42–44; I. Ingelbrecht, "Le féminisme et le femme témoin," *Revue politique et parlementaire* 23, no. 68 (February 1900): 382; Andreea Dimitriu, "Le Féminisme Roumain et ses Affinités avec le Féminisme Français (1918–1940)," PhD diss., Université d'Angers, 2011, 55–56, 126.

77 Bucur, "Negruzzi, Ella," 363–365.

78 Marion Röwekamp, *Die ersten deutschen Juristinnen. Eine Geschichte ihrer Professionalisierung und Emanzipation (1900–1945)* (Cologne: Böhlau, 2011), 25–60.

79 Exceptionally, a few women were apparently admitted to their bar associations without great difficulty, such as Adolphine Kok (1879–1928), admitted to the Rotterdam bar in 1903, and Elise Sem (1870–1950) in Norway in 1902–1904. On Kok: G. Chr. Kok and F.A. Arnbak-d'Aulnis de Bourouill, "Mevrouw mr. A.E. van den Hoeck-Kok (1879–1928); De eerste vrouwelijke advocaat in Nederland in 1903," in *Rotterdamse juristen uit vijf eeuwen*, ed. ibid (Hilversum, 2009), 157–162; Clark, *Women and Achievement*, 230. On Sem: Thordis Støren, *Justitias døtre. De første kvinnelige jurister i Norge* (Oslo: Universitetsforlaget, 1984); Thordis Støren, *Justitias gode tjenere: de første kvinnelige advokater* (Oslo: Dreyer, 1987). See Klotz, "Women Lawyers in Europe," 33–34.

80 Inga Dahlsgård, *Women in Denmark: Yesterday and Today* (Copenhagen: Det Danske Selskab, 1980), 112.

81 Albisetti, "Portia ante Portas," 837; Klotz, "Women Lawyers in Europe," 33–34.

82 Lidia Poët (1855–1949) sued for her rights; Teresa Labriola (1874–1941) was the first to practice. Klotz, "Women Lawyers in Europe," 33–34. On Labriola: Piero Addeo, *Eva togata* (Naples: Rispoli, 1939); Zara Algardi, *La donna e la toga* (Milan: Giuffrè, 1949); Vittorio Oligati, "Professional Body and Gender Difference in Court: The Case of the First (Failed) Woman Lawyer in Italy," in *Women in the World's Legal Professions*, 419–436; Fiorenza Taricone, *Teresa Labriola: biografia politica di un'intellettuale tra Ottocento e Novecento* (Milan: FrancoAmgeli, 1994). On Poët: 'Dolores,' "Les Femmes Avocats," *Bulletin de L'Union Universelle des Femmes: Revue Mensuelle* 7 (July 15, 1890): 9–12.

83 Krassimira Daskalova, "Maria Zlatareva," in *Biographical Dictionary of Women's Movements and Feminisms*, 620–623; Papp, *Feminismus in Ungarn*, 411–417.

84 "Women in the Legal Profession," *Women Lawyers' Journal* 3, no. 1 (1913): 2.

85 L. Qvam, "Official reports. Norway. The First Woman Judge," *Jus Suffragii: International Women's News* 8, no. 1 (1913): 7; "Norges første kvindelige assessor," *Nylaende: tidsskrift for kvindernes sak* 35, no. 19 (1921): 299; Albisetti, "Portia ante Portas," 837; Klotz, "Women Lawyers in Europe," 33–34.

86 "Women Judges," *Jus Suffragii: International Women's News* 11 (1917): 154.

87 "Ireland. Four Women Magistrates Appointed," *Jus Suffragii: International Women's News* 14, no. 5 (1920): 75.

88 "Reports from Auxiliaries. A Women Judge in Lithuania," *Jus Suffragii: International Women's News* 20, no. 4 (1926): 57; "Feminist Notes: Sweden's First Woman Judge," *Equal Rights* 14, no. 21 (1927): 162 chapter 10 (Röwekamp).

89 "Feminist Notes: Training Women to be Judges," *Equal Rights* 16 (1931): 224; Schultz and Shaw, *Women in the World's Legal Professions*, 389.

90 "Zum ersten weiblichen Richter in Dänemark," *Die Frau* 42 (1930): 54; "Feminist notes: Denmark Appoints Woman Judge," *Equal Rights* 19, no. 33 (1933): 262.

91 Patrick Polden, "The Lady of Tower Bridge: Sybil Campbell, England's First Woman Judge," *Women's History Review* 8, no. 3 (1999): 505–526; Brenda Hale, "Heilbron, Dame Rose (1914–2005)," in *Oxford Dictionary of National Biography*, ed. Lawrence Goldman (Oxford: Oxford University Press, 2009; online ed., January 2015), accessed July 6, 2015, http://www.oxforddnb.com.ezproxy.depaul.edu/view/article/96231.

92 On France see Sara L. Kimble "No Right to Judge: Feminism and the Judiciary in Third Republic France," *French Historical Studies* 31, no. 4 (2008): 609–641; and Sara L. Kimble, *Women, Feminism and the Law: Justice Redressed* (New York: Routledge, forthcoming).

93 Röwekamp, *Juristinnen in Deutschland*, 364.

94 This organization, established in 1928, had varied names. Currently: Fédération International des femmes des carrières juridiques (FIFCJ or International

Federation of Women in the Legal Careers) and historically: La Fédération Internationale des Femmes Magistrats et Avocats (FIFMA).

95 Marcelle Kraemer-Bach, "Federation internationale des femmes avocats," *La Française* (November 9, 1929); Tamul, "Poska-Grünthal, Vera," 450–451.

96 WIBA was spearheaded by Catharine Waite (1829–1913), the Illinois suffragist and lawyer who in 1886 founded *The Chicago Law Times*. Marcelle Kraemer-Bach, *La Longue Route* (Paris: La pensée universelle, 1988), 243–244. Marcelle Kraemer-Bach, *Les Inégalités légales entre l'homme et la femme* (Paris: Presses Universitaires de France, 1927), 2.

97 The League of Nations, *Supplement to Handbook of International Organisations* (Geneva: League of Nations, 1929), 20.

98 Esther Jaffe Mohr, "Women Lawyers in Central Europe," *Women Lawyers' Journal* 23 (1936/1937): 6–9.

99 Daniel Gorman, *The Emergence of International Society in the 1920s* (Cambridge: Cambridge University Press, 2012), 12, 58.

100 Sara L. Kimble, "Women, Law and Friendship: Activities of the International Federation of Women in Legal Careers Between the Two World Wars," paper presented at the Social Science Historical Association Conference, Minneapolis, November 5, 2006.

101 Julie Fette, *Exclusions: Practicing Prejudice in French Law and Medicine, 1920–1945* (Ithaca, NY: Cornell University Press, 2012); Liora Israël, *Robes noires, années sombres: avocats et magistrats en résistance pendant la Seconde Guerre mondiale* (Paris: Fayard, 2005); Frank Mecklenburg, "The Occupation of Women Emigrés: Women Lawyers in the United States," in *Between Sorrow and Strength: Women Refugees of the Nazi Period*, ed. Sibylle Quack (New York: German Historical Institute and Cambridge University Press, 1995), 289–299; Röwekamp, *Juristinnen in Deutschland*, 636–734.

102 For example: Ann Taylor Allen, Anne Cova, and Jane Purvis, "International Feminism," *Women's History Review* 19 (2010): 492–501; Bonnie S. Anderson, *Joyous Greetings: The First International Women's Movement, 1830–1860* (Oxford: Oxford University Press, 2000); Gisela Bock, *Women in European History* (Oxford: Blackwell, 2002); Oliver Janz and Daniel Schönpflug eds., *Gender History in a Transnational Perspective. Biographies, Networks, Gender Orders* (New York/Oxford: Berghahn Books, 2014); Kathryn Kish Sklar and James Brewer Stewart eds., *Women's Rights and Transatlantic Antislavery in the Era of Emancipation* (New Haven: Yale University Press, 2007); Ida Blom, *Medicine, Morality, and Political Culture. Legislation on Veneral Disease in Five Northern European Countries, c. 1870–c. 1995* (Lund: Nordic Academic Press, 2012); Margaret McFadden, *Golden Cables of Sympathy: The Transatlantic Sources of Nineteenth-Century Feminism* (Lexington, KY: University Press of Kentucky, 1999); Myra Marx Ferree and Aili Mari Tripp eds., *Global Feminisms: Transnational Women's Activism, Organizing, and Human Rights* (New York: New York University Press, 2006); Christine von Oertzen, *Science, Gender, and Internationalism: Women's Academic Networks, 1917–1955* (New York: Palgrave Macmillan, 2014); Offen, *European Feminisms*; Offen, *Globalizing Feminisms*; Leila Rupp, *Worlds of Women: The Making of an International Women's Movement* (Princeton, NJ: Princeton University Press, 1997); Bonnie G. Smith ed., *Global Feminism Since 1945* (London: Routledge, 2000); Bonnie G. Smith, *Women's History in Global Perspective*, 3 vol. (Urbana: University of Illinois Press, 2008); Bonnie G. Smith, *The Oxford Encyclopaedia of Women in World History*, 4 vol. (New York: Oxford University Press, 2008); Patricia Ward D'Itri, *Cross Currents in The International Women's Movement, 1848–1948* (Ohio: Bowling Green State University Popular Press, 1999).

103 Anne Cova, "The National Councils of Women in France, Italy and Portugal. Comparisons and Entanglements 1888–1939," in *Gender History in a Transnational Perspective*, 46–76, 69.
104 See Offen, *European Feminisms*, 151–154.
105 On 1900, see *Deuxième congrès international des œuvres et institutions féminines*, 2 vol. (Paris: Blot, 1902).
106 By 1912, the International Council of Women (ICW) created a pioneering report, *Women's Position in the Laws of the Nations*, edited by the Frenchwoman Mme d'Abbadie d'Arrast, that was an effort to insist that women's problems in the law, especially married women's status, transcended national boundaries.
107 "Vérone, Maria," in *Encyclopedia of Women Social Reformers*, 724–725. See also Sara L. Kimble, "Politics, Money, and Distrust: French-American Alliances in the International Campaign for Women's Equal Rights, 1925–1928," in *Practiced Citizenship: Women, Gender and the State in Modern France*, ed. Nimisha Barton and Richard Hopkins (Lincoln: University of Nebraska Press, forthcoming).
108 The book by Dieter Gosewinkel, *Schutz und Freiheit? Staatsbürgerschaft in Europa im 20. und 21. Jahrhundert* (Berlin: Suhrkamp, 2016) will contain a comparative chapter on married women's nationality.
109 See Rupp, *Worlds of Women* for histories of international activities for ICW, IAW, WILPF.
110 Mary Ellen O'Connell, *The Power and Purpose of International Law: Insights from the Theory and Practice of Enforcement* (Oxford, New York: Oxford University Press, 2008), 14.
111 For the "invented tradition of Grotius," see John T. Parry, "What Is the Grotian Tradition in International Law," *University of Pennsylvania Journal of International Law* 35, no. 2 (Winter 2013–14): 299–378.
112 Gorman, *The Emergence of International Society*, 12, 58.

Part I

Gender and Family Law

1 Adaptation, Emulation, or Tradition?

Greek Family Law and the Courts in the First Decades of the Modern Greek State

Evdoxios Doxiadis

The history of Greek family law in the nineteenth century, though thoroughly addressed in both legal and feminist studies by scholars like Eleni Varikas, Efi Avdela, Angeliki Psarra, Alexandra Bakalaki, and others, is surprisingly unexplored at an empirical level and strangely focused in the final quarter of the century.[1] Even as the preceding Ottoman period is increasingly well understood, the emergence of the modern legal framework in Greece, and especially its treatment and impact on women, has been dealt with primarily through the use of contemporary and late nineteenth century legal and feminist debates rather than through an examination of the activities of the courts at the time. It is this absence of empirical data that this examination will attempt to redress by an examination of the way the mid-nineteenth century Greek courts actually dealt with women and a comparison of their approach to earlier courts during the Ottoman period. This chapter will argue that the Greek courts of the time, while consciously operating under a European framework and well aware of European legal developments, were not afraid to continue to place an emphasis on customary law in matters of family law despite condemnations of customary law by contemporary Greek legal scholars. At the same time, these legal scholars promoted certain European ideas regarding statehood, such as centralization, and, in essence, were willing to diverge from blind acceptance of customary law by creating a unique mixture of traditional and modern jurisprudence that survived much longer than earlier scholarship has suggested.

Greece emerged in 1830 as an absolute monarchy at the insistence of the European Great Powers, although in 1843 the young Bavarian king Otto was forced to accept a fairly liberal constitution. Greece until 1862 was limited to the Peloponnese, the Cyclades, and a small part of the mainland, roughly a third of its current size. My empirical data for 1860 comes from the Appeals Court of Athens (*Efeteio Athinon*), one of two appeals courts in Greece, situated in the capital and responsible for much of the state at that time. Because of the debate regarding the use or avoidance of customary law in the modern Greek judicial system, the use of the Appeals Court, which draws cases from several regions, gives insights into this issue and also allows us to confirm what the highest legal authorities thought at the time, since reversals at the Supreme Court (the *Areios Pagos*, also situated in Athens) were noted next to the decision of the Appeals Court with extensive notes regarding the rationale of the Supreme Court. This examination uses 275 cases dealing with women presented in front of the Appeals Court between January 27 and October 9 of 1860, as well as 195 legal documents from the communal courts of Naxos and Mykonos, two Aegean islands that became part of the modern Greek state following the Greek War of Independence, for the period from 1750 to 1829, as a counterpoint to the legal situation in Ottoman Greece prior to the establishment of the modern Greek State. I will also use other notarial documents from the regions mentioned above as well as from the region of Leonidio for the period 1750–1850. Before I begin the discussion of the data, however, I must briefly review the existing historiography on the question of civil law in nineteenth century Greece. The question is complicated because despite numerous efforts, the Greek state did not produce a comprehensive Civil Code until the mid-twentieth century, and thus, there was a long and quite lively debate on the principles upon which courts should pass judgment.

Before the Greek War of Independence of 1821, which eventually produced the modern Kingdom of Greece almost a decade later, the areas that formed the latter were part of the Ottoman Empire and thus enjoyed a very flexible and multifaceted judicial environment. The Ottomans had, of course, created a fairly comprehensive network of courts, each with its Islamic judge or *kadi* who based his decisions on *Shari'a*, the Sultanic decrees known as *Kanuns*, and local custom, but Christians and Jews also had other options available to them. As a result of the *millet* system, religious minorities had the right to set up their own courts under their religious leaders in which to settle disputes among themselves. Indeed, ecclesiastical and rabbinical courts proliferated during the Ottoman Empire, mostly dealing with what we would today call civil cases and, of course, family law, their decisions being enforceable by Ottoman authorities.[2]

Non-Muslims, however, quickly recognized that on certain occasions using the *kadi* courts might be to their benefit, and throughout the Ottoman period, Greek Christians used those courts extensively.[3] Women, for instance, frequently sought divorces in the *kadi* courts even though divorce was theoretically available in Orthodox ecclesiastical courts.[4] The many reasons for this include easier grounds for divorce in the *kadi* courts, their lower cost, questions of custody of children, and possible financial benefits.[5] Wives in fact continuously braved the denunciations of their own religious leaders to the point that the Greek Orthodox Church gradually loosened grounds for divorce to ensure that its flock would not venture beyond the institution of its faith.[6]

Beyond the ecclesiastical and *kadi* courts, some areas developed what can best be described as communal courts that also dealt with civil matters (and on occasions even penal cases), particularly regarding questions of property.[7] This was primarily done in areas that had received the right from the Sultans to retain laws and traditions, a right usually bestowed in the peaceful incorporation of a region to the Empire, as was the case with the Cyclades, most of which lacked any Muslim presence and thus often lacked a *kadi*. These courts were primarily composed of local notables who also wielded significant political and economic authority and may have included the local Ottoman official (*zapit*, etc.) or the local bishop.[8] Ottoman officials could also judge criminal and civil cases; even Christian officials like the Dragoman of the Fleet, who was usually a Greek Phanariot from Constantinople, frequently stood in place of the *Kapudan* Pasha in such cases.[9] Furthermore, through the so-called Capitulations that the Ottoman state had signed with various European powers, foreign consuls and ambassadors had received judicial authority over their subjects in the Ottoman Empire, and as the numbers of Greeks with foreign nationality proliferated in the latter part of the eighteenth century, many sought to involve the various consuls in civil matters.[10]

It is evident that the judicial system of the Ottoman Empire was anything but simple, and it was further complicated by the different sources of law used. Leaving aside the *kadi* courts, both ecclesiastical and communal courts claimed to have been implementing Byzantine legislation, in essence, Roman law. However, the question was which Roman law they were attempting to implement, since unlike continental Europe, where Justinian's *Corpus Juris Civilis* had become accepted as the standard, Byzantine emperors had continued to legislate to the very end of the Empire in 1453, almost a millennium after Justinian. Both ecclesiastical and communal courts often claimed to be using a thirteenth century collection called the *Exavivlos* by noted Byzantine legalist Constantine Armenopoulos, an example of the collections called *Nomocanons* that combined Roman and Canon law.[11] Even that, however, is problematic, not only because we know that at certain periods other collections were more popular, such as the later *Nomocanon* by Manuil Malaxos, especially in the ecclesiastical courts,[12] but also because it is almost certain that none of the communal courts actually had copies of any such collections. Instead, they based their decisions on what we may call customary law, which over the centuries of Ottoman rule diverged significantly from the original and from place to place.[13]

Regardless of the various local differences that existed, however, there were certain similarities regarding these courts that should be emphasized. First of all, they were local, and their decisions, much like the decisions of the *kadi* courts, were more or less final without an established principle of appeal.[14] They were also fairly informal and lacking professional jurists or lawyers. The notables who composed them simply listened to the cases as presented by the various parties and reached their decision, sometimes after soliciting the opinion of experts or after calling upon additional witnesses. Furthermore, like the *kadi* courts again, these courts were apparently quite affordable, as evidenced by the small claims cases with which they often dealt. One outcome of these characteristics was that all members of society, including poor people and women who may otherwise have been excluded, used these courts regularly.

Communal courts differed significantly from the professional courts of Europe in another crucial factor. These courts did not simply try to apply the law as stated in a code but strove toward compromise as the preferred solution, on occasion completely ignoring the law in order to achieve what they considered to be a more socially just outcome in order to forestall an escalation to violence that was a possibility in the honor-based society of Ottoman Greece.[15] Such cases not only often involved particularly disadvantaged individuals such as widows, the elderly, or people with disabilities, but they also involved disputes between local people and outsiders where the locals were invariably favored.[16] Outsiders were, of course, doubly disadvantaged by lacking knowledge of the local customary laws as well as by discrimination in favor of local individuals.

The records from Ottoman Greece, those few that exist,[17] are too fragmentary to make precise statements about the participation of women in litigation. However, research has shown that women were active in Ottoman *kadi* courts, including Christian and Jewish women, defending their property rights, seeking divorces, defending themselves against many types of accusations, or even pursuing men in what we would call paternity suits or accusing them of defloration and even rape.[18] The same can be seen in the customary courts of Ottoman Greece, though again the records are fragmentary. Women, like men, quite frequently abused the court systems either by playing one system of law against another or by manipulating circumstances to their benefit or even the benefit of their families, often with remarkable success.[19] Far from the image that still persists among scholars,[20] women were actively involved within the judicial systems, often in litigation against their relatives, brothers, parents, and even husbands.

On the other hand, the tendency to generalize from the evidence of certain regions has to be resisted, because as I mentioned previously, customary laws and practices differed dramatically. Even in such basic concepts as the dowry, child custody, or inheritance, each region differed from the next, covering nearly the entire spectrum of possibilities. Regarding the dowry, for example, we have a region like Mani in southern Greece where some scholars have argued for the presence of bride price and the near absence of dowry,[21] while in other regions like the island of Karpathos, firstborn women could receive the bulk of the family's wealth as dowry.[22] Similarly, in some regions, widows automatically became the guardians of their underage children, while in others, a family council or the brothers of the deceased husband assumed the responsibility with or without the participation of the widow.[23]

Despite these differences, we can draw some broad conclusions regarding family law and the place of women in such matters. First of all, upon marriage women were normally supposed to be dowered by their fathers or their parents, the responsibility in some cases also falling to brothers if the father or parents were no longer living or capable of dowering the women. Dowries were inalienable, and although the husband had managed the dowry for the duration of the marriage, it had to be returned intact to the woman at the time of the marriage's dissolution. Women could, in extreme circumstances, seek to replace their husbands as managers of their dowries, but such cases were rare. In some regions of continental Greece, husbands had to provide their wives with a "premarital gift" (*progamiaia dorea*), in essence a dowry, but the practice was far from universal. Women's properties were often augmented through inheritance, which, following Canon law, was supposed to be equal among all offspring whether male or female, although in many regions, dowered daughters were excluded from inheritance.

Divorce was possible and increasingly easy during the Ottoman period, though our information about divorce primarily comes from examinations of *kadi* courts or ecclesiastical directives and proclamations by the Patriarchs of Constantinople. Although this matter was supposed to be within the responsibility of the ecclesiastical authorities, and presumably the bulk of such cases were dealt with in the ecclesiastical courts, there has been no in-depth examination of ecclesiastical records; thus, our knowledge is rudimentary. It does appear, however, that communal courts also played a role following the severing of the marital bond in settling possible financial disputes.[24] By the end of the Ottoman period, even consensual divorces had become possible.[25]

Financial disputes, divorces, and even the death of a husband often raised another issue, that of custody of children. There does not seem to have been a universally accepted outcome, especially in matters of divorce, even though fathers may have been favored; at least, that is the implication behind some women's seeking divorce through the *kadi* courts. Significantly, fathers were responsible for the support of children regardless of whether they had custody or not, although there is evidence that even that was negotiable. Fathers may have been responsible for the support of illegitimate children as well, and the inclusion of such children in last testaments may indicate certain rights of inheritance, but the issue is often obscured by the fact that women frequently went to court to pursue damages for defloration rather than support for illegitimate children even if the outcome seems to point to the latter.[26]

In cases of the death of the father, mothers almost everywhere assumed the authority of the *pater familias* to some degree, at least, and became responsible for the support, upbringing, and dowering of their children. Usually, they also assumed control of the property of their late husbands, now inherited by their children, until the maturity of their offspring, though often only for as long as they did not remarry. Furthermore, their control over that property was on occasion limited to management, and they could not sell it without the approval of a family council, although again, there was considerable regional variation.

Second marriages were far from rare and generally not seen favorably, although this was not nearly as objectionable as was often found in other parts of Europe, and in some regions those that remarried to previously unmarried individuals had to compensate them with a financial gift, called *agriliki* or *pallikariatiko* for men and "for virginity" (*gia parthenia*) for women. When the first marriages had produced children, the situation was even more complex, and frequently the family of the deceased spouse would intervene regarding the custody of such children in order to protect their inheritance rights.[27]

This was a very broad outline of the legal situation when the Greeks revolted against Ottoman rule in 1821 and were immediately confronted with the problem of creating a judicial system for their state-to-be. Europe, of course, was already seen as the "paragon of civilization," as Paschalis Kitromilidis has put it,[28] and immediately, the Greeks sought to create a state that would measure up to modern European examples.[29] The *kadi* and rabbinical courts were wiped out along with much of the Muslim and Jewish populations, but the leaders of the Greek revolt in the immediate post-revolutionary period were unsure regarding which legal system to adopt, especially with respect to civil law. They all shared a goal—to create a modern and European state, which essentially meant to imitate existing structures found in Europe and in particular, in such archetypal European states as France and Britain.[30] From the very first years of the revolt, the revolutionary authorities passed decrees regarding the establishment of a new, centralized judicial system in Greece with a new Ministry of Justice, but although lawyers did appear for the first time in modern Greek history, the reality of the conflict meant that nearly all of these courts failed to materialize and their duties were assumed by the existing communal courts.[31] Significantly, there was no real debate regarding the desirability of creating a judicial structure similar to that found in European states of the time, and the failure to develop one was more due to the circumstances of the war than any real opposition to the idea.

The same cannot be said regarding the legal codes upon which these courts were supposed to base their decisions. There was little dispute regarding the commercial code, which was in essence a translation of the French Commercial Code that was already more or less used by Greek ship-owners and merchants in the Mediterranean,[32] but the civil code was something else entirely. The early revolutionary authorities passed contradictory decrees regarding this issue; for example, the General Charter of the Peloponnese in July 1821 recognized three existing sources of law: natural law, local custom, and the *Exavivlos* of Armenopoulos, which were to be supplemented by newly enacted legislation.[33] Other regional charters recognized only the authority of the laws of the Byzantine emperors,[34] and the topic was not clarified by the ensuing constitutional assemblies. The First National Assembly in Epidaurus in 1822 determined that until new codes could be produced for civil and penal matters, the Byzantine legislation would take effect, and for commercial matters, the French code would be used, a position reiterated at the Second National Assembly in Astros in 1823. The Third National Assembly at Troezina in 1827, however, stated that the parliament that was to be elected should publish new civil, penal, and military codes based upon the French laws, though until then, Byzantine legislation would be in effect.[35] The very next year, 1828, the new Governor of Greece, Ioannis Kapodistrias, issued a decree that recognized specifically the *Exavivlos* as well as the French commercial code[36] but then proceeded to establish the equality of law and custom with complementary recourse to the French *Code civil*.[37] Thus, several conflicting positions emerged in a struggle that would last almost throughout the nineteenth century.

One of the most powerful bodies regarding law in the revolutionary period and up to the time of Kapodistrias was the Orthodox Church, and thus several bishops became ministers for religion, justice, and internal affairs in the revolutionary governments. These men quite naturally attempted to impose the formal Byzantine law that they were familiar with on the new state.[38] Starting with Kapodistrias, however, and especially after the arrival of the Bavarian Regency that included the noted legal scholar Georg Ludwig von Maurer among its members, the role of the Church in the developing judicial system was limited to matters pertaining to marriage and divorce.[39] The influence of the Church was particularly diminished following the break with the Patriarchate of Constantinople, which persisted until 1850, and the confiscation of much of the monastic property during the Bavarian Regency and early years of King Otto.

With the role of the Church curtailed, the discussion regarding legal matters in Greece became limited to the emerging legal scholars, most of whom had concluded their studies in European universities. Some of these scholars advocated the wholesale adoption of the Napoleonic Code, and this concept was even incorporated in the decrees of the National Assemblies of the revolution, as mentioned above. Unfortunately for them, the Napoleonic Code had had no impact in Greece, with the exception of the Ionian Islands, which had come under brief French and later British control (and which would not become part of the Greek state until 1863).[40] Nonetheless, proponents of this adoption seemed to be gaining ground with the establishment of the state,[41] and some of the most prestigious legal scholars were commissioned to provide a translation of the *Code civil* in 1837–1838.[42] Many of the earliest Greek jurists and most of the first professors of the newly established Law School in Athens, like Georgios Mavrokordatos, had studied in France and considered the Napoleonic legislation as the most comprehensive and modern approach in Europe, a view shared by many other European scholars, since the Napoleonic Code was introduced in a number of other states.[43]

Other legal scholars disagreed with this option because they rightfully recognized that it had no resemblance to existing practices in Greece, especially as far as family law was concerned. Many, therefore, preferred the option of trying to create a new civil code from the existing practices, recognizing that the customary laws then practiced in Greece would be recognizable and understood both by the population and those that would sit in judgment. This was not necessarily a "traditional" approach but reflected another strand of European legal thought most prominent in German-speaking areas known as the Historical School. This view held that customary law contained the spirit of the people and should, therefore, be promoted and defended.[44] Among these scholars was Maurer himself, who designed and published the final commercial and penal codes and jurisprudence, as well as the organizational law for the modern Greek judicial system.[45] The development of a civil code, however, was far more difficult since customary laws varied dramatically from region to region and creating a unified code was a Herculean task. Maurer attempted it by dispatching two questionnaires to every single community in Greece requesting details regarding the local practices, but the effort floundered after his recall.[46] In any case, the difficulty of crafting such a unified law may have been beyond the capacities of the state, as even in a more stable society such as Germany, similar efforts took decades to complete. Nevertheless, this position was solidified through a decree in 1830 that stipulated the collection of customary laws in anticipation of the development of a new civil code.[47]

The dispute between these two groups resembles a similar debate that was taking place in Germany at that time between the proponents of the *Code civil*, as exemplified by Anton Friedrich Justus Thibaut, and their rivals, such as Friedrich Carl von Savigny.[48] To complicate matters further, however, a third group of scholars advocated something quite different. Originally led by Georgios Rallis and Markos Renieris, this group included Pavlos Kalligas, possibly the most influential legal mind of nineteenth century Greece. Kalligas believed that the creation of the modern state was a great opportunity to assert the true legal character of the Greek nation, freed from the additions, corruptions, and abuses of the Ottoman and even the later Byzantine period.[49] In essence, these men advocated a return to the pure form of *Corpus Juris Civilis* with whatever modern additions and changes were deemed necessary. In their view, such an action would deliver a single comprehensive code, well within the authentic Greek heritage.[50]

Inevitably, the final outcome was a compromise. Customary practice was accepted, if the courts could confirm it. In other cases, the judges had the right to seek guidance in Byzantine legislation until such a date when the Greek state would produce a new civil code for their use. Legal scholars have claimed that this compromise undermined customary law, since most judges, especially at the Appeals and Supreme Court levels, were ignorant of customary law, having been formally trained at the new law school of the University of Athens and often concluding their studies at foreign universities, originally mostly French but increasingly German ones.[51] The most recent noted legal scholar Nikolaos Pantazopoulos has even claimed that the early scholars Rallis and Renieris, through methodical misinterpretation, undermined the idea of equality between law and custom and that Kalligas followed in their footsteps.[52] Pantazopoulos also claimed that Kalligas undermined the use of Armenopoulos' collection, specifically named as a valid source up to the period of Kapodistrias, by interpreting the 1835 decree, which had established the principle of equality between custom and law and recognized the validity of the civil laws of the Byzantine emperors, as implying the adoption of the law contained in the *Corpus Juris Civilis* rather than later collections.[53] Furthermore, by using the German collections and commentaries of *Juris Civilis*, Kalligas and his followers were not only reverting to the roots of the Greek legal tradition, as they were claiming, but they were also Europeanizing it by accepting a western European textual history of Roman Law to match the European judicial structure established by the Bavarian Regency.

I should note, however, that Kalligas and his cohort were not blindly trying to emulate Europe as the supporters of the *Code civil* were doing. Nor were they simply trying to turn back the clock through their rejection of centuries of legal development. Kalligas had no objection to innovation and progress, but he held in contempt everything that had transpired since the heyday of Byzantium while strongly supporting the European orientation of Greek law. His viewpoint regarding the 1830 testamentary law is exemplified by the claim that those who composed that law, "feeling unequal to the task of producing their own work, unfortunately did not rely on the more perfect laws of France or those of Austria, but looked to the Ionian islands adopting the practice of Venice."[54]

Furthermore, unlike similar debates in France, England, or Germany, questions of gender roles and rights never entered into these discussions in Greece. The Greek legal scholars were not unaware of the issues, as for example the nationality of a married woman,[55] questions of parental authority,[56] and so on, but such issues were tackled functionally without any references to ideological constructs or beliefs. There was no defense or condemnation of patriarchy, not even consideration of existing conditions. The discourse was supremely theoretical, abstract, and detached from any consideration of the possible effects such changes would have with regards to gender roles and rights. That is not to say that Greece as a whole did not engage in such discussions, the field of education being hotly contested—especially the education of women—[57] but in legal scholarship such arguments are surprisingly absent.

Kalligas's view has been inadvertently supported by feminist historiography that examined the early feminist movement of Greece. As Eleni Varikas showed, early Greek feminists echoed in their first journals the debates seen in much of Europe at the time regarding the lack of access to education for women, their inability to control their property in marriage, and so on.[58] This image contrasts dramatically with the situation of women in many parts of Ottoman Greece and thus lends credence to the idea that in the second half of the nineteenth century, Greek women had, in fact, lost many of the property and family rights they had enjoyed in the Ottoman period and were experiencing the same problems and difficulties as their European counterparts. Certainly by the twentieth century, women had lost the ability to protect their dowry, now seen by many as part of a common conjugal fund. Further rights were also eroded, including the right to divorce, which was severely curtailed in 1922 with a reform that abolished, among other things, consensual divorce.[59] Revealingly, the legal scholar who drafted the 1922 law on divorce also produced a paper explaining his rationale for the need for these new restrictions, claiming that his purpose was to protect women whose husbands divorced them after exhausting their dowry, leaving them without property at an advanced age. In fact, he argued that his goal was to bring equality between the sexes, since under the current system the law was favorable to men and resulted in increased divorces, especially in towns. To strengthen his argument, he explored both Byzantine regulations on divorce as well as contemporary laws in Europe, particularly those of France, Germany, and Switzerland.[60]

A reading of nineteenth century legal works by influential scholars like Paparrigopoulos or Kalligas certainly gives the impression that radical changes had taken place in the practice of law in Greece. Consciously or unconsciously reflecting French Revolutionary discourse,[61] Kalligas argued, for example, that the Orthodox Church had only assumed control over marriage at the end of the Byzantine era, especially during Ottoman times, arguing for the assertion of the role of the state with respect to marriage.[62] Kalligas saw the husband as having absolute control of the material aspects of the household as well as absolute authority regarding the upbringing and disciplining of children. He clearly stated that the mother could not limit the authority of the father and could not even appoint representatives unless she was already in possession of "paternal" authority: that is, if the husband were dead or in some legal fashion incapacitated.[63] Only in one area did Kalligas recognize the significance of the mother: "As a rule, the supervision of the upbringing of minors includes the moral upbringing and education that as a work of affection and spiritual care belongs *ex officio* to the mother."[64]

Similarly, with a nod to the *Code civil*, Kalligas tied the concept of citizenship to sex, declaring that a woman assumed the nationality of her husband, losing Greek citizenship if she married a foreigner, and was obliged to follow him to his place of residence even if that was beyond the borders of the state.[65] These ideas had been enshrined as early as 1835 and reflected concepts developed in Europe and often found in works on natural law in the first half of the nineteenth century.[66]

Paparrigopoulos, in his turn, claimed that a poor or undowered widow could lay claim to a share of her husband's property, clearly contradicting earlier practices that did not allow one spouse to inherit the other's property, a stipulation that was not necessarily extended to widowers, who are not mentioned.[67] Kalligas further noted that illegitimate children had neither support nor the right to inheritance from their father, leaving the mother solely responsible for their needs, a position that was eventually supported by the courts and fully in accordance with the stipulations of the *Code civil*.[68] Finally, Kalligas continued the attack on customary laws, targeting their malleability and the fact that courts had to prove the existence of a custom before passing judgment. For Kalligas that indicated the inferiority of customary laws to published laws that, according to him, became widely disseminated through publication and thus removed confusion and uncertainty.[69] This last argument, as well as his insistence that ignorance of law was unacceptable, is particularly revealing because it shows that Kalligas had a very limited segment of the Greek population as active participants in the judicial system in mind, since in Greece at the time nearly all women and most men were illiterate.[70]

This picture, however, reflects neither the impressions of contemporary foreign travelers to Greece nor the evidence from the courts. The German criminalist Gustav Geib commented on the absence of the concept of common conjugal property, while Arthur de Gobineau, the infamous author of the *Inequality of Human Races* and representative of a powerful anti-modern current in Europe, who served as ambassador in Greece between 1864 and 1868, favorably commented on the customary practices of Greece and found their compulsion to legislate and copy western laws unfortunate.[71] The French novelist Edmond About found the relative absence of prejudice regarding illegitimacy as well as the ease of dissolving marriages, especially among the lower classes, refreshing and admirable.[72] There were, of course, negative images as well: Geib noted the "widespread" use of practices such as abortion, infanticide, and pederasty in Greece, while About lamented the absence of the rule of law in the country.[73]

The structure of the new judicial system certainly worked to physically exclude women from its midst. The hierarchical nature of the system, from the justices of the peace to the Courts of First Instance to the Appeals Courts and finally to the Supreme Court, extended the temporal duration of a dispute and required travel to the various locations of the courts. In a country rife with banditry and with few roads, such travel was particularly prohibitive for women, who had to safeguard their moral standing in an honor-based society such as Greece. Thus, women frequently assigned men to represent their interests in court, unlike the practice in the Ottoman period when women vigorously defended their rights in person, as I have argued elsewhere.[74] The cost of a legal dispute also rose steeply, not only due to the repeated trials but also due to new costs, such as the need for a lawyer mandated by law. This was necessary because of the new language and procedural requirements of a modern case. At a time when the monthly salary of a teacher was a mere 50 *drachmas*, court expenses awarded were significantly higher.[75] Even so, the costs of travel and accommodation necessary for an individual to be present at every stage of the trial, coupled by the social constraints placed upon women, contributed to the rare personal appearance of women in their court cases.

Furthermore, the population shifts and urbanization of society in the nineteenth century[76] removed women from their familiar framework of customary law, often taking them to areas where they were not knowledgeable about the local customs. To make matters worse, women were less likely to know their rights, since changes in new legislation were disseminated in print, just as Kalligas wanted, and women, despite the pledges of the new state, increasingly lagged behind men in terms of literacy and education. In 1834, approximately 10% of all students were female, and even a generation later girls composed only 20–22% of students at the primary level. While in 1837, women and men were almost universally illiterate (91% of men and nearly all women), fifty years later, the rate of illiteracy had dropped for men to 69%, but was still 90% for women.[77] Such findings are confirmed by contemporary observers, who noted the discrepancy between the numbers of boys and girls attending school.[78] Part of the reason was the different function of education for each sex, which was meant to provide employment opportunities for boys and good housewife skills for girls, as the different subjects of study also indicate.[79] Ironically, as early as the period of the Greek War of Independence, the Greek state assumed the burden of providing primary education to both boys and girls, an obligation that became law (making primary education for both boys and girls mandatory) in the modern Greek state. However, financial restraints would not allow the state to meet that pledge, and women's education suffered the most neglect. Urbanization also led to the increasing monetization of the dowry, since ancestral fields were of little value to people in far-away cities. Furthermore, the imposition of a stamp duty on notarized dowries may have driven poorer families to compose oral dowry contracts that were not defensible in court, since an 1836 law recognized only dowry contracts drafted by a public notary.[80]

Thus, although the early modern Greek governments attempted to create a modern and European judicial structure modeled after existing European systems while retaining the regional customary legal practices as far as civil and family law is concerned, the effect seems to be the undermining of the traditional rights of women. These new circumstances reduced Greek wives to the position that married women found themselves in throughout much of western Europe: unable to control their wealth, gain access to education, or be employed in most professions. While such demands gave rise to the first wave of feminism in most of Europe, this was not the case in Greece, as the small number of female feminists and their rather conservative demands indicate. Moreover, early Greek feminists did not frame their critiques in terms of denunciations of the existing legal structures but offered them as social critique, often within the dominant paradigm of Greek nationalism.[81] However, most of this discussion relies on secondary sources rather than evidence from the courts themselves, and it is to that evidence that I will now turn my attention.

From 27 January 1860 to 9 October 1860, the Appeals Court of Athens heard 652 civil cases and petitions. Of those, 275, or 42%, involved women.[82] As can be expected, the vast majority of these cases involved property disputes, but several also dealt with issues of fraud, divorce, marital difficulties, and even marital violence. The significant presence of women indicates that a generation after the establishment of the modern Greek State, women were present in the judicial system and were still actively defending their rights, if not necessarily in person. There were, however, some interesting differences as well as similarities from the earlier period.

First of all, despite the efforts of the learned jurists I mentioned before, custom continued to play a significant role in 1860, as many decisions specifically mentioned the validity of local customs. Repeatedly, the courts refer to customary practices of inheritance, dowries, and so on.[83] Even when a custom was in apparent conflict with the established law, the court did not dismiss it but demanded further investigation regarding the validity of said custom.[84] At the same time, the court did not simply accept any claim of custom, and in some cases rejected the use of existing customs. One example of this could be if the custom in question was from regions outside the Greek state even though the case involved Greek citizens.[85] In another example, the court refused the validity of a custom entirely. In that case, an argument was presented by the relatives of two women that had converted to Christianity regarding the custom that Muslim converts to Christianity lost their rights to inheritance, but there, the court decided that according to the law, a custom had to be proven to be of long duration and without interruption (*polychronon kai adiakopon*), whereas conversion to Christianity from Islam was only possible since the Greek revolt of 1821. Instead of custom, the court decided to apply "Byzantine" laws in this case.[86]

Frequently, the court postponed discussions of the case until the existence of a custom could be investigated,[87] and they often reverted to the use of Byzantine-Roman law when custom was absent or impossible to determine.[88] What is more interesting are the references to the *Code civil* found among the decisions of the court, which in theory should not have had validity in Greece.[89] In one case, the matter involved two Catholic subjects of Greece from the island of Syros where the Court of First Instance refused to use local customs because the deceased husband was a French citizen, though a resident on the island. The appeal was on the basis of common conjugal property, absent in Greek law, but the argument was that since the husband was a French citizen so was the wife, and thus, the *Code civil* was the appropriate law. The case ended up in the Supreme Court of Greece, which overturned all previous decisions, sending the case back to the Appeals Court with a demand to examine if there was a custom among the Catholic population of Syros regarding common conjugal property.[90] The *Code civil* is referenced in other cases as well. The first had been initiated at the Greek consulate of Constantinople (Istanbul), though the decision did not turn on it.[91] A second case was that of a French Philhellene who had stayed in Greece after the Greek War of Independence, becoming a Greek citizen and serving as a doctor first in the Greek army and then in the Greek navy. The Court of First Instance apparently based its decision on the Napoleonic Code and rejected the pension claims of his widow against the state, but the Appeals Court reversed the decision.[92] What these cases indicate is that the judges of the Appeals Court were quite aware of the stipulations of the *Code civil* and the limitations it imposed on women with regards to property. They were also willing to accept the possibility of implementing those provisions in Greece but only within the context of the *Code civil* being applied as the customary law of a minority, as the Catholic population of some islands were perceived, or to foreign nationals. In both the examples above, the courts, after some initial confusion, rejected the disadvantages the *Code civil* would have imposed on the women in question, thus affirming their rights to property and pension.

Many of these cases regarded disputes dealing with women's dowries, as had been the case in the pre-independence period. However, almost fifty women with disputes arising from the latter's inheritance of their fathers' properties appeared before the court in their capacity as natural guardians or custodians of their underage children, and another four were present as court-appointed guardians.[93] The almost non-existent presence of family councils in the record[94] seems to indicate that mothers had gained the undisputed right to act as guardians for their underage children, a right also recognized and supported by contemporary legal authorities,[95] who saw a significant role for the mother in the upbringing of children, even if in the duration of the marriage that role had mere moral and no legal validity.[96]

In cases of dowry and inheritance, it seems clear that the law of the land was customary law, including such stipulations as the right of a husband to use dowered properties as collateral[97] or the exclusion of a dowered individual from inheritance.[98] The significance attached to custom is best exemplified in a case where a woman argued that her brother had received a dowry and should thus be excluded from the inheritance. This "dowering" of sons at the time of their marriage was a custom in many Greek islands during the Ottoman period, even though their dowries did not have the same legal protections as a woman's dowry. Furthermore, the concept of a male dowry is absent in Roman law, whether Byzantine or otherwise, but in this case, the Appeals Court found in favor of the woman, reversing an earlier decision by a lower court, again signifying the importance assigned to customary law.[99]

Divorces and annulments, as was the case in Ottoman times, were still a matter for the Church to deal with, due to the religious character of the topic; however, on occasion, and in extraordinary circumstances, they did appear in front of the Appeals Court. In such cases, custom played no role, but it is interesting to see the use of Armenopoulos's *Exavivlos* side by side with *Corpus Juris Civilis* in the decisions of the court, despite the condemnations of the former by Kalligas and other leading scholars of the time.[100] More interestingly, these extraordinary divorces were fairly well balanced, with five women seeking to divorce their husbands and five men seeking to divorce their wives. Four women and one of the men stated that their lives had been endangered by their spouses, a valid cause for divorce under Byzantine law, but the women also added the lack of material support by their husbands. All the men, on the other hand, accused their wives of infidelity or of leading a dissolute life by "going out to theaters and entertainments," with three of the men[101] adding that their wives had left the marital home and were living with other men. The court granted three of the divorces initiated by the men and found in favor of three of the women, though it did not issue divorces but rather sent the cases back to the Courts of First Instance to examine witnesses. The court rejected two of the cases brought by the men, on one occasion because the husband who was accusing the wife of having left the marital home had, in fact, abandoned the home himself, and his wife had sought employment at the home of the British ambassador.[102] In the final case, the court accepted the separation of the spouses but did not deem the causes serious enough to merit a divorce.[103] Interestingly, even in the cases where the court found in favor of the men seeking a divorce, it split the court expenses between both litigants in all cases but one, which, judging by the names of the litigants, probably involved foreign-born individuals.[104] These cases are not indicative of the frequency of divorce in Greece, since most cases would have been handled by the Ecclesiastical authorities and not the judicial system, but they do show that unlike most European states of the time, Greek women as well as men could initiate divorces and were willing to exercise this right. Though we cannot talk of equality since the causes for divorce clearly favored men, the courts certainly recognized women as independent legal persons separate from their husbands.

The case of Zoi Mourouzi is particularly interesting because she not only sued her husband in order to get a divorce but also in order to force him to provide her with compensation. Apparently the husband, Ioannis Vasileiadis, was called to military service and left his wife with her parents without providing her with financial support and simply instructed her to get money from the various individuals who were in debt to him. Upon his return, however, he sued her and her parents and refused to join her in the marital home. Zoi had won all of her points at the Court of First Instance, but the Appeals Court wanted further proof that she was indeed without income.[105] This and all the divorce cases seen at the court do not rely on customary law, of course, but rather on Canonical and Byzantine legislation as they, on occasion, state directly. The involvement of the courts in matters of marriage, however, is a new phenomenon since until then such matters were left to the Church.

There are other new elements in the cases seen at the Appeals Court, especially involving new legislation. For instance, in the trial between the village of Plessa in Doris versus the State regarding the traditional rights of pasture in communal lands as recognized by Ottoman stipulations, the State was able to prove that Ottoman laws as well as traditional rights no longer applied as a result of legislation enacted in 1833–1834, transforming all communal lands to state lands. Even in this case, however, we can see the enduring power of traditional rights, since among the village signatures that brought the case to the courts, we find eight widows acting as heads of households as both tradition and the new laws gave them the right to do.[106] Women were also able to use the court to make claims that were previously difficult, if not impossible, for example, requesting a portion of the deceased husband's wealth in cases of extreme poverty.[107] Significantly, the widow in my example did not base her request on custom but simply stated that she was legally entitled to receive two-fifths of her husband's property.

A similar case involved a dispute between the widow Maria and the two men acting as guardians for her three children with the deceased Andreas Koromilas, with one of the guardians being Pavlos Kalligas, the prominent legal scholar I discussed above. According to the law as stated in the decision, since the husband died without a will, his widow was entitled to a quarter of his property, and the earlier decisions had been in her favor. The guardians of her children, however, claimed that she had received a dowry, and in any case, they wanted her barred from entering a second marriage according to a "long and continuous" custom in Athens. The court did not make a decision but gave both parties a two-month period to try to prove whether Maria was in fact poor.[108]

An interesting case of women utilizing the opportunities presented by the new courts is the case of Aikaterini, widow of Lambros Dagklis, who demanded 25,500 *drachmas* from Kosta Kedro: 15,000 as compensation for the murder of her husband and the rest as money stolen.[109] Such a case is not outside of the realm of customary law, and in fact, we have examples of similar cases from the Ottoman and Revolutionary periods.[110] What is interesting about this case is the fact that Kedros had stood trial in a penal court and been found innocent, but the widow used the opportunities presented in the new system to pursue a civil suit against him. In other cases, a woman took a man who had been convicted for rape but pardoned by the king to civil court,[111] while a court-appointed guardian sued a man for seducing his ward and infecting her with venereal diseases, demanding that he would either marry her or compensate her with 5,000 *drachmas*.[112] Clearly, women and their guardians were not reluctant to use the civil courts even for what were technically penal matters if they felt that the penal courts had not resolved the case to their satisfaction.

It bears pointing out, however, that almost no woman was physically present in the courtroom at the time of the hearings. Instead, lawyers and other men, usually family members, represented women, a finding in accordance with my earlier findings from the town of Leonidio for the period 1830–1850.[113] Men also used lawyers but rarely delegated their authority, giving power of attorney to third individuals the way women did. Thus, although the court system was clearly used by women, it was done by proxy, and women were usually physically absent from the deliberations. This reluctance to present themselves in court fits with the emerging ideas regarding the roles of women as well as the custom in some towns, including Athens, that limited the presence of women in the public space, including such areas as the marketplace.

An interesting point regards whether the court used contemporary ideas about gender in their decision-making or if we can glean such ideas in the language and decisions of the court. The evidence on this point is far from clear. There is no specific mention in these cases about gender roles or ideas about gender, and invariably, the passages that state the court's decisions were succinct to the point of being laconic. Of course, ideas regarding gender permeated the courts through the beliefs and convictions of the judges, but rarely do we catch glimpses of such beliefs. The most obvious one is the apparent acceptance that the husband is responsible for the material support of his wife and the belief that women in general were presumed not capable of supporting themselves.[114] This is primarily seen in the handful of divorce cases as well as in the court's treatment of widows, who are seen as being in a disadvantaged position, economically as well as socially, and thus in need of state assistance. However, in extraordinary circumstances, such as the divorce case I mentioned above, the court was not critical of married women who sought to support themselves when abandoned by their husbands but rather was understanding of their need. Women also seem closely associated with the concept of motherhood in the eyes of the court, at least in the sense that the concept was raised repeatedly by the court as well as women themselves who found it useful in advancing their cases, especially where children were concerned.

There is, however, a disconnect between the court record described above and the rhetoric of late nineteenth century middle- and upper-class Greek feminists like Kalliroe Parren, who, among others, demanded the right of women to manage their property and have custody of their children in the event of either divorce through the fault of the husband or widowhood.[115] These demands seem out of place when the courts appear to actually be enforcing them. Furthermore, we should not consider unwritten customary law to be open to arbitrary decisions by judges. Clearly the courts took great effort to determine the local practice and to base their decisions upon it, a process reinforced and supervised by the Appeals court and the Supreme Court, as the examples mentioned thus far illustrate. More and deeper research is needed here, but a possible explanation could lie in the divergent experiences of middle- and lower-class women. With the exception of a handful of women, nearly all women in the court record were described as "*penites*" (paupers). Though hardly surprising considering the economic conditions of Greece and the widespread poverty of Greeks at the time, the near complete absence of middle-class women,[116] or at least of women not referred to as poor, is interesting because one tends to assume that wealthier individuals would make more frequent use of the courts due to their higher standards of education, not to mention wealth, as is often seen in other states.[117] Although the definition of "pauper" is not provided in the record, its overwhelming use may be indicative of different social practices among lower- and middle-class women in nineteenth century Greece.

The apparent absence of middle- and upper-class women from the courts may imply the earlier penetration of new ideas regarding gender roles from Europe among those classes that were more exposed to them through their education and social circumstances, a fact noted by some contemporary foreign observers.[118] Unlike the great majority of Greek women, middle- and upper-class girls had access to education, and by 1860, there were several schools, including the famous *Arsakeio*, catering to their needs, some run by foreign missionaries while others were set up by wealthy benefactors to train young girls to become good wives and mothers.[119] These schools looked to western Europe for inspiration in their curricula and eagerly embraced contemporary ideas regarding domesticity and the glorification of motherhood, sprinkled with a strong dose of nationalism.[120]

The surprising absence of middle-class women from the courts could, therefore, reflect the penetration of European ideas regarding domesticity and new concepts regarding gender roles. These merged with local concepts regarding female modesty and propriety, perhaps reinforced by the formation of an Orthodox Christian awakening movement in the last quarter of the nineteenth century, to severely curtail the public role, in fact the public presence, of women in Greece.[121] Education was the obvious area where this merging could take place, and thus, female education became a battleground in nineteenth century Greece, especially after the 1860s.[122] Feminism in particular attracted much condemnation and was attacked as a foreign import.[123] For the critics of emancipation, and modernity as a whole for that matter, the West was "a stronghold of degeneration, corruption and the flowering of all sorts of materialist theories capable of polluting Hellenism, imposing on it models of social organization that were opposed to both the natural and the divine order of things."[124] These ideas, though challenged at the time, in part by stressing the idea of patriotic motherhood,[125] became fused with concepts of domesticity to mandate the exclusion of women from the public and their isolation within the private sphere. Modern anthropologists working in the 1960s and 1970s noted the strong association of men with the public and women with the private realm, where women could in fact hold a position of real power,[126] and the suspicion toward women who ventured into the public sphere, a suspicion that had strong sexual and moral overtones.[127]

This idea that women should be limited to the private realm was also reflected in the writings of the legal scholars of the time like Kalligas. His writings certainly assumed that women would be limited to the domestic sphere. This idea, among others, is reflected in his opinions regarding citizenship that I mentioned above.[128] As a strong advocate for the "purification" of Greek law from the influences of the Ottoman and even later Byzantine periods, Kalligas's push for a return to the more pure forms of Byzantine-Roman law, coupled with his undoubted prestige and influence, has convinced many modern scholars that customary law was quickly eliminated from the Greek courts, which increasingly accepted Roman law as the law of the land. Perhaps many among the emerging middle class in Greece already shared such views, but it was far from universal. The evidence from the courts shows the continuation of the use of customary law with only a handful of allusions to Roman law and most of those referring to later Byzantine law rather than the *Corpus Juris Civilis* that Kalligas favored.

In all of these matters, the influence of contemporary European ideas, such as common conjugal property, was evident and already making timid appearances in the records of the Appeals Court of Athens.[129] Between 1860 and the first decades of the twentieth century, the ideas advocated by Kalligas, Paparrigopoulos, and others who wanted a return to more "classical" Roman-Byzantine law had influenced Greek law and transformed the practices of the courts. However, for the first decades of the Greek judicial system and despite the pressure of the academic legal scholars, the Greek courts managed to maintain the flexibility that had been the hallmark of the Ottoman-era courts and continued to apply primarily customary law in civil disputes. Women's concerns continued to have a significant presence (at least by proxy) in the courts, since nearly half the cases at the Appeals Court involved women, and in most respects, the law defended their rights. In fact, changes in society may have preceded legal ones, as the possible absence of middle-class women may indicate. Bourgeois women would have been exposed to the new concepts regarding gender roles, duties, and rights, the whole cult of domesticity so prominent in nineteenth century Europe, and thus their absence from the courts may be due to social pressure or shared beliefs.[130]

The contrast with contemporary Europe can, therefore, be striking. At the time when poor Greek women were still defending their rights in courts and middle-class women were retreating to their domestic environment, European middle-class women were beginning to bemoan the lack of separate properties in marriage and their husbands control over their own wealth.[131] The campaign for marriage law reform, which was initiated in England in the 1830s by Caroline Norton regarding property as well as child custody laws, did not see fruition until the end of the century in Europe, though admittedly as early as 1854 in the United States.[132] The Greek Revolution ultimately did not challenge the existing legal system unlike the French Revolution, which deliberately challenged the patriarchy of the *ancien regime.* In France, early revolutionary legislation legalized divorce and reduced the power of the father in matters of marriage and inheritance only to see reversals in a conservative backlash, first under Napoleon and then with the Bourbon Restoration that once more outlawed divorce and reestablished much of the power of the father and husband over their families.[133] In contrast, in the mid-nineteenth century, the Greek courts, despite their claims and the rhetoric of nearly all contemporary legal scholars, followed neither tradition nor blind emulation of European developments but were attempting a novel approach of marrying modern structures with traditional and familiar systems, a process that allowed the bulk of the population to accept and to use the new courts as eagerly as they had done in Ottoman times. The mere fact that the Appeals Court of Athens, one of two such courts, had a caseload of over 650 cases in under eight months in a country with one million inhabitants, indicates both the litigiousness of Greeks in the nineteenth century and their acceptance of the new courts.

Life, however, was not as optimistic for women in Greece, nor did the courts simply continue the practices of the Ottoman period. As Efi Avdela has argued, the importance of kinship in almost every aspect of Greek society at the time led to "legal prescriptions in respect to the rights and duties of different family members toward one another and to the community at large," leading to the exclusion of women as a "natural consequence of their subordinated position in the family."[134] However, as she also makes clear, before the civil code of 1946 there was considerable legal ambiguity, leaving the legal position of wives in the family undefined and thus allowing the courts great flexibility. This ambiguity allowed women to exercise some agency, as we clearly saw in the above court examples.

Perhaps it is for this reason that the first feminist stirrings in Greece came so late and did not target the judicial system but focused almost exclusively on matters of education and employment. Greek women did not have a *Code civil* or a dower act to galvanize them in opposition. The target of the early feminists and their publications, starting with the journal *Thaleia* in 1867, was the societal model that limited their education and constrained them within the home.[135] Unsurprisingly, many of the early Greek feminists were school teachers, one of the very few professions available to women, but it should be noted that nearly all feminists of the time fully embraced the nationalist aspirations of the Greek state, and many women went to teach and to promote the Greek nationalist cause in areas still occupied by the Ottoman Empire, especially Macedonia.[136] The most influential of feminist publications, the *Efimeris ton Kyrion*, deliberately embraced the concept of patriotic motherhood, though some feminists had an ambivalent vision of motherhood, as has been noted by other scholars.[137] Furthermore, although the involvement of women in the disastrous Greek-Ottoman War of 1897 galvanized hundreds of middle- and upper-class women to offer their services in the war effort, which proved crucial for broadening their networks to foster the development of a women's movement,[138] the early twentieth century wars and conflicts (Balkan Wars of 1912–13, World War I, and Asia Minor War of 1920–1922) in essence suffocated the feminist movement of Greece, which would only reemerge as a significant force in the 1970s.[139] There were, of course, some feminist organizations in the interwar period that continued to raise questions regarding female employment in general and increasingly in state employment in particular, and some raised demands for changes in family law with particular focus on the rights of unmarried mothers.[140] However, the early vigor, which was not that powerful to begin with, had been spent. In fact, the demands of the Greek feminists changed significantly in the twentieth century, even though the legal framework remained more or less the same, as Avdela has shown, with the focus shifting to demands for equality regarding divorce, abolition of state regulated prostitution, and so on.[141] The principle of equality was only included in the Greek Constitution in 1975, two decades after women gained the right to vote, while the 1946 Civil Code was reformed in 1982 with a new Family Law enacted by the first Greek socialist government.[142] Ironically, much of the post-World War II reforms were spurred by external factors; for example, the ratification of the UN Convention for Human Rights by Greece in 1952, which led to the easing of restrictions on female employment and eventually to the granting of the right to vote[143] and the ascension of Greece to the European Economic Community in 1981.

In conclusion, the Greek courts of the nineteenth century appear remarkably pragmatic, and despite the urgings of nearly all legal scholars of the time, they maintained a reasonable attitude toward customary law that allowed both women and men to make widespread use of the judicial system despite the inherent hostility such modern hierarchical structures presented to women. This emulation of the structures of the modern European judicial systems while maintaining the traditional practices of customary law made the Greek courts of the nineteenth century fairly open and approachable for the population at large and in particular for lower-class women and men who often found themselves excluded elsewhere. Nevertheless, the twentieth century saw the triumph of legal scholars who eventually produced new codes to supplant the unwritten customary ones, severely curtailing the flexibility of the courts. Ironically, this emulation of the West came at the time when those original or model Western codes were being rewritten to allow women more rights and greater access to the judicial system across Europe. Greece would eventually emulate these changes itself but with a considerable time lag and often under political pressure from its ascension to various international bodies and organizations. It is still a question for further investigation, however, if this legislative history represents the reality found in the courts themselves, and if the nineteenth century is an indication, the legal framework and its ideological imperatives in modern Greece do not always reflect the legal experience of the population.

Notes

1 See, for example, Alexandra Bakalaki, "Gender-Related Discourses and Representations of Cultural Specificity in Nineteenth-Century and Twentieth-Century Greece," *Journal of Modern Greek Studies* 12, no. 1 (1994): 75–106; Marie Elizabeth Handman, "Astikos Kodikas kai Ethimiko Dikaio," in *Oikogeneia kai Periousia stin Ellada kai tin Kypro*, ed. Colette Piault (Athens: Vivliopoleioo tis Estias, 1994), 239–252; Roula Kaklamanaki, *I Thesi tis Gynaikas stin Oikogeneia, stin Koinonia, stin Politeia* (Athens: Paideia, 1979); Nota Kyriazis, "Feminism and the State of Women in Greece," in *Greece Prepares for the Twenty*

First Century, ed. Dimitris Constas and Theofanis G. Stavrou (Baltimore: Woodrow Wilson Center Press, John Hopkins University Press, 1995), 267–301; Jane Lambiri-Dimaki, "Dowry in Modern Greece: An Institution at the Crossroads between Persistence and Decline," in *The Marriage Bargain*, ed. Marion A. Kaplan (New York: Harrington Park Press, 1985), 165–178; Dimitra Samiou, "To Feministiko Kinima stin Ellada (1860–1960)," in *I Ellada ton Gynaikon*, ed. Eytychia Leontidou and Sigrid R. Ammer (Athens: Enallaktikes Ekdoseis/Gaia, 1992), 57–63; Eleni Varikas, "National and Gender Identities in Turn of the Century Greece," in *Women's Emancipation Movements in the 19th Century*, ed. Sylvia Paletschek and Bianka Pietrow-Ennker (Stanford, CA: Stanford University Press, 2004), 263–279; Margaret Poulos, "The Burden of History," *Aspasia* 1 (2007): 176–196; Efi Avdela and Angelika Psarra, "Engendering 'Greekness': Women's Emancipation and Irredentist Politics in Nineteenth-Century Greece," *Mediterranean Historical Review* 20, no. 1 (2005): 67–79; Efi Avdela, "Between Duties and Rights," in *Citizenship and the Nation-State in Greece and Turkey*, ed. Thalia Dragonas and Faruk Birtek (New York: Routledge, 2009), 117–143; Angelika Psarra, "A Gift from the New World: Greek Feminists between East and West," in *Ways to Modernity in Greece and Turkey*, ed. Anna Frangoudaki and Caglar Keyder (New York: I.B Tauris 2007), 150–175.

2 Rossitsa Gradeva, "Orthodox Christians in the Kadi Courts: The Practice of the Sofia Sheriat Court," *Seventeenth Century Islamic Law and Society* 4, no. 1 (1997): 41.

3 Ibid., 55.

4 Ronald C. Jennings, "Divorce in the Ottoman Sharia Court of Cyprus, 1580–1640," *Studia Islamica* 78 (1993): 160; Ronald C. Jennings, "Zimmis (Non-Muslims) in Early 17th Century Ottoman Judicial Records: The Sharia Court of Anatolian Kayseri," *Journal of Economic and Social History of the Orient* 21, no. 3 (1978): 275.

5 Gradeva, "Orthodox Christians in the Kadi Courts," 58.

6 Dimitrios S. Ginis, *Oi logoi Diazygiou epi Tourkokratias* (Thessaloniki: Aristoteleio Panepistimio Thessalonikis, 1960), 242, 256; Eleftheria Sp. Papagianni, *I nomologia ton Ekklisiastikon Dikastirion tis Byzantinis kai metabyzantinis periodou se themata perousiakou Dikaiou* (Athens: Ant. N. Sakkoula, 1997), 120.

7 Nikolaos I Pantazopoulos, *Apo tis "Logias" Paradoseos eis ton Astikon Kodika* (Thessaloniki: Aristoteleio Panepistimio Thessalonikis, 1965), 105–107; Eleni Koukkou, *Oi Koinotikoi Thesmoi Stis Kyklades Kata tin Tourkokratia* (Athens: Istoriki kai Ethnologiki Etaireia tis Ellados, 1980), 168; Gradeva, "Orthodox Christians in the Kadi Courts," 57; Menelaos Tourtoglou and Lydia Paparriga-Artemiadi, *I Symvoli ton Dragoumanon tou Stolou stin Proagogi tis Dikaiosynis ton Nision tou Aigaiou* (Athens: Akadimia Athinon, 2002), 10, 98–100.

8 See among many General State Archives, Naxos Notarial Archive (GAK Naxos) F98/5, July 27, 1805; GAK Naxos F98/15, October 22, 1805; GAK Naxos F98/66, September 9, 1815; see also Themistoklis N. Filadelfeos, *Istoria ton Athinon* (Athens: Notis Karavias, 1902), 253.

9 The *Kapudan* Pasha, the Ottoman admiral, had extensive authority over the Aegean islands, including the right to hear complaints by the population, but he usually delegated that right to his invariable Christian and usually Greek *dragoman* or translator.

10 Nikolaos I Pantazopoulos, "To Dikaion tis Tourkokratias," *Epistimoniki Epetiris Scholis Nomikon kai Oikonomikon Epistimon* 9 (1975): 872; Manouil Io Gedeon, *Vracheia Simeiosis peri ton Ekklisiastikon imon Dikaion* (Constantinople: Patriarchiko Typografeio 1909), 132–133.

11 Ruth Juliana Macrides, "Nomos and Kanon on Paper and in Court," in *Kinship and Justice in Byzantium 11th–15th Centuries*, ed. Ruth Juliana Macrides (Brookfield: Ashgate, 1999), VI, 64–67.

12 Nikolaos J. Pantazopoulos, *Church and Law in the Balkan Peninsula during the Ottoman Rule* (Thessaloniki: Institute for Balkan Studies, 1967), 45.
13 Koukkou, *Oi Koinotikoi Thesmoi stis Kyklades*, 25–53, 89.
14 One could consider as an appeal the ability of individuals to seek justice with Ottoman officials, such as the various Pashas or even the Sultan himself, but such actions were rare and strongly resisted by the notables of each region who considered them as challenges to their own authority. Also, in some respects, the appeal to *kadi* courts after a case had been judged by ecclesiastical courts can be seen as a process of appeal (Gradeva, "Orthodox Christians in the Kadi Courts," 59).
15 Evdoxios Doxiadis, "Property and Morality: Women in the Communal Courts of Late Ottoman Greece," *Byzantine and Modern Greek Studies* 34, no. 1 (2010): 69.
16 Evdoxios Doxiadis, *The Shackles of Modernity, Women, Property, and the Transition from the Ottoman Empire to the Greek State* (Cambridge: Department of Classics, Harvard University, 2011), 199–200.
17 In addition to the loss of records due to wars and other disasters, most of Ottoman Greece, with the exception of the islands and the city of Athens, did not have a notarial culture, so few records outside the Ottoman *kadi* courts survive (Iakovos T. Visvizis, *I Politiki Dikaiosyni kata tin Ellinikin Epanastasin mechri tou Kapodistriou* [Athens: Aristom. G. Papanikolaou, 1941], 194).
18 Sophia Laiou, "Christian Women in an Ottoman World: Interpersonal and Family Cases Brought Before the Shari'a Courts During the Seventeenth and Eighteenth Centuries," in *Women in the Ottoman Balkans*, ed. Amila Buturovic and Irvin Cemil Schick (New York: I.B. Tauris, 2007), 243; Gradeva, "Orthodox Christiansen the Kadi Courts," 55–56; Jennings, "Zimmis (Non-Muslims)," 251, 275; Marc Baer, "Islamic Conversion Narratives of Women: Social Change and Gendered Religious Hierarchy in Early Modern Ottoman Istanbul," *Gender & History* 16, no. 2 (2004): 426.
19 See Evdoxios Doxiadis, "Legal Trickery: Men, Women, and Justice in Late Ottoman Greece," *Past and Present* 210 (2011): 129–153; Doxiadis, "Property and Morality," 61–80.
20 See, among others, Helen Angelomatis-Tsougarakis, "Women in the Greek War of Independence," in *Networks of Power in Modern Greece*, ed. Mark Mazower (New York: Columbia University Press, 2008), 47–48; Efi Avdela, "Gender and Citizenship in Greece 1864–1952," in *Citizenship and the Nation-State in Greece and Turkey*, ed. Faruk Birtek and Thalia Dragonas (New York: Routledge, 2005), 120.
21 See Eleftherios P. Alexakis, "Ta Geni kai I Oikogeneia stin Paradosiaki Koinonia tis Manis," PhD diss., University of Athens, 1980.
22 Giorgos Michailidis-Nouaros, "Paratiriseis sto Klironomiko Ethimo tis Karpathou," *Etaireia Karpathiakon Meleton* 3 (1984): 11.
23 Papagianni, *I nomologia ton Ekklisiastikon Dikastirion*, 140, 142; Georgios Men. Valassis, "Tina peri Patrikis Exousias kata to Dikaion tou Meta tin Alosin Ellinismou," in *Themata Genikis Theorias kai Philosophias tou Dikaiou*, ed. S. I. Stavropoulos (Athens: 1970), 532–548.
24 General State Archives, Mykonos Notarial Archive (GAK Mykonos), F18/058, April 18, 1754.
25 Ginis, *Oi Logoi Diazygiou*, 255.
26 Menelaos A. Tourtoglou, *Parthenofthoria kai Evresis Thisavrou, Byzantio, Tourkokratia, Metepanastatikoi Chronoi Mechri tou Kapodistriou* (Athens: Athenai, 1963), 97–98.
27 See Panagiotis I. Zepos, "Pallikariatikon I Agriliki," *Peloponnisiaka* 5 (1962): 322–347.
28 Paschalis M. Kitromilides, "Europe and the Dilemmas of Greek Conscience," in *Greece and Europe in the Modern Period: Aspects of a Troubled Relationship*, ed. Philip Carabott (London: Centre for Hellenic Studies King's College, 1995), 3.

29 Georgios Varouxakis, "The Idea of Europe in Nineteenth Century Greek Political Thought," in *Greece and Europe*, 19.
30 John Anthony Petropoulos, *Politics and Statecraft in the Kingdom of Greece 1833–1843* (Princeton, NJ: Princeton University Press, 1968), 61.
31 Iakovos Visvizis, *I Politiki Dikaiosyni*, 20, 26, 30.
32 Nikolaos I Pantazopoulos, *Apo tis "Logias" Paradoseos*, 157–159, Nikolaos S. Papantoniou, *To Idiotiko Dikaio ton Ellinon kata tin Epanastasi tou 1821* (Thessaloniki: Aristoteleio Panepistimio Thessalonikis, 1977), 19.
33 Pantazopoulos, *Apo tis "Logias" Paradoseos*, 130–131.
34 Ibid., 132, 136.
35 Alexandrtos Svolos, *Ta Ellinika Syntagmata 1822–1875/1986* (Athens: Stochastis, 1998), 119, 131, 145, 149.
36 Pantazopoulos, *Apo tis "Logias" Paradoseos*, 160.
37 Nikolaos I Pantazopoulos, "I Entaxi tis Elladas stin Evropaiki Koinotita, i Symvoli tis Antivasileias kai tou Othona (1833–1843)," in *I Krisi ton Thesmon tou Kratous*, ed. Petros I Pararas and Faidonos Th. Vegleris (Athens: Ant. N. Sakkoulas, 1988), 572.
38 Pantazopoulos, *Apo tis "Logias" Paradoseos*, 121, 123.
39 Visvizi, *I Politiki Dikaiosyni*, 13; Pantazopoulos, "I Entaxi tis Ellados," 563–565.
40 Zelio Lada-Varvaresou, *I Thesis tis Gynaikos kata ton Ionion Politikon Kodika* (Athens: N.P., 1973), 6.
41 Pantazopoulos, *Apo tis "Logias" Paradoseos*, 236.
42 Pantazopoulos, "I Entaxi tis Ellados," 579–580.
43 Nikolaos I Pantazopoulos, "Georg Ludwig von Maurer, I pros Evropaika Protypa Oloklirotiki Strofi tis Neoellinikis Nomothesias," *Epistimoniki Epetiris Scholis Nomikon kai Oikonomikon Epistimon* 13 (1968): 1464; Pan. I Zepos, *I Neotera Elliniki Epistimi tou Astikou Dikaiou* (Athens: Ioannis Zacharopoulos, 1954), 14–15; Suzanne Desan, *The Family on Trial in Revolutionary France* (Berkeley: University of California Press, 2004), 308–309.
44 Stavros I Stavropoulos, *Themata Genikis Theorias kai Philosophias tou Dikaiou* (Athens: N.P., 1970), 101–102.
45 Pantazopoulos, "Georg Ludwig von Maurer," 1366.
46 See Georg Ludwig von Maurer, *O Ellinikos Laos* (Athens: Afoi Tolidi, 1976).
47 Pantazopoulos, *Apo tis "Logias" Paradoseos*, 165–167.
48 Pantazopoulos, "I Entaxi tis Elladas," 597.
49 Pantazopoulos, *Apo tis "Logias" Paradoseos*, 252, 254.
50 Pavlos Kalligas, *Systima Romaikou Dikaiou* (Athens: Andreas Koromilas, 1878), vol. A, viii, xi.
51 Zepos P., *I Neotera Elliniki Epistimi*, 22.
52 Pantazopoulos, "I Entaxi tis Ellados," 580.
53 Ibid., 577, 580.
54 Pavlos Kalligas, *Systima Romaikou Dikaiou* (Athens: Andreas Koromilas, 1876), vol. E, 252.
55 Kalligas, *Systima Romaikou Dikaiou*, vol. A, 214, 215; Kalligas, *Systima Romaikou Dikaiou* (Athens: Georgios Fexis and Yios, 1930), vol. D, 67.
56 Kalligas, *Systima Romaikou Dikaiou*, vol. D, 176, 213, 223.
57 Bakalaki, "Gender-Related Discourses," 79.
58 Eleni Varikas, *I Exegersi ton Kyrion, I Genesi mias Feministikis Syneidisis stin Ellada 1833–1907* (Athens: Katarti, 2004), 299.
59 Georgiou S. Maridaki, *To Astikon Dikaion eis tais Nearais ton Byzantinon Aftokratoron* (Athens: G. I. Vasileiou, 1922), 92.
60 See Konstantinos L. Triantafyllopoulos, "Ekthesis kai Proschedion Nomou peri ton Logon tou Diazygiou kai SynepeionTtinon Aftou," in *Ypourgeio Dikaiosynis, Epitropi tou Astikou Kodikos* (Athens: Ethniko Typografeio, 1918).
61 Desan, *The Family on Trial*, 27.

62 Kalligas, *Systima Romaikou Dikaiou*, vol. D, 15.
63 Ibid., 176, 213, 223.
64 Ibid., 249. In all this one must note the similarity with the *Code civil*, which restored the father's authority in the family following the challenge of the French revolutionary legislation (Desan, *The Family on Trial*, 175).
65 Kalligas, *Systima Romaikou Dikaiou*, vol. A, 214, 215; Kalligas, *Systima Romaikou Dikaiou*, vol. D, 67; Desan, *The Family on Trial*, 301.
66 B. K. Nikolopoulos and A. I. Kakoulidis eds., *Syllogi Apanton ton Nomon, Diatagmaton, Egkyklion, Odigion, kai Eidopoiiseon ton Ypourgeion kai Synthikon tis Ellados meta ton Allon Ethnon* (Athens: Ch. Nikolaidou Filadelfeos, 1860), vol. 2, 364. This concept was also stated in Albert Fritot's treatise on natural law that had been translated into Greek in 1836. Significantly, among the subscribers to this edition one finds the most famous legal scholars of Greece, including Paparrigopoulos, Mamoukas, Soutzos, Kambouroglou, Ragvis, Mavrokordatos, Tertsetis, Renieris, Metaxas, Filimon, Vamvas, and so on (Albert Fritot, *Didaskalia Peri tou Fysikou Dikaiou* [Athens: Andreas Koromilas, 1836], 77, 128).
67 Pavlos Paparrigopoulos, *To En Elladi Ischyon Astikon Dikaion* (Athens: S. K. Vlaston, 1875), vol. 8, 186.
68 Kalligas, *Systima Romaikou Dikaiou*, vol. D, 178; Maridakis, *To Astikon Dikaion*, 83; Desan, *The Family on Trial*, 217.
69 Kalligas, *Systima Romaikou Dikaiou*, vol. A, 145, 319.
70 Varikas, *I Exegersi ton Kyrion*, 77.
71 Gustav Karl Geib, *Parousiasi tis Katastasis tou Dikaiou stin Ellada* (Athens: Govosti, 1990), 78; Arthur de Gobineau, *Sto Vasileio ton Ellinon* (Athens: Periplous, 1999), 150.
72 Edmond About, *I Ellada tou Othonos* (Athens: Afoi Tolidi, 1992), 139, 149.
73 Geib, *Parousiasi tis Katastasis*, 110; About, *I Ellada tou Othonos* 164, 166.
74 Evdoxios Doxiadis, "Standing in their Place: The Exclusion of Women from the Judicial System in the First Decades of the Modern Greek State, 1821–1850," *Journal of Modern Greek Studies* 25 (2007): 89.
75 Dimitris A. Sakkis, *Neosystato Elliniko Kratos 1833–1848* (Athens: Giorgos Dardanos, 2001), vol. A, 41. In one case that did not involve travel, the awarded court expenses were 68 *drachmas* (Society of the Friends of the People, Chrysospathis Archive (EFL Chrysospathis) BV/2, no. 78, June 22, 1853). Others that had dragged on longer and involved travel and more witnesses could be two or three times that.
76 The population shifts were partly caused by the ten year war itself, when thousands of refugees from areas that had risen in rebellion but eventually remained within the Ottoman empire (Psara, Chios, Crete, etc.) were settled in the new Kingdom of Greece, partly by the circumstances of the new state where populations moved to occupy the lands formerly held by Muslims, and partly by the emergence of new urban centers (or old urban centers that gained new prominence) like Athens, Ermoupoli, Piraeus, and so on.
77 Varikas, *I Exegersi ton Kyrion*, 76–77.
78 Henri Belle, *Taxidi stin Ellada 1861–1974* (Athens: Istoritis, 1993), vol. A, 194–195
79 Varikas, *I Exegersi on Kyrion*, 57, 77; Belle, *Taxidi stin Ellada*, 196.
80 Kalligas, *Systima Romaikou Dikaiou*, vol. D, 76.
81 Angelika Psarra, "A Gift from the New World," 152.
82 There is a remarkable similarity to the percentage of court cases involving women that I found in the Appeals Court for 1860 and those found by Angeliki Laiou in the surviving Byzantine records of Peira (36%), Chomatianos (71%), MMI (35%), and MMII (42%), which, alongside the fragmentary records of the Ottoman period, point to a continuous presence of women in the courts (Angeliki E. Laiou, *Gender, Society and Economic Life in Byzantium* [Brookfield: Ashgate, 1992], 234).

83 General State Archives, Appeals Court of Athens Archive, Civil Case Rulings (GAK Efeteio), vol. 119, pg. 29, no. 17770, February 2, 1860; GAK Efeteio, vol. 119A, pg. 281, no. 17935, March 16, 1860; GAK Efeteio, vol. 119A, pg. 313, no. 17937, March 19, 1860; GAK Efeteio, vol. 120, pg. 1109, no. 18165, June 4, 1860; GAK Efeteio, vol. 121, pg. 653, no. 18258, June 18, 1860; GAK Efeteio, vol. 121, pg. 1393, no. 18329, September 10, 1860.
84 GAK Efeteio, vol 120, pg. 149, no. 18071, May 7, 1860.
85 The case in question involved Greek citizens who came from the city of Smyrna (now Izmir) (GAK Efeteio, vol. 119A, pg. 973, no. 17995, April 13, 1860).
86 GAK Efeteio, vol. 119A, pg. 725, no. 17974, March 25, 1860. See also GAK Efeteio, vol. 121. Pg. 2281, no. 18419, October 8, 1860.
87 GAK Efeteio, vol. 121, pg. 1, no. 18201, May 28, 1860.
88 GAK Efeteio, vol. 120, pg. 9, no. 18060, April 30, 1860. Interestingly, on one occasion, the Supreme Court overturned a decision of the Appeals Court of Athens that had been based on "Roman Law" as modified by the new codes of jurisprudence using a different interpretation of Roman law (GAK Efeteio, vol. 121, pg. 345, no. 18229, June 11, 1860).
89 In fact, the courts frequently had to determine what law was applicable, the most interesting case involving the validity of sales of property in Athens during the Greek War of Independence. Athens had switched hands several times during the Greek War of Independence, and the conclusion of the war found Athens under Ottoman occupation. In fact, Ottoman troops remained in Athens until 1832, well past the establishment and international recognition of Greece as an independent state. An enterprising lawyer, however, claimed that a sale in 1832, while Ottoman troops still controlled the town, should be considered under Ottoman law and not under the laws of the new state. Unfortunately for him, the Appeals Court rejected this claim (GAK Efeteio, vol. 121, pg. 309, no. 18227, June 18, 1860). A similar confusion is seen in a commercial case when the court uses the new commercial code, although there was an argument asking for the application of Byzantine law, as the events of the case predated the publication of the new commercial code (GAK Efeteio, vol. 119, pg. 539, no. 17822, February 3, 1860).
90 GAK Efeteio, vol. 119A, pg. 483, no. 17954, March 12, 1860 (Supreme Court decision no. 128, June 2, 1860).
91 GAK Efeteio, vol. 119A, pg. 152, no. 18050, April 20, 1860.
92 GAK Efeteio, vol. 119A, pg. 177, no. 17924, March 18, 1860.
93 GAK Efeteio, vol. 121, pg. 1509, no. 18342, September 10, 1860; GAK Efeteio, vol. 121, pg. 473, no. 18240, June 18, 1860; GAK Efeteio, vol. 120, pg. 189, no. 18076, April 16, 1860; GAK Efeteio, vol. 119, pg. 943, no. 17846, February 27, 1860.
94 For the period in question, there was only one mention of a family council.
95 Kalligas, *Systima Romaikou Dikaiou*, vol. D, 177.
96 Ibid., 249.
97 GAK Efeteio, vol. 119A, pg. 949, no. 17993, March 28, 1860.
98 GAK Efeteio, vol. 119, pg. 29, no. 17770, February 2, 1860; GAK Efeteio, vol. 119A, pg. 281, no. 17935, March 16, 1860; GAK Efeteio, vol. 121, pg. 1509, no. 18342, September 10, 1860.
99 GAK Efeteio, vol. 121, pg. 2041, no. 18395, October 1, 1860.
100 GAK Efeteio, vol 120, pg. 813, no. 18135, May 25, 1860; GAK Efeteio, vol 120, pg. 833, 18137, May 25, 1860, GAK Efeteio, vol 120, p. 1329, 18183, June 8, 1860; Kalligas, *Systima Romaikou Dikaiou*, vol. A, 48, 153.
101 GAK Efeteio, vol. 120, pg. 813, no. 18135, May 25, 1860.
102 GAK Efeteio, vol. 121, pg. 851, no. 18277, June 24, 1860.
103 GAK Efeteio, vol. 121, pg. 791, no. 18271, June 21, 1860.

104 Although the names were spelled in Greek, their origin is probably German and French. The wife was called Theresa Krouboller, her husband Christos Velier, and her presumed lover Sigel (GAK Efeteio, vol. 121, pg. 771, no. 18268, June 3, 1860).
105 GAK Efeteio, vol. 121, pg. 1973, no. 18389, September 27, 1860.
106 GAK Efeteio, vol. 121, pg. 1207, no. 18307, June 25, 1860.
107 GAK Efeteio, vol. 121, pg. 157, no. 18214, June 15, 1860.
108 GAK Efeteio, vol. 120, pg. 897, no. 18145, May 14, 1860. The presence of guardians is a bit confusing in this case, considering the absence of a will, and it may have to do with the question of remarriage of the widow.
109 GAK Efeteio, vol. 119, pg. 1143, no. 17862, March 2, 1860.
110 GAK Mykonos 97/140, 7, September 13, 1826.
111 GAK Efeteio, vol. 121, pg. 2185, no. 18408, October 4, 1860.
112 GAK Efeteio, vol. 121, pg. 2241, no. 18413, October 4, 1860.
113 Doxiadis, "Standing in their Place," 76.
114 This is fully in agreement with the expectations of Roman Law but not with the reality of the past, when husbands habitually relied on their wives to conduct their affairs in their absence and where widows frequently headed households often with considerable skill (Historical and Ethnological Society of Greece, Mykonos Notarial Archive (IEEE Mykonos), No. 22321, November 16, 1808; IEEE Mykonos, No. 22326, January 22, 1809; IEEE Mykonos, No. 22558, October 22, 1817; IEEE Mykonos, No. 22537, May 22, 1817; IEEE Mykonos, No. 22539, May 27, 1817).
115 Avdela, "Between Duties and Rights," 123.
116 The use of the term middle-class may be problematic for Greece at the time because the implications of wealth, capitalism, and so on may be quite misleading. According to statistics of the time, of the non-agricultural population that can be classified as middle-class, 9,928 were employed by the state (public and municipal functionaries, professors and teachers), while only 3,160 were not (merchants, artists, lawyers, newspaper writers, medical men, apothecaries), plus another 29,044 who could be classed as petite bourgeois (shopkeepers and artisans), nearly as many as the total number of workers (32,801). The rest of the population was engaged primarily in agriculture as proprietors (16,122), agriculturalists (147,507), shepherds (38,953), or drivers and carriers (2,307). A significant number belonged to the clergy (5,102), the merchant marine (19,303), or worked as manservants (12,651). The only women mentioned as employed were midwives (832) and female servants (7,724), as well as 9,035 female students (as opposed to 42,680 male). These numbers indicate the unique character of the Greek middle class, which was heavily dependent upon the state rather than the private economy. (Demetrius Bikelas, "Statistics of the Kingdom of Greece," *Journal of the Statistical Society of London* 31, no. 3 (1868): 292.
117 Desan, *The Family on Trial*, 129.
118 About, *I Ellada tou Othonos*, 54, 134.
119 Frederic Thiersch, *I Ellada tou Kapodistria* (Athens: Afoi Tolidi, 1972), vol. B, 105–106; Nikolopoulos and Kakoulidis, *Syllogi*, vol. 2, 206; Belle, *Taxidi stin Ellada*, vol. A, 83. The prevalence of middle-class girls in such schools is indicative of the professions of their fathers, who were primarily merchants, ship captains, and professionals, as well as by the fact that most female students are found in urban settings while fewer or often no girls attended schools in rural areas. (Sakkis, *Neosystato Elliniko Kratos*, vol. A, 113, 120–121, 127–128).
120 Nikolopoulos and Kakoulidis, *Syllogi*, 213. The period also saw the translation of several books regarding the proper upbringing of girls, such as Madame de Lambert's *Avis d'une mère à sa fille*, Jean Nicolas Bouilly's *Conseils à ma fille*,

and Fenelon's book on the upbringing of girls (Paschalis Kitromilides, *Enlightenment, Nationalism, Orthodoxy, Studies in Culture and Political Thought of Southeastern Europe* [Hampshire: Aldershot Variorum, 1994], 47–49, 52–53; Fenelonos, *To Peri Agogis Korasion* [Athens: Th. Nikolaidou Filadelfeos, 1857], Greek version of François Fénelon, *Fenelon's Treatise on Education of Daugthers* (London: H. Ruff, 1805)].

121 Effi Gazi, " 'Fatherland, Religion, Family': Exploring the History of a Slogan in Greece, 1880–1930," *Gender & History* 25, no. 3 (2013): 701; Maria Anastasopoulou, "The Inception of Feminism in Nineteenth-Century Greece," *The Classical Bulletin* 80, no. 2 (2004): 175; Varikas, *I Exegersi ton Kyrion*, 46.

122 Avdela, "Between Duties and Rights," 121; Bakalaki, "Gender-Related Discourses," 77.

123 Psarra, "A Gift from the New World," 150.

124 Ibid., 153.

125 Ibid., 152.

126 Ernestine Friedl, "The Position of Women: Appearance and Reality," *Anthropological Quarterly* 40, no. 3 (July 1967): 97.

127 Juliette duBoulay, *Portrait of a Greek Mountain Village* (Oxford: Clarendon Press, 1974), 130–131.

128 Kalligas noted that foreign women who married Greeks become Greek, and that in general, marriage changes the nationality of a woman (Kalligas, *Systima Romaikou Dikaiou*, vol. A, 214–215). This principle became law in Greece on October 29, 1856 (Kalligas, *Systima Romaikou Dikaiou*, vol. D, 67).

129 Ibid., 65; Maridakis, *To Astikon Dikaion*, 166.

130 Desan, *The Family on Trial*, 12; Bonnie G. Smith, *Ladies of the Leisure Class. The Bourgeoises of Northern France in the Nineteenth Century* (Princeton, NJ: Princeton University Press, 1981), 54; Michael Anderson, *Approaches to the History of the Western Family 1500–1914* (London: The Macmillan Press, 1980), 46–47; Ruth H. Bloch, "American Feminine Ideals in Transition: The Rise of the Moral Mother," *Feminist Studies* 4, no. 2 (1978): 101; Varikas, *I Exegersi ton Kyrion*, 39, 42, 46, 55, 68–69; Bakalaki, "Gender-Related Discourses," 91.

131 Caroline Norton, *English Laws for Women in the Nineteenth Century* (Westport, CT: Hyperion Press, 1981), 163.

132 Marry Lyndon Shanley, *Feminism, Marriage, and the Law in Victorian England 1850–1895* (Princeton, NJ: Princeton University Press, 1989), 17, 103; Ellen Carol DuBois, *Feminism and Suffrage* (Ithaca, NY: Cornell University Press, 1978), 42.

133 Desan, *The Family on Trial*, 3, 6, 303.

134 Avdela, "Between Duties and Rights," 119.

135 Samiou, "To Feministiko Kinima stin Ellada," 57.

136 Varikas, "National and Gender Identities," 267.

137 Samiou, "To Feministiko Kinima," 58; Varikas, "National and Gender Identities," 274.

138 Avdela and Psarra, "Engendering 'Greekness'," 72.

139 Kyriazis, "Feminism and the Status of Women in Greece," 271.

140 Samiou, "To Feministiko Kinima," 61.

141 Avdela, "Between Duties and Rights," 125.

142 Anna Karamanou, "The Changing Role of Women in Greece," in *Greece in the Twentieth Century*, eds. Theodore A. Couloumbis, Theodore Kariotis, and Fotini Bellou (London: Frank Cass, 2003), 280.

143 Ibid., 285.

2 Family Law, Legal Reforms, Female Lawyers, and Feminist Claims in Spain, 1868–1950

Gloria Nielfa

Introduction

This chapter considers the alternation of advances and setbacks that characterize the legal history of women over a long period in contemporary Spain with regard to family law, showing the influence of political changes, the pressure from women's movements, and the actions of female lawyers, who in turn are also studied in the process of access to the profession. The aim of this research was to review and contribute to the existing historiography. To achieve this, family legislation in the different periods has been consulted in the official journals of both the Spanish state and Catalonia during its brief period of self-government during the Second Republic (1931–1939).[1] These journals also provide information about some women in certain professional positions within the official legal sphere. The study of the laws enacted was complemented by reading documentation from the press in order to understand how these laws and their implementation affected society, and some academic records were also consulted. Additionally, it was vital to consult the works of female authors who have left us evidence of the legal situation of women in the periods studied.

To put this process in context, we need to be aware of the main developments in the political evolution of Spain during this period. In the middle of the nineteenth century, there was a formally liberal monarchy in a clearly oligarchic society. In 1868, a coalition of progressive, democratic, and republican parties, which supported freedom of association, assembly, and conscience, as well as universal male suffrage, carried out a triumphant revolution that resulted in the dethronement of Queen Isabel II. Thus began the period known as the *Sexenio Democrático* (Six Years of Democracy, 1868–1874), during which the country enjoyed the greatest degree of freedom up to that point.[2] At the end of 1874, the Bourbon Restoration began, and in 1890, universal male suffrage was re-established, having previously been in force between 1868 and 1873. Between 1900 and 1930, there was a considerable increase in literacy rates and urbanisation. In 1910, women gained the right to enroll at university without the need for special authorisation. Spanish society was modernizing amidst considerable turbulence.

In 1923, the uprising by General Primo de Rivera caused the suspension of the Constitution of 1876, which was accepted by King Alfonso XIII, and the establishment of a dictatorship that lasted until 1930. In 1931, the Second Republic began, a new, democratic constitution was drafted, and a Republican-Socialist coalition carried out intensive reforms between 1931 and 1933: the recognition of women to participate in the legislature as well as separation of church and state, agrarian reform, approval of the Statute of Autonomy of Catalonia, and the extension of education. After the electoral victory of the centre-right, the reforms were halted in 1934 and 1935, though this was subsequently reversed following the victory of the *Frente Popular* in February 1936. The military uprising against the government in July 1936, backed by the most conservative sectors, marked the start of a civil war in which the insurgents were assisted by the totalitarian powers, Nazi Germany and Fascist Italy. This ended in 1939 with the establishment of the Franco Dictatorship and lasted until 1975, during which time all the Republican legislation was repealed. The lengthy dictatorial regime continued against the backdrop of different international contexts, such as the Second World War and the subsequent isolation in the 1940s, and that of international recognition in the frame of the Cold War in the following decades.

Parliamentary Monarchy

In nineteenth century Spain, as in other European countries, a codifying effort took place as an attempt to build articulate and systematic legal systems to substitute for the varying and conflicting existing legislation. Nevertheless, a civil code was not approved until as late as 1889. The issue of marriage was the cause of that delay, as a result of the confrontation between conservatives and liberals with regard to the role of the Catholic Church in their regulation.[3] The Civil Code of 1889 was heavily influenced by the French Civil Code of 1804, as was the case in other Latin countries.[4] Other sources of inspiration for its elaboration were the records of customary Spanish law, such as the *Leyes de Partidas* (thirteenth century) and the *Leyes de Toro* (sixteenth century).[5]

As a preceding law, then still in force, it is worth mentioning the *Ley de Enjuiciamiento Civil* (Civil Procedure Law) passed in 1855, which showed a clear preference for men as opposed to women in holding the position of a guardian or trustee to look after the interests of a disabled person or a minor who had lost his/her parents. Additionally, with the establishment of legal separation procedures, judges could order a woman to be placed outside her husband's house, in a family member's house, or in a convent under the charge of someone other than the husband. This was a temporary measure called a *depósito* (deposit).[6]

Criminal treatment of adultery was clearly discriminatory against women in the 1870 Criminal Code, as with the 1848 Code. It was defined only as the crime committed by a married woman and the man with whom she had intercourse, he being aware of her marital status, and it was punished with simple imprisonment; there was no legal conception of adultery by the husband against his wife. For the husband's infidelity to be condemned the fact must be continuous and well known; nevertheless, the sentenced penalty for this crime, called *amancebamiento* was minor.[7] On the other hand, the 1870 Criminal Code reproduced the 1848 provisions with regard to the husband who killed his wife, or the other man, after discovering her guilty of adultery; penalty was banishment and he would be exempt from punishment if the resulting injuries were not serious (Article 438).

As far as the influence of the Church is concerned with regard to marriage law, it is sufficient to recall that even the Provisional Act on Civil Marriage, approved in 1870 during the *Sexenio Democrático*, established that marriage was by nature a perpetual and indissoluble bond.[8] Under the 1889 Civil Code, married women's rights were notably restricted within wedlock, for it declared that wives owed obedience to their husbands and were under the obligation to follow their spouses wherever they took up their residence. Moreover, men were the managers of marital property and wives were not allowed to accept or reject any inheritance, go to court, or purchase goods without their husband's authorization.[9] Furthermore, parental authority was attributed to the father and, in the case of this one failing, to the mother (Article 155). If a widowed mother remarried, she would lose parental authority over her children, unless her deceased husband had otherwise provided special dispensation from the law (Article 168). In the case of single women, notwithstanding that full legal age was established at 23, a woman under 25 years of age could not leave her parents' home without her father's or mother's permission, unless it was for contracting marriage or becoming a religious figure, or otherwise because her father or her mother had married subsequently (Article 321). In addition, women were not allowed to be witnesses to a will, except in cases of epidemics (Articles 681 and 701). According to the jurist Francisco Tomás y Valiente's view, one of the goals laid down in this code would be "to regulate a specific conception of marriage and family in conformity with what the Church hierarchy preached and what the affluent and wealthy bourgeoisie demanded."[10]

Some feminist female writers pointed out the inconsistency provided by the civil law that considered women as morally and intellectually inferior to men in coexistence with the criminal law that imposed the same punishment in case of offense. Significant examples of the above are some writings of Concepción Arenal (1820–1873) and Carmen de Burgos (Colombine) (1867–1932). Arenal had attended classes in the Faculty of Law at the University of Madrid in 1842 by masking her female identity in male dress; she wrote many works dealing with criminological subjects and about the situation of women in Spain.[11] Carmen de Burgos, a teacher at a normal school, writer, and journalist, succeeded in developing a career by moving to Madrid with her daughter after her marriage ended.[12]

The discrimination toward women as far as marriage was concerned was heightened by the fact that absolute divorce did not exist; indeed, in the civil code the word divorce was simply used to refer to any separation that only implied cessation of cohabitation, though it did not allow one to enter into marriage again. This so-called 'divorce' was based on the guilt principle, which said that the innocent spouse was the only one able to sue; the judge might set alimony for the woman and children during the trial process; and finally children were kept under the authority and care of the innocent spouse.[13] In 1903, the aforementioned Carmen de Burgos launched a campaign for the enactment of a divorce act. She conducted a survey about this issue from the column that she published daily in the Madrid newspaper *Diario Universal* and the results were edited in a book. In this way, the writer asked some well-known figures of the intellectual world, as well as readers of the newspaper, their views about this question, resulting in the majority being in favour of it.[14]

The creation of several groups, such as the Asociación Nacional de Mujeres Españolas (ANME) (National Association of Spanish Women) in 1918 and the Cruzada de Mujeres Españolas (Spanish Women's Crusade) in 1920, gave impetus to the campaign in favour of legal reform regarding civil and political women's rights through the submission of petitions to the authorities.[15] Though many aspects were similar in both programs, ANME's was a little more moderate. The petition from the Cruzada, submitted in 1921, was supported by 800 signatures. Recently, it has been labelled as a request for "a renegotiating of the *sexual agreement* in a truly equal direction."[16] President of the Cruzada, Carmen de Burgos, also drew some attention to the subject matter in her works of fiction, such as *El artículo 438* (Article 438), which alludes to the aforementioned Criminal Code's article, or *La malcasada* (The Mismarried), about the indissolubility of marriage.[17] These and other works by Carmen de Burgos have been analysed from the feminist theory point of view by Anja Louis in a work that deals with literature and law from an interdisciplinary perspective. She points out that these kinds of books provided a means of political propaganda in order to raise the issue of women in the public domain, as well as the fact that they must be studied jointly with her theoretical essays, such as *La mujer moderna y sus derechos* (The Modern Woman and Her Rights).[18]

The First Female Jurists

The 1920s was the decade in which we began to see women working in the practise of law professionally in Spain, with María Ascensión Chirivella Marín (1893–1980) being the first woman admitted to the bar.[19] She was accepted in Valencia in 1922, after graduating the previous year, and the news featured prominently in the press.[20] Her acceptance into the bar association was permitted despite the fact that a medieval law that prevented women from doing this job was still in force. The Madrid Bar Association and the Barcelona Bar Association, in anticipation of that state of affairs, established in their statutes in 1920 and 1921, respectively, that women could be admitted to exercise the profession, an example that was to be followed by other Spanish bars.[21] The two first female lawyers whose work would achieve a remarkable prominence were Victoria Kent Siano (1892–1987) and Clara Campoamor Rodríguez (1888–1972). In their student days, both women had belonged to the Juventud Universitaria Feminista (JUF) (Feminist University Youth), an organization created in 1920 by women of the ANME to assemble a group of female students, graduates, and doctors. Their aim was to expand the movement among female students. That association was soon affiliated with the International Federation of University Women (IFUW).[22] Kent was the first female lawyer to act in the court of Madrid, in 1925, and furthermore the first woman to act in a court-martial in the Supreme Court, where in 1931 she defended Álvaro de Albornoz, a member of the Revolutionary Committee.[23]

Campoamor also began practising law in 1925, following her admission to the Royal Academy of Jurisprudence and Legislation the previous year, in which she was deeply involved. She focused on issues related to the legal incapacity of married women and the determination of paternity, and in 1926 she won a case before the Supreme Court on this latter issue. Among the many activities that she undertook in those years, one worth mentioning is the preparation for the 12th IFUW Congress that took place in September of 1928 in Spain, as well as her work as President of the JUF beginning in 1929. Furthermore, she was part of the committee alongside other women of different persuasions that was set up for the purpose of erecting a monument in memory of Concepción Arenal supported by grassroots donations. This monument would mean the celebration of a symbol for feminism and criminology alike. Campoamor was, along with Marcelle Kraemer-Bach (1896–1990) and Agathe Dyvrande-Thévenin (1885–1977) from France, Vera Poska-Grünthal (1898–1986) from Estonia, and the attorney Margarete Berent (1887–1965) from Germany, one of the founders of the Fédération International de Femmes de Carrières Juridiques (FIFCJ) (International Federation of Women in Legal Careers), created in Paris in 1928.[24]

Among the women that were members of the Royal Academy of Jurisprudence and Legislation in the 1920s, one can also cite Matilde Huici (1890–1965) and Concepción Peña Pastor (1906–1960).[25] Having accomplished her legal and education studies, Matilde Huici went to the United States and to several European countries to get acquainted with the penitentiary system with regard to marginalized children, an issue that was a source of constant concern for her throughout her life and that led to her participation in the Juvenile Court.[26] She was with Kent and Campoamor in JUF, and also in the Lyceum Club, a space of female sociability that was created in 1926 to become the meeting place for feminists of various organizations, together with non-militant women and others affiliated with several political parties, especially the Republican ones.[27] All three female jurists were included as founding members of the Spanish branch of the International Institute for Intellectual Cooperation and in the International Federation of Intellectual Unions, linked to the League of Nations. The close collaboration between Campoamor and Huici was also expressed in 1927 in several acts of protest against Article 438 of the criminal code as well as in the Lyceum Club campaign against Article 57 of the civil code, which determined the wife's obligation to obey her husband. Additionally, they participated in the foundation of the Liga Femenina Española por la Paz (Women's Spanish League for Peace) in 1929 in connection with the Women's International League for Peace and Freedom (WILPF). Both women were part of the executive committee.[28]

These activist women were Republicans and also influenced by liberal humanism. The influence of the Institución Libre de Enseñanza (ILE) (Free Teaching Institution) is also apparent; we can recall, for example, that both Kent and Huici stayed in the Residencia de Señoritas (Residence for Young Ladies), an educational centre with liberal and humanist leanings supported by the Junta para Ampliación de Estudios e Investigaciones Científicas (JAE) (Committee for Extension of Studies and Scientific Research).[29] It is important to stress that despite being outstanding figures, these women had to reconcile their private law practise with other professional jobs as their means of livelihood.[30] In addition, "[they] had also to defend themselves against the prejudices and the arrogance of a patriarchal justice system, extremely out of date and aggressive."[31]

Within the Catholic and conservative wing, we should mention Carmen Cuesta del Muro (1890–1968), who was the first woman to receive a doctorate in law in Spain (1928). She was closely involved with the Institución Teresiana (Teresian Institution), aimed at the training of Catholic female educators, and led its Female University Residence. During the dictatorship of General Primo de Rivera, she was one of the thirteen women appointed to as a member of the Asamblea Nacional Consultiva (Consultative National Assembly), in which she also served in one of the four Secretariats. In her assembly interventions, she called for the extension of civil rights for unmarried women and widows, though she defended the husband's authority with regard to married women, according to her Catholic orientation of thought.[32]

In 1924, Carmen López Bonilla, a woman with a degree in law, submitted an application before the Presidency of the Military Council requesting the publication of a decree under which women could be allowed to sit examinations to become a notary, property registrar, etc. Her petition was denied based on the contradiction it represented concerning the limitations on the rights of all women, who were not allowed to be witness of a will, and particularly the special situation of married women, who were required to have marital authorization for a number of acts.[33] In 1928, several female law students brought the same petition to the minister of justice, but the issue was not resolved then either.[34]

The Second Republic

The establishment of the Spanish Second Republic in 1931 meant great legal progress for women, both in terms of civil rights and political rights, and therefore it began a critical period for female citizenship.[35] In spite of the fact that, as we have already seen, those same rights had been claimed by women's organizations such as ANME or the Cruzada de Mujeres Españolas since the second decade of the twentieth century, a change in the regime was necessary for those reforms to become a reality. In addition, the profound involvement of some of those women who had an associative activity background was necessary. Those first female lawyers in the 1920s, such as Campoamor and Kent, were also among the first to be Members of Parliament and General Directors in Spain. Huici was appointed member of the Criminal Law Sub-Commission of the Comisión Jurídica Asesora (CJA) (Advisory Legal Committee) to develop a draft of the constitution, though the government did not endorse it.[36] More effectively, Campoamor participated in the parliamentary commission that drew up the constitution draft to be discussed in parliament. She played a key role in the inclusion of egalitarian principles in the Republican Constitution of 1931 as far as gender equity was concerned, and in particular for the establishment of universal suffrage through a woman's right to vote on the same terms as men. This action was supported by several associations of women, which distributed leaflets in Congress in favour of equality for electoral rights and organised a reception in honour of Campoamor and her fight for women's suffrage on November 15, 1931.[37] On her side, Kent, who carried out significant penitentiary reform as a first female General Director of Prisons, was for the delay of women's suffrage, according to her party position.[38]

The Constitution of 1931 stated that marriage had to be based on the equal rights of both genders and therefore could be dissolved by mutual dissent or by a request of either of the spouses as long as a fair cause claim was submitted (Article 43), which opened the way to the elaboration of a divorce law. As a member of parliament, Campoamor was actively involved in its debate and demanded that it should be based on freedom and secular principles. Likewise, Huici, as a member of the CJA, set out an individual opinion, giving rise to the need to elaborate a family statute to regulate the economic relationships as well as the individual rights of women in marriage. She argued that according to Article 43 of the constitution, the gender equity approach required the amendment of the civil code.[39] Eventually, the Act of 1932 established the mechanisms for granting divorce at the request of both spouses by mutual agreement, or one of them in cases such as adultery, bigamy, abandonment, attempt by the husband to prostitute his wife, an attempt by one spouse on the life of the other spouse or the children, domestic violence, contagious and serious venereal disease, de facto separation for three years, and insanity. In the case of spousal fault, the children would remain with the innocent spouse and, save a ruling to the contrary, children under the age of five would remain in the care of the mother. Parental authority would correspond to the spouse granted custody of the children; the judge would dictate the manner in which the other spouse should contribute to their sustenance—non-compliance would be punished by imprisonment or fines—and would also establish the manner in which he/she could communicate with them and oversee their education. If the innocent spouse did not have sufficient resources for his/her own sustenance, he/she could demand the payment of alimony from the other spouse. Likewise, it was established that if the spouse who had custody of the children remarried, this would not alter the situation, save a reasoned ruling to the contrary.[40] This law is often regarded as one of the more progressive divorce laws of that period, as it admitted dissolution of marriage by mutual agreement. According to the statistics about its implementation in the following years, it was women who applied for divorce in more than half of the cases.[41]

The next step in the family law reform was the enactment of a law that established civil marriage as the only legally valid form of marriage, whereby civil jurisdiction became the only one to exclusively deal with matters such as validity or nullity of marriage. On the other hand, sentences rendered by ecclesiastic courts did not produce any legal effect. Certain changes were introduced with regard to particular aspects in the form of the celebration of marriage. For instance, from then on, it did not include the reading of Article 57 of the civil code that imposed on married women the obligation to obey their husbands.[42] According to the testimony of Huici, the aforementioned CJA produced a draft of a bill about "the woman's legal capacity and the juridical regulation of marriage" that was presented in parliament when Álvaro de Albornoz was Minister of Justice, but it did not reach discussion.[43] A few months later, the Ministry of Justice established that, by analogy with that which was set forth in the divorce law with regard to divorced women, widows who remarried would not lose parental authority over their children.[44] Despite this, in 1934 when a widow who, after remarrying, claimed parental authority, a judge ruled that Article 168 of the civil code remained in force, as it had not been reformed.[45] As part of the adaptation of the civil code to the Republican Constitution, the CJA drafted a bill about filiation and paternity proceeding.[46] This bill, according to Article 43 of the constitution—which also outlawed discrimination between legitimate and illegitimate children—paid attention to the individual opinion presented by Huici. Recorded in the minutes of the parliamentary sessions was the request of Deputy Campoamor, who appealed for the urgent submission of a bill regarding this issue in June of 1933. The information about this bill appeared in the press a week later following the conclusion of the Council of Ministers, but in the end it did not pass.[47]

The Republic in 1932 also brought reform to the 1870 Criminal Code for the purpose of adapting it to the contents of the new constitution, as well as to humanise its precepts, leaving the task of drawing up a new code until later.[48] The CJA, with the participation of Huici, was tasked to elaborate that reform, and when it was discussed in parliament, the proposal made by Campoamor about the suppression of adultery and *amancebamiento* was passed, along with the elimination at the same time of the aforementioned Article 438 to implement the principle of non-discrimination of gender laid down in Article 25 of the constitution.[49]

In April of 1931, the Republic's Provisional Government issued a decree under which women were allowed to be contenders for the candidacy to become a notary public and a registrar of property, and they subsequently were granted access to the post of local judicial secretary, and later on, to that of *procurador* (a member of the legal profession who carries out procedures before the court).[50] However, two years after the instauration of the Republic, women had not yet seen an open door to the practise of all the professions related to the world of law; hence, Campoamor made a plea in June of 1933 to the Ministry of Justice asking for the admission of women to all professional careers deriving from a law degree. One year before, this question had been a matter of attention in a report by the journalist Josefina Carabias, which pointed out that the number of women qualified as lawyers in Spain was less than twenty, and those practising the profession were less than ten. Furthermore, the report included a comparison with other countries and the views for and against women practising law by different leading figures of the judicial world.[51]

The outcome of the elections in November of 1933, favourable to the centre-right wing, meant the defeat of the reformist coalition that had been in power since 1931, and therefore the freeze-up of several bills that had not yet been approved. As far as women practising the legal profession were concerned, in 1934 a law graduate named Teresa Argemí Meliá requested from the Ministry of Justice a declaration as to whether women were allowed to take the exams to become prosecutor, judge, and legal secretary. In defence of this, she put forward a number of articles of the constitution, as well as the aforementioned regulations, but the result was an order denying the access of women to prosecution and judicial posts.[52] Regarding notaries public and property registrars, there is no evidence of any woman taking those posts in the brief period of the Republic, though records do exist of two women who took the exams to become property registrars in 1936.[53]

In 1932 the Statute of Autonomy of Catalonia was approved according to the regional system provided for in the constitution. It was followed by subsequent elections to form the autonomous parliament elections that resulted in the victory of the political party named Esquerra Republicana de Catalunya (ERC) (Republican Left of Catalonia). This political framework in Catalonia, different from the rest of Spain, was the base to facilitate the promulgation in 1934 of a law recognising the same civil legal capacity of women and men, which stated that marriage did not change said capacity.[54]

Civil War: Two Conflicting Areas, Two Conflicting Models

As soon as the electoral triumph of the Frente Popular (Popular Front) in February 1936, was known, the preparations for a military uprising against the Republican Government started.[55] The uprising eventually took place in July 1936 and led to a division of the territory in two areas: one loyal to the government, where the constitution and the Republican institutions were to be maintained, and one controlled by the rebels, where they were gradually dismantled.

In the Republican zone, there was an intense mobilization on the part of women, resulting in several changes in their way of life and activities. Nevertheless, the patriarchal gender patterns still carried a lot of weight in society. Agrupación de Mujeres Antifascistas (AMA) (Union of Antifascist Women) and Mujeres Libres (Free Women) were the main women's organizations. AMA gathered women of the different political parties that integrated into the Frente Popular as well as other women who supported the antifascist struggle, and was headed by communist women. Although it paid some attention to the issue of education and culture for women, generally speaking, the real demands of feminists were pushed into the background in relation to the main concern: antifascism. As for Mujeres Libres, this organization was formed by anarchist women concerned with the emancipation of women from a working class perspective.[56]

President Francisco Largo Caballero, a socialist, carried out the government's reorganization at the beginning of November of 1936 in a critical moment for the Republic due to the arrival of Franco's troops just outside of Madrid. It included the appointment of four anarchist ministers to the Cabinet, among them a woman, Federica Montseny, in the Ministry of Health and Social Assistance. A decree from the Ministry of Justice, headed by Juan García Oliver, also an anarchist, developed the egalitarian principles with regard to marriage that were contained in Article 43 of the 1931 Constitution, building on several reforms already analysed, and that were introduced from the beginning of the Republic in the Civil Code of 1889.[57]

At this same stage, the Catalonian self-government, formed by a coalition of republicans, communists, and anarchists, issued a decree on the artificial interruption of pregnancy with the purpose of fighting against problems derived from clandestine abortion.[58] This measure tied in with the anarchist movement on sexual reform that had been developing in earlier decades. Their position was that abortion should be carried out in hospitals and clinics prepared to perform the operation, and therapeutic, Neo-Malthusian, eugenic, or ethical reasons should be required, being exclusively the decision of the affected woman to take the initiative in this respect. The low number of abortions performed under the decree regulations and the continued practise of clandestine abortion shows the failure of the measure due to a number of factors, such as the reluctance of physicians, the continued existence of a condemnatory mindset on abortion, and the difficulty in maintaining the anonymity of the women who had a legally performed abortion.[59]

It was also in Catalonia where the competences regarding justice had been transferred, and in a revolutionary situation, where the appointment of a woman as judge was made for the first time at the end of 1936 under the mandate of Andreu Nin, Regional Minister of Justice, who belonged to the Partido Obrero de Unificación Marxista (POUM) (Worker's Party of Marxist Unification). This woman was Mª Llüisa Algarra Coma (1916–1957), who had not yet obtained her law degree—she obtained it in 1938—and she had been the Secretary of the Revolutionary Committee, which occupied the Palace of Justice in Barcelona during the summer of 1936, and was a playwright. She was appointed to fill the post as judge in the Court of First Instance and Instruction of Granollers (Barcelona), and Nin declared to the press that her appointment "broke the anachronistic mould constraining the administration of justice" by excluding women.[60] Nevertheless, the political changes in the Catalan Autonomous Government led to her removal from office when the Regional Ministry of Justice was occupied by Rafael Vidiella, who was a member of the Partido Socialista Unificado de Cataluña (PSUC) (Unified Socialist Party of Catalonia), very akin to Partido Comunista de España (PCE) (Communist Party in Spain). Later on she took a post as an administrative assistant.[61]

A different case is that of Elvira Fernández Almoguera (1907–1938), as she was the first woman to legally occupy a position in the Public Prosecution Service.[62] She was president of the Socorro Rojo Internacional (International Red Aid) in Albacete, and under the mandate of Juan García Oliver as Minister of Justice, referred to earlier, she was appointed to become prosecutor of the People's Court of Granada, based in Baza.[63] Later, she was assigned to the Higher Regional Court of Albacete when the republican Mariano Ansó headed the Ministry of Justice.[64]

Another woman, Julia Álvarez Resano (1903–1948), also held the post of judge in Alberique (Valencia) and then even of magistrate in the Central Court of Espionage and High Treason, though very briefly; she resigned due to her husband's serious illness.[65] She was a teacher and a socialist lawyer who defended the workers when she was in the legal advice department of the Federación Nacional de Trabajadores de la Tierra (FNTT) (National Federation of Land-based Workers), which belonged to the socialist trade unions Unión General de Trabajadores (UGT) (General Union of Workers). She was also elected to parliament as deputy of Frente Popular in February of 1936, and prefect of the province of Ciudad Real from July of 1937 to March of 1938, the first woman in Spain to hold this post.[66] In addition, two women, the aforementioned Matilde Huici and Luz le Boucher Villén, were appointed as judges of Juvenile Court in August 1937.[67] In view of all this, it can be stated that women holding positions as judges and prosecutors during this period was extremely unusual.

In the territory dominated by insurgents, gradually increasing throughout the war as Franco's troops were advancing, the situation appeared to be moving in the opposite direction. There, the gender relationship pattern based on the traditional roles of male authority and female submission was defended. The women of the Sección Femenina de Falange (SF) (Feminine Section of Falange) assumed that model, which was antagonistic to the egalitarian and secular measures that the Republican governments had adopted.[68] Thus, in March of 1938 the first government of Franco enacted the *Fuero del Trabajo* (Labour Charter) that was inspired by Mussolini's *Carta di Lavoro*. It declared: "The State [. . .] will free women from the workshop and the factory."[69] A few days before, the processes and trials of divorce and separation under the Divorce Law of 1932 had been suspended.[70] In that same month, the Civil Marriage Law from 1932 was repealed, and Title IV referring to marriage from Book 1 of the 1889 Civil Code was declared as the legislation applicable in that respect. In this way, all the republican reforms of this matter were suppressed.[71] In addition, Article 22 of the civil code was declared in force with regard to the obligation of married women to take their husband's nationality; in any case, the Dictatorship did not pay attention to the League of Nations debates about the topic.[72]

In July of 1938 a new law saw the light under which the family allowances were established. The reforms were promised in the aforementioned *Fuero del Trabajo*. The objective of the law was to prevent mothers who would be compelled to look for a salary "to deviate themselves from their supreme and irreplaceable role of preparing their children, the weapon and the foundation of the Nation."[73] The subsidy would be paid to the "head of household," although in particular circumstances it could be paid to the mother or on her behalf.[74] A few months later, an order from the Ministry of Trade Union Action and Organization reaffirmed that the "trend of the New State is to ensure that women devote their whole attention to the household and separate themselves from jobs," and raised the possibility of prohibiting married women from employment in the event that the husband's income reached a certain upper limit.[75]

Early Francoism[76]

The progression of the Civil War and the later defeat of the Republic on April 1, 1939, resulted in the exile of 500,000 people from Spain, initially to France and North Africa, where they were confined in refugee camps by the French authorities, and later on to Latin American countries. Among them were most of the women who had worked in the practise of law during the 1920s and 1930s, cases in point being the aforementioned examples of Chirivella, Kent, Campoamor, Peña, Huici, Algarra, and Álvarez Resano. With the end of the war, Franco's dictatorship extended to the whole territory, and the task of repealing the Republican legislation went on. For instance, that same year all the laws, provisions, and doctrines adopted in Catalonia's Parliament were withdrawn.[77]

Policy with regard to the family was one of the main concerns of the new regime, both for outright anti-feminist ideological reasons as well as for demographic reasons. Consequently, in September 1939 under the Head of State Law, the Divorce Law of 1932 was repealed, as it was considered "radically opposed to the deep religious feeling of Spanish society." So, the final divorce sentences pronounced under the repealed law were declared invalid, as were any civil marriages subsequently entered into by the divorcees, while at the same time the complete validity within civil law of the sentences from the ecclesiastical courts regarding annulments of marriage was recognized.[78] In addition, legislation was adopted against abortion wherein the penalties to the health and pharmaceutical staff members who collaborated in the operation and to women who had an abortion were harsher. Moreover, contraceptive propaganda and the distribution, displaying, or marketing of any contraceptive product were also criminalized.[79] These provisions were in force throughout the regime period. In 1942, another law that amended several articles in the criminal code was enacted that raised the penalties relative to infanticide and the abandonment of children, as those established for abortion had equalled them.[80] Adultery and *amancebamiento* offences were re-established in the criminal code that same day, justified on the necessity to assure that the Republican code, which did not punish those offences, "does not prevail even for a single second more."[81] These and other changes were introduced in the "criminal code, recast text of 1944."[82] Furthermore, under the Labour Agreements Act of 1944, which repealed that of 1931, married women needed authorisation from their husbands to conclude a service provision agreement, except in cases of de facto or legal separation, where it was assumed as granted (Article 11). Even more, the express opposition of the husband could prevent his wife from cashing by her own paycheck (Article 58).[83]

As far as women's professional activity is concerned, the provisions of the *Estatuto de Funcionarios* (Staff Regulations) from 1918 were invoked in order to sustain the idea that not all jobs in the State Administration were appropriate for women.[84] Moreover, the professional opportunities that had opened up for women in the Republican period were gradually closed, and not only because a high percentage of posts in the Public Administration were reserved for "disabled gentlemen" and veterans.[85] Women were soon excluded from the opportunity to compete to enter the state legal profession, as was expressed in the modified notice of the open competition of 1940.[86] In 1941, women were also excluded from the diplomatic corps[87] Also in 1941, women were excluded by omission from candidacy for positions as judges and prosecutors and, in 1943, these competitions were limited to men.[88] As for competition to become a notary public, the 1944 call introduced this requirement, which differed from the previous regulation that explicitly admitted women since it asked for a certificate showing that the *Servicio Social* (Social Service) had been completed in the case of a female applicant.[89] In fact, there were fourteen women among the more than 1,400 male applicants to notary offices in 1943.[90] A transitory provision authorised women who had appeared as accepted candidates in the lists for previously held competitions to apply again for up to a maximum of two examination sessions. Thus, three women obtained the post and began their practise in the 1940s, before that possibility was closed to the rest, and retained the post until their retirement: Consuelo Mendizábal Álvarez was notary public in 1942, Margarita Baudin Sánchez in 1944, and Carolina Bono Huerta in 1947.[91]

As far as property registers are concerned, male exclusivity regulations were delayed, and so we know of seven cases of women who obtained these posts between 1941 and 1948; however, the examination requirements of October 1948 established that only men could apply, which was rectified a month later to include female candidates during a transitory period, thus following the precedent of the notaries.[92] There are records of women as property registrars who reached the professional practise in those years—Beatriz Blesa Rodríguez, Mª de los Ángeles Torcida Fuente, Celia Puente Ojea, Carmen Bono Huerta, Mª Teresa Guerreira Marcos, Ana Mª Viola Sauret, and Carmen Gomá Roger—and it happened that indeed some of them were the same ones who entered the competitions for notaries in 1943.[93] Thus, paradoxically, the Republic provision that opened notaries public and property registers to women in 1931, and inspired some of them to study law, was effective in the first stage of the Franco regime before a reversion to the earlier situation.[94] On the other hand, perhaps the progressive closure of qualified professional opportunities throughout the 1940s is related to the remark made by Christine Lavail, who points out the drop in the appreciation of university women in the review *Medina* (one of the SF media) in 1943.[95] Until those years, Falangist discourse concerning what was acceptable or not for women was wider than it had been since then, as "national Catholic" aspects gradually overtook "national unionism," especially since the end of World War II.[96]

In the post-Spanish Civil War period, women's membership to any bar association was exceptional. Notably, however, in 1950, Mercedes Formica became a member of the Bar Association of Madrid. Years later, in the 1950s, Formica would be the promoter of the reform of the civil code with regard to marriage. She was joined by another female lawyer, María Telo, who would take up the baton in the 1960s and 70s, still under the Dictatorship.[97] Even the SF itself was aware of the need for certain changes. But the pressure of the feminist movements during the Democratic transition (1975–1981) was necessary in order to finally achieve egalitarian family law and for the normalization of the practise of the legal professions by women in Spain.[98]

Conclusion

The Liberal Period in Spain saw the emergence of discriminatory legislation toward women, in particular with regard to marriage, as had occurred in other countries, especially in those that followed the tradition of French Civil Code. In the nineteenth century and the beginning of the twentieth, the voice of some women rose up against this legislation, first in isolation and later on through associations and organized claims. But it was not until the brief period of the Second Republic when changes toward equality appeared, such as the divorce and civil marriage laws and the reform of the Criminal Code, promoted by female lawyers who had previously been members of feminist organizations. Therefore, in order to achieve these reforms, a change was necessary in the political regime, along with an élite of qualified women who claimed a new pattern of relationships between men and women. However, not all the objectives could be accomplished. Because of the short time that the reformist coalition was in power (1931–1933), some projects in relation to the legal capacity of women in marriage and the question of parentage and paternity never became laws; this issue, namely, the limited scope of reforms, is an area where this chapter has offered new information. In the sphere of the legal professions, women were permitted to become notaries public and property registrars, as well as clerks of court, but not judges or public prosecutors.

The Civil War (1936–1939) was a time of intense mobilization of women, when Republican women understood that while they defended the legitimate government they also defended the continuity of the progress achieved for them. In the Republican zone, a decree was enacted establishing the equality of spouses within marriage, in accordance with the Constitution of 1931, and the Autonomous Government of Catalonia authorized abortions performed in public hospitals. As evidence of the change that was taking place, for the first time women were appointed as judges and public prosecutors. Meanwhile, in the area controlled by insurgents, the abolition of equality laws began and the traditional model of gender relationships was reintroduced, characterized by male domination and women's subordination, and supported by the female Falangist organization, SF.

The role of a woman as wife and mother was praised as the prototype of womanhood, and the previous discriminatory provisions were reestablished in the civil code and the criminal code. Likewise, professional opportunities for women, especially in the legal sphere, were increasingly limited once Franco's victory led to the establishment of a dictatorship throughout the territory, though a few women managed to obtain positions as notaries publics and property registrars during these early years (but not the judiciary or the district attorney's office, which were considered to be of greater significance) and retain these posts through the Francoist period. The very existence of these few cases has been relatively unknown to date, and they are of interest due to the paradox that it was Republican-era laws that made them possible. It would be almost two decades before some reforms began to be made in the regulation of marriage.

This study arrives at two main conclusions. First, the history of family law and of women's access to legal professions in Spain has taken place in an international context, but has been strongly influenced by political changes in Spain throughout the twentieth century. For this reason, I have decided to examine the liberal era here, which culminates with the reforms of the Second Republic, the brief period of civil war, and the early stages of the Franco regime, up to the year 1950. In that year, women's situation was back to that in which they found themselves prior to the Republic, as regards both family law and opportunities to enter legal professions. This was followed, in Spain, by another period of struggle in favour of legal equality between men and women during the Franco regime, from the 1950s to the 1970s, and this continued during the democratic transition. Its chronology coincides at certain points with events under other dictatorships in southern Europe. Second, in the 1920s and 1930s, female jurists in Spain took the lead in combating the obstacles they suffered as professionals who were unable to accede to legal positions under equal conditions with men, and at the same time, some of them, who had previously been linked with women's movements, played a major role in promoting legal reforms in areas that affected all Spanish women, such as family law, during the Second Republic. The result of the civil war and the establishment of a dictatorship aborted the process, although it was to re-emerge many years later.

Notes

1 In Spain, the official journal where the government provisions are published has adopted several names through different periods: *Gaceta de Madrid, Gaceta de Madrid: Diario Oficial de la República, Gaceta de la República: Diario Oficial* (all of these are henceforth referred to as *Gaceta), and Boletín Oficial del Estado* (henceforward, *BOE*) (www.boe.es). The Catalan autonomous government's official journal was successively named *Butlletí Oficial de la Generalitat de Catalunya* (henceforward, *Butlletí*) and *Diari Oficial de la Generalitat de Catalunya* (henceforward, *Diari*) (www.gencat.cat/docg).

2 In 1873, the First Republic was proclaimed, but it lasted less than one year.

3 Pilar Muñoz López, *Sangre, amor e interés. La familia en la España de la Restauración* (Madrid: UAM y Marcial Pons, 1991), 40.

4 Regarding differences between Common Law systems and the Latin model, see Mariette Sineau, "Law and Democracy," in *History of Women in the West*, vol. 5, ed. Françoise Thébaud (Cambridge, MA: Harvard University Press, 1994), 497–526.

5 Josefina Alventosa, "Situación jurídica de la mujer en el ámbito del Derecho Civil español," in *Mujeres y Derecho*, ed. Paloma Durán y Lalaguna (Valencia: Ajuntament de Valencia, 1998), 37.

6 *Ley de Enjuiciamiento Civil de 1855*, official editing, Ministry of Mercy and Justice, second part, Title III, arts. 1245–1246, and Title IV, arts 1277–1311.

7 *Código Penal de 1848*, Title X, arts. 349 and 353, *Gaceta*, 21 to 28-III-1848; *Código Penal de 1870*, Title IX, arts. 448 and 452, *Gaceta*, 31-VIII-1870.

8 *Ley provisional de Matrimonio Civil*, 18-VI-1870, *Gaceta*, 21-VI-1870. On the debate about this law, see Gloria Espigado Tocino, "Revolución burguesa, Estado liberal y género. La Ley de matrimonio civil de 1870," *Alcores* 13 (2012): 43–61.

9 *Código Civil de 1889, Gaceta*, 25 to 27 VII, 1889, arts. 57–62 and 995.

10 Francisco Tomás y Valiente, "Los supuestos ideológicos del Código Civil: el procedimiento legislativo," in *La España de la Restauración: política, economía, legislación y cultura*, ed. José Luis García Delgado (Madrid: Siglo XXI de España Editores, S.A., 1985), 371.

11 Concepción Arenal, *La mujer del porvenir* (Sevilla: Eduardo Perié, Madrid: Félix Perié, 1869); re-issued: *La mujer del porvenir. La mujer de su casa* (Barcelona: Ediciones Orbis, 1989), 13. Regarding Arenal see: María Campo Alange, *Concepción Arenal, 1820–1893: estudio biográfico documental* (Madrid: Revista de Occidente, 1973); Mª José Lacalzada, *Mentalidad y proyección social de Concepción Arenal* (El Ferrol: Cámara de Comercio, 1994).

12 Text previously mentioned: Carmen de Burgos, *La mujer en España: conferencia pronunciada en la Asociación de la Prensa Italiana en Roma el 28 de abril de 1906* (Valencia: Sempere, 1906), 45–46. Regarding de Burgos: Concepción Núñez Rey, *Carmen de Burgos, Colombine, en la Edad de Plata de la literatura española* (Sevilla: Fundación José Manuel Lara, 2005).

13 *Código Civil de 1889*, arts. 104, 107, 68, 73.

14 Carmen de Burgos, *El divorcio en España* (Madrid: Viuda de Rodríguez Serra, 1904). Carmen de Burgos, without legal training but acquainted with the legal issues she addressed, may be considered a link between the legal profession and the general public, since she made use of her position as a reporter to inform about these questions. Anja Louis, *Women and the Law: Carmen de Burgos, an Early Feminist* (Woodbridge: Tamesis, 2005), 34.

15 Geraldine M. Scanlon, *La polémica feminista en la España contemporánea (1868–1974)* (Madrid: Ediciones Akal, S.A., 1986), 138–139; Concha Fagoaga, *La voz y el voto de las mujeres. El sufragismo en España, 1877–1931* (Barcelona: Icaria, 1985), 127–139, 152–155.

16 Marta del Moral Vargas, "Persiguiendo el reconocimiento de la igualdad: la petición de la *Cruzada de Mujeres Españolas* a las Cortes (31-V-1921)," *Arenal, Revista de historia de las mujeres* 16, no. 2 (2009): 379.

17 Carmen de Burgos, *El artículo 438* (Madrid, Prensa Gráfica: 1921); re-issued in *Mis mejores cuentos* (Barcelona: Editoriales Andaluzas Unidas, 1986), 35–67; *La malcasada* (Valencia: Sempere, 1923).

18 Louis, *Women and the Law*, 18; Carmen de Burgos, *La mujer moderna y sus derechos* (Valencia Sempere, 1927); re-issue: ed. Pilar Ballarín (Madrid: Biblioteca Nueva y Ministerio de Educación y Ciencia, 2007).

19 José S. Yanes Pérez, *Mujer y Abogacía. Biografía de María Ascensión Chirivella Marín* (Santa Cruz de Tenerife, Valencia: Ilustre Colegio de Abogados de Valencia, 1998).

20 A photograph in *Blanco y Negro* features her wearing the toga, 11-XII-1921, 10.

21 Yanes, *Mujer y Abogacía*, 82–83.

22 Concha Fagoaga y Paloma Saavedra, *Clara Campoamor. La sufragista española* (Madrid: Instituto de la Mujer, 2006); Fagoaga, *Voz y voto*, 143–152.

23 Zenaida Gutiérrez Vega, *Victoria Kent: una vida al servicio del humanismo liberal* (Málaga: Universidad de Málaga, 2001); Mª Dolores Ramos, *Victoria Kent, 1892–1987* (Madrid: Ediciones del Orto, 1999). The Revolutionary Committee had been created in the summer of 1930, its objective being to establish the Republic in Spain.

24 Fagoaga y Saavedra, *La sufragista*, 70; Sara L. Kimble, "Women, Law and Friendship: Activities of the International Federation of Women in Legal Careers between the Two World Wars," paper presented at the Social Science History Association Conference, Minneapolis, November 2–5, 2006, 3. (Consulted by author's courtesy.)

25 Peña's activities must have been rather well-known, since she was termed in a magazine "fashionable criminologist," *La Esfera*, 26-VII-1930, 24–26; see also:

Regina, "La mujer y la República. Una entrevista con Concha Peña," *La Voz*, 20-VI-1931.
26 Ángel García-Sanz Marcotegui, *Matilde Huici (1890–1965). Una "intelectual moderna" socialista* (Pamplona: UPNA, 2010).
27 Concha Fagoaga, "El Lyceum Club de Madrid, élite latente," in *Les Espagnoles dans l'histoire. Une sociabilité démocratique (XIXe–XXe siècles)*, ed. Danièle Bussy Genevois (Saint Denis: Presses Universitaires de Vincennes, 2002), 145–167; Shirley Mangini, "El Lyceum Club de Madrid, un refugio feminista en una capital hostil," *Asparkia* 17 (2006): 125–140. They all, Kent, Campoamor, and Huici, appear briefly interviewed in a report entitled "El feminismo en marcha. Las 'abogados' de España, contentas con su profesión," *Estampa*, 21-II-1928.
28 Fagoaga y Saavedra, *La sufragista*, 88–95.
29 Carmen de Zulueta y Alicia Moreno, *Ni convento ni college: la Residencia de Señoritas* (Madrid: CSIC, 1993); *Mujeres en vanguardia. La Residencia de Señoritas en su centenario (1915–2015)* (Madrid: Residencia de Estudiantes y ACE, 2015); *La Residencia de Señoritas y otras redes culturales femeninas*, ed. Josefina Cuesta, María José Turrión y Rosa María Merino (Salamanca: Ediciones Universidad de Salamanca, Fundación José Ortega y Gasset-Gregorio Marañón, 2015). The *Institución Libre de Enseñanza* was a private pedagogical institution of liberal nature created in 1875 that was very important for the educational renovation in Spain in the final decades of the nineteenth century and the first of the twentieth century.
30 Mercedes Montero, *La conquista del espacio público. Mujeres españolas en la Universidad (1910–1936)* (Madrid: Minerva, 2009), 124.
31 Federico Vázquez Osuna, "Las primeras mujeres juezas y fiscales españolas (1931–1939)," *Arenal, Revista de historia de las mujeres* 16, no. 1 (2009): 134.
32 Susanna Tavera ed., *Mujeres en la Historia de España: enciclopedia biográfica* (Barcelona: Planeta, 2000), 486–488; Montero, *Conquista del espacio*, 77–95.
33 Orden 24-IV-1924, *Gaceta*, 27-IV-1924.
34 "Las mujeres españolas quieren ser 'Jueces', 'Notarios', 'Registradores'," *Estampa*, 17-IV-1928.
35 Mary Nash ed., *Ciudadanas y protagonistas históricas. Mujeres republicanas en la II República y la Guerra Civil* (Madrid: Congreso de los Diputados, 2009); Mª Gloria Núñez Pérez, "Políticas de igualdad entre varones y mujeres en la segunda república española," *Espacio, Tiempo y Forma*, serie V, Historia Contemporánea 11 (1996): 393–445.
36 The CJA, created by the Republic's Provisional Government in May 1931, was the organ that prepared the bills to be submitted to the Parliament.
37 *Constitución de la República Española*, 9-XII-1931 (arts. 25, 36), *Gaceta*, 10-XII-1931. Fagoaga y Saavedra, *La sufragista*, 111–238; Rosa Mª Capel ed., *Historia de una conquista: Clara Campoamor y el voto femenino* (Madrid: Ayuntamiento de Madrid, 2007).
38 María Telo Núñez, *Concepción Arenal y Victoria Kent: las prisiones. Vida y obra* (Madrid: Instituto de la Mujer, 1995); Judith Keene, " 'Into the Clear Air of the Plaza': Spanish Women Achieve the Vote in 1931," in *Constructing Spanish Womanhood: Female Identity in Modern Spain*, ed. Victoria Lorée Enders and Pamela Beth Radcliff (Albany: SUNY Press, 1999), 325–347.
39 J. M. Simal: "Hablando con doña Matilde Huici. Los trabajos de la Subcomisión de Leyes Civiles. El divorcio y la capacidad jurídica de la mujer casada," *La* Voz, 12-II-1932 (reproduced in García-Sanz, *Matilde Huici*, 304–306).
40 *Ley relativa al divorcio*, 2-III-1932, *Gaceta*, 12-III-1932.
41 Ana Aguado, "Entre lo público y lo privado: sufragio y divorcio en la Segunda República," in *República y republicanas en España*, ed. Mª Dolores Ramos, *Ayer* 60, no. 4 (2005): 105–134; Mary Nash, "Forjar la ciudadanía en femenino:

igualdad y derechos de las mujeres durante la II República y la Guerra Civil," in *Ciudadanas y protagonistas*, 22–49; Aurora Morcillo Gómez, "Feminismo y lucha política durante la II República y la Guerra Civil," in *El feminismo en España: dos siglos de historia*, ed. Pilar Folguera (Madrid: Editorial Pablo Iglesias, 1988), 57–83.

42 *Ley de matrimonio civil*, 28-VI-1932, *Gaceta*, 3-VII-1932.

43 Matilde Huici, "Los derechos civiles de la mujer y su ejercicio," *Mujeres. Portavoz de las mujeres antifascistas*, no 1, 1-X-1937, 2ª época (reproduced in García-Sanz, *Matilde Huici*, 334–336). The draft law was given a reading in Parliament, and was then passed to the corresponding Commission for it to give its verdict, *ABC*, 7-VII-1933.

44 Orden 4-X-1933, *Gaceta*, 5-XI-1933.

45 *ABC*, 23-IX-1934.

46 It is one of the claims laid down in the ANME programme and so in the petition of the *Cruzada*.

47 García-Sanz, *Matilde Huici*; Fagoaga y Saavedra, *La sufragista*, 248; "El Consejo de Ministros de ayer," *ABC*, 1-VII-1933: 17–18.

48 *Código Penal reformado*, 27-X-1932, *Gaceta*, 5-XI-1932.

49 García-Sanz, *Matilde Huici*; Fagoaga y Saavedra, *La sufragista*, 246. During the dictatorship of Primo de Rivera a Criminal Code was elaborated in 1928, introducing some changes regarding punishment of adultery and *amancebamiento*, as well as penalties for the spouse who committed the killing of the adulterer, *Código Penal de 1928*, 8-IX-1928, *Gaceta*, 13-IX-1928. As was the case with other laws passed in the dictatorship period, the Republic's Provisional Government repealed the Criminal Code of 1928 in 1931.

50 Decreto 29-IV-1931, *Gaceta*, 30-IV-1931, ratified as law: Ley 30-XII-1931, *Gaceta*, 8-I-1932; Decreto 13-V-1932, *Gaceta*, 15-V-1932; Decreto 6-V-1933, *Gaceta*, 11-V-1933.

51 Josefina Carabias, "Las mujeres van a ser jueces, notarios, registradores . . .," *Estampa*, 9-IV-1932: 3–6. The author had a law degree and she was a member of the Royal Academy of Jurisprudence and Legislation and had a thorough knowledge of the judicial sphere of the time.

52 Orden 16-XI-1934, *Gaceta*, 20-XI-1934. Ten years later, in 1944, already during the Franco dictatorship, Teresa Argemí had a position as a teacher in a Graduate School of Barcelona, *La Vanguardia*, 29-VII-1944. She would later serve as lawyer for many years, *La Vanguardia*, 3-VIII-1994.

53 Directorate General for Justice. List of candidates accepted to take the competitive exams for Property Registrars, 20-I-1936, *Gaceta*, 21-I-1936.

54 Ley 19-VI-1934, *Butlletí*, 20-VI-1934.

55 *Frente Popular* was a coalition of bourgeois and workers' parties opposing the rise of fascism.

56 Mary Nash, *Rojas. Las mujeres republicanas en la Guerra Civil* (Madrid: Taurus, 1999).

57 Decreto 3-II-1937, *Gaceta*, 4-II-1937.

58 Decreto 25-XII-1936, *Diari*, 9-I-1937. The regulations for its implementation were fixed in Orden I-III-1937, *Diari*, 5-III-1937.

59 Nash, "Forjar la ciudadanía," 36–40; Nash, *Rojas*, 233–247.

60 Orden 2-XII-1936, *Diari*, 4-XII-1936; *La Vanguardia*, 4-XII-1936, *La Humanitat* (publication medium of the ERC), 4-XII-1936, *La Batalla* (publication medium of the POUM), 4-XII-1936.

61 Vázquez, "Primeras mujeres juezas," 142–143.

62 Ibid., 143. She had finished her law studies in 1928, at the *Universidad Central*, Archivo General de la Universidad Complutense de Madrid (AGUCM) DE-287, 1.

63 Orden 30-IV-1937, *Gaceta*, 5-V-1937. Regarding the *Socorro Rojo Internacional*, see Laura Branciforte, *El Socorro Rojo Internacional (1923–1939). Relatos de la solidaridad antifascista* (Madrid: Biblioteca Nueva, 2011). The People's Courts were created by the Republican Government to impose order in the judicial sphere following the revolutionary events which occurred at the start of the war; they were directed by law professionals and they also had representatives of the political forces, Raúl Cancio Fernández, *Guerra civil y tribunales: de los jurados populares a la justicia franquista (1936–1939)* (Cáceres, Universidad de Extremadura, 2007), 55–58.

64 Orden 17-I-1938, *Gaceta*, 19-I-1938. Her early death was reported in the press, which highlighted "her great abilities and Republican enthusiasm," *Defensor de Albacete*, 15-VIII-1938.

65 Orden 16-VII-1938, *Gaceta*, 17-VII-1938; Orden 3-VIII-1938, *Gaceta*, 4-VIII-1938; *Solidaridad Obrera*, 5-VIII-1938. Regarding the mentioned Central Court, Cancio, *Guerra civil y tribunales*, 78–84. The resignation was accepted by means of Orden 3-IX-1938, *Gaceta*, 4-IX-1938; Vázquez, "Primeras mujeres juezas," 144.

66 Fermín Pérez-Nievas Borderas, *Julia Álvarez Resano. Memoria de una socialista navarra (1903–1948)* (Pamplona: Pamiela, 2007).

67 Orden 22-X-1937, *Gaceta*, 24 -X-1937.

68 *Falange Española*, FE (Spanish Falange) was a political movement of totalitarian orientation that was founded by José Antonio Primo de Rivera, dictator Miguel Primo de Rivera's son, in October of 1933. During the Civil War, where it played a basic role in the insurgent area, it became the Spanish Traditionalist Falange and the JONS (FET y de las JONS) under the decision of Franco who took over the head of movement. *Sección Femenina*, a group of women that supported their male comrades, was founded in 1934, and Pilar Primo de Rivera, Miguel's daughter and José Antonio's sister, was its National Chief until 1977 when it was dissolved. Regarding *Sección Femenina*, Mª Teresa Gallego, *Mujer, falange y franquismo* (Madrid: Taurus, 1983); Kathleen Richmond, *Women and Spanish Fascism: The Women's Section of the Falange 1934–1959* (London: Routledge, 2003). A controversial point of view on the SF can be found in Victoria Lorée Enders, "Problematic Portraits: The Ambiguous Historical Role of the *Sección Femenina* of the Falange," in *Constructing Spanish Womanhood*, 375–397.

69 *Fuero del Trabajo*, 9-III-1938, Title II, 1, *BOE*, 10-III-1938.

70 Decreto 2-III-1938, *BOE*, 5-III-1938, fulfilled by the Order 9-XI-1938, *BOE*, 12-XI-1938.

71 Ley 12-III-1938, *BOE*, 21-III-1938.

72 Decreto 24-V-1938, *BOE*, 31-III-1938. Regarding the League of Nations debates on nationality of married women: Carol Miller, " 'Geneva—The Key to Equality': Interwar Feminists and the League of Nations," *Women's History Review* 3, no. 2 (1994): 219–245; Karen Offen, *European Feminisms, 1700–1950. A Political History* (Standford: Standford University Press, 2000), 341–359; Catherine Jacques, "Des lobbys féministes à la SDN: l'exemple des débats sur la nationalité de la femme mariée (1930–1935)," in *Femmes et relations internationales au XXᵉ siècle*, ed. Jean-Marc Delaunay and Yves Denéchère (Paris: Presses Sorbonne nouvelle, 2006), 267–277.

73 Ley 18-VII-1938, *BOE*, 19-VII-1938.

74 A comparison of the trend to pay out benefits to the father in dictatorships and the trend to pay them to the mother in democracies favouring their independence is examined by Gisela Bock and Pat Thane eds., *Maternity and Gender Policies. Women and the Rise of the European Welfare States. 1880s–1950s* (London and New York: Routledge, 1991).

75 Orden 27-XII-1938, *BOE*, 31-XII-1938.

76 For a general overview, see Gloria Nielfa, "Mujeres y política en el franquismo: el régimen y la oposición," in *Ciudadanas, militantes, feministas: mujer y compromiso político en el siglo XX*, ed. Ángeles Egido y Ana Fernández Asperilla (Madrid: Eneida, 2011), 163–198.
77 Ley 8-IX-1939, *BOE*, 30-IX-1939.
78 Ley 23-IX-1939, *BOE*, 5-X-1939.
79 Ley 24-I-1941, *BOE*, 2-II-1941.
80 Ley 11-V-1942, *BOE*, 30-V-1942.
81 Ley 11-V-1942, *BOE*, 30-V-1942.
82 Decreto 23-XII-1944, *BOE*, 13-I-1945.
83 Ley de Contrato de Trabajo, Decreto 26-I-1944, *BOE*, 24-II-1944.
84 Orden 27-IX-1939, *BOE*, 3-X-1939.
85 Ley 25-VIII-1939, *BOE*, 1-IX-1939.
86 Orden 16-VII-1940, *BOE*, 17-VII-1940; Complementary rules, 17-VII-1940, *BOE*, 23-VII-1940.
87 Decreto 6-XII-1941, *BOE*, 30-XII-1941.
88 Decreto 17-V-1941, *BOE*, 24-V-1941.
89 Decreto 14-X-1942, *BOE*, 23-X-1942. *Servicio Social* consisted of the provision of services during a six-month period that was set by the State for single women and childless widows from 17 to 35 years old; it was necessary to demonstrate compliance in order to receive official titles, to participate in public contests and competitions, to take administration posts, to work in public companies, and to occupy public charges. Decreto 7-X-1937, *BOE*, 11-X-1937. Later on, it was also requested to obtain passport or driving licence. 1944's call for notaries public' posts: Decreto 2-VI-1944, *BOE*, 7-VII-1944.
90 List of applicants issued in the *BOE*, 25-I-1943.
91 Regarding Mendizábal: *ABC* (Andalusian edition), 25-VI-1942 and 18-XI-1942. Regarding Baudín see *BOE*, 11-X-1944; 2009 interview, in *Notario del Siglo XXI, Revista on line del Colegio Notarial de Madrid* 25 (May–June 2009), http://www.elnotario.com; *ABC* published the news of her wedding, 27-X-1944: 10. Regarding Bono: *BOE*, 16-IX-1947 *La Vanguardia*, 16-VII-1947.
92 Call for Property Registrars' posts 23-X-1948, *BOE*, 31-X-1948; Orden 18-XI-1948, *BOE*, 25-XI-1948.
93 *BOE*, 28-IX-1941, 24-VIII-1942, 31-XII-1942, 2-VI-1946, 4-VI-1946, 5-VI-1946.
94 Some examples are the following: Torcida, Registrar of Property, completed her studies during the period of the Republic; others, such as the notaries Baudín and Bono and the Registrar Guerreira, had also initiated their studies during the Republic, but finished them after the Civil War (Archives of the Faculty of Law, Universidad Complutense, records 4485, 4624, 7050 and 4573, respectively.)
95 Christine Lavail, "L'étudiante et ses représentations dans la revue *Medina* (1941–1945): tentative de typologie et d'interprétation," *Imaginaires et symboliques dans l'Espagne du franquisme. Bulletin d'Histoire Contemporaine de l'Espagne* 24 (1996): 107–129.
96 Carme Molinero, "Historia, mujeres, franquismo. Una posible agenda de investigación en el ámbito político," in *Memoria e historia del franquismo. V Encuentro de Investigadores del franquismo*, ed. Manuel Ortiz Heras (Cuenca: Ediciones de la Universidad de Castilla-La Mancha, 2005), 171–172.
97 Rosario Ruiz Franco, *¿Eternas menores? Las mujeres en el franquismo* (Madrid: Biblioteca Nueva, 2007).
98 For further reading: Carmen Martínez Ten, Purificación Gutiérrez López and Pilar González Ruiz eds., *El movimiento feminista en España en los años 70* (Madrid: Cátedra, 2009); Monica Threlfall, Christine Cousins and Celia Valiente eds., *Gendering Spanish Democracy* (London and New York: Routledge, 2005).

3 Democracy at Home

Debating Family and Marriage Law in the First Czechoslovak Republic, 1918–1938

Melissa Feinberg

On January 22, 1919, the interim (or "revolutionary") National Assembly of the new state of Czechoslovakia met to debate a new municipal voting law. The proposed statute would abolish the complicated Habsburg era curial voting system and grant equal voting rights to all adult men and women in municipal elections. The law was widely praised for its progressive stance on political equality. The bill's proponents presented it as a significant and necessary step in the creation of the new Czechoslovak Republic. In their introduction to the text, the law's authors characterized their work as part of the "wave of democracy" that had swept Europe after the end of the First World War. In keeping with this trend, they said, "The idea of equality is becoming ever more a part of the moral consciousness of cultured nations."[1] The municipal voting statute would help bring Czechoslovakia into compliance with this new moral standard.

The "debate" over the bill was more like a chorus of praise for it and for the infant Czechoslovak Republic. The mood in the assembly hall was ebullient as legislators congratulated themselves on entering the ranks of "cultured nations." They waxed particularly eloquent on the subject of women's suffrage. One representative from the National Democratic Party, Bohuslav Franta, declared that "every friend of progress" would rejoice at women's new political equality. In his speech in favor of the law, Franta regretted that women had not been granted equal rights with men during the French Revolution, when the chance was there. He approvingly mentioned men who had championed women's equality, like Condorcet and John Stuart Mill. While these early pioneers were ridiculed, he said, now "the whole nation recognizes women's right to vote and be elected to public office."[2] Franta's sentiments were echoed by his colleague from the left, Social Democrat Antonín Němec. According to Němec, the new republic had no choice but to recognize the principle of women's equality. As he declared, "It would not be a true democracy if women were not in public life, in political life, and placed on a completely equal social level with men!"[3] As Němec spoke, shouts of "excellent!" rang out in the chamber as other deputies expressed their approval of his words.[4] After Němec spoke, Cyril Horáček, from the more right-leaning Agrarian Party, joined the chorus: "Justice demands that we give women the right to vote," he declared, once again to shouts of "excellent!" and "so it does!"[5] And so it went—as the debate moved on to a second day, not one speaker raised objections to women's suffrage on an equivalent basis with men.

This enthusiastic consensus on women's right to vote was amazing, even for this revolutionary moment in European history. While women across Central Europe gained the right to vote after the end of the First World War, the reaction in Czechoslovakia was unique.[6] In the speeches of Franta, Němec, Horáček, and others, women's political equality was taken to be one of the constitutive elements of democracy. Women's suffrage was a sign that democracy had been achieved and was, therefore, a cause for general celebration. But, as a 1921 article titled "Democracy and Women" suggested, the right to vote was only the first step toward true legal equality between men and women. The author, František Dvořak, declared that democracy must transform the family as well as the voting booth. As he noted, "It is not democracy if the husband makes decisions autocratically."[7] Czechoslovak feminists certainly agreed. They made changing Czechoslovakia's family law one of their top priorities. It quickly became clear, however, that removing gender specificity from Czechoslovakia's civil law was much more contentious than extending voting rights to women. Feminists argued that legal equality must be absolute and unlimited. But many others believed that political equality could comfortably co-exist with a legal reliance on gender difference, especially when the law dealt with relations between wives and husbands. In this essay, I examine the debates over family law in interwar Czechoslovakia. My analysis is based on extensive archival research, including the papers of the largest Czechoslovak feminist organization, the National Council of Women (Ženská Národní Rada), the papers of the Czechoslovak Ministries of Justice and Unification, the archives of the Czechoslovak Parliament, the published debates of the Czechoslovak Parliament, and an extensive survey of the interwar Czech-language press, particularly periodicals associated with women's organizations of all political persuasions.[8] In the first section of this essay, I show how gender equality became a marker of democracy and progress during the founding of the Czechoslovak Republic. I then consider how proposals to revise Czechoslovakia's Civil Code forced Czechoslovaks to define more precisely what they meant by "equality." I argue that the project of revising family law in Czechoslovakia ultimately failed because there was no consensus over the meaning of women's equality and no agreement over the extent to which democratic ideals should mandate actual changes in Czechoslovak civil law.

Feminism, Czech Nationalism, and the Law after 1918

The Republic of Czechoslovakia was created in the aftermath of the First World War from pieces of the Habsburg Monarchy. Czechoslovakia had not been a distinct territorial unit before 1918, and its population was a complicated multinational mix of peoples. The larger part of the new country—composed primarily of the provinces of Bohemia and Moravia—had been administratively in the Austrian half of the Monarchy. The largest ethnic group in this region was the Czechs, but there was also a large German-speaking minority, comprising over twenty percent of the new country's population. The eastern part of Czechoslovakia—the territories of Slovakia and Ruthenia—had been part of the Hungarian half of the Habsburg Monarchy, administered from Budapest rather than Vienna. The largest ethnic group in this region was the Slovaks, who spoke a Slavic language similar to Czech but distinct from it. There were also substantial Hungarian and Ruthenian minorities.[9] This ethnic and administrative diversity meant that there were few pre-existing "Czechoslovak" national, legal, or institutional traditions from before 1918 for the new state's founders to draw upon. A majority of those founders, however, identified themselves as Czechs and had been part of the pre-1918 Czech national movement. Specifically Czech nationalist ideals predominated at the founding of the Czechoslovak Republic and greatly influenced the attitudes of (often also Czech-identified) state officials toward democracy and gender equality.

Czech nationalism before 1918 was a multifaceted movement that encompassed a wide variety of political opinions. But in 1918, the national ideology associated with Tomáš Garrigue Masaryk achieved some prominence. Masaryk was a progressive democrat, and he believed that the Czech nation was, by virtue of its history, particularly oriented toward democracy. Masaryk was the person most responsible for identifying both the Czech nation and the Czechoslovak state with democracy. Even today, if people in the West associate anything with interwar Czechoslovakia, it is most likely the idea that the country was the last bastion of democracy in interwar continental Europe. This longstanding belief is due both to Tomáš Masaryk's ideas and his political acumen.[10] Masaryk was forced to flee Prague in 1914 to avoid arrest, and he spent the war years lobbying the Western powers for Czech independence within a Czechoslovak state. He successfully convinced Allied leaders that the Czechs were a modern, progressive, and democratic people worthy of statehood (with their brother Slovaks). He returned home in triumph to be appointed Czechoslovakia's first president, a position he would hold until forced to resign due to bad health in 1935.

Writing about democracy in the years before the First World War, Masaryk described it as more than a republican government based upon universal suffrage. For him, democracy indicated a society based on the values of freedom and equality more generally. As he wrote in 1913, "Universal suffrage does not guarantee democratic attitudes; a true democrat will not only be such in Parliament, but in the community, in a political party, in a circle of friends, in the family; he will feel and act democratically everywhere."[11] As the quote implies, Masaryk believed that democracy required equality between men and women. A society that allowed men to rule over women, in his judgment, did not meet the definition of democracy. In essays and lectures from the turn of the century onwards, Masaryk declared that women and men were equally intelligent and equally capable. He advocated not only for political rights for women but also for their economic independence and admittance into all arenas of professional life.[12] Masaryk's beliefs about women's rights were included in the Washington Declaration, the blueprint for a Czechoslovak state that he co-authored and presented to the Western Allies in a bid to convince them that an independent Czechoslovakia would be a more worthy ally than the Habsburg Monarchy. The Washington Declaration promised that in Czechoslovakia, women would be "placed on a level with men, politically, socially and culturally."[13]

Before the First World War, there was solid support for women's suffrage within the Czech nationalist movement, especially among Masaryk's supporters and on the left, but many Czech nationalist politicians remained opposed to the idea.[14] By 1918, however, this resistance had evaporated. The period just after the founding of Czechoslovakia was a triumphant moment for advocates of women's rights. Women's suffrage was taken as such a self-evident given that even before elections were held, eight women were asked to join the provisional National Assembly that would govern in the interim. Women also gained unprecedented access to higher education, including admission to all universities and secondary schools except for schools of theology.[15] The so-called *celibát*, which denied married women employment in the civil service (a category that included everything from postal clerks and teachers to bureaucrats), was abolished as well.[16] Czech feminists, seeing these rapid and remarkable gains, initially believed that their battle for equality was over. One woman, writing in the magazine *Ženský obzor* (Women's Horizon) in early 1919, exclaimed "Today the Czech woman is free," later remarking that this had happened so suddenly it was "as if by magic."[17]

But although the enthusiasm around women's suffrage was real, the debate over women's equal rights in Czechoslovakia was not over. The terms had simply changed. Suffrage was no longer an issue; men and women were equally accepted as political actors. But other crucial questions remained. Chief amongst them was the following: did democracy demand a legal code that treated men and women as genderless individuals in all areas? Or was it acceptable to see citizenship as a gendered category, with different rights and duties tied to the different social roles played by men and women, especially as mothers and fathers, husbands and wives? As if to point out this conundrum, the new Czechoslovak Constitution, enacted in 1920, provided justification for both conceptions of citizenship. Two articles of the constitution pertained directly to this issue. The first, §106, declared, "Privileges of sex, birth and occupation will no longer be recognized."[18] This article suggested that Czechoslovak laws had to be egalitarian in spirit and could not allow one sex to be treated more advantageously than another. But §126 of the constitution proclaimed, "Marriage, motherhood and the family are under the protection of the law."[19] The wording of the article strongly suggests that it was intended to promote a traditionally gendered family, where the spouses had very different duties and power was not distributed equally between them. The Czechoslovak Constitution seemingly required egalitarian laws that also protected traditional gender roles and hierarchies.

The debate among the drafters of the constitution over §106 shows that they were aware of this contradiction. The men who worked on this document believed that women should be active citizens and voters. But they weren't sure whether or not this meant that women always had to have the same legal rights as men. Some were clearly afraid of what might happen to society if women exercised their equality as citizens. At the meeting to discuss the draft of §106, several legislators objected that it would be wrong to legally bind the state to a policy of not recognizing sexual privilege, arguing that this might have unintended consequences. One, František Weyr, said that "privileges of sex do exist. I would not want §106 to change the civil code, which assigns a husband certain privileges . . . that we do not want to destroy."[20] For Weyr, marriage was not a contract between equal citizens but a social institution based on the natural differences between men and women. Another committee member, Jiří Hötzel, worried that legal equality between the spouses would have dramatic and harmful effects on marital harmony. He remarked, "I cannot imagine marriage if the law was to legalize anarchy within it. . . . Where there is a society of two people, one of them must make the decisions."[21] While democratic procedures worked for legislatures, families could not follow such principles. Building on Hötzel's comments, the representative Josef Dolanský noted, "We cannot institute something which is against reality. 'Birth' [he was referring here to social categories determined by birth, such as the nobility] is a creation of societal orders, but sex is given by nature."[22]

But other committee members disagreed. Theodor Bartošek argued that women were already taking on new roles in the working world and in political life, however much other members of the committee might want to stop them. These social developments would soon make it impossible to justify the privileges given to husbands in existing civil law; Czechoslovakia needed a constitution that was prepared for the realities of the future. This argument about the legality of so-called "sexual privileges" in a democracy was never really resolved. The committee eventually voted five to three to accept §106, but some of those who voted in favor only did so because they thought the wording was ambiguous enough to preclude any truly dramatic changes to the established gender order in the family.[23]

Divorce and Democracy

At the time of its founding, Czechoslovakia did not have a unified code of civil law. Bohemia and Moravia fell under the jurisdiction of the Austrian Civil Code of 1811, while Slovakia and Ruthenia used Hungarian civil law, which dated largely from 1894. The task of unifying these two systems fell to a special commission established in 1920 under the jurisdiction of the ministries of justice and unification.[24] As the unified code was to be based on the 1811 Austrian law, my comments refer exclusively to that code and later proposals to modify it for Czechoslovakia. The Austrian Civil Code of 1811 was based on Roman law. Its sections dealing with marriage and the family were similar to other European civil law codes from the early nineteenth century, such as the Napoleonic code.[25] Like the Napoleonic code, Austrian law gave the husband the title of head of the household, granting men the power to legally represent their wives and children, administer their property, and make decisions about their future. Wives, like children, did not have the status of full legal persons; their legal status was inextricably tied to their husbands. Husbands could compel their wives to live in their residence, forbid them to work outside the home, and take their earnings if they did work. Wives, in return, had a right to subsistence. Women had no rights over their own children and could not contest their husband's decisions about a child's education or marriage. A father could even will custody of his children to a guardian other than their mother in the event of his death, leaving her with no legal connection to her own offspring.[26]

In their debate over §106, the framers of Czechoslovakia's constitution worried that the civil code might soon come under scrutiny for the decidedly unequal way it allocated rights to husbands and wives. Family and marriage law did soon preoccupy the National Assembly but in a rather different context. In May 1919, the Assembly began to consider a bill that legalized divorce and civil marriage in the Czech lands. In Habsburg Austria, the state deferred to religious conventions with regard to marriage law and the responsibility for registering marriages was left with religious authorities.[27] As a substantial majority (over ninety percent) of the population was at least nominally Catholic, this had made divorce impossible for most people in the Czech lands. In the context of the time, this proposal to legalize divorce was framed as a means of removing the Habsburg influence from the Czechoslovak legal system, as the Habsburg dynasty was closely identified with Catholicism. The Czech nationalist politician Alois Hajn, for example, called the monarchy "a veritable El Dorado of Roman Catholicism." Hajn criticized the Habsburg government, not only for granting privileges to the Catholic Church but also for the practice of deferring to religious law more generally. A "modern" state, said Hajn, should have one code of laws for all citizens; it should not have different rules for those who adhered to different faiths. Hajn advocated for complete state control over marriage, including mandatory civil marriage and the legalization of divorce for all.[28] As the newspaper *Národní politika* (National Politics) put it, the issue was one of "modern culture, freedom, and justice." The point, according to the paper, was for all citizens to be truly equal under the law.[29]

While some Czech nationalists decried the Catholic Church as "Habsburg" and "Austrian" and believed that creating an independent democratic Czechoslovak Republic required attacking the Church, most of the country's population was Catholic. Some organized politically as Catholics and resisted the idea that they could not be good democrats or good Czechs if they did so.[30] In 1919, the focus of their objection was the idea of mandatory civil marriage. Catholics did not want to see religious ceremonies lose their legal validity.[31] They defended the religious content of marriage, calling a civil ceremony a sacrilege. Church leaders denied that having marriage under the control of organized religion went against the ethos of the new Czechoslovakia, claiming that the moral values of the Church did have a place in Czechoslovak society. The Catholic press also spoke out against the legalization of divorce, claiming that this would result in thousands of abandoned, penniless wives, discarded by their husbands in favor of younger and prettier brides.[32]

Catholic politicians were successful in having mandatory civil marriage taken out of the proposed legislation. The new marriage law that was debated on May 20–21, 1919 made civil marriage possible but did not require it, allowing religious ceremonies to retain legal validity. The new law did, however, make divorce legal for citizens of all faiths. While Catholic leaders vigorously objected, most of the members of the Assembly saw the marriage law as a means of modernization and democratization. They claimed that part of the task of creating a republic was separating church and state and rewriting laws to realize the mandate of legal equality for all citizens. As one representative, the National Democrat Josef Matoušek, said, "If we accept the most modern form of constitution, where we demand the absolute equality of every human being before the law, we must allow equality and not judge a Catholic and a Protestant differently because they belong to different faiths."[33] Or, as his colleague from the Czech Socialist Party, Theodor Bartošek, remarked, "The union of a democratic state which recognizes only the rule of the people with the absolute monarchy of the Pope is a legal and political monstrosity and would be a diseased phenomenon and a curb on all cultural and political progress in our Republic."[34] Democracy, it seemed, required divorce.

Those who spoke in favor of legalizing divorce were careful to note that they did not intend to undermine the family as an institution. Speaker after speaker emphasized the family's crucial social role, especially in educating and nurturing future generations. A marriage, they claimed, would ideally never be dissolved. But not every family was functional, and unhappy couples should not be forced to remain together. Josef Černý of the Agrarian Party claimed that divorce could even improve children's lives. He asked, "What kind of effect does the unhappiness of the parents have on the children? Dear Sirs, certainly a pernicious and even immoral one. How can the children of such a marriage become useful members of human society?"[35] If their parents could divorce and happily remarry, then this dysfunctional family could be transformed into two socially useful ones.

The marriage law of 1919 passed easily. But despite the initial consensus around its legalization, divorce did not become as widely accepted as women's suffrage. The 1919 legalization of divorce had been hastily organized by nationalist politicians who primarily wanted to remove Church influence from the laws of the new Czechoslovak Republic. It was not the result of feminist agitation, and women's organizations were not given the opportunity to negotiate the provisions of the legislation. The legal grounds for divorce were, in the words of one legal scholar, "complex."[36] Spouses could sue for divorce if their partner had committed an offense such as adultery, leading a dissolute life, committing a serious crime, etc., or if he or she was responsible for the complete breakdown (*hluboký rozvrat*) of the marriage. It was also possible to get a divorce on the grounds of incompatibility (without assignment of guilt), generally if preceded by a legal separation of at least one year.[37] The law of 1919 did not itself provide new grounds for alimony or child support. The practice of determining levels of spousal or child support was also complex, but women judged as the guilty party in divorce suits usually forfeited all rights to spousal support.[38]

Given the disastrous economic consequences divorce often had on women, a wide variety of Czechoslovaks from different political persuasions began to favor making divorce harder to obtain. Catholic politicians and Catholic women's groups remained staunchly opposed to divorce and hoped that it would be banned altogether.[39] Some feminists also came to oppose existing divorce laws, arguing that they allowed men to abandon wives and children to poverty.[40] Members of the National Council of Women, the largest feminist organization in Czechoslovakia (founded in 1923), were divided on the issue of how easy it should be to obtain a divorce. Some believed that divorce laws should be liberal, allowing either spouse to petition for divorce after a two-year separation. Others thought divorce should only be granted for cause (like adultery, etc.), and that a spouse who had committed a divorceable offense should never be allowed to divorce the "innocent" party (presumed to be the woman) against her will.[41] Revising laws on alimony to improve the economic situation of divorced women was also a matter of concern, although some feminists believed that in the spirit of egalitarianism, women should also be required to provide support to indigent ex-husbands.[42]

In the popular media, divorce was often portrayed as problematic. A number of articles published in 1924, for example, bemoaned the fact that after only five years of legal divorce, there were already 60,000 divorced women in Czechoslovakia. One article claimed that there were seventeen-year-old divorcees and expressed the hope that media coverage of the often impoverished state of divorced women would cause couples to think more carefully before deciding to either make or break a marriage.[43] Another also quoted the figure of 60,000 divorced women and focused on the creation of an organization to promote their interests. This author saw the creation of such a group as immoral and thought that divorced women should spend their time pondering why their marriages failed rather than organizing to get more money out of their ex-husbands. What's next, he wrote, "an advice center for the more efficient monetization of prostitution, an advice center for ‘hoodwinked’ husbands and the education of calculating women, or an organization devoted to putting marriage on a commercial basis?” Divorced women should not agitate for greater alimony or child support but “roll up their sleeves and work to provide their children with the basic necessities. That will be an example for frivolous women!”[44]

The plot of a novella entitled *Rozvodová advokátka* (Female Divorce Lawyer), first published in installments in the women’s magazine *Pražanka* (Prague Woman), is a telling example of popular attitudes toward divorce. This novella, later published as a book, told the story of Šarka Melianová, whose poor opinion of men had led her to become a lawyer specializing in divorce. Šarka is young, beautiful, and intelligent but also cold and unforgiving, especially when it comes to male fidelity. When the novella begins, Šarka has a successful career and a charming boyfriend, the car dealer Leo Janák, who will soon become her fiancé. But things are not going well in her family. Šarka’s father is in disgrace for cheating on her mother, and her parents are living apart. Šarka soon discovers that her sister Líba’s husband Milan is also being unfaithful. Šarka counsels Líba to get a divorce. Líba refuses, saying she loves Milan and will not abandon him. Disgusted with what she considers her sister’s weakness, Šarka cuts off all contact with Líba and insists that her mother do so as well. Around this time, her father begins corresponding with her mother, saying that he is sorry for the pain he has caused her and wants to come home. Šarka forbids her mother to reconcile with her father, as she considers his sins to be unforgiveable. Unbeknownst to Šarka, her parents plan her father’s secret return while she is gone on her honeymoon with Leo.[45]

Before this can happen, however, Šarka discovers during a visit to Leo’s apartment that it is Leo’s own sister, Irena, who has been having an affair with her brother-in-law, Milan. Leo has even covered for Irena by telling her husband that she was with him during the time she was having a tryst with Milan. Horrified that Leo would be a party to adultery, Šarka breaks off their engagement. She returns home to a note from her mother informing her that her father has taken ill in Slovakia, and she has gone to nurse him. Šarka finds the pile of letters detailing her parents’ reconciliation and falls into despair over the weakness and immorality around her. As time passes, both her parents and her sister and Milan work out their troubles and regain their marital happiness. Šarka tries to absorb herself in her work, which had previously given her so much pleasure and purpose. But she is consumed with thoughts of Leo and cannot regain her former happiness. While on vacation in the Alps, she realizes that perhaps she had been wrong to counsel so many women to divorce their husbands immediately after discovering they had been wronged. She goes home to Prague, quits her job, reconciles with her family, and lives happily ever after.[46]

The point of this admittedly pulpy story was clear. Šarka, the independent professional, was not a woman to be envied or emulated. She was beautiful and brilliant but hard and uncompromising, ultimately lacking precisely the qualities women needed most: self-sacrifice and unconditional love. Her career was no substitute for a successful marriage and the warmth of her family. In the novella, women were happiest as wives and divorced at their peril. Even if their husbands were unfaithful, they were better off staying in their marriage. *Rozvodová advokátka* suggested that even if divorce were legal, women were foolish to attempt it, no matter their husbands' sins. The magazine in which this novel was serialized, *Pražanka*, was a mass-market publication that usually had features on fashion, cinema, and travel, as well as more traditional topics like recipes and children. But it also occasionally published more serious articles with a feminist bent, and shortly after *Rozvodová advokátka* was completed, the magazine ran a series of articles by Marie Tippmannová advocating for changes in Czechoslovak family law to equalize the legal relationship between husbands and wives.[47] In the pages of *Pražanka*, the messages about gender equality were mixed. Women might ask for more equality within marriage, but they also should beware the consequences of renouncing their feminine roles as wives and mothers.

A New Czechoslovak Civil Code?

The special commission called in 1920 to create a unified civil law code for all of Czechoslovakia published its first results in 1924. In the area of family law, the commission's proposal incorporated the marriage and divorce law of 1919 but made few other changes to the old Austrian code of 1811. The extensive rights granted to husbands as the head of the household remained intact: wives and children did not gain the status of legal persons nor were wives allowed control over their own property nor a legal say in their children's lives. Wives were still required to take their husband's name, obey his wishes in domestic matters, and contribute their labor to the household.[48] The few substantive changes the commission proposed in 1924 tended to actually limit married women's legal rights even more. For example, the proposed new law would expand a wife's legal obligations by mandating that "if the husband is not able to provide for himself, it falls to his wife to provide him with a decent standard of living." In the "spirit of mutuality," wives would now be legally bound to support husbands who were not capable of earning a living. However, if a woman did have to take over the role of provider for her family, she did not get to assume the title or rights of the "head of the household." Even after assuming her husband's responsibilities, she would still be obliged to follow his orders and abide by his decisions.[49]

The 1924 proposal was only a draft that had been published for the purpose of public discussion. Unfortunately for its authors, few seemed to find it acceptable. For Czechoslovak women's activists, the government's family law proposal was a disgrace. In their view, it did not meet the needs of contemporary women nor did it uphold the mandate of §106 of the Czechoslovak Constitution. As the prominent Social Democrat Betty Karpíšková remarked, "What is expressed [in the 1924 proposal] is fundamentally the old law of men, his arrogant position in the family and alternatively for women, blind obedience and submission to the 'masters'."[50] On the other hand, Catholic activists were similarly disappointed with the proposal, as its most substantive changes were to fully incorporate the 1919 laws on civil marriage and divorce into the civil code.

Many women's groups took an active interest in the revision of Czechoslovak family law. The feminist effort to revise the civil code was headed by the National Council of Women (NCW). The NCW was a federation of pre-existing women's organizations created after independence in 1923 to coordinate campaigns for women's equality. Avowedly feminist, the NCW was non-partisan, allowing it to join together women from an array of different political parties, albeit never from the Catholic-oriented People's Party or the Communist Party.[51] Its founder and president was Františka Plamínková, a stalwart of the Czech feminist movement, and after 1925, a Czechoslovak senator for the National Socialist Party.[52] Plamínková's clout, along with that of other female politicians who worked with the NCW, gained the group extensive access to government officials.[53]

In most instances, the NCW advocated for legal equality between men and women. Its members took a position similar to Tomáš Masaryk and declared that Czechoslovakia could not have a democratic state if it did not democratize the family. Marriage had to be transformed from a dictatorship into a partnership, where spouses shared decision-making authority.[54] NCW activists did not deny the existence of gender difference or that tasks within the family might be gendered. But they did embrace an egalitarian brand of citizenship that demanded men and women be treated as legal equals, even within the family. For the NCW, egalitarianism was not a threat to family stability but rather the means of modernizing the family for a new, democratic age.[55]

The NCW's legal section developed its own ideal family law code to use in negotiations with the Ministry of Justice. The NCW proposal treated all adult family members as legal persons, endowed with the same fundamental rights and privileges. Husbands and wives would legally become "spouses," with an equal right (or responsibility) to legally represent their family, to determine their place of residence and their married name (which would not need to be the husband's name), and to provide for each other and their children. Both wives and husbands would have the freedom to work outside the home as they saw fit, and housework would no longer be considered a wife's legal responsibility. Recognizing that dual-earner couples were not the norm in interwar Czechoslovakia (although they were becoming more prevalent), the NCW's proposal would legally grant spouses who devoted their time to unpaid household work a right to half of the salary of their partner. While at the time this would realistically only benefit women, the NCW was careful to use gender-neutral language, allowing for the possibility that men might also someday receive a wage for housework in this fashion. The NCW's enthusiastic pursuit of gender-neutrality in civil law even led them to advocate rules that could disadvantage women. For example, they suggested that in a divorce, all property gained in marriage should be divided equally and the spouse with the lower income be granted a right to alimony from the other, whatever that spouse's sex might be.[56]

The NCW's striking endorsement of gender equality in civil law could not have been more different from the Catholic position on the issue. The NCW organized its campaign for revising Czechoslovak family law around §106 of the Czechoslovak Constitution and argued that democracy required that all citizens receive equal treatment under the law, even when they were acting as husbands and wives.[57] Catholics took their inspiration from §126 of the constitution, which declared the importance of family, marriage, and motherhood to the state. For Catholic women activists, families did not follow the same rules that democracies did; family members looked instead to nature's law to guide their behavior. Family harmony required a clearly gendered division of labor and power in the home. Without this, family life would be destroyed by the same kind of petty conflict and strife that plagued democratic legislatures.[58]

The primary organization for Catholic women in Bohemia and Moravia was the Federation of Catholic Women and Girls. This group was also one of the largest women's organizations in interwar Czechoslovakia, with over 300,000 members.[59] The Federation of Catholic Women and Girls urged their government to assign rights on a gendered basis, at least in the realm of family law.[60] For these Catholics, the goal of political action was to protect and defend the family's gendered roles. In contrast to the NCW, the Federation of Catholic Women and Girls wanted the civil code to retain the husband's status as the head of the household, requiring men to remain responsible for making the family's financial and legal decisions so that their wives could focus on domestic tasks. The goal of their activism was not to help women achieve greater mobility outside the family but to increase their power and security within its confines.[61] They believed that women were directed by their God-given nature to this domestic life; secular legal codes should not give them the right to deny this natural calling. As another author in *Křesťanská žena* noted, "a woman does not have a right to her body, she is inseparably tied to the company of the family and the nation, she does not answer only to herself, but above all to God."[62] Czech Catholic women activists did not think married women should have the right to paid employment (and economic independence). For a family to function properly, women had to be homemakers and men breadwinners. Turning husbands and wives into mere "spouses," as the NCW proposed, would, they believed, destroy the very essence of the family.[63]

Catholic women also wanted to revoke the legalization of divorce and civil marriage. As characterized by the Federation of Catholic Women and Girls, divorce was "the biggest evil and unhappiness of every state. It disrupts its foundations, destroys peace in families, rips the bonds of marriage, and does not even stop in front of the fearful little faces of the children and moves like an avalanche, dragging with it everything that stands in its path."[64] Divorce was like a knife held to the throats of all good women who only wanted to be wives. Who, divorce opponents asked, could dedicate themselves to having and raising a family if they could never be sure that their husband would not suddenly abandon them for a new bride? And what young woman would want to become a mother if she could never be sure whether or not her husband would throw her out on the street with several small children to feed? As a lasting impediment to the creation of stable and fertile families, Catholic activists believed that divorce was a threat to the survival of the Czech nation.

A Body Without a Heart

In 1926, the Czechoslovak government formed a new commission (the "super-revisory" commission) to review responses to the draft of a new civil code and make further changes as necessary. This super-revisory commission worked for six years and published a new revised draft in 1931. This latest version, however, did little to satisfy critics on any side. In the area of family law, the 1931 draft continued to designate the husband as the head of the household and to deny his wife the power to be her own legal person.[65] The commission justified this decision by echoing the argument made by Jiří Hötzel during the discussion of §106 of the Czechoslovak Constitution: if a husband could not put his foot down and end a dispute with his wife by fiat, family harmony would disappear. "It is easy," the commission wrote in its report, "to say that husband and wife should have the same position in the family, that is, the same duties and the same rights."[66] But equality between the spouses would bring chaos and anarchy to the family. Couples, constantly arguing over petty matters, would be forever turning to the courts to arbitrate disagreements over where they would live or how to allocate household earnings. The super-revisory commission believed that leaving decision-making power with the husband was the only way to avoid this disruptive discord.

Feminists from the National Council of Women were incensed by the super-revisory commission's family law proposal, especially since they had negotiated personally with representatives from the Ministry of Justice about the new family law in 1929 and had believed that their meeting would bring the results they wanted.[67] As an article in their journal *Ženská rada* (Women's Council) asked, "Do the leaders of the Republic really want a true democracy? Do they want it from internal conviction that it is the correct path for our nation? If they want it, they cannot want, they are not allowed to want a family law which would come outside the democratic spirit of equality between spouses and between parents."[68] Their protests did reach some sympathetic ears at the highest levels of government. In 1932, the Minister of Justice, Social Democrat Alfréd Meissner, remarked in a speech that "the super-revisory commission's proposal does not completely satisfy this demand [of equality] and it will be necessary to revise many of its statutes. For example, the mere sentence that the 'husband is the head of the household' is in many cases a mere fiction."[69] The NCW legal committee again tried to influence the process of revising the law; it spent months going over the 1931 draft and coming up with a detailed set of proposed changes to it.[70] After petitioning the Justice Ministry, the organization was able to set up a private series of meetings between NCW officer and lawyer Milada Horáková and senior Justice Ministry official Dr. Srb in September 1935. At these meetings, Horáková argued the NCW case and demanded that the principle of gender equality be inserted into Czechoslovak family law.[71]

But feminists were not the only ones trying to influence the proceedings. The super-revisory commission placed mandatory civil marriage into their 1931 proposal, arguing that any modern nation should have just one set of administrative procedures for registering marriages. The commission claimed that it was not trying to infringe on religious freedom or attack the Catholic Church, noting that religious marriage ceremonies could still occur, provided that the obligatory civil ceremony also took place.[72] Catholics did not agree. The Federation of Catholic Women and Girls was incensed at the prospect of mandatory civil marriage, claiming that it was a pernicious practice responsible for suicides, unhappiness, pain, and misery. They associated civil marriage with divorce, broken homes, and miserable children.[73] The Federation sponsored protest meetings, pilgrimages, and masses, including a rally on March 15, 1932 attended by Cardinal Karel Kašpar. In his speech that day, Kašpar declared that civil marriage was not marriage at all; it was, in fact, "nothing but concubinage." For Catholics like Kašpar, making marriage into a civil institution took away its power. Civil bonds would never be as strong as religious ones, and civil marriages would be prone to divorce. The family would be broken and children would suffer. Kašpar tried to argue in patriotic terms rather than religious ones, claiming that strong families were the foundation of the Czechoslovak nation. Catholics loved their nation, he said, much more than those who were trying to violently institute mandatory civil marriage.[74]

After its publication and the vociferous public response, the super-revisory commission's draft for a new civil code was debated by the various branches of Czechoslovak government in closed sessions. In the fall of 1935, the super-revisory commission was recalled to make changes based on those discussions. The commission finished its work a year later. The now final text was not released to the public until it was presented to the National Assembly for preliminary debate in April 1937. However, to the shock and disappointment of the legislators, the new civil code they were supposed to discuss was not complete: the section on family and marriage law was missing. In a speech to the Senate, Ivan Dérer, the new Justice Minister, admitted that the family law codes were left out of the proposal because the government had not been able to come to an agreement on the issues of mandatory civil marriage and divorce.[75] According to the Federation of Catholic Women and Girls, it was the People's Party that had held up negotiations and continued to do so. Government leaders were not willing to break their coalition over the matter, and so they simply delayed making any decision.[76]

The other portions of the civil code were briefly debated in both houses of the National Assembly before being sent to committee for more detailed discussion. Speakers in the Assembly heralded the long-deferred arrival of a unified Czechoslovak civil code, which they hoped would help to knit the country's regions and peoples more firmly together.[77] They also lamented the incomplete status of the bill at hand. Representative Ladislav Rašín noted that if the family was the foundation of the state, without family law, "the entire structure of the civil code will crumble."[78] Representative Oldřich Suchý from the Agrarian Party charged that the civil code without its family and marriage sections was "like a trunk without a head—even, I think, without a heart."[79] A final version of the family and marriage law sections of the civil code was not released during the existence of the first Czechoslovak Republic.

Even the truncated version of a new Czechoslovak civil code never actually became law. It remained in committee as Europe lurched closer to war. In October 1939, Czechoslovakia was forced by the signers of the Munich Agreement to cede part of its territory to Germany. This trauma spelled the end of the first Czechoslovak Republic. After a brief interlude during which leaders tried to reorganize the state on a federal basis, the country was invaded by Nazi Germany and broken into two parts: an independent Slovak Republic and the Protectorate of Bohemia and Moravia, which remained under German rule. It was only after the war ended that the reconstituted Czechoslovak government returned to the issue of its civil code, but the project would only be completed after the imposition of a Communist dictatorship in 1948. Passed by the National Assembly in 1949, this first unified code of Czechoslovak civil law acceded to feminist demands and placed spouses on an equal legal footing in the family.[80] However, the political realities of the postwar world meant that this long-sought legal equality was realized in a country that had done away with the political freedoms that characterize democracy.[81]

Conclusion: Gender and Citizenship in Interwar Czechoslovakia

The failed project to create a new Czechoslovak civil code reveals two competing and ultimately irresolvable beliefs about the relationship between gender and citizenship in interwar Czechoslovakia. Czech feminists believed that citizenship was a relationship between equal individuals. While they admitted there might be a few instances where laws should take gender into account (in providing for paid maternity leave, for example), they generally rejected the idea that rights should be allocated to citizens on a gendered basis. Especially in the months and years shortly after the establishment of the Czechoslovak Republic, this egalitarian vision of citizenship was widely supported in Czechoslovak politics. Many echoed Tomáš Masaryk and linked women's equality with modernity and progress. In the debates over the 1919 municipal voting law, legislators characterized their actions as a necessary part of the process of creating a democracy. In that debate, one of the women appointed to that first National Assembly, Božena Ecksteinová, declared, "We entered the National Assembly without a fight, not only cast by a wave of democratism but recognized on account of our equal humanity."[82] The Czechoslovak Constitution itself seemed to echo this feeling in its §106.

But while Czechoslovaks did enthusiastically welcome women as voters, there was no such general agreement when it came to the issue of civil equality. Tomáš Masaryk had famously said that a real democrat would act as such even within the family. The NCW hoped to make that into a legal reality. Its proposals for a new civil code included the possibility of wives who supported their husbands economically, removed the responsibility of housework from women, and even threw the idea of a wife taking her husband's name into doubt. The feminists in the NCW did not see their proposal as radical; they believed it was mandated by the Czechoslovak Constitution and by the ideological requirements of any democratic state. As NCW president Plamínková declared in a speech to the Senate in 1937, revising the civil code was "not about conservative or progressive [legal] opinions." In her view, the government's draft proposals for a new civil code "simply did not respect the spirit of the democratic constitution in basic, foundational elements."[83] Some, including Justice Ministers Meissner and Dérer, were sympathetic to the NCW's position. Indeed, it is telling that in negotiations with the NCW, Czechoslovak government officials did not attempt to challenge their constitutional argument for civil equality. But they also refused to accede to their demands.

For groups like the Federation of Catholic Women and Girls, the kind of equality the NCW took as self-evidently necessary was dangerous. In their view, the family was indeed essential to the state, but it was not governed by the same laws or bound by the same legal norms. The family was the province of nature rather than constitutions and it did not need equality within it. Civil law should respect men's and women's essential differences and assist them in realizing their natural roles in the family. Some of the very framers of the Czechoslovak Constitution agreed with this view and hoped that the constitution's seeming mandate of equality would not be taken to the lengths that the feminists wanted.

Those who remember Czechoslovakia as the democratic exception in fascist Central Europe are not wrong. In the 1930s, democracy was more popular (and more functional) in Czechoslovakia than elsewhere in the region.[84] But even though much of the population supported "democracy," there was no general agreement on the kind of legal system democracy entailed. Debates over issues like revising the civil code showed the limits of the political consensus on democracy in Czechoslovakia. There was simply no agreement on the proper legal relationship of gender to citizenship, or, to put it more broadly, the relationship of political equality to civil rights. As the case of the civil code shows, these disagreements were so fundamental that they could not be resolved during the lifespan of the First Czechoslovak Republic.

Notes

1 Tisk #302/1919 ("Zpráva ústavního výboru o předloze řádu volení do obcí"), accessed December 20, 2013, http://www.psp.cz/eknih/1918ns/ps/tisky/t0302_01.htm.
2 Speech of Bohuslav Franta, January 22, 1919 meeting of the Czechoslovak National Assembly, accessed December 20, 2013, http://www.psp.cz/eknih/1918ns/ps/stenprot/019schuz/s019002.htm.
3 Speech of Antonín Němec, January 22, 1919 meeting of the Czechoslovak National Assembly, accessed December 20, 2013, http://www.psp.cz/eknih/1918ns/ps/stenprot/019schuz/s019003.htm.
4 Ibid.
5 Speech of Cyril Horáček, January 22, 1919 meeting of the Czechoslovak National Assembly, accessed December 20, 2013, http://www.psp.cz/eknih/1918ns/ps/stenprot/019schuz/s019004.htm.
6 Women gained suffrage in Germany, Austria, and Poland in 1918 and had limited suffrage in Hungary after 1921 (it was less restricted from 1920–21). On this period in European feminism, see Karen Offen, *European Feminisms, 1700–1950: A Political History* (Stanford, CA: Stanford University Press, 1999), 257–310.
7 František Dvořak, "Demokracie a žena," *Ženské noviny* 3, no. 3 (1921): 1–2.
8 A more complete account of this research is contained in Melissa Feinberg, *Elusive Equality: Gender, Citizenship and the Limits of Democracy in Czechoslovakia, 1918–1950* (Pittsburgh: University of Pittsburgh Press, 2006).
9 In this region, bilingualism, especially for Czech and German speakers, was common and language use was not necessarily a marker of national identification. While after 1918, many people claimed a fixed national or ethnic identity (as Czech, German, Slovak, etc.), some continued to move fluidly between national groups. There is an enormous literature on this phenomenon. Just a few of the key titles in English include: Tara Zahra, *Kidnapped Souls: National Indifference and the Battle for Children in the Bohemian Lands, 1900–1948* (Ithaca: Cornell University Press, 2008); Chad Bryant, *Prague in Black: Nazi Rule and Czech Nationalism* (Cambridge: Harvard University Press, 2007); and Jeremy King, *Budweisers into Czechs and Germans* (Princeton, NJ: Princeton University Press, 2002).
10 On the success of Masaryk's mythmaking about Czechoslovakia, see Andrea Orzoff, *Battle for the Castle: The Myth of Czechoslovakia in Europe, 1914–1948* (New York: Oxford University Press, 2009).
11 Tomáš Garrigue Masaryk, *Nesnáze demokracie*, excerpted in Koloman Gajan ed., *Tomáš Garrigue Masaryk o demokracii* (Prague: Melantrich, 1991), 48.
12 For Masaryk's views on women, see Tomáš Garrigue Masaryk, *Mnohoženství a jednoženství* (Prague: Čin, 1925), *Masaryk a ženy* (Prague: Ženská Národní Rada, 1930); also Feinberg, *Elusive Equality*, 13–20.

13 It was called the Washington Declaration because it was released in Washington, DC. Tomáš Garrigue Masaryk, Edvard Beneš, and Milan Štefánik, *Washingtonská deklarace* (Brno: Moravský Legionař, 1925). On Masaryk's activities in Washington, see Orzoff, *Battle for the Castle*, 37–56.

14 Jitka Malečková, "The Emancipation of Women for the Benefit of the Nation: The Czech Women's Movement," in *Women's Emancipation Movements in the 19th Century: A European Perspective*, ed. Sylvia Paletschek and Bianka Pietrow-Ennker (Stanford, CA: Stanford University Press, 2004), 167–188; Katharine David, "Czech Feminists and Nationalism in the Late Habsburg Monarchy," *Journal of Women's History* 3, no. 2 (1991): 26–45; Feinberg, *Elusive Equality*, 20–28.

15 "Ženy v naší české republice nabývají nových oprávnění," *Ženský obzor* 17, no. 1 (1919): 25.

16 Marie Tippmanová, "Vdaná žena ve veřejném povolání," *Žvěstování* 1, no. 35 (1919): 2. On the interwar controversy over married women in the Czechoslovak civil service, see Feinberg, *Elusive Equality*, 99–128.

17 Krista Nevšimalová, "Žena ve státě československém," *Ženský obzor* 17, no. 3 (1919): 66.

18 Czechoslovak Constitution of 1920 (č.121/1920 Sb), accessed June 11, 2014, http://www.psp.cz/docs/texts/constitution_1920.html.

19 Ibid.

20 Stenograph from 110th meeting of the Constitutional Committee, Archiv Federálního Shromáždění ČSR, Prague, box 31.

21 Ibid.

22 Ibid.

23 Ibid.

24 Protocols from initial meetings of commission, March 6, 1920 and June 16, 1920. Národní Archiv, Prague (hereafter NA), fond Ministerstvo Spravedlnosti (hereafter MS), box 302.

25 On the issue of gender in the Napoleonic Code, see Jennifer Ngaire Heuer, *The Family and the Nation: Gender and Citizenship in Revolutionary France, 1789–1830* (Ithaca: Cornell University Press, 2005), 121–192.

26 On Czechoslovak family law, see Marie Mikulová, *Žena v právním řádě československém* (Prague: self published, 1936). Mikulová was one of the first female lawyers in Czechoslovakia. Her book is an indispensible compilation of interwar Czechoslovak law and legal practice as it particularly relates to women.

27 Civil marriage and divorce had been legalized in the Hungarian Kingdom in 1894 in a process similarly driven by liberals who wanted to remove the influence of the church from the state. The 1919 legislation would not be valid in Slovakia, which remained under the 1894 Hungarian civil code. On the Hungarian reforms, see Robert Nemes, "The Uncivil Origins of Civil Marriage," in *Culture Wars: Secular Catholic Conflicts in Nineteenth-Century Europe*, ed. Christopher Clark and Wolfram Kaiser (New York: Cambridge University Press, 2003), 313–335.

28 Alois Hajn, "K reformě práva manželského," *Nová síla* 1, no. 2 (1919): 2–3.

29 "První den rokování o reformě manželského práva," *Národní politika*, May 21, 1919.

30 On Czech Catholics and Czech nationalism, see Cynthia Paces, *Prague Panoramas: National Memory and Sacred Space in the Twentieth Century* (Pittsburgh: Pittsburgh University Press, 2009), especially 87–114.

31 "Pro rozluku manželství a proti kněžskému bezženství," *Lidové noviny*, May 21, 1919.

32 B. N., "Mravní význam nové úpravy manželského práva," *Zvěstování* 1, no. 23 (1919): 1–2.

33 Speech of Dr. Matoušek, 52nd meeting of the Czechoslovak National Assembly, May 21, 1919, accessed December 20, 2013, http://www.psp.cz/eknih/1918ns/ps/stenprot/052schuz/s052009.htm.
34 Speech of Dr. Bartošek, 53rd meeting of the Czechoslovak National Assembly, May 22, 1919, accessed December 20, 2013, http://www.psp.cz/eknih/1918ns/ps/stenprot/053schuz/s053001.htm.
35 Speech of Dr. Černý, 52nd meeting of the Czechoslovak National Assembly, May 21, 1919, accessed December 20, 2013, http://www.psp.cz/eknih/1918ns/ps/stenprot/052schuz/s052006.htm.
36 Zdeňka Králíčková, "Developments in Marriage and Marital Law in the Czech Republic," in *Marriage and Quasi Marital Relationships in Central and Eastern Europe*, ed. Lynn Wardle and A. Scott Loveless (Provo: Brigham Young University Academic Publishing, 2008), 178.
37 For a complete breakdown of the grounds for divorce and the state of legal praxis in divorce cases, see Mikulová, *Žena v právním řadě československém*, 62–69.
38 Ibid., 137–145.
39 This was a common theme in the Catholic women's press. As one example, see "Rodinné právo," *Křesťanská žena* 19, no. 32 (1937): 1. See also notes 46, 49, and 50.
40 For example, an article in the journal of the National Council of Women took this position. Jaromír Růžička, "Nutnost reformy manželského práva," *Ženská rada* 5, no. 9 (1929): 126–127.
41 Minutes from meeting of commission on women's legal position, March 15, 1932, NA, fond Ženská Národní Rada (hereafter ŽNR), box 22. Also Františka Plamínková, "Budiž jasno!," *Ženská rada* 11, no. 10 (1935): 186–187.
42 Papers of the NCW commission on women in the law (1923–1937), NA, fond ŽNR, box 22 and 23.
43 Anna Ziegloserová, "Hlídka sociální—60,000 rozvedených žen," *Ženský obzor* 19, no. 3–4 (1924): 61.
44 Fr. Roman Jírman, "Sekretariát rozvedených žen," *Člověk* 1, no. 10 (1924): 1–2.
45 Vlasta Sternová, *Rozvodová advokátka* (Prague: Rodina, 1933); serialized in *Pražanka* 7–8, nos. 364–381 (1931–1932).
46 Ibid.
47 Marie Tippmanová, "Ženské stanovisko k reformě rodinného práva," *Pražanka* 8, no. 384 (1932): 5; Maru, "Ženské stanovisko k reformě občanského zákoníka," *Pražanka* 8, no. 389 (1932): 2; Maru, "Ženské stanovisko k reformě občanského zákoníka," *Pražanka* 8, no. 391 (1932): 21.
48 Bruno Kafka, *Právo rodinné (Návrh subkomitétu pro revisi občanského zákoníka)* (Prague: Ministry of Justice, 1924), 14; Mikulová, *Žena v právním řádě československém*, 40–47.
49 Kafka, *Právo rodinné*, 81.
50 Betty Karpíšková, "Do nového zákona—staré otroctví," *Ženské noviny* 6, no. 44 (1924): 1.
51 The People's (or Populist) party (*Československá strana lidová*) was the party of Czech political Catholicism.
52 The Czech National Socialists were a leftist and nationalist party that had absolutely no relation to the German NSDAP. On the history of the party, see T. Mills Kelly, *Without Remorse: Czech National Socialism in Late-Habsburg Austria* (Boulder, CO: East European Monographs, 2006).
53 On the NCW, see Jana Burešová, *Proměny společenského postavení českých žen v první polovině 20. století* (Olomouc: Universita Palackého, 2001), 59–88.
54 "Občanský zákoník a jeho novelisace," NA, fond ŽNR, box 32.
55 Ibid. The NCW's basic perspective on family law did not change throughout the interwar period. It is a constant throughout the papers of the NCW commission on women in the law (1923–1937), NA, fond ŽNR, boxes 22 and 23.

56 "Subkomitétu pro revisi občanského zákoníka," *Ženská rada* 1, no. 6 (1925): 5–7.
57 This is a summation of their basic position, but for a specific example, see Luisa Landová-Štychová, "Právni postavení československých občanek v manželství a rodině," *Ženská rada* 1, no. 5 (1925): 10–12. This article was continued in *Ženská rada* 1, no. 8 (1925): 9–11 and *Ženská rada* 1, no. 9 (1925): 3–5.
58 Lup., "Krise manželství zkázou rodiny," *Křesťanská žena* 17, no. 9 (1935): 1–2.
59 "Rozmach a Síla—Svazu katolických žen a dívek," *Křesťanská žena* 19, no. 17 (1937): 1–5; Burešová, *Proměny společenského postavení českých žen*, 261.
60 The Federation of Catholic Women and Girls heartily approved of women having equal political rights with men. For example, "Žena a politika," *Moravská žena* 1, no. 1 (1919): 1; "Žena a politika," *Křesťanská žena* 17, no. 4 (1935): 1–2. This was the same journal under different titles.
61 "Život rodiny," *Křesťanská žena* 17, no. 33 (1935): 2–3.
62 Bohumila Wiererová, "O pravé a nepravé emancipaci," *Křesťanská žena* 19, no. 25 (1937): 1–2.
63 Ibid. Similar examples include "Krise manželství zkázou rodiny," and "Dnešní sňatky," *Křesťanská žena* 19, no. 21: 5–6.
64 "Občanský sňatek," *Křesťanská žena* 14, no. 4 (1932): 1–2.
65 Superrevisní komise, *Zákon, kterým se vydává všeobecný zákoník občanský* (Prague: Ministerstvo spravedlnosti, 1931), 32–33. See also the analysis in Mikulová, *Žena v právním řádě československém*, 47–48.
66 Quoted in Mikulová, *Žena v právním řádě československém*, 43.
67 "Ze Ženské Národní Rady— Valná schůze ŽNR," *Ženská rada* 5, no. 4–5 (1929): 59.
68 M. Košková, "Řídí se veřejní činitelé naší republikánskou ústavou," *Ženská rada* 10, no. 7 (1934): 128–130.
69 Quoted in ald, "Min Dr. Meissner o osnově občanského zákoníka," *Národní osvobození*, March 26, 1932.
70 Minutes from meeting of the NCW presidium, March 28, 1935, NA, fond ŽNR, box 6. For specifics on these discussions, see the papers of the commission on women in the law, NA, fond ŽNR, box 22.
71 NCW notes from meetings of Králová-Horáková and Srb on September 20, 25, and 27, 1935, also minutes from the November 1, 1935 meeting of legal committee. NA, fond ŽNR, box 6 and Srb's file notes on the meetings (dated October 1, 1935), NA, fond MS, box 1963.
72 DK, "Z chystaného nového čs. občanského práva," *Lidové noviny*, January 1, 1932.
73 "Občanský sňatek," 1–2.
74 "Velká manifestace katolíků proti chystaným povinným laickým sňatkům," *Lidové listy*, March 16, 1932. Kašpar's remarks about civil marriage being equivalent to concubinage sparked a number of public protests.
75 "Ministr Dr. Dérer na obranu občanského zákoníku," *Národní listy*, April 21, 1937.
76 "Rodinné právo," *Křesťanská žena* 19, no. 32 (1937): 1.
77 Speech of Dr. Stránský, April 15, 1937 meeting of the Czechoslovak National Assembly, accessed December 20, 2013, http://www.psp.cz/eknih/1935ns/ps/stenprot/092schuz/s092005.htm.
78 Speech of Dr. Rašín, April 15, 1937 meeting of the Czechoslovak National Assembly, accessed December 20, 2013, http://www.psp.cz/eknih/1935ns/ps/stenprot/092schuz/s092008.htm.
79 "Předběžná rozprava o občanském zákoníku skončena," *Národní listy*, April 16, 1937.
80 Alexej Čepička, *Šťastná rodina, šťastný národ* (Prague: Ministerstvo informací a osvěty a Ministerstvo spravedlnosti, 1949).
81 On the immediate postwar era, see Feinberg, *Elusive Equality*, 190–222.

82 Speech of Božena Ecksteinová, January 23, 1919 meeting of the Czechoslovak National Assembly, accessed December 20, 2013, http://www.psp.cz/eknih/1918ns/ps/stenprot/020schuz/s020002.htm.

83 "Řeč Senátorky F.F. Plamínkové v plénu senátu 11 prosince 1937," *Ženská rada* 14, no. 1 (1938): 18.

84 That is not to say that Czechoslovak democracy was perfect. For critical assessments of the First Republic, see Feinberg, *Elusive Equality*; Orzoff, *Battle for the Castle*; Peter Bugge, "Czech Democracy 1918–1938: Paragon or Parody?," *Bohemia* 47, no. 1 (2006–2007): 3–28; or, for a rather over the top interpretation, Mary Heimann, *Czechoslovakia: The State that Failed* (New Haven: Yale University Press, 2009).

4 Equality at Stake

Legal and National Discourses on Family Law in Czechoslovakia, 1918–1931

Jana Osterkamp

In independent Czechoslovakia, the initiation of women as citizens and equal members of society was accompanied with applause, even with praise. After the revolutionary year 1918, while building up a new democracy on the ruins of the Habsburg monarchy, women's suffrage had high political priority. New voting laws enfranchising women would be passed in the very first moments of the new state in 1920.[1] The unanimous welcoming of women to political life formed an important part of the Czech national euphoria and self-understanding. By 1918, the women's movement had become an intrinsic part of a Czech nationalism that dated well before the failed revolution of 1848.[2] The historical past of the Hussites in Bohemia informed a new Czech political narrative in which—according to the well-known women's rights activist Františka Plamínková—there had been days when "a real brotherly and sisterly relation of the two sexes to each other actually existed [. . .], an equality of strength and determination in the work for justice, for liberty of conscience and later for the liberty of the nation."[3] Cooperation between Czech feminists and representatives of Czech nationalists first focused on an improved girls' education and later extended to the campaign for universal suffrage.[4] In 1907, universal suffrage was introduced to the Lower House (Abgeordnetenhaus) within the Austrian bicameral system, but it was denied to women. Only representative suffrage to the Upper House (Herrenhaus) based on property included noble women.[5] On the local level, women were admitted to some form of franchise; in Bohemia, twenty percent of all voters on the municipal level were women.[6] However, attempts had failed to extend these rights to the provincial and national levels. Czech women's activists like Plaminková claimed that older provincial voting laws were gender neutral, providing women with "the oldest rights of suffrage in the whole world."[7] The case of the Czech nationalist writer Božena Vitková-Kunětická, whose election in 1912 was, shortly afterwards, declared void by the Provincial governor, mobilized many Czechs.[8] Women's suffrage became a symbol for "the resistance to Vienna."[9] It formed part of the broader Czech national discourse, which reproached the imperial government for its oppressive policies toward aspiring national groups.[10] Moreover, Czech public opinion had endorsed the women's rights movement as a political claim, which meshed with the even more popular call for democracy.[11]

These initial successes of the women's rights movement after 1918 vested Czechoslovak women with political self-confidence.[12] Furthermore, like the Austrian or the Constitution of Weimar, the new Czechoslovak Constitution of 1920 established the principle of gender equality and "did not recognize any gender privileges."[13] In the euphoric setting of the first months of Czechoslovak independence, it seemed that political leaders would respond to feminist claims for equality. As Plamínková put it in 1920: "The position of women in the Czechoslovak Republic today with respect to political rights may be regarded as the realization of the boldest hopes of those who have labored for the civic rights of women and of the hopes of all who have desired to see civic equality forming the basis of the state [. . .]. The consciousness of the equality of rights of men and women in this political collaboration is growing day by day."[14] One of the governing ideas of the new Czechoslovak Constitution was indeed the granting of comprehensive individual equal rights, not only with regard to gender issues, but by also abolishing social, national, and confessional inequalities and injustices.[15] Yet, despite the fact that democracy on an individual basis was one of the key contributions of the Czechoslovak Constitution, when it came to everyday politics, severely conflicting collective loyalties and identities undermined this egalitarian approach. National, confessional, class, and occupational loyalties also effectively hindered the emergence of a unified and cross-ethnic women's movement in Czechoslovakia.[16]

This fact raises the question of whether the history of gender in Czechoslovakia is to be regarded as one divided by "nationality." The main sources presented here are the proceedings of the German Lawyers' Association in Czechoslovakia, a conference of legal professionals of the German national minority living in Czechoslovakia. While Melissa Feinberg presents the Czech perspective in her illustrative book *Elusive Equality: Gender, Citizenship, and the Limits of Democracy in Czechoslovakia, 1918–1950*, quoting mainly from Czech sources,[17] this chapter reveals a perspective typical to German legal scholars in Czechoslovakia. In several political and legal fields of nationalities' policies, the boundaries between these two nationally conflicting groups were becoming almost unbridgeable during the interwar period.

However, national boundaries were not dominating legal discourse on gender equality. A result of this chapter is the insight that the leading legal discourse on gender equality was Western-bound. It divided Czechs and Germans living in the Western Bohemian Lands from Slovaks inhabiting the Eastern part of the country. Even if the Slovak legal system disposed of a more progressive approach to gender equality in family law, it had nevertheless been virtually excluded from Czech and German legal discourses. Quite in contrast to the contemporary assumption of "Westernization" as "modernization," that self-restriction of legal scholarship at least contributed to the fact that the reform of family law in Czechoslovakia had been retarded.

The National and the Legal Setting

Interwar Czechoslovakia consisted of three major "nationalities": Czechs, Germans, and Slovaks, none of which formed an absolute majority in the new state. Additionally, there were other important "national" or ethnic groups, such as Magyars, Ruthenians, Poles, and Jews. According to the preamble of the constitution, only the Czechs and the Slovaks, officially referred to as "Czechoslovaks," were regarded as the two national groups leading the nation-state, whereas other groups, without regard to their actual number, were bestowed only with the legal status of national minorities. The framers of the international treaties after World War I recognized this nation-state character of Czechoslovakia despite its multinational character, but they emphasized the establishment of individual democracy and egalitarian minority policy. In a sense, Czechoslovakia had inherited the national, social, economic, and religious heterogeneity that had been characteristic of the deceased Habsburg monarchy. With calling Czechoslovakia a nation-state, a hierarchy of "nations" developed with a numerical superiority of Czech and Slovak inhabitants, which was in blatant conflict with the internationally and constitutionally granted legal equality of all nationalities. Official discourse held that Czechs and Slovaks were entangled to such a high degree by language and culture that they formed an indivisible nation. Within the logic of Czech and Slovak national politics, Czechoslovakia as a nation-state appeared as the successful result of the national movement and fight against "Vienna" throughout the nineteenth century.

The political narrative of common language, culture, and history shared by Czechs and Slovaks was just one aspect, however. Before the Revolution in 1918 that brought about the new Czechoslovak democracy, these two parts of the state were neither ruled by the same laws nor administered by the same political body even though both had belonged to the Habsburg Empire. The Bohemian Lands in the West were dominated by the imperial center in Vienna that relied on the German-speaking population as their leading "nation," whereas Slovakia was governed by Magyar elites from Budapest. The underside of an allegedly common Czechoslovak cultural realm and identity was a huge diversity in the sphere of law. There existed a sharp legal boundary between the Western part of Czechoslovakia, the Bohemian Lands, and the Eastern part, formed by Slovakia and Ruthenia.

With regard to the private law system in the dual monarchy, the Bohemian Lands had been subject to the Viennese codification efforts that had resulted in the Austrian General Civil Code of 1811 (ABGB). However, in nineteenth century Hungary, which Slovakia had been part of, the ABGB had been repealed after being in force for just a decade. The emerging Hungarian legal culture was paying only lip service to the central Austrian administration in Vienna. Instead, in the early 1880s, a collection of national Hungarian laws were passed and complemented with a common law structure.[18] Interwar Czechoslovakia imported both legal systems. In the Western part of the country the former ABGB was adopted with only a few modifications, whereas the former Hungarian Common Law System applied to Slovakia.[19] A whole ministry for "unification" was then established to see to these differences and to replace them with unitary laws. Obviously, there was a strong economic and political need for legal unification.[20] At the ministry, the Revisory Commission for the new Civil Code began work in 1920 and produced a first final draft in 1931. These efforts and drafts were never put into practice. Until 1938, when Czechoslovakia ceased to exist as a consequence of the Munich Agreement and Hitler's expansion plans, the legal division of Czechoslovakia was not yet overcome.

Members of the Revisory Committee had soon agreed that the tradition of the former Austrian Civil Code should serve as a model for the new Czechoslovak civil law, whereas the civil law regime from Slovakia and Ruthenia had been rejected. The tasks of the Commission then became twofold: first, to translate the codification from the original German version into the new official state languages of Czech and Slovak, and second, to reform the Civil Code in accordance with the new Czechoslovak Constitution and to respond to social, economic, and political needs. However, the longer the work of revision continued, the more it became obvious that the plan to change the Civil Code so as to ensure gender equality was meeting with widespread resistance. Women were not granted direct access to the commission's work.[21] So even if some of the positions and arguments of the Czech women's movement, most importantly the Czechoslovak National Council of Women (*Ženská národní rada*) were theoretically accepted by the ministries, they were not put into practice and did not become part of the revisory works. Melissa Feinberg, who has depicted this fight over women's equality, comprehensively summarizes the less-than-modest results: "The non-partisan super-revisory commission defended its choice to leave a husband's powers in his household essentially intact by ignoring the issue of constitutionality. Instead, they claimed that they made the only practical choice [. . .], they argued for the stability of the family and its importance to the nation and the state."[22]

The difficulty of reforming the family law system in the direction of equality of the sexes became one of the main reasons that no political consensus about private law reform was ever achieved.[23] Gender roles had changed drastically in the course of World War I. The war experience had torn to pieces traditional social bonds within the family and had undermined conventional gender roles. As a young female legal scholar put it in 1931, if there was anything valuable about the war, it was the possibility for women to demonstrate and develop their abilities without being hindered by gender prejudices, even though they were forced to do so by sheer economic need.[24] The long-term absence of men had forced women to take men's jobs and assume their roles. After the end of World War I, the clocks could not be turned back. Legally, however, gender roles within family law remained essentially unchanged.

Research Questions

This chapter starts with the significant contrast between the rather modern Czechoslovak Constitution and the civil codes, statutes, and laws that preserved gender principles and rules established over a century ago. Why was it that gender equality could not be implemented in private law, even though in the constitutional field gender equality was granted almost simultaneously with the establishment of the new state? What made it harder to accept a more egalitarian family law? Family law reform had to struggle not only with gender stereotypes. In fact, there was an intrinsic gap between professionals of the private law sphere and the constitutional law sphere, and I will discuss the different logics of constitutional legal thinking and of private law argumentation. However, in addition to an allegedly fortunate past of gender equality under the Hussites' movement, one has also to wonder about Czechoslovak specificities: Did the predominant national discourses have an impact on gender discourses? This question is complicated by the fact that two different legal systems were operating in Czechoslovakia.

As I have indicated above, the politically mobilizing power in favor of universal suffrage and thus gender equality in the public arena had been overwhelming. In the realm of family law, the public campaign for the abolition of the Catholic Church's control of marriage (and divorce) law that dated back to 1905 had a comparable impact. Divesting marriage law of denominational control was made statutory law in the very first weeks of the newly founded state; it was the first legal proposal that passed the National Revolutionary Assembly.[25] However, the introduction of civil marriage and the reform of divorce law did not leave women better off but rather significantly increased their risk of poverty. The fight for a reformed civil code that would establish financial equality of spouses and would abolish gender discrimination in a more comprehensive manner found less support.

There was an obvious gap between a wife's new position in the public political sphere and within her private home, between her rights and duties as laid out in public law versus private law. This gap was sustained by legal scholarship that had drawn sharp boundaries between the constitutional law sphere and the private law sphere.[26] The possible ways of reconciling the two conflicting spheres did not prove successful. On the one hand, there was the possibility to harmonize the private laws in accordance with the constitution by simply allowing the constitution to legally annul contradictory statutes. The constitution itself declared contradictory statutes as void.[27] However, the history of the Czechoslovak Constitutional Court, which in fact had been established to ensure this principle of constitutionalism, illustrates the reluctance among politicians, courts, and scholars to take the constitution as a law with prevailing force seriously.[28] Still in the 1920s and 1930s, apart from some avant-garde legal scholars, constitutional law was generally not regarded as "paramount" to statutory law.[29]

The Conference of the German Lawyers' Association on Gender Equality in 1931

These boundaries between public law and private law were seldom made explicit. To reconstruct these antagonisms and ignorance, this chapter takes one of the bi-annual meetings of the Deutscher Juristentag in der Tschechoslowakei (German Lawyers' Association in Czechoslovakia) as an example. The 1931 session put the legal position of women in Czechoslovakia on its agenda, and for the first time, women were included among its discussants.[30] This conference was intended to bring together legal scholars of both constitutional law and private law to discuss the issue of gender equality. Questions of constitutionality of family law formed an important part of the agenda. This approach was innovative within Czechoslovak legal scholarship for that time. Only a few years earlier, a young legal professor had noted, "neither in practice nor in theory is it common to refer to the impact of the Constitution on the positive norms of the Civil Code."[31] The choice of topic and time was deliberate. With regard to private law, the year 1931 was expected to become a cornerstone of the reform and unification of family law (even though these expectations would ultimately be disappointed). The Revisory Commission for the Reform of the Civil Code was expected to present its final draft to the public. With regard to constitutional law, the late 1920s and early 1930s had seen a huge upturn of constitutional arguments. Both in Czechoslovakia and in the neighboring states of Austria and the Weimar Republic, equal rights were provided with more practical legal dogmatism. By that time equality arguments were on the way to be taken into account by scholars of private law, even if they were still far from being taken seriously by the general public.

The German Lawyers' Association in Czechoslovakia had become the leading forum for German-speaking lawyers, judges, and legal scholars. Indeed, the bi-annual meetings of the German Lawyers' Association (which organized parallel sections on constitutional or administrative law, on private law, and on criminal law) became a model for similar conferences of Czech and of Slovak lawyers. Among German-speaking lawyers and legal scholars in Czechoslovakia, the conference was highly esteemed as a forum where one could tap into the latest legal discussions, and where the gap between legal scholars and practitioners could be bridged. The conference was loosely linked to its holding organization in Germany, the German Lawyers' Association (Deutscher Juristentag), and thus was regularly visited by leading legal scholars from the new German and Austrian republics. Due to its inherently comparative approach, the impact of the bi-annual meeting of the German Lawyers' Association was not restricted to Germans living in Czechoslovakia. Czechoslovak governments and Czech and Slovak legal scholars regularly referred to the opinions and arguments provided and published by the Association.

Legal Discourse on Gender Equality at the German Lawyers' Association in Czechoslovakia

The first major presentation at the German Lawyers' Association in Czechoslovakia in 1931, titled "The Legal Position of the Wife," was given by Egon Weiß, a civil law professor at the German University of Prague.[32] As one of few Germans, Weiß was taking part in the work of the Revisory Commission for a new Civil Code and became an influential member of the sub-commission for a revision of family law. He did not exclusively present his own legal opinion, but rather represented the arguments of the Revisory Commission. Initially, Weiß summed up the legal framework of the former Austrian Civil Code that applied to the Western parts of Czechoslovakia.

He pointed out that from an economic perspective the Austrian Civil Code of 1811 had incorporated some progressive features, at least in the context of its time of codification. He gave as an example the fact that wives were *in principle* allowed to manage their financial matters on their own, and that marriage did not deprive women of their financial powers. Additionally, Weiß pointed out, marriage law *in principle* was built on the idea of marriage as a contract between equal persons equipped with personal autonomy. These principles would have meshed with the new constitutional notion of gender equality. However, they were weakened, if not turned upside down, by the further stipulations of Austrian family law.

Results of the Revisory Commission's Work on a Reform of Family Law

According to the Austrian Civil Code, the family, as a small community, was seen as an economic unit, establishing a strong and unequal bond between the spouses. Since it seemed to be unthinkable that an economic unit would function without leadership, men were regarded as "heads of the household," men alone could represent the family and were not accountable for their decisions or expenses. As another consequence, it was assumed that men administered the assets and finances of their wives, unless wives explicitly protested and revoked this authority. A wife had the legal obligation to assist in her husband's business and to see to the household chores. It was not taken into account whether a wife would wish otherwise or whether she had the opportunity to pursue a professional career of her own, possibly with an even better income. Quite the opposite: a wife who did not quit her job at the request of her husband could be sued for divorce for not fulfilling her wifely duties.[33] At an earlier moment, Weiß had explicitly approved of this privileged role of a husband.[34] In personal matters, too, wives were largely dependent on their husbands. The husband chose the family's place of residence. The family's surname must be that of the husband with no exceptions. With concern to the upbringing and education of the children, it was the man who had the power to decide whenever disagreements would arise. As a kind of reward to wives who fulfilled their duties, men had the obligation to provide for them.

The years of the Revisory Commission's work as presented by Egon Weiß made only some changes to this family law system. Almost the only, albeit important, concession the Revisory Commission made to modern times was abolishing the legal fiction that financial acquisitions during the time of marriage belonged to the husband only. There was a fiction proposed that both spouses should equally benefit from the acquisition of marital assets, the so-called matrimonial separate property regime or "*le régime des acquêts*" (or *Errungenschaftsgemeinschaft* or *Zugewinnstgemeinschaft*). Many welcomed this rule as an important step toward gender equality. The Revisory Commission had, however, initially rejected this proposal and agreed to it only reluctantly after Slovak legal scholars were given access to the commission's work in 1926.[35] However, Weiß criticized this new legal fiction as not reflecting reality. According to him, in the case of divorce or death of a spouse, the courts should decide about the just distribution of earned assets. A rather surprising argument he put forward was the fact that women regularly earned less for the same kind of employment.[36] He implied that women were not therefore entitled to half of the assets if they were regularly bringing home less than their spouses. Alternatively, the Commission proposed that a woman should be obliged to provide for her husband, if he was unable to do so for himself. However, a wife's duty to support her husband was designed as an exceptional case, whereas a husband was obliged to provide for his spouse without regard to her financial situation.[37]

The only case in which Weiß invoked the constitution concerned the wife's duty to use the husband's surname after marriage. Weiß claimed that this privilege of gender could not be constitutionally upheld. If a woman had an economic interest in retaining her name, e.g., because she was a successful physician, a writer, or an actress, she should be allowed to use her surname as she wished. Apart from that, the wifely duty to obey the husband's will and the men's role as "head of the household" remained unquestioned.[38]

Referring to the constitutional principle of equality only once, Weiß remained reticent to challenge the principles of husbandly prerogatives embedded in the Austrian Code. His report paid homage to the private law tradition, in fact to the Roman law tradition that had established a husband's authority over his wife. To scholars of private law, this was of comparable, or of even greater, importance than responding to the challenges of the new Czechoslovak Constitution.[39] This way of legal thinking in the private law tradition remained unhindered by the potential legal impact of the Czechoslovak Constitution.

Different Logics of Public Law and Private Law Systems

Apart from the possibility of legal reform, it was questionable whether the Czechoslovak Constitution itself provided any means to invalidate contradictory laws and statutes. The constitution declared as void every legal norm that contradicted constitutional principles. Thus, legal scholars pondered whether the constitution declared those parts of the Civil Code void that were obviously in conflict with its principles like gender equality.[40]

In the new Czechoslovak state, the newly established idea of the constitution as "paramount law," an idea familiar to American legal scholars since the famous decision of the Supreme Court in *Marbury v. Madison* in 1806, took its time to find acceptance within the legal thinking of interwar Czechoslovakia.[41] In the former Austrian empire, the idea of an equal legal value of constitutional and statutory laws had been popular and widely accepted among legal scholars. Only with the younger generation that had been educated in Czechoslovakia was this paradigm of legal thinking gradually losing influence and eventually replaced by the idea of a legally prevailing constitution.[42] As a consequence, until the 1930s constitutional principles such as equal rights were regarded as a political program for the future rather than accepted as hard legal norms that must be met.[43]

This was the background for the second presentation at the German Lawyers' Association in Czechoslovakia in 1931, with the title "The Position of Woman According to the Public Law within the Czechoslovak Republic."[44] The speaker was a second professor from the Prague German Law Faculty, public lawyer Heinrich Rauchberg, an expert on minority rights who was above all an expert on the nationalities' question.[45]

Rauchberg laid open the different logics of the public law sphere and the private law sphere. He attested the private law system was slowed down by "inertia." It would answer social changes reluctantly and only under severe political pressure.[46] Legal institutions of private law, he indicated, were so intertwined with each other that they had evolved an existence of their own irrespective of any sociological basis.[47] In contrast, public law was not hindered in responding to changing political and social circumstances.[48] Rauchberg stated that "it is one of the greatest tasks of our time to resolve the conflict between women's legal position according to the public law and according to the private law, and to grant women equal rights like men in every respect, as far as their bodily condition allows."[49] Rauchberg's statement was a plea for legal reform of private law in the light of the Czechoslovak Constitution.

As a public lawyer, however, he highlighted the problem of married women's nationality as the most pressing. Women were automatically losing Czechoslovak citizenship due to marriage if their husband was not Czechoslovak. The wife's citizenship was inevitably bound with the husband's citizenship. For women, losing Czechoslovak nationality and thus citizenship could have harsh social and economic consequences. They would be forced to give up their jobs as public school teachers, as advocates, or as administrators.[50] After divorce, there was no easy way back to Czechoslovak citizenship. Restrictive citizenship laws of a husband's home country that did not automatically award spouses with citizenship, like the Cable Act passed by the United States in 1922, would even make them stateless.[51] Also in the neighboring countries, which were mostly newly founded states established after the dissolution of the Habsburg monarchy, citizenship laws were regularly restrictive. Czechoslovak citizenship law itself was entangled with nationalistic policies.[52] It did not even meet the rather weak legal standards of The Hague Nationality Convention that was signed the previous year. At the Lawyers' Association in 1931, Rauchberg proposed extensive amendments for the likely reform and supported women's right to opt for their nationality.[53] However, the expected reform never came into being, and by 1938 the Czechoslovak citizenship law for women remained one of the most restrictive in the world.[54]

The Constitutionality of a Husband's Prevailing Role According to Family Law

Despite his criticism, Rauchberg handled the question of the constitutionality of citizenship laws for women differently. In comparison with his colleague Egon Weiß from the private law section, Rauchberg was ready to name as unconstitutional the law that forced a wife to follow her husband to his place of residence and to adopt his citizenship because he was seen as "head of the household." He pointed out that this one-sided dependency of the wife on her husband's choice of where and how to live contradicted not only with the constitutional principle of gender equality, but also with the constitutionally granted freedom of movement and freedom of trade.[55] He then considered the possibility that the constitution takes precedence over these strictures, given the fact that the constitution declared contradicting statutes as void.[56] However, this radical argument was still premature within Czechoslovak public law discourse, which did not yet accept the arguments for legal superiority of the constitution over existing and conflicting statutes and regulations. Rauchberg interpreted the constitutional principles thus only as an "important item on the agenda for the renewal of our marriage law."[57] With regard to the legal validity of wives' residence and citizenship law, Rauchberg said, "One cannot assume that the builders of the Constitution had the intent [. . .] to take one brick out from the wall of the edifice of marriage law that was in force at that time."[58]

The whole edifice of marriage law, however, was built upon the principle of a dominant role for men. This outdated gender privilege, according to Rauchberg, had been responsible for several residual forms of women's discrimination within the sphere of public law. He asserted that sex discrimination within public law was above all a reflection of the minor position of wives in the Civil Code. Rauchberg did not leave any doubt that the

Revisory Commission for the Civil Code must accept the principle of gender equality and thus eliminate the privileged role of men as "heads of the households."[59] His presentation opposed the conclusions reached in Egon Weiß's paper, which had defended the established order of private law.

The general discussion of the papers given by Weiß and Rauchberg was opened with a contribution by Arthur Lenhoff, Judge at the Austrian Constitutional Court, professor at the University in Vienna and at the Law School for Women in Vienna.[60] Lenhoff had the first Austrian chair for Industrial law and was thus well acquainted with the overlap of public law and private law. Although he had occasionally dealt with women's equality issues in his minor writings, at the German Lawyers' Association in Czechoslovakia conference he had demanded an examination of the constitutionality of family law in light of the constitutional guarantee of gender equality.[61] To everyone's surprise, however, he backed the conclusions presented by Egon Weiß.

Lenhoff took up the question of whether or not the constitutional guarantee of gender equality would necessarily lead to the annulment of contradicting provisions in private law. He invoked the implications of other constitutional rules for the interpretation of gender equality. The Czechoslovak Constitution, like the Constitution of the Weimar Republic, stated in Article 126 that marriage, family, and motherhood were under the special protection of the laws. Only recently (in the 1920s) did Weimarian legal scholars propose a solution to address constitutional statements that were obviously not meant to provide subjective political rights; these special guarantees were interpreted as so-called institutional guarantees. Carl Schmitt, who had promoted this dogmatic approach in his textbook about the Constitution of Weimar, had written that constitutional institutional guarantees had the aim to make the deletion of the respective institutions impossible by way of statutory laws.[62] Actually, this did not necessarily imply that they were meant to preserve a certain legal status quo and were not to be altered at all.[63] However, institutional guarantees were regularly used to conserve an allegedly "objective order."[64]

Lenhoff applied this model to the Czechoslovak Constitution in a conservative and restrictive manner. Lenhoff stated that the institutional guarantee of marriage and family in the Czechoslovak Constitution was, for the time being, bound to the family law model that was valid when the constitution was enacted in 1920. He claimed that the constitution itself had implicitly accepted the place of gender roles in family law based on the former Austrian Civil Code.[65] Lenhoff even criticized the formulation of Article 106 on gender equality as misleading: "The wording of Article 106 const. is a failure, since it does not express that differences in treatment [of gender] are not rejected by the constitution, if the nature and the character of the legal institutions require such a differentiation."[66]

Lenhoff's concept of marriage as cooperative led him to the conclusion that statutes were not constitutionally hindered in establishing a division of labor within family, that is, a division of gender roles. He was convinced that different gender roles were naturally given and that they were part of the institutional guarantee in Article 126. Since he regarded household chores and raising of the children as the "natural profession of women," he concluded that women should pursue a professional career only in cases of financial need.[67] Lenhoff's interpretation of Article 126 as an institutional guarantee corresponded perfectly with the intuition of the two most important Czech public law scholars—Jiří Hoetzel and František Weyr—that a husband's privileges were not meant to be destroyed by the constitution.[68]

Nevertheless, even Lenhoff admitted that gender discrimination created some problems. From his own professional field he criticized the restriction on women workers within labor law. Female public servants such as teachers were condemned to celibacy and would be fired automatically in the event of marriage.[69] His criticism extended also to the relationship between parents and their children. Here he praised the results of the Thirty-Third German Lawyers' Association and the forthcoming presentations at the Thirty-Sixth German Lawyers' Association in Lübeck.[70] Furthermore, Lenhoff promoted the right of a child to bear the surname of the mother, adopting an argument advanced decades earlier by Marianne Weber.[71] Not least, he agreed with Rauchberg that women's citizenship should be handled separately from their husband's.[72]

Gender Issues in Family Law Presented by Women at the German Lawyers' Association in Czechoslovakia

Following the debates on public law, the conference discussion turned to concrete questions of family law and gender equality. Whereas women like Marianne Weber, Marie-Elisabeth Lüders, Margarete Berent, Marie Munk, and Emmy Rebstein-Metzger were included among the key speakers at the bi-annual meetings of the Lawyers' Association in Germany that dealt with gender equality, at the German Lawyers' Association in Czechoslovakia in 1931 women participated for the first time, and only in the discussions.[73]

Käthe Spiegel, a representative of the women's association Women's Progress (Frauenfortschritt), was among the participants. While the above-mentioned Czechoslovak National Council of Women (NCW/Ženská národní rada) was narrowly, albeit not exclusively, related to the Czech national movement and to women of Czech nationality, Women's Progress represented women of German nationality within Czechoslovakia.[74] As a principal representative of that association, Spiegel gave papers at international and national women's congresses, spoke on the radio, and wrote for newspapers. Spiegel had grown up in a liberal German-Jewish home in Prague. By profession she was a historian, renowned for her cultural history of the United States of America.[75] Additionally, she had studied law for several semesters, and was skilled in legal practice as a result of her work as a secretary to her father, the famous public law professor at the Prague Law Faculty of the German University, Ludwig Spiegel, a founder of the German Lawyers' Association in Czechoslovakia.[76]

At the German Lawyers' Association in Czechoslovakia in 1931, Käthe Spiegel focused her criticism first on the private law section presented by Egon Weiß. She stated that the planned new Civil Code, especially the family law section, still presumed different intellectual capabilities of women and men. Whereas a man had to prove his incapacity to exercise a certain right or function, a woman, on the contrary, had to prove her capability to perform it. These questions were relevant for decision-making related to the raising of children or for minor powers related to household duties. Spiegel claimed that this inequality with regard to the burden of proof was not justifiable with gender differences given by nature.[77] She rejected gender difference of intellectual capabilities in general, yet she admitted the appearance of difference (with qualifications): "We want to admit that at the moment we perhaps face a situation when women cannot be regarded as equals to men, a situation when the not-employed, inexperienced woman might not equally be able to grasp the matters of the outer world. But, there is a growing circle of women standing firmly on the grounds of real life."[78] Leaving the track of legal arguments by diving into sociological assertions, she paved the way for Weiß's reply. He claimed that a "moderate priority" of a husband's role within the private law was justified by "reality," since "the majority of women, as the revisory commission had depicted them, is still seeking affection," and only the "highly-educated women" would regard this attitude as a kind of discrimination.[79]

It was obvious however, that Spiegel was far less interested in systematic questions of private law than in social causes. With regard to law of inheritance and divorce law she demanded amendments that would establish equality between women who were dedicated to the household chores and those who were employed. This claim was similar to the argument presented by Emmy Rebstein-Metzger at the German Lawyers' Association in Lübeck.[80] In contemporary Czechoslovak legal literature, criticism had been leveled at the fact that employed women found themselves in a financially better position than housewives, even though household chores were sometimes more demanding.[81] The risk of poverty for women, especially with children, had risen significantly after World War I.[82] Yet legislation had still not acknowledged that fact. According to Spiegel, the inheritance system should provide widows who had been housewives for a long time with a retirement pension, and divorce law should take into account the material value of household chores. In favor of the Revisory commission's plans to delete the legal fiction within the Civil Code according to which financial acquisitions during marriage belonged to the husband only, Spiegel put forward a different argument. She pointed out that the husband's work and his income regularly benefited from and depended upon the domestic work undertaken by the wife.[83]

Spiegel's emotional involvement in the debate shows that her primary intention was not just to strengthen the legal position of housewives. Spiegel almost became furious about Lenhoff's opinion that wives should be allowed to work only in the event of financial necessity. To Spiegel, women "who did not feel inclined to emphasize their abilities as a cook" should have the right to choose their profession freely, without any conditions, and according to their own will.[84] Still, years later at the International Congress for Suffrage and Equal Citizenship of the International Alliance of Women in 1935 in Istanbul, Spiegel made the same case both for women to choose their profession freely and for their marital financial independence.[85] The freedom to choose one's career was, in her views, one of the essential features of individual self-determination. As a consequence, she argued, wives should also contribute financially to the common household. At the German Lawyers' Association in Czechoslovakia, Spiegel reiterated the fact that occupational liberty for women was intrinsically bound to contract law; after their marriage, wives were not allowed to conclude a contract on their own. Spiegel stirred up the typical contemporary prejudices of her male peers as she made her case for freedom of contract for wives; hecklers interrupted her with the question: "But what if they conclude unreasonable contracts?"[86] As another lawyer put it later, even if the statistics clearly indicated that a majority of women were employed and doing well, they were still expected to lack the necessary abilities to do so.

Marie Munk was the second of the two women who spoke at the Lawyers' Association on gender equality in Czechoslovakia; she brought her own experience and perspective to bear in the discussion. In Germany, Munk had been among the first female law students, among the first female applicants for public legal professions, and she had become one of the first female judges in Prussia.[87] Since the 1920s she had become one of the most renowned female legal scholars on German family law. With a contribution to the proceedings of the Thirty-Third German Lawyers' Association in 1924 that promoted separate property with an equal share of the gained assets to spouses, Munk had a lasting influence on the legal development of marital property. Even so, in Germany her proposals were not put into practice until 1957.[88]

Munk was less critical than Spiegel about Czechoslovak family law, since she initially had to admit, "Today again I had to see with regret, how backward we appear in Germany in comparison with your so much older codification; actually I have to say how lucky we were to call your marital property regime our own."[89] In accordance with her commitment to a reformed family law within German-Weimarian legal debates, Munk promoted the idea of a mandatory statutory matrimonial property regime (*Zugewinnstgemeinschaft*). This idea had been proposed by the Czechoslovak Revisory Commission in 1931, but it had been rejected by Egon Weiß. According to Munk, every spouse should be entitled equally to benefit from the assets that were gained during the marriage.[90] Munk rehearsed the somewhat old-fashioned character of marriage as an economic unit as it had been presented by Weiß when she chose small businesses, pubs, corner shops, and the like as examples to show how often both spouses cooperated and contributed equally to the family income, without having the same entitlement to the fruits of their work in case of divorce or death. In many cases, Munk suggested, a statutory matrimonial property regime would make concurring claims for maintenance unnecessary, since women would then be rewarded with financial means to re-enter their profession, to start a new career, or to open another small business by themselves.[91]

A "Moment of Inertia": Final Propositions of the German Lawyers' Association

At the end of its conferences, a lawyers' association passes guidelines and propositions on the discussed topic in the event of agreements among the speakers and audiences. It was a remarkable sign of courtesy that Käthe Spiegel and Marie Munk were appointed to participate in the preparatory work for the guidelines of the Revisory Commission for a new Civil Code in Czechoslovakia given the fact that neither had presented on the topic at the Association. The outcome, however, did not favor reform. On the constitutional level, Rauchberg's crystal-clear plea for more gender equality within the family law system was rejected. Rather, it was Lenhoff's conservative approach that succeeded. By arguing with institutional guarantees meant to conserve a certain legal status quo and by depicting marriage as cooperative with a fixed legal framework of gender roles, Lenhoff had effectively placed the then current marriage law in a hierarchy above the gender equality granted by the constitution. Accordingly, the ensuing guidelines stated that the legal position of spouses could only be altered if the purpose of the matrimonial cooperative would require so. Constitutional gender equality was thus severely restricted, since it was further held that gender equality within family law had to take into account different kinds of duties that arise with respect to the given purpose of the matrimonial cooperative.[92] It is remarkable that a judge of a Constitutional Court who was supposed to serve as a guardian of the constitution brought about the favoring of the existing family law model over the constitutional principle of equality.

However, with regard to spouses' citizenship and their place of residence, the guidelines recommended that the legal position of women be modestly improved to prevent problems such as statelessness. Even so, strict equality of both sexes was not proposed.[93] In economic respects, the recommendations of the Lawyers' Association went a little further. Both spouses should be entitled to represent the common household, and both had to contribute to its maintenance; housework now was explicitly mentioned as being of the same value and importance as professional employment.[94] However, Munk could not convince her colleagues to adopt her model of equal benefit from the gained assets during the time of marriage (*Zugewinnstgemeinschaft*). Nevertheless it was stated, even if in a rather vague way, that wives should share in the common property accumulated during the time of marriage.

Rather unexpectedly, a controversy arose about the legal assumption of the older Austrian Civil Code that the husband would be entitled to manage and to make use of the financial assets of his wife. The small committee that prepared the guidelines had unanimously stated that this special function of the "husband as head of the household" should be abolished. During previous discussion this position was criticized as a "bolshevization of marriage."[95] The respected lawyer now proposed to uphold the original version; whereas the day before his claim had met with resistance from the audience, now they approved it.[96]

The proceedings of the German Lawyers' Association in Czechoslovakia in 1931 that dealt with gender equality reveal both the struggle to overcome gender stereotypes and the interests in upholding some of the discriminatory legal measures that were presumed to correspond to a given female or matrimonial "nature." This fight was exercised on uneven grounds, since a husband's position after marriage, along with the position of men in general, was subject to several legal privileges and since men at key political and scholarly positions were reluctant to make much effort to clear these positions, even in the name of constitutional gender equality.

To mix public law and private law discourses apparently made little difference to the resulting discussions on gender equality. However, this was not only due to private law scholars' deafness to constitutional arguments, but due to conflicting interpretations of gender equality within public legal scholarship as well. Whereas Rauchberg presented constitutional arguments to strengthen women's equality within family law, Lenhoff pushed forward the idea of marriage as an institutional guarantee with a legally given set of gender roles. Thus, he followed the logics of the private law track. This interpretation restricted the importance of Article 106 on gender equality to a minimum and almost rendered it meaningless. The "inertia" and the unwillingness to make fundamental changes that Rauchberg had criticized as being typical for the private law sphere thus spread to constitutional dogmatic thinking. It muted the power of the constitution to abolish the inequalities aligned to gender.

Gender Equality and the National Discourse

At the proceedings of the German Lawyers' Association in Czechoslovakia, the nationalities' question was mentioned only once. Lenhoff had dealt with family names briefly and promoted the idea that each spouse should be entitled to decide for him or herself which surname he or she wished to have. According to him, a child should be entitled to decide for him or herself at the age of fourteen, when the child also was legally entitled to choose his or her own religion, another idea that went back to a book by Marianne Weber.[97] The possibility that a family could be expected to have one or two different surnames had met with strong resistance among his conservative colleagues. Lenhoff's reaction shows the national-symbolic value of family names: "Here [in Czechoslovakia] one would expect more understanding. After all, that question goes along with national issues. I just intended to vest a child with the right to choose its family name, for example, if the mother has a German surname, whereas the father has a Slavonic one. I assume that this argument is convincing [. . .] that my argument is very worth it to be considered."[98]

This quotation reveals the tense relationship between the nationalities at the beginning of the 1930s, where nationalities' politics aimed at "reclaiming children for the Nation," as Tara Zahra has put it.[99] Czechoslovakia had established a nationalities' policy on "objective" grounds in the interwar period; in the course of it, all citizens lost the possibility to make a free choice of their own national affiliation. Instead, nationality became a term that was ascribed by official census takers who tended to disregard national indifference or bi-nationalities.[100] Lenhoff suggested that the freedom to choose one's surname would provide for at least a symbolic substitute.

The East-West Divide in the Legal Reform Debate

Legal discourse about gender equality within the family reveals a lot about otherwise hidden national hierarchies that had determined the legal reform debate. These hierarchies contradicted the official national narrative of a leading Czechoslovak state-nation. Once the official committee for civil law's reform had agreed on the fact that the new Czechoslovak civil code was to be based largely on the old Austrian system of the General Civil Code, the Slovak private law system with its peculiarities mattered little.[101] This development was undoubtedly accelerated by the fact that contributions by Slovak legal scholars were comparatively few. Even more telling is that during the first decisive years until 1926, there were not any Slovak legal professionals participating in the work of the Revisory Committee for a Reform of the Civil Code.[102] Rather, there had been a professional alliance established between Czech and German legal scholars. Regarding their quotation practice, they almost exclusively referred to each other and to the private law discourse in Austria, Switzerland, or Germany.[103] Their mental map of private law in Czechoslovakia was Western-bound.

This initial absence of Slovakia in the debates about a new family law fits the broader picture of interwar politics. Quite frequently, the Slovakian part of the country was considered a somewhat socially, politically, and economically backwards region. Although Czechs and Slovaks officially formed a state-nation, everyday political culture was Czech-dominated and characterized by sheer ignorance of the Eastern part. Thus, the pattern of an alleged European West-East divide with regard to its modernization standards was applied to internal East-West differences within Czechoslovakia.[104] Peter Haslinger has described this minor interest in Slovakia as a consequence of the fact that Czech national discourse had never really accepted Slovakia as being an integral part of the national "imagined territory;" after 1918, identification and interests of Czech politicians did not reach over the former Austrian-Hungarian inner borders.[105]

This "self-restraint" of legal thinking in Czechoslovakia set limiting and unhelpful boundaries to the reform debates about family law. As a lawyer living in Slovakia pointed out: "The common law system always presents broader opportunities to adapt itself to modern conditions than does a codex that turns the law into a stationary system." With regard to the ongoing legislation work he added, "If the means of unification efforts consist on the one hand of an old codex, and on the other hand of a common law system, the latter should be considered seriously because of its more progressive character."[106] After the abolition of the class character of the Slovak private law system in 1918 (the originally Hungarian private law system had had special rules for members of aristocracy and public service, and members of the middle and lower classes), private law in Slovakia was in many respects seen as being more progressive.[107] This assessment holds true especially for family law.

The Ignored Modernity of Slovak Family Law

One important feature of family law in Slovakia was its laic character; in 1894 the Hungarian part of the Empire had introduced civil marriage law in response to modern European developments.[108] By contrast, family law of the former Austrian Civil Code that now applied to the Czech lands had a clear denomination basis.[109] Thus, whereas in the Czech lands civil marriage was introduced with high political costs due to a strong opposition of the Catholic Church, and therefore of Catholic People's Parties, in Slovakia, civil marriage had been obligatory for two decades. In the Czech lands, as in the new Austrian Federal Republic, Church interests intensified the debates about family law reforms.[110] The Catholic Church protested against any legal limits to their control over marriage and stamped them as a "product of indifferentism."[111] This rather illiberal position was also promoted by Catholic women's associations.[112] The adoption of civil marriage laws in addition to a religious ceremony was perceived as a product of political anticlericalism. Demands for a separation of state and religion had culminated in the officially tolerated demolition of religious memorials.[113] As a compromise with the Catholics, the new law had been extended to Slovakia where only civil marriage was possible.[114] In Slovakia, this compromise was consequently seen as regressive.[115] At first Slovak registrars denied the legal validity of religious marriages.[116] Similar conflicts arose with the modernization of divorce law.[117]

The initial ignorance of Czech and German legal scholarship in Czechoslovakia was striking when it came to the regulation and distribution of financial benefits gained during marriage. Apart from being an issue of gender equality, the mandatory matrimonial separate property regime was one essential means of preventing poverty risks for women, especially for housewives and for women with children, after their marriage had come to an end. The Slovakian version of matrimonial property law had established elaborate and encompassing rules, including matrimonial property after divorce, separation, or death; claims by spouses to common property; claim to special funds by one spouse, etc.[118] Some experts considered the Slovakian version as a more modern position.[119] Hungarian legal scholars described this system as being superior not only in comparison to the Czech Lands, but within the European legal framework. It did not recognize the highly hierarchical legal principles of either Roman *manus* (a husband's authority over his wife) or of German *mundus* (a husband's guardianship over his wife), which had characterized European legal relations between spouses.[120] Spousal equality and mutual independence formed the dominant scholarly ideal of Hungarian family law even if judicial practice did not always reflect this approach.[121] However, the Revisory Committee rejected this model as unsuitable to the systematic framework of the ABGB, since "this would mean a complete reversal of the development of the law in the lands of former Austria [the Czech lands]."[122] Only after the protests of Slovak legal scholars in 1926 that criticized the planned "unification of the law" as a legal colonization of Slovakia, and after Slovak scholars became members of the Revisory Committee, was the regime of marital separate property with an equal share for spouses to the accumulated assets proposed by the Czechoslovak Revisory Commission for the new Civil Code in 1931. This approach was almost identical to the claim made by Marie Munk at the German Lawyers' Association in Czechoslovakia. However, the idea to distribute gained assets equally between spouses still met with resistance. Among German legal scholars, Lenhoff and Weiß with their statements at the Lawyers' Association rejected Munk's recommendation; among Czech scholars, the influential Jaromír Sedláček claimed that an equal share in the gained assets "would just complicate the relations during marriage."[123]

Although the Slovakian property system served as a model for the new Civil Code by 1931, it is surprising that it did not become part of the discussion at the Lawyers' Association. Any possible references were swept away in advance by Lenhoff, who stated that the Slovakian, formerly Hungarian, civil law system had been a two-class model unworthy of consideration or emulation.[124] One of the most frequently repeated arguments against a statutory matrimonial property regime at the Lawyers' Association was its impracticability and the fact that it was allegedly not in use at all (in the Czech lands).[125] The resistance from legal scholars did not even diminish when the Revisory commission finally accepted the Slovakian model for the new Czechoslovak Civil Code.[126] A comparison with legal discourse in Germany on the matter implies that it was easier to discuss that model of separate property and equity for property held in common promoted by Munk and others in a system, where it was entirely new. In Czechoslovakia, the adaptation of that model turned out to be more difficult, even if it had been already practiced in the (allegedly backwards) Slovakian region. To most Czech legal scholars it did not matter that the model of spousal equality in gained assets was the most popular model of financial regulation of marriage in Slovakia, or that the Slovakian model responded better to the constitutional claim of gender equality.[127]

Conclusion

The 1931 session of the German Lawyers' Association in Czechoslovakia that brought together public law scholars and private law scholars to discuss gender equality in the family reveals the rather conservative character of the legal discourse in Czechoslovakia on gender questions by that time. Even if everyone admitted to the fact that gender roles had changed drastically and that statutes did not meet reality anymore, typical gender stereotypes labelled through the terms "women's nature" or "nature of things" ran through all contributions. The presumption that women were impulsive, inexperienced, and undereducated was intended to determine their legal position. Thus, the legal setting of the former Austrian Civil Code, with its inflexible gender roles, remained fundamentally untouched. Core competencies of a husband's role as "head of the household," encompassing the right to financial administration of the family's and the wife's funds, were still supported by a majority. Women's financial position was modestly strengthened in circumstances where marriages ended.

That these proposals were far from being sufficient to put gender equality into practice was pointed out by representatives of public law scholarship. However, their interpretation of gender equality guaranteed by the constitution was not unanimous. Private law scholars used the "institutional guarantee" to support their conservative approach. The fact that the constitution put the family under special protection of the laws was interpreted as an approval of the historically given civil law with its normative set of gender roles. This argument reveals a Western-bound self-restraint of legal scholarship in Czech lands. In fact, this argument of an "institutional guarantee" conserving a legal status quo did not apply to one certain family system with its gender roles. In the realm of the Czechoslovak Constitution there was not one civil law, but two.

In contrast to the codification of the ABGB that applied to the Czech lands, in the Eastern part of Czechoslovakia, Slovakia, a modernized common law system was in practice with a comparatively progressive marriage law based on spouses' independence. From the beginning, the political stereotype that Slovakia was a backwards region compared with the Czech lands hindered legal scholars from regarding the Slovakian peculiarities. This attitude contributed to a delay of the reform, and the uneven distribution of gender roles within the Czechoslovak family law remained widely unchanged. The final reform draft of the Ministry of Justice in 1938 was thwarted by Nazi-German occupation. Significantly, the history of family law reform had been obstructed before due to the persistence of gender stereotypes and also to national prejudices and scholarly ignorance.

Notes

1 Compare Jiří Klabouch, *Manželství a rodina v minulosti* (Prague: Orbis, 1962), 163.
2 Jitka Malečková, "Nationalizing Women and Engendering the Nation: The Czech National Movement," in *Gendered Nations: Nationalisms and Gender Order in the Long Nineteenth Century*, ed. Ida Blom, Karen Hagemann and Catherine Hall (Oxford, New York: Berg, 2000), 293.
3 Františka Plamínková, *The Political Rights of Women in the Czechoslovak Republic* (Prague: Gazette de Prague, 1920), 7.
4 Compare Karen Johnson Freeze, "Medical Education for Women in Austria," in *Women, State, and Party in Eastern Europe*, ed. Sharon L. Wolchik and Alfred G. Meyer (Durham: Duke University Press, 1985); Jana Malínská, *Do politiky prý žena nesmí—proč? Vzdělání a postavení žen v české společnosti v 19. a na počátku 20. století* (Prague: slon/libri, 2005), 21, 23, 30; Marie Bahenská, *Počátky emancipace žen v Čechách: Dívčí vzdělávání a ženské spolky v Praze v 19. století* (Prague: slon/libri, 2005), 132–134; Melissa Feinberg, *Elusive Equality: Gender, citizenship, and the Limits of Democracy in Czechoslovakia, 1918–1950* (Pittsburgh: University of Pittsburgh Press, 2006), 26–28.
5 Brigitte Bader-Zaar, "Rethinking Women's Suffrage in the Nineteenth Century. Local Government and Entanglements of Property and Gender in the Austrian Half of the Habsburg Monarchy, Sweden, and the United Kingdom," in *Constitutionalism, Legitimacy, and Power. Nineteenth-Century Experiences*, ed. Kelly L. Grotke and Markus J. Prutsch (Oxford: Oxford University Press 2014), 107–126, 111.
6 Bader-Zaar, "Rethinking Women's Suffrage in the Nineteenth Century," 107–126, 107, 114.
7 See Plamínková, *Political Rights*, 16; compare also Richard J. Evans, *The Feminists: Women's Emancipation Movements in Europe, America and Australasia 1840–1920* (London: Croom Helm, 1979), 95–96.
8 For a short biography, compare Dana Musilova, *Z ženského pohledu: Poslankyně a senátorky Národního shromáždění Československé republiky 1918–1939* (Hradec Králové: Veduta, 2007), 118–119.
9 The writer Božena Viková-Kunětická pointed that out in a session on voting laws in June 1912, quote cited in Musilova, *Z ženského pohledu*, 27.
10 Feinberg, *Elusive Equality*, 28.
11 Ibid., 39.
12 Jana Burešová, *Proměny společenského postavení českých žen v první polovině 20. století* (Olomouc: Univerzita Palackého, 2001), 40.
13 Article 106 of the Czechoslovak Constitution, adopted February 29, 1920, stated: "Privileges based on sex, birth, or profession are not recognized." For the (lack of) impact of the constitutional changes in the German lands, compare Marion Röwekamp, *Die ersten deutschen Juristinnen. Eine Geschichte ihrer Professionalisierung und Emanzipation 1900–1945* (Cologne: Böhlau, 2011), 244. See also Feinberg's chapter in this volume.
14 Plamínková, *Political Rights*, 1, 16. For a short biography of Plamínková, compare Musilová, *Z ženského pohledu*, 110–111.
15 Article 128 of the Czechoslovak Constitution states: "All citizens of the Czechoslovak Republic are entirely equal to each other before the law and they are entitled equally to the same civic and political rights without regard to their race, language, or religion."
16 Bruce M. Garver, "Women in the First Czechoslovak Republic," in *Women, State, and Party in Eastern Europe*, ed. Sharon L. Wolchik and Alfred G. Meyer (Durham: Duke University Press, 1985), 78–79.
17 Feinberg, *Elusive Equality*, 10, 53.

18 Anna Loutfi, "Legal Ambiguity and the 'European Norm': Women's Independence and Hungarian Family Law 1880–1913," in *Women's Movements: Networks and Debates in post-communist Countries in the 19th and 20th Centuries*, ed. Edith Saurer, Margareth Lanzinger and Elisabeth Frysak (Cologne: Böhlau, 2006), 510.

19 Compare Renata Veselá, "Vývoj rodinného práva v meziválečném období," in *Československé právo a právní věda v meziválečném období (1918–1938) a jejích místo ve střední Evropě* 2, ed. Karel Malý and Ladislav Soukup (Prague: Karolinum, 2010), 791.

20 Josef Singer, *Das in der Slowakei geltende Recht: 2. Teil enthaltend das slowakische (ehemals ungarische) Privatrecht* (Prague: Mercy 1924), IX.

21 Burešová, *Postavení českých žen*, 68–69.

22 Feinberg, *Elusive Equality*, 70.

23 Compare Feinberg, *Elusive Equality*.

24 Gisela Tauber, "Die rechtliche Stellung der Frau," *Prager Juristische Zeitschrift* 11, no. 10/11 (1931): 364–365.

25 Compare Klabouch, *Manželství a rodina*, 154–160, and Legal draft, printed matter no. 1/1918 by the National Czechoslovak Assembly, proposed by PhDr. Bouček and others, accessed August 5, 2014, http://www.psp.cz/eknih/1918ns/ps/tisky/t0001_00.htm.

26 Jaromír Sedláček, "Ústavní listina a občanský zákoník," in *Naše právo a stát: Sborník k šedesátému výročí založení spolku československých právníků "Všehrd"*, ed. by František Čáda (Prague: Všehrd, 1928), 88, 93–94.

27 Article I paragraph 1 of the statute that introduces the Czechoslovak Constitution, no. 121/1920: "Statutes that contradict the Constitution, its parts, or other laws, that amend or alter the Constitution, are invalid."

28 Jana Osterkamp, *Verfassungsgerichtsbarkeit in der Tschechoslowakei (1920–1939): Verfassungsidee, Demokratieverständnis, Nationalitätenproblem* (Frankfurt am Main: Klostermann, 2009), 111.

29 One has to be careful not to apply a contemporary understanding of the Constitution to the interwar period, as does, I fear, Natali Stegmann when stating that she regards the Czechoslovak Constitution of 1920 as a "state institution" and as a "normative text with legally binding formulations and with thus having direct impact on the political dealings of the state;" see Natali Stegmann, "Gleichheitspostulat und innere Differenzierung: Geschlechtliche und andere Hierarchisierungsmuster in der tschechoslowakischen Politik bis 1948," in *Geschlechterbeziehungen in Ostmitteleuropa nach dem Zweiten Weltkrieg*, ed. Claudia Kraft (Munich: Oldenbourg, 2008), 108.

30 Rudolf Schranil, "Der fünfte deutsche Juristentag," *Prager Juristische Zeitschrift* 11, no. 14 (1931): 499.

31 Sedláček, "Ústavní listina," 93.

32 Egon Weiß, "Die rechtliche Stellung der Ehefrau," in *Fünfter Deutscher Juristentag in der Tschechoslowakei: Gutachten*, ed. by Deutscher Juristentag in der Tschechoslowakei (Prague: Sudetendeutscher Verlag, 1931), 135.

33 Obviously, jurisdiction later changed in that matter; compare the statement of Franz Kraus, *Fünfter Deutscher Juristentag in der Tschechoslowakei: Verhandlungen* (Prague: Sudetendeutscher Verlag, 1931), 310.

34 Egon Weiß, "Die Reform des allgemeinen bürgerlichen Gesetzbuches," in *Erster Deutscher Juristentag in der Tschechoslowakei: Gutachten*, ed. by Deutscher Juristentag in der Tschechoslowakei (Prague: Verlag der Prager Juristischen Zeitschrift, 1923), 7.

35 Bruno Kafka, *Právo rodinné: Návrh subkomitétu pro revisi občanského zákoníka pro Československou republiku* (Prague: Nákladatelství Ministerstva Spravedlnosti, 1924), 98–99; Jaromír Sedláček, *Rodinné právo* (Brno:

Nakladatelství Československého Akademického Spolku Právníků, 1934), 77, and Jaromír Sedláček, *Reforma manželského práva* (Prague: Linhart, 1938), 51.
36 Weiß, "Stellung der Ehefrau," 142.
37 Ibid., 138.
38 Ibid., 139–141.
39 Compare Sedláček, *Reforma*, 45, and Egon Weiß, "Griechen und Römer," in *Das Institut der Ehe im Altertum*, ed. Ludwig Wahrmund (Weimar: Böhlau, 1933), 126.
40 Compare Heinrich Rauchberg, "Die öffentlich-rechtliche Stellung der Frau in der Tschechoslowakischen Republik,"in *Fünfter Deutscher Juristentag in der Tschechoslowakei: Gutachten*, ed. by Deutscher Juristentag in der Tschechoslowakei (Prague: Sudetendeutscher Verlag, 1931), 150–151, and, Ulrich Scheuner, "Die Gleichheit vor dem Gesetz im tschechoslowakischen Verfassungsrecht," *Prager Juristische Zeitschrift* 11, no. 10/11 (1931): 391, 394, 400–402.
41 Compare the Report of the Constitutional committee about the Czechoslovak Constitution from January 16, 1920, printed matter no. 2421/1920 of the National Czechoslovak Assembly, accessed August 5, 2014, http://www.psp.cz/eknih/1918ns/ps/tisky/T2421_01.htm.
42 Osterkamp, *Verfassungsgerichtsbarkeit*, 111, 195.
43 This interpretation dates back to a formulation of the Czech legal scholar Jiří Pražák, *Rakouské právo ústavní, vol. III: Říšská ústava* (Prague: jednota právnická, 1902), 42, also quoted in Jaroslav Krejčí, *Základní práva občanská a rovnost před zákonem* (Prague: Moderní stát, 1929), 167.
44 Rauchberg, "Stellung der Frau," 145.
45 Heinrich Rauchberg, *Die Reform des Minderheitenschutzes* (Wrocław: Kern's Verlag, 1930).
46 Rauchberg, "Stellung der Frau," 147.
47 Ibid.
48 Ibid.
49 Ibid., 145–146.
50 Tauber, "Stellung der Frau," 368.
51 Feinberg, *Elusive Equality*, 77–78.
52 Ibid., 74.
53 Rauchberg, "Stellung der Frau," 154.
54 Feinberg, *Elusive Equality*, 97.
55 Article 108 of the Czechoslovak Constitution.
56 Rauchberg, "Stellung der Frau," 145–146, 150.
57 Ibid., 151.
58 Ibid.
59 Ibid., 161–162.
60 Abbo Junker, "Der Einfluß von Arthur Lenhoff (1885–1965) auf das Arbeitsrecht im deutschsprachigen Raum," in *Der Einfluß deutscher Emigranten auf die Rechtsentwicklung in den USA und in Deutschland*, ed. Marcus Lutter, Ernst C. Stiefel and Michael H. Hoeflich (Tübingen: Mohr Siebeck, 1993), 268.
61 Arthur Lenhoff, "Marianne Beth: Das Recht der Frau," *Zeitschrift für soziales Recht* 3 (1930): 208.
62 Carl Schmitt, *Verfassungslehre* (Berlin: Duncker & Humblot, 1927), 170.
63 Ibid., 171.
64 Michael Stolleis, *Geschichte des öffentlichen Rechts in Deutschland: Weimarer Republik und Nationalsozialismus* (Munich: Beck, 2002), 111.
65 Lenhoff, *Fünfter Deutscher Juristentag in der Tschechoslowakei: Verhandlungen* (1931), 260–261.
66 Ibid., 261.
67 Ibid., 271.
68 Compare Feinberg, *Elusive Equality*, 35–37, and, Krejčí, *Rovnost*, 172–175.

69 Lenhoff, *Verhandlungen*, 262.
70 Ibid., 267. The debates with contributions by Marianne Weber and Marie Munk were much more fundamental than the one at the *Juristentag in der Tschechoslowakei*; compare *Verhandlungen des sechsunddreißigsten Deutschen Juristentages* (Berlin, Leipzig: de Gruyter, 1932), 80–142.
71 Lenhoff, Verhandlungen, 329, and Marianne Weber, *Ehefrau und Mutter in der Rechtsentwicklung: Eine Einführung* (Tübingen: Mohr, 1907), 420–421.
72 Idid., 295–296.
73 Röwekamp, *Erste Juristinnen*, 598–599; Schranil, "Der fünfte deutsche Juristentag," 499.
74 Feinberg, *Elusive Equality*, 53–54, and Burešová, *Postavení českých žen*, 71.
75 Käthe Spiegel, *Kulturgeschichtliche Grundlagen der amerikanischen Revolution* (Munich, Berlin: Oldenbourg, 1931).
76 Gerhard Oberkofler, *Käthe Spiegel: Aus dem Leben einer altösterreichischen Historikerin und Frauenrechtlerin in Prag* (Vienna: Studienverlag, 2005), 25, 31, 39.
77 Spiegel, *Fünfter Deutscher Juristentag in der Tschechoslowakei: Verhandlungen* (1931), 307.
78 Ibid., 308.
79 Weiß, *Verhandlungen*, 313.
80 Compare Röwekamp, *Erste Juristinnen*, 600.
81 Tauber, "Stellung der Frau," 368.
82 Compare Veselá, *Vývoj rodinného práva*, 804.
83 Spiegel, *Verhandlungen*, 308–309.
84 Ibid., 309.
85 Oberkofler, *Käthe Spiegel*, 92–98.
86 Spiegel, *Verhandlungen*, 309.
87 Compare Marion Röwekamp, *Juristinnen: Lexikon zu Leben und Werk* (Baden-Baden: Nomos, 2005), 276–277; see also Marion Röwekamp, "Doing Gender, Doing Law, Doing Biography: Marie Munk (1885–1978)," *Bios* 23 (2011): 100–102; Marion Röwekamp, *Marie Munk: Rechtsanwältin, Richterin, Rechtsreformerin* (Berlin: Hentrich, 2014).
88 See Röwekamp, *Erste Juristinnen*, 587–588; Dagmar Coester-Waltjen, "Die fachliche Arbeit der Deutschen Juristentage und ihre Wirkungen auf dem Gebiet des Familienrechts," in *150 Jahre Deutscher Juristentag. Festschrift Deutscher Juristentag 1860–2010*, ed. Ständige Deputation des Deutschen Juristentages (Munich: Beck, 2010), 132–134, 144–145; Jens Lehmann, *Die Ehefrau und ihr Vermögen: Reformforderungen der bürgerlichen Frauenbewegung zum Ehegüterrecht um 1900* (Cologne: Böhlau, 2006); and Jörg Offen, *Von der Verwaltungsgemeinschaft des BGB von 1896 zur Zugewinngemeinschaft des Gleichberechtigungsgesetzes von 1957* (Frankfurt am Main et al.: Peter Lang, 1994), 7–9, 34–35.
89 Marie Munk, *Verhandlungen*, 320.
90 Ibid., 320.
91 Ibid., 321.
92 Grundsätze, *Verhandlungen*, 333.
93 Leitsätze, *Verhandlungen*, 333–334.
94 Ibid., 335.
95 Stradal, *Verhandlungen*, 326.
96 Leitsätze, *Verhandlungen*, 335, 337.
97 Weber, *Ehefrau und Mutter in der Rechtsentwicklung*, 420–421.
98 Lenhoff, *Verhandlungen*, 329.
99 Tara Zahra, *Kidnapped Souls: National Indifference and the Battle for Children in the Bohemian Lands, 1900–1948* (Ithaca and London: Cornell University Press, 2008), 106.
100 Ibid., 106–108.

101 As a good example of this Western-bound thinking, see Kafka, *Právo rodinné*, and Weiß, *Reform*.
102 Veselá, *Vývoj rodinného práva*, 810, 817.
103 For an example, compare again Kafka, *Právo rodinné*. Kafka was member of the Revisory committee. As the responsible referent for the new family law, he published the commission's first draft with remarks. These refer almost exclusively to the Austrian, the German, the French, and the Swiss systems. The Committee simultaneously published a German version of its draft: *Das bürgerliche Gesetzbuch für die Čechoslovakische Republik. Übersetzung des Entwurfes der Kommission für die Revision des ABGB*, ed. Justizministerium der Čechoslovakischen Republik (Reichenberg: Stiepel, 1924).
104 Peter Haslinger, *Nation und Territorium im tschechischen politischen Diskurs 1880–1938* (Munich: Oldenbourg, 2010), 312.
105 Ibid., 440–444.
106 Singer, *Recht der Slowakei*, VIII.
107 Sedláček, *Reforma*, 46–47.
108 Loutfi, "Hungarian Family Law," 812.
109 Helmut Slapnicka, *Österreichs Recht außerhalb Österreichs: Der Untergang des österreichischen Rechtsraums* (Vienna: Verlag für Geschichte und Politik, 1973), 13.
110 With regard to Austria, compare Ulrike Harmat, *Ehe auf Widerruf? Der Konflikt um das Eherecht in Österreich 1918–1938* (Frankfurt am Main: Klostermann, 1999), 121, 449.
111 Johannes Schlenz, *Das tschechoslowakische Ehegesetz vom 22. Mai 1919 nach dem geltenden bürgerlichen und kirchlichen Rechte erläutert* (Reichenberg: Volksbundverlag 1930), 13.
112 Musilova, *Z ženského pohledu*, 69.
113 Martin Schulze Wessel, *Revolution und religiöser Dissens: Der römisch-katholische und der russisch-orthodoxe Klerus als Träger religiösen Wandels in den böhmischen Ländern und in Russland 1848–1922* (Munich: Oldenbourg, 2011), 120–122.
114 Musilova, *Z ženského pohledu*, 70.
115 Klabouch, *Manželství a rodina*, 166.
116 Veselá, *Vývoj rodinného práva*, 798.
117 Musilova, *Z ženského pohledu*, 69.
118 Vladimír Fajnor and Adolf Záturecký, *Nástin súkromného práva platného na Slovensku a podkarpatskej Rusi* (re-print of the edition 1935, Šamorín: Heuréka, 1998), 435–438; Singer, *Recht der Slowakei*, 194–199; and Sedláček, *Reforma*, 46–47.
119 Veselá, *Vývoj rodinného práva*, 812.
120 Loutfi, "Hungarian Family Law," 814.
121 Idid., 815–817.
122 Kafka, *Právo rodinné*, 95, 98.
123 Sedláček, *Reforma*, 52.
124 Lenhoff, *Verhandlungen*, 272.
125 Sedláček, *Reforma*, 52.
126 Käthe Spiegel, "Die Frau und der Entwurf des neuen bürgerlichen Gesetzbuches," *Die sudetendeutsche Frau. Unabhängige Monatsschrift. Offizielles Organ des Verbandes deutscher Frauenvereinigungen in der Tschechoslowakischen Republik* 13, no. 2 (1938), re-print in Oberkofler, *Käthe Spiegel*, 147.
127 Singer, *Recht der Slowakei*, 195.

Part II

Women in the Legal Professions

5 The Rise of "Modern Portias"

Feminist Legal Activism in Republican France, 1890s–1940s

Sara L. Kimble

Introduction: Feminism and the Legal Profession in Historical Perspective

In 1900, when French women gained access to the legal profession in France, Jeanne Oddo-Deflou (b. 1856), leader of the French Group for Feminist Studies (Groupe français d'études féministes), expressed optimism that "great progress" could be realized now that "women themselves can plead their own cause if not before the [French] Parliament then at least in the courts."[1] She was correct that women's rights would be advanced as a result of women's entrance into the legal profession.[2] The pioneering female lawyers, beginning with Jeanne Chauvin (1862–1926), supported the organized feminist movement. Chauvin spearheaded the campaign to open the profession for women in France and she allied with feminist groups with whom she formulated draft legislation to reform women's individual rights.[3] She also reclaimed the history of women's intellectual achievements through her writing.[4] However, the controversy she engendered by raising the question of women's access to the bar reignited a smoldering debate about the future of women's rights in French society. During the debates in the Chamber of Deputies, Deputy Joseph Massabuau, a closet anti-semite and independent republican, argued that female lawyers and their feminism would spell the end of traditional marriages, result in the triumph of free unions, and culminate in women's total equality in civil, political, and economic terms.[5] The bill's sponsor, feminist supporter and independent socialist Deputy René Viviani, replied that Massabuau's "zealous" diatribe against feminism suggested "to those who do not know you better that you harbor indelible grievances against women."[6] While Viviani's retort undercut Massabuau's comments, they were met with general amusement by the assembly (presumably approbation), the very fact of the arduous protest signaled the cultural weight attached to "*la femme avocat*" and the ways in which this new opportunity for women raised important questions about the gendered organization of French society.

When the Chamber of Deputies voted on June 30, 1899, to admit women to the bar, they approved the measure by 319 votes against 174. When the

Senate finally took its vote on November 13, 1900, the bill passed by 172 in favor and 34 against, a wider margin.[7] The resulting law of December 1, 1900, permitted qualified women to join the bar but implicitly refused to authorize them to serve in other positions, such as judges, notaries, solicitors, or court clerks.[8] The possibility that women might receive equal treatment was conceived in a legislative committee but never formally proposed or debated.[9] Nevertheless, the ultimate compromise legislation was a first in Europe and marked a change in judicial interpretation after similar claims by women and their advocates had been rejected in Italy (1884) and Belgium (1888).[10] Chauvin's success in France echoed beyond its borders, especially in countries where the Napoleonic *Code civil* (1804) influenced other national laws. After France's decision, women were officially admitted to the bar in Romania (1901), the Netherlands (1903), Norway (1904), and Denmark (1906). Countries such as Britain, Germany, Italy, and Belgium, however, would not admit women to practice law until the 1920s.

Evidence of women's challenges to male dominance in the judicial system exists in the revolutionary origins of republican France. Between 1789 and 1793, women demanded the right to equal political participation in their *cahiers de doléances* (grievance lists) and petitioned for the appointment of female judges.[11] Even Chauvin, who was not a trained historian, was able to unearth evidence of women from the Third Estate who had requested the right to education, to development of their intellect, and to work.[12] During the French Revolution, women did serve on the bench in the arbitration courts.[13] This was an exceptional opportunity at a historic moment when rights for all were debated, but equality was not extended.[14] These appeals gained wider recognition only in the second half of the nineteenth century, when other texts, such as Ernest Legouvé's *Histoire morale des femmes* (1848), Julie-Victoire Daubié's two-volume *La femme pauvre au dix-neuvième siècle* (1866–1869), and John Stuart Mill's influential *The Subjection of Women* (1869) defended women's intellectual capacity and argued in favor of women's expanded rights to work. In 1870, Maria Deraismes and Léon Richer's Association for Women's Rights (L'Association pour le droit des femmes) demanded equality for women in the family and work, access to secondary education, and the establishment of professional education. By 1889, the idea that women had the intellectual capacity to train as lawyers and that they should have the right to work in the legal profession was in evidence among women's rights supporters at the French and International Congress of Women's Rights.[15] Chauvin's own law thesis, *Étude historique sur les professions accessible aux femmes* (Historical Study on Professions Accessible to Women, 1892), argued for the logic of opening all professions—where merit was the criteria for admission—to women in a democratic and meritocratic society.[16] These academic arguments found fulfillment in practical terms only when leaders in the French and Belgian women's rights movements stood behind Chauvin and her reformist ambitions to put pressure on the French legislators in the 1890s.[17]

The controversy over women's entrance into various realms of law (including university study, the legal profession, legal administration, and professional associations) was the consequence of the meanings associated with law in society and particularly the relationship between law and authority in its various manifestations. Sociologist Carol Smart reiterated in *Feminism and the Power of Law* that law is powerful because it shapes the social construction of the sexes in ways that affect men's and women's economic positions, their status in legal discourse, and legally prescribed roles within the family structure.[18] The law is one of the most important sites for the enforcement of the patriarchal order, and it functions coercively in society, as philosopher Michel Foucault illustrated in *Discipline and Punish*.[19] Moreover, the law contributes to the realization of a particular political, economic, and moral order. The courts act as arbiters in the mediation of the community's evolving ideas of what is moral and just. Once women were granted the right to plead cases and participate in the legal sphere in the French Third Republic (1870–1940), they approached the opportunity to experience and to advocate for greater gender equality in practical and symbolic terms. Women's participation in this milieu brought with it social and cultural capital and thus cemented their place in the social elite. Following Pierre Bourdieu's theory on the reproduction of the elite, those women born into families where men already worked in the legal profession were likely to possess the necessary capital to be successful in the field newly opened to them.[20] Chauvin's father was a notary, and her brother, Émile, worked as a lawyer, law professor, and was elected to the Chamber of Deputies. Agathe Dyvrande-Thévenin's father was a judge. Even those few women who benefited from law as a familial profession worked against the grain of the dominant social mores governing the appropriateness of such work for women of the bourgeoisie.

This chapter argues that women's entrance and subsequent participation in the legal profession in France was a landmark event for the *belle époque* (1880–1914) women's rights movement and the status of women. *Avocates* (female attorneys) represented the intellectual, social, and political potential of "*la femme nouvelle*" (the new woman) of the era, and their appearance contributed to the destabilization of gender roles. Their participation in women's rights and women's professional associations raised the level of debate and strengthened the connections between their own groups and the *hommes politiques* (political men) operating on the national and international level. In a bid for social acceptance, *avocates* appropriated the values of the patron saint of lawyers, Saint Yves de Tréguier (Brittany). Like St. Yves, these pioneering women vowed to defend the rights of the underclass: the poor, widows, and orphans.[21] Indeed, their disproportionate work in the juvenile justice system would become well known.[22] At the time, devotion to the downtrodden fit well with the generally socially acceptable expressions of women's maternalism expressed by feminist lawyers as they defended women's right to work in the legal system as an extension of women's traditional or so-called "essential" female talent for nurturing.

In France, female attorneys also entered the profession at a politically auspicious moment when support for republicanism was the norm. The heyday for the so-called "republic of lawyers" ran from 1877 to 1914, when young lawyers promoted republican values and policy.[23] Regarding this, Philip Nord wrote that the legal profession was the self-styled "school of liberal statesmanship" and that "there was no better preparation for a career in parliamentary politics than a stint at the Palais" [de Justice].[24] Moreover, he commented that the bar taught the primary virtues of public service: "independence of mind, eloquence in defense of principle, devotion to self-government."[25] This training would prove beneficial to politically engaged men, and later, women, of the *belle époque*.

This history of female lawyers and their activism was drawn from varied manuscript and printed documents by two generations of active female attorneys who joined the bar before or immediately after the First World War (1914–1918). This chapter focuses on the activism of republican feminist women who endeavored to empower others through their casework, participated in political associations, and disseminated legal knowledge to the public. Among the most significant impacts made by these activist-lawyers (*avocates engagées*) was their role in popularizing feminist thought and social criticism in multiple settings, including their newspaper columns, popular lectures, and participation in legal aid venues. These figures called themselves "modern Portias" and believed that they combined the warmth of their "hearts" with their erudition in order to provide useful and often altruistic legal services to others.[26] In the use of this term, Marcelle Kraemer-Bach (1896–1990) drew on the maternalist tradition within the French women's rights movement, which justified women's entrance into the civic, charitable, or political world on the grounds that their contributions as women were unique. In 1928, Kraemer-Bach co-founded the International Federation of Women in Legal Careers (Fédération International des femmes des carrières juridiques or FIFCJ) to consolidate the power of French lawyers and connect them to the broader rights movement among European women during the interwar years.[27]

The consequence of this political engagement was a contribution to the disruption of conventional gender roles through their professional work and the advancement of women's rights. Viewed collectively, French female lawyers' activism forms a pattern of activity that I have termed "political uses of the law" to describe women's participation in legal discourse and legal processes to advance women's rights and foster reform.[28] This concept allows us to see coherence among otherwise seemingly disparate activities by women in the profession in the early twentieth century, and to illuminate this collective process, this chapter highlights the major strategies, tactics, and achievements that characterize the ways *avocates* challenged the status quo. This analysis underscores efforts through which women's activism contributed to changing social roles and relations of power, particularly as structured by law and legislation. The content addresses, briefly, a history of gender and the legal profession from a theoretical standpoint before then engaging with the significance of women's entrance into the legal profession through examples of their participation in political reform.

Gender and the Legal Profession

A theoretical framework of both gender and law guides this analysis of women's history in the French legal profession. The social construction of gender, that is, the meaning assigned to being male or female, influenced women's admission to the legal profession, their experience within it, and their political impact. Historian Joan W. Scott has argued that "gender is the social organization of sexual difference," not fixed but variable at different moments and within different social groups. Sexual difference is a function of "knowledge" about the body and of the meanings assigned to sexual difference.[29] Scott notes that such attributions of meaning belong to "something that will always elude definition."[30] While instability remains with the subject, gender can be defined within specific contexts, constructed at specific times and places, and is, thus, subject to change. Women in *belle époque* French society were subordinate to men in the formal organization of society as well as in private life. Under the law, married women endured the yoke of the civil code that prescribed the obedience wives owed to their spouses and dramatically curtailed their civil autonomy. While scholars recognize the diversity of human experience as mediated by such forces as religion, social class, and politics, this acknowledgement does not negate the fact that as women, they lived under legal and social structures and expectations that restricted their opportunities. As women, they were denied equal education and political rights for the first half of the twentieth century. As married women, authority over their personhood, their property, and their children belonged to the male head of household. The development of the possibility of the self-reliant figure of the *femme nouvelle* (or her predecessor the *éclaireuse*) expanded the restrictive dichotomy formulated by what Pierre-Joseph Proudhon (1809–65) called the traditional roles of "housewife or courtesan."[31] While the *éclaireuse*, an emancipated career woman who pursued her own ambitions and pleasures, made inroads in French *belle époque* popular culture, conventions governing cultural change continued to hold fast in the law and other more conventional sectors of society.

Female lawyers, who actively broke barriers in the pursuit of professional employment, were also met by the expectation that they would be different in their legal practice particularly by enacting greater nurturing or maternalist tendencies. Women themselves reinforced this expectation. In an 1899 interview, Chauvin claimed that her first priority in work was to help unfortunate and socially disinherited children.[32] Such a claim shaped a maternalist role within the work of lawyering. The connotation of women with motherhood and mothering was not *a priori* disadvantageous. Rachel Fuchs' research in *Contesting Paternity* illustrated the ways in which mothers often successfully appealed to the justice system on behalf of their children born outside of marriage.[33] Female civil servants also deployed maternalist strategies to pursue nontraditional careers, as Linda Clark has shown.[34] Whether playing the role of supplicants or agents on behalf of others, women found ways of taking action for the purposes of changing their own or others' circumstances despite formal restraints on their exercise of power. In France and beyond, Karen Offen has argued, "motherhood became a 'political strategy' for feminist activism" where women established institutions to empower women as mothers and push for nations to prioritize issues of human welfare.[35] Indeed, French feminism in the *belle époque* respected women's relationship to their families and the important place of the family as the primary unit within society. By this they meant a partnership family, not a hierarchical one. By consequence, women who strove to engage in politics did well to frame their work in terms of maternalism. Seth Koven defined "civil maternalism" as a "set of rhetorical strategies, attitudes, and ideas about the ways in which women's motherly capacities to love, nurture, and care for others were linked to the imperative to deploy these gifts within their local communities and municipalities."[36] French female lawyers engaged with their gender in multiple ways, most importantly by valuing sexual difference, rather than negating it, during the pursuit of women's collective interests both locally and beyond.

At the same time that female lawyers derived various strategies involving gender roles to pursue personal and professional success, they were engaged in a process that challenged these same gender roles. Changes in women's roles were well under way at the end of the nineteenth century, but this process accelerated as a result of the new opportunities and disruptions of the First World War, when "all the world was topsy-turvy since the War began" according to a poem at the time.[37] Mary Louise Roberts has argued that out of the confusions of the war, three modes of femininity emerged in cultural discourse during the postwar era to take account of the changing society: the reassuring mother, the disruptive "new woman," and the ambiguous single woman.[38] Women in professions often attempted to skate over the controversies their novelty engendered by emphasizing the utility of their service to others while minimizing their own singularity. The legal profession was a traditionally masculine one where success was framed in terms of the expression of masculine virtues and aptitudes, including analytical reasoning, forceful argument and eloquence, and physical stamina. An attorney's pleading "from exordium to peroration, might well last a full five hours."[39] Women could not compete as "men" in such an environment but rather could made their way by drawing on maternalist rationales to argue for their suitability as women in the quasi-public roles required of advocates. Representations of *avocates*—which they themselves could not readily control—tended to concentrate on the disruptive and even sexual connotation of the *femme nouvelle*.[40] But women themselves attempted to straddle the tension of the masculine professional roles with their own feminine and frequently feminist priorities.

Demographics and Statistics

During the *belle époque* the number of women who joined the legal profession in France was modest. This should not come as a surprise since the legal profession required fortitude and financial resources at all levels of education and career training. Moreover, female students faced a disadvantage at law faculties, since before 1924 their primary and secondary curriculum was not the same as that provided to boys.[41] Consequently, girls had to study privately for the *baccalaureate* during secondary schooling to prepare for the university, and women's limited career opportunities restrained the appeal of this profession. While men with law degrees might pursue careers in civil service, government ministries, or representative politics, such fields were arbitrarily closed to women. Women's opportunities were constrained both by tacit discrimination and structural inequalities. Married women's right to work, even as lawyers, was formally subjected to spousal authority in an era with uneasy tensions between family law and individual rights. Despite this, law school enrollments for Paris show a gradual and modest increase over time. In 1901–1902, 13 women were enrolled at the law school in Paris out of a total enrollment of 4868. By 1910, 117 women and 7824 men studied law in Paris. By 1920, there were 509 female students and 8975 male students.[42]

In the pursuit of a legal career, men and women who had completed law school were consequently required to complete an internship of several years after admission to the bar, during which time they rarely earned a full income. While some of the pioneers could rely on the support of better-paid spouses, this was certainly not always the case. Many early pioneers of the bar worked out of economic necessity. Marguerite Dilhan (1876–1956), who joined the bar in Toulouse in 1903, was an orphan and unmarried. She claimed to work in law for the purposes of defending the "right of the weakest" in society, yet she still needed to earn an income.[43] Chauvin supported herself and her widowed mother through a combination of teaching at the *lycée* level, legal casework, lectures, and a few publications. Maria Vérone, a divorced mother of two children, supported her family and her political causes primarily through her remunerated legal work and journalism. Vérone attested to the fact that earning a salary sufficient to raise one's children was one of the central satisfactions of working in the legal profession. And she had other work experiences upon which to make a comparison; she had previously worked assisting her mother with hat making, within public schools as an adjunct teacher, and also briefly as a dancer.[44] Vérone strategically declared her appreciation for the legal profession because she through it could render services to those less fortunate, demonstrating that women could successfully work in a "man's milieu" while still fulfilling the roles of good wife, mother and citizen. She advised other women that success depended upon the application of their "tenacity, conscientiousness, command of logic, and a little devotion."[45] As Linda Clark has revealed in her study of professional women, some of the French female graduates of law schools pursued careers in civil service, as staff in legal offices, or in other fields that provided a more reliable income than what was available to independent lawyers.[46] Edmée Charrier noted that by 1928, a total of 332 women were inscribed on the lists of active attorneys in France, its colonies, and its protectorates. This group was divided into full-fledged attorneys (109) and those who were still in their initial internship (*stage*) or training period (223).[47] Such numbers would not have included those who were not current on their bar membership fees. Nor would it include outliers such as Flora Rosemberg, an attorney trained in Rennes but who worked in the courts of Shanghai from 1921, the first European woman to do so.[48] While the actual number of women who entered the legal profession before the Second World War was modest, their impact in society was considerable.

Women's Challenges to Institutions

Women's entrance into academia and the liberal and legal professions challenged male exclusivity in these institutions. Men's response to women's arrival varied across a spectrum that ended in violent opposition. Limited documentation suggests that female students who audited courses at the law school in Paris in the 1870s were chaperoned, but their presence was initially tolerated without incident. This relative acceptance demonstrated to the Dean of the Faculty of Law, Henri Berthélemy, that women could "come and go with total freedom without causing any disturbances, or risk becoming the object of regrettable familiarity."[49] Female students may have been tolerated, but women's request to enter the profession was another matter. In medicine, fine arts, and law, male students protested women's claim to the right to work in their fields. In 1884, medical students hung Blanche Edwards-Pilliet in effigy as she attempted to gain access to residency training.[50] Female art students were confronted by "noisy demonstrations and the first candidate for an internship had been burned in effigy."[51] Henri Rochefort, a radical journalist, condemned these protests for their display of "shameful jealousy" while predicting the same outrage at the Palais de Justice.[52] Indeed, male law students disrupted Jeanne Chauvin's thesis defense in July 1892, forcing it to be rescheduled. The second time she did succeed in defending her ideas, but male students again asserted their opposition to gender equality.[53]

The question of Chauvin's right to practice law was also divisive for practicing professionals. On the one hand, Edmond Ployer, the president of the Paris bar, described Chauvin as "charming, very erudite, and truly worthy of exercising the lawyer's tasks. I am convinced that she has a more profound understanding of the law than the average law graduate."[54] Others, however, declared Chauvin's claim illegitimate. Parisian attorney Camille Ducreux asserted that the sexes were indelibly different and unequal and thus granting equal rights was nonsensical. He argued that legal careers were like political careers requiring "an exterior life, public influence, [and] contact with the masses that must be forbidden to women. All this is simply public morality."[55] Ducreux's sentiments reflected conventional bourgeois social mores that opposed women's participation in many public venues and professions.

When Chauvin sought admission to the formal oath ceremony for admission to the internship period for new attorneys Edmond Bertrand (1842–1929), the *procureur général* (who represented the state), barred her access. Bertrand would argue in the Appeals Court that Chauvin, was ineligible to take the necessary attorneys' oath because women were excluded under Roman, Justinian, and French law. He insisted that under ancient Roman law, the legal profession was a "virile" one where women were excluded as court advocates because of the offense caused by Gaia Afrania (d. 48 CE), with her allegedly "shrewish," "impudent," and "litigious" behavior.[56] This exclusion was reinforced by the fifth century Justinian Code, when women were to be forbidden from "all public and civil offices," prohibited "to be judges, to plead, to intervene in law on behalf of another, to be procurators."[57] The 1810 regulations governing the bar made no mention of women at all, but Bertrand argued that the subordinate position of married women under the civil code should guide legal interpretation and support women's exclusion from the bar and the judiciary. After all, wives under the code were treated as minors. In other words, the civil inequality of married women was to be applied to all women regardless of their actual marital status.[58]

The Court of Appeals in Paris, presided over by Samuel Périvier (1828–1902), sided with Bertrand's reasoning but left the door open to legislative reinterpretation. The judges acknowledged that all citizens, without distinction of sex, were due their "*liberté du travail*" (right to work). The Court would not act on this concession, however, because only the legislature had the power to desegregate the bar. Two judges encouraged legislators to take up the question of women's right to work in light of "social progress" and the "evolving state" of French mores.[59]

The legislative debates that followed considered not only women's rights but also the potential consequences of women's expanded professional opportunities on French society itself. The majority of representatives in the Chamber of Deputies and in the Senate voted in favor of a narrowly written bill that provided women access to the legal profession as attorneys only, not as notaries, clerks, judges, or other formal positions. The bill was justified as a way to put into action "the grand principles of liberty and equality in education and in work for all women as it is for all men."[60] Rhetorically at least, women's right to work as lawyers was conceived as a matter of fulfilling republican and democratic principles. Objections in the

Senate conflated women's right to work as attorneys with the right to admit women to government positions, an act that would be characterized by one opponent as the equivalent to "high treason."[61] Such hyperbolic objections to the bill aside, a legislative majority made the law of December 1, 1900, possible, formally admitting women to work in the legal profession as "*avocats*," eligible to represent clients and to plead cases in all jurisdictions in France and its overseas territories.

The fact that the legislation admitting women to the "*avocature*" excluded them from the "*magistrature*" (position of magistrate) was not lost on women's rights advocates. As I have argued elsewhere, the history of women and the judiciary in France pivoted on the ways in which women's second-class citizenship restrained their fundamental right to work.[62] Those who argued that the "right to judge" belonged only to those with full political rights (which, until 1944, meant only men) opposed women's entrance into the judiciary. Women's inferior civil, political, and social status rendered them theoretically ineligible for the bench. Activist lawyers engaged in a decades-long campaign to secure job opportunities in the legal profession and the judiciary, and to defend women's right to equal treatment under the law. Agathe Dyvrande-Thévenin (1885–1977), president of a French female lawyers' solidarity group, criticized the law of 1900 for "establishing an inequality, prejudicial to women, between *avocats* of the two sexes; it closes the door by which women have already entered into the sanctuary of justice itself."[63] Feminist attorney Suzanne Grinberg (1889–1972) made claims in 1909 for women's rights, including participation on juries, admission to the judiciary, elimination of married women's inequality under family law, and political rights.[64] She would become active in the major national suffrage association (French Union for Women's Suffrage or UFSF) and the International Women's Suffrage Alliance (IWSA). In 1922, she argued that the assertions that justified the inferiority of women were founded in the same type of prejudice launched against "Jews, blacks, communists or clericals, royalists or radicals" and equally indefensible.[65] Individual protests of this type became a collective movement when, in 1929, Dyvrande-Thévenin, then president of the FIFCJ, organized a delegation to the minister of justice.[66] Consequently, legislation was introduced to permit women's nomination to the judiciary in 1930.[67] The opposition argued that granting women judicial rights before suffrage was "illogical and premature" and to do so failed to respect the gradual "stages" of women's "civic education."[68] It was an easy excuse to effectively forestall change.

The opposition to female judges persisted despite the creation of the new juvenile court system in 1912, where women's participation was considered more appropriate, and again after the First World War, when the profession suffered from the paucity of male candidates. Feminists argued that women might find a place in the juvenile courts as a stepping-stone to other jurisdictions. However, this campaign stalled despite the role of women in the growing field of social work and the international examples of female judges (in Europe and North America). In the legal profession, the question of women's access to the judiciary did not hinge on whether women were qualified but rather on their lack of political rights. At a meeting of the French National Association of Lawyers (*Association nationale des avocats*, or ANA), for example, attorney Vérone was acknowledged as "a worthy opponent," one of the best orators of her generation, and well-suited for the judiciary.[69] Nevertheless, the association collectively opposed women's entrance into the judiciary at a time when women's voting rights were rarely off the political agenda, and the Senate repeatedly defeated voting rights bills that had met with approval by the Chamber.[70] Only when women themselves served as political representatives would they ram through legislation to secure equal access to the judiciary (law of April 1946). Up to that point, the debate over women's "right to judge" had pivoted on women's citizenship rights and the question of female authority.[71] The issue of women's authority remained problematic in the French colonies, where breaches in gender conventions met with tenacious resistance.[72]

Although French women's admission to the bench did not occur until after the Second World War, women had made gradual inroads into the administration of the legal profession in earlier decades. In particular, women gained access to the young lawyers' association, which was, in Gilles Le Béguec's analysis, part of the bar's own administrative "aristocracy" that centered on honorary appointments and elections to professional institutions that functioned as part of the profession's self-regulation.[73] When in Bordeaux in 1921, Madeleine ("Manon") Cormier (1896–1945) was elected as a secretary to the young lawyers' association, she seized upon this honor to speak on the trial of the revolutionary Madame Roland (1754–1793), a topic that reclaimed women's role in the French Revolution and women's place in politics.[74] Paris followed suit in 1922 with the election of Jeanne Rospars (b. 1895).[75] She recalled feeling honored to work: "It was very difficult, very awe-inspiring. But I had been well prepared by my boss Léouzon Leduc; I was not excessively intimidated."[76] Despite her modesty and the rhetorical deference to credit a man with her success, Rospars' admission signaled the erosion of women's marginalization in the profession.

The promotion of known feminists within the legal administration was another sign of women's acceptance in the profession. After the twenty-fifth anniversary of women's admission to the bar, Suzanne Grinberg was the first woman to be elected to the central council of the ANA. At the same time, she defended women's expertise with the legal needs of women and children: "What genre of affairs do *avocates* plead? Above all, they plead—and the judicial assistance is a valuable apprenticeship—divorce, separation, and guardianship of children. In the correctional courts, they assist with the delinquents of all genres, thieves, swindlers, those accused of violation of trust, assault and battery, outrages against an authority, etc. . . . They often contribute to the defense of *enfants coupables;* the place of women is very important in the courts for children."[77] Grinberg became well known for popular articles in the French press on legal matters and books on women's history or rights, including *The Rights of Widows and War Orphans* (1916), *Feminine Careers* (with Alice La Mazière, 1917), the *History of the Suffragist Movement since 1848* (1926), *Women's Rights and New Constitutions* (1935), and with Odette Simon, *The New Rights of the Married Woman* (1938).[78] She was active in many associations, and on the occasion of the 1926 International Federation of University Women conference in Amsterdam, Grinberg reported on women's right to work and the legal status of married women based on comparative research into the status of women in 33 countries. The work drew attention for "the need for having women jurists as members of the Federation in all countries since many of the questions concerning the rights of women were in reality legal matters."[79] Such an occasion underscored the value of female lawyers for the defense of women's rights and reinforced the need for a collective advocacy of women's access to legal knowledge. No matter the specific association within which she worked, Grinberg's overarching political goal was to abolish the idea of "dominance or submission" in gender relations and replace this binary with true cooperation between men and women.[80]

The defense of women's rights within the broader framework of human rights was an important aspect of feminist lawyers' thought. When, in 1927, Juliette Veillier-Duray was elected to a selective position in the Paris bar association's lawyers' conference, she used her position to lecture on civil disobedience in the social movement of Mohandas Gandhi, the attorney and leader who led the downtrodden in demonstrations for human rights in British India. Veillier-Duray was active in the French Association of University Women (*Association Française des Femmes Diplômées des Universités*, or AFFDU) as vice president and later president (1931–1936), where she defended women's right to work and their access to employment. She was publically critical of the civil code's antiquated restrictions on married women's rights to autonomy and called for reform in national and international forums.[81]

The pinnacle of women's achievement in France may have been signaled by their admission to the Legion of Honor, where this admission required both a nomination and excellence in one's field. The Legion institution, founded by Napoleon in 1802, reasserted distinctions in French society, but since the mid-nineteenth century recognized expertise and heroism irrespective of sex.[82] Among the female attorneys honored during the interwar era were Jeanne Chauvin (1925), Marie-Thérèse Moreau (1927), Marguerite Dilhan (1933), and Maria Vérone (1936).[83] Chauvin was nominated to the Legion by none other than Raymond Poincaré, president of the French Republic (1913–1920). Feminist groups founded an association of women decorated by the Legion to prove the *civisme* (civic virtue) of the French female elite.[84] Feminist groups did not accept, however, the exact timing of women's induction as a sign of recognition of women's achievement. Vérone's induction in 1936 was regarded by her supporters as long overdue.[85] Regardless of delays, the recognition was important to women who demonstrated their allegiance to the French Republic by acknowledging such honors as the success of meritocracy.[86]

These examples illustrate the complexity of the interwar period, when women's civil status and their position in society underwent considerable flux viewed through the lens of gender. In the 1920s, there was also a general acknowledgement of women's social emancipation, yet the growing socioeconomic crises of the 1930s led to tensions between progressive and regressive definitions of the feminine.[87] In Europe, more broadly, many countries had granted women voting, educational, and professional rights such that by the 1930s, as Christine Bard argues, "militant feminism" suffered a decline because their "successes" led to complacency in the context of the emerging consumerist culture. By the mid-1930s, sex-segregated political societies were a bit passé as the Popular Front encouraged greater comradeship among women and men.[88] The advantage for feminist lawyers at this moment was the fact that they were better able to participate in mixed-sex philanthropic societies, legal or academic conferences, or political associations where they were increasingly accepted as normal rather than exceptional representatives of their fields.[89]

Lawyers, Feminism, and Politics

Social acceptance of women's expanding roles outpaced the extension of their legal rights. The French women's rights movement of the *belle époque* prioritized education, civil, political, and economic rights. The elimination of gender inequalities enshrined in the civil code and the improvement of women's material conditions were especially important. As Gisela Bock observed, "The demand to eliminate *puissance maritale* [marital power], *pouvoir paternelle* [paternal power], and the ban on *recherche de la paternité* [paternity suits] would later become the most important issues for the French women's movement."[90] These legal priorities coexisted with the need for women's enfranchisement. Women's rights activists understood well the substance behind René Viviani's comment that "legislators make the laws for those who make the legislators," meaning that those who do not vote do not count, politically speaking.[91]

Historians have recognized that in the women's rights movement, each feminist group had its own lawyer or group of lawyers who were active in leadership circles.[92] These lawyers were spread out across the left and center of the political spectrum, and some were also affiliated, to the degree that it was possible, with political parties.[93] While feminist lawyers' involvement in the women's rights movement—particularly for suffrage and reform of the civil code—has been well documented, the scope and diverse expression of their legal activism has not been adequately recognized. In practice, this included such action as teaching legal education clinics or courses, writing newspaper articles or columns, publishing legal treatises, drafting and supporting new legislation, and advocating for women's rights in official forums. They used their legal knowledge and political acumen to advance women's rights. Feminist lawyers, through their engagement in critical legal discourse and political processes, intended to foster reform and pinpoint the ways the law impinged upon women's social freedoms.

Briefly, let us note the contextual background that frames women's political deployment of legal knowledge and criticism of the law. Such activism was facilitated by the sea changes in the French Third Republic that liberalized the press (1881), institutionalized compulsory and free public education for boys and girls (1880s), and granted the freedom of association (1901). Such efforts were part of the apogee of the "republican moment" when republicanism was consolidated and the state bureaucracy expanded.[94] At the same time, the legal profession was itself a politicized community. The Paris bar association, with its opportunities for election to positions for professional self-governance, functioned as a training ground for political office. In 1910, 37 percent of elected representatives in the French National Assembly were lawyers. Between 1898 and 1940, legal professionals represented more than 26 percent of French deputies.[95] Given their predominance as a political force, this era earned the moniker "the republic of lawyers."[96]

Although women were formally excluded from political representation, exemplary figures among them nonetheless engaged in political service. Acting as citizens regardless of their lack of formal rights, female lawyers pursued political ends through their activism inside and outside the courtroom. In the 1890s, when Chauvin argued that women with law degrees had a right to practice law, she used individualist feminist arguments in the court to advance women's rights. Chauvin's claim that "*all humans* have the undeniable right to live, to think, and to work freely" was the basis of her cause célèbre.[97] She made arguments about the meaning of republicanism itself, stating that discrimination against women was the "last vestige of prejudice" in a society still influenced by the Judeo-Christian tradition. A truly modern, secular, and meritocratic society, she argued, would not be structured by patriarchy but rather by equality. She believed that progress was the "spread of right" by which the reforms championing equity would triumph over "abuses of power."[98] Chauvin used the press to promote women's rights and their intellectual achievements as part of a larger dedication to the women's rights movement. Simultaneously, Chauvin advocated for the legalization of paternity suits and the expansion of women's rights within the family.[99] Collaborating with Jeanne Schmahl and her political association, L'Avant Courrière (The Forerunner), they would secure women's right to serve as witnesses in civil acts (1897) and grant wives control over their earned incomes (1907).[100] These modest reforms were important advances in the process of dismantling married women's legal inequality. Moreover, Chauvin's use of her legal expertise and authority for the purposes of legal reform demonstrated the political utility of women's education in a republican society.

The tradition of the politically engaged female lawyer (*avocate engagée*) that originated with Chauvin was embraced by other pioneers who also saw the value of representing women's interests through social and political means. Maria Vérone (1874–1938) was the major exemplar of this tendency. Before joining the bar association, Vérone had worked as a public school assistant teacher and then as a journalist for a variety of Parisian newspapers.[101] She wrote on legal topics for the all-women's paper *La Fronde* under the pseudonym "Thémis," Greek goddess of good counsel. As an editor of *Le Droit des femmes*, Vérone had a special platform from which to engage the public. Her participation as a journalist was influential in an era when, as Evelyne Sullerot put it, "feminism was so combative, its organs of the press so numerous, and its journalists so prolific that none could ignore it."[102]

Vérone gained a considerable reputation as an activist lawyer in the first years of her career by arguing an antimilitarism case (1907) and defending women's right to run for election (1908). In this latter case, Vérone argued on behalf of Jeanne Laloë, a candidate for municipal office in Paris. Laloë was put up as a publicity stunt for the newspaper, *Le Matin*, where she worked as a reporter. Yet Laloë's campaign became politically important as Vérone advocated for women's right to run for elections, to cast ballots, and to use public property for political assemblies.[103] In the end, Vérone succeeded by facilitating the first electoral campaign of a female candidate in twentieth-century France.

Vérone came to the women's rights movement through her political associations with free thinkers and mutualists.[104] She joined the influential French Women's Rights League (LFDF), first as the general secretary under the presidency of teacher and feminist Maria Bonnevial (1841–1918), and then became LFDF president upon Bonnevial's death. Vérone served as LFDF president for two decades to advocate for women's rights. Before 1918, her most important contribution to the transformation of the judiciary was her campaign, with LFDF, to create the juvenile court system for France.[105] Through the International Council of Women (ICW), her work took an international turn, and she would lead the League of Nations Women's Consultative Committee on Nationality in the 1930s and compose reports to advise officials, notably on creating an universal law governing married women's nationality rights.[106]

In their feminist jurisprudence, *avocates* engaged with discourses on gender particularly by refuting the premise of women's incapacity. When Vérone represented a young woman accused of counterfeiting coins, for example, she argued that the state itself was to blame for creating the wretched socioeconomic conditions that impoverished the underclass, including her client. The right to vote, Vérone insisted, would give disadvantaged women the opportunity to voice their needs and assert a stake in their nation's future.[107] Vérone also advocated for single mothers by reprimanding the state for its inadequate assistance to indigent women and children and encouraging women to take pride in their autonomous maternal skills under the difficult circumstances imposed by single motherhood.[108]

Female lawyers came to represent the paradigmatic modern women or *éclaireuses* in popular French culture. The *éclaireuse*, as playwright Maurice Donnay termed her, was "a woman who prepares the path for other women to follow in view of a larger movement, in this play, the feminist movement."[109] In a 1913 event featuring the "*vrai éclaireuses*," Vérone and Grinberg were invited to represent real attorneys' experiences.[110] Female lawyers continued to be important authorities on feminist thought and functioned as representatives of women's modern experiences. After the First World War, several lawyers wrote long-running newspaper columns that publicized potential changes to legal codes and legislation, articles that functioned as an "everywoman's guide" to family and civil law. Their purpose was to help average women gain a sense of how their legal status shaped their opportunities and the circumstances of their lives and to keep readers informed about the women's rights movement.[111]

The political campaign to reform the civil code to abrogate those elements that "incapacitated" adult women in civil terms upon marriage gained strength during the interwar years. In 1924, feminists succeeded in catalyzing the creation of an extraparliamentary commission to rewrite the civil code on married women's rights. Eminent lawyers, judges, and jurists served in the group, which included Kraemer-Bach and Grinberg (but excluded Vérone for reasons not yet known). The resulting commission, associated with Minister of Justice René Renoult (1867-1946), attempted to overturn married women's inequality from the inside. On the commission, *avocates* and their allies in the women's rights movement criticized the status of women under the civil code and constitution to promote a vision of women's citizenship that recognized their social role as wives and mothers, which served to justify women's rights to individual liberties. By 1932, the commission presented draft legislation that proposed the modification of seventy-one articles of the civil code and the abrogation of twenty-four others to restore to wives their civil capacity.[112] Their recommendations went to the National Assembly, where the political process eviscerated the original proposals. The resulting legislation finally passed in 1938 made only minor changes to women's rights. Although the requirement of wives' obedience in Article 213 was eliminated, the male head-of-household structure remained intact. Symbolic progress was achieved, but feminists continued to campaign for comprehensive reforms.

During this political movement to alter the code affecting women, female lawyers attempted to disrupt social passivity regarding gender relations. International law expert Marcelle Kraemer-Bach encouraged women to conceive of themselves as an oppressed class with potential for political rebellion. Writing in ways that echoed Abbé Sièyes's revolutionary document, "What is the Third Estate?" (1789), Kraemer-Bach asked: "Apart from the specialists, which woman understands the principles of the law? *None!* Who are the women interested in knowing the law? *All!* All women without exception: Mothers and wives, unmarried women and female citizens [*citoyennes*], all working women, [whether] bureaucrats and employees, teachers and workers, industrialists and businesswomen, artists and liberal professionals, proprietors, renters, the financially independent. . . . Ignorance of law and jurisprudence is often the cause of ruin."[113] Kraemer-Bach was a prolific writer and popular speaker, and she started her own newspaper, *L'Information féminine*, on women's legal topics to fill the void in women's knowledge. The popular appeal of such legal questions, however, was limited for a population confronted at every turn by inequality, distracted by consumer culture, and strained by economic vicissitudes.

Feminist jurists and lawyers understood the law as a reflection of social customs and the means through which the doctrine of gender inequality had been legitimized. To reach the public with their message of code reform, *avocates* translated abstract notions into terms of lived experiences. To protest married women's civil incapacity, they emphasized the consequences of women's inequalities when wives must demonstrate spousal authorization to work, to make contracts, to open bank accounts, and to apply for passports. In an increasingly mobile economy, they underscored the ways in which married women's civil autonomy was hobbled in the event of spousal absence. *Avocates* publicized cases where women's ability to act on behalf of their families—such as traveling to aid a sick child or husband—was hampered, or denied, by the exigencies of their civil incapacity. In her text *The Legal Inequalities between Man and Woman* (1927), Kraemer-Bach argued for the abolition of the civil code articles requiring female subordination in marriage in order to permit married women the same social rights as men, such as the right "to travel and work freely, as a man does," but also to permit her authority over the children, the domicile, and her earned income.[114] Despite small advances for women, such as the 1907 law granting married women property authority over their salaries, the assumption that husbands could or should control all aspects of decision making for his wife and children persisted. In a polemical essay, Kraemer-Bach argued that contemporary women already rejected the "protections" offered by the marital law articles of the civil code and demanded their "liberty." Moreover, she observed that regarding women's rights, "The laws lagged behind life's requirements and must be put in accord with mores."[115] Kraemer-Bach and others publicized cases of harm to husbands when wives were unable to function independently in what was a shrewd strategy that deployed women's familial role (that is, service to others) to argue for women's civil autonomy.[116]

At the same time that these *avocates* argued for the improvement of women's rights within France and its overseas empire, they also participated in the rise of the internationalist movement. The League of Nations provided activist lawyers with new opportunities to push for women's rights through international agreements. In the interwar years, activists worked on specific projects, such as establishing equal pay for equal work in principle, abolishing human trafficking and government-regulated prostitution, aiding economically vulnerable children, and securing independent nationality for married women under international law. As Carol Miller noted, access to the international delegates in Geneva was seen as the "key to equality."[117] Among the most important campaigns of the interwar years was the right of married women to their own nationality, a concern of an increasing number of women due to the upheavals of the war and its aftermath, when migrations and international marriages increased.[118]

The question of married women's nationality rights was not new; it had been placed on the platform of the French Women's Rights League in 1878.[119] Since 1900, the ICW debated how to address the problem of nationality, but they stumbled over the intractable problem of the conflict of laws.[120] Linda Kerber has illustrated that influential international legal communities failed to address the inconsistencies across nations that could result in such problems as women's statelessness, their involuntary expatriation, the possibility of double nationality, and other denials of rights.[121] The First World War exacerbated the situation. Scottish barrister Chrystal Macmillan (1872–1932) asserted that "it is insulting to a woman to assume that she can transfer her allegiance without her consent."[122] She campaigned from 1917 for an international solution to protect women's rights to their nationality. Individual nations, including the United States (1922) and France (1927), reformed their nationality laws, but inconsistencies remained.

Women's associations recognized both the importance of engaging in international law debates and that the average activist was not necessarily suited for the task. The International Federation of University Women (IFUW) declared that "lawyers of each national federation" should weigh in on the nationality question.[123] Female lawyers from Europe an countries and the United States demanded to speak to delegates at the 1930 The Hague Codification of International Law conference.[124] When lawyers Macmillan, Vérone, and the National Women's Party's Doris Stevens finally secured the opportunity to speak to The Hague delegates, they emphasized that nationality was a fundamental human right for women as well as men. Vérone requested that the delegates endorse equality in nationality law to "prove that woman is no longer a chattel which the owner may dispose of as he thinks best, but a human being who, like a man, is entitled to justice, freedom, independence, and I would say, the primary right of the human being: the right to a fatherland."[125] Despite women's passionate arguments, the delegates ultimately agreed only to encourage nations to study the possibility of introducing "the principle of equality of the sexes in matters of nationality."[126]

This work on women's nationality continued with the historic and unprecedented creation of the League of Nations' Women's Consultative Committee on Nationality.[127] The sixteen-member Consultative Committee made recommendations to the League's Committee of Experts. The reports, written largely by Vérone, urged that "the principle of equality must be laid down in international legislation."[128] Reinforcing this message, FIFCJ lawyers Marcelle Renson (1894–1988, Belgium) and Kraemer-Bach collaborated on a landmark study, *Le Régime matrimonial des époux dont la nationalité est différente* (*Matrimonial Law for Spouses of Different Nationalities*), where they argued for a universal code of private law as a solution to the problem of married women's nationality status.[129] While their solution was radical and support for women's autonomy was still a minority position, these women were part of a broader conversation about using global governance to provide legal protections for individuals. Women's access to the League mattered, as they voiced their priorities to this multinational body and found there some allies—even if not always from their own countrymen. The League was important because, as Susan Pedersen notes, it was part of "the shifting boundaries between state power and international authority in this period."[130] As a result of women's actions, League members were convinced that women's position in society could be construed "as a problem for international attention" forever disrupting "the notion that the status of women was a purely 'national' issue."[131] Many years later, and after many setbacks, Renson and Kraemer-Bach's efforts were credited with advancing the groundwork for eventual reform achieved by the UN Convention on the Nationality of Married Women, ratified on January 29, 1957, and effective on August 11, 1958.[132]

Conclusion and Continuities

The tactics employed by French feminist lawyers in the early twentieth century included the use of the courts, political organizing, raising of public awareness of gender inequality through the press and testimonials, and participation in official commissions. Their methods included lobbying officials from within professional and political associations, disseminating knowledge to the public, engaging in persuasive campaigns, and working on politically tinged trials. Forward thinking female jurists and lawyers contributed to significant legal reforms, including: women's right to bear witness in civil affairs (1897), admission of women to the bar (1900), married women's control over their salaries (1907), the creation of the juvenile courts (1912), the decriminalization of paternity suits (1912), married women's nationality rights (1927), the revision of married women's civil rights (1938), women's right to vote (1944), and women's right to serve in the judiciary (1946). Integral to these campaigns, and their related political engagement, was the articulation of feminist jurisprudence that contributed egalitarian language and rationales for the reforms. All of this was a product of the vibrancy of the women's rights movement and the culture of the bar that fostered connections to political life. While such efforts did encounter resistance, this fact should not eclipse the value of the struggle for equality.

This research illustrates ways in which the history of women's involvement in the legal profession in France during the early twentieth century was interwoven with the history of the women's rights movement. The entrances of women into the French legal profession in 1900 and later into the judiciary in 1946 were part and parcel of the larger advancement of gender equality in France. While excluded from formal political rights, female lawyers defended the rights of others. Indeed, activist female lawyers pinned down precise elements of law and legislation to determine the ways in which it caused harm and proposed means to alleviate the inequality that such legal structures engendered. Feminist lawyers envisioned and sought to secure the incorporation of women into all aspects of society on equal terms—whether in education, employment, the family, political realms, legal institutions, or processes. At the same time, these republican militants sought social harmony. Vérone, for one, wanted men and women to work together: "It is not the battle of the sexes, but their collaboration that our feminism desires."[133] Indeed, her association for women's rights, LFDF, was not a segregated one. Vérone's second husband, Georges Lhermitte (d. 1943), demonstrated his advocacy for women's rights by writing for her paper, *Le Droit des femmes*, and serving as the association's president after her death in 1938.[134]

Recently, the public has begun to recognize these feminist lawyers as humanists whose legacy represents the best of the democratic tradition. In 2006, the Paris city council chose to rename a street for Vérone to honor her promotion of "human rights."[135] Commemorations in the form of street signs, the renaming of public school buildings, and plaques installed in other French cities recognize other female attorneys, including Chauvin, Dilhan, and Cormier.[136] These public acknowledgements signal a broader shift in the valuation of women's history that has spread from academia into popular culture and indicate ways in which women's history is in the process of being reclaimed for the future of France.

Notes

1 Jeanne Deflou, "Chroniques: France," *Revue de Morale sociale* 2, no. 6 (June 1900): 260–261.
2 Sara L. Kimble, *Women, Feminism, and the Law in Modern France: Justice Redressed* (New York: Routledge, forthcoming).
3 Jeanne Chauvin, "La capacité légale des femmes," *La Fraternité. Journal hebdomadaire. Organe des intérêts d'Haïti et de la race noire*, May 3, 1893. Gaston Petit, *Le droit de la femme mariée sur les produits de son travail. Thèse pour le doctorat*, Université de Paris. Faculté de droit (Paris: A. Rousseau, 1899), 151–156.
4 Jeanne Chauvin, "La femme," *La Revue de France* (November 1884), n.p. in Bibliothèque Marguerite Durand (hereafter BMD), *Dossier Chauvin.*
5 France. Assemblée nationale (1871–1942). Chambre des députés. *Annales. Débats parlementaires*, vol. 2, Séance du 30 Juin 1899 (Paris: Imprimerie du journal officiel, 1900), 1738–1764.
6 "Le Parlement. A la Chambre," *Le Matin*, July 1, 1899.
7 Senat, Année 1900, Session Extraordinaire. *Journal officiel de la République française. Lois et décrets* (November 14, 1900), 7555; André Daniel, *L'Année politique 1900* (Paris: Charpentier, 1901), 324.

8 See Sara L. Kimble, "No Right to Judge: Feminism and the Judiciary in Third Republic France," *French Historical Studies* 31, no. 4 (2008): 609–641.
9 Archives Nationales de la France (hereafter AN), 6th Legislature, series C//5595, dossier 1892.
10 Mary Jane Mossman, *The First Women Lawyers: A Comparative Study of Gender, Law and the Legal Professions* (Portland, OR: Hart, 2006). See also the chapter by Eva Schandevyl in this volume.
11 See Paule-Marie Duhet ed., *Cahiers de doléances des femmes en 1789: et autres textes* (Paris: Des femmes, 1981); and Karen Offen, *European Feminisms, 1700–1950: A Political History* (Stanford, CA: Stanford University Press, 2000), 55.
12 Jeanne Chauvin, "Conférence sur le féminisme en France," (speech, Salle du Globe, Paris, March 23, 1898), manuscript 620 025, Bibliothèque Historique de la Ville de Paris, Paris, 10–11.
13 "Accès des femmes à la magistrature. Débats de l'Assemblée consultative provisoire," *Journal Officiel* 42 (1945): 1092–1095.
14 On gender and republicanism, see Judith F. Stone, "The Republican Brotherhood: Gender and Ideology," in *Gender and the Politics of Social Reform in France, 1870–1914*, ed. Elinor Accampo, Rachel G. Fuchs, and Mary Lynn Stewart (Baltimore: Johns Hopkins University Press, 1995), 28–58.
15 *Congrès français et international du droit des femmes* (Paris: E. Dentu, 1889). See Popelin's argument in particular, 238–245.
16 Jeanne Chauvin, *Étude historique sur les professions accessible aux femmes: Influence du sémitisme sur l'évolution de la position économique de la femme dans la société* (Paris: Giard et Brière, 1892).
17 Julie Carlier, "Moving Beyond Boundaries: An Entangled History of Feminism in Belgium, 1890–1914," Doctoral thesis, Department of History, Ghent University, Ghent, Belgium, 2010, 72–79.
18 Carol Smart, *Feminism and the Power of Law* (London: Routledge, 1989), 66.
19 Michel Foucault, *Discipline and Punish: The Birth of the Prison*, trans. Alan Sheridan (New York: Vintage Books, 1979).
20 Pierre Bourdieu and Jean-Claude Passeron, *Reproduction in Education, Society and Culture (La reproduction, engl.)*, trans. Richard Nice (London, Beverly Hills: Sage, 1977).
21 Andrew MacErlean, "St. Ives," *The Catholic Encyclopedia*, vol. 8 (New York: Robert Appleton Company, 1910), accessed September 10, 2013, http://www.newadvent.org/cathen/08256b.htm.
22 Christine Machiels, "'Protégeons la jeunesse!' Maria Vérone, une avocate féministe face à la prostitution des mineur(e)s (1907–1938)," *Revue d'histoire de l'enfance 'irrégulière'* 10 (2008): 119–137.
23 Yves Gaudemet, *Les juristes et la vie politique de la III Republique* (Paris: Presses universitaires de France, 1970).
24 Philip G. Nord, *The Republican Moment: Struggles for Democracy in Nineteenth-Century France* (Cambridge: Harvard University Press, 1995), 117.
25 Ibid., 117.
26 Marcelle Kraemer-Bach, "La Fédération Internationale des Femmes Magistrats et Avocats," *Bulletin du Soroptimist-Club* (January 1935): 5.
27 Marcelle Kraemer-Bach, *La Longue route* (Paris: La pensée universelle, 1988). The name of this association varies; early variation: International Federation of Women Lawyers and Magistrates.
28 Kimble, *Women, Feminism, and the Law in Modern France* (forthcoming).
29 Joan Wallach Scott, *Gender and the Politics of History* (New York: Columbia University Press, 1988), 2.
30 Joan Wallach Scott, *The Fantasy of Feminist History* (Durham, NC: Duke University Press, 2012), 6.

31 Mary Louise Roberts, "Making the Modern Girl French: From New Woman to *éclaireuse*," in *The Modern Girl around the World: Consumption, Modernity, and Globalization*, ed. Alys Eve Weinbaum and The Modern Girl Around the World Research Group (Durham, NC: Duke University Press, 2008), 77–95. On Prudhon see Simone Debout-Oleszkiewicz, "Utopia and Counteruptopia: Women in the Works of Charles Fourier," in *Political and Historical Encyclopedia of Women*, ed. Christine Fauré (New York: Routledge, 2003), 185.
32 Paul Lefranc, "Cher Maître!" undated newspaper clipping in Dossier Chauvin, BMD.
33 Rachel G. Fuchs, *Contested Paternity: Constructing Families in Modern France* (Baltimore: Johns Hopkins University Press, 2008).
34 Linda L. Clark, "Feminist Maternalists and the French State: Two Inspectresses General in the Pre-World War Third Republic," *Journal of Women's History* 12, no. 1 (2000): 32–59. Linda L. Clark, *The Rise of Professional Women in France Gender and Public Administration since 1830* (New York: Cambridge University Press, 2000).
35 Offen, *European Feminisms*, 239.
36 Seth Koven, "Borderlands: Women, Voluntary Action, and Child Welfare in Britain, 1840 to 1914," in *Mothers of a New World: Maternalist Politics and the Origins of Welfare States*, ed. Seth Koven and Sonya Michel (New York: Routledge, 1993), 108.
37 Jessie Pope, "War Girls," written 1916, quoted in Sandra Gilbert, "A Soldier's Heart: Literary Men, Literary Women, and the Great War," in *No Man's Land: The Place of the Woman Writer in the Twentieth Century*, ed. Sandra M. Gilbert and Susan Gubar, vol. 2 (New Haven: Yale University Press, 1988), 293.
38 Mary Louise Roberts, *Civilization without Sexes: Reconstructing Gender in Postwar France, 1917–1927* (Chicago: University of Chicago Press, 1994).
39 Nord, *Republican Moment*, 118.
40 See Kimble, *Women, Feminism, and the Law* (forthcoming), chap 4. Juliette Rennes, Femmes en métiers d'hommes (cartes postales, 1890–1930). Une histoire visuelle du travail et du genre (Saint-Pourçain-sur-Sioule: Bleu Autour, 2013).
41 Karen Offen, "The Second Sex and the *Baccalauréat* in Republican France, 1880–1924," *French Historical Studies* 13, no. 2 (Autumn 1983): 252–286.
42 *Annuaire statistique de la ville de Paris, 1901* (Paris: Imprimerie nationale, 1903), 574; *Annuaire statistique de la ville de Paris, 1910* (Paris: Imprimerie nationale, 1912), 451–452; *Annuaire statistique de la ville de Paris, 1920* (Paris: Imprimerie nationale, 1924), 359.
43 J. L., "A Paris, les avocates fêtent la jubilé de leur doyenne," *L'Ouest France*, March 7, 1929.
44 James F. McMillan, *France and Women 1789–1914: Gender, Society and Politics* (London: Routledge, 2000), 213–215.
45 Jane Misme, "Votre profession vous plaît-elle? Offre-t-elle un avenir aux femmes?" *Le Matin*, August 12, 1911.
46 See Clark, *Rise of Professional Women*, on obstacles faced by female lawyers: 105, 164–65, 170, 196, 205.
47 Edmée Charrier, *L'évolution intellectuelle féminine* (Paris: Albert Mechelinck, 1931), 351–352.
48 Frouma (dite Flora, née Grenberg) Rosemberg. Untitled Note, *Journal officiel de la République française. Lois et décrets* (October 17, 1929), 11608; "French Woman is Chinese Lawyer," *Reading Times* (Pennsylvania), June 16, 1930; Suzanne Grinberg, "Une avocate française à Shanghai," *La France Judiciaire* (July 10, 1932): 598.
49 Henri Berthélemy, "L'Ecole de droit," *Revue des deux mondes* 36 (November–December 1926): 329–330.

50 Mme Astié de Valsayre was harassed at the École de Molière by hostile students who expressed a horror for all "*femmes de lettres*," in *Calendriers d'un bourgeois du quartier latin du 1 janvier 1888 au 31 décembre 1900*, ed. Henri Dabot (Paris: Péronne, 1905), 124. Charrier, *L'Évolution intellectuelle féminine*, 442 qtd. in James C. Albisetti, "Portia Ante Portas: Women and the Legal Profession in Europe, ca. 1870–1925," *Journal of Social History* 33, no. 4 (Summer 2000): 825–857.

51 Eugen Weber, *France, fin de siècle* (Cambridge: Belknap Press, 1986), 95–96. Tamar Garb notes that the "most visceral protest" against women in the *Ecole des Beaux-Arts* was not until May 1897. See Tamar Garb, *Sisters of the Brush: Women's Artistic Culture in Late Nineteenth-Century Paris* (New Haven: Yale University Press, 1994), 70–104.

52 Henri Rochefort, "Le Métier d'avocat," *Midi*, September 19, 1897.

53 Dabot, *Calendriers d'un bourgeois*, 103–104.

54 "Doctoresse. Une visite au bâtonnier de l'Ordre des avocats," *L'Éclair* (October 10, 1897): 1.

55 Camille Ducreux, *Les droits de la femme dans la société française. Discours à rentree de 1897. 20 November 1897* (Paris: Alcan-Lévy, 1898).

56 Senator Licinius Buccio was Afrania's husband. On Afrania and other women advocates (i.e., Amasia Sentia, called Androgyne, and Hortensia, daughter of Quintus Hortensius), see Valerius Maximus, "Memorable Deeds and Sayings," 8.3. in Mary R. Lefkowitz and Maureen B. Fant, *Women's Life in Greece and Rome: A Source Book in Translation* (Baltimore: Johns Hopkins University Press, 1992). Louis Frank confirms that Afrania's behavior was the excuse used for a general prohibition against women speaking in tribunals and courtrooms in "The Woman Lawyer: In View of Mlle. Popelin," trans. Mary Greene, *Chicago Law Times* 3 (1889): 80–81.

57 "The text of the law 18, Cod. II, 12 (12) (*de procuratoribus*), plainly affirms this principle: *Alienam suscipere defensionem virile est officium, et ultra sexum muliebrem esse constat*" according to Frank, "The Woman Lawyer," 81–82.

58 *Dalloz Périodique. Jurisprudence générale* (Paris: Librairie Dalloz, 1899) (Part 2, 1898), 185–195, 191.

59 "L'Actualité. La Décision de la cour dans l'Affaire Jeanne Chauvin," *L'Éclair* (December 2, 1897): 1.

60 *Annales de la Chambre des députés. Documents Parliamentaires*. No. 3145. March 22, 1898. vol. 54 (Paris, 1898), 924.

61 Quoted in Charrier, *L'Évolution intellectuelle*, 244. See *Journal Officiel*, Débats parlementaires, Sénat, November 14, 1900, 836.

62 Kimble, "No Right to Judge," 609–641.

63 Mme. [Ghénia] Avril de Sainte-Croix ed., *Dixième congrès international des femmes. Œuvres et institutions féminines, droits des femmes; 2 juin 1913, Paris* (Paris, 1914), 396.

64 Suzanne Grunberg [sic], "Les femmes jurés," *La Revue Judiciaire* 2, no. 12 (December 25, 1909): 353–354.

65 Suzanne Grinberg, "Féminisme," *Mercure de France* 154, no. 569 (March 3, 1922): 475.

66 "Les femmes juges," *La Française*, November 23, 1929.

67 *JO, Débats parlementaires, Chambre des députés*, April 5, 1930, 1559–1561.

68 *JO, Débats parlementaires, Chambre des députés*, April 5, 1930, 1561.

69 Maria Vérone, "Le Congrès de Marseille," *Le Droit des femmes* (December 1930): 298–300. *Le Congrès d'Alger de l'Association nationale des avocats (22–24 avril 1930), Bulletin de l'Association nationale des avocats inscrits aux barreaux de France, des colonies et pays de protectorat* (Paris: [ANA], 1930), 111–112.

70 Siân Reynolds, *France Between the Wars: Gender and Politics* (New York: Routledge, 1996).

71 Anne R. Epstein, "Gender and the Rise of the Female Expert During the Belle Époque," *Histoire@Politique* 2, no. 14 (2011): 84–96.

72 Kimble, "No Right to Judge," 638; Anne Boigeol, "Les Femmes et les cours. La difficile mise en œuvre de l'égalité des sexes dans l'accès à la magistrature," *Genèses* 22 (March 1996): 107–129.

73 Gilles Le Béguec, "L'aristocratie du barreau, vivier pour la république. Les secrétaires de la conférence du stage," *Vingtième Siècle. Revue d'histoire* 30 (1991): 22–31.

74 Cormier's *discours* December 12, 1921. "Conférence du Jeune Barreau de Bordeaux," *Les Announces de la Seine*, June 13, 2012, http://www.annoncesdelaseine.fr/index.php/2012/06/13/6141/

75 "Secrétaires de la Conférence," *Le Figaro*, July 13, 1922.

76 Geneviève Bardot, "La première femme qui . . .," *Le Monde illustré* (July 25, 1936): 631.

77 Suzanne Grunberg [sic], "Avocates," *La Renaissance politique*, 2, no. 6 (February 7, 1914): 426–427.

78 Suzanne Grinberg, *Les Droits de veuves et des orphelins de guerre* (Paris: A. Michel, 1916); Suzanne Grinberg and Alice La Mazière, *Carrières féminines* (Paris: Larousse, 1917); Grinberg, *Historique du mouvement suffragiste depuis 1848* (Paris: H. Goulet, 1926); Suzanne Grinberg and Odette Simon, *Les Droits nouveaux de la femme mariée commentaire theorique et pratique de la loi du 18 fevrier 1938* (Paris: Sirey, 1938).

79 The International Federation of University Women, *Report of the Fourth Conference, Amsterdam, July 28 to August 2 1926* (London: IFUW, 1926), 35. I. C. W. Standing Committee on Laws Concerning the Legal Position of Women; with an introd. by Mme. d'Abbadie d'Arrast, *Women's Position on the Laws of Nations. A Compilation of the Laws of Different Countries* (Karlsruhe: Braunsche Hofbuchdruckerei, 1912).

80 Suzanne Grinberg, "À travers les faits du mois. En France et à l'étranger," *L'Etat Moderne* (June 1930): 553–556.

81 "Women Find Land of Dons Also Changing," *Chicago Tribune*, March 31, 1931. Antoinette Quinche, "Le congrès du Conseil international des femmes," *Le Mouvement féministe* (Geneva) 22 (July 28, 1934). The French Federation of University Women (AFFDU): 290 active members and 1500 affiliated members in 1925 under presidency of Mme Marie Octave Monod. (See Françoise Blum, Colette Chambelland, and Michel Dreyfus ed., "Les mouvements de femmes (1919–1940). Guide des sources documentaires," *Vie sociale* (November–December 1984): 614.

82 Haryett Fontanges, *Légion d'honneur et les femmes décorées* (N.p.: Alliance Coopérative du Livre, 1905); Danièle Déon-Bessière, *Les femmes et la Légion d'honneur: depuis sa création* (Paris: Officine, 2002).

83 Chancellery records are incomplete and inconsistent with the contemporary press. See Archives Nationales, base de données Léonore (Légion d'honneur), dossiers Grinberg, Suzanne (b. 1888/01/25); Dilhan, Marguerite (b. 1876/09/17); Moreau, Marie-Thérèse (b. 1883/05/06).

84 Christine Bard, "Les Femmes et le pouvoir politique dans la France de l'entre-deux-guerres," in *Les Femmes et La Politique*, ed. Armelle Le Bras-Chopard and Janine Mossuz-Lavau (Paris: Editions L'Harmattan, 1997), 46.

85 "La Légion d'honneur à Mme Maria Vérone," *Le Mouvement féministe* (Geneva) 24 (February 1, 1936): 11.

86 Uniquely, Marie-Thérèse Moreau, a Parisian lawyer admitted to the association of World War I veterans because she had been a civil hostage and wartime nurse,

built on her unimpeachable reputation to advocate for women's rights through Catholic organizations. "Petites nouvelles," *Le Temps*, October 28, 1923. See also Cheryl Koos and Daniella Sarnoff, "France," in *Women, Gender and Fascism in Europe: 1919–45*, ed. Kevin Passmore (New Brunswick, NJ: Rutgers University Press, 2003), esp. 176–182.

87 Angela Kershaw and Angela Kimyongür, "Women in Europe between the War: A Culture of Contradictions," in *Women in Europe between the Wars: Politics, Culture and Society*, ed. Angela Kershaw and Angela Kimyongür (Aldershot: Ashgate, 2007), 1–22.

88 Christine Bard, "La crise du féminisme en France dans les années trente," *Les cahiers du CEDREF*, 4–5 (1995), published online October 1, 2009, accessed February 24, 2014, http://cedref.revues.org/291.

89 See Kimble, *Women, Feminism, and Modern France* (forthcoming).

90 Gisela Bock, *Women in European History*, Allison Brown, trans. (Malden, MA: Blackwell Publishers, 2001), 64.

91 McMillan, *France and Women, 1789–1914*, 215.

92 See Paul Smith, *Feminism and the Third Republic: Women's Political and Civil Rights in France* (Oxford: Clarendon Press, 1996) and Sara L. Kimble, "Portia's Sisters: Transatlantic Networks for Women in the Legal Professions," paper presented at the Annual Meeting for the American Historical Association, Chicago, IL, January 5–8, 2012.

93 Female lawyers were involved with the French Section of the Workers' International (Germaine Picard-Moch and Simone Weiler), the Republican Radical Party (Marcelle Kraemer-Bach), and the Popular Democratic Party (PDP) (Germaine Poinso-Chapuis). The PDP was the precursor to the Popular Republican Movement (MRP).

94 For lawyers within this context, see Nord, *Republic Moment*, 115–138.

95 Maria Malatesta, *Professional Men, Professional Women: The European Professions from the Nineteenth Century until Today* (London: Sage, 2011), 10–11.

96 Gaudemet, *Les juristes*, 78. Physicians were also elected in considerable numbers to the National Assembly during the Third Republic. See Jack D. Ellis, *The Physician-Legislators of France: Medicine and Politics in the Early Third Republic, 1870–1914* (Cambridge: Cambridge University Press, 1990).

97 Jeanne Chauvin, "Les femmes à l'école des beaux-arts," *Revue encyclopédique Larousse*, vol. 6 (November 1896): 853.

98 Chauvin, *Étude historique sur les professions accessible aux femmes*, 288.

99 Fuchs, *Contested Paternity*, 148.

100 Jeanne Chauvin, *Proposition de loi sur la capacité des femmes mariées de disposer du produit de leur travail ou de leur industrie personnels* (Paris: Publications de l'Avant-courrière, 1893).

101 Sara L. Kimble, "Popular Legal Journalism in the Writings of Maria Vérone," *Proceedings of the Western Society for French History* 39 (2011): 224–235.

102 Evelyne Sullerot, *La Presse féminine* (Paris: Armand Colin, 1963), 37.

103 See Steven C. Hause and Anne Kenney, "Women's Suffrage and the Paris Elections of 1908," *Laurels* 1, no. 41 (1980): 21–32.

104 Jacqueline Lalouette, *La Libre pensée en France: 1848–1940* (Paris: Bibliothèque Albin Michel Histoire, 1997), 93.

105 Kimble, "No Right to Judge," 614–618; Christine Bard, s.v., "Maria Vérone," in *Dictionnaire Biographique du Mouvement Ouvrier Français* ed. Jean Maitron (Paris: Editions Ouvrière, 1993), 162–163.

106 Candice Lewis Bredbenner, *A Nationality of Her Own: Women, Marriage, and the Law of Citizenship* (Berkeley: University of California Press, 1998), 219.

107 Mary M. Lilly, "The French Women Lawyers," *Case and Comment* 21 (October 1914): 431–433.

108 Maria Vérone, "Pour empêcher l'avortement. Respectons les mères," *L'Oeuvre* July 6, 1922.
109 Maurice Donnay quoted in Mary Louise Roberts, "Making the Modern Girl French: From New Woman to *éclaireuse*," 87.
110 "Le déjeuner des 'vrai éclaireuses,'" *Le Petit Parisien*, March 22, 1913.
111 Kimble, "Popular Legal Journalism in the Writings of Maria Vérone," 224–235.
112 Marc Ancel, "Le Projet français sur la capacité de la femme et les enseignements du droit comparé de l'université de Paris I," *Annales de l'Institut de droit comparé de l'Université de Paris I* (1934): 145–168.
113 Emphasis in original. Marcelle Kraemer-Bach and Robert Moreaux eds., *L'Information féminine. Première revue française du droit et des intérêts féminins* no. 1 (May 1927), n.p.
114 Marcelle Kraemer-Bach, *Les Inégalités légales entre l'homme et la femme* (Paris: Presses universitaires de France, 1927), 10.
115 Marcelle Kraemer-Bach, "L'incapacité civile de la femme," *Les Cahiers des Droits de l'homme* 27 (October 30, 1928): 627–630.
116 "Informations," *Le Figaro*, January 1, 1938.
117 Carol Miller, "'Geneva—the Key to Equality': Inter-War Feminists and the League of Nations," *Women's History Review* 3, no. 2 (1994): 219–245.
118 Bredbenner, *A Nationality of Her Own*, 198; Ellen Carol DuBois, "Internationalizing Married Women's Nationality: The Hague Campaign of 1930," in *Globalizing Feminisms, 1789–1945*, ed. Karen Offen (London: Routledge, 2010), 204–216.
119 *Congrès international du droit des femmes. Ouvert à Paris, le 25 juillet 1878, clos le 9 août suivant. Actes et Compte-rendu des séances plénières* (Paris: A. Ghio, ca. 1878); René Viviani in *Cinquante-ans de féminisme: 1870–1920* (Paris: Ed. de la LFDF, 1920), 11.
120 *Congrès international de la condition et des droits des femmes* (Paris: Impr. des Arts et Manufactures, 1901), 205.
121 Linda Kerber, "Presidential Address: The Stateless as the Citizen's Other: A View from the United States," *American Historical Review* 112, no. 1 (February 2007): 1–34.
122 Chrystal Macmillan, "Nationality of Married Women: Present Tendencies," *Journal of Comparative Legislation and International Law* 7, no. 4 (1925): 144, 153. Also see her earlier articles in *Jus Suffragii* (July 1917, June 1918).
123 International Federation of University Women, *Report of the Fifth Conference, Geneva, August 7 to August 14, 1929* (London: International Federation of University Women, 1929), 134.
124 Ibid., 134.
125 League of Nations, *Acts for the Conference for the Codification of International Law* [Held at the Hague from March 13 to April 12, 1930. Minutes of the Committees. Vol. II. Minutes of the First Committee. Nationality] vol. II. Official no. C351 (a). M. 145(a) 1930 V., 180.
126 *Acts for the Conference for the Codification of International Law*, 253.
127 Bredbenner, *A Nationality of Her Own*, 219.
128 1932 Report, quoted in Louise C.A. van Eeghen, "Maria Vérone," *Equal Rights* (September 1, 1938): 318.
129 Marcelle Kraemer-Bach and Marcelle Renson, *Le Régime matrimonial des époux dont la nationalité est différente: rapport presente à la Fédération Internationale des Femmes Magistrats et Avocats en 1934 et 1935* (Paris: A. Pedone, 1939). Sophie Grinberg-Vinaver, "The Status of Women throughout the World," *Marriage and Family Living* 17, no. 3 (August 1955): 197–204.
130 Susan Pedersen, "Back to the League of Nations," *American Historical Review* 112, no. 4 (October 2007): 1092.

131 Miller, "'Geneva—the Key to Equality,'" 238.
132 Convention on the Nationality of Married Women, 309 U.N.T.S. 65. Agathe Dyvrande-Thévenin, "La Fédération International des femmes magistrats et avocats," *La Vie judiciaire*, November 10, 1934. See also Catherine Jacques' chapter in this volume.
133 Maria Vérone, "Barreau et féminisme," *L'Oeuvre* (July 1925): 15 [copy from the Bibliothèque Historique de la Ville de Paris (BHVP), Fonds Bouglé, Manuscrits, Articles de journaux, Maria Vérone, Boite 3 (2)].
134 Kimble, "Popular Legal Journalism in the Writings of Maria Vérone," 224–235.
135 City of Paris, Délibération 18.2006.15, *Compte rendu du conseil d'arrondissement du lundi 16 janvier 2006*, accessed February 16, 2014, http://www.mairie18.paris.fr/mairie18/document?id=14707&id_attribute=127.
136 There are streets named for Jeanne Chauvin in Paris (13th arrond.) and Provins, near her hometown of Jargeau (Loiret); and Maria Vérone has been honored with streets in Paris and the working-class city of Le Creusot (Saône-et-Loire), in Montauban (Tarn-et-Garonne), and a public school named in Villebarou (Loir-et-Cher). Dilhan's former Toulouse residence has a plaque, as does Cormier's in Bassens, Aquitaine.

6 Women and the Courts in Twentieth-Century Belgium

An Historical Perspective

Eva Schandevyl

Introduction

The phenomenon of women participating in the justice system is relatively recent in most western countries. In Belgium, women's access to the courts was achieved only in 1948, after decades of fierce discussion and negotiation concerning the specificity and legitimacy of women's possible role in the judicial process. Today, women represent half of the entrants into the legal profession and half of the law students in most European universities. There is no longer any doubt about the added value of women's representation within the judiciary: since they adopt a woman's perspective, the reasoning often goes, women will make decisions that are meaningful and acceptable to all, women included. Many scholars do indeed believe that women in law offer a distinctive contribution and that women's voices differ from those of men in that their ethic is one of care as opposed to a male ethic of justice. In this, the majority of authors agree with the thesis of Carol Gilligan, the American apologist of difference feminism.[1] Apart from their greater sensitivity to, and advocacy of, for example, human rights and youth protection, women seem inclined to promote fundamental justice. Research suggests that women do tend to choose a more interdisciplinary approach, avoiding the rigid application of universal rules and doctrinal notions. Yet opinion does remain divided as to the question of whether female lawyers and judges *really* do think and act differently than men.[2] Less ambiguous is the fact that barriers to actual equality for women in the law still exist. In most European countries, for example, there is a more or less pronounced glass ceiling that limits women's access to top judicial careers, the highest and most authoritative positions in the judiciary, such as magistrates in appeal courts or first chairmen or presidents of courts: here the figures—a ratio of about 1:5 in Belgium *and* throughout Europe—speak for themselves.[3] *Formal equality* in the judiciary was reached in 1948 when Belgian female jurists gained access to the courts, but their entrance did not eliminate (sometimes self-imposed) gender stereotypical reasoning that still persists. *Real equality* between men and women in the legal world has not yet been completely reached; an historical perspective of the problem allows us to identify and contextualize the reasons.

This chapter assesses the historical trajectory of women's access to the legal profession in Belgium, revealing both the successes and the roots of present-day barriers to gender equality in legal careers, specifically to careers in the judiciary. Belgian women were granted access to the bar by law in 1922 but were denied admission to the judiciary until after the Second World War. In Belgium, as elsewhere in Europe, both these professions were historically reserved for men. The structure of these professions and their deontology were developed without taking into account female perspectives on justice. The culture of these professions was thus implicitly constructed around the image of the married man who was fully dedicated to his public function, while his wife was in charge of the family-related and household duties. These characteristics were "naturalized" in the course of the nineteenth and twentieth centuries. The masculine identity revolved around strength and reason—only men were intended to assume public responsibilities—while women, emotional as they were and utterly lacking self-control, were confined to domesticity.[4]

These gender stereotypes determined the functioning and the perception of the Belgian judicial apparatus. And also the law itself has always influenced the social relations between the sexes by legitimizing prejudiced cultural attitudes and justifying unequal practices.[5] Here lies an essentially major contradiction: justice, as a central pillar of democracy, appeals to the ideal of an egalitarian society, at least as it concerns equality before the law. But in practice, the gender-difference factor has always counted and has led to gender discrimination. Opposing this, organized feminist resistance has grown since the end of the nineteenth century. Feminists questioned anti-women legislation and the "traditional" sex roles. The battle for access to the legal profession was important to them, not least because professional opportunities with a major symbolic value in the public sphere were at stake.

In the historical development toward greater equality between women and men in the judicial field in Belgium, individual women and men who first questioned the male monopoly of the judicial professions often took the initiative.[6] Their campaigns for state intervention in favour of a more women-friendly legal system concentrated at two key moments during the twentieth century: in the early years during the first quarter of the century and again after the Second World War. Both phases took place against a background of social democratization and changing ideas about the public and private spheres. From the end of the nineteenth century on, a small but growing number of women stepped into the public sphere and were increasingly likely to attend university, study law, enter the labour market, and demand access to the legal profession. This did not occur "automatically" or "naturally": the history of these women's access shows to what extent the women's movement played an important role in that process. It was the result of a battle in which two fundamentally different images of society (that reached well beyond the judicial world) stood against one another.

These ideological debates and worldviews are analyzed in this chapter. Sources for exploring these questions are numerous and rich. I drew on the words of men and women in parliamentary debates proceedings (*Annales parlementaires*), literature on the administration of justice, as well as writings on Belgian feminists engaged at the national and international levels. Both the men's arguments on the basis of which women were denied access are discussed in this chapter, as well as the arguments and strategies that were used and are still being used by pro-feminist reformers. Although Belgium is a "bi-cultural" country, with a French speaking population in the south and a Dutch (or Flemish) speaking population in the north, most of the action on this question was centred in Brussels and writings were published in French.

The Flemish political figures participating in these debates were uncommon for several reasons. Flanders was largely Catholic and conservative toward gender relations in society. Furthermore, its politicians for the majority identified themselves with the ruling parties that were dominantly French speaking at that time. Public life everywhere, and especially in Brussels, almost exclusively ran in French. Only at the end of the nineteenth century was a modest start made in organizing the law, administration, and higher education in Dutch, too, and this under the pressure of a growing Flemish movement. From 1930 onwards, the state university of Ghent was the first to offer (law) degrees exclusively in Dutch; the private universities of Louvain and Brussels would in the long run also offer courses in Dutch, but they remained predominantly French speaking until 1968–1969, when both of them split into two autonomous Flemish universities. Within the Belgian state, the centre of political and intellectual power resided in Brussels, where the freethinking Université libre de Bruxelles—counterpart of the Université Catholic de Louvain—played an important part. The Université libre de Bruxelles was the first university in Belgium to open its door for women. Here also lay a centre of Belgian feminism that was predominantly supported by the liberal movement.

A first phase in the antidiscrimination movement aimed at justice and the law from the end of the nineteenth century on was focused on access to the bar. When Belgian female lawyers were finally granted this right in 1922, they soon demanded also—as Sara L. Kimble has phrased it—the "right to judge."[7] They found allies in the reformers of youth law who advocated the presence of female professionals with a so-called natural caring function in everything involving the protection of minors. These early pleas for a general access to the judiciary were, however, thwarted by the argument that all women were unfit to deliver a judgment because of their legal and political incapacity. After the Second World War, new campaigns began for equal rights between men and women in the labour market as well as on the political level. Just as has been demonstrated by Kimble for France, in Belgium, too, the strong historical relation that existed between political rights for women and their access to the judiciary meant that women could only gain access when they also gained the right to vote.[8] Even so, the feminization of justice was not yet completed, as the promotion of women to the highest official functions continued to be problematic throughout the twentieth century. That is why the last part of this contribution discusses the quota regulations that have been proposed during the last ten years and that aim at a fair representation of both women and men in Belgium's highest courts. The different phases on the road to equality within the Belgian judiciary will be chronologically treated below.

Portia Ante Portas: Popelin before the Closed Doors of the Bar

Marie Popelin (1846–1913) caused the first breach in the masculine judicial establishment, running from the courts of first instance to the Court of Cassation. Belgium's justice system is organised as a pyramid based on the justice of the peace courts, the courts of first instance, labour courts, and commercial courts at the lowest level. The higher courts consist of five courts of appeal, where judges debate the grounds of a case for a second time. The court of highest instance in Belgium is the Court of Cassation, which is the court of last resort in Belgium and whose jurisdiction and powers are similar to those of its French counterpart: appeal to the Court of Cassation is only possible against judgments against which no ordinary appeal is possible anymore. The Court of Cassation can only confirm these judgments or annul them; it is responsible for verifying the interpretation of the law, but it does not re-examine the facts of a case. As well as the usual law courts and courts of appeal, there are two other legal panels that have a supervisory role: the Council of State and the Court of Arbitration. The 1948-established Council of State is responsible for suspending and annulling administrative acts—individual and statutory—that are contrary to the legal rules in force. The Constitutional Court owes its existence to the development of the Belgian unitary state into a federal state since 1970, where the legislative power is divided between the federation and the federated regions, each with legislative bodies. The 1984-established Court of Arbitration, later renamed Constitutional Court, was given the task of demarcating the boundaries of each legislative authority and of reviewing the division of competences between them.

During Marie Popelin's lifetime, Belgium was still a unitary state where French was dominant in law, politics, and intellectual life. And in Belgium's capital of Brussels, the Université libre de Bruxelles would often serve as a pioneer in the field of human rights and fundamental rights: obviously in its resistance against the German occupier during the Second World War and also in relation to women's rights from the nineteenth century onwards. From the moment it opened its doors to women in 1876, the Université libre de Bruxelles would always be the university in Belgium with the highest number of female students, most of them from the petty bourgeoisie (teachers and civil servants).

Popelin, who was initially a teacher in Brussels, decided at the age of thirty-seven to study law at the Université libre de Bruxelles. In 1888, Popelin became the first Belgian woman to earn a degree in law. However, when she applied to register with the male-controlled bar association, her request was refused.[9] In theory, there was no law preventing women from taking their place at the bar (nor in the judiciary), but in practice, the exclusion of women was a tradition in almost all European countries. The declaration in the 1831 Belgian Constitution that "Belgians are equal before the law" nevertheless logically required that these offices should be accessible to all those who, without distinction of sex, met the conditions expressly set out in the law; the exclusion of Belgian women from the legal profession was thus founded on the gap that existed between the spirit of the law and its interpretation, as would be pointed out repeatedly by feminist parliamentarians during the 1946–1948 parliamentary debates on women's access to the judiciary, during which the Popelin case was invoked.[10] Following a decision in the Brussels Appeals Court in 1888, Popelin took her case to the Court of Cassation. But this court also rejected the admission of female lawyers. The judges argued that women were not fit to exercise the profession "because of their innate frailty, the fact that they had to be protected, the demands of motherhood and the education that they have to give to their children; because of their household duties, they are not properly adjusted to the specific demands of the bar and its constraints."[11] During the Popelin trials, there were repeated references to the incapacity of women—married women specifically—and a woman's submission to her husband following marriage: these arguments were also used against (the unmarried) Popelin. Women's incapacity was not only situated on the legal level, but also on the political level, as they had no voting rights. Both these aspects were closely linked to one another, as opponents argued that, *no matter how*, women should be excluded from the legal profession as long as they were not politically emancipated, i.e., not citizens in the political sense.[12]

Women remained excluded, but Popelin did not give up and continued the fight for equal rights. In this, she enjoyed the support of a Brussels lawyer of Jewish origin, Louis Frank (1864–1917), a university companion of Popelin and later the author of a book (first published in 1888 as a brochure) on the discrimination encountered by female lawyers: *La femme-avocat: exposé historique et critique de la question* (1898). This work was preceded by his *Essai sur la condition politique de la femme* (1892) and by *Le grand catéchisme de la femme* (1894).[13] Frank entered at length into the subject of the purported and the civil incapacity of women, and during the academic year 1884–1895, he also lectured "*sur la législation feminine*" at the Université libre de Bruxelles. Frank was an inspirational force behind the middle-class feminism of the day, and around the turn of the century, he conducted a wide correspondence with fellow supporters of advanced women's rights: male and female activists, suffragettes, publishers of women's journals, and female lawyers all over the world.[14] *La femme-avocat* provides an insight into the status of women with regard to the legal professions at the end of the nineteenth century; it was a call for legal reforms that would achieve equal rights for women. Frank's book contains a comprehensive account of the evolution of this legal and social status in the principles of civil law (including Ancient Greek and Roman law), in common law in the period preceding the French Revolution, and finally, of the acknowledgement in revolutionary France in 1791, that everybody, without distinction, should be able to pursue the profession of his or her choice. In his arguments for permitting women access to the bar, Frank emphasized that in the Civil code women are *not explicitly* excluded from legal practice, which he said should be interpreted as de facto consent.[15] The second edition of Frank's book was also intended as a polemic in support of the French lawyer Jeanne Chauvin (1862–1926), who took her demand for the right to take the lawyer's oath to a Parisian court in 1897. Chauvin was thus the first woman in France to contest the exclusively masculine character of the bar through the courts with success. The French legislature finally enabled women to join the bar in 1900. In this achievement, Chauvin's contact with influential male colleagues—jurists—had been crucial. It was through the intervention of sympathetic members of parliament and influential deputies and senators, such as Raymond Léon Poincaré, Léon Bourgeois, and René Viviani, that the legal profession was opened to women. The defenders developed the mentality that began to take hold in France in the wake of the Dreyfus affair, to the effect that radical changes in French society were needed and that women's rights were a crucial element. The political context of the Third Republic allowed more state intervention in favour of more professional opportunities for women.[16]

Chauvin succeeded in using her professional legitimacy as a female lawyer to aid the struggle for equal rights through her work in women's associations and networks as well as through publications and lectures.[17] Hopes were high that her case would convince the Belgian legislators to open the profession to women there, too. Because of the great similarity between both countries in politics and in the field of law, Frank assumed that the French example would have repercussions in Belgium and that Popelin would thus stand a new chance—already his first edition of *La femme-avocat* had come out in support of Popelin. A bill was introduced to that effect in 1901 by socialist and liberal parliamentarians in the Belgian Parliament, in which the French example was extensively cited,[18] but minds had not yet evolved in that direction and the proposal was defeated. That the French legislature passed a law allowing women such as Jeanne Chauvin to practice law while the Belgian legislature did not follow suit for Popelin has everything to do with their respective composition at the time. In the wake of conflicts over the introduction of secular elementary schools around 1880, the Catholic conservative party held an unbroken legislative majority in Belgium until after World War I.

Thus, Belgian women with law degrees at the beginning of the twentieth century would continue to work on the periphery of the legal profession without having a fully-fledged statute or access to the bar. Popelin exercised the profession of lawyer but without the possibility to plead in court. In an 1894 interview with the journal *La Réforme*, she stated, "There has to be a place for women at the bar; as a proof of this I can cite the number of women who came to me for advice or for an intervention, although they know I am not authorised to plead."[19] Popelin possessed her own law office at her family's house, where she acted as legal advisor to many women but was not allowed to bear the official title. As a result of this continuing injustice, some Belgian female jurists would shift their attention to the international women's movement for equal rights.

The legal tug of war surrounding Marie Popelin was a turning point in the Belgian feminist movement. The case received enormous press publicity; public opinion was aroused, and Popelin subsequently developed much greater interest in all facets of women's emancipation.[20] The Popelin affair had made it clear that more was needed than education and training in order to remove the existing inequalities between women and men; in particular, women's access to the legal profession and to the parliamentary system were necessary to improve legal rights for women.

In response to this new awareness, various new organizations of a middle-class feminist nature and from different political tendencies were founded from the end of the nineteenth century on. The first one to be created was the Ligue belge du droit des femmes, of which Popelin served as the president. Together with Louis Frank, she founded it in a classroom of the Université libre de Bruxelles in 1892. This was the first feminist organization in Belgium. Over the years, it would have about three hundred members. The Ligue's program contained three main demands: to abolish the principle of husband's authority and to achieve legal parity between husband and wife within marriage; to grant women the right of access to all professions, positions, and employments; and to allow women to participate in the management and settlement of public affairs. On the occasion of her first international feminist congress (from which other Belgian women remained absent), it became clear to Popelin and the other Ligue members to what degree Belgian feminist organizations were divided and thus inefficient. From then on, their goal was to achieve unity between the different feminist organizations by following a well-defined program. After various attempts, the National Council of Belgian Women (NCBW) was finally created in 1905, and quickly affiliated with the ICW. Popelin acted as its president and secretary until she died. Under Popelin's guidance, the National Council of Women put forward various legislative initiatives and participated in the surveys and activities of the International Council of Women (founded in 1888).[21]

Up until World War I, these Belgian feminists would assist in the introduction of a series of different laws that would improve women's position in the law; all were based on the NCBW's preparatory legal work. Popelin also succeeded in winning over male politicians to her cause: besides Louis Frank, these were notably socialist lawyers Henri La Fontaine and the then newly graduated Emile Vandervelde, later one of Belgium's foremost socialist leaders (he became the first member of the Belgian Labour Party to serve as a Minister). Both were co-founders of the Ligue belge du droit des femmes. After the war ended, Vandervelde would submit the bill that formed the basis of the law of November 7, 1922, which, after decades of struggle and polemics, gave women the right to exercise the legal profession.[22]

A Changing State of Mind in the 1920s

Originally, in 1901, Vandervelde, together with parliamentarians Hector Denis, Georges Hubin, and Paul Janson, had introduced such a bill in the Belgian Parliament.[23] A verbal dispute between proponents and opponents had followed in the *Journal des Tribunaux*, during which Henri La Fontaine called on the Fédération des Avocats belges to support this bill. Upon his call, some Belgian lawyers did indicate their support for women's access to the bar.[24] In parliament, however, the opponents were in the majority. In successive parliamentary committees, the proposal was stalled and eventually rejected in 1912. Hoping for a more favourable mental climate, Vandervelde would wait another eight years before re-introducing his proposal, this time in his capacity as Minister of Justice. In his text, he referred to the law of May 15, 1910 (introduced in 1901 by Hector Denis) that had created the possibility for women to vote and to sit in labour courts, and which, according to Vandervelde, annulled the legal objections to women's access. To appease opponents, he kept in his proposal the provision that married women needed the consent of their husbands to practice as a lawyer. Moreover, he stated that only a small group of women—well-to-do daughters of the bourgeoisie—would enjoy the opening up of the legal profession to women. They would thus hardly compete with their much more numerous male colleagues. After the debate in parliament, the proposal was almost unanimously accepted by a legislature in which Belgian socialists were now (since 1919) well represented.[25] After the granting of voting rights in local elections to women one year earlier, this law suited the broader reform movement (of which justice formed a part), which sought to offer a solution to the diverse social problems arising in Belgian society at the time. Popelin and other feminists had created the conditions for change by forcing the legal profession to make explicit the reasons for excluding women. Thus, women's access to the legal professions ultimately became a problem that had to be resolved in law.

After 1922, female lawyers in Belgium were able to join the bar and argue a case in court. Yet even by the 1950s, only half of the Belgian women with law degrees—about ten times fewer than the men—actually pursued a career in the legal profession. As lawyers, they were often subcontracted to male lawyers, preparing their cases as clerks and doing secretarial work, or they acted as legal advisers for female clients on matters of marriage and divorce.[26] In addition, the doors to the courts and the judiciary remained closed to them. In the 1920s and 1930s, women's access to the judiciary was requested by feminists and others involved in the protection of minors because their "ethics of care" approach to juvenile justice and/or social work meant that women "naturally" demonstrated the "maternal" skills or "feminine" competency needed in the field. In 1912, when Belgium had adopted the country's first law on child protection, the opening of the juvenile judge position to women had not yet been discussed. Those new judges would be recruited from magistrates in office, who at that time were all men. Notwithstanding intensive lobby work, the proponents of women's access had to wait until 1935, when a socialist minister of justice created a commission to study the ways women could contribute to the domain of youth protection. Under the presidency of the juvenile court judge Paul Wets, the feminists Paule Lamy, Marcelle Renson, and Jeanne Vandervelde were seated in the commission next to several male lawyers and Aimée Racine, a female lawyer who specialized in juvenile delinquency. After two years of deliberation, the commission presented a proposal that supported women's access to juvenile courts. The National Council of Women, of which some members were seated in the youth protection commission, insisted that the minister of justice introduce that very year a law to create a female police corps as well as to grant women access to courts of law (they could already sit in the labour courts). However, after several cabinet reshuffles, the Catholic Charles du Bus de Warnaffe shot down these proposals, which were opposed by the First Chairmen (Premier Président) of the courts of appeal on the grounds that women's political incapacity was a major obstacle to granting them access to this public office.[27]

The Opening of the Courts to Women

After the first wave of Belgian feminism and its achievements, new developments in society were needed to give the struggle for women's rights a new impetus. The exceptional context of the aftermath of World War II ensured that the principal feminist demand, that of women's suffrage, would be granted in 1948.[28] The opening up of the judiciary to women was an immediate consequence. On this occasion, too, activists in the women's movement played an important role. As they had always done from the beginning, the NCBW continued to call for new legislation, based on the preparatory legal work of its members that would advance women's rights. In 1945, the National Council of Women launched a survey asking female lawyers if women should be granted access to the judiciary and, if so, why. Predictably, the conclusion was that they should: many thought it simply "unjust" that only men could judge, especially in cases of divorce and assignment of guardianship of children.[29]

After World War II, Georgette Ciselet (1900–1983) played a key role in further opening the judicial profession to women and demanding immediate voting rights. In 1923, she became the fourth woman in Belgium to take the oath as a lawyer, and she quickly specialized in divorce cases. In the 1930s, on the basis of her own experience, she published her first texts on the discrimination against married women and the comparative study of law, along the lines of Louis Frank's work thirty years earlier. She wrote the following: "Women have to know where they stand, what marriage does to them legally, what they can and cannot do in relation to political participation, divorce, money and children."[30] In the meantime, she adhered to the women's section of the liberal party and, after the war, chaired its judicial commission. In 1963, she left Belgian politics and became the first woman named to the Council of State. In the years preceding this, Ciselet had tirelessly devoted herself to women's political, social, and family rights. She was also a member of the board of the National Council of Women and participated in its committee on the law, where she devoted herself to women's access to the judiciary and to the notarial profession.[31]

In 1946, as a senator and the first female liberal member of the Belgian Parliament, Ciselet took the lead in increasing the pressure on the Ministry of Justice to make changes. Within the judiciary, the main opponents from earlier times had given way to reformers. The then attorney general to the Court of Cassation, Léon Cornil, held the view that an explicit act of law was necessary in order to change "so long-established a custom."[32] Proponents repeatedly referred to France, where the law of April 11, 1946, granted women access to the judiciary; it was passed with minimal discussion in the National Assembly. France was the country to which Belgian feminists looked most often, as it had essentially the same legal system since the 1800s.

The French deputy Marianne Verger, a member of the Resistance during World War II who had been elected to the French Parliament, had introduced the bill that settled the question. Her text had been co-signed by all the female deputies, a unique event in the history of the French Parliament.[33] Women's heroism during the war was used as an argument, just as in the debates on granting women national voting rights. The same would happen in Belgium. The French parliamentary proceedings read as follows: "The good and beautiful French *citoyennes* who by their active patriotism have shown themselves dignified when sent to Ravensbrück and having suffered there tortures and the torments of the Nazi hell; those who by their martyrdom have equalled the well-known heroines of Antiquity legends, and the greatest saints of the holy script; those new saints of our country have bought with their agony and with their blood the right to judge and to render justice in name of the French people."[34] Immediately after the French law was passed, a first appointment to the French Court of Cassation followed. Eight women were subsequently appointed to the courts of first instance and to district courts.[35]

Next to the arguments connected with the post-World War II political context, the opening of the judiciary to women was presented in terms of principal rights that were, however, always rooted in a differentialist approach. In Belgium, just as in France, supporters invoked the specific qualities of women who, "for certain matters" were "more appropriate than men," as in cases of juvenile delinquency, protection of the family, and so on.[36] It is true that the discourse of "women's specificity" can be a double-edged sword. It functions as an argument to promote the integration of women in the judiciary, but it can also justify the limitation of their competences to one specific field, as the anti-essentialist French sociologist of law Anne Boigeol has pointed out: once women in France had won access to the judiciary, they mainly targeted the bench and juvenile courts rather than the public prosecution service, which remained an exclusively male bastion for many more years. The feminization of the judiciary had indeed undermined the differentiation between men and women in some areas, but it also displaced the distinction to others. Men developed new strategies based on the accumulation of cultural and financial capital at a time when not only was the judiciary becoming feminized but also the social status of judges had begun to lose prestige. Boigeol also points to the phenomenon of the "extra-professional mobility" of judges as a part of an on-going male struggle to distinguish themselves in a feminizing profession.[37] The greater involvement—which continues even today—of male judges in the intellectual arena and in public debates about the relationship between justice and politics can be interpreted as a strategy to distinguish themselves from the "junior judges."[38] Equality between women and men has been a legal fact since 1946, but at the same time, this feminization of the judiciary has precipitated new forms of "distinction."[39]

In this, Belgium followed France's lead. As a first measure after World War II, it was decided in 1947 that women could appear as counsellors and as lawyers in the Court of Cassation. The general and complete opening of the judiciary to women finally took place a year later.[40] A bill put forward by Georgette Ciselet, co-signed by the Catholic Paul Struye,[41] the socialist Henri Rolin,[42] and the communist Jean Fonteyne,[43] would provide the basis for the Law of February 21, 1948, which opened up all of Belgium's judicial posts to women. Male champions of women's emancipation supported the bill. Moreover, cross-party cooperation soon led to a consensus. As chair of the Justice Commission in the Senate, Henri Rolin had mollified conservatives and the remaining supporters of traditional gender roles by declaring that "women's domestic vocation would not be weakened" by the bill: women would continue firstly to aspire "to marriage and motherhood." However, experience showed—and Popelin probably provided an example—that "not all women can achieve this ambition."[44] The reasoning was thus, in fact, as follows: even though there were "well-founded psychological or biological reasons" *not* to do so, the judiciary should be opened to women *on principle* "since men and women were of equal value."[45]

Discussion of the proposal in the Senate was remarkably brief. In her argument, Ciselet limited herself to examples from abroad. She reminded conservative senators in the Catholic group of their responsibility, given the fact that equal treatment of the sexes had been a part of their election manifesto. In the House of Representatives, Ciselet was supported by the new Catholic deputy and advocate Marguerite De Riemacker-Legot,[46] and her solidarity with the women's cause outweighed submission to the hardliners in the Catholic party. To Fonteyne's argument that a modernized and, therefore, female-friendly legal system was necessary to the future of democracy in Belgium, Justice Minister Struye added a reference to the past. Just as had happened in the French Parliament, he defended the bill as a "just tribute" to the role played by Belgian women during the war and the model of "civic virtue" they had offered. Struye expressed this as follows: "This bill is a just homage to the eminent role played by Belgian women, not least in the recent years of our troubled history, and during the tragic period of the occupation. It is beyond doubt that our women, from whatever category of the population, have given a magnificent example of civic virtue. I am quite convinced that they can and would exercise the virtues of the hearth and civic virtues side by side."[47] The liberal deputy Charles Janssens[48] would later also point to Belgian justice's deviations in the punishment of collaboration after World War II as an argument (e.g., the inconsistencies in the judgments and sentences passed), urging that the appointment of female judges would give Belgian justice "a more honourable and human face." During the debate, he noted, "Observing the sometimes disappointing way in which justice is delivered in our country, particularly in the matter of the purging of the administration, I have come to believe that if women were represented in the courts martial or the military court, the repression of collaborators would perhaps not have led, as now, to shameful outbursts of public opinion."[49]

After a near-unanimous vote in the Senate, the debate in the House of Representatives was much more contentious. Against the arguments of his fellow Catholic Riemacker-Legot, Marcel Phillipart[50] consigned the proposal firmly to the wastebasket. Philippart evoked the by now conventional conservative Catholic resistance to female professional activities, which threatened to remove the wife from the home and the family. These (very) few opponents rehearsed "the innate moral and intellectual failings of many women" whose "typically feminine intuition and emotion" were the antithesis of "rational logic," "impartial judgment," and "other male characteristics, such as self-control, tenacity and calm."[51] In his argument, Philippart referred extensively to a fiercely discussed speech delivered at the opening of the 1946 judicial year by the advocate general Delwaide, who was a leading member of Liège legal circles and the very incarnation of conservatism in the Belgian judiciary. His speech offered a classic example of gender-differential reasoning on the distinction between the private and public spheres. The exercise of judicial office was associated with a vocation comparable to that of the priesthood. The courts and the judiciary—"manly offices"—were a part of "the unmistakable masculinity of public functions."[52] The admission of women created not only the specter of competition within the service, but also an attack on the fundamental image of the judiciary as a "manly function." A binding law admitting women was also seen as an attack on the independence of the profession and its powers to determine the admissibility of candidates. For some older judges like Delwaide, the admission of women meant the end of a *gendered* ideal of "professional honor."[53] By this time, however, these sexist and timeworn arguments represented a marginal opinion. The majority of members of the Belgian Parliament received such claims with disapproval.

Neither Delwaide nor Philippart was able to turn the tide. The law granting Belgian women access to the judiciary was adopted with 139 votes for and 19 against.[54] This took place more or less contemporaneously with the Law of March 27, 1948, which gave women the right to vote in elections for the House of Representatives and the Senate. The legitimacy of women's suffrage was no longer in doubt in the political context of the liberation, when women's rights made a leap forward in the global movement toward equality, democracy, and human rights. This had the effect of neutralizing opponents and making the vote of the laws granting women voting rights and access to all law courts possible. In both cases, only a minority objected. In both cases, the arguments had focused on the courage and patriotism of Belgian women during World War II.[55] Because of the war and the role women had played during German occupation and in the resistance, it had become impossible to deny them the political rights they had demanded for so long. The access to professions profited from this trend toward gender justice and recognition of women's competency and their sense of moral judgment.[56]

Thus from 1948 onwards, women finally held the right to judge. However, marital consent was still required for married women working as judges. This only ended with the revision of the Civil code in 1958, which in turn was partly the result of a bill proposed a decade earlier in the Senate by Ciselet to reform the existing law on reciprocal duties and rights within marriage. In 1946, she had introduced a proposal that intended to establish full equality of the rights of husbands and wives. Two years later, the socialist Isabelle Blume once more introduced a proposal that would abolish conjugal consent and grant married women their full legal capacity. None of these proposals were immediately taken up by parliament, but they did lead to the creation in 1948 of a commission with the responsibility to reform the system of reciprocal duties and rights within marriage and regarding marital property. The commission's proceedings resulted in the law of April 30, 1958 that finally abolished conjugal consent and the incapacity of married women.[57]

The Feminization of the Belgian Judiciary in Practice

Less than a year after the promulgation of the law of February 21, 1948, Geneviève Pevtschin (1915–2002), an advocate in the Brussels *commune* de Saint-Gilles, was appointed to the Court of First Instance in Brussels.[58]

She thus became the first female judge in Belgium. The first female public prosecutor did not follow until 1953. Pevtschin was the daughter of a Brussels businessman of Russian Jewish descent. In 1937, she completed her studies at the Université libre de Bruxelles, and soon afterwards, she was admitted to the city's bar association. As an advocate, she was also working for the *Journal des Tribunaux*. When her career was interrupted by the German ordinance of October 1940 concerning the removal of Jews from their offices and posts, she applied to join the resistance. She let it be known that she wanted "to do something" by way of resisting the occupier, and she became active in the intelligence and escape network known as "Zéro." She also worked for the underground paper *La Libre Belgique*. In 1943, she was arrested by the Gestapo and taken to a military prison and two months later deported to Germany (the fortress at Anrath) and finally to Dachau. She was eventually freed in 1945 after an exhausting forced march. For her services to the resistance and her courage during imprisonment, she was honoured by the Belgian state. In April 1946, she was made an Officer of Belgium's Order of the Crown, awarded a *Croix de Guerre* (military cross) with palms, and promoted to the rank of captain ARA (Agent de Renseignement et d'Action). For many, she personified the fact that Belgian women, as much as men, could be supporters and servants of the nation.[59] This distinction certainly influenced her subsequent career. In 1946, as the first woman in the history of the Belgian law courts to serve as keynote speaker at the Conférence du Jeune Barreau de Bruxelles, she chose as her topic "Pierre Brachet and the Defence of Liberty," eulogizing a young lawyer who had been killed at the front in the Spanish Civil War in Madrid in 1936 and who, as she put it, "realized that when the bell tolled for the end of the freedom in Spain, it also tolled for that in Belgium."[60] The *Journal des Tribunaux* later reported "she achieved greatness in the profound silence of a deeply moved audience."[61]

Pevtschin practiced at the bar until her nomination as magistrate. While mainly welcomed by her superiors, she was made to work hard, six days a week.[62] A couple of years after her appointment, Pevtschin married the lawyer Marcel Janssen, who had also been a member of the resistance and a political prisoner during World War II. During her career, Pevtschin dealt mainly with civil cases and especially those relating to intellectual rights at the Brussels Appeal Court to which she was appointed in 1973. Between 1981 and 1985, she was president of the Second Chamber of this court. This was the highest level that she reached in the Belgian judiciary. While serving in the Brussels law courts, Pevtschin also put her legal expertise at the disposal of the European Commission on Human Rights, to which she was appointed as its first Belgian member in 1954 and as one of its very few female members. In 1972, she became Belgium's expert at the European Council in Strasbourg and was instrumental in the establishment of the new Court for Human Rights.[63]

For a long time, Pevtschin remained an exception at the top. For although there was no shortage of female law students, by 1961, there were still only

17 female judges (1% of the total); in 1979, there were 177, and in 1995, just 575 (30% of the total).[64] From the start, women have, in their analysis of the difficulties that blocked professional mobility, emphasized the opposing elements in the organizational structure and culture of the judicial system. A female public prosecutor testified, during a gender study day in the Belgian Senate several years ago, regarding the difficulties she had encountered upon her nomination in the mid-1980s as the only woman and as youngest of the staff. Her male colleagues certainly did not welcome her; her ability to bear the responsibility of her function was constantly questioned, and she had to work twice as hard as her male colleagues.[65] Similar stories came up in many testimonies. In addition to such examples of institutional sexism in Belgium, there was also the fact that until 1998, no gender neutral and objective selection procedures existed for nominations in the judiciary. In Belgium, unlike in France where recruitments depend on competitions, nominations depended on the minister of justice and were inevitably politically coloured.

In fact, the change in numbers only came about in the 1970s. It was not until 1970 that a woman first reached the level of the Court of Appeal, and the doors of the Court of Cassation did not open until 1975. From 177 female magistrates in 1979 to 575 in 1995, this group grew in 2008 to 1103 female magistrates on a total staff of 2459.[66] The judiciary has gained a more equal gender representation in recent years—the number of female judges now fluctuates around 45%—but just as is the case in France too, this does not apply in the upper echelons of the judicial system, where a glass ceiling still hinders women from reaching the top jobs and decision-making positions. At the top, the judiciary remains a male bastion. In Belgium's higher courts there remains even today a striking discrepancy between the numbers of women and men. The number of women in comparison with that of men amounts today to 13% at the Court of Cassation, 25% at the Council of State, and in the five different appeal courts, between 15% and 35%. Of the 264 magistrates in the appeal courts of which 94 are women, 78 of them are councillors and 16 are heads of chamber.[67] None of them are first chairmen.

In the lower ranks, the picture looks entirely different. Among the chairmen of the courts of first instance, women represent 10%, among the chairmen of the commercial courts 13%, and at the labour courts 33%.[68] Women are best represented in the courts of first instance. There, they represent almost half of the staff. For the labour courts, this number is 55%, and in the justice of the peace courts 31%.[69] In sum, there remains a great gap between the appearance of equality and equality in reality. Yet, as Marie Popelin suggested over a century ago, the democratic nature of the institutions and the law demands a balanced representation reflecting the composition of society. Contemporary Belgian feminists point out that without that balance, the unspoken impression remains that politics and justice—two important vectors of democracy—are, and always have been, a world of and for men.[70]

To increase the number of women in the Belgian higher courts, the association of Christian-Democratic Women pleads for a quota, an approach that is supported by many female parliamentarians. The reasoning here is that a quota can improve a social reality that historically has been askew and that it can function as a crowbar to fight any form of conscious and unconscious discrimination. Since 2003, several bills have been introduced in the Belgian Senate to guarantee, by way of a quota, a balanced presence of men and women in the Constitutional Court, the Court of Cassation, the Council of State, and the appeal courts. However, none of these or the later proposals made it onto the agenda of the Commission of Justice, nor were they discussed in parliament. This lack of debate on democratic parity through quota in the judiciary lags behind the developments on the international level.[71] Indeed, the International Criminal Court Statute has built in measures for a balanced composition in its organization. It prescribes that the states, in their choice for judges to compose the Court, not only have to respect a geographical balance and a balance between the different law systems and traditions in the world, but also a fair balance between men and women.[72]

The fact that in the Belgian judiciary there exists little support for quotas is also illustrated by a recent statement of the First Chairman of the Court of Cassation in a Belgian newspaper, saying that there are too few qualified female candidates for top functions since they are hindered by their family duties.[73] The argument that qualified women for high positions are unavailable is a classic one that displaces the responsibility onto the women themselves. It is certainly true that women's distribution in the various courts is also partly the result of self-selection, as women *do* often target safe and predictable positions such as the bench and *do* often limit their competences to gender sensitive areas such as juvenile courts. Yet women, in their analysis of obstacles in their careers, *do* emphasize the role of opposing elements in the professional structure and the culture of the organization: the corporate culture of the judiciary provides that an empty space is often filled with more of the same, those already present—thus, mostly men.[74] One can also ask why the question of "qualification" only comes up when talking about women.

Proponents of positive actions agree that quotas in the judiciary are not only desirable for the sake of equality but also for reasons of suitability: a sector like the Belgian judiciary, often characterized by its rigidity and traditionalism, cries out for change and diversity, by which additional aspects of a case can be taken into account. A critical mass of women can introduce women-sensitive (and often neglected) policy concerns such as, for instance, domestic violence. Advocates of quotas conclude that the absence of women in judicial deliberations undermines the representative character of the judicial institutions. Moreover, without respect for equal treatment and gender balance within its own organization, the judiciary can hardly act as a role model for rightfulness and social justice.[75]

Conclusion

The equal representation of women and men in the legal field has been pursued in various ways and with varying degrees of success. From qualified jurists without a fully-fledged statute or access to the bar, women evolved to *professionals* that nowadays in Belgium occupy half of the judiciary. Legal professions transformed from being solely men's business to being open to both sexes.

Over the years, progress was never made spontaneously but always under the influence of the grassroots or from outside the legal profession by binding law. Certainly in the early days, the actions of individual women, supported by the women's movement, were crucial. Through the combination of their social position—these were independent women from the urban middle class—and their political engagement or feminist commitment, Marie Popelin, Georgette Ciselet, and Geneviève Pevtschin were pioneers in effecting more diversity in the masculine world of Belgian law.

In Belgium—as in most countries—Catholic governments, public prosecution departments, and judges in place were the main obstacles to women's admission to judicial professions. In view of the number of judgments and political statements claiming that women were "unfit" to exercise such positions, the only road for women to achieve access lay in changing the legislation via parliament.[76] Popelin and later Ciselet took action for state intervention in favour of a more women-friendly legal system. They achieved success by gaining the support of influential colleague-jurists and by involving themselves in various feminist organizations and legal commissions that acted as pressure groups on the authorities.

Once they were granted access to the bar, women also demanded the right to judge. Their protest against gender discrimination in the legal field intrinsically encompassed the demand for equal citizenship and voting rights, as was illustrated by Ciselet's commitment. Opponents experienced this demand as an assault on the traditional sex roles and the power balance of social relations between men and women. They deployed the powerful argument that, without political emancipation, women could not and should not speak about the law. For antifeminists, it was very convenient to present women's access to the judiciary as "premature," as women did not yet possess voting rights.

Nonetheless, already in the interwar period, women were, as an exception, present in labour courts and commercial courts. What's more, a host of legal experts were convinced that the absence of women, "with their natural maternal instincts," would even obstruct the efficient operation of the newly created youth courts. Arguments in favour of women becoming judges drew on women's specificity or gender "essentialism"—i.e., that women had inherent characteristics that made them better suited than men to work in family and juvenile courts.

But when women after World War II at last gained the right to judge, this did not happen as the recognition of their "exceptional qualities" or as the result of a global striving for equality. It was principally presented as a token of esteem for the role they had played during the war and the suffering they had experienced during those years. The same arguments were used, almost simultaneously, to grant Belgian women the right to vote in 1948. Women's access to the judiciary was the result of continuous feminist activism that benefited from reform-minded post-war politics. Likewise, women's access to the bar had indirectly profited from World War I, as this had radically influenced parliament's composition: 1919 saw the introduction of the first socialist parliamentarians in the Belgian legislature, some of whom sympathized with the women's cause (yet on the whole, women's issues were marginalized by socialist party politics). Women in Belgium, as well as in France, became lawyers before they won the right the vote. That situation persisted for just one generation in Belgium, but for two in France. Yet in many countries, a strong argument against admitting women to the bar was that such a step meant an inevitable and essentially immediate opening of suffrage. No such immediate prospect existed in interwar Belgium: during this period, the socialist party had continued to support women's exclusion from voting rights. This party feared that in predominantly Catholic Flanders women would most certainly vote for the Catholic party.

With the 1948 law, formal equality in the courts was achieved, but in the following decades, the progress toward feminization of justice was excruciatingly slow, and women did not succeed in reaching the top positions in the same numbers as men did. In sum, the admission of women to the legal professions in Belgium did not indicate the final point where true equality could finally be achieved. In this, the Belgian example does not stand out as an exception in Europe where there did—and still does—seem to exist a difference between common law and civil law in countries regarding women's entry to and career progression within the judiciary. This may be due to the fact that, as a rule in civil law countries, success in examinations determines access to the judiciary. In common law countries, by contrast, judges are chosen from experienced legal practitioners, and in this professional visibility, evaluations of professional achievement, and access to networks are of crucial weight.[77]

Yet it seems that whatever procedure is applied, there is one feature that remains in place: namely that stereotypical perceptions of masculinity and femininity continue to play an important part. It thus appears that the progression of women to the top of the judicial structure remains a complicated problem about which opinions are divided as to causes, remedies, and responsibilities. If the judicial system itself appears unable to resolve this problematic professional flow, a task is reserved here for government and parliament. At least that is the strategy that had been followed more than one hundred years ago by Popelin and Chauvin, with eventual success.

Notes

1 Ulrike Schultz and Gisela Shaw, "Introduction: Gender and Judging: Overview and Synthesis," in *Gender and Judging*, ed. Ulrike Schultz and Gisela Shaw (Oxford: Hart Publishing, 2013), 29–33; Carol Gilligan, *In a Different Voice: Psychological Theory and Women's Development* (Cambridge, MA: Harvard University Press, 1982).

2 Tracking down and providing evidence for effects of difference due to the gender of the lawyer or the judge is of course difficult because male and female gender always intersects with other aspects of difference, such as age, family background, class/social stratum, and religion, as well as an individual's personal qualities. See: Schultz and Shaw, "Introduction," 29–33.

3 Although the judiciary has gained a much more equal representation in recent years, this does not apply to the upper echelons of the judicial system, which remain a male bastion. Recent European studies show that the higher the level in the hierarchy, the proportion of female judges in higher courts still tends to decrease. The majority of women are gathered in lower judicial positions. See: European Commission for the Efficiency of Justice (CEPEJ), *European Judicial Systems: Efficiency and Quality of Justice. An Overview*, August 1, 2014, http://www.coe.int/T/dghl/cooperation/cepej/evaluation/2012/Synthese_Version_finale_en.pdf. See also: Marianne de Rooij, "A Woman is the Judge. 60 jaar vrouwelijke rechters in Nederland," *Nederlands Juristenblad* 39 (2007): 2474–2481.

4 Eva Schandevyl, "Portia ten tonele: de feminisering van de Belgische magistratuur," in *Histoire du droit et de la justice: une nouvelle génération de recherches*, ed. Dirk Heirbaut, Xavier Rousseaux and Alain Wijffels (LLN: Presses Universitaires de Louvain, 2009), 565–577.

5 Sara L. Kimble, "No Right to Judge: Feminism and the Judiciary in Third Republic France," *French Historical Studies* 31, no. 4 (2008): 610.

6 Eva Schandevyl, "De toegang van vrouwen tot het gerecht: enkele sleutelmomenten en-figuren in de Belgische geschiedenis," *Historica* 31, no. 1 (2008): 16–18.

7 This phrase is from Kimble, "No Right to Judge," 609–641.

8 The parallels with the French case, as described by Sara L. Kimble, are striking.

9 On Marie Popelin, see: Eliane Gubin, Catherine Jacques, Valerie Piette and Jean Puissant eds., *Dictionnaire des femmes belges. XIXe et XXe siècles* (Brussels: Editions Racine, 2006), 459–462; Françoise de Bueger-Van Lierde, "A l'origine du mouvement féministe en Belgique. L'affaire Popelin," *Belgisch Tijdschrift voor Filologie en Geschiedenis* V (1972): 1128–1137; Jean-Pierre Nandrin, "Le femme-avocate. Le long combat des féministes belges (1888–1922)," *Sextant* 19 (2003): 131–142; Jean-Pierre Nandrin, "De vrouwelijke advocaten," in *Vrouwenzakenvrouwen. Facetten van vrouwelijk zelfstandig ondernemerschap in Vlaanderen, 1800–2000*, ed. Leen Van Molle and Peter Heyrman (Ghent: Provinciebestuur Oost-Vlaanderen, 2001), 165–172.

10 Belgian Senate, Parliamentary Documents, no. 132, October 23, 1946; Belgian House of Representatives, Parliamentary Documents, no. 159, January 21, 1948.

11 *Pasicrisie belge*, 1889, *II partie: arrêts des Cours d'Appel* (Bruxelles: Bruylant, 48–50); *Journal des Tribunaux*, no. 577, 16 décembre 1888, col. 1476–1478; *Belgique judiciaire*, no. 1, janvier 1889, col. 15–17.

12 *Journal des Tribunaux*, no. 577, 16 décembre 1888, col. 1465–1478. This Belgian Civil code was based on the 1804 French (Napoleonic) Civil code, which was imposed onto the Southern Netherlands (that is, today's Belgium) by French occupants in 1795 and which remained in force in Belgium throughout the 1800s. Like the Code Napoleon, according to the Belgian Civil code, marriage reduced the wife to legal incapacity.

13 Louis Frank studied law and philosophy in Brussels and in Bologna. His commitment to the feminist cause began early; he defended the rights of women in his academic work, at conferences, and in many pamphlets, in which he called for a thorough revision of the Civil code. Initially he could count on a wide audience, but he was gradually forgotten. Gubin et al., *Dictionnaire des femmes belges*, 252–254.

14 Royal Library of Belgium, Department of Manuscripts, Correspondence of Louis Frank. On Louis Frank, see also: Françoise de Bueger-Van Lierde, "Louis Frank, pionnier du mouvement féministe belge," *Belgisch Tijdschrift voor Nieuwste Geschiedenis* IV, no. 3–4 (1973): 377–392.

15 Louis Frank, *La Femme-avocat. Exposé historique et critique de la question* (Brussels: F. Larcier and Bologna: N. Zanichelli. 1888). Reprinted in Paris by Giard et E. Brière, 1898; translated by Mary A. Greene and reprinted in the USA as "The Woman Lawyer," *Chicago Law Times* 3 (1889): 74–86, 120–140, 253–268, 382–411.

16 Mary Jane Mossman, *The First Women Lawyers: A Comparative Study of Gender, Law and Legal Professions* (Portland: Hart Publishing, 2006), 241; Eva Schandevyl, *Tussen revolutie en conformisme. Het engagement en de netwerken van linkse intellectuelen in België 1918–1956* (Brussels: ASP, 2011), 16.

17 Anne Boigeol, "French Women Lawyers (*advocates*) and the 'women's cause' in the First Half of the Twentieth Century," *International Journal of the Legal Profession* 10, no. 2 (2003): 193–207.

18 Belgian House of Representatives, Proceedings, January 24, 1901.

19 *La Réforme*, October 4, 1894.

20 On the many echoes of the Popelin case in the Belgian and foreign press in 1888–89 and also in Belgian feminist publications at the end of the nineteenth century, see de Bueger-Van Lierde, "A l'origine du mouvement féministe en Belgique," 1131–1136.

21 On the women's rights movement in Belgium, see: Eliane Gubin and Leen Van Molle eds., *Des femmes qui changent le monde: histoire du Conseil international des femmes 1888–1988* (Bruxelles: Racine, 2005); Julie Carlier, "Moving Beyond Boundaries: an Entangled History of Feminism in Belgium, 1890–1914," PhD diss., University of Ghent, 2010.

22 Nandrin, "Le femme-avocate," 131–142.

23 Belgian House of Representatives, Proceedings, January 24, 1901.

24 Nandrin, "Le femme-avocate," 131–142.

25 Belgian Senate and House of Representatives, Parliamentary Documents and Proceedings, 1919–1922.

26 Martine Hissel, "Etudiantes et diplomées en droit à l'Université libre de Bruxelles de 1882 à 1940," MA thesis, Université libre de Bruxelles, 1980, 82–85.

27 Catherine Jacques, "À l'assaut d'un bastion masculin. L'accès des femmes à la magistrature," *Les Cahiers de la Fonderie* 39 (2008): 51–55; Aurore François and Christine Machiels, "From Philanthropists to Juvenile Judges: Women dealing with Juvenile Delinquency. International Debates and Local Practices in Belgium (1890–1960)," in *Women in Law and Law Making in Nineteenth and Twentieth Century Europe*, ed. Eva Schandevyl (London: Ashgate, 2014), 34. First chairmen are called the presidents of the Court of Cassation, of the courts of appeal, and of the labour courts; at the level of the public prosecutor, the courts of appeal are presided over by the prosecutors-general.

28 Boigeol, "French Women Lawyers," 204.

29 Jacques, "A l'assaut," 52.

30 Georgette Ciselet, *La Femme: ses droits, ses devoirs et ses revendications* (Bruxelles: L'Eglantine, 1930).

31 Gubin et al., *Dictionnaire des femmes belges*, 100–103.
32 Belgian Senate, Parliamentary Documents, no. 132, October 23, 1946.
33 *Dossier documentaire "Magistrats"* (349 MAG) at the *Bibliothèque Marguerite Durand*, Paris.
34 Anne Boigeol, "Les femmes et les Cours. La difficile mise en oeuvre de l'égalité des sexes dans l'accès à la magistrature" *Genèses* 22, no. 22 (1996): 107–129.
35 Belgian Senate, Proceedings, July 10, 1947.
36 Ibid.
37 Anne Boigeol, "Les magistrats 'hors les murs'" *Droit et Société* 44–45 (2000): 225–248.
38 Anne Boigeol, "La contribution des magistrates au débat sur la justice," in *Intellectuelles. Du genre en histoire des intellectuels*, ed. Nicole Racine and Michel Trebitsch (Brussels: Editions Complexe, 2004), 271.
39 Anne Boigeol, "Male Strategies in the Face of the Feminisation of a Profession: The Case of the French Judiciary," in *Women in the Legal Professions*, ed. Ulrike Schultz and Gisela Shaw (Oxford: Hart Publishing, 2003), 401–418.
40 Jacques, "À l'assaut," 51–55.
41 Paul Struye (1896–1974) was a lawyer, a professor at Leuven, a Catholic senator, and the Minister of Justice between 1947 and 1948.
42 Henri Rolin (1891–1973) was a lawyer, a professor at Brussels, a socialist senator (1932–1968), and the Minister of Justice in 1946.
43 Jean Fonteyne (1899–1974) was a lawyer and a communist senator from 1946 to 1949.
44 Belgian Senate, Parliamentary Documents, no. 214, June 26, 1947.
45 Belgian House of Representatives, Parliamentary Documents, no. 159, January 21, 1948.
46 Marguerite De Riemacker-Legot (1913–1977) was a lawyer, a Catholic MP, and a minister for family and housing during the 1960s.
47 Belgian Senate, Proceedings, July 10, 1947; House of Representatives, Proceedings, February 5, 1948.
48 Charles Janssens (1898–1982) was a lawyer, the mayor of Ixelles (1956), a liberal MP (1939–1965), and a member of the European Parliament (1958–1965).
49 Belgian House of Representatives, Proceedings, February 5, 1948, 18.
50 Marcel Philippart de Foy (1884–1966) was a lawyer and a Catholic MP from 1936 to 1958.
51 Belgian House of Representatives, Proceedings, February 5, 1948, 14–15.
52 *La femme magistrat? Mercuriale de M. le Procureur Général ff. L. Delwaide à l'audience solennelle de rentrée du 16 septembre 1946 et dont la Cour a ordonné l'impression* (Liège: Liège Appeal Court, 1946).
53 Ibid.
54 Belgian House of Representatives, February 5, 1948.
55 Leen Van Molle and Eliane Gubin, *Vrouw en politiek in België* (Tielt: Lannoo, 1998), 39–40; Catherine Jacques, *Le féminisme en Belgique de la fin du 19e siècle à 1970* (Bruxelles: Cahiers du CRISP, 2009).
56 Boigeol, "Les femmes et les cours," 107–129.
57 Nandrin, "De vrouwelijke advocaten," 165–172; *De vrouw in de rechtsbedeling. Rede uitgesproken door de H. Charles Colard, Advocaat Generaal, ter plechtige zitting van 15 september 1949 en waarvan het Hof het drukken bevolen heeft* (Brussels: Court of Cassation, 1949).
58 Moniteur belge, November 12–13, 1948, 9133.
59 Gubin et al., *Dictionnaire des femmes belges*, 447–448.
60 Geneviève Pevtschin, André Delvaux, and Jean Renkin, *Pierre Brachet et la défense de la liberté. Discours prononcé par G.P. à la séance solonnelle de rentrée*

à la conférence du Jeune Barreau de Bruxelles le 23 novembre 1946 (Brussels: Larcier, 1946).

61 Jacqueline Wiener-Henrion, "Geneviève Janssen-Pevtschin," *Jewish Movement Archive*, August 1, 2014, http://jwa.org/encyclopedia/article/janssen-pevtschin-genevieve.

62 Ibid.

63 Pierre Lambert, "*In memoriam* Geneviève Janssen-Pevtschin," *Revue trimestrielle des droits de l'homme* 13, no. 49 (2002): 3–4.

64 Nicole Berns-Lion, "Le monde des magistrats en Belgique," *Courier hebdomadaire du CRISP* 852 (1979): 15–21 ; information provided by the Service public fédéral Justice.

65 Belgian Senate, Proceedings, May 4, 2010, 60.

66 Berns-Lion, "Le monde des magistrates," 15–21.

67 Instituut voor de Gelijkheid van Vrouwen en Mannen, *Vrouwen aan de top 2012*, August 1, 2014, http://igvm-iefh.belgium.be/nl/binaries/65%20-%20Vrouwen-aan-de-Top-NL_tcm336–224819.pdf.

68 Ibid.

69 Ibid.

70 Van Molle and Gubin, *Vrouw en politiek in België*, 25.

71 It also lags behind the measures applied in Belgian politics. In the 1990s, a first quota law was voted in the Belgian Parliament. It stipulated that on electoral lists for national elections, only three fourths of the candidates could belong to the same sex. Later this number was raised to two thirds. As difficult as it had been for this first quota law to be debated and eventually voted and accepted in the Parliament, it was conversely very easy for it to be later further severed by the condition that those lists should count as many male as female candidates and that the zipper principle had to be applied for the first two positions on those lists. The political quota was also extended to the level of the regional and the EU elections in Belgium. See: Eva Schandevyl, Alison E. Woodward, Elke Valgaeren and Machteld De Metsenaere, "Genderquota in de wetenschap, het bedrijfsleven en de rechterlijke macht," *Res Publica* 55, no. 3 (2013): 359–374.

72 Ibid.

73 "Meer vrouwen nodig aan de top," *De Standaard*, November 10, 2009, http://www.standaard.be/cnt/ds2hpdqq

74 Eva Schandevyl, "An Introduction to Women in Law and Law Making in Nineteenth and Twentieth Century Europe," *Women in Law and Law Making*, 4, 17–19.

75 Ben Sloot, "Afspiegeling, quota en de samenstelling van de rechterlijke macht (Afscheidsrede aan de Open Universiteit op 16 maart 2012)," *Open Universiteit*, April 8, 2014, http://www.ou.nl/web/promoties-en-oraties/afscheidsredes.

76 James C. Albisetti, "Portia Ante Portas: Women and the Legal Profession in Europe, ca. 1870–1925," *Journal of Social History* 33, no. 4 (2000): 825–857, here 844.

77 Schultz and Shaw, "Introduction," 5–6, 15–16, 20.

7 The First Lawyers and Attorneys

The Struggle for Professional Recognition of Women's Rights in Yugoslavia (1918–1953)

Gordana Stojaković

Introduction

This chapter offers an overview of the history of the first female attorneys in Yugoslavia by focusing on the life and work of Katarina Lengold-Marinković (1904–1974) and Neđeljka (Neda) Božinović (1917–2001), two attorneys whose lives and professional choices are intertwined with the history of the women's rights struggle in Yugoslavia.[1] The time frame for this survey is the period from 1918–1953, beginning with the creation of the Kingdom of Serbs, Croats, and Slovenes (*Kraljevini Srba, Hrvata i Slovenaca*, the Kingdom of SHS), and ending with the cessation of the Women's Antifascist Front of Yugoslavia (AFŽ) in socialist Yugoslavia.[2] This was a period of great historical and social upheaval that led to a huge transformation of the status and role of women in society. For this analysis, I am drawing on the work of contemporary newspapers, the archive of the Lawyers' Association of Vojvodina, as well as on secondary literature and my own previous work on the biographies of famous women in Novi Sad and women's organizations in Novi Sad and Vojvodina from the nineteenth century to the end of 1953.[3] I am also drawing on the biographies of two female lawyers to analyze how women's roles in the social and political context of that period were redefined. Such analysis involves the recuperation of the professional work, activism, and personal choices of Božinović and Lengold-Marinković. The critical resources here include a biography of Božinović that I published in 2002, which is largely based on an oral history interview that I conducted with her shortly before her death in 2001. For the life of Lengold-Marinković, I am relying on the testimony of Milorad Botić (1913–2007), a lawyer from Novi Sad who knew her, as well as on contemporary publications.[4]

By singling out the life and work of Lengold-Marinković and Božinović, I hope to include not only part of the history of women's entrance into the legal profession but also the story of women's rights in Yugoslavia. Lengold-Marinković's activism was related to the civic women's organizations based in Novi Sad and Belgrade; Božinović's professional and activist work was significant more broadly in Yugoslavia though especially in Belgrade. Using a chronological approach, I will follow their professional and private lives (to the degree possible) to reconstruct their role in the broader context of women's rights in Yugoslavia in the period from 1918–1953. By combining a biographical approach with the context of the legal position of women, I hope to be able to provide a better understanding of the strategies of women's activist organizations, particularly feminist and communist ones, and the scope of their struggle. These two women's lives represent two different stages of women's history in Yugoslavia. Their professional experiences, their activism, and their life choices were interwoven with the history of women's struggle for their rights in Yugoslavia. Lengold-Marinković's significant role in the Women's Movement Alliance (hereafter Alliance) and in the Yugoslav Federation of University Women (YFUW) is highlighted below. My intention in the following analysis of these two female lawyers is to undertake a history of women in the legal profession and demonstrate their centrality to the Yugoslav women's rights movement. I also illustrate the vulnerability and instability of women's rights over time.

The professional history of female lawyers in Yugoslavia, especially connected to the general women's rights history, is little researched. What is known is that the first female lawyer appeared at a time of the Kingdom of Yugoslavia and that just before World War II there was a mass entry of girls to the University Law School in Belgrade.[5] The appearance of female judges and prosecutors through their entry into the Supreme Court and the Constitutional Court took place immediately following World War II after the Constitution of the Federal People's Republic of Yugoslavia was adopted.[6] At the same time, women and men became equal legally in all aspects of life and work.

In the first section of this chapter, I will contextualize the first female lawyers and jurists within the socio-political context in which they appeared. This was also an important moment for the establishment of feminist women's organizations. The second section is dedicated to the purposes and methods of the Alliance and Youth Section of the Women's Movement (Youth Section), including the collaboration and differences among these organizations to which Lenglod-Marinković and Božinović belonged. The third and the fourth sections demonstrate Lenglod-Marinković's and Božinović's professional and personal choices. In the concluding section, I argue that there was a significant legacy from the struggle for women's rights that was led by feminist civic organizations before World War II. This history is still not as well known as it merits. At the same time, since the legacy of women in socialist Yugoslavia is subject to historical revisionism, it is important that the testimony given by Božinović few weeks before her death be recorded and analyzed.

Yugoslavia and the Legal Position of Women, 1918–1953

World War I brought a dramatic change to the areas later known as Yugoslavia. While the war caused immense suffering, it also propelled these regions into the twentieth century. Politically, a shift occurred in 1919 when the monarchy headed by the Karađorđević dynasty was replaced by a constitutional monarchy with the creation of the Kingdom of SHS.[7] The old patriarchal society slowly cracked under the onslaught of new ideas and new social forces, which demanded change with a compelling insistence. Women's voices were among the many claiming reform. Legally and by custom, women in different parts of the Kingdom of SHS were subject to different levels of oppression, and some were among the most oppressed of all women in Europe. After the war efforts that had fallen heavily on the shoulders of women, the leaders of the women's movements hoped that the new state would recognize their war efforts and thus enact equality of the sexes as had happened in some European states.

There seemed to be some hope when in 1921 the Vidovdan Constitution of the Kingdom of SHS (St. Vitus's Day Constitution) was adopted and introduced the basic principles of democracy: the parliamentary system; civil rights and civic freedoms; and liberal, civic, political, and social organizations.[8] A study of lived experiences, however, illustrates that these constitutional and legislative provisions were often disregarded.[9] This was the case for voting rights. Under the provisions of the Vidovdan Constitution, active and passive voting rights were set by age. Article 70 of the constitution stipulated that a separate, special law was to regulate women's suffrage. But eventually, this law provided only for men to have a right to vote and also did not establish any other equal legal rights for women.[10] This relative freedom ended when on January 6, 1929 King Alexander[11] dismissed parliament and banned all political parties, trade unions, and national and religious organizations and imposed censorship on the press. The result of the so-called Sixth January Dictatorship (*Šestojanuarska diktatura*)[12] was the proclamation of a new constitution in 1931, the so-called *Oktoisani*,[13] which formally abolished many civic freedoms and civil rights. Women were still deprived of the basic political right, the right to vote, and they were not allowed into public service (i.e., the state administration) as judges or prosecutors.[14] The Law on Lawyers of the Kingdom of SHS that passed in 1928 and went into effect in 1929,[15] however, permitted women to practice law (i.e., to be attorneys). But the Law on Judges of the Regular Courts, in accordance with the new constitution, still stated in Article 2, Paragraph 2: "Females cannot be judges."[16] The Law on Public Prosecutors (1931) embodied the same discriminatory attitude toward women.[17]

Thus it was only in the late 1920s that women could begin to practice law officially. Before, however, there were some exceptions; for example, a certain Miss Roknić became the first female attorney candidate for the bar in Belgrade in 1911.[18] Little is known about her, but she must have received her legal education outside of Serbia[19] because the first woman graduated at Belgrade University only in 1914.[20] Considering that women could not officially exercise the legal professions, the number of female law students was relatively high before the Law on Lawyers of the Kingdom of SHS was passed in 1928. The University Law School in Subotica had, for example, in the first academic year of 1921–1922, 496 students registered from all over the Kingdom of SHS; among them were twelve women, who constituted 2.5% of the registered student population.[21] The number rose quickly after the law of 1928–1929 was passed. There were one thousand young women among four thousand students of the University Law School in Belgrade shortly before World War II.[22]

The prevailing notion in Yugoslav society was that women should not participate in political life or deal with public professions other than ones in the educational, medical, and clerical fields. Nevertheless, in 1923, Jelena Mihalović-Đorić, Smilja Jovanović-Krikner, and Ruža Vinterštajn-Jovanović passed the examination for judges and lawyers in Belgrade in the hopes of joining the profession.[23] At the time, however, women were denied the right to become judges. On the exclusion of women from the position of judges, Milica Vlajić, a member of the Alliance organization in Belgrade, explained that the laws that discriminated against women occurred in a society that supported the overall subordination of women.[24] The women's movement organized a protest against the exclusion of women from the profession of judges.[25] But still the Appeals Court for Croatia-Slavonia and Međumurje based in Zagreb in 1925 denied two supporting female judicial officers their right "to declare in criminal matters"[26] because women could not be judges, nor could they represent clients unless the clients were their husbands and only then in disputes involving values up to 500 dinars.[27]

By contrast, in 1929, women seemed accepted into the legal profession. According to women's rights advocate Milica Vlajić, women were "relatively easily allowed to be lawyers" because the private law practices were held in low regard and the prevailing attitude was that the lawyer's job was "so compromised that the women will not ruin it more."[28] Vlajić offers two reasons for the devaluation of private law practice: the possibility of abuse and the poor financial status of judges, so "all went to the attorneys."[29] The poor perception of the attorney's job led to a provision called "the new legal project" that planned seven years of internships for lawyer trainees.[30]

The area of the Kingdom of SHS was ethnically, religiously, politically, economically, and culturally strongly divided and as a result, civil and family law were also quite diverse, yet everywhere women experienced inequality under the law and in customs. In the Kingdom of Serbia, and later in the respective part of the Kingdom of Yugoslavia where the Serbian Civil Code had been adopted in 1844, Montenegro had its own customary law. The Austrian Civil Code of 1811 was in force in Croatia and Slavonia and other parts, while the Hungarian Civil Code covered the Vojvodina, and Sharia Law was in effect in Bosnia and Herzegovina.[31] The new state, however, allowed for all regions to maintain their own family codes, so there was a wide range of different regulations concerning marriage, divorce, and alimony, etc. But as a common basic denominator, it was evident that in all legal areas the law sanctioned the inequality of the sexes. This was still the case when Julka Chlapec-Gjorgjević, one of the leading feminists, wrote her review of Ferdo Čulinović's book *Žena u našem krivičnom pravu*,[32] a 1934 cross-section of the state of women's rights in all legal areas of the Kingdom of Yugoslavia. She stated that a woman, as a human being, was subordinate as far as the law was concerned since "she had no legal capacity equal to that of a man."[33] This was especially pronounced in families where the newly proposed, unified Civil Code of the Kingdom of Yugoslavia still allowed for a husband to be "the head of the family, to give a woman her family name, determine her domicile, manage the household and the entire life of his family."[34] As far as hereditary rights were concerned, the regional differences based on the customary law were still observed. This meant that women were still subject to traditional patriarchal domination. It was not until 1946 that a unified marriage law was established and women became the legal equals of men.[35]

Women faced considerable discrimination in work, society, and the family in the 1920s. Female teachers, for example, were only given the right to marry by choice in 1924.[36] They were prohibited from the position of the gymnasium (high school) director though and neither could become school administrators. Female civil servants could not rise to administrative heads of ministry departments. Female teachers could not become school administrators, and female clerks could not rise to administrative heads of ministry departments.[37] After the Kingdom of SHS was created in the 1920s, the mode of operation of women's civic organizations changed as well. Women started joining forces according to the ideas and goals of their organizations rather than by their religion and ethnicity. Belgrade, Zagreb, and Ljubljana became centers for women's activist organizations, where women's magazines based on their new activist agenda were printed. In this discriminatory climate, different women's societies and feminist groups unified in 1919 into the National Women's Alliance of the Kingdom of Serbs, Croats, and Slovenes (*Narodni ženski savez u Kraljevini Srba, Hrvata i Slovenaca*), a group which represented 205 organizations by 1921. The Feminist Alliance of the Kingdom of SHS was established in 1923. The organization was made up of the women's movement's organizations in Belgrade and Sarajevo, the Association of Yugoslav Women from Zagreb, and the General Women's Organization from Ljubljana. Since 1926, just the women's movement organizations constituted the Women's Movement Alliance (Alijansa ženskih pokreta u Kraljevini SHS).[38] The Alliance organizations in Vojvodina gained more power in the period from 1937 to 1940.[39] One of the leaders of the organization was the lawyer Katarina Lengold-Marinković. She lived in Novi Sad, far from Belgrade, the epicenter of the struggle for women's rights. Nonetheless, the contemporary women's newspapers and journals reported on events and followed the activities of the Alliance.[40] According to a report for 1926, the Alliance in that year was "gradually winning [the fight against] many prejudices"[41] and furthering women's rights.

The goals of the Women's Movements Alliance included equality with men in private and public life, equal education and professional opportunities, and equal pay for equal work. They also worked for reforms in marital rights, such as civil marriage in all regions, paid household work for women, child custody, and pension rights. The Alliance coordinated events with other national women's groups in the region, such as in Athens in 1926, to discuss the rights of female clerks at the Congress of the "Women's Little Entente," a regional organization consisting of Yugoslavia, Czechoslovakia, Romania, Bulgaria, Greece, and Poland.[42]

Between the two World Wars, the Alliance continued the practice of monitoring legislation regarding women's rights.[43] The Belgrade organization of the Alliance engaged "women jurists and lawyers" to provide comments on the design of any new legislation related to women's rights.[44] The philosopher and feminist, Dr. Ksenija Atanasijević,[45] wrote that it was the feminist organization that, "among all of the Yugoslav women's associations, was struggling to secure women's rights"[46] and to address the overall subordination of women in society. She stressed how difficult it was to fight against the "theory of the inferiority of women and the naturalness of her subordinate position."[47] In such circumstances, the feminists of the Alliance thought that the struggle for women's voting rights was the most important goal, and when all women won political rights they would be able to occupy all positions equally with men.[48]

The Secretariat of Women Socialists,[49] a part of the Socialist Workers' Party of Yugoslavia,[50] was established in 1919 with the aim of raising women's awareness about the necessity of fighting for women's rights, particularly political rights. Prohibition of activities of the Communist Party of Yugoslavia (KPJ) caused the communists to join the trade unions and women's organizations in order to continue political work. Communist women, mainly students, joined the Alliance, and there they established in 1935 a separate wing known as the Youth Section.[51] Božinović, then a law student, was a member. Based on the directives of the KPJ, the communist members of the Youth Section went to the factories to organize the special women's sections of the trade unions. Some trade unions established female sections: the Association of Banking, Insurance, Commercial, and Industrial Clerks (SBOTIČ) and the Union of Textile Workers.

The female intellectuals had their own association, the Yugoslav Federation of University Women (YFUW), founded in 1928 in Belgrade. This organization cooperated with the International Institute of Intellectual Cooperation in Paris and the International Labour Organization in Geneva.[52] This association operated until the beginning of World War II and it was the only feminist civic organization that renewed its work in socialist Yugoslavia in 1951.[53] Božinović was instrumental in the re-establishment of this organization.[54]

The complexity of the Serbian (and Yugoslav) women's political front between the two World Wars, in a situation where few women (mostly those who were college-educated) were politically active, resulted in many women getting involved in two or more organizations.[55] Thus, Lengold-Marinković, a lawyer by profession, was one of the leaders of the feminist Alliance in Vojvodina and a member of the YFUW, whereas Božinović was a member of the Youth Section under communist control as well as the YFUW.

Women's rights concerns took a subordinate place in the state priorities of the Kingdom of Yugoslavia. The leaders of the newly emerging state were preoccupied with the problem of uniting diverse and often reluctant cultural, ethnic, and political groups. As a result, the women's movement made very little progress in its struggle for equal rights. Women continued to be subordinate to men and subject to localized and domestic forms of patriarchy, which varied according to the ethnic, cultural, and religious characteristics of the group.

With the fascist occupation in April 1941, the years of the constitutional monarchy were over. The armed uprising by the KPJ began in July of the same year when the first partisan units were formed. The People's Liberation Struggle (NOB) included many ethnic communities, as well as a great number of women who participated in it as partisans in the People's Liberation Army (NOV) or as members of the illegal groups in the cities and as members of the Antifascist Women's League (AFŽ) of Yugoslavia.[56] The AFŽ was established in 1942 in Bosanski Petrovac, a town in western Bosnia and Herzegovina, and became the women's mass organization during and after World War II. In the period between 1942 and 1945, women participated in resistance activism by carrying arms and serving as couriers, doctors, and nurses and in other kinds of service roles. In some areas women were active in leading bodies of the NOV, in the so-called "People's Liberation Committees." Barbara Jančar-Webster concluded in her book on female partisans that the transformation of women's status in Yugoslavia during the four years of World War II occurred rapidly, unlike the interwar era. By the end of the war, women achieved the right to enter into society "on male terms."[57]

When World War II ended in May 1945, women demanded equal rights based on their contributions during the war, especially emphasizing their role as partisans, and invoked the platform of equality that the KPJ had adopted before the war. The Constitution of the Federal People's Republic of Yugoslavia was passed on January 31, 1946 and defined the new state as a "Federal People's Republic, a community of equal nations where the people have sovereignty."[58] Women gained the right to vote and the constitution (Article 24) guaranteed the equality of women: "Women are equal to men in all fields of state, economic and socio-political life. For equal work, women are granted equal pay as men and they enjoy special protection in employment. In particular, the state protects the interests of a mother and her child by the establishment of nurseries, kindergartens and children's homes, as well as the mother's right to a paid leave before and after childbirth."[59] Laws effecting personal and family life also corresponded to the constitution. For example, possessions acquired by the economic activity of a husband or wife during marriage would henceforth be owned in common, and women could keep their maiden name. Mothers had the same custody rights as fathers, and in case of the father's death, the mother was the legal guardian of her children.[60]

Despite women's high rate of illiteracy, they became engaged in the political life of the country in socialist Yugoslavia.[61] This was possible because many women became involved in the activities organized by the AFŽ, which was regarded as the organizational form of the KPJ for work among women. In fact, the massive appearance of women in the public sphere in the period from 1945 to 1950 was one of the key features of political and social life of socialist Yugoslavia. According to the census of 1948, the country had 15,842,000 inhabitants, 8,227,000 of whom were women. Out of the total 3,163,000 who were illiterate, 34.4% were women, with the lowest rates in Slovenia (2.5%) and Vojvodina (15.5%) and the highest in Kosovo and Metohija (78.4%).[62] In the first post-war elections in socialist Yugoslavia, 88% of women voted, and twenty-two women were elected members of the National Parliament.[63] In the Supreme Court of the People's Republic of Serbia in 1948, four women were seated as judges. In 1946, legal obstacles were removed to permit women to serve in the judiciary on an equal basis with men.[64]

The KPJ's ideology called for an active role for women in the social and economic spheres: they became workers with exemplary achievements, members of cooperatives, politicians ("socio-political workers"), and economically independent women who had mastered various professions. Introducing women to the new legislation, however, was a problem in rural and underdeveloped areas despite the importance of reforms to address infanticide, abandonment of children born out of wedlock, and maternity leave. Women were ill-informed of their legal rights. After the Second Congress of the Serbian AFŽ (1948), Vojka Demajo, a judge of the People's Republic of Serbia's Supreme Court, suggested that the "Mother and Child" section of the AFŽ should provide legal assistance to women to help them understand the rights that the law provided to women.

The social and political involvement of women began to decline in 1950 when the workers' management system was introduced. The social welfare provisions intended for children and mothers implemented before had become an expensive project almost overnight. Women were offered a high child care allowance, so many of them left work. Only rural women were still getting special support because the project of the socialist transformation of the villages had still not been completed.[65]

In terms of the women's movement, however, the new socialist state dissolved the earlier women's organizations. Until 1953, the AFŽ was the most important women's organization and it enjoyed support from women across the social strata. The organization dedicated itself to the rebuilding of the country and society, focusing on welfare before feminism. From 1950 to 1953, however, AFŽ activities subsided. Vague directives given at the

Third Congress of the AFŽ (1950) contributed to the members' disorientation. At the time, women in the AFŽ debated important questions, such as the double burden of women and how to channel women's activism. The AFŽ was formally abolished at the organization's Fourth Congress in 1953. At that last congress, Neda Božinović spoke on the legal status of women in marriage and family. She complained that the laws and principles of socialism were incomprehensible to people in Yugoslavia, where the patriarchal tradition was far stronger than communist ideology.[66]

The Ideological Trenches: Revolution vs. Reform

Feminist organizations attempted to change the situation of women within the patriarchal society through reform efforts such as lobbying, campaigns, and petitions. On the other side, communist women fought against capitalism to change the socio-political system. For communists, the women's issue was an integral part of the working class struggle that should be resolved by the revolution.[67] At its Fifth National Conference in 1940, the KPJ defined women's issues both separate from and also integral to the struggles of the working class. Women's separate and special demands were pointed out in the fields of suffrage, equal pay for equal work, abolition of nighttime work for women, paid maternity leave, prostitution and double moral standards, protection of children, and equality of children born in and out of wedlock.[68] All these issues were advocated also by Božinović.

Katarina Lengold-Marinković, on the other hand, promoted the ideas presented by Alojzija Štebi, one of the leaders of the Alliance, in her article entitled "Our Requirements" (1938).[69] These demands were broadly conceived: women's suffrage and full legal capacity for women, compulsory civil marriage and civil jurisdiction of the courts in matrimonial disputes, equality of spouses in marriage and child custody as well as complete equality of illegitimate children. She wanted women to have the same rights in inheritance and property law as well as to establish women's household work as paid labor. She proposed equal wages in civil service; the promotion of women in the Labour Inspectorate to control the "social welfare and social hygiene regulations; and extension of insurance rights to cover periods of illness, accident, old age, and death for the population of both sexes working in agriculture."[70] If we analyze the demands of the feminists and the communists in the Alliance, we can see that this was a unique platform in its reference to equality of men and women in domestic, personal, and political life.

The KPJ program delineated the different approaches to addressing women's issues: "Feminism sets common requirements of all classes of women separate from the requirements of the working people by emphasizing women's common requirements in conflict and in fighting against men. Feminism hides class under women's issues, and thereby deters women of the masses from the struggle against capitalism and against class society in general. [. . .] Feminism in our ranks should be marked as a right-wing opportunistic effort to help the civic women's movement by spreading the illusion that some reforms could supposedly solve the problem in the class society."[71]

These ideological differences were first manifested in different ways of understanding the struggle for women's rights. Ksenija Atanasijević considered that despite the criticism that the Alliance's struggle for women's rights was slow and inactive, one must take into account that the women's liberation confronted very conservative conditions. Thus the greatest effects would be achieved if the women's liberation actions were carried out cautiously and in stages.[72]

In addition to accusations of slowness and tepidity, the feminists of the Alliance were criticized for lack of leadership and avoidance of political parties. Atanasijević argued that they should avoid demagoguery, the imposition of leaders, and all the methods used by men, such as aggression and imposition.[73] The differences between the communist and feminist women's organizations proved to be insurmountable.

The first mass action for women's suffrage had been organized in 1935 and led by the feminists of the Alliance. In Novi Sad, Belgrade, Zagreb, Užice, Šabac, Ljubljana, Banja Luka, Skopje, and other towns, they organized women's conferences and passed the declarations favoring the active and passive voting rights for women.[74] The declaration was addressed to the legislative authorities of the Kingdom of Yugoslavia. Their demands were rejected by the political elites who participated in the parliament. The second action for women's suffrage was led by the communist members of the Youth Section in 1939 who edited the newspaper *Žena danas* (Woman Today) in which they launched a national campaign to collect signatures for women's suffrage.[75] Without coordination with the leaders of the Alliance, they invited women to organize the committees, conferences, and rallies.[76] This event precipitated the open conflict between the Youth Section's members and the leadership of the Alliance. The management of the Alliance advocated that, due to the outbreak of World War II and the "extraordinarily difficult conditions,"[77] a delegation composed of representatives of the Alliance, the Yugoslav Women's Association, and the YFUW should submit demands for women's suffrage to the Deputy Prime Minister Vlatko Maček and the Minister of Justice Lazar Marković. On several previous occasions, such demands had been rejected on the grounds that women were politically unreliable and that "the present time is not favorable for experiments."[78] After the failure of direct lobbying, the Alliance leaders decided to collect signatures for women's suffrage through its organizations in locations where there were no women's movement's organizations sponsored by the Yugoslav Women's Association. At the same time, they decided to organize a conference in Belgrade with the participation of the representatives of the Alliance from several towns. Božinović recalled that the two organizations intended their events to be complementary. Cooperation, however, was not the norm.[79]

The first of these two conferences for women's suffrage was held in Belgrade on November 23, 1939 with the participation of many women's organizations, including the Alliance, the YFUW, the Women's League for Peace and Freedom, and others. Among the participants was Olga Alkalaj,[80] a law student and a representative of legal apprentices, and Božinović, a law student.[81] The communists and members of the Yugoslav Communist Youth League (SKOJ) dominated among the speakers. Three days later the Alliance held another conference for women's suffrage at the same place where feminist leader Lengold-Marinković spoke first. Of all the speakers, only one was a communist.

These kinds of parallel actions were an introduction to the upcoming conflicts of the Youth Section members with the leaders of the Alliance regarding the form the struggle for women's rights should take. The Youth Section members did not agree to settle for partial actions like women's gatherings and lobbying for women's suffrage as proposed by the leaders of the Alliance. They rejected changes within the patriarchal structure but advocated for a general change in the system with no fear of repercussions.

Through these two parallel events for women's suffrage in Yugoslavia, hundreds of thousands of women's signatures were raised.[82] They did not change the political status of women, but the mass action for women's political rights successfully channeled women's demands and gave women the experience of working collectively across class lines.[83] The general public did not approve. Some of their prominent opponents were members of the right-winged student organization, The Rally,[84] which denigrated the participants as "Jewish communist propagandists" and advocates of "free love."[85] Such labels often caused feminists problems in their workplaces and in their private lives. That was why the majority of female activists opted for milder forms of demonstration for women's rights, which the Youth Section named "pale methods and anemic measures."[86] In fact, it claimed that the Alliance was suffering a "depoliticization of the women's movement," which was leading to its self-destruction. Consequently, the Youth Section left the Alliance in 1940 and founded the Young Girls Cooperative.[87]

Katarina Lengold-Marinković (1904–1974): The Experience of Struggle in Patriarchy

Katarina Lengold-Marinković represents the intertwined history of women's access to the legal profession and the feminist movement that avoided political parties within the larger context of the rise of communism in Yugoslavia. Lengold-Marinković was a female lawyer from a lower middle class family. Božinović came from a family where her father was a lower-level tax official and her mother a housewife. The two biographies describe female lawyers' fight from two different political, local, and cultural backgrounds to reach a common goal by choosing different methods.

By concentrating on their biographies, the struggles come alive and acquire individual faces.

Lengold-Marinković was born in Petrovaradin, now a southern part of Novi Sad. She graduated from an elementary and high school for women in Novi Sad.[88] In 1923, she enrolled in the Law Faculty in Subotica and graduated in 1927. At the time of her studies, women were not allowed to work as lawyers. After 1929, women could become lawyers but not judges. According to memories of Milorad Botić, a well-known Novi Sad lawyer of an older generation, Lengold-Marinković's decision to practice law was acceptable to her colleagues within a few years. He remembered that no one had anything against female lawyers in courts, since they were well versed in law, agile, accurate, conscientious, and persistent. Botić, who knew Lengold-Marinković since her apprenticeship, remembered that she was a proper young lawyer appointed to his office by one of the most respected lawyers in Novi Sad, Dr. Oscar Cipris. She did part of her apprenticeship in the District Court in Novi Sad. The "Directory of Lawyers" of the Vojvodina Lawyers' Association (001–1200) states under number 9/1932 that "the Examination Committee confirms that the trainee lawyer Lengold Katarina, maiden name Marinković, passed her final (bar) exam on 25 February 1932 and got trained as a lawyer, so her certificate was issued and delivered to her on this occasion."[89] She took the bar oath on September 2, 1933. Lengold-Marinković was the only female lawyer in the 1930s who practiced law in Novi Sad until World War II. Despite the common prejudice that the legal practice was a "man's profession" and ill-suited to women,[90] she was appreciated and respected by her colleagues. According to Botić's testimony, most of her cases were in the field of civil law, and most of her clients were women who hired her for matters involving divorce, property division, and other situations related to marriage and family law.

During World War II Novi Sad was occupied by the Hungarian Army, allies of the Germans. Occupation authorities organized a new system of government, administration, and judiciary that excluded all persons who were not politically and ethnically eligible. Lengold-Marinković turned out to be one of the lawyers prohibited from working. But immediately after the liberation she was appointed "Guardian of the Lawyers' Association of Vojvodina" due to her professional reputation and honorable conduct during the occupation, which included the preservation of the archives and the books of the lawyers' association.[91] Lengold-Marinković held the office of a guardian for two years, until 1946. The "Directory of Lawyers" recorded that, upon her own request, she was taken off the list on March 15, 1949, at the age of only 45. Due to a lack of written accounts and records I must rely on the memories of Milorad Botić, who testified that she was disappointed by the attitude of the new authorities who appointed only Communist Party members to the decision-making positions in the lawyers' association. Until her retirement in 1956, Lengold-Marinković practiced law in Belgrade and Novi Sad as a lawyer. After retirement, she lived withdrawn in Sremski

Karlovci, a small town near Novi Sad and "still enjoyed a high reputation among her colleagues."[92]

Lengold-Marinković was fully engaged in the struggle for women's rights throughout her whole career as a lawyer until 1941. By her own orientation, her activist engagement supported liberal feminism. She was the leader of the Alliance in the Vojvodina and a member of the YFUW. She organized branches of the Alliance in the town of Sombor and Petrovgrad (today Zrenjanin). But Lengold-Marinković's activist work is difficult to track because she was not a scholar, nor was she a woman who recorded her own activism.[93] It is evident though that her life and work were tied to the Vojvodina, the northern part of Serbia, which until 1918 was part of the Habsburg monarchy and after that of the Kingdom of SHS (1918–1941), and finally of socialist Yugoslavia (from 1945 until her death in 1974). The Vojvodina had actually been the forefront of the struggle for women's rights;[94] from early on women had participated in the election rallies demanding the right to vote, had set up their own magazines, opened women's libraries, and had been active in the international women's conferences for women's suffrage.[95] In the Vojvodina, women gained (for a short time) the right to vote in 1918, and seven women were elected to the Grand National Assembly only to vote for the unification with the Kingdom of Serbia.[96] Lengold-Marinković's professional and personal choices were rooted in a solid foundation in her women's activism in the Vojvodina, which even spawned a Women's Party founded in 1928.[97]

According to contemporary witnesses she showed a "dignified, fair and strong performance" as a lawyer and was pioneering in opening the space for other women entering the legal profession.[98] Each segment of the professional path of Lengold-Marinković was a struggle to prove that women could accomplish the tasks involved in education, apprenticeship, and work as a lawyer. Similar to the first female physicians who could work only as gynecologists[99] or pediatricians, the first female lawyers had to fight to conquer other specialist fields within the profession besides civil law.

An important part of Lengold-Marinković's career happened in a patriarchal society in which women struggled for their personal, familial, and political rights. Thus feminism was central to her work primarily because she belonged to a small number of women of her time who had experienced divorce in an environment that saw divorced women through patriarchal lenses. Even Lengold-Marinković's choice of profession and "living from her own work," without the help of family or husband, can be interpreted as a rebellion against the socially constructed roles for women whereby women gained economic security through marriage. Furthermore, to start studying law at a time when women could not be lawyers or judges was not only courageous, but it was a political statement claiming women's equal rights with a new set of skills acquired at the law schools. On March 12, 1938, for example, she gave a lecture titled "On the Rights of Women: Personal,

Family and Political" at the celebration of the International Women's Day in the hotel Sloboda in Novi Sad.[100] Lecturing to women on their rights and raising legal questions within the women's organization set a new pattern in the fight for women's equal rights fight involving the special competences the female lawyers.

Besides her fight for women's equal rights in the family and political area, her most important contribution to women's rights was the conquest of economic independence through the lawyer's profession before the concept of women's economic independence became an important factor in the process of women's emancipation under socialism. Her bequest to women had lasting effects and perhaps she could have done even more, but in 1974 she died in a car accident in Zagreb on her way to the meeting of the International Federation of University Women. There is little data about her personal life. It is known that she was married for a short time and that she had no children.

Božinović Neđeljka Neda (1917–2001): The Biography of the Yugoslav Communist

The case history of Neđeljka (Neda) Božinović shows the connection between the communist and feminist civic organizations before and after World War II, the AFŽ, and the heritage of women in socialism. Božinović believed that women's emancipation could not happen just by solving class conflicts.

Božinović was born in Topolo, a village seventy kilometers away from Dubrovnik (now Croatia). She finished elementary school in Ston, her first year of high school in Stolac, and the rest of her high school in Kotor. In 1935 she enrolled in the Law Faculty in Belgrade and finished her studies in 1939. Speaking about the situation of girls studying in Belgrade, Božinović testified as follows:

> Before World War II in Yugoslvia,[101] the atmosphere was terrible. All women who attended school—high school, for example—were considered to be prostitutes. Not to be misunderstood: all without exception. The most advanced layer of the civil society tried to suppress it, but their way of life, at the same time, often provided the material to treat women in this way. It was very difficult to find a way of life and expression which was in line with emancipation, and which would at the same time make you get accepted by a wider class of people.[102]

A left-wing student herself, she actively participated in the work of women's and students' organizations: the Youth Section, the Association of Students of Belgrade University, the Students' Legal Society, the SKOJ, and the YFUW. She belonged to the communist liberal stream[103] that advocated cooperation with women's civic organizations, despite the fact that within the communist party feminism was characterized as a backwards movement:

> I would say that the civil women's movement always had a limit to which it is allowed to go, but could not go any further than that because of its male partners. This was very typical of the Youth Section of the Women's Movement. We were balancing three movements: the women's, peace[104] and, towards the end of the forties, the Youth Section of [the] Women's Movement. . . . The supporters of the peace movement were mostly young men and women from a bourgeois background. We had a lot of trouble with those coming from the workers' classes, because their aspirations were somewhat different. It took some time to convince each other on—why equality for women was necessary. It was accepted in a manner that was not always fruitful.[105]

Božinović became a member of the KPJ in 1939, and in 1941 she participated in the NOV both as a partisan and as a political activist. She was a member of the District and the County Committee of the KPJ in Nikšić, a Deputy Political Commissar of the Nikšić Third Battalion, and the first in rank in the political department (Politodel) of the Kozara[106] Fifth Brigade and the First Proletarian Division. By the end of World War II she achieved the rank of a major in the NOV. From 1945 and until her retirement in 1974,[107] she held a number of political offices in socialist Yugoslavia: Organizational Secretary of the Committee of the SKJ in Belgrade, Instructor of the Central Committee of the Communist Party of Serbia, Deputy Chairperson of the Commission for the State Control (in the Federal People's Republic of Yugoslavia), Assistant Minister of Labor of the Federal People's Republic of Yugoslavia, Secretary and Vice President of the Veterans' Association of Yugoslavia, Secretary of State for the General Administration Tasks and Budget of the Federal Executive Council of Yugoslavia, a member of the Federal Parliament (1958–1963), and a Judge of the Constitutional Court (1963–1972). Some of the decorations and awards she received included the Partisans' Memorial Medal of 1941 and the golden wreath of the Order of Brotherhood and Unity.

Unlike the civic feminist approach to which Lengold-Marinković belonged, Božinović was among the leaders of a project which mobilized huge masses of women from villages and towns, young and old, educated and illiterate, politically active and politically inactive.[108] All of them participated in the project of women's emancipation that began by educating women for various jobs, providing reading classes,[109] organizing conferences,[110] and working in different sections of the AFŽ. This work resulted in women's involvement in economy and political life. In socialist Yugoslavia, the emancipation process meant not only equality between men and women by diminishing women's economic independence through their "participation in socially productive work," but also by providing the conditions that each woman had the opportunity to be educated, employed with equal pay as men.[111]

Božinović's life path was also a struggle. Before World War II, as a law student and a communist, she was politically active within the Youth Section. Her status was dangerous because an affiliation to the KPJ was considered the greatest threat to the monarchist system.[112] Nevertheless, there was great solidarity among the members within the KPJ, where female members held important and responsible positions. Božinović's political activity and her organization of life and work were both part of a collective plan and support created by the communist women. The solidarity among the KPJ members was transferred and developed during the NOB, and as a result Božinović conquered new roles: that of a partisan (a major in their ranks) and a political commissar of the brigades during World War II.

After the liberation, Božinović worked on a comprehensive women's emancipation project until 1953. This work was ideologically and politically planned by the KPJ and coordinated by the AFŽ's organizations on the federal, regional, and local levels. It was a broad effort of continuous education actions in relation to women's rights, including mass agitation for women's voting campaigns, women's participation in government organizations, projects for women's education, and women's involvement in the economy and rural agricultural cooperatives within the years of 1945–1953. At the same time, a battle against the brutal conditions and backwardness of women in some parts of socialist Yugoslavia was fought by educating women on infanticide, contagious diseases, abortion (which was criminalized) the necessity of giving birth in maternity wards, and establishing nurseries and kindergartens. It was also fought by enlightening these women on laws such as the law that prohibited wearing a "*feredža*" or a "*zar*"[113] (Muslim veils) (1951 Serbia).

During the breakup and fall of the Socialist Federal Republic of Yugoslavia (1990–1991), Božinović re-engaged in the work of the women's organizations and anti-war peace groups such as: the SOS Hotline for Women and Children Victims of Violence, the Center for Antiwar Action, and the Women's Parliament. However, her activism was mostly associated with the Women in Black peace group. In addition to her important work as an activist, the publicist work of Božinović includes important writings all published in Belgrade.

There Once Was a Country: For Not to Forget

In my book on Božinović, *Neda—A Biography*, I used the phrase "There Once was a Country" to stress the importance of the socialist period in relation to the fundamental improvement of the legal and social status of Yugoslav women. Božinović's testimony revealed a much wider and deeper aspect of our precursors' struggle for women's rights, which provides insights on communist history, and on women's civic and feminist organizations as well as their agents and the possibility for women to make a professional career as Božinović did. This legacy was fairly unknown, just as the legacy of women in socialist Yugoslavia may remain unknown to future generations.

The analysis of the socio-political context in which Lengold-Marinković and Božinović started their careers as attorneys shows that theirs were bold steps forward for women entering the public sphere. Those were no easy or certain plans, for their aspirations were not in alignment with the standard female roles, which meant in the patriarchal society of Serbia that women were restrained by the patronage of a father and a husband. Between the Vojvodina in the north and the rest of Serbia, there were significant cultural differences regarding the roles of women in Serbian society. Women in the Vojvodina, as was the case with Lengold-Marinković, had a better starting position than those south of the Sava and Danube rivers.[114]

The analysis of the professional work and activism of Lengold-Mariković and Božinović shows the continuity of struggles for women's human rights, both through the efforts of feminist and communist women's organizations and personal life choices. These two are parallel lines: activism and a feminist testimony by living one's own life along unexplored paths.

Based on the biography of both attorneys it is evident that the immersion in the ideological framework and the constructed role of women in the socio-political context were not the only coordinates for the path to female emancipation. Change on a personal and family level occurred slowly if at all. Neither Božinović nor Lengold-Marinković spoke about their personal choices regarding family, reflecting the broader social taboo against exposing the private sphere. The political and professional engagements of Lengold-Marinković and Božinović reflect their responses to the socio-political context and their own ideological beliefs and show how intertwined ideological choices and career chances for women were in socialist Yugoslavia.

The results of the broadly planned women's emancipation project in socialist Yugoslavia could be measured according to the criteria assessing the position of women in the society, including the legal provisions and the extent of women's participation in the political and economic life of the country. In this context, women in socialist Yugoslavia made significant progress from 1945 to 1953. By introducing equal rights for women and special protection of mothers and children, socialist Yugoslavia did provide legal equality for women. However, there were major differences in the potential exercising of these rights depending on the regional differences throughout the country, as well as whether women lived in rural as opposed to urban areas.

The personal and professional trajectories of Lengold-Marinković and Božinović exemplify two steps in the Yugoslav women's emancipation project. Lengold-Marinkovic's trajectory signals a personal struggle and professional development in the field of law aimed at making even the smallest advances by setting a personal example and working professionally. Božinović's example implied that education in a legal profession would become operational in a plan with a wider political platform, that of legal equalization of men and women, and a social one, that of a collective effort to educate women to get qualified enough for their massive entry into the public sphere. Their lives echo the broader narrative of women's expanding liberty in the early twentieth century: that of the right to practice a profession, to be politically active, and to control their private lives.

Acknowledgments

Parts of this chapter were adapted from Stojaković, Gordana, ed. *Neda—jedna biografija*. Novi Sad : Futura publikacije. 2002 and Stojaković, Gordana, ed. *Znamenite žene Novog Sada I*. Novi Sad : Futura publikacije. 2001, 42, 57, 215–217.

Notes

1 The term "Yugoslavia," without determinants, is a geographical one: it includes the area of the current independent states of Slovenia, Croatia, Bosnia and Herzegovina, Montenegro, Macedonia, and Serbia. Before the breakup of the Socialist Federal Republic of Yugoslavia, there were the following countries in this area: the Kingdom of SHS (1918–1929), the Kingdom of Yugoslavia (1929–1941), the Democratic Federal Yugoslavia (1943–1946), the Federal People's Republic of Yugoslavia (1946–1963), and the Socialist Federal Republic of Yugoslavia (1963–1992).

2 AFŽ Yugoslavia was abolished in 1953 by a political decision of the Yugoslav Communist League (SKJ). The Yugoslav Communist League before 1952 was the Communist Party of Yugoslavia (KPJ).

3 Gordana Stojaković ed., *Znamenite žene Novog Sada I* (Novi Sad: Futura publikacije, 2001); Gordana Stojaković, "Skica za studiju: Počeci feminističkog pokreta u Vojvodini (1748–1941)," in *Znamenite žene Novog Sada I*, ed. Gordana Stojaković (Novi Sad: Futura publikacije, 2001), 17–23; Gordana Stojaković, "Skica za potret: Antifašistički front žena Vojvodine 1942–1953," in *Partizanke, žene u Narodnooslobodilačkoj borbi*, ed. Daško Milinović and Zoran Petakov (Novi Sad: Cenzura, 2011), 13–38; Gordana Stojaković, *Rodna perspektiva u novinama Antifašističkog fronta žena (1945–1953)* (Novi Sad: Zavod za ravnopravnost polova, 2012).

4 The data about Katarina Lengold-Marinković I received from Milorad Botić based on discussions we had in late 1999 and based on the text that Botić had written about Lengold-Marinković for the *Enciklopedija Novog Sada* (1999). Milorad Botić (1913–2007) was a prominent member of the Lawyers' Association of Vojvodina (established as the Lawyers' Association of Novi Sad in 1921) and editor of the *Glasnik Advokatske komore Vojvodine* (1952–1972). Milorad Botić, "Katarina Lengold-Marinković," in *Enciklopedija Novog Sada*, ed. Dušan Popov no. 12 (Novi Sad: Novosadski klub 1999), 320–321.

5 *Istorijat Fakulteta*, last modified 2012, accessed June 29, 2012, http://www.ius.bg.ac.rs/istorijat/default_cir.htm. Marija Milutinovic-Punktatorka (1810–1875) was among the first female lawyers in Belgrade in 1847 in a pre-professionalization era (see Stojaković, *Znamenite žene Novog Sada I*, 74–75.

6 Ivana Pantelić, *Partizanke kao građanke* (Beograd: Institut za savremenu istoriju / Evoluta, 2011), 71.

7 According to the census of 1921, the Kingdom of SHS had 11,984,919 inhabitants, with around two million of them being ethnic minorities: Germans,

Hungarians, Romanians, Poles, Czechs, Russians, Albanians, and others. Branko Petranović, *Istorija Jugoslavije 1918–1978* (Beograd: Nolit, 1981), 29.

8 The Constitution was adopted in 1921 on a Serbian religious holiday, Vidovdan (June 28). Vidovdan is also the day when the Battle of Kosovo took place on June 28, 1389.

9 Ljubomirka Krkljuš, "Pravni položaj žene u Vojvodini pre Drugog svetskog rata," in *Zbornik Matice srpske za društvene nauke*, ed. Stojanov Mladen, no. 88 (Novi Sad: Matica srpska, 1990), 96.

10 Ibid.

11 Aleksandar Karađorđević (1888–1934).

12 The January 6th Dictatorship (*Šestojanuarska diktatura*) began on January 6, 1929 and lasted until September 3, 1931 when the Oktoisani Constitution entered by force into the Kingdom of Yugoslavia.

13 Adopted by a decree "from higher instances."

14 Krkljuš, "Pravni položaj žene," 97.

15 The Law on Lawyers of the Kingdom of SHS was passed in December 1928 (Krkljuš, "Pravni položaj žene," 97). The Secretary of the Lawyers' Association of Vojvodina, Dejan Ukropina, gave me the information that the mentioned law was passed in 1928 and came into force on March 17, 1929. *Advokatska komora Srbije*, accessed June 29, 2012, http://www.advokatska-komora.co.rs/vojvodina.

16 Krkljuš, "Pravni položaj žene," 97.

17 Ibid.

18 "At the Belgrade lawyer Mr. Nikola Nikolić's request the Belgrade Trial Court allowed Miss. Roknić, an accomplished lawyer, entry in the list of law trainees. This is (?) the first Serbian female attorney candidate. The Court will decide later whether she will become a lawyer." *Ženski svet* 5 (1911): 118.

19 Miss Roknić probably completed her law studies outside of the Kingdom of Serbia at another European University. The faculty of law in Zagreb was established in 1776 but contains no information on female law students and graduates on its official website. *Pravni Fakultet*, http://www.pravo.unizg.hr/. The faculty of law in Ljubljana was established in 1920. Barbara Jančar-Webster, *Women and Revolution in Yugoslavia 1941–1945* (Denver, CO: Arden Press, Inc, 1990), 13.

20 The faculty of law in Belgrade was established in 1841; the first female graduated in 1914. *Istorijat Fakulteta*.

21 *Pravni Fakultet u Subotici*, accessed June 29, 2012, http://www.gradsubotica.co.rs/pravni-fakultet–u-subotici/.

22 *Istorijat Fakulteta*.

23 Milica Vlajić, "Žene advokati," *Ženski pokret* 8 (1923): 338.

24 "Žene, koje imaju i koje će imati kvalifikacije za sudije i volje za taj poziv, biće udaljene od tih poziva, sve dok i poslednji protivnik ne odboluje predrasude, sve dok se ne isčeprkaju i svi poslednji mogući i nemogući razlozi protiv postavljenja žena za sudije i dok se najzad ti razlozi ne pobiju i kod nas . . ." Vlajić, Ibid., 339.

25 Ibid., 338. This was a notice of protest, but there was not a record in the feminist journal *Ženski pokret* that the event took place.

26 Nikolić Lazar, "Institucija vlasti muža: istorijsko pravni aspekti," in *Mapiranje mizoginije u Srbiji: diskursi i prakse*, ed. Marina Blagojević, no. 1 (Beograd: AŽIN 2000), 261.

27 Ibid.

28 Vlajić, "Žene advokati," 338.

29 Ibid., 339.

30 Ibid.

31 The Austrian Civil Code (without novelties from 1914, 1915, and 1916) was in force in Croatia, Slavonia, and a part of the Military District in the Vojvodina (in the District Courts in Novi Sad, Bela Crkva, Kovin, Uljma, and in Pančevo where some provisions of the Hungarian Civil Code were also valid), the area of the

district courts in Kastav, Krk, Rab, Pag, Čakovec, and Prelog. The Austrian Civil Code with the novelties (from 1914, 1915, and 1916) was in force in Slovenia and Dalmatia and partly in Istria and Prekomurje. The Hungarian Civil Code was in force in the Vojvodina without the areas mentioned above. The Serbian Civil Code was in force in the former Kingdom of Serbia. The Montenegrian Property Code was in force in the former Kingdom of Montenegro. The Austrian Civil Code and the Sharia Law for Muslims were in force in the territory of Bosnia and Herzegovina. Ana Božić, *Položaj žene u privatnom pravu kroz istoriju do danas* (Beograd: Beogradski univerzitet/ Pravni fakultet, 1939), 10–15.

32 Ferdo Čulinović, *Žena u našem krivičnom pravu* (Beograd: Globus, 1934).

33 Julka Djordjević-Hlapec, "Žena u našem krivičnom pravu prikaz knjige dr Ferde Čulinovića," in *Život i rad—isocijalno književni časopis*, ed. Milan L. Rajić (Beograd: Mlada Srbija, 1935), 276.

34 Ibid.

35 A. G. Chloros, *Yugoslav Civil Law: History, Family, and Property* (Oxford: Clarendon Press, 1974).

36 Atanasijević Ksenija, "Položaj žene u našem javnom životu," in *Etika feminizma*, ed. Ljiljana Vuletić (Beograd: Helsinški odbor za ljudska prava u Srbiji, 2008), 46; Neda Božinović, *Žensko pitanje u Srbiji u XIX i XX veku* (Beograd: Devedesetčetvrta, 1996), 80.

37 Ksenija Atanasijević, "Izveštaj sa Treće konferencije Male Antante Žena, održane od sedmog do trinaestog decembra 1925. g. u Atini," *Ženski pokret* 1–2 (1926): 37.

38 For Barbara Jančar–Webster the name of the organization was the Alliance of the Women's Movement. See Jančar–Webster, *Women & Revolution in Yugoslavia 1941–1945*, 35; for more information on the women's movement see also part two: The Interwar Era, World War II, and the Socialist Era, in the anthology *Gender Politics in the Western Balkans. Women and Society in Yugoslavia and the Yugoslav Successor States*, ed. Sabrina P. Ramet (Pennsylvania State University Press, 1999); "Women's History in Yugoslavia," in *Writing Women's History: International Perspectives*, ed. Karen Offen, Ruth Roach Pierson and Jane Rendall (Bloomington: Indiana University Press, 1991), 417–421.

39 In that time the Vojvodina was the part of the Dunavska banovina in the Kingdom of Yugoslavia.

40 *Ženski pokret*, Beograd (1920–1937); *Glas Narodne ženske zajednice*, Beograd (1928–1933), *Jugoslovenka žena*, Beograd (1931–1934), *Glasnik Jugoslovenskog ženskog saveza*, Beograd (1935–1940) and *Žena danas*, Beograd (1936–1940).

41 Dara Marodić, "Izveštaj Ženskog Pokreta za 1926.g.," *Ženski pokret* 9–10 (1923): 455–461.

42 Atanasijević, "Izveštaj sa Treće," 36–43. At the Congress of the International Alliance for Women's suffrage (IAW) in Rome (1923), The Woman's Petite Entente (Mala Antanta Žena in some sources Mala Ženska Antanta) was founded with a mission to gather feminist organizations in Yugoslavia, Poland, Czechoslovakia, Bulgaria, Romania, and in Greece in the struggle for peace and women's political and economic rights. *Ženski pokret* 9–10 (1923): 423.

43 The Serbian National Women's Union was monitoring the status of women's rights before World War I.

44 Atanasijević, "Izveštaj sa Treće," 37.

45 Philosopher Dr. Ksenija Atanasijević (1894–1981), the first woman to earn a PhD from Belgrade University (1922), was one of the Women's Movement Alliance's leaders. She was a prominent member of the Yugoslav League of Women for Peace and Freedom and the Yugoslav Federation of University Women.

46 Ksenija Atanasijević, "Povodom poslednje skupštine beogradskog Ženskog pokreta," *Zivot i rad* 4 (1931): 277.

47 Ksenija Atanasijević, "Pravo glasa žena u ideologiji Žen. (skog) pokreta," *Ženski pokret* 9 (1932): 122.

48 Ibid., 122–123.

49 Sekretarijat žena socijalista (komunista).

50 In 1920, The Socialist Workers' Party of Yugoslavia (Communists)—Socijalistička radnička partije Jugoslavije (komunista) changed its name to the Yugoslav Communist Party (KPJ). In the same year, the Government of the Kingdom of SHS banned the KPJ and communist activity was declared a criminal activity by a government proclamation. Thus the work of the members and supporters of the KPJ had to be illegal. Gordana Stojaković, CD *AFŽ Vojvodine 1942–1953* (Novi Sad: izdanje autorke, 2007).

51 Omladinska sekcija Ženskog pokreta.

52 Stojaković, *Znamenite žene Novog Sada I*, 43; Andrea Feldmann, "Der Verband universitätsgebildeter Frauen Jugoslawiens (1927–1939)," in *Frauenmacht in der Geschichte*, ed. Jutta Dalhoff, Uschi Frey, and Ingrid Schöll (Düsseldorf: Schwann, 1986), 125–133.

53 From 1950, the KPJ's main goal was political work with rural woman. For most women there was a possibility of working in the humanitarian mother and child organizations. Working women were supposed to gather in the union, and for the most educated women, the Federation of University Women was re-established. These were the plans of women's activism that were offered instead of the AFŽ. Stojaković, CD ROM-*AFŽ Vojvodine 1942–1953*.

54 Gordana Stojaković ed., *Neda-jedna biografija* (Novi Sad: Futura publikacije, 2002), 46.

55 The circulation rate of the *Ženski pokret* (Women's Movement) newspaper may serve as an illustration of the number of women active in the civic feminist movment. The circulation in 1921 was 1,200 copies, and its distribution was the following: Belgrade (371 copies), Bosnia and Herzegovina (292), the old borders of Serbia (138), Banat and Bačka (129), Croatia and Slavonia (113), Montenegro (66), Srem (fifty-nine), "Old Serbia and Macedonia" (23), Slovenia (6), the Czech Republic (1), Vienna (1), and London (1). *Ženski pokret* 12 (1922): 35. Vojvodina consists of Banat, Bačka and Srem.

56 Ruža First, "National Liberation Struggle and Women in Yugoslavia," in *National Liberation and Women's Liberation*, ed. Matia Mies and Rhoda Reddock (The Hague: Institute of Social Studies, 1982), 53–63; Jelena Batinić, *Women and Yugoslav Partisans: A History of World War II Resistance* (New York: Cambridge University Press, 2015).

57 Jančar–Webster, *Women & Revolution in Yugoslavia 1941–1945*, 4.

58 Branko Petranović, *Istorija Jugoslavije 1918–1978* (Beograd: Nolit, 1981), 394.

59 Blaženka Mimica, "Ravnopravnost žene u Ustavu Federativne Narodne Republike Jugoslavije," *Žena danas* 38–39 (1946): 1–3.

60 Neda Božinovic ed., *Položaj žene u FNRJ* (Beograd: Savezni odbor Socijalistickog saveza radnog naroda Jugoslavije, 1953), 10–12; Stojaković, CD-*AFŽ Vojvodine 1942–1953*; Susan L. Woodward, "The Rights of Women: Ideology, Policy, and Social Change in Yugoslavia," in *Women, State, and Party in Eastern Europe*, ed. Sharon L. Wolchik and Alfred G. Meyer (Durham: Duke University Press, 1985), 234–256.

61 Bogdan Denitch, "Women and Political Power in a Revolutionary Society: The Yugoslav Case," in *Access to Power: Cross-National Studies of Women and Elites*, ed. Cynthia Fuchs Epstein and Rose Laub Coser (London: George Allen and Unwin, 1981) 115–123; Ana Devic, "Redefing the Public-Private Boundary: Nationalism and Women's Activism in Former Yugoslavia," *The Anthropology of East Europe Review* 15, no. 2 (1997): 31–41.

62 Božinović, *Žensko pitanje u Srbiji u XIX i XX veku*, 238.

63 Stojaković, CD ROM—*AFŽ Vojvodine 1942–1953*.

64 Pantelić, *Partizanke kao građanke*, 71.

65 During the AFŽ's prominance, special attention was paid to women in rural communities in the form of education (literacy, political education, introducing new technologies in agriculture, education about childcare and upbrining of children, women's health). Stojaković, CD ROM-*AFŽ Vojvodine 1942–1953*; Lydia Sklevicky, "Emancipated Integration or Integrated Emancipation: The Case of Post-revolutionary Yugoslavia," in *Current Issues in Women's History*, ed. Arina Angerman et al. (New York: Routledge, 1989), 91–109.
66 Neda Božinović "O radu komisije za porodične odnose—izveštaj Nede Božinović," *Žena danas* 112 (1953): 25.
67 Božinović, *Žensko pitanje u Srbiji u XIX i XX veku*, 127; Neda Božinović, "Key Points in the History of the Women's Movement in Former Yugoslavia," in *What Can We Do for Ourselves? East European Feminist Conference, Belgrade, June 1994*, ed. Daša Duhaček and Jasmina Lukić (Belgrad: Center for Women's Studies, Research and Communication, 1995), 13–18.
68 Ibid., 127–128.
69 *Žena danas* 14 (1938): 3–4.
70 Ibid.
71 Božinović, *Žensko pitanje u Srbiji u XIX i XX veku*, 128.
72 Atanasijević, "Pravo glasa žena u ideologiji Žen.(skog) pokreta," 122–123.
73 Atanasijević, "Povodom poslednje skupštine beogradskog Ženskog pokreta," 277–280.
74 Božinović, *Žensko pitanje u Srbiji u XIX i XX veku*, 118.
75 The occasion was the establishment of new rules of the parliamentary elections.
76 Božinović, *Ženski pokret u Srbiji u XIX i XX veku*, 123.
77 Ibid., 122.
78 Ibid., 122.
79 Ibid., 124.
80 Olga Alkalaj (Beograd, 1907—Beograd, 1942) was a lawyer, a member of the Youth Section of the Women's Movement, and one of the first members of the *Žene danas* editorial board. She had been a member of the KPJ since 1937. Harriet Pass Freidenreich, "Yugoslavia," in *The Jewish Women's Archive*, last modified 2014, accessed June 29, 2012, http://jwa.org/encyclopedia/article/yugoslavia.
81 Bosa Cvetić ed., *Žene Srbije u NOB* (Beograd: Nolit, 1975), 73–74.
82 Božinović, *Žensko pitanje u Srbiji u XIX i XX veku*, 124.
83 Anonim "Akcija za pravo glasa žena—Sada će reći glasovi iz 1939," *Žena danas* 36 (1945): 12. Retrieved from Žena danas 26 (1940): 12.
84 The "Rally" (*Zbor*) was a conservative nationalist organization with a strong anti-communist and anti–Semite ideology. It was founded in 1935 by Dimitrije Ljotic (1891–1945). See Jozo Tomasevich, *War and Revolution in Yugloslavia, 1941–1945. Occupation and Collaboration* (Stanford, CA: Stanford University Press, 2001), 186–189.
85 Jovanka Kecman, *Žene Jugoslavije u radničkom pokretu i ženskim organizacijama* (Beograd: Institut za savremenu istoriju/Narodna knjiga, 1978), 343.
86 Ibid., 344.
87 The Belgrade Women's Movement's management offered the Youth Section of the Women's Movement to take over leadership but the latter group refused. Božinović, *Žensko pitanje u Srbiji u XIX i XX veku*, 125–126. Based on Mitra Mitrović's memories, Barbara Jančar-Webster has recorded the same situation but differently: the feminists of the Women's Movement in Belgrade "discreetly and elegantly" informed the communists of the Youth Section of the Women's Movement that they were "warned" that the Youth Section's communists should change the strong connection and affinity for the Soviet Union, and when the Soviet Union invaded Finland the split between the feminists and the communists was formally completed. Jančar-Webster, *Women and Revolution in Yugoslavia 1941–1945*, 25.

88 The education of female children in the Vojvodina and Novi Sad has a long tradition. In Novi Sad, the Serbian Higher Girl's School has been in operation since 1874. Novi Sad Girl's School with education in Hungarian was established in 1876. In the State Women's Real Gymnasium in Novi Sad, the first female students were enrolled in 1919. Stojaković, *Znamenite žene Novog Sada I*, 17–23.

89 Stojaković, *Znamenite žene Novog Sada* I, 215–217.

90 Writing about Katarina Lengold-Marinković, Milorad Botić described the conditions in which she began a career as the first female lawyer in Novi Sad: "There was conviction that the law practice is not a profession for women." See Botić, "Lengold-Marinković Katarina," 320–321.

91 Novi Sad was liberated on October 23, 1944 by the Yugoslav People's Liberation Army and the Red Army.

92 Botić, "Lengold-Marinković Katarina," 321.

93 Ibid.

94 Stojaković, "Skica za studiju: Počeci feminističkog pokreta u Vojvodini (1748–1941)," 5–58.

95 Gordana Stojaković, "Prilog za istoriju ženskog pokreta u Vojvodini i Srbiji u 19. i 20. Veku," in *Uvod u rodne teorije*, ed. Ivana Milojević and Slobodanka Markov (Novi Sad: ACIMSI i Mediterran Publishing, 2011), 63–81.

96 Gordana Stojaković, "Milica Tomić," in *Women's issue. Magazine Žena-Milica Tomić*, ed. Vesna Nedeljković Angelovski (Novi Sad: City Museum, 2012), 34.

97 The Women's Party was established in Belgrade in 1927 and in Novi Sad in 1928. The Manifesto and the Program of the Women's Party stated that "for the cultural, economic, moral and healthy survival of our country it was necessary for women to fully participate in the organization and life of the state. The Women's Party paid a lot of attention to their struggle for realization of professional equality for women, regardless of whether they worked in public service or in private companies. Once the January 6th Dictatorship had been introduced in 1929, the Women's Party and all the odher political parties and organizations stopped operating, but the Women's Party never again resumed its work. See Bozinović, *Žensko pitanje u Srbiji u XIX i XX veku*, 115; Stojakovic, *Znamenite žene Novog Sada I*, 38.

98 Botić, "Lengold-Marinković Katarina," 321.

99 Gordana Stojaković, "Pioneer Serbian Women Physicians and Their Activist Role in Women's Rights," in *Serbian Studies: Journal of the North American Society for Serbian Studies* 24 (1–2), ed. Ljubica D. Popovich and Lilien F. Robinson (Bloomington: Slavica Publisher, Indiana University Press, 2012), 109–125.

100 Gordana Stojaković, *Znamenite žene Novog Sada* I, 216.

101 The testimony of Neda Božinović primarily related to cities and areas in which she lived and worked.

102 Stojaković, *Neda-jedna biografija*, 53.

103 Božinović's cooperation with some representatives of the feminist movements that began by her activism in the Youth Section of the Women's Movement continued after World War II by collaboration with members of the feminist movements that were involved in the Yugoslav Federation of University Women. See Stojaković, *Neda-jedna biografija*, 46.

104 In 1928, the Yugoslav League of Women for Peace and Freedom was founded. Its President was Danica Zečević. Stojaković, *Uvod u rodne teorije*, 71.

105 Stojaković, *Neda-jedna biografija*, 54–55.

106 Kozara is a mountain in Bosnia.

107 The withdrawal from political life is the result of removing the "liberals" from political life in Serbia. The liberals were in positions of power over the Serbian

Communist Party in the period between 1969 and 1972. See Sonja Biserko, "Srpska elita i realizacija srpskog nacionalnog programa," in *Kovanje antijugoslovenske zavere*, ed. Sonja Biserko (Beograd: Helsinški odbor za ljudska prava 2006), 12–13.

108 In 1948, there were four hundred thousand women in the Vojvodina, out of whom 340,000 were in the AFŽ and 290,000 were members of the People's Front. About fifty thousand women were employed in companies, and 6,348 of them were Union officials. *Slobodna Vojvodina*, March 7 (1948), 1. The daily newspaper, *Slobodna Vojvodina*, were printed in Novi Sad as the voice of the People's Front for Vojvodina (Narodni front za Vojvodinu). The circulation rate of the AFŽ's magazines in Serbia (*Žena danas, Zora, Glas žena, Dolgozó Nő, Vajdasági Dzolgozó Nő)* was around 100,000 copies in the period between 1948 and 1950. Stojaković, *Rodna perspektiva u novinama Antifašističkog fronta žena (1945–1953)*, 40.

109 A very popular form of women's gathering were the so-called women's reading groups, which in rural areas were also like traditional women-only gatherings during which women would spin wool jointly while talking, singing, and socializing. Women would bring their handiwork, and one of them would read to the others, usually articles from the AFŽ's women's press. Reading groups were also organized in factories and cities. It was a mandatory activity through which women and men acquired political knowledge.

110 The AFŽ's most common initiatives were the conferences, mass gatherings of women during which their results were summed up and the platforms for their future activities were set.

111 Vida Tomšič, "Uloga žene u socijalističkoj izgradnji," *Žena danas* 93 (1952): 1.

112 Communist activities in the cities were carried out according to strict rules of conspiracy, and that meant that members of organized groups generally knew two or three people that they worked with directly only by their nickname (conspiratorial name). When arrested, they could be severely tortured in prisons. See Andrija Radenić, "Metodi nemačke i kvislinške strahovlade u Beogradu 1941," *Godišnjak grada Beograda* no. VIII (Beograd: Beogradske novine, 1961), 327–363.

113 Traditional headscarves covering Muslim women's faces fully or partially. Names of Muslim veils are given as the original name used in socialist Yugoslavia.

114 Božinović, *Žensko pitanje u Srbiji u XIX i XX veku*, 21–23. According to Ana Božić's doctoral thesis, women's position in private law was better in the Vojvodina than in Serbia because it was located in the cultural, juridical, and political milieu of the Habsburg monarchy until 1918, Božić, *Položaj žene u privatnom pravu kroz istoriju do danas*, 150–157.

8 Bulgarian Women in Legal Education and the Legal Profession During the First Half of the Twentieth Century

Krassimira Daskalova

This chapter presents the history of women in the juridical professions in Bulgaria during the first half of the twentieth century. It deals with the history of legal education and tracks the establishment of the first Bulgarian university in 1888 and women's admittance there in 1901. The text articulates the struggles by women with law degrees for the realization of their professional ambitions, for not until 1945 could female law school graduates practice their profession. A special emphasis in my text is the creation of women's solidarity groups and especially the role of the Bulgarian Association of University Women (with its section of female lawyers) and the Bulgarian Women's Union (BWU). The last part of the chapter presents case studies where I focus on the life trajectories of female lawyers and on the stories of two leaders of the women's movement who had earned law degrees. It shows how women's personal problems were entangled with their public struggles for a better life. This chapter illustrates how the personal is political and how private matters are actually politically determined. The text is based on various kinds of sources, both archival and published: materials from the personal archival collections of feminist leaders Dimitrana Ivanova (1881–1960) and Vera Zlatareva (1905–1977); the documents of organizations of Bulgarian lawyers, kept at the Bulgarian Historical Archive (in the National Library Cyril and Methodius) and the State Historical Archive in Sofia; feminist publications of the time; and secondary sources, which include publications by women and gender historians in the country as well as scholars publishing on the history of law.

Historical Context

The Bulgarian nation-state was established in 1878 after five centuries of Ottoman rule. It was designed as a constitutional monarchy (with a foreign—German—dynasty), which lasted until 1947. Bulgaria then became, and until 1989 was, a state-socialist "people's" republic with a one-party system. After 1878, exposure of the agrarian Bulgarian society to the standards and values of the dynamic urban, industrial, and liberal Western culture—a process that had begun within the Ottoman Empire—intensified. The new political elites of the nation-state introduced a Western-style liberal constitution and civil code, and one of their main goals was to modernize the country. The society was exposed to Enlightenment and liberal ideas about progress, freedom, equality (understood as fraternity), and emancipation. The majority of the population, however, was peasants (seventy-five percent in the early 1940s).[1]

Citizenship was slow in coming to women. The Bulgarian experience with women's educational, professional, and political rights confirms that women and men were differently integrated into the national project and that, for most of the modern era, the concept of "citizen" should be understood in masculine terms. Article 86 of the first Bulgarian Constitution—*Tŭrnovo*—of 1879 introduced electoral rights for "all Bulgarian citizens" above 21 years of age. Its Article 54 defined "Bulgarian citizens" as all people born in Bulgaria to parents who were Bulgarian subjects (and who did not possess another citizenship). In the context of suffrage, however, (and, as we will see, in that of the professional rights of people with law degrees as well) the term "citizen" was interpreted as referring only to men. This was not the case in other contexts. As Bulgarian citizens, for example, women had to obey the law regarding free and compulsory primary education; they also had to pay taxes and had the right to establish unions and associations. The gender of the term "citizen" was thus ambiguous: its scope was not determined by the constitution and laws but by tradition—that of a peasant patriarchal society without parliamentary practices.[2]

Women's Organizations, Legislation, and Women with Education in Law

The first Bulgarian institution of higher education—*Vissheto uchilishte* (the Higher School)—was founded in Sofia in 1888. It was renamed a university in 1904.[3] Women, however, were not admitted there initially. The formal reason for this discrimination was the difference between the programs of boys' and girls' high schools. Actually, the largest and best-known national feminist women's organization, BWU, was born as a reaction to the limitations imposed on women's university education.[4] Women had to campaign for many years until they were allowed to enter the university, first as just auditors during the second half of the 1890s and as full time students only in 1901 (after a special law on women's education equalized girls' high schools with those for boys in 1897). Paradoxically, in the time before women were allowed to study in Bulgaria, the Bulgarian Ministry of (People's) Education gave stipends to women to study abroad, and up until 1944 many Bulgarian girls graduated from foreign universities. The first women were admitted to Sofia University's law department in the 1902–1903 academic year.[5] By 1946, 507 women graduated from that department and twelve female Bulgarian citizens obtained their juridical education abroad.[6]

In 1905, as the first women who had entered Sofia University at the beginning of the twentieth century were about to graduate, the fourth congress of the BWU asserted, with a special resolution, that women have professional rights in all sectors of the labor market.[7] This resolution regarding the admission of women to the liberal professions mostly concerned the situation of female legal professionals. After the graduation of the first female lawyers, their professional realization became a serious problem, as was the case with highly educated women with prestigious professions everywhere at the time.

In 1907, one of the first women to graduate from the faculty of law of Sofia University wrote to the minister of justice asking to be allowed to practice in court. The minister answered that she did not have, according to his interpretation of the law, such a right, nor was she allowed to practice in a law firm.[8] In principle, the opponents of women's admission to the bar connected it with the political rights of women and especially with women's suffrage.[9] Other interpretations, however, given by some male lawyers who were supporters of women's rights, emphasized that neither the first Bulgarian Law on Lawyers from November 1888, nor its amendment from December 1897, nor the Law on the Structure of the Courts of 1883 and its amendment from 1898, forbade women with law degrees to practice their profession.[10]

To summarize, before 1945 women were not admitted to the bar, although Bulgarian legislation did not contain any restrictive language to this effect. Similar to the situation with suffrage, it was neither the constitution, nor the Law on Lawyers, nor the Law on the Structure of the Courts that barred women from practicing law, but rather patriarchal tradition and politicians' strong but unspoken material interests. More than that, Article 65 of the *Tŭrnovo* Constitution guaranteed all Bulgarian citizens the right to hold positions in the state, societal, or military structures.[11] In this case the constitution did not actually use the term "citizens" but rather "Bulgarian subjects" (*podanitsi*); however, it is clear that according to these constitutional provisions women had the right to take judicial (*sŭdebni*) positions.

The amendments to the Law on Lawyers from 1897 and to the Law on the Structure of the Courts from 1898 listed the conditions for being a lawyer as including: Bulgarian citizenship, the exercise of civil and political rights, university juridical education, a two-year certificate of judicial training, proof of passing the state examination, and registration at the circuit courts under the Law on Lawyers.[12] According to the texts of these laws, there were no formal obstacles for women with legal education to become lawyers. Most of the politicians and powerful conservative jurists of that time, however, interpreted the above-mentioned conditions in a way that excluded women (women did not possess voting rights, which in these interpretations were understood as political rights), and therefore women were not allowed to become interns in a law firm, which was one of the preconditions for practicing law.[13]

As already mentioned, from the very beginning of the twentieth century and up to 1944, the leaders of the BWU supported all actions of female students in law and women with law degrees. The Union appealed to the legislators' sense of justice and insisted on women's rights to practice their profession as freelance attorneys and to be appointed as judges in court.[14] In their well-argued documents, female students in law showed that neither the existing law for the judiciary nor the law on lawyers contained any stipulations that barred female lawyers from practicing as judges or attorneys.[15]

The case of female lawyers was guided by interpretations that paralleled those faced in the struggle for women's political rights. Although the constitution did not contain any restrictive clauses concerning women's rights as citizens, the interpretations provided by the dominant male lawyers—due to their overriding material interests and their fear of competition from women—excluded female law professionals from the category of citizens of the Bulgarian nation-state.[16] Indeed, even the most modest rights for the "second sex" (for example, a woman's opportunity to be employed by the telegraph and telephone administrations or the railway administration) required special parliamentary decisions.[17] Here was the real paradox: according to the general conditions of the Bulgarian Constitution, women were not specifically excluded from the rights of Bulgarian citizens; on the other hand, however, in practice they did not have the same rights as male citizens. As Nira Yuval-Davis' authoritative critique of writings on gender and nationhood has shown, women are often excluded from the collective "we" of the body politic and remain in positions of being objects rather than subjects. (Thus the construction of womanhood has the characteristics of "otherness.")[18]

When in 1909 the Bulgarian Parliament discussed the new amendment to the Law on the Structure of the Courts,[19] female students from the law department of Sofia University sent another petition to parliament asking for "the right to practice the profession of an attorney and to serve as judges."[20] At the same time, on behalf of the BWU, its current leader Julia Malinova (1869–1953) signed a letter to the MPs supporting the petition of the female students in law and insisting on women's right to sit in the courts.[21] The petition of the female lawyers and the demands of the women's movement activists were supported by several MPs, all of whom belonged to new political formations: three Democrats, one representative of the Radical-Democratic party, and one from the Agrarian party.[22] The majority of the MPs, however, voted against the petition.[23]

Clearly, only a tiny proportion of the MPs supported equal citizenship for women. The only parliamentary group that unconditionally supported the demands of female lawyers and the organized women's associations was that of the Agrarian party. Another illogical circumstance was the position (emblematic of Bulgarian culture) of some well-known Europeanized intellectuals. For example, Stoyan Mihailovski, a misogynist man of letters educated in France who was known as a fighter against "tyranny and entrenched power," was also an obsessive anti-feminist. He addressed the parliament and asked the MPs "in no way" to allow female lawyers to take positions of attorneys or of judges. He even insisted on forbidding women to practice any profession, thereby defending "male dominance and women's subordination,"[24] as one feminist activist put it.

The anti-democratic appeals of Mihailovski and people like him were countered by the "open letters" written and spread by Anna Karima (1871–1949)[25] and Zheni Bozhilova-Pateva (1879–1955),[26] who were the most prominent leaders of the women's movement at the time. The anti-democratic appeals were also countered by a series of resources and protests of women's associations from around the country and by information published in the official organ of the BWU, the newspaper *Zhenski glas* (Women's Voice),[27] about the status of women in the judiciary throughout the world.

From 1910 to 1911, female students of law and the BWU tried once more to introduce a bill supporting the professional rights of female lawyers, but without success. Because one of the major arguments of the opponents of women's right to be lawyers was that in order to practice their profession women should first obtain political (voting) rights, the BWU and the new women's association *Ravnopravie* (Equal rights)[28] aimed their struggles at gaining political rights for women while at the same time continuing to plead the cause of female lawyers. These two organizations defended women's rights not only on the pages of their organs (the newspapers *Zhenski glas* and *Ravnopravie*) and the pages of other periodicals published in the country (such as Zheni Bozhilova-Pateva's feminist journal *Grazhdanka*, or Woman Citizen),[29] but they also organized numerous public meetings trying to mobilize more women, both in the capital Sofia and in smaller provincial towns. Thus in January 1912, in connection with the expected changes in the electoral law, the BWU organized a large rally in support of women's political rights with the participation of a number of male politicians and lawyers—professors from Sofia University.[30]

Although during the Balkan Wars (1912–1913) and World War I (1914–1918) women's professional struggles were put on hold, the number of women who studied law was considerable. In 1916 and 1917, female law students sent new petitions to the parliament but the MPs ignored them. In 1917, the parliament debated a bill for an amendment to the Law on the Structure of the Courts.[31] One of the most outrageous points in the text was the suggestion made by male politicians that people without a special education in law be allowed to take positions in the court administration on the grounds that there were not enough lawyers. Women who had the necessary education, supported by the women's movement in the country, insisted that they should fill this gap. In the fall of 1917, the BWU organized another huge rally in Sofia and invited male supporters of women's causes.[32] Their speeches were published in a special brochure. Female activists succeeded in convincing some MPs to support a bill that would allow women to practice their profession. Among the supporters of the new amendment were men from a range of political parties. Although most of them belonged to leftist parties, some politicians were affiliated with more conservative political structures.[33] In 1918, these MPs proposed additions to Articles 103 and 115 of the Law on the Structure of the Courts and to Article 4 of the Law on Lawyers, respectively. The change envisioned by both men and women was for women to be appointed to the sphere of the judiciary and as attorneys.[34]

According to some publications of the time that opposed women's emancipation struggles, however, the Bulgarian legal system was not "well worked out and was not yet well developed" and because of that "it was dangerous" to let women enter this sector.[35] As if in the realms of education, telegraph and telephone, banking, state or municipal administrations, industry, construction work, or agriculture, everything was perfectly arranged, sarcastically commented Bulgarian feminists—for women were allowed to work in these sectors. However, continued the feminist periodicals, nobody would think of contesting women's participation in those difficult segments of the economy where they worked for a meager wage.[36]

Since the very beginning of the twentieth century, immediately after the first women graduated from Sofia University's law department, women's rights activists had been organizing and participating in various actions against this pronounced injustice. During World War I, however, the discussion about the professional rights of female lawyers was displaced by other, supposedly "more urgent" issues, only to reappear with new intensity immediately after the war was over. But, as it became clear, the progressive male lawyers never stopped supporting the struggle for female professional rights.

In the interwar period, the rights of female lawyers continued to be among the major professional struggles of women. In 1920, under the Agrarian party government, the Minister of Justice Yossif Fadenhecht and his administration drafted a new Law on the Structure of the Courts, which envisioned women gaining the right to become advocates. The Sŭyuz na bulgarskite advokati, (SBA, Union of the Bulgarian Attorneys, UBA), was established in 1921. In the 1920s, all congresses of the UBA continued debating and voting on suggestions related to the issues of the professional rights of female lawyers and especially to their right to work as attorneys. The first general assembly of attorneys, held in 1921, entrusted the board to prepare a preliminary project about advocacy. The text drafted by the board—the result of the collective work of several lawyers—envisioned (in its Article 4) that "people from both sexes can become attorneys."[37] The project would be discussed during the second congress of advocates, but that gathering of Bulgarian advocates decided to postpone the debates. After the approval of the project by the codification commission, the proposal was sent to all advocates in the country in order to, as they put it, be able to draft "an excellent" bill that could serve as a "stable foundation of the future law for attorneys."[38] All attorneys and judges in the country were expected to speak to the question of whether or not it was time to give female legal professionals the right to practice their profession in court. Nobody, however, answered this question, and at the end, the codification commission—against the wishes of the union of attorneys—proposed its own project in which only men had the right to be attorneys. This was the text voted for by the Third Congress of Attorneys, held in December 1923, with a minimum majority of only 10 votes. Its negative result notwithstanding, the vote also showed that a lot of male politicians did support the women's demands.[39]

It is clear that, because there were not enough people supporting women's rights among the politically powerful men at the time and because there were no women elected to the parliament who could defend their own rights, the numerous initiatives of female legal professionals, of female law students, and of various feminists and women's rights activists in the country failed. No wonder, then, that the large general gathering of female lawyers held in Sofia on December 23, 1923 made the decision to organize all female lawyers to defend their professional rights and interests. The editors of the newspaper *Zhenski glas* began to create a database of all female lawyers living both in Sofia and in provincial towns in an effort to unite and mobilize them for action.[40]

The opponents of the change put forward some very strange argumentation in the journal *Advokatski pregled* (Attorneys' Review), which actually echoed the decision of the Third Congress of Bulgarian Attorneys.[41] They believed that the "woman" should first obtain "full equality with man in terms of civil rights, after that she should get political rights on equal terms with men and only after that should she aspire for the right to be an attorney."[42] As Dimitrana Ivanova, the editor in chief of *Zhenski glas* and the leader of the BWU from 1926 to 1944, mentioned, this formulation did not follow any logical or historical reasons since the right to be an attorney is a professional right: it is a right to make a living and should not be dependent on political rights.[43] Just as there are female teachers, doctors, workers, employees, etc., there should be female attorneys, Ivanova commented. She continued: it is clear that Bulgarian "democrats" do not want to let women take such a strong professional position:[44]

> But nothing can stop life going on and deny life's demands—if not today, tomorrow you will be pushed to admit this right to women; with today's refusal you will only leave a document showing to the future generations that advocates—the supporters of the rule of law—had acted as opponents of a right articulated by life, only because this right of women affected their material interests. [. . .] Let us remind you, that we, women, have the right to study law. And is there a greater absurdity than to prevent us from using our knowledge?![45]

Moreover, the shorthand record of the Bulgarian Parliament from 1925 and the periodical press of the time also reported a confusing episode in the work of this ostensibly most democratic Bulgarian political institution. Thus in 1925, during the third reading of the bill of attorneys, Angel Vŭlchev (from the Democratic Party) and an MP from the town of Nikopol moved that the right to practice the profession of attorney be granted to all Bulgarian citizens, irrespective of their sex.[46] Vŭlchev's proposal was even put to the vote and the majority of the MPs supported it.[47] However, Minister of Justice Tsviatko Boboshevski opposed this result and threatened to withdraw the bill if the already voted decision was accepted by the parliament. The Chairman of Parliament, Dr. Boris Vazov, instead of accepting the already voted decision (after more than half the MPs had supported the rights of female lawyers), decided to put the issue to the vote once again. Some well-known lawyers, Professor Fadenhecht, for example, urged all MPs to vote according to their consciences. However, in order to please Minister Boboshevski, some of the voters who had previously supported women's rights refrained the second time.[48]

After years of discussions, however, as mentioned, in July 1925 the parliament finally voted on the new Law on Lawyers, which again left female lawyers without the possibility of practicing law. This document stipulated a mandatory training period for candidates to be authorized to work as lawyers, the requirements of admission of the candidates to training, the length of the training period, its course, its end, and the rights and duties of the trainee-lawyers. In order to practice their profession, the lawyers had to register at the bar association and receive a certificate from the bar council. The new law preserved the rights of the "status quo lawyer practitioners" under the Law on Lawyers from 1888, and for the first time it explicitly postulated that women could not practice law.[49]

At the Seventh Congress of the Union of Bulgarian Attorneys (UBA), held on July 7 and 8, 1928 following the decision of both the UBA and that of the Union of Bulgarian Judges (UBJ), which had gathered at a joint meeting in 1927, delegates spent a lot of time discussing the rights of women with law degrees to practice their profession as attorneys. Fourteen male attorneys spoke in support of the right of women to be attorneys, and seven of the speakers at the congress were against women's professional rights. The BWU published a special brochure on the topic presenting the entire history of this controversy.[50] The leader of the Democratic Party, Alexander Malinov, spoke at the congress of the UBA explaining his motives to vote for the rights of women with law degrees to become attorneys and judges.[51] In December 1929 at the session of the Twenty-Second Ordinary National Assembly, Professor Georgi Danailov introduced his own agenda for a bill giving female lawyers rights to be attorneys.[52] Representatives from all parliamentary groups supported this motion. Dr. Todor Kulev, then Minister of Justice, also supported the project. The Congress of the International Alliance of Women for Suffrage and Equal Citizenship held in Berlin at the same time sent a telegram in support. The motion was voted on at first reading, but because there was a new minister—Kuncho Milanov—who was against this measure, the bill was neither discussed in the parliamentary committee of justice nor ever voted on in parliament.[53]

In May 1924, Bulgarian female university graduates established their own organization: the Association of Bulgarian Women University Graduates (ABWUG, Druzhestvo na bŭlgarkite s visshe obrazovanie), later known also as Bulgarian Association of University Women (BAUW).[54] Most of its members were teachers, lecturers at Sofia University, lawyers, writers, artists, architects, and medical doctors from Sofia, representing the entire intellectual and scientific elite in the capital. In July 1925, the ABWUG became a member of the International Federation of Women Graduates, later known as the International Federation of University Women (IFUW). Four sections were formed within its framework over time: those of female lawyers, female artists, female writers, and female students. About fifteen percent of the members of this organization had been educated abroad (mainly in France, Germany, Switzerland, and Austria-Hungary). Most had received their education at Sofia University in Bulgaria, at the Academy of Arts, or at the Music Academy. One-third of the members had doctoral degrees and most knew foreign languages, sustained extensive contacts with female activists and intellectuals abroad, and participated in the meetings of the IFUW.[55]

The major goal of the ABWUG was to secure favorable conditions for professional women in Bulgaria. Its lawyers' section was formed first in 1928 and turned into the biggest corporate organization of Bulgarian women's elite, with about 150 members during the 1940s.[56] The leaders of the section of lawyers were authoritative and internationally recognized jurists. Over the years, the section was led by three women. The first (between 1928 and 1934) was Maria (Manja) Girginov(a), who in 1930 was also elected a member of the Council of the International Federation of Women in Legal Careers created in 1928 in Paris (known by its French acronym FIFCJ).[57] The second (between 1934 and 1936) was Velisslava Radulova, who specialized in commercial law in Italy and had been a delegate (in 1921) to the Italian-Bulgarian Mixed Arbitration Court in Rome.[58] In 1936, she was elected to the board of the FIFCJ and in 1938 she was nominated to the Commission on the Status of Women at the League of Nations. The third chairwoman of the section of lawyers (from 1936 until 1948) was Teofana (Fany) Kesyakova, whose career was typical for Bulgarian female jurists: after her graduation from the Sofia University law department (in 1920), Kesyakova worked as a secretary for private companies and foreign diplomatic missions in Sofia.[59]

The struggles for the professional and political rights of Bulgarian women with law degrees were the major focus of the lawyers' section of the ABWUG. The FIFCJ provided support on the issue of women's professional rights as early as 1929, but, of course, it was not in a position to change the situation in the country, as the powerful Bulgarian male politicians saw this issue as a problem in constitutional law rather than a labor issue. That is why the section of lawyers at the beginning initiated a juridical dispute against the Law on Lawyers and at the same time aimed—with political support—at amending the Law on the Structure of the Courts.[60] In 1934, after a military coup d'état and the establishment of an authoritarian regime in Bulgaria, along with banning all political parties, the new government refused to discuss the case of women lawyers with their section within the ABWUG. At that point female lawyers changed their strategy and concentrated specifically on women's suffrage. They believed that once they became full citizens with voting rights, women with a legal education could also hold positions in the legislature. This brought them very close to the agendas of other women's organizations (apart from BWU) prior to World War I, such as the small suffragist formation Ravnopravie (Equal Rights, known as the Union of Progressive Women, as well).[61]

As shown earlier, the struggles of female lawyers to obtain their professional rights were supported by many Bulgarian attorneys and many members of the UBA. After the restoration of parliamentary regime, women obtained the right to participate in local (communal) and parliamentary elections. In 1937, women were granted—in accordance with the dominant nationalistic demographic concerns of the time—voting rights for local elections if they were mothers in a legal marriage, i.e., as reproducers of the nation. In 1938, the new electoral law defined all Bulgarian subjects as voters, including both men and women twenty-one years of age and older—the latter, however, only if married, divorced, or widowed. Voting was obligatory for male voters; it was optional for women voters.[62] The parliamentary elections in 1938 were the first after the restoration of the constitution. Judging from the results reported in the periodical press, only 1,563,188 women obtained the right to vote. In the 1937 local elections, only 434,633 of those women participated, while in the parliamentary elections in 1938 their number rose to 764,550 voters.[63]

The lawyers' section of the ABWUG sharply criticized the regime because the new electoral laws did not treat women and men as equals. Female lawyers argued that it was completely inappropriate to make civil status dependent on such criteria as "marriage" or "maternity" and to deprive of active suffrage various categories of women including adoptive mothers, women with children born out of wedlock, childless women, and single women. After married, divorced, and widowed women got suffrage rights, however, female lawyers were still not able to practice their profession, even the married ones among them. The persistent efforts of Dimitrana Ivanova, the leader of the Bulgarian Women's Union in the interwar period, and Vera Zlatareva, one of the most active members of the lawyers' section of the ABWUG, offer stellar examples of women's activism, but I will come back to these cases later.

Since in 1938, married, divorced, and widowed women in Bulgaria received the right to vote in parliamentary elections, the major objection of the opponents of the rights of female lawyers—that female lawyers could not practice their profession because they did not have political rights—was eliminated. Immediately after the first elections with women's participation, representatives of the BWU—among them Dimitrana Ivanova, Rada Petrova, and Dr. Vera Plocheva—met with Minister of Jurisprudence Ivan Kuzhuharov. The latter promised that women would only earn the right to serve as attorneys through an amendment to the Law on Lawyers. At the same time, women's insistence that the new law of juvenile courts envisioned the possibility for women to take positions as judges there met the resistance of the minister, who said that it was untimely to ask this when women did not yet have the right to be attorneys. However, the minister did allow a representative of the BWU to participate in the committee preparing the law on juvenile courts; this was the jurist Fany Kesyakova, member of the ABWUG and chairwoman at that time of its section of lawyers.[64]

In October 1940 the Ministry of Justice introduced a bill for changing Article 1 of the Law on Lawyers, which dealt with the admission of women to the bar. The changes supported by the then-Minister of Justice Vassil Mitakov would allow female lawyers to become attorneys. The following text was also added in the law: "Persons of the female sex, although they do not have political rights according to the laws of the country, can be attorneys, if they meet all the other conditions, written in the previous article. They also have the right to train in a law firm."[65] In the end, however, female lawyers only obtained rights equal to those of men when the communists came into power within the antifascist government established on September 9, 1944.

I would like to present here some available statistical information about all (male) lawyers in the Bulgarian nation state during the period 1878–1944. According to the preserved official data, by the end of December 1885 in the principality of Bulgaria, there were 358 lawyers; among them, only fifteen had completed juridical education. The largest number of lawyers (fifty) was registered at the Sofia court district because of the larger population in Sofia and their needs and also because of the existence of a court of appeal there.[66] In 1904, there were 823 attorneys in the country, only 289 among them with law degrees. In 1911, there were 1,106 attorneys, 656 among them with university law degrees and 107 with doctorates. In 1918, the number of lawyers in Bulgaria was 1,170; 876 among them had legal education and ninety-two had doctorates. In 1925, the number of lawyers was 2,394; in 1932, 2,821; in 1936, 2,596; and in 1941, 2,981. These lawyers were working as attorneys, judges, public prosecutors, notaries, secretaries, etc.[67]

Only shortly after the September 9 coup d'état the new communist dominated government issued a decree from October 13, 1944 that introduced the full equality of people from both sexes.[68] This law established the equality of women and men in all spheres of economic, state, cultural, social, and political life. After several decades of struggles, women obtained the right to be attorneys, district attorneys, and judges. The Law on Lawyers from October 1947 significantly changed the provisions in the regulation of the legal profession and legal defense in accordance to the new socialist Dimitrov Constitution.

Two Emblematic Case Studies: Dimitrana Ivanova (1881–1960) and Vera Zlatareva (1905–1977)

The aforementioned Dimitrana Ivanova, leader of the BWU, studied philosophy at the University of Zurich in Switzerland.[69] Due to family misfortunes, she was forced to return home when she had only the final examination to complete. She then found work as a teacher. Well-educated and with a keen sensitivity to sexual inequality, having more than once encountered discrimination because of her sex, her involvement in the women's movement seems only logical. She was the leader of the association *Dobrodetel* in her native town of Rousse and one of the most visible activists of the national women's movement. In the early 1920s—while married with three young children—she decided that an education in law would enable her to do more for the women's cause. She tried to enroll at the law faculty of Sofia University but was rejected on the grounds that she "did not have a complete secondary education" (all high schools in Bulgaria by then had eight grades, while she had—during the 1890s—needed to complete only six). It was then that, as she wrote in her autobiography, "the conviction became deeply seated in me that I should fight formalism and injustices against women."[70] After completing her eight-year high school education by taking the necessary final exams (at the same high schools where she had been teaching for sixteen years), Ivanova enrolled in the law faculty and graduated in 1927. In 1928 she founded, and for two years edited, the journal *Zhenata* (The Woman), which specialized in legal aspects of male domination and women's subordination. From 1920 to 1944 she was the editor in chief of *Zhenski glas*, the organ of the BWU, and from 1926 until the communist takeover in September 1944, she also served as chairwoman of the BWU. In 1929, Dimitrana Ivanova applied to practice law as an attorney. The case required the intervention of Sofia's Council of Attorneys (SofCA [Sofiiski Advokatski Sŭvet, SAS]), the Supreme Council of Attorneys (SCA [Visshia Advokatski Sŭvet, VAS]), and the Supreme Cassation Court (SCC [Vŭrhovnia Kasatsionen Sŭd, VKS]). All these institutions were expected to take a position on the question of women's rights to be defense lawyers/attorneys. SofCA and SCA explained their negative opinion about female lawyers' rights by pointing out that women did not have political (i.e., voting) rights. According to the answer of the SCC, the question of women's political rights was irrelevant to women's professional rights; it justified its judgment with the already-cited new Law on Lawyers, approved in 1925, which denied women the right to make a living by practicing their profession.[71]

Under Ivanova's leadership, the BWU continued its campaign for the professional rights of female lawyers. Edited by her, the newspaper *Zhenski glas* reported all social actions and feminist pressure on the government and parliament on this issue. Thus, for example, in 1926 the BWU made a proposal to the Minister of Justice, Todor Kulev, regarding the juridical rights of women and the rights of female lawyers in particular. The activists' suggestions concerned numerous important issues: among them, equalizing property rights of spouses and family property; introducing civil marriage parallel to the religious one with the proposal that divorces be dealt with by civil courts (and that the reasons for divorce be the same for both women and men); introducing a law for identifying the father of a child born out of wedlock, for child support money, and for children's rights (as well as support for the mothers of such children); asking for guarantees for protection of the underage girl and her honor; equalizing inheritance rights of girls and boys for uncovered unmovable property; demanding state or communal support of poor widows and their children; insisting that the Law on Lawyers envision a text regarding women's rights to be attorneys; and asserting that women with legal education have the right to be judges, and all laws be revised and all limitations imposed on women be removed, thus guaranteeing full equality between women and men.[72]

Under Dimitrana Ivanova's leadership, the Bulgarian suffragists did achieve partial success by participating in local elections in 1937 and in parliamentary elections in 1938. In the 1920s and 1930s, Ivanova demanded equality between the sexes in the sphere of education, reacting against government attempts to establish different types of schools for girls and campaigning for the right of female jurists to appear as defense lawyers in courts—commitments that were intimately informed by her personal life. Ivanova actively participated in the activities of the International Alliance of Women for Suffrage and Equal Citizenship (IAWSEC) and, in the second half of the 1930s, was a board member of that organization (elected in 1935 by the congress in Istanbul). The advent of the communist regime, however, was a turning point in her life. Initially, she became a victim of personal revenge like other socially prominent figures of the "ancient regime." She narrowly escaped a death sentence—i.e., an arbitrary decision to execute her without a trial—in the manner of the new regime dominated by communists. Dimitrana Ivanova's life story, like the history of the women's movement in Bulgaria, was shaped by powerful political trends—leftist, nationalist, and authoritarian—as well as by the particular political situation. The compulsory end of her public activities in 1944 marked the end of the autonomous women's movement in Bulgaria, her life story merging once again with the broader fate of the Bulgarian women's movement.[73]

Vera Zlatareva, the secretary of the lawyers' section of the ABWUG, was born into a teachers' family in a small village a hundred kilometers east of the Bulgarian capital Sofia. After finishing the local village school, Zlatareva graduated from the middle and high schools in Plovdiv, the second largest city in the country.[74] She graduated from the law school of Sofia University in 1929, where in 1931 she would also be granted a doctorate. In 1936 she married Mihail Genovski (1903–1996), a lawyer, journalist, politician, and later professor at Sofia University. Vera Zlatareva never took her husband's name. In a brochure published in 1945, she wrote that the change of name signified "the property relation that a man has over his wife."[75] The couple had two children, a daughter and a son. Zlatareva struggled continuously against the exclusion of Bulgarian female lawyers from the bar and won some concessions to her case. Thus in May 1938, the SofCA allowed Zlatareva to begin training at the law firm of her husband Mihail Genovski, where she worked as an attorney for a probationary period. But the public prosecutor in Sofia (supported by some members of the SofCA and the prosecutorial supervision at the Sofia District Court) contested the decision, and it was subsequently annulled by the SCA.[76] In 1942, following the Bulgarian invasion of Macedonia in 1941, the Council of Defense Lawyers in Skopje allowed Zlatareva and a colleague of hers to practice in Skopje. But it was again the SCA in the capital of Bulgaria that put a stop to this.[77]

In October 1940, Zlatareva also applied for a position as a professor of labor and social law at Sofia University, but due to the existing sexist statute of the university—it allowed women to apply for a university position only if there was no male candidate—she failed.[78] The only successful female candidature at the Sofia University's faculty of law before 1944 was Luksa G. Danailova, appointed as an assistant professor in 1941. She was the daughter of Georgi Danailov, one of the very well known Bulgarian lawyers and professors at the university.[79]

The protests of female lawyers across Bulgaria were, as Zlatareva's life story shows, reflections of these women's personal struggles with the male legal profession and a direct articulation of their experience as they persistently came up against obstacles to their professional development. These experiences evoked the passion and anger that fueled Zlatareva's actions as secretary to the female lawyers' section of the ABWUG.

Vera Zlatareva was a prolific researcher of various social issues. She published extensively on prostitution in Bulgaria, as well as on the status of illegitimate children and juridical factors affecting Bulgarian women's status, including labor, property and family relations, alcoholism, and gambling. Zlatareva and her husband were both active members of the Bulgarian Agrarian party (the peasant party), and together they edited the agricultural journal *Zemia i trud* (*Land and labor*). For many years, Zlatareva was president of the Bŭlgarski neutralen vŭzdurzhatelen sŭjuz (Bulgarian Independent Temperance Union). She was also an active member of the previously mentioned ABWUG.

In the second half of the 1930s, Zlatareva became active in anti-prostitution campaigns. She was an official Bulgarian delegate to the First International Congress on Social Morality held in Budapest in October 1934 and, from January 1935, she maintained contacts with the Internationaler Verein Freundinnen junger Mädchen (International Union of Friends of Young Girls) based in Neuchâtel, Switzerland. In May 1937, Zlatareva attended the International Abolitionists Congress in Paris, presenting a paper on prostitution in Bulgaria. In this, as in all her research on prostitution, she paid particular attention to social, economic, psychological, moral, and juridical factors, and spoke out against prejudiced "explanations" of prostitution as a product of "women's nature." She was well informed regarding contemporary debates on prostitution and the history of abolitionist campaigns in Western Europe, especially regarding the prominent role of the abolitionist leader Josephine Butler (1828–1906).

Female lawyers would only win the right to practice law in Bulgaria after the introduction of communist legislation in October 1944, which granted women equal rights with men. Zlatareva was the first woman to become an attorney in 1945. After World War II, Zlatareva remained a public figure as a lawyer and MP (a representative from the agrarian party). In the late 1940s, she participated in various parliamentary committees that drafted socialist laws. She was particularly committed to laws granting women and men equal rights and, from 1947, to the Socialist constitution project. Zlatareva insisted that equality between women and men be clearly stated in statute in order to prevent the discriminatory interpretations of law that she had personally experienced under the "old regime."[80]

Afterword

Between 1944 and 1989 the number of female lawyers would gradually rise and, during the last twenty years of transition to political pluralism and a market economy after 1989, they began to outnumber men. In 2001 there were 1,567 female and 1,923 male members of the Sofia Bar Association. The number changed in 2004 to 2,323 women and 2,247 men.[81] This, however, does not mean that female lawyers could access the highest power in the country. The glass-ceiling effect is still present in today's Bulgaria.

Notes

1 Roumen Daskalov, *Bulgarskoto Obshtestvo 1878–1939*, vol. 2 (Sofia: Guttenberg, 2006).
2 Krassimira Daskalova, "Women's Suffrage in Bulgaria," in *The Struggle for Female Suffrage in Europe. Voting to Become Citizens*, ed. Blanca Rodriguez-Ruiz and Ruth Rubio-Marin (Leiden and Boston: Brill, 2012), 321–337.
3 From now on I will use the term "university."
4 *Bŭlgarski Zhenski Sŭyuz.*
5 Dimitrana Ivanova, "E li dostatuchno iziasnen vŭprosa za advokatskoto pravo na zhenite?," *Zhenata* 1, no. 9–10 (December–January 1930): 214–218.
6 Georgeta Nazŭrska, *Universitetskoto obrazovanie I bŭlgarskite zheni 1879–1944* (Sofia: IMIR, 2003), 206.
7 Ivanova, "E li dostatuchno iziasnen vŭprosa," 214–215.
8 Ibid., 214–218, esp. 214–215.
9 B-va P-va, "Zakonoproektŭt po sŭdoustroistvoto I bŭlgarskata zhena," *Zhenski glas* (December 5, 1909): 1–4; "Izlozhenie na Bŭlgarskia Zhenski Sŭyuz po zakonoproekta za dopulnenie niakoi chlenove ot sŭdosustroistvoto," *Zhenski*

glas (December 17, 1909): 1–2; "Petitsia na studentkite pri juridicheskia fakultet v Sofia do Narodnoto sŭbranie," *Zhenski glas* (December 5, 1909): 5.

10 See the laws in Petko Dobchev ed., *The Sofia Bar Association 1878–2005* (Sofia: Sibi, 2005), 15–18.

11 On the texts of this constitution, see: Vesselin Metodiev and Lŭchezar Stoyanov eds., *Bŭlgarski Constitutsii I Constitutsionni Proekti* (Sofia: Dŭrzhavno izdatelstvo "Petŭr Beron," 1990).

12 Dobchev, *The Sofia Bar Association*, 17.

13 Ivanova, "E li dostatuchno iziasnen vŭprosa," 214–218.

14 B-va P-va, "Zakonoproektŭt," 1–4; "Izlozhenie na Bŭlgarskia Zhenski," 1–2.

15 "Petitsia," 5.

16 Ivanova, "E li dostatuchno iziasnen vŭprosa," 214–218, esp. 214 and 215; Georgi Danailov, "Davaneto na advokatski práva na zhenite-juristki v Bŭlgaria: Motivi kŭm predlozhenieto," *Zhenata* 1, no. 3 (1929): 51.

17 B-va P-va, "Zakonoproektŭt," 1.

18 Nira Yuval-Davis, *Gender and Nation* (London, Thousand Oaks and New Delhi: Sage Publications, 1998), 47.

19 In Bulgarian—*Zakonoproekt za izmenenie I dopŭlnenie na Zakona za sŭdoustroistvoto.*

20 Ivanova, "E li dostatuchno iziasnen vŭprosa," 214.

21 About Malinova, see: Krassimira Daskalova, "Julia Malinova," in *A Biographical Dictionary of Women's Movements and Feminisms. Central, Eastern and South Eastern Europe, 19th and 20th Centuries*, ed. Francisca de Haan, Krassimira Daskalova, and Anna Loutfi (Budapest and New York: CEU Press, 2006), 293–295.

22 Krŭstiu Mirski, At. Kraev, and Milev from the Democrats; K. Siderov from the Radical-Democratic party; and Alexander Stamboliiski from the Agrarian party supported these women.

23 Ivanova, "E li dostatuchno iziasnen vŭprosa," 214.

24 Jenny, "Konkretni zhenski iskania pred sŭda na obshtestvenoto mnenie," *Zhenski glas* (December 17, 1909): 3–4.

25 About Karima, see: Krassimira Daskalova, "Anna Karima," in *A Biographical Dictionary of Women's Movements*, 235–240.

26 State Archive of the town of Bourgas, Collection 814 к (Zheni Bozhilova-Pateva); for a short presentation of Bozhilova-Pateva's life in German, see: Wolf Oschlies, "Ženi Božilova-Pateva (1878–1955). Leben und Werk der bulgarischen Volksbildnerin und Demokratin," *Südost-Forschungen* 32 (1973): 192–210. See also my article about her published in Bulgarian: " 'Grazhdankata' Jeni Bojilova Pateva (1878–1955)," in *Beati Possidentes*, ed. Antoaneta Totomanova and Tsvetanka Pancheva (Sofia: Natsionalna biblioteka Sv. Sv. Kiril I Metodii, 2012), 445–459.

27 "Po davane prava na juristkata," *Zhenski glas* (January 1, 1911): 1–2; D., "Svoboda na profesiata," *Zhenski glas* (February 1, 1911): 2–4; Zl. D. Raikova, "Chirpanskoto zhensko druzhestvo v otgovor na G-n Mihailovski," *Zhenski glas* (January 1, 1910): 2–3; Jenny, "Zhenata v advokaturata," *Zhenski glas* (January 1, 1910): 4–5; D., "Dopushtane na zhenata do advokatskata profesia. (Iz spisanie. „Die Frau"na Helene Lange)," *Zhenski glas* (December 7, 1910): 6.

28 Established in 1908 with Anna Karima—the former president of the *Bŭlgarski Zhenski Sŭyuz*—in charge and specifically struggling for women's political rights.

29 "Vuprosut za juristkite v Nar. Sŭbranie," *Grazhdanka* 1, no. 3 (March 1911): 71–72.

30 Among them Dr. Nikola Sakarov, Prof. Dr. Stefan Kirov, Prof. Georgi Danailov, and Tseko Brŭshlianov.

31 *Zakonoproekt za izmenenie I dopulnenie na zakona za ustroistvoto na sŭdilishtata.*
32 Ilia Yanulov and Dr. Nikola Sakarov among them.
33 *Zakonodatelno predlozhenie* (a bill allowing women to serve as judges and advocates). Among the MPs who proposed this bill one can see the names of Ilia Yanulov, Dr. Nikola Sakarov, Alexander Tsankov, B. Lissev, Dr. Petŭr Dzhidrov, Dr. Yossif Fadenhecht, Stoian Kostourkov, and P. Stanchov. A great number of the MPs signed the bill, Prof. Georgi Danailov and Prof. Dr. Danev among them. Ivanova, "E li dostatuchno iziasnen vŭprosa," 216.
34 Among the proponents of this idea were Ilya Yanulov, Dr. Nikola Sakarov, Alexander Tsankov, P. Lissev, Dr. Petŭr Dzhidrov, Dr. Yossif Fadenhecht, Stoyan Kosturkov, and Ts. Stanchov, and they were supported by T. G. Danailov, P. Paskalev, Yanko Kutsarov, Ivan Georgov, Todor Lukanov, Georgi Kirkov, Vasil Kolarov, Stoyan Omarchevski, and Hristo Kabakchiev. See about this: "Iskaneto na zhenite juristki I otgovorite po nego na Predsedatelia na Narodnoto sŭbranie I na Ministŭra na pravosŭdieto," *Zhenski glas* (January 15, 1924): 4–5.
35 "Absurdŭt ne e dokazatelstvo," *Zhenski glas* (July 15, 1918): 2.
36 Ibid., 2–3.
37 The jurists who worked on the project were Zgurev, Vladimir Mollov, Dr. Yossif Fadenhecht, Dr. Boris Vazov, Velyu Kyuchukov, and B. Ierusalimov. For more information, see: *Advokatite v zashtita na advokatskite prava na zhenite. Iz VII Kongress na Sŭyuza na advokatite v Bŭlgaria 7–8 yulii 1928* (Sofia: Bŭlgarski Zhenski Sŭyuz, 1930), 5.
38 Ibid., 5.
39 These included Prof. Alexander Tsankov, Alexander Malinov, Prof. Georgi Danailov, Prof. Yossif Fadenhecht, Prof. Venelin Ganev, Dr. Petŭr Dzidrov, and Dr. Nikola Sakarov. R. Madzharov, then a minister of justice, also supported women's rights. The Bulgarian Women's Union immediately protested against this decision, organized another rally, and conducted an inquiry among the leaders of various political parties. "Kŭm deputatite-advokati," *Zhenski glas* (February 10, 1924): 1.
40 "Vŭtreshna hronika. III Razni: Zhenite juristki se organizirat," *Zhenski glas* (January 15, 1924): 7.
41 "Za zhenite advokati," *Advokatski pregled* 8 (December 16, 1923): 111.
42 See: "Pravoto na advokatstvo na zhenite. Iziavlenie na g. ministura na pravosudieto g. R. Madjarov I Mnenie na Prof. Dr. Yossif Fadenhecht (dadeno po pokana na redaktsiata na v. *Zhenski glas*)," *Zhenski glas* (February 10, 1924): 1; Dimitrana Ivanova, "Pak za zhenite advokati," *Zhenski glas* (January 15, 1924): 4.
43 About Dimitrana Ivanova, see: Krassimira Daskalova, "Dimitrana Ivanova," in *A Biographical Dictionary of Women's Movements and Feminisms*, 182–184; Krassimira Daskalova, "The Women's Movement in Bulgaria in a Life Story," *Women's History Review* 13, no. 1 (2004): 91–103.
44 For comparison, in the United States, women had the right to be attorneys since 1869 but obtained suffrage only in 1920; in France, women were allowed to practice as attorneys in 1900 but got political citizenship only in 1944; Switzerland allowed female lawyers to be advocates in 1922 but women got political citizenship very late—after WWII. From these examples it is clear that there is no strict relation between women's political and professional rights. After WWI, in 1919, Italian women got access to the advocate profession; in 1920, the constitution of the new state of Czechoslovakia equalized the labor rights of women and men; and in 1923, women in Czechoslovakia got the right to practice in the courts and full rights of judges in 1930. Women in Germany were allowed to be advocates in 1922. During the same year, Great Britain and all countries from the British Commonwealth—Ireland, Egypt, India, New Zealand, and Canada—gave women the right to be barristers plus the right to be notaries. Also in 1926,

Sweden and Norway allowed women to practice as judges. Women in Belgium, Spain, Mexico, Chile, Argentina, China, and Japan obtained rights to be advocates also in the 1920s. Bulgaria and Albania were the only countries in the Balkans where female lawyers had no professional rights until 1944. In Greece, female lawyers got such rights in 1926; in Yugoslavia this happened in 1927; in Turkey, in 1928; and in Romania, in 1929. The data are cited in [Dimitrana Ivanova] "Delegatsia na Suyza pri Ministura na pravosudieto," *Zhenski glas* (July 20, 1938): 3.

45 Ivanova, "Pak za zhenite advokati," 4.

46 P. Stefanov, "Kamarata I advokatite: Predlozhenie da se dade na zhenite pravo da advokatstvat," *Advokatski pregled* 7, no. 1 (1926): 9.

47 This suggestion was supported by jurist Alexander Malinov as well. He was an MP, the leader of the Democratic Party, and husband of Julia Malinova, who until 1926 was the chairwoman of the *Bŭlgarski Zhenski Sŭyuz, BZhS*. About this, see: D. Ivanova, "Pravoto na advokatstvo na zhenite v Narodnoto sŭbranie," *Zhenski glas* (July 1, 1925): 2.

48 A publication in the official organ of the Bulgarian Union of Advocates, however, contains another version of this story: the author, P. Stefanov, insists that because the proposal of Angel Vŭlchev was made during the third hearing and against the statute of parliament, which said that no changes could be made during the third hearing of a bill, the suggestion of MP Vŭlchev was turned down. This was the formal reason for turning it down!

49 Petko Dobchev ed., *The Sofia Bar Association 1878–2005* (Sofia: Sibi, 2005), 19.

50 Among the supporters were Alexander Malinov and Dr. Todor Kulev, Minister of Jurisprudence, and delegates from Sofia (Dr. G. Lipovanski, Dr. T. Mihailov, Dr. Minchev, Dr. Papazov, P. Boyadzhiev, Ts. Panchev, S. Petkov, and Ivan Runevski); Stara Zagora (S. Georgiev); and Elhovo (I. Popyanchev). The final vote of the congress of advocates was 71 "for" and 81 "against" the right of female lawyers to serve as advocates. Those who voted "for" insisted that women had the necessary education and qualities to enter advocacy and that only male egoism, selfish material interests, and fear of women's competition prevented their opponents from voting for justice and proving to be real supporters of the rule of law and human justice. Among the conservative supporters of the status quo one can read narrow-minded and biased opinions about women's "nature" and their role in the society and family and their potential qualities to corrupt male judges. See: *Advokatite v zashtita na advokatskite preva na zhenite. Iz VII Kongress na Sŭyuza na advokatite v Bŭlgaria 7–8 yulii 1928* (*Po sluchai vnasianeto v Narodnoto sŭbranie na zakonodatelno predlozhenie za davane na advokatski prava na zhenite juristki v Bŭlgaria*) (Sofia: Bulgarski zhenski suyuz (Pechatnitsa "Pravo"), 1930), 23.

51 Alexander Malinov, "Advokatskoto pravo na zhenite yuristki: Rech, durzhana v kongressa na Advokatskia suyuz prez july 1928 g pri debatite po vuprosa za advokatskoto pravo na zhenite," *Zhenata* 1, no. 1 (1929): 4–9.

52 Danailov, "Davaneto na advokatski," 49–51.

53 Ivanova, "E li dostatuchno iziasnen vŭprosa," 214–218.

54 Nazŭrska, *Universitetskoto obrazovanie*, 156–164.

55 Ibid.

56 Georgeta Nazŭrska, "The Bulgarian Association of University Women, 1924–1950," *Aspasia* 1 (2007): 153–175, esp. 162.

57 Later known as the International Federation of Women in the Legal Careers (FIFCJ). She was the sister of Alexander Malinov (a lawyer, the leader of the Democratic Party, and three times Bulgarian Prime-Minister) and was married to Alexander Girginov. They were also activists of the Democratic Party. See: "Maria Girginova," *BAUW*, 2010, accessed May 13, 2014, http://bauw-bg.com/?page_id=146.

58 She graduated from Sofia University Law department in 1914. See: "Velislava L. Radulova," *BAUW*, 2010, accessed May 13, 2014, http://bauw-bg.com/?page_id=148.
59 Teofana (Fani) Kesyakova was born in 1891 in the town of Plovdiv into the family of Todor Kesyakov, a lawyer and politician. She studied at the American College for Girls in Istanbul, Turkey; she then studied music in Paris and later graduated from the Sofia University Law Department (in 1920). *Bulletin of IFUW* 12 (1930): 66. See: "Teofana Kesyakov," *BAUW*, 2010, accessed May 13, 2014, http://bauw-bg.com/?page_id=150.
60 Central State Archive, f. 1752k, op. 1, a. e. 791, l. 1–2.
61 Daskalova, "Women's Suffrage in Bulgaria," 321–337, esp. 326.
62 For more details, see: Daskalova, "Women's Suffrage in Bulgaria," 321–337.
63 See: Krassimira Daskalova, *Zheni, pol I modernizatsia v Bulgaria, 1878–1944* (Sofia: Sofia University Press, 2012), 331.
64 [Ivanova], "Delegatsia na Suyza pri Ministura na pravosudieto," 3.
65 Vassil Mitakov, "Po vuprosa za priznavane advokatski prava na zhenite juristki," *Advokatski pregled* 23, no. 19 (1943): 218.
66 Petko Dobchev ed., *The Sofia Bar Association, 1878–2005* (Sofia: Sibi, 2005), 40.
67 Dobchev, *Bŭlgarskata advokatura*, 121–123, esp. 162.
68 *Dŭrzhaven vestnik* 227 (October 16, 1944). See also: Petko Dobchev, *Bŭlgarskata advokatura 1878–2000* (Sofia: Sibi, 2003), 168.
69 Daskalova, "Dimitrana Ivanova," 182–184; Daskalova, "The Women's Movement in Bulgaria," 91–103.
70 Dimitrana Ivanova's "Memoirs," an unpublished handwritten manuscript of several hundred pages, are contained in her personal archival collection: National Library Cyril and Methodius-Bulgarian Historical Archive, f. 584, a. e. Cited in Daskalova, "The Women's Movement in Bulgaria," 96.
71 Dobchev, *The Sofia Bar Association*, 19.
72 "Iskania na Bŭlgarski zhenski sŭjuz pred g. Ministŭra na pravosŭdieto," *Zhenski glas* (May 1, 1926): 1.
73 Daskalova, "The Women's Movement in Bulgaria," 91–103.
74 About Zlatareva, see: Krassimira Daskalova, "Vera Zlatareva," in *A Biographical Dictionary of Women's Movements and Feminisms*, 620–623. The Central State Archive keeps the personal archival collection of Vera Zlatareva, as well as a lot of documents related to her struggles for professional rights. See: Central State Archive, f. 1752k (Vera Zlatareva).
75 Vera Zlatareva, *Pravnata zashtita na zhenata* (Sofia: Bŭlgarski Naroden Zhenski Sŭjuz, 1945).
76 The *Vissh Advokatski Sŭvet, VAS* (Supreme Council of Attorneys, SCA) was established in 1925 as a supreme institute of Bulgarian attorneys. The SCA elaborated all rules related to the profession. Its aim was "to supervise" and "discipline" Bulgarian attorneys and raise the prestige and ethics of attorneys. See about the SCA the documents kept in the Central State Archive, f. 997 (Vissh Advokatski Sŭvet). This archival collection contains correspondence and other materials related to the "Zlatareva" case: Central State Archive, f. 997, a. e. 46. See also: "Kŭm vŭprosa za dopushtane na zhenite-pravnichki da uprazhniavat advokatska profesia," *Advokatski pregled* 18, no. 19 (June 16, 1938): 260–267.
77 Central State Archive, f. 997 (Vissh Advokatski Sŭvet), a. e. 46; Central State Archive, f. 1752k (Vera Zlatareva).
78 Georgeta Nazŭrska, "Dostŭpŭt na zhenite do bŭlgarskata universitetska nauka (1918–1944)," *Istoricheski pregled* 5–6 (2005): 116–147.
79 Nazŭrska, "Dostŭpŭt na zhenite," 140–141.
80 Daskalova, "Vera Zlatareva," 620–623, esp. 622.
81 Dobchev, *The Sofia Bar Association*, 164.

9 "The Napoleonic Civil Code is to Blame for My Decision to Study Law"

Female Law Students and Lawyers in the Second Polish Republic (1918–1939)

Iwona Dadej[*]

Could an antifeminist code of law or a collection of authoritarian regulations and normative provisions concerning marriage dating back to the early nineteenth century[1] have inspired and incited women to study of law? That does appear to be a distinct possibility and not necessarily in only one isolated instance if we consider the example of Zofia Majmeskuł-Mastalerzowa,[2] who in 1923 became the first female student to receive a doctorate in law from the University of Cracow (Uniwersytet Jagielloński):

> I chose to study law thanks to Caesar Napoleon I. . . . One day I found the Napoleonic Civil Code in our home library . . . the book interested me. Since I wasn't able to understand much, I asked my grandma to read and translate it for me. I learned about the suffering of women, and that one day I would have to obey a strange man, i.e. my husband, and that, if he didn't allow me to go to the theatre, I would have to stay at home, and that he would manage my money, etc. I was an only child, and I felt indignant about that. I was thinking about these things, and I dreamt of one day becoming a lawyer and writing a code myself. It was my first encounter with the law. At about that time I saw a judge in a gown and wig, and I started to play court. I put on a black dress of my mom's and a piece of cotton wool on my head—and thus I became a judge.[3]

In her memoirs, the author describes her preoccupation with the *Code civil* and her indignation over rules and laws codified in the 1807 Polish version of the Napoleonic document that were still in force in parts of partitioned Poland. Cracow's first female lawyer points to all of this as the source of her motivation to study law at Poland's oldest university. This experience of the oppressive social norms and rules that kept women under close watch was undoubtedly a source of inspiration and motivation to break such gender-based rules and, ultimately, to change them. The games of Zofia's early childhood, in which she dressed up as a judge and pronounced judgments before the household pets, developed over time into youthful dreams of becoming a judge or lawyer. These went hand-in-hand with her initial contemplation of the essence of law and injustice, specifically as they were inflected by gender. Similar experiences motivated several of the women discussed in this study to devote themselves to the law, and for many of them, choosing to study law was a more or less "natural" and logical consequence of their socialization in homes where there was a long tradition of fathers and brothers in the legal profession. Often, however, it was misogynistic texts, publications, or legal provisions that were the source of motivation and the catalyst for that first group of female law students and lawyers who still had to fight against the opposition of parents, universities, and society at large for the right to study law.

The struggles of the first female lawyers, and what those struggles contributed to the development of jurisprudence in Poland, have left barely a trace in historic research or collective memory. Typical in this regard is this central notion behind a biographical lexicon of Polish lawyers: "Nothing can spiritually/intellectually bring a young lawyer to **his** knowledge more than the reading of biographies of great lawyers and masters," according to the multi-volume edition of a biographical lexicon of Polish lawyers published in the 1980s, a work that covers the last two centuries with more than 500 biographical profiles and yet contains not a single biographical reference to any of the many lawyers who were women.[4] This language of exclusion chosen by the editorial committee, referring as it does to male lawyers only, comes as no surprise—it is, after all, an excellent illustration of the metanarrative that continues to prevail in Polish legal historiography. This becomes even clearer in the Polish language as it does have masculine and feminine noun genders. The overarching notion that the history of Polish jurisprudence is a man's business or the domain of men remains popular and widespread, both in historical writing and in the collective memory of society.

The topic of female lawyers turns up in law-related historical studies sporadically and usually only as a point of secondary interest. Until now, no inquiry-based body of research literature on this professional group has existed. Instead, the history of female legal professionals is told in a style that might be better described as that of amateur popular social science, which depicts this professional group as a more or less exotic oddity.[5] All such published writings are unanimous in emphasizing the obstacles and problems, the "difficult and bumpy road" that women had to overcome to gain entry to the legal professions and to obtain juridical appointments. Even the historical sketch of Polish legal advocacy during the Second Republic (1918–1939), which mentions the first female lawyers only in passing, deals with this subject in a marginal way.[6]

The present chapter analyzes a cadre of female lawyers of Poland who have been excluded from collective notice, historical research, and both ordinary and legal discourse. It represents the results of a preliminary search for evidence of a forgotten professional group, special attention being devoted to the connections between the women's movement and the political commitment and professional activities of the first female lawyers.[7] Also central to this contribution are considerations of how these students' early interest in women's rights issues were reflected in their later professional activities and in their own professional and women's rights organizations.

Information on the first female legal professionals, the number of female law students, and the presence of female lawyers in Polish public life in the Second Polish Republic can be found in the pamphlets, periodicals, and publications of the women's movement and in the internal analyses of the feminist organization of female university graduates, the Polish Association of University Women (Polskie Stowarzyszenie Kobiet z Wyższym Wykształceniem, hereafter PSKzWW).[8] These are supplemented with an analysis of the matriculation records of the universities in Cracow and Warsaw to estimate the number of female law students.[9] Also analyzed are women's reminiscences.[10] The texts on the female lawyers' association in Poland, the Polish Association of Female Lawyers, (Związek Kobiet z Prawniczym Wykształceniem, hereafter ZKzPW), which survived the destruction of the Second World War in only fragmentary form in the Central Archive of Modern Records in Warsaw (Archiwum Akt Nowych*)*, also constitute an important body of source material.

The present contribution is divided into six areas. The introduction covers the political context, current research findings, and the available source materials. The second section describes the cohort of female students consisting of aspiring lawyers in the Second Polish Republic. The third part is devoted to the protagonists' involvement in women's rights issues. A brief discussion of the struggle to open up the legal professions follows in the fourth part, while the fifth portion examines the professional careers of the first women to work in the Polish legal system and in Poland's civil service. Finally, the history of the organization of female lawyers and its concerns are traced.

The following conclusions can be drawn from my research. The study of law for women was, among other things, a product of the fights for recognition that the women's movement had been leading since 1900. From 1919 on, the first generation female law students benefited from the women's movement's achievements as well as from the regulations of the (newly) established Polish state. But getting a paid position in legal work remained a difficult task. In this area, the interdependency between the interests and aims of the legal professions and the professional women's movement proved to be extensive. It is evident that the women's legal organizations reinforced the traditions and the emancipatory goals of the women's movement.

"All Citizens—Without Distinction as to Sex—are Equal."

The changes in the political context in November 1918 resulted in legislative changes for Polish women.[11] The Polish state that reemerged in November 1918, after the century-long period of partitions by Prussia, Austria, and

Russia, guaranteed the right "of all citizens—without distinction as to sex—to passive and active participation in elections," as decreed by the new heads of the Polish state Marshal Józef Piłsudski, Prime Minister Jędrzej Moraczewski, and Minister of Home Affairs Stanisław Thugut.[12] The equality of voting rights between the sexes was emphasized particularly in Articles 1 and 7. The March Constitution of 1921 subsequently confirmed this provisional legal order, giving it constitutional force through Articles 12 and 96 of the Polish Constitution of March 17, 1921, which provided that "The right to election is granted to any Polish citizen, without distinction as to sex, who by the day on which the elections are announced has reached the age of 21 and is entitled to all civic rights. . . . All citizens are equal under the law. Public offices are for all and in all measures for those entitled to them."[13] The constitutional articles introduced at the dawn of Poland's independence provided a generally applicable instrument and a vague description of the democratic basis for the newly created Polish Republic, which afforded its male and female citizens equal rights. For various reasons, however, the result for women continued to be "unequal opportunities," whether political, social, or economic.[14] A further deterioration in substantive opportunities in Poland's public and political life occurred a decade later. The increasingly authoritarian aspirations of those in power in the 1930s were reflected in, among other things, legislation and the ruling party's negative and destructive attitude toward civil society and democratic institutions in the political and social realms. At this time, relations between the sexes suffered a setback, one that was embodied at its most extreme in the new Polish Constitution. This new document, ratified in April 1935, made no mention of equality between the sexes; instead, it merely expressed, in Article 7, what might be described as wishful thinking: "The rights of no person should be limited on the basis of his nationality, religion, or sex."[15] Women, whether as individuals or in organized groups, now had no advocate to stand up for their rights in the parliament or other bodies. This state of affairs can be attributed to legislation that had deep roots in the nineteenth century, to a lack of modernization in the status of women in society and politics, and to provisions in newly enacted laws or in laws still in force from the days of the partitions that had been formulated with insufficient precision. The Polish matrimonial law exemplified the gulf between the carefully crafted and aspirational sections of the new constitution and other documents of established civil and criminal law. It had been subjected to several attempts at codification during the two decades of the Polish Republic (1918–1939) but it never passed legislation. It proved, according to Claudia Kraft, to be a failed project insofar as the rights of women were concerned.[16] The March Constitution, ratified in 1921 with the hope of establishing equality between the sexes under the law, had been an expression of the political will of nearly all of Poland's leading political camps. In practice, however, the constitution proved to be an unobserved "law on paper" within which all other documents, orders, and legal regulations were manifestly inconsistent.

The incongruity between constitutional declarations of equality and certain exclusionary rules governing the legal profession will be discussed in greater detail in the following sections on the educational and professional careers of female lawyers.

Admission of Women to the Study of Law in Poland: The Case of the University of Warsaw

"To receive the right to study, one must enroll as a [male] student or [female] student or as a [male] auditor or [female] auditor. Submission of the graduation examination certificate from one of the state secondary schools is the condition for acceptance into the student body."[17] This was according to the provision governing the system of higher education that was passed on July 13, 1920 as a part of the reforms of the educational system during the Second Polish Republic. What seems especially important here is the law's inclusive language, which guaranteed women access to all faculties at the state universities and legitimated the earlier semi-formal decisions on admission policies. The provision of 1920 legitimized the lengthy efforts of the Polish women's movement to secure for women entry to all faculties as students who merited equal treatment. This section will analyze only events that occurred at the re-established University of Warsaw. For reasons of space, it will not cover the study of law by Polish women at foreign universities and the turbulent struggles for the right to study in the part of partitioned Poland that was under Habsburg rule: Galicia (e.g., University of Cracow and in Lvov). The Law Faculty opened to women at the University of Warsaw simultaneously with the university's re-establishment in 1915 under wartime conditions and the aegis of the German occupational authority.[18] In 1917, the university was placed under Polish administration. In January 1919, it attained the status of a state university under a decree issued by the new Polish state.[19]

Among the first women to enroll in the law school in November 1915 were Irena Brodzińska, Elżbieta Dawidsohnówna, Blanka Morgenstern, and Janina Sokołowska. In a group in which 230 of their fellow students were male, they accounted for 1.7% of the first law students.[20] The first female students were required to meet strict standards: "The university is pleased to open its doors to female students. However, they are to conduct themselves properly and with dignity and apply themselves seriously to completing their studies."[21] Such words of welcome were an echo of the social debates taking place throughout Europe concerning the "moral" status of female students; it quickly became clear that the aforementioned "new element" or new category in university life—women—was neither viewed in light of unbiased ideas about what constitutes "moral life" nor admitted to a course of study without reservation.

By the second academic year, 1916–1917, nineteen women, who accounted for 3.4% of the entire student population, had already signed up for the law school. Joining the ranks of the first four female law students of the previous year were the following: Irena Kaliska, Maryla Fuksówna, Aniela Berlinerblau, Helena Rappaport-Kahan, Maria Langbartówna, and Stefania Mieczyńska.[22] Also to be mentioned are Irena Wortmannówna, Eugenia Schlichtertówna, and Halina Luksembourżanka, who became law students in the years following.[23] According to the admission rules, all persons from the Kingdom of Poland, and only such persons, were allowed to enroll for study if they were able to submit the required documents to the enrollment commission. These were to include both a certificate of good moral conduct and any previous educational certificates. According to internal university statistics, female law students and other women from the philosophical and medical faculties accounted for approximately 9% of all registrants for the newly established university in the 1915–1916 academic year: of the university's 1,039 students when it resumed operations, ninety-four were women, four of whom were the law students mentioned earlier.[24] A few years later, in 1918, there were 473 women who constituted nearly 20% of the University of Warsaw's student population.[25]

Despite the new university management's fundamental misgivings about having women as students, all three faculties were opened to them. The precedent set by the first enrollments quickly became a customary right for all who came after. The lively and vigorous interest that young women took in studying owes much to the work and mobilization efforts of women's rights advocates and of the Warsaw women's movement. These advocates took their cue from European debates on the subject of women's education, and they had been propagating similar postulates on their own soil since the early 1890s. They also used their own resources to prepare interested women for formal study: for example, prior to 1914 the Association for Equal Rights for Polish Women (Związek Równouprawnienia Kobiet Polskich) offered courses designed to prepare women for the entrance qualification examinations necessary for registration at the universities. Thus, the combined strands that resulted in the relatively "unspectacular" inclusion of women among university students issued directly from the work accomplished by the women's movement, the discussions that took place in Warsaw concerning women's access to higher education, the sympathetic attitude of some university administrators, and, not least, the will and "thirst for knowledge" that existed among these young women. The leading roles that Warsaw assumed after 1918 were as a political center, the main locus of all central institutions of power in Poland (legislative, executive, and judicial) and one of Poland's largest cities, with a corresponding share of the *inteligencja* as a percentage of its population as a whole, is evident. The factors that accounted for the relatively large number of women who enrolled in the study of law also resulted in a substantial group of women in Warsaw's law faculty throughout the two decades of the Second Polish Republic's continued existence. The data for 1938, gathered by the statistical commission of the Congress of Women for Social and Civil Society Work, show that, from 1923 to 1934, a total of 1,389 women received degrees from law schools in Poland.[26] The number of law school graduates from the University of Warsaw in the period between 1920 (hence five years after enrollment for a regular course of studies) and the outbreak of the Second World War in 1939 amounts—according to my statistics—to roughly 1,300 degrees as a "qualified master of law" (*dyplomowana magister praw*).[27] The percentage of women among the legal professionals in Warsaw was rising: while in the 1923–1924 academic year, fifty-three female law school graduates received degrees that accounted for 16.5% of the total number of degrees, by 1934–1935, there were already 183 women who had obtained doctorates, thereby constituting 19.1% of the total population of law students.[28] In comparison to the German universities, where the percentage of female law students remained at no more than 5%,[29] the number of Polish women studying law increased rapidly. That put women in law schools in third place—after female graduates from the philosophical and medical schools, at 54.5% and 30% respectively—on the scale of women completing a course of study at a university.[30]

Warsaw's leading role in admitting women to the study of law constitutes a phenomenon that I refer to as the "Warsaw school of female lawyers." This informal group, of which no more detailed record exists, was comprised of more than 1,300 female law students in Warsaw during the period from 1915 to 1939. These students were more heavily involved in women's rights activities than the graduates of other universities, and they appear to have become active in various legal professions in greater numbers than graduates of other universities.

Such a phenomenon could not have come about but for the friendly and unbiased reception these students met with from law professors. Some of the instructors whom female law students in Warsaw encountered in the course of their studies were liberal in outlook and sympathetic to women, and they did their part to create a friendly climate for the aspiring female lawyers in the early years of these women's studies. Among them was one of the university's founders, Stanisław Bukowiecki, along with the professors Karol Lutostański[31] and, most notably, Leon Petrażycki.[32] As a proponent of political and civil rights for women, he published a pamphlet containing articles that dealt with the social, political, and economic inequality of women in Polish society. "For the rights of women" (*O prawa kobiet*), which appeared in 1919, offered a harsh criticism of the prevailing conditions and a sober prognosis of the changes to come.[33]

The first group of female lawyers was relatively homogeneous as far as its social origins were concerned. These women belonged to the *inteligencja* stratum of Polish society. They were daughters of families that valued education and traced their origins both to the petty nobility (*ziemiaństwo*) and to the Jewish entrepreneurial class. In the nineteenth century, owing to their (usually university-level) education, both of these groups were the proponents and begetters of new values and standards—based on the fundamental principle of education.[34] Consequently, the young women of the *inteligencja* possessed the social and intellectual (and for the most part the economic) capital they needed to venture into what until then had been foreign territory for women: university studies and the practice of law. A considerable portion of prospective female lawyers came from families that were already well versed in the law, families in which the male members—as lawyers, judges, notaries, law professors, etc.—concerned themselves with legislation, legal interpretation, and jurisprudence. They were, therefore, familiar from childhood on with the duties of such a profession, and they grew up with the social prestige that those working in the law enjoyed and with the associated ethos of the *inteligencja*: civic engagement, responsibility for society, and helping to shape the cultural and intellectual life of the local community. It does not appear to be a particularly Polish characteristic that one's experiences in the home environment might themselves provide the incentive to follow in one's father's footsteps. From about 1900, however, the female emulators steadily became independent and active members of the *inteligencja*.[35] By dint of their own active efforts, they earned the educational qualifications that made them active members of the *inteligencja* stratum.

One can say that the nearly 20% of law students who were women presented an imposing figure, especially in comparison to other European countries. As always, however, legal studies took last place in the choice of disciplines for women, trailing at a considerable distance behind the medical and philosophical faculties. The first generation of female law students at Polish universities was a thoroughly national product: most of them studied Polish law at state universities, and it was at the national level that they proved themselves with their skills and services. The University of Warsaw assumed an exceptionally important role in the training of female lawyers.

The First Female Lawyers' Political Commitment to Women's Rights

"Women, nowadays enjoying the full scope of their civil and legal rights, are not aware of how much effort it took and how many obstacles had to be overcome by their predecessors in order to gain these very rights,"[36] the lawyer Maria Stypułkowska wrote in the 1990s. In her essay, she acknowledged the importance of the role of women already working in the law who from the beginning had championed the cause of women. These interests had crystallized as early as their own years of study, when they organized female students' associations such as the Circle of Female University Students (Koło Akademiczek Uniwersytetu Warszawskiego) in Warsaw, or the students' association Jedność in Cracow.[37] The Warsaw legal study pioneers Irena Kaliska, Maryla Fuksówna, and Irena Wortmannówna[38] went, after their studies, from being members of the Koło Akademiczek to membership in such women's organizations as the Progressive Political Women's Club (Klub Polityczny Kobiet Postępowych) and, later on, the Association of Female Lawyers (ZKzPW).

Apart from their activities as students, the first prospective female lawyers exhibited, during their student years, an interest in campaigns and agitation in the political or civil spheres along with an interest in active participation in voluntary associations in the Second Republic.[39] After their years of study, female lawyers also attempted to take their place in the public arena and to make the broader masses of society familiar with the phenomenon of the "female lawyer" and her concerns. The legally trained women's rights advocates postulated multiple changes in the law in the Polish partition sectors as early as the beginning of the twentieth century.[40] Particularly worthy of mention is September 1917, when, on the eve of the resurrection of the Polish state, several hundred women's rights advocates from the three partition sectors met in Warsaw for a women's convention.[41] The lawyers Helena Rappaport, Jadwiga Pyrowiczówna, and Maryla Fuksówna expressly formulated in their papers the objective shared by all women for the attainment of political and civil rights:[42]

> The law should always reflect the given era. . . . It should never stay in one place but be responsive to social evolution so that employers would follow the development of the whole social context by bringing the legal norms in line with the requirements of life. In actual fact, however, it happens otherwise, which creates conflict between the requirements of life and the law, which becomes dead. The foremost example of this can be observed in the legal position of women in Poland. . . . I am expressing not only hope but the strong conviction that the creators and editors of the new Polish Codex, the most distinguished and enlightened Polish lawyers—following the *Zeitgeist* as well as the requirements of life—will implement the rule of 'equality under the law.'[43]

Another example of political commitment in pursuit of women's rights is the work of Janina Podgórska-Jurkiewiczowa, a pioneer in the law.[44] With her specialized knowledge, she lent her support to women's organizations in Warsaw and voluntarily held regular consultation hours and consultation courses for women in which legal questions concerning the status of women before a court of law and in jurisprudence could be discussed in full. Janina Podgórska's counseling and information service, which was offered through and on the premises of the Association for Equal Rights for Polish Women as well as in her own law offices, stands as one of the first such initiatives in Poland managed by a knowledgeable female professional.[45] In her journalistic work and her direct counseling activities, she enlightened many women about their rights under the legal documents in force, criticized the Napoleonic Civil Code that had never been abolished as it related to the status of women, and involved herself in the struggles for the vote. Her goal, as she defined it herself, was the "prevention of the wretchedness that befalls women as a result of ignorance and lack of understanding of their rights, along with help in the legal enlightenment of women about their status."[46] Podgórska's work as an energetic operator of a consultancy office for women and their legal questions served as a pilot project for subsequent legal consultation offices serving Polish women.

The female lawyers offered their skills and professional knowledge for the benefit of women's rights and the women's movement, both during legal studies and in professional life. As speakers at political, academic, and professional gatherings or at conventions of the women's movement, they postulated the introduction of political rights and the acknowledgement of women as legal persons. As directors or proprietors of consultancies for women, they enlightened broader circles of women about their rights. As publicists and journalists, they reached the reading public with their articles on the status of women and, thereby, contributed to educational and informational work. At the same time, they presented the new and previously unknown profile of the women's rights advocates to the broader public: knowledge and expertise in the law, supported by educational qualifications. The female lawyers' entry into the women's movement and their general political actions and postulations in the women's rights arena mark a preliminary stage in the struggle and mobilization strategies for the admission of women to the legal professions.

The Struggle to Open the Legal Professions to Women

In the beginning, women's rights-related lawyering gave Polish women a certain legitimacy in their efforts to enter the profession. Some female lawyers attempted to become established in the legal profession by questioning the prevailing legal norms and making new policy proposals to advance the rights of women or speaking out knowledgeably on the position, role, and importance of women as a category in specific areas of the law. Undoubtedly, the law was also attractive to women because it promised opportunities to take on the norms and institutions that were responsible for inequality. With their interest in and commitment to the politics of women's rights, they wished to seize a prime opportunity to have a hand in developing procedures and institutions and the recoding of life. The women's associations supported individual female lawyers and the entire, steadily growing group of female law school graduates in these exchanges with the competent bodies and ministries. The arguments the female lawyers used to advocate opening up these male redoubts cannot be neatly fitted or categorized into the models of difference-based or equality-based feminism. The arguments that were based on sexual differences—that, among other things, a woman's special role in the law derives in part from her profound psychological knowledge and the abilities that, by virtue of her sex and the feelings associated with it such as motherliness and empathy, enable her to interact on an intuitive and profound level with juveniles who are subject to punishment—were used and propagated in alternation with the assertion that both sexes were equally predestined for judicial work. Not infrequently, both premises were used even in one and the same line of argument.[47] The years of struggle to open up the judicial profession provided the best example of interpenetration and mixing of these arguments, which were not necessarily contradictory in the context of the time.

The admission of women to the various areas of legal practice (as attorneys and judges) had to be provided for in separate documents. Opening up the legal profession appears to have been less problematic than the campaign for the first appointment of a woman as judge or the nationwide integration of the judicial profession in Poland. Women were admitted to the bar with relatively little restriction in the Second Republic. The rules governing the legal profession as promulgated by decree had gone into force with the formation of Poland's reemerging statehood on December 30, 1918. It abolished the sex-based restrictions on admission to the bar.[48] Helena Kononowicz-Wiewiórska,[49] however, did have to remove an additional hurdle on her way to becoming the first professional female lawyer. Although she obtained her doctorate in Saint Petersburg, Russia, she was barred from practice as a lawyer in Poland. The three-year probationary training period provided in the decree lasted twice as long in her case before she finally received, in 1925, authorization from the Warsaw bar to practice in law.[50] With this approval, she achieved a certain breakthrough and facilitated a shift in the legal profession.

The struggle to open up the judiciary was far more drawn out and intense as the opposition from judges and the ministry of justice was immense. The wording in the decree of February 8, 1919 concerning the probationary judicial training period defined a clear prohibition against admitting women to training or to positions in the court: "A judicial trainee is a male citizen of Poland who has graduated from the faculty of law at the state university. Women can serve an apprenticeship for the occupation of lawyer under Article 14 of the temporary Polish Palestra statute."[51] It was not until a decade later that this law was abolished, along with other discriminatory provisions, as a consequence of the overhaul of Polish jurisprudence. The regulation that went into effect on February 8, 1928 repealed a total of forty-four decrees and statutes that had, among other things, substantially limited the admission of women to the legal professions.[52] With its nearly 300 articles, the document provided for, among other things, entry into all levels and areas of the judicial profession.

In legal and feminist circles, however, the preparations for reform had sparked a vigorous discussion beginning around 1925, which concerned the admission of women to practice in jury courts (*sąd przysięgły*). The minister of justice's proposals for new rules governing the ordinary law courts did much to appease conservative groups and movements in the legal realm, containing as it did a clause stating that "only a person of the male sex may be appointed judge in a jury court," expressly excluding women from these socially prestigious areas of judicial practice.[53] The resulting conflict of interest separated those old legal organizations that expressly wished to have no female members in the jury courts (and that had submitted to the parliament a draft bill to that effect) from the organized or individual female lawyers who were able to call upon the strong mobilized and organized support of the entire feminist community, which harshly criticized such exclusionary practices in the legal professions. The Women's Section of the Association of Trainees/Candidates for the Legal Profession (Sekcja Kobieca Zrzeszenia Aplikantów Prawniczych) coordinated communication with ministries, parliament, and the judiciary. Women's organizations of every persuasion joined female lawyers to form an alliance to protest against such regulatory proposals and to exert pressure on the ministry of justice, the government, and the parliament.[54] Their arguments used against the proposals invoked the March Constitution of 1921 and called for the observance of the rights the constitution guaranteed to women and accused the legislature of incompetence in constitutional interpretation. They also emphasized the injustice and inequality in the judiciary's treatment of women, who, as defendants, were perceived to be at a disadvantage before the all-male juries.[55] The women's movement failed, however, in its campaign on the issue of the jury courts. It took the previously mentioned organizational reform of the Polish justice system to bring women, in 1929, some measurable success.

The event I have referred to as "halfway successful" was the nomination and confirmation of Wanda Grabińska-Wójtowicz as a judge in 1929.[56] The first female Polish judge's jurisdiction was limited exclusively to sentencing youthful offenders; she continued to be denied ordinary jurisdiction over adults. Despite the fact that a woman had been appointed to serve in a supposedly less prestigious capacity in the judicial profession, the women's movement and female lawyers were for the moment content, not least because the discriminatory mechanisms and exclusionary approaches had been removed for the first time from the regulatory regime governing the judicial profession. The women's organizations that had endorsed her candidacy stressed that she had a special gift for interpreting the criminal code by virtue of her sex. As a woman, she was said to be better able to understand delinquent youths (especially girls) and, by virtue of such "innate" gifts as empathy, to be absolutely predestined for the profession. As a woman, accordingly, she was said to have the ability to "bring the noblest values to the profession and, through direct and intuitive contact with under-age defendants, deliver well-reasoned judgments, always with a concern for such under-age defendants' future and welfare."[57]

The protracted struggle to open the judiciary to female lawyers had received widespread exposure in the media, and it was waged on multiple fronts. The struggles to secure for women the right to practice professionally in the courtroom stood as examples, and in the press, assumed symbolic significance for other judicial and legislative areas that female law school graduates wished to apply themselves to and participate in.

The Polish "Portia ante portas"[58]—Fields of Employment for Women in the Law

In 1929, an embittered female Polish journalist wrote of the first years of female employment in the various disciplines within the law:

> It would appear, judging by the number of women reading law, that this type of profession is known and familiar to them. This, however, is not the case: law is an area that has not yet been completely mastered by women. . . . The majority of ladies graduating from law schools, having received a pompous master's degree and gotten high on its very grandeur, soon falls rather hard and helplessly into the everyday grind of office work, leaving the lofty convictions about their own brilliance behind and remaining in this state until marriage or some other, equally crucial, milestone.[59]

Helena Wiewiórska quickly became a model for several dozen women who aspired to work as lawyers. The legal profession's relatively open attitude toward women is reflected in the words of welcome with which a Warsaw periodical for lawyers greeted the first woman to practice law: "On April 1 of this year [1925] Mrs. Helena Wiewiórska took her oath to the Warsaw bar association. She consequently became the first female lawyer in Poland, thereby assuming a permanent place in the history of the women's movement. Mrs. Wiewiórska is a clear example of the fact that the Polish woman is not about to be satisfied with equality on paper, but aspires to positions and professions that in the past have been the exclusive privilege of men. We have no doubt . . . but that Mrs. Wiewiórska is bringing a new quality to the legal profession," particularly in dealings with female clients.[60] This marked a breakthrough within the Polish legal system: a woman with a law degree had been accepted into the association and professional organization of lawyers.[61] According to data released by the Polish Institute of Statistics and the PSKzWWs' own estimates, there were approximately 100 women working as self-employed lawyers in 1931. By 1937, there were already as many as 212 female lawyers and 440 female lawyers-in-training.[62] Overall, female Polish lawyers as a group represented less than 10% of the entire population of lawyers in Poland.[63] More than half (138) of the female lawyers worked in Warsaw; in other major cities in Poland, the number of women practicing as lawyers was in the two-digit range (18 in Cracow, 28 in Lvov).[64] Among the female lawyers who established their law practices in Warsaw were, apart from Helena Wiewiórska, other graduates of the Warsaw school of female lawyers, such as Irena Kaliska, Halina Luksembourżanka, Aleksandra Stypułkowska, Stanisława Hermelin, and Maria Magdalena Haydenowa. In Cracow, there were the sisters Janina and Stanisława Ściężko, along with Aniela Berlinerblau-Steinsberg; in Lvov, there was Bronisława Reiter-Silberschlagowa.[65] Some of these female lawyers established and independently managed their own law offices. A considerable number pursued their legal careers as a family enterprise (usually with a husband or father). Not surprisingly, one of the most popular fields of practice for female lawyers, in which they represented the interests of female clients, was family and matrimonial law. Divorce law and inheritance law, along with the defense of clients in criminal proceedings, were also among the most frequent sources of work for female lawyers.[66] Apart from these areas of practice that had a genuinely "feminine" connotation, a relatively small portion of female lawyers devoted themselves to work associated with the political process, such as lawyers for the political opposition or as defense counsel for supporters of the communist party or the workers' movement.[67]

Access to civil service in the chief public prosecutor's office (*Prokuratoria Generalna*) was generally not denied to female lawyers under the rules of employment.[68] Chief public prosecutor Stanisław Bukowiecki's liberal and benevolent attitude and his "women-friendly" personnel policy made such access even easier.[69] My investigations identified five female lawyers who served as employees of the public prosecutor's office (i.e., as officials in the lower pay grades): one was Maria Fuksówna, mentioned briefly in the previous section, who for more than two decades, beginning in the early 1920s, worked there as legal counsel (*radca prawny Prokuratorii Generalnej*), and, from 1927 on, as department head.[70] Others who worked for Bukowiecki were Eugenia Schlichtertówna,[71] Grażyna Szmurłowa, Izabela Chojecka-Boniecka, and Zofia Gawrońska-Wasilkowska, all of them from the Warsaw school of lawyers.

A dramatic reversal in the political situation in Poland and in the political culture associated with it occurred a decade later. The economic and political crisis of the 1930s also gave rise to debates about whether employed and married women should be excluded or driven from professional and public life. For this reason, Izabela Chojecka-Boniecka's candidacy for a public prosecutor's position was rejected by the minister of justice on the basis of the candidate's sex, and she was only allowed to hold the position of a junior civil servant.[72]

It was not until 1929, with the nomination of Grabińska-Wójtowicz as juvenile court judge, that the judiciary was opened to women. But by no means did the ministerial order allow women unrestricted entry into the judicial profession. In the beginning, women could only be found as judges in juvenile court (*sąd dla nieletnich*), a local trial court (*sąd grodzki*), or a labor court (*sąd pracy*). Between the 1929 appointment of the first female judge for juvenile criminal matters and the outbreak of war, in all of Poland, only seven women served in local trial, juvenile, and labor courts. After Grabińska-Wójtowicz joined the courts, the other "female Warsaw lawyers" served in local trial courts or juvenile courts: Maria Hasińska, Wanda Kamińska, Helena Lepiarzowa, and Irena Wojnikonis.[73] The ratio between practicing female judges and female law school graduates is a clear indication of the structural and psychological barrier for women in the field of legal adjudication. For this reason, Grabińska-Wójtowicz, judge and penologist, became iconic for a feminine sense of justice and empathy. A pioneer in the courtroom, she also fulfilled the hopes and expectations of the women's movement by addressing the concerns of women who had been excluded, marginalized, or penalized. In her judicial work, Grabińska-Wojtowicz advocated for, among other things, the development of social institutions, especially for rehabilitating female juvenile offenders. In addition, she wrote papers and expert opinion pieces for the Sejm (the Polish parliament) among which was a bill to improve the status of children born out of wedlock and a proposal for a legal battle against prostitution and the trafficking of women (especially that of underage girls), including a draft proposal for re-socialization programs for the latter.[74] As an established judge, she had been actively involved since the late 1930s in the legal reforms enacted to curb prostitution and diminish sexually transmitted diseases. Working closely with the members of the Sejm, she presented draft proposals for the reform of legislation relating to this topic to the public at large and to the codification commission. As an expert in this area, she represented the Polish government in the Social Commission of the League of Nations from 1930 to 1939.[75]

One area of the law from which women were excluded during the 1920s and 1930s was the profession of a notary, the rules for which were recodified in 1933.[76] Not a single female lawyer succeeded in establishing herself as a notary during this time. The reason for this was that notaries were organized on the basis of the Napoleonic tradition and that the profession was taken up as "a vocation of social trust," or that of a "public official" (*funkcjonariusz publiczny*), to which only select male citizens, with the background to match, had entry.[77]

The lion's share of the nearly 1,400 female law school graduates, however, went into the state administrative service. Female lawyers were to be found in ministries, national and local authorities, state-owned enterprises such as the Institute of Statistics, insurance companies, local and national tax offices, and several administrative posts in the Polish *voivodeships* (hence at the highest level of the territorial subdivision of the Polish state).[78] With approximately five thousand of them employed in public service in Poland in the 1930s, women accounted for 8% of the entire workforce employed in the machinery of state. That number also included female lawyers and their services as lawyers and advisors in various ministries. One should note, however, that women were assigned to jobs at the lowest salary levels. With a total of twelve salary levels in public service, most female employees were confined to levels six to twelve, level one being the highest. Only a few individuals in the aforementioned group—roughly 200—were placed in salary levels four and five, hence the highest grade for an official that a woman could achieve in public service.[79] One also finds cases of unemployment among female law school graduates, which presumably are attributable to the fact that the women concerned lacked the "cultural capital" to help them along. By that I mean, among other things, having the benefit of one's father's or husband's legal, social, or professional networks or the financial means to develop an independent livelihood through self-employment.[80]

To complete the picture, mention should also be made of academic careers at the universities and the first women to be accepted into the law schools, not as students, but as academic personnel. The university statistics are sobering, and they reflect in a certain way the prestige of the law schools and of university professorships and lectureships. Throughout the 1920s in the Second Polish Republic, academic positions in law schools remained the exclusive preserve of men: in the years from 1919 to 1939, not a single woman achieved a post-doctoral teaching qualification at any of the five Polish universities. The remaining choices tended to be rather marginal positions or composite positions combining the position of a private lecturer (adjunct) with that of a secondary school teacher or that of an employee in the public prosecutor's office or in a ministry with that of a private lecturer at a university. Among the fifty-eight members of the non-professorial academic staff in the law schools, there was only one female employee, Wolna Wszechnica Polska, who was not explicitly employed by the university as such, but by the College for the Social and Political Sciences.[81] Zofia Rynkiewicz, a specialist in civil law, was also employed by this college as a lecturer as early as 1926, along with other recognized legal scholars, such as Leon Petrażycki, in its Institute for Politics and the Social Sciences.[82]

A law degree afforded women no protection against exclusionary practices in hiring or recruitment for civil service positions where categorical consideration of gender constituted a genuine exclusionary practice. The general conviction that legal studies guaranteed social prestige and a civil service appointment, along with the attendant financially and professionally lucrative career, did not apply to women. Instead, a disparity arose between the number of female law school graduates and the number of employees on the first four salary levels in the Polish government and judicial service. As a result of the crisis in the 1920s, stiff competition in the labor market, and a persistent bias against women who were employed and aspired to the higher positions, this field also cannot be described as affording much success. Relatively few women were able to achieve independent professional success in the Polish judicial system as lawyers or judges.

A Professional Organization of Their Own: Związek Kobiet z Prawniczym Wykształceniem 1929–1939

The March Constitution (1921) introduced gender equality in principle, however, Teodora Męczkowska would argue a decade later that cooperation among women's advocates was necessary to realize this ideal. Such was the rationale behind the creation of the Polish branch of the International Federation of University Women (1926). Moreover, Męczkowska suggested that stronger cooperation between women's rights and women's professional associations was essential to raise the status of women in society.[83]

> A woman with the trade of a doctor, advocate, teacher or office worker meets on daily basis . . . with a range of questions of a completely unprofessional nature, just because she is a woman. Where are these offices, companies, etc., that admit women? Where are the posts they occupy? The lowest official levels and lowest salaries are accessible to women, but they are constantly denied better positions. . . . It is fair to state that little has changed in the position of women, and important articles of constitutions, such as §96 [section of Poland's March Constitution that guaranteed the equality of both sexes] and others announcing the full equality of rights is just a fiction on paper.[84]

A few new professional organizations for women were formed in the Second Republic. Female university graduates in general had been organized since 1926 in the PSKzWW; female doctors had had their own Association of Female Polish Doctors since 1925.[85] The formation of the Association of Female Lawyers, ZKzPW, can be described as the logical consequence of the work of female lawyers in women's rights matters. It would be founded in 1929 as a consequence of the women's struggle against "theoretical or fictitious equal rights."[86] The goal of the association was defined in its by-laws as "to defend the rights and interests of female lawyers and to exert influence upon the social and legal rules governing public life, with special consideration given to the rights and interests of women."[87] The Association of Female Lawyers arose as a result of the vigorous discussions taking place between the women's movement and the Polish government, represented by the minister of justice, concerning calls to open the judicial profession to women—discussions that ended only after the discriminatory rules were abolished in 1929. The women who had participated in that dispute organized themselves from then on in the association of female lawyers.

The association's founding mothers were the previously mentioned pioneers, Helena Wiewiórska and Wanda Grabińska-Wójtowicz, and Maryla Fuksówna and her involvement in the Association of Female Lawyers also played an important role in the organization's founding and continuing existence.[88] The founding committee immediately transformed itself into the regular executive board, which consisted of the following members: Wanda Grabińska-Wójtowicz as the board's chairman and Helena Wiewiórska as its deputy chairman, Warsaw lawyer Halina Luksembourżanka[89] and judicial trainee Helena Lepiarzowa,[90] along with Maria Lutostańska[91] later on, who became the association's recorders or secretaries. Maria Roszkowska[92] and Aleksandra Stypułkowska,[93] both prospective lawyers, were appointed members of the executive board.[94] Others among Warsaw's female lawyers, such as Grażyna Szmurłowa, Zofia Szulcowa, and Maria Czarnecka, would join the executive board later on.[95] By 1937, the founders continued to serve the association in a management capacity: Grabińska-Woytowicz served as chairman, along with Fuksówna as chairman's deputy. All of the founders had already amassed a wealth of experience in civil society organizations—in several female students' associations, in women's rights-related organizations, and in the Polish Association of University Women. Thus, the association had on its board and among its members a number of media-savvy trailblazers for women seeking higher education or work in the justice system, and the print media were receptive to them, often granting them interviews on the subject of their experiences as women or lawyers.[96] A safe estimate of the number of members puts them in the two-digit range, between thirty and no more than sixty women in Poland as a whole. Geographically, the association was based in the center of Warsaw, presumably in the offices of one of the women members. All public announcements, topical accounts, or reports relating to participation in national or international gatherings and conventions were issued through the bulletin of the Association of University Women, *Komunikat Zarządu* (Minutes of the Managing Committee of PSKzWW) or through the print organ *Kobieta Współczesna* (The Modern Woman). How the ZKzPW conducted itself in its relations with the Polish Association of University Women is relatively unclear. It is to be surmised that the ZKzPW belonged to the PSKzWW as a constituent member. The cooperation between the PSKzWW and the ZKzPW appears to have been fluid and without friction. The Association of Female Lawyers was represented on the main executive board of the Polish Association of University Women by Helena Kononowicz-Wiewiórska, while Irena Wortmannówna[97] was elected to the executive board of the Polish Association of University Women-Warsaw group.[98] Other female lawyers, such as Irena Kaliska, are to be found among the regular members of the PSKzWW.[99] In the other women's organizations, the female lawyers enjoyed the status of experts on the new rules governing public and private life. As advisors, they introduced several subject areas, most notably Helena Kononowicz-Wiewiórska on "Civil marriage and divorce in the three former partition sectors of Poland" in the Progressive Political Women's Club, Halina Luksembourżanka on "Criminal proceedings for termination of pregnancy," Irena Wortmannówna on matrimonial law with the subject of "Civil rights of a married woman," and Maria Fuksówna with her "Sketch of the professional situation of the first female lawyers."[100] Grabińska-Wójtowicz had close ties with the Alliance of Women's Work for the Civil Society (ZwiJunta para Ampliaciónzek Pracy Obywatelskiej Kobiet, ZPOK), before which she read papers with Helena Wiewiórska on women's civil rights as part of a continuing education program. Irena Wortmannówna served in this association as an education consultant for women acting as information disseminators in the provinces, who took an interest in the criticisms and the proposals for more equal treatment of women in connection with the codification processes.[101] Grażyna Szmurłowa wrote for the journal of the ZPOK some articles explaining to readers of *Praca Obywatelska* the rules and mechanisms of the Polish codification commission and clarifying and commenting on the commission's regulatory projects relating to women's issues, such as a married woman's citizenship status, divorce laws, etc.[102] The Association of Female Lawyers came under the scrutiny of the interior ministry in the 1930s, when it submitted its slightly amended bylaws for approval. A routine exchange of information concerning the association ensued between the foreign office and the interior ministry.[103]

The Polish female lawyers and their organization ZKzPW felt themselves to be part of the European community of female lawyers. In their arguments and political agitation, they were strongly influenced by their French colleagues and, later, by the work of the International Federation of Women in Legal Careers (with French acronym FIFCJ).[104] "The International Federation of Women in Legal Careers and our association have set themselves the goal of furthering professional support for its members and supporting the further development of professional solidarity among women," states the founding document of 1929.[105] The members of the board of the Polish Association of Female Lawyers, along with sympathetic female lawyers, were keen and active participants in the gatherings of the FIFCJ that occurred every other year. The dynamic contacts with various women's committees abroad, as well as close personal relationships, had come about as early as the women's law school days or in connection with international women's conventions. The private character of these acquaintanceships developed over the years into institutional or semi-official connections and professional networks.[106] These close contacts and exchanges with the international organization for female lawyers arose in the 1930s and survived both the war years and the transformed political reality in Poland after 1945 when a communist government took power.[107] Within the international umbrella organization of female lawyers, Polish women travelled to meetings of the federation's council and its conventions, and they were elected to the internal committees during the conventions, as well as to the executive board and federation council. Grabińska-Wójtowicz was elected deputy executive board chairman at the International Female Lawyers' convention in Vienna in 1936 and, along with Fuksówna, was also appointed to the federation council.[108] As delegates from the Polish Association of Female Lawyers and other women's organizations, the female lawyers served at the meetings of a League of Nations commission for women and children and represented Polish women's organizations at the conventions of the international women's organizations.[109] Particularly outgoing and indefatigable were Maryla Fuksówna, Wanda Grabińska-Wójtowicz, Helena Wiewiórska, Maria Lutostańska, and Grażyna Szmurłowa, who have been mentioned repeatedly at the national level and who were active in international feminist legal circles only during the one decade of the ZKzPW's existence, from 1929 until the outbreak of war in 1939. The subject areas discussed at the female lawyers' professional conventions concerned for the most part the status of women under the legal systems of the various nation-states. Through this comparative approach and their determined joint efforts, the female lawyers attempted to create a universal model that, ideally, might have been accepted and introduced by all European states. The problem of citizenship for married women and the legitimation and status of children born out of wedlock were continually recurring themes in the international consultations.[110] Female university graduates and lawyers also made efforts to portray their concerns and struggles in their home countries to the female half of the European public. They published reports concerning the legal situation of women in Poland and the first generation of female lawyers. These appeared in French and English in the magazine *la femme polonaise*.[111] Polish women and Polish affairs received further exposure in the organizational structures of the League of Nations and elsewhere, through the study by Grażyna Szmurłowa, published in 1937, on current Polish law and the situation of women in Poland.[112] This was a compilation of the Polish laws in which women are mentioned as a category. The study was intended as a report on women's rights in Poland for the Secretariat of the League of Nations and as a compact information source for interested organizations abroad. As published in its original language, Polish women used the study to gain an overview of the statutes of Polish legislation.

The Second World War and the later consequences of the ensuing political decisions brought an abrupt halt to relations and relationships on the European continent. Nevertheless, the assumption that there was an absolute isolation of, and strict political separation between, the organizations that, according to the geopolitical situation, belonged together before the war must be critically questioned in several respects. The extent to which female Polish lawyers were also able to influence or prevail in the perpetuation of their personal and professional contacts, given the restrictive political conditions, is questionable. One thing that remains certain is that female Polish lawyers were represented in politics in the post-war period. Zofia Gawrońska-Wasilkowska, for example, a former "Warsaw female lawyer" in the Second Republic, became a role model for survivors of the first generation of female Polish lawyers and those who remained in Poland. Gawrońska-Wasilkowska's entry into politics in 1945 and her tenure as a minister of justice (1956–1957) followed her political interests and her commitment during the Second Polish Republic, when her sympathies lay very much with the communist political movement.[113] As a functionary in the machinery of state (she sat for decades as a judge of the nation's highest court) and in the women's organization, but above all as a practicing lawyer, she represented the People's Republic of Poland at the International Congress of Women in the Law in 1961 in Paris, where discussions centered on, among other things, the rights of children and adoption rights from an internationally comparative perspective.[114] At that time, the ZKzPW no longer existed, having been dissolved in the late 1940s along with the PSKzWW as a result of the increasing Stalinization of political life in Poland. It is interesting to note that female lawyers from Poland were the only ones in the entire

"Eastern Bloc" who had a voice of their own, albeit one that remained loyal to their government, at the Paris Congress in 1961. The specific concerns and associated legal reforms that the congress drafted as a proposal for the European states in regard to adoption law was also one of the main preoccupations of the Paris delegate Zofia Gawrońska-Wasilkowska. Even if this continuity in the cultivation of international contacts seems fragile, especially after the Second World War, the contacts and networks with female lawyers from other European countries (especially from countries at the core of the women's movement) that were so vigorously pursued during the interwar years, and that were sometimes gained on a basis of friendship, were in certain ways a matter of course for Polish women. Both at the time when contacts were made in the 1920s and 1930s and after 1945, under political conditions that were obviously altered and more difficult, they remained intent on pursuing them.

The ZKzPW is to be regarded as a professional organization with a strong legal profile, one that both looked after the interests of the organized members within its own sorority of lawyers and publicly commented on political and legal topics, partly by assisting in legislation with a special concern for relations between the sexes. Beyond national borders, its leaders quickly became part of the international community of female lawyers and representatives of both Polish women and the Polish state before the institutions of the political order and women's political committees.

Conclusion

The Polish women portrayed in these biographical sketches are trailblazers in the legal professions. Their protracted struggles with social norms and sex-specific codes of conduct, their campaigns over many years to open the universities, and their turbulent admission efforts to the legal professions made them self-assured pioneers and members of the Polish *inteligencja*. The female lawyers I have described were likewise indomitable people who labored, for their own recognition as persons and as women, both in the family and as legal persons in the society, and who thereby generated social transformations and modernizing processes. They are deserving of a place in history and collective memory.

"All citizens, without distinction as to sex, have the right to vote," proclaimed Marshal Józef Piłsudski's order on those November days in 1918, and this guaranteed women's participation and involvement in the political and social events of the re-emergent Polish state. It elevated women who had previously been "without rights" to the status of citizens with the same rights as Poland's male citizens. That these legal provisions tended to be illusory in practice, an indication in several respects of the great disparity between the laws and their incomplete social application, has been examined through the struggles waged by the female lawyers. As both a professional group and a unit actively engaged in political matters of concern to women, the female lawyers failed to achieve a full change of heart on the part of society as a whole as far as equal rights for women were concerned. Even the efforts to integrate female lawyers into the community of Polish lawyers met with only limited success. For several centuries, the great social esteem and prestige enjoyed by judges and lawyers, along with their usually financially lucrative careers, characterized the generally accepted image of a male lawyer. Accordingly, the attempt made in the early twentieth century—in unison with the efforts of the women's movement—to establish the first women in the legal system met with a considerable resistance on the part of the legal profession. The male-dominated law-related professional associations wished to preserve the *status quo*, with its homogeneity in terms of sex and social stratum, and perpetuate it as an elite professional group, "unspoiled" by the intrusion of new "strangers" into its ranks.

This essay on Polish women in the law has afforded a first look at the history of this professional group. In their struggle for the right to study and practice law, female lawyers traveled a long and difficult road between the late nineteenth century and the outbreak of the Second World War. An examination of the legal fields in which female lawyers worked, and of the socio-political causes to which they devoted themselves in the associations of female lawyers, complete the picture and make one thing very clear: contrary to the historical Polish metanarrative of old, women were an active part of the legal community, but at the same time, fell victim to its internal exclusionary mechanisms. The fates of the female lawyers must be looked at differently and do not lend themselves to measurement against masculine career models. For the contributions they made, however, they belong both in the master narrative of Polish national history and the transnational history of women's political efforts toward emancipation.

Notes

* I am very grateful to PD Dr. Dietlind Hüchtker and Prof. Claudia Kraft for their suggestions and comments.

1 The Napoleonic *Code civil* was imposed by the French authorities on the Polish territories in 1807, and some sections of it remained in effect in various regions of Poland for the remainder of the nineteenth century and as late as the 1960s, cf., inter alia, Artur Korobowicz and Wojciech Witkowski, *Historia ustroju i prawa polskiego 1772–1918* (Kraków: Zakamycze, 2002). It was a reminder of the imposed codification and a symbol of the legal subjugation of women, cf. Anna Rosner and Katarzyna Sójka-Zielińska, *Kodeks Napoleona. Historia i współczesność* (Warszawa: Lexis Nexis 2008).

2 Zofia Majmeskuł-Mastalerzowa (1899–1984) earned a "doctor iuris" in 1923 at the Jagiellonian University in Cracow, the first woman to do so. She was unable to fulfill her dream of writing a constitution that guaranteed gender equality, or to become established in a legal profession as a lawyer or judge. Following her studies, marriage, and again after her divorce, she worked for various authorities of the *voivodeship* of Cracow (in Zakopane and Cracow) and in the Polish tax offices. She wrote her memoirs for the six-hundredth anniversary of the university in 1964. The publishers of an anthology, who found them "very

feminine and emotional, though engaging," did not accept them for inclusion, however, and it was not until 2006 that they were published separately, cf. Zofia Majmeskuł-Mastalerzowa, "Moje wspomnienia," ed. Urszula Perkowska, *Krakowski Rocznik Archiwalny* 12 (2006): 217–232; Urszula Perkowska, *Studentki Uniwersytetu Jagiellońskiego w latach 1894–1939. W stulecie immatrykulacji* (Kraków: Secesja, 1994).

3 Majmeskuł-Mastalerzowa, "Moje wspomnienia," 223.

4 *Słownik biograficzny adwokatów polskich* (Warszawa: Wydawnictwo Prawnicze, 1980–1988). Emphasis mine.

5 Roman Łyczywek ed., *Szkice z dziejów adwokatury polskiej* (Warszawa: Wydawnictwo Prawnicze, 1976); Stanisław Milewski, "Zanim kobieta została adwokatem," *Palestra. Pismo adwokatury polskiej* 56, no. 1–2 (2002): 98–106.

6 Małgorzata Materniak-Pawłowska, *Adwokatura II Rzeczypospolitej. Zadnienia prawno-ustrojowe* (Poznań: Wydawnictwo Naukowe UAM, 2009); Małgorzata Materniak-Pawłowska, "Ustrój adwokatury w Polsce w świetle regulacji prawnych z lat 1918–1939," *Czasopismo prawno-historyczne* 58, no. 2 (2006): 51–85; Lech Krzyżanowski, *Sędziowie w II Rzeczypospolitej. Okręgi apelacyjne: krakowski i katowicki* (Katowice: Wydawnictwo Uniwersytetu Śląskiego 2011), 255–260; Maria Stypułkowska, "Trudna droga kobiet do wykonywania zawodów prawniczych," *Palestra. Pismo adwokatury polskiej* 48, no. 9–10 (1994): 139–149.

7 For more detailed research, see Iwona Dadej, "Die Frau von morgen." Frauenpolitisch tätige Akademikerinnen in Deutschland und Polen, 1918–1939," PhD thesis, Freie University Berlin, 2015.

8 See, inter alia Polskie Stowarzyszenie Kobiet z Wyższym Wykształceniem, *Polskie Stowarzyszenie Kobiet z Wyższym Wykształceniem w latach 1926–1936* (Warszawa: Drukarnia B-ci Drapczyńskich, 1936); Teodora Męczkowska, *Do czego dążymy: Działalność Polskiego Stowarzyszenia Kobiet z Wyższym Wykształceniem* (Warszawa: Drukarnia "Kobiety Współczesnej," 1931); the journal *Kobieta Współczesna* [The Modern Woman] for the years 1927–1938, as well as the journal *Komunikat Zarządu Głównego Polskiego Stowarzyszenia Kobiet z Wyższym Wykształceniem* [The bulletin of the Polish Association of University Women, hereafter "*Komunikat Zarządu*"] for the years 1930–1938. About the IFUW see Edith C. Batho, *A Lamp of Friendship. A Short History of the International Federation of University Women 1918–1968* (Eastbourne: Sumfield & Day, 1968); Christine von Oertzen, *Strategie Verständigung. Zur transnationalen Vernetzung von Akademikerinnen 1917–1955* (Göttingen: Wallstein 2012); see also Dadej, "Die Frau von Morgen."

9 Teczki doktorskie, Jagiellonian University Archive in Cracow; Teczki studenckie Wydziału Prawa, Warsaw University Archive.

10 Majmeskuł-Mastalerzowa, "Moje wspomnienia," 217–233; Zofia Gawrońska-Wasilkowska, "Wspomnienia 1930–1939," in *Wydział Prawa w relacjach i wspomnieniach pracowników i studentów 1918–1950*, ed. Grażyna Bałtruszajtys, *Studia iuridica* 17 (1990): 57–62; Janina Bogucka-Ordyńcowa, *Cyganeria i polityka: wspomnienia krakowskie 1919–1939* (Warszawa: Czytelnik, 1964).

11 November 11, 1918 marked a new phase in the development of Polish society when, after twelve decades as a partitioned country (where Poland's citizens and society functioned as a "nation without a state"), the Polish independence movement created a sovereign state. Bianka Pietrow-Ennker, "Frau und Nation im geteilten Polen," in *Geschlecht und Nationalismus in Mittel- und Osteuropa 1848–1918*, ed. Sophia Kemlein (Osnabrück: fibre, 2000), 125–142; Michael G. Müller and Rudolf Jaworski, *Eine kleine Geschichte Polens* (Frankfurt am Main: Suhrkamp, 2000); Adam Zamoyski, *The Polish Way: A Thousand-Year History of the Poles and Their Culture* (New York: Hippocrene Books, 1994).

12 "Dekret o ordynacji wyborczej do Sejmu Ustawodawczego z 6 grudnia 1918 roku," *Dziennik Praw Państwa Polskiego* nr. 18, poz. 46, art. 1 (1918).
13 Konstytucja Rzeczpospolitej Polskiej, Ustawa z dnia 17 marca 1921 roku in Dziennik Ustaw nr 44 poz. 267 (1921); see also Wanda Sudnik, *Prawo polityczne Rzeczypospolitej Polskiej 1918–1939. Wybór źródeł* (Warszawa: Wydawnictwo Sejmowe, 2002), 60.
14 The expression "equal rights but unequal opportunities" stems from the observations of Anna Żarnowska and Andrzej Szwarc regarding the legal and social position of Polish women in the interwar years; see Anna Żarnowska, and Andrzej Szwarc eds., *Równe prawa i nierówne szanse. Kobiety w Polsce międzywojennej* (Warszawa: DiG, 2000), 5–7.
15 Konstytucja Rzeczpospolitej Polskiej, Ustawa z dnia 23 kwietnia 1935 roku, in Dziennik Ustaw nr 30, poz. 227 art. 7 par. 2; see also in: Sudnik, *Prawo polityczne Rzeczypospolitej Polskiej*, 91–92.
16 Claudia Kraft, "Das Eherecht in der Zweiten Polnischen Republik (1918–1939) und das gescheiterte Ideal gleichberechtigter Staatsbürger," in *Zwischen Kriegen. Nationen, Nationalismen und Geschlechterverhältnisse in Mittel- und Osteuropa 1918–1939*, ed. Johanna Gehmacher, Elisabeth Harvey and Sophia Kemlein (Osnabrück: Fibre, 2004), 63–82.
17 Ustawa o szkołach akademickich z dnia 13 lipca 1920, in: Dziennik Ustaw Rzeczypospolitej Polskiej, nr. 72 poz. 494, art. 2. and art. 85.
18 Cf. Andrzej Garlicki, *Dzieje Uniwersytetu Warszawskiego 1915–1939* (Warszawa: PWN, 1982), 18–23.
19 Dziennik Urzędowy Ministra Wyznań Religijnych i Oświecenia Publicznego nr 1 poz. 5 z 1 lutego 1919 roku.
20 "Kalendarz uniwersytecki. Uniwersytet Warszawski 1915/1916," ed. Jan Muszkowski (Warszawa: Księgarnia Hoesicka, 1915), 142–149.
21 "Kalendarz uniwersytecki," 83.
22 "Kalendarz uniwersytecki. Uniwersytet Warszawski 1916/1917," ed. Jan Muszkowski (Warszawa: Księgarnia Hoesicka, 1916), 113–120.
23 Teczki studenckie Wydziału Prawa, Warsaw University Archive.
24 Kazimierz Konarski, *Dzieje szkolnictwa w byłem Królestwie Kongresowem 1915–1918* (Kraków: Książnica Polska w Warszawie, 1923), 107; Jerzy Halbersztadt, "Kobiety w murach Uniwersytetu Warszawskiego 1915–1939," in *Kobieta i kultura. Kobiety wśród twórców kultury intelektualnej i artystycznej w dobie rozbiorów i niepodległym państwie polskim*, ed. Anna Żarnowska and Andrzej Szwarc (Warszawa: DiG, 1996), 107–126.
25 Konarski, *Dzieje szkolnictwa*, 245.
26 *Komunikat Zarządu* 8, no. 12 (1938): 11.
27 Ibid., 11; Teczki studenckie Wydziału Prawa, Warsaw University Archive.
28 Kongres Społeczno- Obywatelskiej Pracy Kobiet, opr. Podkomisja Statystyczna Kongresu pod kierunkiem Haliny Siemieńskiej, Archiwum Jędrzeja i Zofii Moraczewskich, file 63, Central Archive of Modern Records in Warsaw; *Komunikat Zarządu* 8, no. 12 (1938): 3–14.
29 Marion Röwekamp, *Die ersten deustchen Juristinnen: eine Geschichte ihrer Professionalisierung und Emanzipation 1900–1945* (Cologne: Böhlau, 2011), 99.
30 *Komunikat Zarządu* 8, no. 12 (1938): 11.
31 Karol Lutostański (1880–1939), Polish lawyer, professor at the University of Warsaw, authored the new civil code provisions concerning the legal status of married women in the former territories of the Kingdom of Poland, effective in 1921. The 36 sections were a prelude to the new provisions concerning matrimonial law that were adopted later, which incorporated immediate and necessary changes, cf. *Ustawa w przedmiocie zmiany niektorych przepisow prawa cywilnego obowiazujacych w b. Krolestwie Polskim dotyczacych praw kobiet,*

in: Dziennik Ustaw RP 1921 nr. 64 poz. 397; Edward Muszalski, "Karol Lutostanski," *Polski Słownik Biograficzny* 18 (1973): 158–160; on matrimonial law see, inter alia, Kraft, "Das Eherecht," 64.

32 Krzysztof Motyka, *Leon Petrażycki. Challenge to Legal Orthodoxy* (Lublin: Towarzystwo Naukowe KUL, 2007); Karl Berthold Baum, *Leon Petrażycki und seine Schüler. Der Weg von der psychologischen zur soziologischen Rechtstheorie in der Petrażyckigruppe* (Berlin: Duncker & Humblodt, 1967); Krzysztof Pol, *Poczet prawników polskich* (Warszawa: C.H. Beck, 2000), 731–740.

33 Leon Petrażycki, *O prawa kobiet*, trans. Jadwiga Petrażycka-Tomicka (Lwów: Wydawnictwo Polskie, 1919); Małgorzata Fuszara, "Leon Petrażycki's Theory and Women's Rights," *Societas/Communitas* 7, no.1 (2009): 37–45.

34 Maciej Janowski, Jerzy Jedlicki and Magdalena Micińska, *Dzieje inteligencji polskiej do 1918 roku. Tom 3: Inteligencja na rozdrożach 1864–1918* (Warszawa: Neriton, 2008); Denis Sdviskov, *Das Zeitalter der Intelligenz. Zur vergleichenden Geschichte der Gebildeten in Europa bis zum Ersten Weltkrieg* (Göttingen: Vandenhoeck & Ruprecht, 2006), in Polish: *Epoka inteligencji: historia porównawcza warstwy wykształconej w Europie* (Warszawa: Neriton, 2010); Bodan Cywiński, *Rodowody niepokornych* (Paris: Spotkania, 1985).

35 The origins and biographical sketches of female lawyers, such as Aniela Berlinerblau-Steinsbergowa, Maria Estericher, Maria Lutostańska, Wanda Grabinska-Woytowicz, and many others provide confirmation of this assumption, cf. also Janowski, Jedlicki, and Micińska, *Dzieje inteligencji polskiej*, 25.

36 Stypułkowska, "Trudna droga," 148.

37 Jadwiga Suchmiel, *Polskie Stowarzyszenie Studentek Uniwersytetu Jagiellońskiego "Jedność" w Krakowie 1910–1939* (Częstochowa: Wydawnictwo Akademii Jana Długosza, 2005).

38 Teczki studenckie Wydziału Prawa: Maria Fuksówna, Irena Wortmannówna, Irena Kaliska, Warsaw University Archive.

39 Some were socialists, communists, pacifists, or national conservatives, see inter alia Agnieszka Janiak-Jasińska, Katarzyna Sierakowska, and Adrzej Szwarc eds., *Działaczki społeczne, feministki, obywatelki . . . Samoorganizowanie się kobiet na ziemiach polskich po 1918 roku (na tle porównawczym)*, vol. II (Warszawa: Neriton, 2009); Dobrochna Kałwa, *Kobieta aktywna w Polsce międzywojennej. Dylematy środowisk kobiecych* (Kraków: Historia Iagiellonica, 2001).

40 For the Austrian partition sector of Poland, Galicia, see, inter alia, Birgitta Bader-Zaar, "Bürgerrechte und Geschlecht. Zur Frage der politischen Gleichberechtigung von Frauen in Österreich, 1848–1918," in *Frauen in der Geschichte des Rechts. Von der Frühen Neuzeit bis zur Gegenwart*, ed. Ute Gerhard (Munich: C.H. Beck, 1997), 547–562.

41 The convention of Polish feminist circles from all partition sectors was intended to create a unified front for the attainment of women's rights including suffrage, cf. *Pamiętnik Zjazdu Kobiet Polskich w Warszawie w 1917 roku*, ed. Justyna Budzińska-Tylicka (Warszawa: Składnica Główna, 1918).

42 cf. *Pamiętnik Zjazdu Kobiet Polskich*, 2.

43 [Helena] Rappaportowa, "Koreferat do wystąpienia Jadwigi Pyrowiczówny," in *Pamiętnik Zjazdu Kobiet Polskich w Warszawie w 1917 roku*, ed. Justyna Budzińska-Tylicka (Warszawa: Składnica Główna, 1918), 86–89.

44 Janina Podgórska-Jurkiewiczowa (born circa 1880 and died after 1945) studied in Paris, then by 1909, worked in law firms in Petersburg and later in Warsaw. Following her marriage in 1919 to Stanisław Jurkiewicz, a notary and later minister for social affairs, she withdrew from professional and political life. Even as early as her return to Warsaw around 1909 she was perceived and acclaimed as the "first Polish female lawyer," cf. Janina Podgórska, "Informacje prawne," in *Kalendarz kobiety polskiej za rok 1910*, ed. Związek Równouprawnienia Kobiet

Polskich (Warszawa: Biuro Związku 1910), 110–111; P. K. R., "Sprawa adwokatek w Radzie Państwa," *Ster. Organ Związku Równouprawnienia Kobiet Polskich* 6, no. 3 (1913): 3; Dionizja Wawrzykowska-Wierciochowa, *Od prządki do astronautki. Z dziejów kobiety polskiej jej pracy i osiągnięć* (Warszawa: Wydawnictwo Związkowe, 1963), 388.

45 Z., "O kobietach prawniczkach," *Kalendarz Kobiety Polskiej za rok* (1910): 110–111; Janina Podgórska, "Informacje prawne," *Kalendarz Kobiety Polskiej za rok* (1910): 170–175.

46 Romana Pachucka, "Zrzeszenia równouprawnienia kobiet," *Kalendarz Kobiety Polskiej za rok* (1910): 17.

47 Zofia Miszewska, "Kobieta sędzią. Wywiad z sędzią Wandą Grabińską," *Bluszcz. Pismo tygodniowe ilustrowane dla kobiet z* 62, no. 16 (1929): 10–11.

48 Dekret w przedmiocie statutu tymczasowego Palestry Państwa Polskiego z dnia 30 grudnia 1918 roku in Dziennik Praw Państwa Polskiego, nr 22. poz. 75, Art. 3.

49 Helena Kononowicz-Wiewiórska (1889–1967) studied law in Petersburg around 1909, where she became involved in the student organization "Spójnia" and other charitable and women's rights organizations. In 1913, she married Jerzy Wiewiórski. During World War I, she worked in Petersburg and Odessa, returning to Poland in 1919, where she completed her probationary training period and became the first female attorney in Poland in 1925. She was co-founder and board member of the female lawyers' association, in the ZPOK in the legal section, and continued working as a lawyer after 1945, cf. *Z życia studentek Polek w Petersburgu* (Warszawa: Jan Cotty, 1929), 17; Stanisław Łoza ed. *Czy wiesz kto to jest?* (Warszawa: Główna Księgarnia Wojskowa, 1938), 798; Wawrzykowska-Wierciochowa, *Od prządki*, 389; Akta Ministerstwa Spraw Zagranicznych, file 2332, Central Archive of Modern Records in Warsaw.

50 "Pierwsza kobieta adwokat," *Palestra. Pismo Adwokatury Polskiej* 2 (1924): 754.

51 Dekret o aplikacji sądowej, in Dziennik Praw Państwa Polskiego, 8 lutego 1919, nr 18 poz. 225, art. 1.

52 Prawo o ustroju sądów powszechnych. Rozporządzenie Prezydenta Rzeczypospolitej, in Dziennik Ustaw, 6 lutego 1928 nr 12 poz. 93 art. 297.

53 Prawo o ustroju sądów powszechnych. Rozporządzenie Prezydenta Rzeczypospolitej, in Dziennik Ustaw, 6 lutego 1928 nr 12 poz. 93 art. 214.

54 Sylwia Bujak-Boguska ed., *Na straży praw kobiety. Pamiętnik Klubu Politycznego Kobiet Postępowych 1919–1930* (Warszawa: Jan Ulasiewicz i Syn, 1930), 70–71.

55 Bujak-Boguska, *Na straży praw kobiety*, 72.

56 Wanda Grabińska-Wójtowicz (1902–1980), the first female judge to be appointed for juvenile sentencing, employee in the Ministry for Social Affairs, delegate to the Social Commission of the League of Nations, co-founder and chairman of the female lawyers' association, in exile after 1945, cf. Teczki studenckie: Wanda Grabińska, Warsaw University Archive; Akta Ministerstwa Spraw Zagranicznych, file 2332, Central Archive of Modern Records in Warsaw; Miszewska, "Kobieta sędzią," 10–11; Jacek Piotrowski, *Dzienniki czynności Prezydenta Rzeczpospolitej Polskiej Władysława Raczkiewicza 1939–1947*, 2 vol. (Wrocław: Wydawnictwo Uniwersytetu Wrocławskiego, 2004), 55, 176; Wanda Grabińska, *Let us try. Podręcznik języka angielskiego. 1 rok nauczania* (Katowice: Universum, 1946).

57 Miszewska, "Kobieta sędzią," 11.

58 James C. Albisetti, "Portia Ante Portas: Women and the Legal Profession in Europe, ca. 1870–1925," *Journal of Social History* 33, no. 4 (Summer 2000): 825–885.

59 Zofia Miszewska, "Jak pracują kobiety, cześć II: prawniczki," *Bluszcz. Pismo tygodniowe ilustrowane dla kobiet* 62, no. 17 (1929): 17.

60 "Pierwsza kobieta adwokat," 754.

61 Łoza, *Czy wiesz kto to jest?*, 798.

62 *Komunikat Zarządu* 8, no. 12 (1938): 4–6.
63 The estimates were derived from sampling in the journal of *Palestra, Pismo Adwokatury Polskiej*, ed. Naczelna Rada Adwokacka, in the years 1925–1939. This contained notifications of registrations for the bar by male and female lawyers-in-training; Perkowska, *Studentki*, 169.
64 *Komunikat Zarządu* 8, no. 12 (1938): 7.
65 Perkowska, *Studentki*, 169; Agnieszka Biedrzycka, *Kalendarium Lwowa 1918–1939* (Kraków: Universitas, 2012), 390.
66 Miszewska "Jak pracują kobiety," 17.
67 The work of Aniela Berlinerblau-Steinsbergowa is an exemplar. She and her husband served as defense counsel for Polish communists and workers in the criminal proceedings in Cracow in the late 1930s, cf. Robert Jarocki and Aniela Berlinerblau-Steinsbergowa, *Polski Słownik Biograficzny* 43 (2004–2005): 344–348.
68 Dekret w przedmiocie utworzenia Prokuratorji Generalnej Rzeczypospolitej Polskiej, in: Dziennik Praw Państwa Polskiego, 7 lutego 1919, nr 14 poz. 181, art. 13.
69 Stanislaw Bukowiecki (1867–1944), as a lawyer and long-time chief public prosecutor, was one of the few advocates of opening the legal professions to women and accepting Jewish female lawyers in the civil service. Cf. Stanisław Bukowiecki, *Polityka Polski niepodleglej. Szkic programu* (Warszawa: Wende, 1922); Łoza, *Czy wiesz kto to jest?*, 85.
70 Maria (Maryla) Fuksówna (1893–1967), one of the University of Warsaw's first female law students and law school graduates. Before she had completed her studies, she became one of the leaders in the Polish women's organizations. Beginning in 1921 she was employed in the chief public prosecutor's office as its first female employee. She is considered also to be one of the initiators of the PZKzPW in 1929, which she represented in the transnational gatherings and work projects. Fuksówna, a Jewess, survived the Holocaust and returned after 1945 to her old position in the public prosecutor's office. She was a member of the commission for arbitration proceedings and a specialist in civil law, cf. Teczki studenckie: Maryla Fuksówna, Warsaw University Archive; Akta Ministerstwa Spraw Zagranicznych, file 2332, Central Archive of Modern Records in Warsaw; Stypułkowska, "Trudna droga," 144.
71 Eugenia Schlichtertówna (b. 1899) enrolled as a law student at the University of Warsaw in 1917. She was active in the female lawyers' association and immediately after receiving her law degree found employment in the chief public prosecutor's office; Teczki studenckie: Eugenia Schlichtertówna, Warsaw University Archive; Akta Ministerstwa Spraw Zagranicznych, file 2332, Central Archive of Modern Records in Warsaw.
72 Izabela Chojecka-Boniecka (1908–1939/1940) studied law in the early 1930s at the University of Warsaw, interrupting her studies occasionally because of a tuberculosis infection. From 1936 she was employed in the chief public prosecutor's office, where she held the position of assessor, cf. Teczki studenckie: Izabela Chojecka, Warsaw University Archive; Stypułkowska, "Trudna droga," 142.
73 Bujak- Boguska, *Na straży praw kobiety*, 71–72; "Budżet Ministerstwa Sprawiedliwości w Komisji Senatu," *Głos Sądownictwa. Miesięcznik poświęcony zagadnieniom społeczno-prawnym i zawodowym* 10, no. 3 (1938): 212; "Kobiety sędziami," *Nowiny codzienne warszawskie* 1, no. 174 (1932): 1; Stypułkowska, "Trudna droga," 142.
74 Wanda Grabińska-Woytowicz, *Opieka społeczna nad dziećmi i młodzieżą* (Warszawa: Nasza Księgarnia 1939).
75 Wanda Grabińska-Woytowicz, *Walka z nierządem i chorobami wenerycznymi: w świetle referatów wygłoszonych przez mgr Wandę Woytowicz Grabińską, radcę Min. Opieki Społecznej i dr Stanisława Ostrowskiego, posła na Sejm*

Rzeczypospolitej Polskiej na Sejmowej Komisji Zdrowia Publicznego i Opieki Społecznej w 1938 r. w związku z projektami rządowymi ustaw o zwalczaniu nierządu i chorób wenerycznych (Warszawa: Ministerstwo Opieki Społecznej, 1938); Wanda Grabińska-Woytowicz, *Projekt ustawy o zwalczaniu nierządu* (Warszawa: Druk. Miejska, 1939).

76 Rozporządzenie Prezydenta Rzeczpospolitej z dnia 27 października 1933 roku: Prawo o notariacie in Dziennik Ustaw RP nr 84, poz. 609 rozdz. 2 art. 7.

77 Dorota Malec, *Notariat Drugiej Rzeczypospolitej* (Kraków: Wydawnictwo Uniwersytetu Jagiellońskiego, 2002).

78 Perkowska, *Studentki*, 169.

79 Michał Pietrzak, "Sytuacja prawna kobiet w Drugiej Rzeczpospolitej," in *Równe prawa i nierówne szanse*, ed. Anna Żarnowska and Andrzej Szwarc (Warszawa: DiG, 2000), 79.

80 Perkowska, *Studentki*, 170.

81 Wolna Wszechnica Polska ed., *Sprawozdanie z działalności w roku akademickim 1926/27 w XXI-ym roku istnienia* (Warszawa: Wydawnictwo Wolnej Wszechnicy, 1927), 79; among those who taught there were female scholars who, though they applied many times, never received professorships or lectureships (Józefa Joteyko, Helena Radlińska, Jozefa Kodis- Krzyżanowska, and many others); Andrzej Garlicki, *Encyklopedia historii Drugiej Rzeczypospolitej: 1918–1939* (Warszawa: Bellona, 1999).

82 *Komunikat Zarządu* 8, no. 12 (1938): 44.

83 Jolanta Sikorska-Kulesza, "Teodora Męczkowska," in *Biographical Dictionary of Women's Movements and Feminisms in Central, Eastern, and South Eastern Europe: 19th and 20th Centuries*, ed. Francisca de Haan, Krassimira Daskalova and Anna Loutfi (Budapest: Central European University Press, 2006), 324–326.

84 Męczkowska, *Do czego dążymy*, 4.

85 Jan Bełcikowski, *Warszawa kobieca* (Warszawa: Biblioteka Nowej Cywilizacji, 1930); Dadej, *Die Frau von Morgen*, 164–179.

86 Męczkowska, *Do czego dążymy*, 4.

87 Akta Ministerstwa Spraw Zagranicznych, file 2332, Central Archive of Modern Records in Warsaw.

88 Akta Ministerstwa Spraw Zagranicznych, file 2332, Central Archive of Modern Records in Warsaw.

89 Halina Luksembourżanka (b. 1900), one of the first female law students and lawyers in Warsaw, member of the female lawyers' association, disseminator of information from the association on legal issues to the local groups of Polish women's organizations. Teczki studenckie: Halina Luksembourżanka, Warsaw University Archive; Akta Ministerstwa Spraw Zagranicznych, file 2332, Central Archive of Modern Records in Warsaw.

90 At that time, Helena Lepiarzowa was still a candidate for the judicial profession and was undergoing her probationary training period. It was not until 1932 that she was appointed judge of the local trial court in Lvov, cf. "Kobiety sędziami," *Nowiny codzienne warszawskie* 1, no. 174 (1932): 1.

91 Maria Lutostańska, born 1904 in Warsaw, a "Warsaw female lawyer," became involved in the female lawyers' association and with its executive board, appeared as a representative for Polish concerns at the international conventions. Her family connections with the law professor Karol Lutostański are not established. Lutostański, a Warsaw jurist, did not have children according to his biographical profile, cf. Teczki studenckie: Maria Lutostańska, Warsaw University Archive; Akta Ministerstwa Spraw Zagranicznych, file 2131, Central Archive of Modern Records in Warsaw.

92 Maria Roszkowska, born 1901, was at that time supposedly still a student and a representative of the Warsaw school of female lawyers, cf. Teczki studenckie: Maria Roszkowska, Warsaw University Archive.

93 Aleksandra Rabska-Stypułkowska (1906–1992) came from a family that belonged to the Warsaw *inteligencja* in which the legal traditional went back very far: her ancestor Aleksander Kraushar was one of Warsaw's most famous lawyers around 1890. She likewise belonged to the "Warsaw school of female lawyers." Beginning in the early 1930s, she managed a law firm in Warsaw together with her husband. She did not return to her homeland after 1945, and she involved herself in the political work of Poles living in exile in London, cf. Rafał Habielski, "Aleksandra Rabska-Stypułkowska," *Polski Słownik Biograficzny* 43 (2005): 207–209; Teczki studenckie: Aleksandra Rabska-Stypułkowska, Warsaw University Archive; Aleksandra Stypułkowska, *People's Poland and Poles Abroad* (London: Liaison Comm. of the Polish Women's Organisations in Gt. Britain, 1976); Aleksandra Stypułkowska, "Genealogia grzechu Werblana," *Na antenie. Mówi Rozgłośnia Polska Radia Wolna Europa* quoted here according to: Adam Michnik ed., *Przeciw antysemityzmowi 1936–2009*, vol. 2 (Kraków: Universitas, 2010), 526–532.

94 "Stowarzyszenie Kobiet z Prawniczem Wykształceniem," *Kobieta Współczesna* 3, no. 19 (1929): 16.

95 List przewodniczacej SKzPW do Ministerstwa Spraw Zagranicznych, 1937, Akta Ministerstwa Spraw Zagranicznych, file 2131, Central Archive of Modern Records in Warsaw.

96 Miszewska, "Jak pracują kobiety," 17; Miszewska, "Kobieta sędzią," 11.

97 Irena Wortmannówna (b. 1895) in Warsaw, matriculated in 1918 to study law and from then on was one of the "Warsaw female lawyers" interested in feminist causes. Well qualified for pedagogical activities (before her studies, she was a teacher at a primary school and director of a primary school affiliated with the "Wiedza" society), she visited the female lawyers' association on behalf of the female university graduates' league's local groups, where, among other things, she trained women to give preliminary legal advice to other needy women. Irena Wortmann enrolled in the university as a "Pole of the Jewish faith," for which reason one shudders to think of the fate that presumably awaited her in the Holocaust; Teczki studneckie: Irena Wortmannówna, Warsaw University Archive.

98 "Skład Zarządu Głównego," *Komunikat Zarządu* 1, no. 1 (1930): 1; "Z życia oddziałów: oddział warszawski," *Komunikat Zarządu* 3, no. 5 (1932): 8.

99 Irena Kaliska (1898–after 1961) was one of the first women who enrolled in the University of Warsaw in January 1916 to study law; in the Second Republic and after 1945 she worked as a lawyer. Member of the female university graduates' association SKzWW; Teczki studenckie Wydziału Prawa: Irena Kaliska, Warsaw University Archive.

100 Bujak-Boguska, *Na straży praw*, 60–66.

101 Akta Jędrzeja i Zofii Moraczewskich, file 63, Central Archive of Modern Records in Warsaw.

102 Zofia Moraczewska, *Związek Pracy Obywatelskiej Kobiet* (Warszawa: ZPOK, 1932), 64–66; for a more thorough treatment of the codification commission, see: Claudia Kraft, *Europa im Blick der polnischen Juristen* (Frankfurt am Main: Klostermann, 2002), 80–153.

103 Akta Ministerstwa Spraw Zagranicznych, file 2131, Central Archive of Modern Records in Warsaw.

104 The Féderation internationale des femmes des carrières juridiques (FIFCJ) used several variations on its name; for a detailed analysis of the organization see Sara L. Kimble, *Women, Feminism, and the Law in Modern France: Justice Redressed* (New York: Routledge, forthcoming).

105 "Polskie Stowarzyszenie Kobiet z Prawniczem Wykształceniem," 16.
106 On the solidarity among female university graduates and their connections across the trans-Atlantic region, see: Oertzen, *Strategie Verständigung*, 245–286.
107 Marcelle Kraemer-Bach, *Rapport présenté à la Fédération internationale des femmes magistrats et avocats* (Paris: P.A. Pedone, 1939); the jointly pursued goals and concerns gave rise also to declarations of solidarity and to assistance: immediately following the end of the war in 1945, those who survived received help from the academic women's organizations and individual persons. The post-war contacts were discontinued around the year 1949 because of the increasingly repressive policies of the Soviet occupational authorities, see "Nasz bilans wojenny," *Komunikat Zarządu* 14 (1948): 1–25.
108 Akta Ministerstwa Spraw Zagranicznych, file 2131, Central Archive of Modern Records in Warsaw.
109 "Z prac Zarządu Głównego," *Komunikat Zarządu* 1, no. 2 (1930): 1.
110 Akta Ministerstwa Spraw Zagranicznych, file 2131, Central Archive of Modern Records in Warsaw.
111 "Réponse au questionnaire sur la position de la femme, comparée à celle de l'homme," *La femme polonaise*, 4–5 (1937): 8–11.
112 Grażyna Szmurłowa, *Kobieta w prawie publicznym i prywatnym, Zbiór przepisów obowiązujących w Polsce* (Warszawa: Druk. Zofia Zastowska i S-ka, 1937).
113 Zofia Gawrońska-Wasilkowska (1910–1996) was professionally active in the Second Republic as an employee of the chief public prosecutor's office, a university lecturer, and politically active in socialist circles (PPS). After 1945, she became a Supreme Court judge and then the first female Minister of Justice (April 1956–February 1957). This ministerial position would not be held by another woman until the late 1990s (Hanna Suchocka, 1997–2000 and Barbara Piwnik, 2001–2002). Gawrońska-Wasilkowska was a member of the women's sections of the PZPR and League of Women (Liga Kobiet); cf. inter alia Teczki studenckie: Zofia Gawrońska, Warsaw University Archive; Akta Osobowe Wydziału Kadr KCPZPR, file 5101, Central Archive of Modern Records in Warsaw (AAN). My thanks go to Anna Nowakowska-Wierzchoś for her friendly and knowledgeable assistance in my search for Gawrońska-Wasilkowska's files in AAN, see also Zofia Gawrońska-Wasilkowska, *Prawa kobiet w Polsce ludowej* (Warszawa: Książka i Wiedza, 1952); Zofia Gawrońska-Wasilkowska, *Małżeństwo. Istota—Trwałość—Rozwód* (Warszawa: Wydawnictwo Prawnicze, 1966).
114 "Le 4è Congrès de la Fédération internationale des femmes des carrières juridiques (Paris, 17–22 juillet 1961)," *Revue internationale de droit comparé* 14, no. 1 (1962): 89.

10 Women, Equal Rights, and the Legal Profession in Germany, 1895–1933

Marion Röwekamp

Equality under the law is an ideal that has inspired women's legal reform efforts since the French Revolution.[1] It took the German women's movements, however, over a century after the French Revolution to understand the role the law would take in the fight for equal rights. It was the earliest German female law graduate, Anita Augspurg (1857–1943), who first raised the question of women's rights as a legal question in 1895: "The women's question is to a considerable degree a question of economics, but maybe to an even greater extent a question of culture, [. . .] but first and foremost it is a *legal* question because only upon the foundation of *warranted rights* not the imaginary ones [. . .] can a definite solution even be thought about."[2] She claimed that the fight for every other aspect in the women's question was meaningless as long as women did not have full, legally guaranteed equal rights on par with men. She discounted any other achievement to be simply something private, personal, isolated, and temporary, which could not serve to become the rule for every woman. Thus, she compared the struggle of the women's movement for their various goals with trying to install windows and frames for doors without having built the foundation walls of a house.[3] Augspurg represented the principles of the radical part of the civic women's movement.[4] The conservative women's movement, by contrast, believed that the question of women's rights was primarily based on education and culture. It promoted the notion of women's distinctive "female" talents to improve the fields of medicine and teaching, for example, but also to reform society in general. According to this idea, women were needed in some professions, such as medicine—especially gynecologists—or education, where they would teach the female students who had begun to pursue secondary education in this era. But at least until 1888, when the Bürgerliche Gesetzbuch (BGB, German civil code) came up for revision, no obvious reason existed why the women's movements should need female lawyers. This changed drastically after the women's movements failed in their challenge to alter the gender-discriminative clauses in the new BGB that was finally enacted in 1900.[5] While Anita Augspurg had claimed to open the legal professions for women from the beginning, the conservative wing of the civic women's movement started to understand how important academically trained female lawyers could be in the battle for equal rights only after their defeat on the BGB. Yet the notion of female lawyers was still too far-fetched to find support in the society of Imperial Germany. While the civic women's movement was convinced that all women had all the abilities to become lawyers, to claim especially female judges in public was still a distant dream. In 1900, the pioneering feminist, teacher, and women's rights activist Auguste Schmidt (1833–1902) conceded: "We were convinced that the profession of [. . .] the lawyer could be adequately exercised by women, but we knew that this opinion would not be considered compatible with common sense. Thus we kept quiet."[6] What Schmidt conceived of eventually became a reality. But it took the women's movement more than a decade to address the question in public and still another decade to break the resistance to women's access to legal professions, which was particularly strong in Germany. As late as in 1921, the feminist Marie Stritt (1855–1928) claimed, "Not even against women's suffrage [. . .] especially from the professional circles, has [resistance] ever been so hard and stubborn as on this" issue.[7] Stritt was founder of the Legal Aid Institution for Women and a former president of the Bund Deutscher Frauenvereine (BDF, National Council of German Women), Germany's umbrella organization for most of the middle-class women's associations, which was founded in 1894 as a reaction to the founding of the International Council of Women (ICW) in 1888.

Unfortunately, Marie Stritt was right. Law was a notoriously difficult field for women to break into in Germany, considerably more difficult than women's entry into medicine or academic professions (except theology). The situation in Germany was far more challenging than in most other European countries because its special legal education ensured that all lawyers were qualified, and in turn, guaranteed access to all legal professions, including civil service and the judiciary.[8] A war and a change in regime were necessary to make it possible. Women in the Weimar Republic were finally admitted to practice law as attorneys in 1922, twenty-five years later than in France they still faced limited opportunities to establish themselves in legal careers before 1933, when Nazis excluded them in principle from exercising their profession. At the same time, Germany was one of the few countries in Europe to admit female judges starting in 1922. This was a time when most other European countries had only opened the courts for female attorneys while keeping the judiciary off limits until decades later. Thus, Weimar Germany could boast of a respectable number of female judges before they were banned from the benches by Adolf Hitler's express directive in 1934 or if indeed they had not yet been already dismissed in 1933 due to their Jewish origins. In 1935, the Nazis also restricted the access of women to the bar, but the regime did not dismiss those who remained and were already working as attorneys.[9]

This chapter will explore the struggles by German female lawyers and their allies in the women's movement to gain access to the legal professions as a part of a general struggle for equal rights for women. It will argue that access was achieved so late and the resistance was so "hard and stubborn" compared to other academic professions because of specific issues related to legal studies in the German empire and to the peculiarities of the practice of law in Germany during the imperial period as well as to male fear that female lawyers would directly lead to women's suffrage and undermine the male-headed family. It will particularly focus on the professional development of female lawyers in the Weimar Republic between 1922, the year of their access, and 1933, the beginning of their gradual exclusion, and it will examine their ideas of professionalism and equality. Then it will show how intertwined, almost inseparable, the challenge of the female lawyers became with the women's movement's fight for equal rights—especially in family law. The chapter draws on a variety of primary sources—both archival and published—administrative documents of the German federal and state governments, private archives, women's archives in the United States and Germany, articles from legal and feminist journals, and numerous secondary sources.

The Struggle for Women's Equal Access to the Legal Professions

1895–1918: The First Years of the Struggle for Access to the Legal Professions

The entrance to the legal professions in Imperial Germany was characterized by a strong traditional university-based legal education that trained all its students to qualify as judges, even if most of them became lawyers. This legal training was a highly regulated state institution primarily for the judiciary and civil service; lawyers were expected to serve "the state" rather than represent citizens. When the position of legal advocate became a private profession in 1879, it retained its ties to the state bureaucracy. A German lawyer's tasks were analogous to that of the barrister or solicitor, yet admission to the bar required fulfillment of state examinations and the attorney remained under supervision by the state. The legal profession was constantly supervised by the state, which prevented advocates from fully gaining control over bar admission. At the turn of the twentieth century, legal education typically consisted of four years of theoretical study at a university that ended with the so-called first state exam. This was followed by a three-year period of practical training in the courts and a second state exam. Since all jurists had to go through exactly the same training, the system featured the so-called *Einheitsjurist* (uniform jurist), a jurist who could work, at least theoretically, in any of the legal professions. But the image of the judge or jurist working in the civil service was seen as the ideal legal profession. This legal education was considered fundamental training for everyone with the ambition not only for the judiciary, but also for legislative and administrative state positions, thus spanning all fields that wielded governmental power.[10] Hence, the legal professions at the turn of the century were probably the most powerful professional organizations, and their leaders were keen on keeping their privileges to themselves. The lawyers protecting access to their profession largely occupied civil service structures and consequently could resist the access of women from every conceivable position.

Furthermore, the legal profession was perceived as an exclusively male club. "Women are the representatives of love, just as men are the representatives of law," one encyclopedia stated in 1820.[11] According to this gendered stereotype, the law required objectivity, rationality, and authority, all of which were deemed to be male characteristics and the absolute opposite of the abilities generally attributed to women: that is, motherly love, tenderness, and understanding. In nineteenth-century Germany, the cultural stereotypes that had shaped gender roles for centuries were deeply embedded and difficult to overcome.[12] At the same time, masculinity was not only deemed central to exercise the legal professions, but the law itself was defined according to discriminating gender norms. It legitimized prejudicial cultural attitudes and justified inequitable practices while claiming to be gender-neutral. This was especially evident in family law but also apparent in all the laws that were referred to in order to exclude women from entering legal professions. As law professor Otto von Gierke put it bluntly in 1897, "Men's professions [. . .] must remain men's professions."[13]

To prevent women in Germany from taking the examinations that would open up all the executive and legal power positions in the administration and the judiciary, the individual state Ministries of Justice simply excluded women from state exams, leaving them only the option of finishing university study with a doctorate in law. Thus, the admission of women to study in the law faculties, such as those in Baden in 1900 and Bavaria in 1903, was only a first step. In Bavaria, law student Maria-Delia Schmidbauer, née Droste (1887–?) had even participated without problems in the first state exam and had entered the legal apprenticeship before the Minister of Interior realized the danger of this precedent, intervened in her individual case, and decided on a general ban on women sitting the exams.[14] More controversial was the opening of the Prussian universities to women, which raised the possibility of women's access to the legal and the theological state exams; government officials wondered whether they might establish a quota to limit women to 2/3 of law graduates. It was considered improper, even impossible, that women should accede to state service, especially as judges. While women's entry into other faculties that ended with state examinations, such as teaching and medicine, was also problematic, teachers and doctors did not wield the same influence in their professions as did lawyers. Another reason for opening these professions first came from the argument that women were needed to teach girls and female doctors to treat female patients. These fields were considered to be more "natural" for women than the legal professions.[15] This debate around women and state examinations, in fact, was one of the main considerations that led to the delay of the opening of Prussian universities for women as compared to other German states. In 1908–1909, when women finally got admitted, an explicit proviso barred them from taking the state exams and seeking the apprenticeship in law.[16] In other words, it worked like a closed guild system.

Hence, women had no problems entering the law faculties. Even so, their numbers remained very small; without a career at the end of it, the study of law attracted very few female students. They were far outnumbered by men, and their experiences as the only female student from their faculty were often difficult. Most female lawyers reported hostile behavior by their fellow students and their professors, such as clapping and stamping and being addressed only as "gentlemen." One student reported that during her years of studying, not one fellow student had once spoken to her. In terms of their social background, female lawyers were predominantly from educated middle class families that supported—albeit with some resistance—the higher education of their daughters. A large number of female students came from families in which the fathers or brothers were also lawyers and wanted to follow their footsteps. They were, from childhood on, familiar with the duties and attitudes of the legal professions and often had prospects to go into the family business with the male members of the family.[17]

The first female lawyers started to work in different institutions founded by leaders of the German women's movement. For example, Alix Westerkamp (1876–1944), the first female doctor in law, worked in a legal aid clinic for women, an institution created in Dresden by feminist Marie Stritt in 1894, to give free legal advice to women, mainly those of the lower classes. "These bureaux [sic] are extraordinarily popular, and sought after with us," the German women reported to the International Woman Suffrage Alliance in October 1913.[18] Others found similar employment in schools for social work, Children's Care Committee centers, as women trustees and guardians, in minor positions in men's law offices, or in private or public welfare agencies, as well as in juvenile care. In all of these jobs they were confronted with the injustice of discriminating laws and became sensitized to the precarious situation of women's, and often the poor's, rights in German society.

Many of the female law students had, in fact, chosen to study law because they had witnessed the adverse legal situation of their mothers or other women in their immediate circles as handicapped by the law, and they had set out to change these legal norms by becoming lawyers themselves. Female lawyers usually felt right at home in these jobs, as they felt they could "do good," which had often been their original inspiration to study law. Furthermore, they could at least work in fields that were related to the traditional legal professions.[19] But what they really desired was to work in the legal professions they had been trained for, especially since "the prospects of a practical professional career for women lawyers in Germany are very unfavourable."[20] While female students of the law may have been tolerated, their subsequent requests to enter the legal professions themselves were quite another matter.

The German women's organizations took up their fight to open the legal professions for women in connection with another legal claim—the right of women to serve on juries, especially in the newly established institution of juvenile courts. Within the context of the debates on the revision of the German Code of Criminal Procedure in 1909 and the German Judicature Act in 1910, as well as the German Juvenile Court Act in 1912, the BDF demanded the participation of women as jurors in juvenile courts.[21] The *Jugendgerichtstag*, the congress of all the professions that participate in juvenile trials and deal scientifically with juvenile criminality, supported this claim. Together they launched a petition that was signed by five hundred thousand women.[22] Many of the female law graduates actively participated in these campaigns.[23] In October 1912, the BDF decided on a strategy based on two main pillars: to petition the Reichstag (the parliament) on a regular basis and to launch a major offensive following the earlier example of their protest prior to 1900 against the draft of the revised German civil code. The BDF organized mass rallies in fourteen major German cities that attracted some attention: in Berlin, a hall seating two thousand was not large enough for the audience.[24] But World War I put an end to the campaigns as the BDF, in an outburst of national patriotism, declared a truce with the government to support the war effort with the expectation of being granted full equal rights for their help once the war ended.

In this situation, the female lawyers decided in 1914 in Berlin to found their own professional organization, the Deutscher Juristinnenverein (DJV, German Female Lawyers' Association). Dr. Margarete Berent (1887–1965), Dr. Margarete Muehsam-Edelheim (née Meseritz) (1891–1975), and Dr. Marie Munk (1885–1978), all of whom were from a Jewish background, wanted "to promote the interests, especially the further professional and scientific legal training of women lawyers."[25] The DJV was independent, was non-denominational, and functioned above party lines. As a result of the small number of German women studying law, the DJV remained a tiny organization. In its founding year, it had twenty-eight members, in 1916–1917 it had thirty-five members, and in 1919 it had eighty-five members. Though small, it was a very active organization that played an important role in German women's campaigns for equal rights.[26]

The DJV not only worked on the national level, it also participated in the transnational struggle for equal rights for women. In 1928, in the light of ongoing global claims for legal reforms, female lawyers and judges from all over Europe came together in Paris to form the Fédération International de Femmes de Carrières Juridiques (FIFCJ, International Federation of Women in Legal Careers). The organization was founded when the Estonian lawyer Vera Poska-Grünthal (1898–1986) suggested establishing an international organization to unite female lawyers in the context of the First Congress of

Social Work, held from July 8 to 13, 1928, in Paris. A provisional committee of lawyers was formed that consisted of, besides Poska-Grünthal, the German attorney Margarete Berent, Clara Campoamor (Spain) (1888–1972), Marcelle Kraemer-Bach (France) (1897–1990), and Agathe Dyvrande-Thévenin (France) (1885–1977). It was a goal of the FIFCJ to maintain contacts between European lawyers and to develop strategies to change women's legal status in family law.[27]

But this is getting ahead of the story: in the years after 1914, the DJV's first attempts to demand admission to the state exams were unsuccessful. Based on the interpretation of norms from the German Judicature Act (GVG), the requests by members of the group were rejected. According to §2 GVG, admission to the profession was dependent on passing the two state exams or, according to §4 GVG, was contingent upon holding a fully tenured position as a law faculty member at a German university. None of the paragraphs explicitly made admission contingent upon being male, but common legal opinion and the legislature asserted that women were not included in this right. Additionally, opponents emphasized women's alleged innate gender characteristics that made them unfit to exercise the legal professions.

Female lawyers and their allies in the battle argued first for the opening of the legal professions based on the argument of equal access to higher education as compared with all the other academic professions, which were already open for women, even though they had completed the studies to the extent they were allowed to. At the same time, they emphasized the necessity for professional female legal impetus related to women's rights and insisted on the good that female attorneys and judges could do for other women, for the improvement of justice, and for society as a whole. They argued that a female presence in the judiciary was necessary as a social counterbalance to centuries of male dominance of the legal system. Furthermore, they emphasized that their more intimate knowledge of women's and children's needs, as well as their motherly empathy, made them the ideal fit for the law. They also pointed out the contradiction that on some occasions, the supposedly gender-neutral term "person" was applied to both sexes in the legal codes, notably in criminal and tax law, but whenever it was inconvenient to do so, it was interpreted as excluding women, as in the case of the §§2, 4 GVG.[28]

Thus, they used a rhetorical strategy, attitudes, argumentations, and ideas that were strongly influenced by the German women's movement's idea of "organized motherhood." This term had been coined in 1870 by feminist Henriette Schrader-Breymann and expressed the view that motherhood did not presuppose physical maternity. The BDF took it up later and applied it to demands for women's employment and women's participation in the broader society, arguing that ("spiritual") maternity was, in principle, a quality inherent in all women, and not only in those who bore children.[29] Women's motherly capacities to love, nurture, and care for others were evoked to legitimize using these abilities as a duty that extended beyond the immediate family to the community and society as a whole. Due to these ideas, women were by virtue of their motherly nature equal to men—though different—and just as valuable.

The crux in the development of equality as a political idea is that it had developed simultaneously with the belief that women were fundamentally different from men by nature and thus could not be treated as the same. This belief in the different nature of women was shared by men and women and used by the different groups to stress either the superior or the inferior side of the nature of women. In any case, it also served opponents of women's access to the legal professions to justify their continued exclusion as they argued that the foundation of the legal system would crumble with the entrance of women into its holy halls. "To allow women to enter justice," one judge stated as late as in 1933, "means a strong injustice towards the man and the woman herself. The injustice towards the man culminates in this intrusion into the holy principle of masculinity of the state."[30] The reference to women's nature thus was a twisted argument; it could work both ways: in the hands of the women to justify their autonomy and liberty while claiming womanly virtues at the same time, and in the hands of opponents to justify their explicit exclusion from the "holy" male-dominated legal profession.[31]

At the same time, these ideas of women's nature could also help the individual female lawyers to overcome stereotyped gender roles. The decision to study at university already distanced a woman from her background and the conventional understanding of a woman's role. But the decision to study law represented such a big step that these women needed to be reassured that they could "remain" women and contribute something specifically feminine to masculine professions. This was particularly important to those women who chose to remain single and saw their profession as an alternative to having a family. The public perception that female lawyers must necessarily forfeit their femininity, as it was often expressed in the media, made them very sensitive to this issue. Often they felt compelled to point out the "motherly and caring" aspects of their profession in order to forestall any attack on their femininity.[32]

1918–1922: Final Success in the Fight for Access to the Legal Professions

In the aftermath of the war and the revolution of 1918, German women gained the vote. The new Constitution of Weimar was passed in 1919; in its Articles 109 and 128, it promised legal equality to women—at least in principle. Equipped with these new rights, female lawyers began to make their case based on legal arguments and equality before the law. But their legal position remained weak, as the constitution had stipulated equality only in principle. This principle meant that different treatment of men and women could be justified when the "nature" of the sexes was so different that equal treatment was not possible. Thus, the crucial legal question remained: was it, in the light of the new constitution, still acceptable to understand citizenship as a concept that could entail different rights and duties for men and women? In the light of this legal possibility, the fight around the opening of the legal professions for women now turned overwhelmingly around the question of whether the "different nature" of women made them scientifically unfit to exercise the legal professions, thus legally justifying their continued exclusion.

The opponents of admission dredged up a number of older "scientific" works that purportedly "proved" the different, innate nature of women. In 1872, anatomist Theodor L. W. Bischoff, for example, postulated women's intellectual inferiority based on a study of male and female brains. According to him, women lacked intellectual strength, logical ability, and, especially, the rational judgment to practice law. Some attested that women, especially female lawyers, were too masculine and pointed out that this was also visible in their appearances. The antifeminist psychiatrist Paul Möbius had, in 1900, gone so far as to state that intellectual activity in women would result in a diminution of their capacity to bear children.[33] Male lawyers gratefully endorsed these arguments: they were particularly afraid that women would be too soft on crime, or too hard on other women because of their natural malevolence toward their own sex, or that their presence in court would prove simply distracting. Some feared that women's full participation in the legal professions would not only weaken the stability of the justice system, but also lead to a change in society: that women would cease to be domestic, cease to be supportive to their husbands, and have too little time and will to raise children. And finally, many lawyers also objected because the professions, especially with the return of the soldiers after World War I, were already overcrowded.[34]

Still, the Weimar Constitution embodied a new ideal of full equal rights for men and women, and by establishing this principle, these rights suddenly seemed achievable, and female lawyers, as well as part of the women's movement, were ready to invoke them.[35] Armed with the new constitution as provisions, the female lawyers set out to fight for their right to enter the legal professions. Now that they had voting rights, they were no longer dependent on the formula of petitions to parliaments but were now able to lodge their requests immediately via the new female members of parliament. The option of bringing their demands directly to the legislature increased their fighting options dramatically. Together, the DJV, the female members of the parliaments, the party faction of the German Democratic Party (DDP), the Social Democrats (SPD), and the women's movement gradually achieved success by combining different strategies.

Initially, the individual female lawyers regularly sent petitions to the Justice administrations in order to be admitted to take the state exams. Orchestrated by the DJV, their individual petitions on the executive level were accompanied by the work of the DJV and the women's movement on the legislative level. In one case, female law students at Leipzig's law faculty asked Saxony's parliament to approve admission to the legal exams.[36] But the primary strategy was to petition the Ministry of Justice of each German state to open the state exams for women by changing the interpretation of the laws, while also attempting to influence the outcome behind the scenes. As daughters from usually influential and well off families, they were socially well connected and used their personal connections for advancing their cause. Member of the DJV's board, Marie Munk, for example, went to school with Marie Schiffer, the daughter of the politician and lawyer, Eugen Schiffer, who became a lifelong friend. Himself a legal reformer, Schiffer was inclined to support the claims of female lawyers, as we can see from his actions as a Reichsminister of Justice.[37]

The first petition of the DJV in March 1919 to the Prussian Minister of Justice caused an avalanche of political movement behind the scenes, where the minister asked for the advice of his colleagues about how he should handle this request. While the Prussian Parliament was discussing the request, the other Ministers of Justice simply rejected the individual pleas of female lawyers as well as the request of the female students from Leipzig and of the DJV with the argument that admission to the law exams "had to be considered consistently for the entire empire by the Reichsministry of Justice." This meant the decision must be made at the federal level.[38] Thus, the Reichsministry in April 1919 asked all the states how they wanted to treat the admission of women to legal offices and professions in the future. The states were predominantly united in their opinion that women should be able to function as members of the jury but that they should not be allowed to exercise legal professions, especially not those of judges, as women were by their nature not fit to act as professional lawyers.[39] In November 1919, the Reichsministry of Justice declared for the first time that it did not see any legal obstacles to admitting women to the exams and to apprenticeships. It suggested opening at least the first of the two required state exams for women.[40]

Yet before the standardized admission of women to the legal exams was decided, in May 1919, the Prussian Minister of Justice had passed a decree that allowed women to take the first state exam, although without the accompanying right to participate in legal apprenticeships.[41] Most states followed the recommendation of the Reichsministry of Justice and the example of Prussia and opened the first state exams to women. Baden and Saxony, the more liberal states, even officially permitted women to enter the apprenticeship service. After being a trailblazer, Prussia now joined Bavaria in strong opposition because it was in the unfortunate position that due to its laws everyone who had passed the second state exam had to be appointed to a position in the justice administration.[42] In contrast, the other states still had the option of simply not appointing women as judges. Bavaria, on the other hand, represented the more backwards, Catholic perspective regarding women's status.

Caught in this complex jurisdictional conflict as both the Reich and the states kept denying their jurisdiction in this question, the BDF and the DJV came to the conclusion that changes in the legal situation could not be achieved solely by convincing justice ministries to adjust their interpretations based on the stipulations of the new constitution. A formal change of the existing laws was required and thus a change in strategy to obtain pertinent legislation at the federal and state levels. Priority was now given to bringing in all requests in the parliaments of all the states. A number of motions of the German Democratic Party (DDP) and the Social Democratic Party (SPD) were debated in the Reichstag and the state parliaments. In an unparalleled development, all thirty-two female members of the Reichstag cooperated on an all-party level to request the admission of women to the legal state exams.[43] Unusually active and eloquent for the cause of female lawyers was the DDP member of the Reichstag, the economist Marie-Elisabeth Lüders (1878–1966). She unfailingly questioned and also channeled all requests to the DDP faction and other female Reichstag members. And as a member of the BDF board of executives, she acted as the contact person of the DJV when the association wanted to introduce a new motion via different party factions.

In January 1921, the Prussian Ministry of Justice yielded again to the parliamentary pressure and decided to permit women to participate officially in the legal apprenticeship in the same way as male candidates, but it still did not permit women to take the second state exam. Pressured by Prussia's move, the Reichsminister of Justice addressed all the states again to seek a uniform regulation for the entire Reich.[44] Once again, this attempt did not find many friends, especially in Bavaria and in Hesse, but the smaller states followed the new directive. While the Reichstag, the BDF, and many female lawyers worked together on a draft for a law permitting women to take all the exams, the German Judges' Association expressed its own understanding of the question as the first legal professional group. In March 1921, after a long and agitated debate, the judges voiced their decision with 245 votes against 5 that declared women to be unsuited to practice law.[45] In January 1922, the German Bar Association also disputed the question and proved to be more liberal than the judges. With 43 votes to 32, the board of directors came to the decision that a "woman is not suited to work as an attorney or a judge. Her admission would lead to a damage of the judiciary and is therefore rejected."[46]

Finally, when the social democrat Prof. Dr. Gustav Radbruch, a supporter of women in the legal professions, took over the Reichsministry of Justice, he immediately set out to draft a law permitting women to work in legal careers.[47] Before introducing his project into the Reichstag, he had contacted the governments of the single states and advised them of his plan.[48] "Nobody who is interested in a steady, stable legal development will be able to take the responsibility for this step," Bavaria desperately warned.[49] Other states found the reform draft too "radical" and felt that it would pose "an enormous risk" for the justice system. Yet, the legal draft passed through the Reichstag, and finally, against some more resistance from the German conservative states like Bavaria, it passed through the Reichsrat (State Council). It became law on 11 July 1922.[50]

What had taken the legal professions and the governments so long to relent on this question of the admission of women to the legal professions? Why had the debates in the parliaments and in the legal professional organization become even more heated than on the question of women's suffrage? While opponents constantly pointed out that the legal professions were "overcrowded," it was admitted in papers strictly for intergovernmental use that the number of women about to enter the legal professions was too small to pose a real threat and thus the overcrowding argument was clearly self-serving.[51] But what was at stake was the question of whether women would be able to judge men and to gain access to real positions of power as well as full citizenships rights. The latter concern had been expressed already before World War I: "If women function publicly as attorneys and judges," law professor Ludwig von Bar mused in 1897, "it will be impossible to withhold political rights from them for very long."[52] After women's voting rights were won, the fear of suffrage was replaced by the fear that women might gain equal rights, especially in family law and other areas of the law where discrimination was still strong. But beyond equal rights, there was a widespread fear of women wielding the sword of justice. "It seems, indeed, as if the idea of women with judicial powers and functions was quite unbearable to men in all lands," Marie Stritt stated in 1921.[53] Women as judges, resulting in men being sentenced by women, was seemingly outrageous, as the law represented a system of gendered moral values of which lawyers saw themselves the keepers. After women had gained access to medicine and education, the legal field was the only area besides the church that still upheld exclusive male supremacy. Different also from all other academic professions, lawyers were omnipresent in every niche of society: lawyers not only held influential positions in governments and parliaments but also in the economy, in banks, and in the stock exchange. Women working in the legal professions meant, in the end, the termination of the male-dominated state as it had been understood for centuries, just as the lawyer Erna von Langsdorff (1887–?) had prophesied in 1912/13: "As soon as women exercise judicial functions, the collapse of the masculine state will be imminent."[54]

1922–1933: First Professional Life

To date, historical research on women in the legal professions in Germany before 1945 has focused on their struggle to gain access to the courts and the judiciary and their renewed exclusion after 1933.[55] The working situation of female jurists after their entrée in the years in between 1922 and 1933 has not yet been researched.

The opposition toward women in the legal professions continued after 1922. The same concerns and arguments that were first used to prevent women from entering the legal profession now served to steer them into certain areas of the law for which, allegedly, they were better suited than the men. Divorce, guardianship, and juvenile law were considered to be preferable to criminal law and other areas of civil law, as well as public and administrative law, all of which were considered to be male territory.[56] The women also seemed to have felt some special attraction for those legal fields: "Furthermore practice had shown," wrote judge Marie Hagemeyer in 1932, "that women are especially successful in the fields that require a pedagogical impact, such as guardianship and juvenile law, while the office of a criminal judge for adults or of a prosecutor is less likely to be attractive for women."[57]

I. 3.1 Female Attorneys

In fact, the first women who became attorneys immediately after 1922 started out in the area of family law, but soon, like their male colleagues, they had law offices in all legal areas. Their first clients were usually women, who preferred to use the service of female lawyers whom they trusted more readily than men. They were relieved to unburden their worries with a woman, feeling they could establish an easier rapport.[58] Showing a willingness to see the human side of cases and listen to their clients, the female attorneys did share a different, more "human" working ethos than male attorneys.[59] The relationship between a female attorney and client was described in the following words: "She took care of them."[60] Another duty was—according to attorney Margarete Berent—to change the gendered interpretation of existing laws while pleading.[61]

It appears then that female attorneys often had to do more work than their male colleagues to achieve a secure and equivalent economic position.[62] Very few male colleagues were willing to accept women as partners in their offices; the elder attorneys, especially, were often worried that their clients would meet female colleagues with some disapproval.[63] Since young attorneys usually joined an office to gain a steady salary and learn under the expertise of more experienced colleagues, for women it was far harder to enter the profession.[64] A number of women went into partnerships with family members, often with their fathers but even more often with their husbands.

The first female attorney in Germany, Maria Otto (1892–1977), was admitted to the bar in Munich. In 1924, Elfriede Meißner was accepted at the bar of Dresden; Marie Munk, Edith Sussmann (1892–?), and Edith Hegemann-Springer (1890–1937) were accepted at the bar in Berlin, and Margarethe Esch (1899–1966) was accepted at the bar in Cologne. Every year, the number of female attorneys grew considerably. In 1933, when the national socialists took power and began to limit women's access to legal professions, Prussia counted sixty female attorneys, Saxony ten, and Munich eight female attorneys. Altogether, the number of female attorneys in Germany at that time was around 120. They were for the major part active in the larger cities.[65]

I. 3.2 Female Judges

Obviously, female attorneys and judges shared a common struggle, but compared with attorneys, female judges met with much stronger resistance. To judge, in the eyes of many, was not a function that could be performed by women. Since the appointment of judges was the responsibility of the states, some, like Bavaria or the small state of Oldenburg, simply decided not to appoint women. Female judges in fair numbers were only to be found in Prussia and Saxony. Judges were always first employed in temporary positions; to later gain a lifetime appointment depended on the state and took between six and ten years. Thus, the first female judges with lifetime positions were found only by the end of the 1920s. The first female judge in Germany was Maria Hagemeyer, who had passed her second state exam in October 1924 in Prussia. The Prussian Ministry of Justice first employed her, and in May 1927, she was appointed *Amts- und Landrichterin* (local and regional) judge in Bonn. In June 1928, she was promoted to a lifetime position and received the first established post as a female judge in Bonn.[66] She was followed in 1929 by Dr. Gertrud Cichorius (1897–?) (who was placed in a full post in Chemnitz),[67] by Dr. Gertrud May (1882–?) in Leipzig,[68] and by Elisabeth Krumme (1897–1984) in Essen.[69] In 1930, Marie Hurtzig (1896–?) was appointed in Chemnitz,[70] Marie Munk (who is often wrongly cited as the first female judge) in Berlin, and Hedwig Brann-Frank (1899–1978) in Frankfurt.[71] By 1933, Germany counted an estimated thirteen lifetime female judges and over one hundred female judges in judicial training.[72]

The difference between judges appointed for life and those assigned to fixed-term positions became all too apparent for non-Jewish female judges in 1934. Despite continued prejudice against female jurists (Hitler's personal antipathy toward them was notorious), the few of them with a lifetime position were not dismissed by the Nazis but simply shifted to less publicly visible positions. This was obviously not the case for female judges of Jewish descent; they all lost their professions, following the Law on the Restoration of the German Career Civil Service in 1933.

As I have argued elsewhere,[73] female judges felt they had a special duty as women in their new field: "I always make a point of not disregarding the human side of the trial alongside the legal assessment, and I try to avoid at any cost the arrogant tone common to officials," one female judge reported.[74] When describing their way of sentencing, female judges usually argued that first and foremost they used an objective and logical approach and also a stronger sense of intuition.[75] They more often sought out a differing opinion and tools for mediation than did their male colleagues.[76] Especially in divorce or custody cases, female clients seemed relieved to be heard by a female judge. Female judges felt they could have a special impact on justice; as Judge Hildegard Koll[77] described it:

> What a judge deems to be "equitable," "appropriate," "reasonable," "public policy," or whatever these abstract expressions might be, will mostly depend on his personal world view, his *Weltanschauung*, his character, in short his purely human mental attitude to the matter. Up to the present, all decisions of this kind have been influenced by the male nature. Nobody ever doubted that a sentence flowing from this nature was an objective one. If now—through the admission of women to the legal professions—new views can enter legal decision-making and cases may be judged and decided from angles different than hitherto, then this, according to the previous criteria, is equally legal. The special character of a woman is not altering the law as such; it is merely having a possible impact within the range of the legally granted freedom of discretion, in the same way as differences among individual male judges' characters may result in different judgments about the same case.[78]

As was the case with female attorneys, there is evidence to suggest that female judges worked harder than their male colleagues in order to prove their qualification for their new positions. Even though they were assiduous, positions in higher ranks continued to be assigned exclusively to men.

None of the female lawyers managed to get into the profession of notary, and very few became public prosecutors. The first was characterized as a "public office" and with its restrictive process of selection was still too elitist to allow women to join its ranks; the latter was closely associated with criminal law, a field that was deemed less suitable for women and also related to state employment. Female lawyers who did not sit for exams had made their way into civil service in areas related to guardianship and welfare law; some gained good positions but were also dismissed after 1933. In sum, female lawyers had, despite all the difficulties, a relatively successful professional time in the short period between 1922 and the beginning of the "Third Reich," when they virtually disappeared from the legal professions. Within the two Germanys after 1945, the history of female lawyers was ambiguous. Their formal entry into the justice system ushered in a prolonged reaction of institutional discrimination that has still not entirely been eradicated.

Female Lawyers in the Fight for Equal Rights in Family Law

After German women managed to gain the vote and even the right to enter all the professions, including the legal ones, many other critical women's legal issues remained: such as the question of married women's nationality, the right to legally possess a title to property when married, and especially equal rights within the family.

The institution of marriage has, in fact, served for centuries to consecrate women's inferiority in law in a supposed contract of equals. Minds like Grotius, Locke, von Pufendorff, Wolff, Fichte, Kant, and Rousseau, along with the Catholic and Protestant churches, relegated wives to a subordinate status within marriage. The civil codes of the single German states had discriminating limitations in their marriage laws, but the *Bürgerliche Gesetzbuch* (BGB, German civil code), which was codified in 1900, legislated women almost into the status of legalized slaves or, as Anita Augspurg phrased it, into "bourgeois suicide."[79] Married women had only a limited legal personhood of their own; they could not own their own property if not contracted differently, they had only limited freedom to contract in general beyond their *Schlüsselgewalt* (wife's authorization to purchase necessities for the household), they could only speak in court for themselves in limited cases, they could only work outside of the house with their husband's permission, they had only limited legal authority over their children, and they could not divorce their husbands except for very limited reasons. The man had the decision in all matters concerning their marriage, including the decision on the family's place to live.[80] Lawyer Anita Augspurg had remarked in 1905 somewhat polemically that "for a woman with self-respect who understands the legal effects of civil marriage, it is in my opinion impossible to enter a legitimate marriage: her drive for self-preservation, her self-respect, and her claim to respect from her husband leaves only the option of *extramarital cohabitation*."[81]

Female lawyers had a strong sense of the wrong the law perpetuated against women and children and thus joined the struggle on their behalf. Concern for their protection had been at the core of their professional behavior from the outset and limited itself not only to court cases, but also to legal reforms. Indeed, female lawyers' experiences in social work before their admission to the legal professions in 1922 and courtroom experiences afterwards seem to have increased their compassion and conviction to address their society's social problems. While their names are still almost unknown for researchers of the German women's movement, they had, in fact, played a key role in defining the legal claims of the BDF for the years since, at least, 1918. Research on the role of the women's movement in the Weimar Republic usually emphasizes the decline of the women's movement's strength, but at least in terms of their legal reform claims, their demands were stronger than ever, thanks to the female lawyers. It was actually the first time that professional legal organizations as well as the parliaments and the governments treated claims made by the women's movement seriously.[82]

The Weimar Constitution of 1919 provided a new legal context for legal reform of family law. Art. 119 stated that marriage was predicated upon equality of the sexes. But as was the case in Art. 109 and Art. 128, most lawyers shared the legal opinion that the constitution had no immediate legal effects and that its stipulation on equality of the sexes thus could only be considered as directives to future legislators. Female lawyers, on the other hand, believed that the constitution expressed the prevailing law and thus set out to tackle a variety of discriminatory laws.

The protection of children was a priority for many female lawyers, who made attempts to end the stigmatization of illegitimate children, which was the case in other European countries.[83] Dr. Marie Munk had drafted a reform paper on this question in 1918.[84] She proposed equal treatment for illegitimate children with children born within marriage, child support by the father, and the legal recognition of children born out of wedlock. As in other countries, female lawyers in Germany also advocated better welfare laws for poor women and children and equal pay for equal work. Dr. Margarete Berent had drafted the BDF reform claims for changes in the married women's nationality law that were comparable with the demands all over the world, permitting married women to maintain a nationality of their own. It was introduced to the Reichstag in 1932.[85] Together with Marie Munk in 1920, she wrote suggestions for the draft of a new Judiciary Act, which would include appointing women as lay judges.[86]

But female lawyers prioritized reforms in family law, including equal spousal responsibilities, easier divorce procedures not based on no fault divorce, common custody law, and equal goods acquired during marriage in case of divorce. As a matter of fact, the BDF board decided as early as June 1919 to form a new legal committee to work out a draft for the reform of family law. The committee was headed by lawyer Marie Munk and consisted of the feminists Marianne Weber (1870–1954), Camilla Jellinek (1860–1940), Marie Stritt, and the head of the legal aid institutions for women, Margarethe Bennewiz (1860–1943).[87] Munk invited Berent as a second legal counsel since Berent was not only a specialist in matrimonial property law, but also the head of the legal commission of the women's working committee of the DDP.[88] The first result of Munk's and Berent's joint work was a series of proposals for the different areas of family law, namely matrimonial law, parental care and authority, rights of the illegitimate child, divorce law, and matrimonial property law.[89] The debates generated in the women's movement by this work led to the decision to ask the board to elaborate a family law memorandum, which would meet the new goal of gender equality provided for in the constitution. The memorandum seemed important because the Reich Ministry of Justice had for some time been working on drafts for a reform of family law. The BDF decided not only to petition to the Reichstag, but also to make its demands accessible to the public by publishing the memorandum in book form. Marie Munk was hired to write it. The memorandum was finished in October 1923, mailed to the Reich Ministry of Justice, and later introduced to the parliament.[90] The publication was well received and soon debated within the legal professions and the interested public.

The work of these two female lawyers emphasized the need for reform in matters of divorce. Since it was obvious that the realities of family life were not reflected in the strictly defined current grounds for divorce, which the BGB provided for, Munk and Berent asked for a significant expansion of the possible legal reasons for divorce. They suggested that divorce be possible on account of an irretrievable breakdown of the marriage instead of focusing exclusively on the proof of guilt. Furthermore, Munk proposed in 1923 that a married couple should also be able to divorce if only one spouse filed for divorce on grounds of "insurmountable aversion."[91] This last demand in particular was much disputed within the BDF, as divorce was considered within the women's movement as well as the last possible option when the special duties and recommendations of the social function of a marriage and family were endangered. The BDF board was afraid that overly progressive claims would lead to a split of the organization that was then constituted of more conservative than progressive members.[92] Thus, the BDF concentrated more on the suggestions for a new matrimonial property law, which was politically less controversial. The board suggested the separation of property during marriage combined with a community of accrued gain in case of divorce or death as the new statutory matrimonial property regime.[93]

In the meantime, the legal professions took up the topic and debated it widely. Central to developments were two congresses of the prestigious *Deutsche Juristentag* (DJT) 1924 in Heidelberg and 1931 in Lübeck, in which attorney Marie Munk and attorney Emmy Rebstein-Metzger (1809–1967) gave important presentations suggesting changes in family law that were well received within the community of the legal professions.[94]

Female lawyers not only formulated the legal reform program for the BDF within the years of the Weimar Republic, but also argued within the diverse setting of the BDF for the most progressive and radical legal changes to protect women in family law. Thus, they constituted the legal department of the BDF, pressuring for an all-compassing legal reform without any legal loopholes. Their comprehensive reform plan was pioneering: particularly so at a time when the majority of the right wing and even the moderate women's organizations within the BDF sought agreement on a far more limited set of legal reforms in family law.

Besides becoming the legal experts of the BDF, a number of other female lawyers published their claims for legal changes in prominent legal journals.[95] But they also frequently wrote in daily newspapers and in the women's movement's journals. They gave public lectures for female audiences, and they taught in schools in order to raise young women's awareness of their legal situation and ask for support of their legal reform claims. Thus, they became highly visible figures in the Weimar Republic, the very incarnations of the "new woman" capable of full participation in public life and able to implement citizenship rights to the extent they could.

Conclusion

The purpose of this chapter has been to explore the struggles by German female lawyers and the women's movement to gain access to the legal professions as a part of the struggle for equal rights for women in Germany more generally. I have argued that the fight to open access to the legal professions in Germany was part of the women's movement's struggle for equal rights in the beginning of the twentieth century. For two decades, the BDF and the few female lawyers fought side-by-side for the admission of women to public offices as members of juries and later as professional female lawyers. While the resistance in the first case had been strong, resistance in the latter case was "as strong and stubborn" as hardly any other fight for equal rights for women in Germany. As I have argued in this chapter, the admission of women was achieved twenty years later than in many Western European countries because of the particularities of the German legal education's emphasis on producing jurists as *Einheitsjuristen*, which would also give women de facto access not only to the advocacy, but also to the judiciary and to employment in the highly prestigious and powerful civil service. In most other European countries, such as Russia (1864), Norway (1890), Sweden (1895), Finland (1895), Switzerland (Zurich 1898, resp. other cantons before 1914), France (1900), Netherlands (1904), Denmark (1906), United Kingdom (1918), Portugal (1918), Poland (1918), Italy (1883, resp. 1919), Austria (1920), Belgium (1922), Romania (1923) and Spain (1930), the admission was carried out in two steps. The first step was to the advocacy and the second, often decades later, to the judiciary. Russia admitted women as judges in 1917, Poland in 1928, Czechoslovakia in 1930, Denmark in 1933, and the Republican part of Spain in 1936.[96] In the other European countries, judgeship was only achieved after World War II and often combined with the gain of suffrage. It appears that resistance to women's entry into the legal professions was less about women working as attorneys and more about the objections to admitting women to the public offices of judges, as Sara Kimble has also argued for the case of France.[97] Furthermore and lastly, opponents feared that permitting women to acquire this specialized knowledge and to work in legal professions such as public offices would, in the end, lead not only directly to women's political rights, but also to equal rights in family law, the last stronghold of male authority. They were right to be worried. Indeed, women's quest to enter the legal professions evoked a great struggle for power, both symbolic and factual. It foretold the erosion of men's authority and the end of women's marginalization.

Notes

1 Ute Gerhard, *Frauenbewegung und Feminismus. Eine Geschichte seit 1789* (Munich: C.H. Beck, 2009); Ute Gerhard, *Debating Women's Equality: Toward a Feminist Theory of Law from a European Perspective* (New Brunswick, NJ: Rutgers University Press 2001); Gisela Bock, *Frauen in der europäischen*

Geschichte. Vom Mittelalter bis zur Gegenwart (Munich: C.H. Beck, 2000), 53–118.

2 Anita Augspurg, "Gebt acht, solange noch Zeit ist!," *Die Frauenbewegung* 1 (1895): 4–5.

3 Ibid.

4 The formulation "civic women's movement" had been used by Alice Salomon in 1899 at the Conference of the ICW in London, as Gisela Bock has pointed out. Alice Salomon, "Protective Legislation in Germany," in *Women in Industrial Life. The Transactions of the Industrial and Legislative Section of the International Congress of Women, London, July 1899*, ed. Ishbel Countess of Aberdeen, vol. 6 (London: T. Fisher Unwin, 1900), 37; Gisela Bock, "Begriffsgeschichten: 'Frauenemanziaption' im Kontext der Emanzipationsbewegung des 19. Jahrhunderts," in *Geschlechtergeschichte der Neuzeit. Ideen, Politik, Praxis*, ed. Ibid. (Göttingen: Vandenhoeck & Ruprecht, 2014), 151.

5 Christiane Berneike, *Die Frauenfrage ist Rechtsfrage. Die Juristinnen der deutschen Frauenbewegung um das Bürgerliche Gesetzbuch* (Baden-Baden: Nomos, 1995); Tanja-Carina Riedel, *Gleiches Recht für Frau und Mann. Die bürgerliche Frauenbewegung und die Entstehung des BGB* (Cologne: Böhlau, 2008).

6 Auguste Schmidt, "Juristinnen," *Neue Bahnen* 25, no. 3 (1900): 32.

7 Marie Stritt, "Germany," *The International Woman Suffrage News* (April 1921): 107.

8 See generally, James Albisetti, "Portia ante Portas. Women and the Legal Profession in Europe, ca. 1870–1925," *Journal of Social History* 33, no. 4 (2000): 825–857; also Ulrike Schultz and Gisela Shaw eds., *Women in the World's Legal Professions* (Oxford/Portland: Hart, 2003).

9 Marion Röwekamp, *Die ersten deutschen Juristinnen. Eine Geschichte ihrer Professionalisierung und Emanzipation (1900–1945)* (Cologne: Böhlau, 2011), 638–748.

10 Peter Krause, "Geschichte der Justiz- und Verwaltungsausbildung in Preußen und Deutschland," in *Juristenausbildung in Europa zwischen Tradition und Reform*, ed. Christian Baldus, Thomas Finkenauer, and Thomas Rüfner (Tübingen: Mohr Siebeck, 2008), 95–125; Kenneth F. Ledford, *From General Estate to Special Interest: German Lawyers 1878–1933* (Cambridge: Cambridge University Press, 1996).

11 "Frauen," in *Allgemeine deutsche Real-Encyclopedie für die gebildeten Stände*, Encyclopedia for the Educated Classes, ca. 1820, quoted after Gerhard, *Debating Women's Equality*, 48.

12 Ute Frevert, *"Mann und Weib, und Weib und Mann": Geschlechter-Differenzen in der Moderne* (Munich: C.H. Beck, 1995); Bock, *Frauen in der europäischen Geschichte*, 121–132; Eric J. Hobsbawm, "Kultur und Geschlecht im europäischen Bürgertum 1870–1914," in *Bürgerinnen und Bürger*, ed. Ute Frevert (Göttingen: Vandenhoeck & Ruprecht, 1998), 175–189.

13 "Otto Gierke," in *Die akademische Frau. Gutachten hervorragender Universitätsprofessoren, Frauenlehrer und Schriftsteller über die Befähigung der Frau zum wissenschaftlichen Studium und Berufe*, ed. Arthur v. Kirchhoff (Berlin: H. Steinitz 1897), 26.

14 Röwekamp, *Juristinnen*, 41–60.

15 Albisetti, "Portia ante Portas," 825–828.

16 James Albisetti, *Schooling German Girls and Women: Secondary and Higher Education in the Nineteenth Century* (Princeton, NJ: Princeton University Press, 1988), 248–250; Patricia M. Mazón, *Gender and the Modern Research University: The Admission of Women to German Higher Education, 1865–1914* (Stanford, CA: Stanford University Press, 2003), 104, 106–107.

17 Röwekamp, *Juristinnen*, 111–117.

18 *Jus Suffragii* (Monthly Organ of the International Woman Suffrage Alliance) 8, no. 2 (October 1, 1913): 59.

19 Beatrix Geisel, "'Alle Juristinnen haben ihre Stellung der Frauenbewegung zu verdanken!' Dem langen Kampf um die Robe folgte der noch immer nicht beendete Streit um die Gleichberechtigung," *Ariadne* 30 (1996): 52–59; Erna von Langsdorff, "Die Berufsaussichten der Juristin in Deutschland," *Die Frau* 20 (1912/13): 603–609; Margarete Bernhard, "Vorbildungs- und Berufsverhältnisse der deutschen Nationalökonominnen und Juristinnen," *Volkswirtschaftliche Blätter* 12, no. 5–6 (1913): 54–59.

20 *Jus Suffragii* 8, no. 2 (October 1, 1913): 59.

21 "Zweiter Deutscher Jugendgerichtstag, 29. September–1. Oktober 1910 in München," *Die Frauenbewegung* 16, no. 21 (1910): 169.

22 Herbert Ruscheweyh, *Die Entwicklung des deutschen Jugendgerichts. Schriften des Ausschusses für Jugendgerichte und Jugendgerichtshilfen* (Weimar: Dietsch & Brückner, 1918), 67.

23 Landesarchiv Berlin (LA Berlin), B Rep. 235–12 (BDF), Fiche 2786.

24 BDF, January 1913, LA Berlin, B Rep. 235–12, Fiche 2787; "Kundgebung für die Zulassung der Frauen als Schöffen," *Die Frau* 20 (1912–13): 376; Gertrud Bäumer, "Zwei Kundgebungen zur Einheitlichkeit der deutschen Frauenbewegung," *Die Frauenfrage* 15, no. 1–2 (1913–14): 2.

25 Quote from: Marie Munk, Autobiography, LA Berlin, B Rep. 235–12, IX, 4. On the biographies see: Marion Röwekamp, *Juristinnen. Lexikon zu Leben und Werk* (Baden-Baden: Nomos, 2005), 36–40; 271–274; 275–278.

26 Röwekamp, *Juristinnen*, 546–552.

27 Marcelle Kraemer-Bach, "Fédération internationale des femmes avocats," *La Française*, November 9, 1929; Sirje Tamul, "Poska-Grünthal, Vera (Veera) (1909–1986)," in *Biographical Dictionary of Women's Movements and Feminisms in Central, Eastern, and South Eastern Europe, 19th and 20th Centuries*, ed. Francisca de Haan, Krassimira Daskalova and Anna Loutfi (Budapest: CEU Press, 2006), 450–453.

28 Röwekamp, *Juristinnen*, 219–234.

29 Irene Stoehr, "'Organisierte Mütterlichkeit': Zur Politik der deutschen Frauenbewegung um 1900," in *Frauen suchen ihre Geschichte: Historische Studien zum 19. und 20. Jahrhundert*, ed. Karin Hausen (Munich: CH Beck, 1983), 221–249.

30 Dietrich, "Der Beruf der Frauen zur Rechtsprechung," *Deutsche Richter-Zeitung* 38 (1933): 1255–1259; similar and earlier also Richter, "Die Frau als Richter," *Deutsche Tageszeitung* Nr. 89, 22.2.1922; Otto Loenig, "Die Rechtspflege und die Frauen," *Recht und Wirtschaft* 8 (1919): 197–200; Otto Hartwig, *Die Frau in der Rechtspflege. Systematische Darstellung der Beseitigung der Frau an der Rechtspflege im In- und Auslande* (Detmold: Meyer, 1922), 18.

31 Gisela Bock and Pat Thane eds., *Maternity and Gender Policies: Women and the Rise of the European Welfare States, 1880s-1950s* (London and New York: Routledge, 1991); Ann Taylor Allen, *Feminism and Motherhood in Western Europe, 1890–1970: The Maternal Dilemna* (New York: Palgrave McMillan, 1994); Sonya Koven and Seth Michel, "Womanly Duties: Maternalist Politics and the Origins of Welfare States in France, Germany, Great Britain, and the United States, 1880–1920," *American Historical Review* 95, no. 4 (1990): 1076–1108; Sonya Koven and Seth Michel, *Mothers of a New World: Maternalist Politics and the Origins of Welfare States* (New York: Routledge, 1993), 1–42; Geoffrey Eley and Atina Grossmann, "The Gendered Politics of Welfare," *Central European History* 30, no. 1 (1997): 67–75.

32 Röwekamp, *Juristinnen*, 633, 779; Marion Röwekamp, "First Female Judges in the Weimar Republic in Germany: Reflections on Difference," in *Gender and*

Judging, ed. Ulrike Schultz and Gisela Shaw (Oxford/Portland: Hart Publishing, 2013), 103–121.

33 Theodor L. W. Bischoff, *Das Studium und die Ausübung der Medicin durch Frauen* (München: Literarisch-Artistische Anstalt, 1872), 19, 30; Theodor L. W. Bischoff, *Das Hirngewicht des Menschen: Eine Studie* (Bonn: Neusser, 1880), 154–155; Paul Julius Möbius, *Über den physiologischen Schwachsinn des Weibes* (Halle: Marhold 1900).

34 Röwekamp, *Juristinnen*, 330–368.

35 Marion Röwekamp, "'Männer und Frauen haben grundsätzlich die gleichen staatsbürgerlichen Rechte.' Weimar—Meilenstein auf dem Weg zur Gleichberechtigung der Geschlechter?" in *Die Weimarer Verfassung, Wert und Wirkung für die Demokratie*, ed. Friedrich-Ebert-Stiftung (Erfurt: 2009), 235–264.

36 Ministry of Saxony, March 1919, Bayerisches Hauptstaatsarchiv (BayHStA) MJu 9829.

37 Röwekamp, *Juristinnen*, 264.

38 GStA Rep 84 a Nr. 579 Fiche 12982, 135; "Die Zulassung der Frauen zu den juristischen Prüfungen und zum Vorbereitungsdienst," *Die Frau* 27 (1919–20): 349.

39 Reichsministry of Justice, 4/14/1919, to all State Ministries of Justice, BA Berlin R 3001 4180, 91 ff.; BayHStA MJu 9829; GSTA Rep 84 a Nr. 579, Fiche 12982, 125.

40 Röwekamp, *Juristinnen*, 261.

41 Justizministerialblätter 1919, 288; GStA Rep. 84 a Nr. 579, Fiche 12981, 118; Margarete Berent, "Die Zulassung von Frauen zu den juristischen Berufen," *Die Frau* 27 (1919–20): 332–334.

42 Curt Zimmer and Friedrich Klee, *Die juristische Ausbildung in Preußen. Zusammenstellung der Gesetzes- und Verwaltungsvorschriften über Rechtsstudium, juristische Prüfungen und Vorbereitungsdienst nebst erläuternden Bemerkungen* (Berlin: Preußische Druckerei-. u. Verlags-A.G. 1930), 19.

43 Petition Mrs. Agnes and companions, February 12, 1920, No. 1035, Hearings of the Reichstag vol. 365, printed matter 1035, Reichstag I. election period 1920, 705.

44 Reichsministry of Justice, February 23, 1921, to all State Ministries of Justice, BA Berlin R 3001/4181, 25.

45 "Verhandlungen des 4. Richtertages," *Deutsche Richterzeitung* 13 (1921): 196–206.

46 "Verhandlungen des Anwaltstages," *Juristische Wochenschrift* 51 (1922): 1247, 1255.

47 Handwritten note by Radbruch, March 2, 1922, BA Berlin R 3001/4181, 198.

48 Proceedings of the Reichsgovernment January 2, 1922, BA Berlin R 3001 4181, 200f.

49 Bavaria's Ministry of Justice to Foreign Office, February 17, 1922, BayHStA MJu 9829.

50 *Reich Law Gazette*, 1/51 (1922): 573–574.

51 Besides competition to be mentioned in different archival material, such as, for example, in draft of April 22, 1919, Justice Ministry of Hesse to Reichsministry of Justice, HessStA DA G 21 A 67/3, also in Dietrich, "Beruf," 1255. Informal papers admitting that it was a spurious argument, for example, Ministry of Justice of Saxonia to Reichsministry of Justice, May 16, 1919, GStA I HA Rep. 84 a Nr. 579 Fiche 12983, 245–246, see also Berent, "Frau in der Rechtspflege," 8, in: Margarete Berent Collection, LBI NYC.

52 "Ludwig von Bar," in *Die akademische Frau*, 19.

53 Stritt, "Germany," 107.

54 Erna von Langsdorff, "Die Berufsaussichten der Juristin in Deutschland," *Die Frau* 20 (1912/13): 608.

55 Stefan Bajohr and Katrin Rödiger-Bajohr, "Die Diskriminierung der Juristin in Deutschland bis 1945," *Kritische Justiz* 13 (1980): 39–50; Reglindis Böhm, "Der Kampf um die Zulassung der Frauen als Rechtsanwältinnen und zum Richteramt," in *Frauen in juristischen Berufen. Ein Brevier für Referendare und Referendarinnen*, ed. Ministry of Justice of Hesse (Wiesbaden, 1987), 11–19; Oda Cordes, "Die Frau als Organ der Rechtspflege? Über die historisch wichtigsten Stationen der Zulassung von Frauen in der deutschen Rechtspflege," in *Frauenrecht und Rechtsgeschichte. Die Rechtskämpfe der deutschen Frauenbewegung*, ed. Stephan Meder, Arne Duncker, and Andrea Czelk (Cologne: Böhlau, 2006), 279–301; Deutscher Juristinnenbund, *Juristinnen in Deutschland. Die Zeit von 1900 bis 1998* (Baden-Baden: Nomos, 2003); Barbara Dölemeyer, "Die Zulassung von Frauen zur Rechtsanwaltschaft und ihr Ausschluß in der NS-Zeit," in *"Ins Wasser geworfen und Ozeane durchquert." Festschrift für Knut Wolfgang Nörr*, ed. Mario Ascheri (Cologne: Böhlau 2003), 151–164; Sibylla Flügge, "Der lange Weg in die Gerichte. Von der Männlichkeit des Staates und vom Ende holder Weiblichkeit," *Streit* 4 (1984): 149–153; Hiltrud Häntzschel, "Justitia—eine Frau? Bayerische Positionen einer Geschlechterdebatte," in *Bedrohlich gescheit. Ein Jahrhundert Frauen und Wissenschaft in Bayern*, ed. Hiltrud Häntzschel and Hadumod Bußmann (Munich: Beck 1997), 194–213; Claudia Huerkamp, *Bildungsbürgerinnen. Frauen im Studium und in akademischen Berufen 1900–1945* (Göttingen: Vandenhoeck & Ruprecht, 1996); Heino Schöbel, "Frauen in der bayerischen Justiz. Der Weg zum Richteramt," *Bayerische Verwaltungsblätter* 44, no. 129 (1998): 65–73, 106–110.

56 Sybille Böge, "Geschlecht und 'horizontale' Segmentierungen in der juristischen Profession," in *Die soziale Konstruktion von Geschlecht in Professionalisierungsprozessen. Vom kollektiven Frauenausschluss zur Integration mit beschränkten Möglichkeiten*, ed. Angelika Wetterer (Frankfurt/Main: Jenior & Pressler 1995), 139; Ilse Costas, "Gesellschaftliche Umbrüche und das Verhältnis von Profession und Geschlecht. Die juristische Profession im deutsch-französischen Vergleich," in Ibid., 121.

57 Marie Hagemeyer, "Die Juristin," in *Frauengedanken zum Beruf*, ed. Ina Neundörfer (Münster: Regensberg, 1932), 53.

58 Margarethe von Erffa and Ingeborg Richarz-Simons, "Der weibliche Rechtsanwalt," in *Die Rechtsanwaltschaft*, ed. Julius Magnus (Leipzig: Moeser, 1929), 476; Käthe Gaebel, "Die Berufslage der Akademikerinnen," *Die Frau* 34 (1926–27), 223; Marie Munk, Pioneer Women Judge, Sophia Smith Collection, Smith College/Northampton, SSC, IV, 4.

59 Margarete Berent, "Die Frau in den juristischen Berufen," *Die Frau der Gegenwart* 11 (1917): 157; Erna Haßlacher-Friedenthal, "Die Juristin," in *Das moderne Buch der weiblichen Berufe*, ed. Erich Janke (Minden: Köhler, 1928), 217.

60 Christine Bartlitz, "Justitia ist weiblich. Emmalene Bulling. Bremens erste Rechtsanwältin," in *Buten un Binnen, Wagen un Winnen. Erste Bremerinnen auf dem Weg ins akademische Leben*, ed. Eva Schöck-Quinteros (Bremen: Hedwig Hintze Inst., 1997), 110.

61 Berent, "Frau in den juristischen Berufen," 157.

62 Marie Munk, *Die Juristin* (Berlin: Merkblätter für Berufsberatung der Deutschen Zentralstelle für Berufsberatung der Akademiker, 1928), 7.

63 Erffa and Richarz-Simons, "Weibliche Rechtsanwalt," 476; Haßlacher-Friedenthal, "Juristin," 218.

64 Gaebel, "Berufslage," 223.

65 Röwekamp, *Juristinnen*, 468–470.

66 Röwekamp, *Juristinnenlexikon*, 123.

67 Cichorius, Gertrud, BA Berlin R 3001 053503.

68 May, Gertrud, Staatsarchiv Leipzig, LG 8008.
69 Röwekamp, *Juristinnenlexikon*, 214.
70 Hurtzig, Marie, BA Berlin R 3001 061499.
71 Röwekamp, *Juristinnenlexikon*, 275.
72 Röwekamp, *Juristinnen*, 451.
73 Röwekamp, "First Female Judges," 103–121.
74 Sims, "Erste Kammergerichts-Richterin," in *Der Montag (Lokal-Anzeiger)*, 4/22/1929.
75 Hildegard Koll, "Die Frau im Richterberuf," in *Städtisches Gymnasium und Realgymnasium in der Kreuzgasse zu Köln, 1828–1928. Festschrift zur Jahrhundertfeier der Anstalt 13. bis 15. Okt. 1928* (Cologne: Kölner Görres Haus, 1928), 100.
76 Koll, "Frau im Richterberuf," 103; Munk, LA Berlin, Rep 235–12 (NMM) Fiche 3508, XII, 11.
77 Life dates unknown.
78 Ibid., 100.
79 Anita Augspurg, "Rede vor einer Volksversammlung in Berlin am" 16. February 1896, 1. Draft, *Die Frauenbewegung* 5 (1896): 49–50, cited after *Anita Augspurg. Rechtspolitische Schriften. Kommentierte Studienausgabe*, ed. Christiane Henke (Cologne: Böhlau 2013), 93.
80 Dieter Schwab, "Gleichberechtigung und Familienrecht im 20. Jahrhundert," in *Frauen in der Geschichte des Rechts. Von der frühen Neuzeit bis zur Gegenwart*, ed. Ute Gerhard (Munich: C.H. Beck, 1997), 790–827; Riedel, *Gleiches Recht für Frau und Mann*; Stephan Meder, Arne Duncker, and Andrea Czelk eds., *Die Rechtsstellung der Frau um 1900. Eine kommentierte Quellensammlung* (Cologne: Böhlau, 2010); Stephan Meder et al. eds., *Frauenrecht und Rechtsgeschichte*.
81 Anita Augspurg, "Ein typischer Fall der Gegenwart. Offener Brief," *Europa* 7 (1905): 311–314, newprint *Die Frauenbewegung* 11 (1905): 81–82.
82 Röwekamp, *Juristinnen*, 556–570.
83 Sara L. Kimble, "No Right to Judge. Feminism and the Judiciary in Third Republic France," *French Historical Studies* 31, no. 4 (2008): 615–616.
84 LA Berlin B Rep. 235–01 Fiche 2765.
85 LA Berlin B Rep. 235–01 Fiche 2782, 2783.
86 LA Berlin B Rep. 235–12 Fiche 2787.
87 Letter Alice Bensheimer to Marianne Weber, 10/4/1919, LA Berlin B Rep. 235–01, fiche 2440; letter Alice Bensheimer to Marie Munk, 7/2/1919, LA Berlin B Rep. 235–01, fiche 2149.
88 Letter Munk to Weber, 10/11/1919, LA Berlin B Rep. 235–01, fiche 2150.
89 Meeting of the closer board, 5/29/1921, LA Berlin, B Rep. 235–12, fiche 3127; Munk and Berent, Proposals for a family law change, summer 1921, LA Berlin, B Rep. 235–12, fiche 2763. See also: Marion Röwekamp, "Misjudged and Underestimated. The family law claims of the *Bund deutscher Frauenvereine* on matrimonial property law, 1918–1933," in *Gender Difference in European Legal Cultures. Historical Perspectives. Dedicated to Heide Wunder on the occasion of her 70th Birthday*, ed. Karin Gottschalk (Stuttgart: Franz Steiner Verlag, 2013), 221–234.
90 LA Berlin, B Rep. 235–12, fiche 2762.
91 Marie Munk, *Vorschläge zur Umgestaltung des Rechts der Ehescheidung und der elterlichen Gewalt nebst Gesetzesentwurf. Denkschrift des Bundes Deutscher Frauenvereine* (Berlin: Herbig, 1923), 7.
92 Klaus Hönig, *Der Bund Deutscher Frauenvereine in der Weimarer Republik 1919–1933* (Egelsbach: Hänsel-Hohenhausen, 1995), 88.

93 Margarete Berent and Marie Munk, *Vorschläge zur Abänderung des Familienrechts und verwandter Gebiete*, summer 1921, LA Berlin, B Rep. 235–12, fiche 2763.
94 Röwekamp, *Juristinnen*, 583–588; 598–606.
95 Ibid., 604–606.
96 For Russia see: "Women Judges," *International Women's News* 11 (1917): 154; for Czechoslovakia, see chapter Osterkamp in this volume and "Feminist Notes: Training Women to be Judges," *Equal Rights* 16 (1930): 104; for Denmark see: "Denmark appoints Woman Judge," *Equal Rights* 19 (1933): 262–263. For Poland, see chapter of Iwona Dadej in this volume and "Poland," *International Women's News* 41 (1947): 85; for Spain, see the chapter of Gloria Nielfa in this volume.
97 Kimble, "No Right to Judge," 605–645.

11 Feminism and Criminology in Britain, 1910–1950

Anne Logan

The admission of women aged over thirty to the parliamentary vote in Britain in 1918 was swiftly followed by legislation, the 1919 Sex Disqualification Removal Act, which opened—among other things—the legal profession, the jury box, and the lay magistracy (made up of justices without formal legal qualifications) to women. While the impact on the first two of these institutions was limited in the short term,[1] the changes to the magistracy were more immediate. Although their numbers were small at first, the new female magistrates of England and Wales, many of whom were veterans of the struggle for women's suffrage, sought to reform the justice system through the establishment of the Magistrates Association, the formation of women magistrates' societies, and the re-invigoration of the country's penal reform pressure groups.[2] Within these organizations, volunteer activists developed cultures of professionalism, research, pedagogy, and activism. Consequentially, at a time when criminology still lacked any recognized position as a discipline within British universities, female magistrates in England and Wales played an important, and largely unrecognized, part in research and teaching on criminal justice subjects.[3]

Standard accounts of feminist engagement with criminology focus primarily on the debates of the post-1970 period. Earlier twentieth century developments, associated sometimes with so-called "first wave" or liberal feminism, remain neglected.[4] Yet the British women's suffrage movement of the early twentieth century prompted profound feminist interest in criminal justice issues, such as infanticide, youth crime, and the prison system, the latter having been experienced personally by some campaigners during the course of the struggle for votes for women.[5] The imprisonment of British men (and some of their female supporters) who refused to perform military service on the grounds of conscience during the First World War further raised consciousness about the penal system. These concerns, as I have argued elsewhere, were not merely a source of activism but were also influential in stimulating the first stirrings of a feminist criminology.[6] The purpose of the current chapter is to examine in some detail the philosophical, epistemological, and theoretical underpinnings of feminist criminology in Britain during the so-called "first wave" of feminism in the early twentieth century.

This chapter discusses four related philosophical and epistemological pillars of this pioneering intellectual movement: feminism, humanitarianism, activism, and research. "First wave" feminism is rarely discussed in the context of criminology or criminal justice except during the era of the heightened suffrage struggles prior to World War One. In any case, the metaphor of "waves" has little correspondence with contemporary understanding of women's history. Over the last twenty years, an extensive historical literature has been produced which demonstrates that feminism in Britain did not disappear after the attainment of women's suffrage in 1918 only to reappear fifty years later.[7] In her work on European feminism, Karen Offen suggests an alternative metaphor, that of a volcano, with its "eruptions, flows, fissures, [and] molten lava." She argues that feminism is "a threatening and rather fluid form of discontent that repeatedly presses against . . . weak spots in the sedimented layers of a patriarchal crust."[8] However, notwithstanding the work of Offen and many others, a leading historian of Britain recently argued that "feminism as a coherent political movement . . . virtually disappeared" after 1918, apparently seen off by the British Establishment.[9] So it seems that outside the field of women's history there is still a tendency to think in terms of "waves." However, it is not credible to assume that women (and men) who spent the early part of their lives fighting for women's rights—not just the vote but associated political, social, and economic rights, such as entry to professions and (crucially for this paper) to full citizenship on juries and the magistrates' bench—ceased to be engaged politically after 1918. It is the philosophy and actions of this generation, undeniably shaped by the times they lived in, which this chapter focuses upon. My contention is that rather than receding on the tide as the waves went out, early twentieth century feminist energy was simply redirected. While some former suffragists continued to work primarily for causes readily identifiable as "feminist" (for example, equal pay and employment opportunities or, more controversially, family allowances and birth control), others became engaged unsurprisingly in the general political struggles of their day: for or against fascism, for improved international relations and the maintenance of peace, or for specific social policies. A few became immersed in mainstream politics, securing elected office as members of parliament.[10]

The specific group of feminists discussed here became involved principally in campaigns for the reform of criminal justice, largely as a result of appointment to the magistracy. I have named this group, rather inelegantly, the "feminist-criminal-justice reform network,"[11] as they linked together a disparate range of organizations from penal reform pressure groups to mainstream women's societies. But it must be stressed that this sort of involvement did not represent an abandonment of feminism but rather the practical application of its core principle, the right of women to engage politically on equal terms with men. This network not only actively promoted policies which have been retrospectively summed up as "penal-welfarism,"[12] but they also engaged in criminological research and developed some original perspectives on crime. While often concerned with issues pertaining to young offenders or adult men, individual female activists nevertheless maintained special interest in, and concern for, women in the criminal justice system. While some organizations in the network had women-only membership, others were mixed bodies with strong feminist influence.

This chapter examines the four themes of feminism, humanitarianism, activism, and research to develop an understanding of the nature of feminist women's critique of criminal justice in early twentieth century Britain. Each section traces the most important influences on the feminist-criminal-justice reform network which originated in the years before the granting of women's suffrage (and the introduction of women magistrates) in the United Kingdom and developed thereafter. The themes are developed and illustrated with examples of feminist activism in the field of criminal justice within England and Wales and further afield.

When discussing the "feminist criminology" of the early twentieth century, we have to be careful to define our terms. "Criminology" itself was not institutionalized or academicized as it is nowadays, yet the term was in current use. The appellation "criminologist" could be employed to describe the work of a great many people, from psychiatrists to journalists. For example, the author F. Tennyson Jesse is described as "writer and criminologist" in the *Oxford Dictionary of National Biography*.[13] Criminology did not become a recognized part of the British university scene until after World War Two, when notable landmarks included the provision of the first public funds for criminological research (in Section 77 of the 1948 Criminal Justice Act) and the launch of the *British Journal of Delinquency* in 1950. But members of the feminist-criminal-justice reform network played an important part in the growth of the discipline in Britain before that time, as described below.

Feminism

Many words have been written concerning the meaning of feminism, and it is not my intention to add significantly to them in this chapter. A definition by historian Carol Dyhouse is a useful one: "feminists . . . can be regarded as those who have identified a problem in the social relationship existing between men and women, deriving from an imbalance of power in favor of the former."[14] However, it seems appropriate to qualify this definition by adding the proviso that feminists are also people who decide to take some action, however small, to redress the balance of gender power.[15] In other words, activism—inseparable from either theory or ideology—is of central importance to the definition of feminism employed in this chapter. Inevitably, support for women's suffrage is often regarded as a litmus test for feminism in the early twentieth century, although there are indications that there were not always simple alignments between support for women's enfranchisement and sympathy with other feminist causes.[16] In the case of criminal justice, there were strong links between pro-suffragism and penal policy activism, not least because of the shocking and revelatory experiences of suffragettes imprisoned as a result of their political activity. A broad definition of feminism such as the one suggested here, while not satisfying all viewpoints, at least allows for flexibility in interpretation.

In the years immediately before the outbreak of World War One, a feminist critique of criminal justice in Britain began to emerge. Women's suffrage campaigners became increasingly concerned about the treatment of women in courts and prisons, not only as a result of the experiences of imprisoned, militant suffragettes but also because of a growing resentment of the fact that the police, judiciary, magistracy, and jury members were all male, as well as a suspicion that women could not necessarily expect justice in the law courts. This critique of justice was manifested most strongly in the pronouncements of Britain's third largest suffrage society, the Women's Freedom League (WFL). From 1912 the WFL journal, *The Vote*, ran a regular column highlighting discriminatory treatment of women in the courts under the ironic headline "How Some Men Protect Women."[17] A particular concern was the common practice in British courts of removing any female other than the witness whenever so-called "sensitive" evidence was to be given by a woman or girl. During the hearing of a rape allegation in 1913, *The Vote*'s reporter refused to leave, but the practice of clearing courts of women continued. Some years later, the newspaper went as far as to openly question whether women—as defendants or victims—could expect to receive justice in courts where no other women was present.[18]

Not only did this critique soon inspire activism, but it was widely shared within mainstream women's organizations as well as the more radical suffrage societies. Among the early manifestations of activism were the rotas of volunteers established in provincial towns by the National Union of Women Workers (NUWW) to attend court hearings from 1912 onwards. In an era when women lacked any formal role in court—being unable to be jurors, judges, or attorneys—female volunteers would take turns to attend court sessions to support any women or children who found themselves there as witnesses or defendants. The NUWW, later renamed the National Council of Women (NCW), was a society of highly respectable, middle-class women, devoted to unpaid social work and philanthropy and led by veritable pillars of society in towns and cities across England and Wales.[19] There is some controversy among historians of the British women's movement as to the extent to which the NCW (and its predecessor) can be regarded as an avowedly feminist organization.[20] However, it should be noted that, while before ca. 1909 some of its leaders were associated with anti-suffragist sentiments, in the years leading up to World War One, the official NUWW line was unequivocally in support of the constitutionalist campaign for women's votes.[21] In addition to suffrage, this democratic organization also supported women's professional advancement: at the 1913 NUWW conference, a resolution supporting the admission of women to the legal profession was carried unanimously.

It is possible to interpret the work of the NUWW rotas as "maternalist."[22] Although "maternalism" can be narrowly interpreted in relation to the assumption of women's prowess in matters of child welfare, it has also been applied to middle-class, white women's care and concern for their "sisters" from lower classes or of different races.[23] Writing on maternalism in British colonial policy, Susan Pedersen offers a useful definition which can be satisfactorily applied in the case of the NUWW court rotas: "[maternalism was] a framework for action whereby educated and usually well-to-do women, drawing equally on their faith in women's superior moral and motherly capacities and on long experience of single-sex philanthropic and political work, sought to represent and protect those women and children who were presumed to be less fortunate or more vulnerable."[24] However, there should not be too much focus on the social class differences between the rota organizers and their clients. Court rotas were not established merely as a result of the concerns of a few philanthropic women for their social inferiors, but because the instigators suspected that the overtly masculine criminal justice system was unfair to all women, and because they recognized that something practical needed to be done in response. Rather than being purely rooted in assumptions about middle-class women's prowess in social work (although these were not irrelevant), the rotas grew out of a recognizably feminist critique of the criminal justice system, a prototype feminist criminology. As early as 1886, British feminists argued that it was "the *right* of any woman or girl concerned in a trial to have some friends of her own sex in court when the *assumed* right to exclude women is exercised."[25] While this quotation contains some echoes of separate spheres and maternalist ideologies, these are augmented by overt use of the language of rights.

The two main strands of British feminism in the early twentieth century—the drive for equal citizenship and the crusade for a single moral standard that had originated some forty years earlier in the Victorian campaign against the Contagious Diseases Acts[26]—together helped to stimulate demand for criminal-justice reform. As the United Kingdom went to war in 1914, the feminist-criminal-justice reform network opened up or renewed its campaigns for the appointment of women police and magistrates in the belief that giving power to women in the courts would ultimately promote greater equality. In 1918, the WFL secretary called for at least one woman to be present on every magistrate bench in the country, and in 1919, *The Vote* demanded that women should be present in all cases involving women and girls.[27] Campaigns for the appointment of female magistrates were therefore motivated at least as much by feminist mistrust of the justice system and desire for gender equality as by maternal concern for weaker or less fortunate women and girls.

A large amount of rhetorical ink has been spilt debating the supposed rift in Britain between "Old" and "New" feminism in the 1920s.[28] The former continued to prioritize equal rights while the latter focused less on challenging the established gender order than on trying to achieve specific improvements in women's lives within that order, for example, through the provision of birth control clinics to married mothers. "New Feminism" has perhaps the potential to be regarded as a variant of "maternalism." However, although the split between the two wings of the British women's movement was real and the debates at times vituperative, recent research suggests that it was not necessarily as deep a rift as has sometimes been supposed.[29] Moreover, the women's movement remained a broad church, and its activists were adept at networking even with those with whom they disagreed or who had different emphases. Regardless of where an individual stood on the question of family allowances or birth control, she was able to agree with her opponents over the necessity for women to be present on juries or the magistrates' bench.[30] Even so-called "equal rights feminists" were not above supporting the campaign for women to be made magistrates in juvenile courts by using the argument that women were experienced in dealing with children. But feminist ambitions did not end with maternalist objectives of protecting women and children; rather, they only started there. As Amelia Scott, secretary of the NCW Public Service and Magistrate committee, argued, "The value of women as magistrates in Children's Courts is so obvious, and is so often quoted as an unassailable argument in favor of the appointment of women as justices that, as so often happens, there is a danger that public opinion being narrowed down to one point, namely, that women should be appointed as magistrates in children's courts only."[31]

Similarly, there was broad agreement across the women's movement that availability for empanelment on juries was a matter of human right and a duty, which should not be abrogated by gender.[32] As I continue to argue below, feminist thought on crime and justice was therefore not dominated by maternalist ideology, but rather, it entailed a strong focus on the liberal ideology of equal rights.

Humanitarianism

Concern with women's welfare was at the center of feminist action, and the feminist-criminal-justice reform network of the early twentieth century developed an advanced critique of the treatment of women in prison.[33] Yet the feminists of the early twentieth century did not limit their concerns to women or children, or to individuals within Britain: their world was one in which there was growing awareness of humanitarian need and an enhanced willingness on the part of people from different nations to work together to meet it. Although humanitarianism could be defined in connection with the care of and concern for fellow human beings within a local or national arena, it is often associated with an international context, and that is the sense in which I use it here. While there has been for some time fulsome recognition in feminist historiography of women's social activism within

Britain, only recently has there been a spate of studies on the international humanitarian work of British feminists in the first half of the twentieth century: for example, Susan Cohen on Eleanor Rathbone's efforts to help Jewish refugees from Nazi Germany, Katherine Storr on the links between the women's suffrage movement and aid to refugees in the First World War, and Linda Mahood's recent biography of Eglantine Jebb, co-founder of the "Save the Children Fund."[34]

Humanitarianism was closely allied to a commitment to an international outlook. The feminist generation under consideration in this chapter grew up in a world in which the groundwork for the supra-national organizations of the twentieth century was being laid at events such as The Hague conferences of 1899 and 1907, which were formative in the creation of international law. Some influential members of Britain's feminist-criminal-justice reform network were intimately acquainted with the international political and humanitarian scene. For example, the foremost penal reform activist of the period, Margery Fry, witnessed the second Hague conference firsthand when she visited her lawyer father, Edward, who was a British plenipotentiary there.[35] Later, during World War One, Fry participated directly in humanitarian relief when she ran the operation of the Society of Friends War Victims' Relief Committee (FWVRC) in the Marne region of Eastern France. A pivotal figure in the feminist-criminal-justice reform network, Fry became one of the first female magistrates in England and was a major player in the establishment of the country's Magistrates Association in 1921.

With its roots in the pre-war era, internationalist sentiment among feminists received further reinforcement during the events of 1914–18. As Heather Jones has commented, "the First World War marked a watershed in the professional development of humanitarian action: mass wartime killing was paradoxically accompanied by an outpouring of international aid work."[36] Following the War, the international community made sustained efforts to preserve the peace and improve human welfare globally through the formation of the League of Nations at the Versailles Peace Conference of 1919. Once again, Margery Fry was an eye-witness at the highest diplomatic levels as a member of a delegation of the International Council of Women (ICW, to which Britain's NUWW was affiliated) and the Inter-allied Conference of Women Suffragists, which lobbied President Wilson of the United States in Paris on April 10 on the subject of women's representation in all levels of League organization. Writing to her mother, she described the delegation of seventeen, including women from the victorious powers—England, the United States, Italy, and France. "Most of the speeches were really good," she reported, "I don't think I ever heard a body of people keep so severely to their points."[37]

Although historical accounts produced in the aftermath of World War Two pronounced the League of Nations a failure, more recent analyses have preferred to highlight its successes, not least the maintenance of a sustained focus on the part of its commissions and committees on international social improvement throughout the undeniably difficult times of world-wide economic depression and escalating conflict.[38] As Susan Pedersen points out, through the auspices of the League's so-called technical bodies, leaders of international women's organizations such as the ICW and the International Women's Suffrage Alliance (IWSA) "swiftly mobilized to stake their claim to a role in the postwar order."[39] Feminists in Britain and elsewhere became immersed in League politics: some notable lobbying initiatives involved the suppression of trafficking of women, safeguarding the rights of children, and the instigation of discussions around minimum standards for prisoners (a project outlined in more detail below).

As well as participating in Britain's leading internationalist pressure group, the "League of Nations Union," some interwar feminists championed a special women's peace organization, the "Women's International League for Peace and Freedom" (WILPF).[40] Originating in 1915 in reaction to the bellicosity and militarism prevalent in Europe, WILPF additionally represented a continuation of the internationalizing trend, which had been an integral feature of the women's movement ever since the foundation of the ICW in 1888 and the IWSA in 1904.[41] In Britain, suffrage activists were divided between those who supported the country's participation in World War One and those who flocked to join the anti-war WILPF. While members of the feminist-criminal-justice reform network could be either supporters or opponents of war, there were nevertheless some interesting connections between WILPF and criminal justice-focused single-issue campaigns. For example, when a group was formed in 1923 with the express purpose of opposing the death penalty, its founder members included WILPF representatives.[42] WILPF also took up the issue of prisoners' treatment in support of the Howard League campaign described below, and it can be regarded as one of the organizations that made up the feminist-criminal-justice reform network.[43]

In earlier work, I drew an analogy between feminist campaigning for peace in the interwar period and feminist agitation on crime and justice.[44] I then envisaged these as essentially parallel campaigns. However, I have since discovered that the two causes were directly connected and surmise that both derived their salience with contemporary feminists from their largely humanitarian and internationalist perspectives. Leila J. Rupp has drawn attention to the connection between feminist concerns about warfare and about the issue of rape, both arguably manifestations of masculine violence.[45] But the connections were organizational as well as discursive. A recent historian of Britain's League of Nations Union (LNU) has commented that "the LNU and the women's movement displayed [. . .] some striking similarities."[46] The same could be said of the penal reform campaigns of the inter-war period, and the similarity is unsurprising since the individuals involved in the various causes networked with each other and in some cases, were the very same people.

An example of the inter-connectedness of the peace and prison reform campaigns is the efforts to lobby the League of Nations Assembly to set minimum international standards for the treatment of prisoners. This campaign can be seen as a clear example of what Pedersen refers to as "humanitarian entrepreneurialism."[47] In 1926, spurred by reports of ill-treatment of prisoners in Eastern Europe, former suffragists[48] Gertrude Eaton and Margery Fry, both members of the Howard League for Penal Reform (HLPR) executive committee, launched (together with the Society of Friends)[49] a "prisoners' charter," a statement of minimum rights of prisoners "in all civilized societies." Eaton and Fry soon obtained the backing of the LNU and Eaton represented the latter at a meeting of the International Federation of League of Nations Societies (FLNS), which also resolved to support the Charter.[50] Perhaps significantly, the HLPR pamphlet (titled *An International Convention for Prisoners: an Appeal to the League of Nations*) emotively highlighted the mistreatment of women as well as of men in custody. Men in some countries, it claimed, were "wearing a heavy iron ball chained to their ankle and forced to spend eight hours a day for three months wheeling the ball in a wheelbarrow round and round the prison yard," while women and girls were held in captivity without female staff to attend them and "at the mercy of armed male warders." In the UK Parliament, the campaign was furthered by a question from Frederick Pethick-Lawrence MP,[51] a feminist and former suffrage activist, while Eaton travelled to Geneva to attend the League of Nations' eighth assembly in 1927 and present the FLNS resolution in person.[52]

Thereafter Eaton (often accompanied by Edith Bigland of the Friends' Penal Reform Committee) visited Switzerland every summer as part of an "annual pilgrimage [of] . . . national delegates, claimants, lobbyists and journalists,"[53] lobbying the League's general assembly until in 1937 ill-health presented her from running the HLPR Geneva bureau. Margery Fry took her place the following year. By the late 1930s, humanitarian concern about the treatment of prisoners and detainees had grown considerably in the wake of reports about the treatment of captives in Fascist regimes. Threats to peace and violations of human rights by totalitarian regimes were linked causes for concern. Again, WILPF, as well as the HLPR, expressed active concern and brought news to Margery Fry in 1938 of a reported Gestapo takeover of the International Criminal Police Commission in Vienna. As Margery Fry explained when she raised this matter to Sir Norman Kendal of Scotland Yard, "[w]here methods of torture are applied in connection with political offences a new element of extreme bitterness is added to the struggle of parties, which tends to poison international relations also."[54] Fry also prepared a questionnaire in order to elicit data on conditions around the world. The results were published by the HLPR as *The Accused: an International Survey*, a publication which stands as a meticulously researched criminological text. Fry achieved a breakthrough of sorts in 1938 when penal conditions at last were tabled for discussion by the League, but noted herself that the

19th Assembly—which coincided with the Munich crisis—"dragged its days under such a weight of tragedy that it [was] no wonder that the work of the 5th Commission has had a note of unreality." However, Fry reported that "from the point of view of penal reform, the session was not unhopeful. Two years' sowings have borne some fruit."[55] In the end, the campaign for minimum standards for captives was stalled until after the war and the creation of the United Nations in place of the (by then discredited) League. At last, in 1955, the First United Nations Congress on the Prevention of Crime and the Treatment of Offenders adopted the Standard Minimum Rules for the Treatment of Prisoners for which British feminists had been campaigning since 1927.[56]

The continuous campaigning and criminological investigation by British women in the HLPR and Friends' Penal Reform Committee, supported by WILPF, for international action on prison conditions in the inter-war years exemplifies "humanitarian entrepreneurialism" and indicates that the groundwork for post-World War Two human rights advances was laid prior to 1939 while under the banner of the League of Nations. As Pedersen argues, on the "technical" ground occupied by the League's social sections its reach "proved to be more expansive, and more genuinely global than its security or state-building operations."[57] But the contribution of feminist women, with the time, energy, and skills to engage in vital research and lobbying work, which enabled the eventual fruition of improved human rights, has been largely overlooked. The next section looks more generally at feminist criminal justice activists and focuses on their methods of operation.

Activism

The above case study of international campaigning for minimum standards of penal treatment is a good example of the third theme of this chapter: activism. This section introduces some of the most active women in Britain's feminist-criminal-justice reform network and attempts to analyze the tactics through which their humanitarian philosophy was advanced. In the case of feminism, activism has itself been identified as a significant spur to research during the last forty years.[58] Yet in some crucial respects, the activism of early twentieth century feminists was distinct from that of their post-1970 successors, containing a greater emphasis on philanthropy and arguably giving fuller attention to parliamentary lobbying.

The operating method of feminists in the early twentieth century can be summed up as super-networking. Recent scholarship tends to see networking as a product of the "information age" and of new technologies, but it is clear that networking is a human activity supportable by many levels of technology.[59] As already mentioned, a wide variety of British women's organizations had connections to the feminist-criminal-justice reform network, ranging from broad-based women's societies such as the NCW and Women's Institutes to specific equal-rights pressure groups such as the Six

Point Group and single-issue lobbyists such as the Association for Moral and Social Hygiene (ASMH, which supported the human rights of women involved in prostitution). The network also included organizations which might, at first glance, seem to have less connection with women's rights: for example, the HLPR and the LNU and ones that might appear to have little connection with criminal justice, such as the WILPF. Maintaining such a coalition of interests was obviously not without difficulty, and it involved a steady flow of information back and forward across the network. However, crucially, the women's suffrage campaign of 1906–18 had tutored its activists in broad-based campaigning. Helen McCarthy points out that "organizing across [political] party lines was a natural modus operandi" for inter-war feminists.[60]

Feminist activism in relation to criminal justice was not restricted to women's issues, although network members paid special attention to the aspects of the judicial and prison systems that most impacted women. This is true also of the ostensibly non-feminist bodies such as the HLPR, and it is explained by the remarkably high level of women's involvement in such organizations. The HLPR was in fact created in 1921 by the action of Margery Fry, who engineered the merger of the small pressure group of which she was secretary—the Penal Reform League—with an older, richer, and less radical body, the Howard Association. As soon as the new HLPR was up and running, Fry and her allies turned their attention to the formation of England and Wales' first Magistrates Association (MA), initially focusing their recruitment efforts on the two-hundred odd women who had recently been appointed as justices. As a result, female magistrates accounted for around one-third of individual MA subscribers in 1922, even though they only made up a tiny proportion of the magistracy at that time.[61]

In the late 1920s, another Oxford-educated woman, Cicely Craven, took over as HLPR secretary, but Margery Fry maintained a close relationship with the organization until her death in 1958. During the two decades in which Craven ran the League, women activists were very prominent in its work, and like Fry, Craven retained strong links with other organizations, especially the NCW, with the two bodies frequently proposing resolutions at each other's meetings. Much propaganda work was also undertaken by female penal reform activists as they addressed NCW branches, women's citizens associations, teachers' assemblies, and a host of other organizations up and down the country.[62] In short, the feminist-criminal-justice reform network played a significant part in Britain's civic associational culture of its day, in which local meetings and discussion forums proliferated. In addition to Craven, Fry, and Eaton, the HLPR's leading figures included Cambridge-based suffrage leader and local councilor Dorothea Rackham, women's trade union organizer Madeleine Robinson,[63] barrister Theodora Calvert, author Winifred Elkin, and pioneer psycho-therapist Dr. Marjorie Franklin. Craven remained the HLPR's organizer until 1950, when the pressure group appointed its first fully salaried (and male) secretary, Hugh Klare. Howard

League women were not merely a significant minority among the pressure group's activists as might be supposed. On many occasions in the thirty years after the 1920 merger, women made up the majority of attendees at the League's executive meetings and were prominent among the organization's most diligent and forthright campaigners.

Even though only a small proportion of prisoners were female, HLPR activists actually spent quite a lot of time considering the specific needs and problems of incarcerated women and girls. This was particularly the case during and after the Second World War, when exposés from conscientious objectors and other prisoners (such as Joan Henry)[64] revealed the poor conditions within Holloway Prison, the main jail for women in the south of England. Parliamentary liaison was another characteristic mode of operation for lobbying organizations of this type. The feminist-criminal-justice reform network ensured that the matter of conditions in women's prisons was raised in parliament on numerous occasions by sympathetic MPs (including Eleanor Rathbone and former suffragette Barbara Ayrton Gould).[65]

Aside from prisons, activists applied a feminist critique to the treatment of prostitutes by the police and courts and campaigned for an end to double standards, including the abolition of the legal term "common prostitute." On this issue HLPR members worked closely with the AMSH, a body whose lineage within the women's movement can be traced back to Josephine Butler's Ladies' National Association, which campaigned against the Contagious Diseases Acts in the 1870s. Margery Fry's adherence to feminist discourse concerning moral and sexual double standards was revealed in a contribution she made to the *Howard Journal* in 1943 following a tour of penal institutions in the United States. She criticized "one-sided powers" which led to the imprisonment of women while "the man usually gets a $25 fine and that is deferred so that he probably never pays."[66]

In keeping with their humanitarian principles, campaigners did not confine their activism to the needs of women alone. They highlighted the problems of victims of crime—men as well as women—some time before the period usually associated with the rise of the "victims' movement"[67] and took an interest in general campaigns for penal reform. For example, Marjorie Franklin was known for her promotion of "Q camps," where her concept of "Planned Environment Therapy," described as "an attempt to make more widely available the insights and therapeutic possibilities of [psycho-] analysis," was tried out.[68] Toward the end of her life, Margery Fry instigated a campaign for victims' compensation, while Winifred Elkin published books putting forward arguments for the general reform of British courts.[69]

These activities all stemmed from a core belief of feminists that women had an equal right to involve themselves with the political and social issues of the day. As with the campaign for international minimum standards for prisoners, a human rights discourse was fundamental to feminist-criminal-justice reform activism. Karen Offen has highlighted the "increasing commitment by the leaders of international organized feminist groups to a new terminology of humanism rather than feminism as the menace of fascism and Nazism" became a threat to democratic values by the 1930s.[70] Thus Margery Fry described her philosophy of equality in a broadcast on the BBC's Europe service in 1950, arguing that "neither class nor sex nor color must limit the emergence of all that is outstanding in human nature."[71] Therefore, paradoxically, feminist activism sometimes found its expression in work that was not directly related to the needs of other women per se, but those of the human race as a whole. Yet this did not represent a rejection of feminism or an abandonment of its agenda, but rather a consolidation and expression of its core values.

In addition to skilled networking and assiduous parliamentary lobbying, women's criminal-justice activism in Britain had a third important characteristic, the utilization of skills learned in philanthropy and voluntary social work. Political lobbying and associational networking were therefore often accompanied by practical efforts to alleviate specific difficulties or improve conditions. For example, Margery Fry became the volunteer "honorary" education officer at Holloway women's prison in London shortly after moving to a nearby street in 1918. Some years later, in 1945, another HLPR member, Xenia Field, began arranging lectures and concerts in London jails.[72] In Gloucester, female justices, organized into the Gloucestershire Women Magistrates Society by suffragist Ethel Hartland, raised funds to pay for a prison piano. Elsewhere, women promoted more ambitious experiments for penal reform, including a scheme for female volunteers to visit young offenders in London and a "league of honor" for inmates of Nottingham Prison.[73] These projects and others were discussed and evaluated as penological experiments by the feminist-criminal-justice reform network, the evaluations forming the basis for a kind of proto-criminology, discussed in the next section.

Research

Underpinning all these activities was a developing commitment to criminological research. Almost all the women mentioned in this chapter were, for their times, unusually highly educated. Most had studied at university—usually in a woman's college at Oxford or Cambridge—at a time when women's access to higher education was very limited. Hardly any of them, however, held a university post. Margery Fry worked for part of her life at Somerville College, Oxford, and Birmingham University (all years, with the exception of a short period as principal of Somerville, spent before she took up penal reform), but her roles were connected to administration rather than teaching or research. However, Fry's degree subject was mathematics, and she approached the preparation of evidence for her campaigns in a rigorous, statistical manner. She was rightly described by Terence Morris as "the dominant figure on the penal reform scene for the whole period."[74]

However, she was not a lone figure but was supported by a significant group of like-minded women who had been drawn to her circle, women such as Craven, Calvert, Robinson, and Elkin.

As mentioned in the introduction to this chapter, women in the feminist-criminal-justice reform network played an important but under-recognized role in the development of British criminology in the period before the discipline became institutionalized in universities. Examples of unofficial or "amateur" exercises in criminological research by leading HLPR members—especially the female activists—abound. New schemes and experiments, such as the League of Honor in Nottingham Prison, were widely reported, evaluated, and discussed in a range of publications, including suffrage journals and magistrates' newsletters. In 1921, Margery Fry, as the first secretary of the newly merged Howard Association and Penal Reform League, launched the *Howard Journal*, with the sub-title "a review of modern methods for the prevention and treatment of crime." Much of the copy in early issues was contributed by Fry herself, although speeches by politicians were featured, such as one in the first volume from Margaret Bondfield, later Britain's first woman cabinet member, on "Prisons and the Public."[75]

Several of the group of women identified in the previous section of this chapter can be said to have made significant contributions to criminological literature, at a time when the subject had little or no official presence within the academy. Following Margery Fry's retirement as HLPR secretary, her successor Cicely Craven edited the *Howard Journal* for many years. Dorothea Rackham contributed many articles to the feminist press on the subject of criminal justice, including a regular column titled "The Law at Work" in the suffragist journal *Woman's Leader*, which ran for much of the 1920s. Madeleine Robinson lectured on youth justice, and Winifred Elkin wrote *The English Penal System* and *English Juvenile Courts*, the former published as a definitive study of its subject by Penguin Books.[76] Margery Fry, in addition to several pieces of research into international prison conditions which have already been referred to, was author of many pamphlets published by the Howard League and other bodies, as well as one full-length book, *Arms of the Law*.[77] Theodora Calvert co-authored *The Lawbreaker* with her husband Roy,[78] and after his untimely death, she revised many of his writings on capital punishment. However, with the exception of Fry's work, these women's contributions are often neglected in accounts of British criminology of the period. Even the account by Morris and Martin of the establishment of the *British Journal of Delinquency* in 1950 highlights the three male editors, the psychiatrists Emanuel Miller and Edward Glover and the criminologist Hermann Mannheim, without mentioning the presence of Margery Fry as member of the advisory board or her extensive behind-the-scenes efforts to get criminology officially recognized and funded by the British government.[79]

Members of the feminist-criminal-justice reform network were also instrumental in the promotion of criminology as a research subject in the UK. In addition to doing criminological research themselves, the early feminist activists were keen to see expansion of the subject as a university discipline. Once again, Margery Fry was especially active in this cause, promoting, among others, the career of Leon Radzinowicz, a Polish exile criminologist, despite finding him "a little Niagara-ish"[80] when they met for the first time (by which I presume her to mean "gushing"). After arriving in Britain in 1938 and contacting Cicely Craven, Radzinowicz was introduced to JCW (Cecil) Turner, an HLPR member and Reader in Law at Cambridge University. Together with fellow members of the University's law faculty, they set up a committee "to consider the promotion of research and teaching in criminal science" for which Radzinowicz worked.[81] This was the birth of what is now the Cambridge University Institute of Criminology. Fry also lobbied the British government for public funds to be set aside for criminological research, a proposition which became law in the 1948 Criminal Justice Act. Madeleine Robinson also strongly supported research activity. For example, she advocated for an enquiry into the effects of sentencing decisions.[82]

Crucially, the women examined in this chapter allied criminological research to activism. While principally committed to a political agenda for penal change, they believed that reform campaigns could only be effectively conducted if backed by objective and "scientific" research, yet they understood that this research was also carried out from a consciously adopted political standpoint. In this commitment, their epistemology was remarkably similar to the "second-wave" feminist practice of "standpointism" analyzed by Nancy Hartstock.[83]

Conclusion

It is clear that the four philosophical pillars of early feminist engagement with criminology were closely intertwined and infused with the normative ethical assumption of the time. Radzinowicz (whose own studies had been conducted at Enrico Ferri's Institute of Criminology at the University of Rome) claimed in his memoir that "there was hardly any English criminology in the continental meaning of the word" when he arrived in Britain in the 1930s.[84] While this may be true, there was plenty of criminology of a different variety—which remains largely ignored—and within that genre operated a significant group of women who can also be said to have been practicing a form of feminist criminology.

However, this early feminist criminology was distinct from its "second-wave" successor in several ways. Firstly, it lacked institutional support and its practitioners were officially regarded as gifted amateurs, notwithstanding Radzinowicz's praise for Margery Fry's "unusually refined mind."[85] Although highly educated and intelligent, these women did not have access to university posts, research funding, or the chance to teach what they knew in any but the most informal of contexts. Secondly, their focus on internationalism, equality, and human rights prompted early twentieth-century feminists, perhaps ironically, to turn from exclusive concern about the position of women to seemingly more pressing political matters, especially during periods of international turmoil and warfare. Thirdly, despite their philanthropic experience, early twentieth century feminists in the criminal-justice reform network placed more emphasis on lobbying government and on achieving legislative change than on direct action. Nevertheless, their work demonstrates an ability to bring together practical knowledge, activism, and social theory, a combination which potentially empowers feminists to "understand the world and then change it."[86]

Notes

1 For the legal profession, see Hilary Sommerlad and Peter Sanderson, *Gender, Choice and Commitment: Women Solicitors in England and Wales and the Struggle for Equal Status* (Aldershot: Ashgate, 1998). For the impact of the 1919 Act on juries, see Anne Logan, " 'Building a New and Better Order'? Women and Jury Service in England and Wales, c. 1920–70," *Women's History Review* 22, no. 5 (2013): 701–716.

2 Anne Logan, *Feminism and Criminal Justice: a Historical Perspective* (Basingstoke: Palgrave Macmillan, 2008).

3 For the contribution of selected female magistrates to research, see Anne Logan, "Feminist Criminology in Britain circa 1920–1960," in *Women, Education and Agency, 1600–2000*, ed. Jean Spence, Sarah Jane Aiston, and Maureen M. Meikle (New York: Routledge, 2010), 204–222.

4 See, for example, Ngaire Naffine, *Feminism and Criminology* (Cambridge: Polity Press, 1997); Loraine Gelsthorpe and Alison Morris, "Feminism and Criminology in Britain," *British Journal of Criminology* 28, no. 2 (1988): 93–110; Kathleen Daly & Meda Chesney-Lind, "Feminism and Criminology," *Justice Quarterly* 5, no. 4 (1988): 497–538.

5 June Purvis, "The Prison Experiences of the Suffragettes in Edwardian Britain," *Women's History Review* 4, no. 1 (1995): 103–133; Elizabeth Crawford, "Police, Prisons and Prisoners: the View from the Home Office," *Women's History Review* 14, no. 3 (2005): 487–505.

6 Logan, *Feminism and Criminal Justice*, 9.

7 For example, Cheryl Law, *Suffrage and Power: The Women's Movement 1918–28* (London: I.B. Tauris, 1997), and for a later period, Jessica Thurlow, "Continuity and Change in British Feminism, C.1940–1960," PhD diss., University of Michigan, 2006.

8 Karen Offen, *European Feminisms, 1700–1950: A Political History* (Stanford, CA: Stanford University Press, 2000), 25.

9 William D. Rubinstein, "Britain's Elites in the Interwar Period, 1919–39: Decline or Continued Ascendancy?," *Britain and the World* 3, no. 1 (2010): 10.

10 For example, Eleanor Rathbone. See Susan Pedersen, *Eleanor Rathbone and the Politics of Conscience* (New Haven: Yale University Press, 2004).

11 Logan, *Feminism and Criminal Justice*, 9.

12 "Penal-welfarism" is defined as the characteristic penality of twentieth century welfare states. For a definitive account of its emergence in Britain, see David Garland, *Punishment and Welfare* (Aldershot: Gower, 1985).

13 Raymond Cordero, "Jesse, Wynifried Margaret (1888–1958)," in *Oxford Dictionary of National Biography*, online ed., ed. Lawrence Goldman (Oxford: Oxford University Press, 2004), accessed November 12, 2012, http://www.oxforddnb.com/view/article/39087.

14 Carol Dyhouse, *Feminism and the Family in England, 1880–1939* (Oxford: Blackwell, 1989), 4. See also Karen Offen, "Defining Feminism: A Comparative Historical Approach," *Signs: Journal of Women in Culture and Society* 14, no. 1 (1988): 119–157.
15 Logan, *Feminism and Criminal Justice*, 5.
16 Julia Bush, "'Special strengths for their own special duties': Women, Higher Education and Gender Conservatism in Late Victorian Britain," *History of Education* 34, no. 4 (2005): 387–405.
17 See, for example, *The Vote* (July 20, 1912): 230.
18 *The Vote* (July 25, 1913): 213; (September 5, 1919): 316.
19 The NUWW was affiliated to the International Council of Women (ICW). For a general history of the NUWW/NCW, see Daphne Glick, *The National Council of Women of Great Britain: The First One Hundred Years* (London: National Council of Women, 1995).
20 For the NUWW and anti-suffragism, see Julia Bush, *Women Against the Vote: Female Anti-suffragism in Britain* (Oxford: Oxford University Press, 2007). With regard to the inter-war period, Caitriona Beaumont argues that the NCW and similar organizations promoted citizenship rather than feminism. See Caitriona Beaumont, "Citizens Not Feminists: The Boundary Negotiated between Citizenship and Feminism by Mainstream Women's Organisations in England, 1928–39," *Women's History Review* 9, no. 2 (2000): 411–429. In contrast, the present author argues that the NCW—or at least the active membership of its Public Service and Magistrates Committee—can be designated as a feminist group. See Logan, *Feminism and Criminal Justice*, 25–30.
21 Glick, *National Council of Women*, 15.
22 For definitions and debates about maternalism, see Seth Koven and Sonya Michel, "Introduction: Mother Worlds," in *Mothers of a New World: Maternalist Politics and the Origins of Welfare States*, ed. Seth Koven and Sonya Michel (New York: Routledge, 1993), 1–42; Gisela Bock and Pat Thane, "Introduction," in *Maternity and Gender Politics: Women and the Rise of the European Welfare States 1880s–1950s*, ed. Gisela Bock and Pat Thane (London: Routledge, 1991), 1–20.
23 Marilyn Lake, "Feminism and the Gendered Politics of Anti-racism, Australia 1927–1957," *Australian Historical Studies* 29 (1998): 91–108.
24 Susan Pedersen, "The Maternalist Movement in British Colonial Policy: The Controversy Over 'Child Slavery' in Hong Kong 1917–1941," *Past and Present* 171 (2001): 165.
25 Minute of November 12, 1886, National Vigilance Association Papers, Box 109, The Women's Library, London. Emphasis added.
26 The Contagious Diseases Acts were passed in the 1860s to halt the spread of venereal disease among soldiers. The measures taken under the acts were thought to damage the human rights of women subjected to the law. Many historical works have focused on the Acts, most notably Judith Walkowitz, *Prostitution and Victorian Society* (Cambridge: Cambridge University Press, 1980).
27 *The Vote* (April 15, 1919).
28 See, for example, Harold L. Smith ed., *British Feminism in the Twentieth Century* (Aldershot: Edward Elgar, 1990).
29 Pat Thane, "Women and Political Participation in England," in *What Difference Did the Vote Make? Women and Citizenship in Britain and Ireland*, ed. Pat Thane and Esther Breitenbach (London: Continuum, 2010), 11–28.
30 Anne Logan, "Making Women Magistrates: Feminism, Citizenship and Justice in England and Wales, 1918–1950." PhD diss., University of Greenwich, 2002.
31 *NCW Occasional Paper* 91, July 1920.
32 Logan, "Building a New and Better Order," 710.

33 See Logan, *Feminism and Criminal Justice*, Chapter 4.
34 Susan Cohen, *Rescue the Perishing: Eleanor Rathbone and the Refugees* (London: Vallentine Mitchell, 2010); Katherine Storr, *Excluded from the Record: Women. Refugees and Relief 1914–1929* (Bern: Peter Lang, 2009), Linda Mahood, *Feminism and Voluntary Action: Eglantyne Jebb and Save the Children 1876–1928* (Basingstoke: Palgrave Macmillan, 2009).
35 Margery Fry to her mother, February 26, 1907. Margery Fry Papers (MFP) 7/11, Somerville College Oxford.
36 Heather Jones, "International or Transnational? Humanitarian Action during the First World War," *European Review of History* 16, no. 5 (2009): 697.
37 Margery Fry to her mother, April 11, 1919. MFP 8/6. See also Offen, *European Feminisms*, 262–263.
38 For a review of historical literature on the League, see Susan Pedersen, "Back to the League of Nations," *American Historical Review* 112, no. 4 (2007): 1091–1117.
39 Susan Pedersen, "Metaphors of the Schoolroom: Women Working the Mandates System of the League of Nations," *History Workshop Journal* 66 (2008): 188.
40 For a history of WILPF, see Gertrude Bussey and Margaret Timms, *Pioneers for Peace: Women's International League for Peace and Freedom 1915–1965* (London: George Allen and Unwin, 1965).
41 Leila J. Rupp, *Worlds of Women: the Making of an International Women's Movement* (Chichester: Princeton University Press, 1997).
42 Logan, *Feminism and Criminal Justice*, 32.
43 Bussey and Timms, *Pioneers for Peace*, 124.
44 Logan, *Feminism and Criminal Justice*, 3.
45 Rupp, *Worlds of Women*, 208–209.
46 Helen McCarthy, "Parties, Voluntary Associations, and Democratic Politics in Interwar Britain," *Historical Journal* 50, no. 4 (2007): 891–912.
47 Pederson, "Back to the League of Nations," 1111.
48 Fry was active in the National Union of Women's Suffrage Societies and the NUWW in Birmingham prior to 1914. Eaton, an early supporter of the Penal Reform League (which was founded as a direct result of conditions endured in prison by suffragettes), was on the committee of the Women's Tax Resistance League and personally refused to pay Inhabited House Duty as a protest against women having no parliamentary vote.
49 The Society of Friends (Quakers) in London had established a Penal Reform Committee in 1920. Relations between it and the HLPR seem to have been close, with some overlapping of active membership. Although brought up in a prominent Quaker family, Margery Fry was not a practising member of the Society and resigned her membership in the 1930s.
50 *An International Convention for Prisoners*, in PCOM 7/61. The National Archives, (TNA).
51 *House of Commons Debates*, December 5, 1927, vol. 211, col. 971. For Pethick-Lawrence's contribution to the women's suffrage campaign and later political career, see Brian Harrison, "Lawrence, Frederick William Pethick-, Baron Pethick-Lawrence (1871–1961)," in *Oxford Dictionary of National Biography*, ed. H. C. G. Matthew and Brian Harrison (Oxford: Oxford University Press, 2004), accessed November 12, 2012, http://www.oxforddnb.com/view/article/35491.
52 HLPR Executive minutes, May 31, 1927, MS16B/1/1,Warwick University Modern Records Centre (WUMRC).
53 Pederson, "Back to the League of Nations," 1112.
54 Margery Fry to Norman Kendal, December 9, 1937. MOP3/2074, TNA.
55 Report on HLPR Geneva work, 1938, WUMRC, MS16B/3IN/1/98.

56 United Nations, *Standard Minimum Rules for the Treatment of Prisoners*, August 30, 1955, accessed November 12, 2012, http://www.unhcr.org/refworld/docid/3ae6b36e8.
57 Pedersen, "Back to the League of Nations," 1110.
58 This is especially the case in relation to second-wave feminist victimology and the analysis of male violence, which originated in grass-roots activity, such as the foundation of refuges for victims of domestic violence and rape crisis centres.
59 For discussion of policy networks in relation to criminal justice activism in England and Wales, see Anne Logan, "Policy Networks and the Juvenile Court: The Reform of Youth Justice, c.1905–50," *Crimes and Misdemeanours* 3, no. 2 (2009): 18–36.
60 McCarthy, "Parties, Voluntary Associations, and Democratic Politics," 535.
61 Logan, *Feminism and Criminal Justice*, 34.
62 There are ample examples of these activities in the HLPR minutes: WUMRC, MS16B/1/1.
63 For more on Rackham and Robinson, see Logan, "Feminist Criminology in Britain," 204–222.
64 Joan Henry, *Who Lie in Gaol* (London: Gollancz, 1952).
65 Logan, *Feminism and Criminal Justice*, 120–121.
66 Margery Fry, "Notes from an American Diary," *Howard Journal* 6, no. 3 (1943): 167.
67 For an account of the rise of the victims' movement in England and Wales (including the part played by Margery Fry), see Paul Rock, *Helping Victims of Crime: The Home Office and the Rise of Victim Support in England and Wales* (Oxford: Clarendon Press, 1990).
68 David Wills, "Marjorie Franklin, 1877–1975," *British Journal of Criminology* 15, no. 2 (1975): 110.
69 For Fry's campaigns for victims' compensation, see Logan, *Feminism and Criminal Justice*, 147–157. Elkin's views on criminal justice can be found in W. A. Elkin, *The English Penal System* (Harmondsworth: Penguin, 1957) and *English Juvenile Courts* (London: Kegan Paul, 1938).
70 Offen, *European Feminisms*, 255.
71 Radio Script, "General News Talk" for the BBC European Service, November 25, 1950. MFP, Box 41/4.
72 Logan, *Feminism and Criminal Justice*, 114.
73 These experiments are discussed in greater detail by Anne Logan, "Gender and Voluntarism in the Criminal Justice System: The Campaigning Activities of Women Magistrates in England and Wales, 1920–1960," in *Understanding the Roots of Voluntary Action: Historical Perspectives on Current Social Policy*, ed. Colin Rochester, George Campbell Gosling, Alison Penn, and Meta Zimmeck (Brighton: Sussex Academic Press, 2011), 121–134.
74 Terence Morris, "British Criminology: 1935–48," *British Journal of Criminology* 28, no. 2 (1988): 23.
75 Margaret Bondfield, "Prisons and the Public," in *Howard Journal* 1, no. 1 (1921): 32–35.
76 Winifred Adeline Elkin, *The English Penal System* (Harmondsworth, Middlesex: Penguin Books, 1957); Winifred Adeline Elkin, *English Juvenile Courts* (London: K. Paul, Trench, Trubner, 1938).
77 Margery Fry, *Arms of the Law* (London: Gollancz, 1951).
78 Eric Roy and Theodora Calvert, *The Lawbreaker. A Critical Study of the Modern Treatment of Crime* (London: Routledge, 1933).
79 Morris, "British Criminology," 29; J. P. Martin, "The Development of Criminology in Britain 1948–60," *British Journal of Criminology* 28, no. 2 (1988): 38.

80 Margery Fry to Cicely Craven, May 26, 1939, MSS16/3/IN/1/116,WUMRC. The awe in which Radzinowicz held Margery Fry is indicated in Craven's letter of May 26, where she describes his arranged meeting with Fry as "an invitation to Mount Olympus."
81 Leon Radzinowitz, *Adventures in Criminology* (London: Routledge, 1999), 141.
82 Papers of Lord Templewood, Cambridge University Library.
83 Nancy Hartstock, "The Feminist Standpoint: Developing the Ground for a Specifically Feminist Historical Materialism," in *Feminisms*, ed. Sandra Kemp and Judith Squires (Oxford: Oxford University Press, 1997), 152–160.
84 Radzinowicz, *Adventures in Criminology*, 85.
85 Ibid., 132. For the role of the female amateur in providing British governments with criminal justice policy advice, see Anne Logan, "Women and the Provision of Criminal Justice Policy Advice: Lessons from England and Wales 1944–64," *British Journal of Criminology* 50, no. 6 (2010): 1077–1093.
86 Liz Stanley, *Feminist Praxis: Research, Theory and Epistemology in Feminist Sociology* (London: Routledge, 1990), 12.

12 Attempting to Advocate

Women Entering the Legal Profession in Finland, 1885–1915[1]

Mia Korpiola

Introduction

In Finland in the 1890s, if someone wished to act as the legal representative of another, no exams or formal requirements were required in the first instance courts—except to be male. The man had only to be honest, not under guardianship, and accepted by the presiding judge. Section 15:2 of the Chapter on Procedure of the 1734 Swedish law stated: "Those who may speak and answer for others must be untainted, honest, respectable, and sensible men." This passage remained unaltered even after Czar Alexander II (r. 1855–1881) slightly modified the section in 1873.[2]

This made lay advocacy possible. Almost every man could theoretically act as an advocate (Sw. *sakförare* or *advokat*, Fi. *asianajaja*) in all three instances in Finland: the town courts or the countryside at the local district courts or assizes; the three Courts of Appeals at Turku, Vaasa, and Viborg (Viipurg); and the Judicial Division of the Senate, a predecessor of the Supreme Court. What was more, entry into the legal profession was unrestricted by the requirement of a law degree (or a degree of any kind) or a state examination, or by requiring compulsory membership to a national bar association, which did not even exist before 1919. In Finland, there was no division between barristers and solicitors (as in England), no system of public notaries (as in continental Europe), nor was there a monopoly of trained advocates accredited by a court. However, whether women could act as advocates under the same conditions as men was another question. In many countries, the question of whether or not the female sex proved a hindrance to studying or practicing law hinged on the same interpretative questions. Those advocating the women's cause favored a more liberal interpretation, rationalized by the changing times and the growing number of working and studying women. The conservatives refused to interpret the text broadly, preferring to leave the matter to the legislator to decide. For example, the entry of women to the traditional Inns of Court and the Law Society in order to become barristers or solicitors in England mainly revolved around the interpretation of the word "person" in the Solicitors Act (1843). Traditionally, this referred to men only. The courts, unwilling to create precedents, opined that parliament ought to legislate on the matter. However, this only took place in 1919.[3]

Although the 1734 law spoke of men acting as legal representatives and advocates, by the late nineteenth century, the changing times and entry of women into universities, professions, and offices exerted increasing pressure to interpret the "men" of the law text as "people" or "persons." At least two Finnish women, Anna Åkesson in Viborg and Signe Silén in Helsinki, are known to have practiced law as advocates, being employed by law firms on a small scale around 1895. Moreover, they became internationally known: e.g., in England (in the *Illustrated London News*) as the two Finnish "Portias of Today"[4] and in continental Europe as the first Finnish female advocates through the book *La Femme-Avocat* (1898) by the Belgian Louis Frank (1846–1917).[5]

But in 1897–1898, these two women were abruptly ousted from the courts. Anna Åkesson (1865–1940), one of the two, was denied access to the court as an advocate because of her sex despite her many years of work as a clerk and holder of procuration at the office of an advocate. She appealed the decision, but failed. The Judicial Division of the Finnish Senate refused to grant her a dispensation from her sex even though women had already been getting dispensations in order to hold minor state offices for some years. A decade later, Agnes Lundell (1878–1935), the first woman in Finland to earn a law degree, faced the same problem. She had already practiced law as an advocate when she attempted to get an official dispensation from her sex from the Senate where she had already worked as a clerk. She met with opposition from the Judicial Division, but after considerable toing and froing, Lundell officially became the first female advocate in Finland in 1911, as will be discussed below in detail.

Although the entry of women into the legal professions in England, the United States, Canada, France, and other European countries has inspired research,[6] there are few scholarly studies on women entering the legal profession in Scandinavia. The existing research mainly briefly presents the acknowledged female pioneers biographically and explores their careers in the field of law, but it does these things without putting these women in a larger context.[7] The same applies to previous research in Finland. Apart from some biographical notes, especially on Lundell, the work has neither been thoroughly scholarly nor systematic. In Finland, Pirkko K. Koskinen and Anneli Winter-Mäkinen have done some preliminary studies, while Harriet Silius has focused on the experiences of later female lawyers more from a sociological than historical perspective.[8] Yet, the trajectory for Finnish women entering the legal profession is almost totally unexplored.

In addition to the small number and unsystematic nature of the works on the early female lawyer, Nordic research has a very narrow perception of women practicing law. Only if a woman took the law degree required to become a judge did she qualify as a lawyer. Accordingly, the studies fail to discuss women who took administrative degrees in law faculties—as in

Finland—or who may have practiced advocacy but without a law degree. For example, Eva Andén (1886–1970) has been hailed as the first woman to practice law and the first female advocate in Sweden. Nevertheless, Anna Pettersson seems to have been the first woman to act as an advocate and establish her own law firm in 1904 in Stockholm. Pettersson had worked eleven years as a clerk in the offices of one of the town councilors of Uppsala. In addition, she had some years of work experience in a law firm in Stockholm. Yet, as she had neither studied law nor taken a law exam, her pioneering work is largely unknown nowadays—although her role was recognized in her own time.[9]

In my chapter, I will investigate the early history of Finnish women in law firms and advocacy. I will look especially at the activities of Anna Åkesson, working at a Viborg law firm, and Agnes Lundell, who had earned the law degree a decade after Åkesson had been driven out of the courtrooms. Finland can be taken as an example of a situation in which a more flexible practice by individual judges of accepting female advocates for more than a decade received a setback after the principle was discussed and resolved at an official level. Both cases will be put into the legal context of attempting to monopolize advocacy by restricting and banning lay advocacy in the 1890s. The chapter explains why Lundell achieved what Åkesson had failed to do more than a decade earlier.

Apart from a couple of exceptions, Finnish law journals and the legal literature of the time passed over the "woman question" (*kvinnofrågan*),[10] the competency of women to hold office and enter the legal professions (advocate, judge), with near-total silence. Therefore, I have been forced to draw on other sources that discuss the efforts of women to enter the legal profession and the attitudes toward them. Finnish newspapers from the period form the main source material of the chapter, supplemented by biographical information (e.g., letters written by Agnes Lundell at the Library of Åbo Akademi); summaries of verdicts of the supreme court of the time, the Judicial Division of the Senate; and political debates in the 1890s in the Finnish Diet and again after 1907 in Finland's Parliament.[11] I have also consulted material produced by the Finnish feminist movement, mainly periodicals and annual reports.

The Background: Finland, its Legal Profession, and Women's Work

Finland had been part of the Kingdom of Sweden and had been sharing its legal and administrative system since the Middle Ages. As a result of the Napoleonic wars, Russia invaded Finland in 1808, and the incorporation of Finland into Russia as the Grand Duchy of Finland was confirmed at the Diet of Porvoo the following year. Finland kept its Swedish laws, court system, and a constitution that gave the ruler considerable powers. Conservative policies dominated in Russia until the 1860s, when even the Grand

Duchy of Finland experienced a period of liberalization. New economic legislation was passed in the spirit of increasing liberty of commerce and trade. A decree on freedom of trade and industry was issued in 1879.[12]

What is now called the University of Helsinki (then: Imperial Alexander's University) existed first and foremost to educate government officials.[13] Many exams required for government posts were, in fact, legal.[14] In the course of the nineteenth century, the nobility had taken up law studies, and practicing law became a high-status profession. The administration of the Grand Duchy of Finland was dominated by jurists, so much so that it could practically be called a "juristocracy." Between 1810 and 1917, 86 percent of the higher officials in the ministries under the Finnish Senate had a degree in law or an administrative degree (*kameralexamen*) with a more limited range of subjects. However, between 1810 and 1915 the central administrative agencies were not as dominated by law graduates; lawyers (including those with administrative degrees) constituting only about 24 percent. In the wake of the industrial development of the latter half of the nineteenth century, more and more specialized experts (engineers, architects, etc.) were needed to populate the newly established central agencies.[15]

Male lawyers traditionally had a monopoly on a large number of offices, a privilege they defended jealously, but their time-honored influence and status was diminishing through the need for other, more specialized professional skills. At the same time, many officials in the courts and central administration earned such paltry wages they could not support their families. Many of them had secondary occupations, and officials commonly acted as advocates.[16] The professionalization of the Finnish jurist (e.g., by establishing law societies and journals) was on its way.[17] Thus, attempting to establish a monopoly of advocacy for lawyers seemed the natural next step.

The economic growth of the latter half of the nineteenth century also benefited women. The postal system developed and the number of letters sent in the country almost doubled between 1845 and 1865. The telegraph and railways were changing the infrastructure and creating more job opportunities. The developing educational system also provided employment to schoolteachers. Since the 1860s, Finnish women had started to enter the postal, telegraph, and railway services as well as government offices. At the end of the century it was estimated that about 400 women worked in telephone and insurance companies, banks, and other offices, usually as clerks. Women gained more economic rights, and in 1864 unmarried women were allowed the right to administer their own property once they reached the age of twenty-five.[18]

This does not sound like much, but foreigners, at least, were impressed. By the 1890s, observers like Ethel Brilliana Tweedie (1862–1940), an Englishwoman travelling around Finland in 1896, noted with surprise the number of working women who could choose between a range of occupations. They did well in them, and Tweedie lauded the "marvellous energy and splendid independence of the women of *Suomi*."[19] By the 1890s, observers like the

Spanish diplomat Angel Ganivet (1865–1898) thought women worked like men in Finland: "One is a gymnastics teacher, another a language teacher, someone a clerk to a notary, another a massage instructress, yet another a cashier at a bank."[20]

Overtime, certain jobs became feminized because the salaries were so small that a man could not provide for a family on them. Population growth also kept wages at a low level, and women were becoming a cheap workforce. The family-provider wage system dominated and was invoked as an argument for paying women less for the same work regardless of whether the women had, in fact, other dependents to provide for. This male breadwinner system was perceived as evil by the women's movement, which aimed at improving the condition of women in all fields of life. The Finnish women's movement was organized in 1884 with the establishment of the Finnish Women's Society (FWS) (*Suomen Naisyhdistys—Finska Kvinnoföreningen*), which was inspired by John Stuart Mill's *On the Subjection of Women* (1869). However, because of a combination of personal strife and linguistic and political reasons, the society split in two in 1891, resulting in the establishment of the more liberal and progressive Unionen—Unioni the following year. Both organizations developed regular international contacts with women in Western European countries and the United States. The socialist women established their own society in 1900.

The FWS aimed at women having equal rights and the same opportunities as men to study and earn university degrees and to work in the liberal professions. Women who had earned degrees demanded similar opportunities to enjoy the benefits that their qualifications merited, as well as to earn the same salary for the same work. The FWS worked for the political enfranchisement of women: suffrage and the opportunity to stand for election in governmental, communal, and even ecclesiastical elections.[21] The journals of both these middle-class women's societies tracked closely the international development of the women's cause, publishing, for example, notices and articles on the first female lawyers in various countries.[22] Thus, the Finnish women's movement's journals followed international models by using examples of women's progress in other countries as an argument for change in Finland. Although the various women's societies had different priorities and emphases, at least they collaborated on issues like the struggle for universal suffrage in the early 1900s.[23] Once universal suffrage was introduced in 1906—a great day for the women's movement—modern political parties were established. This caused the women's movement to fragment even more, as each party had its own women's organizations.[24] In the new Finnish Parliament, party loyalties tended to hinder direct cooperation in legal reform.

Women Enter Law Offices

Political developments followed, with some delay, the practices of everyday life. Women were more visible in the public sphere and outside the household working in shops and offices. Already in the 1890s, Diplomat Ganivet testified that the occupation of shop assistant was completely in female hands. He also reported that there were many women in the postal service, customs, banks, and offices.[25] The growing economic and industrial activities in later nineteenth-century Finland caused an increase in litigation—and thus more demand for lawyers. The increasing number of law firms created more job opportunities for female office workers.

The history of Finnish law firms is a poorly researched field, but this lack of research is only partly due to a lack of sources. What little is written mainly describes the various partners and premises with little attention to other members of the staff.[26] However, it seems that often the female clerks were the mainstays of these law firms. For example, the financial officer Karin Hollo worked at Castrén & Snellman from 1900 to 1945 and Mary Snellman was there between 1915 and 1963.[27]

Newspaper announcements in 1910 made it known that a Helsinki law firm wanted to hire a female clerk with tidy handwriting who had mastered "the domestic languages," probably meaning Finnish and Swedish, and in 1908, the law firm of Cedercreutz and von Winther, "office hours 10–3," offered a permanent job to a female clerk, again one who had mastered the "domestic languages."[28] But the advertisements also went the other way, women using the newspapers to actively seek employment. For example, in 1908, S.H.T., with a degree from a commercial school, advertised in the Helsinki-based *Aamulehti* for employment being sought in "the office of a commercial enterprise, law firm or land surveyor or other suitable employment."[29] In England, solicitors had begun to employ women as early as the 1850s, but it took time before they were generally accepted. However, technical progress in the form of typewriters seems to have facilitated the employment of women in law firms as clerks and assistants.[30]

The archive of the law firm Dittmar & Indrenius permits us a glimpse of the role of female employees in growing a successful legal practice. The lawyers Georg Granfelt (1865–1917) and Emanuel Indrenius (1866–1932) went into practice together, establishing a law firm in February 1899. By the autumn, they had so much work that they employed the first female clerk.[31] By 1901, the firm of Granfelt & Indrenius had expanded, employing both a female clerk and a female financial officer, who did the bookkeeping, paid the wages, and billed the clients. Some years later the firm, by then Dittmar & Indrenius, hired the services of a "reserve writer" (*reservskrifverska*) who worked partly for a neighboring bank and partly for them. The expansion of the firm continued, and in 1907, Agnes Zilliacus came to take care of the foreign correspondence.[32] Some law firms advertised which languages they could correspond in and then had to employ staff accordingly. For example, in 1909, the Helsinki firm of Carlson & Hällfors (*Advokat- & inkassoaffär*) made it known that it handled correspondence in Swedish, Finnish, Russian, German, and French.[33]

When a new law firm was established and registered by the board of industry (*industristyrelse*), the holders of procuration of the firm, those members of staff allowed to act in the name of the company, were also registered. The cashiers of the firm—increasingly women—were usually designated as such. Some firms even publicized this in the newspapers to inform other businesses of the authorized persons. For example, in 1909, the new Tampere firm of Einar Ahlman and Yrjö Pulkkinen announced that their lawyer J.K. Koskinen and the female financial officer G. Backman had both been individually granted procuration.[34]

Although writing and copying using pen and ink was still what clerks largely did in Finland, it was observed in England at the turn of the century that "no busy office [can] afford to be without typewriters."[35] This technical innovation took somewhat longer to reach Finland; however, by the 1900s, Finnish newspapers published employment advertisements for typists.[36] A commercial advertisement in 1910 observed that the typewriter "has nowadays become a necessary object for all business and government offices, firms and writers, etc. who wish to follow the times."[37] Dittmar & Indrenius employed its first typist in 1908. However, she was soon given notice as she was discovered to have neither the necessary skills nor the experience. Later that year, Aina Thurman was employed to handle all office work related to bankruptcy cases.[38]

We occasionally learn something of the women working at law firms from other sources as well. For example, Emma Lilius, Harriet Tavast, and Lydia Damstén, three of the women from Viborg who signed the national petition for female suffrage collected by *Unionen* in 1904, titled themselves "advocates' assistants" (*sakförarbiträde*).[39] Similarly, visual evidence also furnishes us with information of the prevalence of female staff in law firms. A rare, early twentieth-century photograph from the law firm of Alfred Holmström, one of the leading firms in Turku, shows ten persons, eight women and two men, in an office. Several of the women are working: reading papers, writing by hand at desks, and possibly using an early copying machine.[40]

It was profitable for firms to hire women rather than men. For example, the average monthly salary of 122 marks for a female clerk was only 68 percent of the salary of a male clerk (180 marks) in 1907.[41] In 1909, a law firm in a "larger provincial town" wanted to hire an experienced female typist. She was offered a salary of 125 marks a month for about six-and-a-half hours of work per day. However, she would be paid for overtime.[42] It was much more expensive to hire (male) lawyers. It was better for the owner(s) of the firm to hire female clerks who could perform some of the same tasks as men but for smaller salaries. Therefore, it is hardly surprising that in some firms the logical next step was to have competent female clerks or cashiers perform increasingly legal tasks and even to use them occasionally as advocates. In 1911, Åkesson published a biographical short story entitled "To the assizes" ("*Till tings*") in which she described a law office, possibly in Viborg, in which three female assistants (*biträden*) worked under the busy and largely absent advocate. The most senior of these female clerks was supremely competent in giving legal advice and drawing up documents for clients.[43]

Thus, when, in 1895, a Helsinki law firm (*sakförarekontor*) sent its financial officer, "Mrs. Fischer," to plead the case of four workers litigating against their employer, several newspapers noted that this was the first time a female advocate (*sakförare*) had appeared at the town court of Helsinki.[44] But Signe Fischer—also known by her maiden name Silén—was not the first female advocate in the country.

Attempting to Advocate: Anna Åkesson and the Legislation of 1898

In 1886, the readers of *Wasa Tidning* read to their surprise of "a lady-advocate in Finland" who had "recently" appeared at the extraordinary assizes of Rantasalmi. The lady's name was not mentioned, but she was said to come from Viborg, the country's second largest town. The paper conjectured that "she is probably the first female in Finland who has pleaded for another person in court" (*inför rätta fört annans talan*).[45] Several years later, in 1893, two Finnish newspapers published a notice that a woman had recently submitted documents in an appellate case to the [Judicial Division of the] Senate. She was Anna Åkesson, employed by the Viborg advocate Ivar Schröder.[46] This was even noted in the annual report of the FWS as a step forward in the cause of women.[47]

Anna Maria Katarina Åkesson (1865–1940) came from an important family in Viborg. Her father Axel Eric Åkesson (1817–1892) was a doctor of medicine and surgery, and her mother Anna Mathilda Boije af Gennäs (1836–1878) came from a noble family. From 1868 until his death, her father held the position of provincial doctor of the Viborg region. Anna Åkesson had three brothers, all of whom studied law at the University of Helsinki and made their careers within the administration or justice system. Anna and her two younger sisters went to a girls' school in Viborg, but none of them took the matriculation exam—the prerequisite for university studies that had first become possible for women with special dispensation in 1870.[48]

If they had been boys, nothing would have been more natural for them than to become lawyers like their brothers, taking exams at the Faculty of Law, undergoing court training, and obtaining suitable positions. Instead, all three got office jobs. One of Åkesson's sisters clerked in a big bank in Helsinki, while the other was employed by the borough finance department (*drätselkammare*) of Viborg. Åkesson started to work as a clerk in a law office.[49] This was the typical pattern among the upper-class families in Finland at the time. The sons were "educated as doctors, engineers, lawyers, and scientists. By contrast, the daughters became nurses, teachers, post officials, and clerks."[50] These female occupations did not require as high a level of education, and not only were they lower-status jobs but they were also paid less.

It was not uncommon for daughters from a well-off family like the Åkessons to seek employment. The nationalist ethos and state-building process of the time encouraged women to do their share in the service of the fatherland either inside or outside of the home. According to foreign observers like Ganivet, young women also wished to earn money in order to be independent from their families and in order to amuse themselves. "The daughter of the judge is a clerk, the language teacher the daughter of a count, the daughter of a doctor or member of the diet managed a wine enterprise."[51] The English Tweedie, after being widowed and taking up writing professionally to provide for herself and her sons, also commented on the fact that in Finland even "daughters of senators and generals take up all kinds of work." Tweedie saw Finland as a model for England as far as the position of women and their access to university and the job market were concerned. But perhaps more perceptively than Ganivet, she attributed Finnish women's wage-earning partly to the poverty of the country and its large families and partly to the democratic nature of Finland, with "no court and little aristocracy."[52] The poem that was read in 1896 at the seventieth birthday celebrations of Adelaïde Ehrnrooth (1826–1905), the grand old lady of the Finnish feminist movement, refers to a sense of freedom and economic independence as important reasons for young women to take up employment. "In schools, banks, / offices, firms, hospitals / we now see the young woman / — taking care of her work. / She can win her own bread herself / and not remain a burden on the family."[53]

The law firm where Anna Åkesson worked for more than twenty years was that of the advocate Ivar Schröder (1848–1907), who practiced law in Viborg for more than thirty years.[54] Schröder was a bold and famous advocate, whose name was regularly in the newspapers, and who occasionally handled big and politically controversial cases apart from the normal civil, criminal, and bankruptcy cases. Perhaps precisely because of this, he belonged to the wealthiest segment of the population of Viborg.[55] Schröder, the busy advocate, was often travelling in towns and the countryside taking care of cases at court. In the meantime, someone had to take care of the office and the simple cases. Åkesson, his trusted holder of procuration, had studied a year in a commercial school, and she was fluent in several languages.[56] It obviously suited Schröder to have her occasionally handle cases at court and deliver documents to courts.

Schröder was not alone in his liberal notions. In his book on legal reforms, judge Karl Ferdinand Forsström (1817–1903) suggested in 1896 that women should be allowed to act as advocates provided they had earned a law degree. He thought that allowing women to act as advocates was a natural step considering that women already worked as doctors and teachers.[57] In addition, all the judges presiding in all the court sessions that Anna Åkesson and Signe Silén attended as advocates—and all the advocates of their opposing parties—tacitly accepted women as advocates by not objecting to their presence and by not challenging their competence. But others had more doubts. In 1895, the female university students debated among themselves whether or not women were suited to pursue the legal profession. The introducer of the debate topic, Alma Söderhjelm, herself the daughter of an important judge, did not consider women suited for the judiciary, whereas they could certainly work as advocates or district registrars. Whether or not all legal professions should be opened up to women divided the opinion of the female students. Unfortunately, the arguments for and against have not survived in the journals of the female students.[58]

However, in October 1896, advocate Hjalmar Hellström (1864–1946) opposed Åkesson acting as advocate in court and denied her the chance to represent her client by virtue of the law and jurisprudence. Put on the spot through the objection raised by the advocate of the opposing party, the Viborg town court refused to accept her as an advocate because of her sex, a verdict criticized by the journal *Wiborgsbladet* with reference to Åkesson's long experience. Obviously, the newspaper considered that her experience weighed more heavily than the disadvantage of her sex. In his reply, Hellström expressed his indignation at the criticism of the verdict in the press, explaining that it was much more demanding to plead in the lower courts than to merely submit papers to the Senate, where there was no oral procedure.[59]

Referring to the recent Åkesson case, Judge Forsström observed that his notion of granting women the right to advocate had "been universally accepted in all the newspapers." Although Åkesson had successfully pleaded at all levels previously, Forsström remained unsurprised that she had been rejected by the Viborg town court, as the letter of the law was unambiguous.[60] Obviously, Forsström saw himself as the herald of a more progressive practice, also confirmed by the more liberal press, but he knew that an expansive interpretation of the law had not yet generally gained ground.

The Finnish feminist organizations—especially the more liberal Unionen—were closely following the Åkesson case. Helena Westermarck (1857–1938), a renowned painter, journalist, and feminist, was writing about it in *Nutid*, the journal of Unionen. In her article entitled "Women and legal interpretation" ("*Kvinnorna och lagtolkingen*") in December 1896, she was incensed about the decision to ban Åkesson from the courtroom because of her sex, observing that Åkesson had already professionally practiced advocacy (*yrkesmässigt varit rättegångsombud*) for several years at various stages and courts. Suddenly, the law was being interpreted in a way that shut her out of her profession. Westermarck considered it a positive sign that newspapers had expressed a desire to reform such outdated sections of the law and that the times were more progressive than was the letter of the law. However, the article's author thought the case showed clearly how "utterly insecure was the ground on which women build their work." The paper also held that this should not "leave any father untouched if his daughter's future lay close to his heart." Mere talk about one profession after another opening up to women was not enough to guarantee equal opportunities, as women's access to many fields depended on dispensations and arbitrariness. Westermarck considered legal reform the only reliable and solid way of remedying women's situation.[61]

Anna Åkesson challenged the ban in the Viborg Court of Appeal, but in February 1897 the court affirmed the lower court's decision. Thus, because she was a woman, Åkesson was barred from acting as an advocate for other people. After this setback, she attempted to obtain a dispensation from the Judicial Division of the Senate.[62] But only some weeks before the verdict of the Viborg Court of Appeal, the Judicial Division had declared that no woman was to be allowed to deliver legal documents to its registry. The principal was allowed thirty days to have the documents redelivered—by a man.[63] Thus, it is hardly surprising that Åkesson's appeal failed in November 1897 when the Senate refused on the grounds that, according to the 1734 law and a decree of 1873, only men would be allowed to advocate and that a dispensation of the chapter on procedure of the law could not be granted.[64] *Hufvudstadsbladet* wrote that the decision might have been formally correct, but that it was based on a very old-fashioned and anachronistic interpretation of the law. The newspaper asserted that sufficiently qualified women ought to be allowed to act as advocates.[65]

Anna Åkesson's case and attempt to obtain a dispensation was discussed by the feminist periodical *Nutid* in several issues.[66] The conclusion was that legal reform was the only remedy possible once Åkesson had finally been denied dispensation by the Judicial Division of the Senate. *Nutid* called for all women to unite behind reform of the law.[67] However, attitudes toward lay advocacy in general were hardening at the time in Finland. There were complaints about their incompetence and the damage they caused to their clients. The courts were accused of laxity because they did not prevent lay advocates of dubious reputation, honesty, and morality from representing others at court. In the 1890s and early 1900s, there were attempts to reform the Finnish court system and its procedural law: "There was a consensus among the experts that a modern court procedure necessitated a learned corps of advocates."[68] As mentioned above, ostensible concerns for the quality of the advocates covered up men's efforts to monopolize advocacy. This would have benefitted the Finnish juristocracy and cemented its financial position through the widespread part-time advocacy of civil servants.

While the reform of the law of procedure was being prepared, Czar Nicholas II (r. 1894–1917) of Russia, Grand Duke of Finland, proposed to the Finnish Diet in 1897 that to remedy the problems purportedly caused by lay advocates and the laxity of judges, henceforth all advocates who wished to pursue their profession at the Judicial Division of the Senate, the Courts of Appeal, and the major town courts were required to have a law degree as well as experience. They had also to be members of an advocates' association.[69]

The Czar's proposition to change the law to ban lay advocates from the most important courts was discussed in the four estates of the Diet. Some liberal voices among the burgher and clerical estates spoke for allowing women to act as advocates, proposing that the law be changed so that women would be allowed to act as advocates (*rättegångsbiträde*). For example, Jaakko Forsman (1839–1899), professor of criminal law, stated that the 1734 law had long been interpreted so that "man" also meant "woman," and that interpreting it as "men only" was regressive. Others agreed, observing that women had long been accepted as witnesses to wills even though the law spoke of "men." The advocacy of women was in fact jeopardized by the current practice of the Judicial Division of the Senate. Other more conservative representatives considered advocacy totally unsuitable for women, whom they deemed incapable of objectivity and led by emotions. Finally, the noble estate and burghers seemed ready to accept women as advocates, but the peasants and the clerical estate were not.[70] The Czar's proposition (that would have amounted to a monopoly of advocates in many cases) did not pass because the peasant and clerical estates opposed it, fearing the costs of such a reform to ordinary people.[71] At the same time the estates discussed whether women ought to be allowed to participate in communal positions of trust or to gain entry to all teaching positions.

What was achieved in 1898 was a reform of section 15:2 of the Chapter on Procedure of the 1734 law. It forbade all persons without a degree in law in the "university of the country" to act as advocates (*oikeudenkäynti-asiamiehenä tahi riitapuolen apulaisena*) in the higher courts.[72] This effectively banned foreigners who lacked a degree from the University of Helsinki. Occasionally notices can be found in the newspapers of non-local men being authorized as advocates in the local court; in 1909, L. L. D. Hermann Friedman from Riga, employee of Fredrik Thuring's Advocate's and Business Office, was granted the right to advocate at the Helsinki town court.[73]

More importantly, however, these debates restricted lay advocacy even before the reform of 1898 came into force. For example, in 1897, the Helsinki town court authorized the "advocate's assistant" (*sakförarbiträde*), former student Berndt Frithiof von Pfaler (1846–1901), to handle only "simpler actions of debt [*fordringsmål*] and registrations, not criminal cases." Nevertheless, he had this authorization for the time being "as assistant of an advocate, accepted by the court and experienced in law" (*biträde åt lagfaren, af rådstufvurätten godkänd sakförare*).[74]

There seems to have been no reason in law why von Pfaler could not have acted as an advocate in the Helsinki town court as before. Admittedly, according to the university enrollment register, he had not studied law but rather had studied in the faculty of science and mathematics.[75] On the other hand, no law degree was required at the Helsinki town court as a first instance court, even after the restrictions of 1898. Nor does it seem that the court mentioned any reason related to von Pfaler's person or respectability that would indicate why his competence should have been curtailed.

These court-ordained restrictions seem not to have been to von Pfaler's liking, as he appealed first to the Court of Appeal in Turku and then to the Senate in 1898. However, both higher instances confirmed the sentence of the Helsinki town court, giving von Pfaler only a limited right to act as an advocate's assistant.[76]

The legislative debates, the decisions of the Justice Department in the cases of Åkesson and von Pfaler, and the reform of 1898 effectively closed the doors of courtrooms to lay advocates of both sexes. For women, their sex rather than their lack of law degree was the major motive. But the trend was the more remarkable as there was no legal justification for banning respectable and honest male lay advocates from the town courts. In the wake of this legislation, men could also face difficulty in pursuing advocacy even in lower courts. Thus, Åkesson suffered both because she was a woman and because she did not have a law degree. The legal (male) status profession, the Finnish juristocracy, was taking precautions and protecting itself against lay competition in the courtrooms by the reform. The attempts to monopolize lay advocacy were part of the defense of the university-trained elite profession; the many-centuries-long tradition of "self-learned" lay advocates in the provinces were hardly in themselves a serious threat to the privileged city lawyers.[77] However, the position of the aristocratic lawyer elite was also being shaken by the need for other professions and the growing numbers of university students, increasingly from the Finnish-speaking lower classes—and increasingly female.[78]

When the leading expert on procedural law Baron Rabbe Axel Wrede (1851–1938) wrote his commentary on the law of civil procedure in 1905, he insisted that being male was a necessary precondition for an attorney. He explained this in a footnote: the law used the word "man." However, he added: "Lately, some courts have probably allowed women to act as representatives. But that such a practice is not common is demonstrated by a court case." Wrede then referred to the above-mentioned case from the Judicial Division of the Senate in 1897.[79] He wrote in a detached way as if the debates of the 1890s had never taken place. He and other conservatives treated the question as a purely technical matter of interpreting a 170-year-old law rather than one of legal policy. A member of the noble estate, Wrede also opposed extending communal suffrage to women.[80] Nevertheless, he had to admit that the practice was changing, as more liberal and progressive courts, judges, and male advocates at the grassroots level could acquiesce to female advocates' professional work. Such a practice eroded the interpretation that "men" was not to be understood as "persons" to exclude women altogether. Change was taking place from the bottom to the top, and this put pressure on the strict policy of the conservatives.

Why had Anna Åkesson decided to challenge the traditionalist interpretation? The answer is probably a mixture of personal and structural reasons. Åkesson had grown up in a liberal Swedish-speaking elite family, and as she had for many years acted as an attorney uncontested, she knew that many lawyers were willing to accept women as advocates. Moreover, women's entry into universities, government posts, schools, and offices made the question of equality of the sexes in access to the professions very topical. Equal opportunities for both sexes to work and obtain posts were among the paramount goals of the Finnish feminist movement, which supported Åkesson. In addition, she was determined and had strong progressive and feminist convictions. For years she was an active member of the Viborg branches of the Unionen and the Konkordia Society that granted scholarships to women wishing to learn skills with which they could support themselves.[81]

Although it has been suggested that the failure of Åkesson's lawsuit "limited the actions of female advocates (*sakförare*) excessively in Finland for more than three decades,"[82] this may be an exaggeration. The public debate on Åkesson's capacity to act as an advocate lasted for some years in the Finnish press, thus preparing the ground for Lundell. When Lundell decided to challenge the interpretation of the law in 1909, fundamental political and legal changes had already taken place.

Becoming an Advocate: Agnes Lundell

In 1899, Agnes Lundell had begun her studies at the Faculty of Law in Helsinki, like dozens of young women before her since 1892.[83] The appearance of women at the university helped to inflate the number of university students, which multiplied in the late nineteenth and early twentieth centuries. Between 1874 and 1913 their number more than tripled from 981 students to 3,195.[84] The university consistory had proposed to the Czar in 1878 that university studies for women be allowed, but his decision in 1882 upheld the necessity for dispensations. The Czar did not wish to create a precedent in Russia. However, in Finland, dispensations were routinely given to all women who had taken the matriculation exam until 1901, when women were allowed to study on the same conditions as men. Whereas women had formed about 15 percent of all students between 1894 and 1896, their number rose rapidly to 39 percent of all students between 1914 and 1916.

Women entered the Faculties of Arts and Medicine first,[85] but their matriculation into the Faculty of Law came in 1892. There seems to have been no public debate about female students at the Faculty of Law either within the legal sphere or in the press. The first female law students, Lucie Rosenius (1872–1939) and Alie Humble (1872–1951), were mentioned by name in the Finnish newspapers in the same way as female pioneers in any field.[86] What came to distinguish Lundell from all of these ladies was her decision to study for a law degree instead of the administrative degrees that many other female law students before her had chosen. Thus, she had earned the law degree required by the reform of 1898 although she was still of the "wrong" sex.

Lundell did not come from an affluent family, and she had to finance her degree at least partly by working as a teacher and through scholarships. She received at least three scholarships from funds for female students managed by women's associations (*Finska Kvinnoföreningen* and *Konkordia*).[87] As mentioned above, women automatically received dispensations to study at the university in the 1890s, and there were no institutional obstacles to women studying for any of the degrees in the Faculty of Law. Lundell first earned a higher administrative degree (*högre förvaltningsexamen*) as other women had before her, but in 1906 she was the first woman to earn a degree in law (*rättsexamen*, *oikeustutkinto*) as well. In 1907, an acquaintance suggested to her that she apply for the post of registrar (*aktuarie*) at the Court of Appeal of Turku. Lundell was disinclined to do this: "How could I leave Helsinki and all plans and interests there," she wrote to a friend.[88]

Remaining in Helsinki, the path that Lundell also initially trod once she had taken her exam had already been pursued by women before her. She obtained the right to become a scribe (*kopist*) at the divisions of trade and industry as well as agriculture of the Economic Division of the Finnish Senate (i.e., the Finnish government). But she aimed higher and soon petitioned for the right to keep minutes at the meetings of the Economic Division—an office no woman had previously held. This proved a much more difficult question, as it created a precedent for women's capacity to hold office—a disputed and yet unresolved question. Lundell's persistent lobbying was finally successful, although the dress code posed extra problems.[89] But Lundell had other aspirations.

In the early 1900s, changes had taken place in Finnish society and political life. As a consequence of the humiliating defeat in the Russo-Japanese war of 1904–1905 and the political unrest in the empire, Czar Nicholas had granted more political rights to the people. The Finnish Diet, based on four estates, was reformed into a one-chamber parliament with 200 seats in 1906. All citizens who were 21 years old had the right to vote and be elected to the new parliament. In 1907, 19 women were elected.[90] Thus, Finnish women were the first in Europe to vote but also to become legislators, as the granting of universal suffrage in Finland in 1906 was a first in Europe.

New groups in parliament brought reforms to the agenda. However, the opportunity of the new parliament to alter and liberalize laws was still severely curtailed by the power of the czar. He repeatedly used his veto to stop liberal reforms that had been endorsed by the Finnish Parliament. In 1907, parliament discussed the question of advocates while also considering the capacity of women to hold office. The proposition to parliament allowed all "respectable and honest persons who were not under guardianship" to act as advocates in court. This would have allowed most men and unmarried women to act as advocates. (As married women were under their husbands' guardianship according to the Code of 1734, this debarred them from working in the profession.) In the general discussion, this new proposal was greeted by four members of parliament (three female and one male) as a welcome innovation. Still, the women wanted to correct the language in the Swedish version of the bill (*person*, *han*) so that there would be absolutely no doubt that women were also intended. Although this bill was endorsed by parliament, Czar Nicholas II refused to allow it to become law.[91]

The same year, two propositions were made by the MPs to extend an equal, or nearly equal, right to competent women to hold government office. The first proposal was put forward by six female MPs of the Finnish Party and the second was proposed by five MPs of the Young Finnish Party (two female and three male). Several of the female MPs were active in the women's movement. Even after 1907, MPs—both male and female—made repeated propositions (in 1908 and 1909) about repealing the 1898 act and granting women the right to become advocates, but each time their attempts were frustrated.[92]

Unable to count on legislative reform to allow women to practice law, Lundell did what her predecessors Åkesson and Silén had done in order to pursue her goal: she presented herself at court with all her credentials. Later, she said in an interview that the head of the Helsinki town court (*justitieborgmästare*) Edvard Loo, who obviously favored a liberal interpretation of the law, had told her in April 1909 that the court would accept female advocates.[93] Lundell's first client was Tyra Strömberg, who claimed that she had been locked in a lunatic asylum unlawfully and involuntarily. The case became a *cause célèbre* for many reasons. Not only was the issue sensational in itself, but it was made even more so by the fact that complaint was brought against four doctors, among whom was professor Christian Sibelius (1869–1922), brother of the composer Jean Sibelius (1865–1957). Moreover, Strömberg's female advocate added to the news value of the case.

The trial lasted many months in the fifth department of the Helsinki town court, presided over by Gustaf Björkman. Neither he nor any of the advocates of the opposing parties contested Lundell's position as advocate because of her sex.[94] Each hearing of the case was closely and avidly covered by almost all the newspapers in Finland. The parties and Lundell gave interviews to the media and their images and photos were printed in the newspapers.[95] After the process, Lundell's name was said to be on the lips of the reading public all over the country.[96]

The feminist journal *Nutid*, published by Unionen, commented on the case under the title "Finland's first female advocate" (*Finlands första kvinnliga advokat*). After giving the basics of the case, the journal observed that the fact that Lundell was accepted without further ado by the court as Strömberg's representative was "the more strange considering that similar rights had previously not been granted to a woman" because of the prescriptions in the Chapter on Procedure. The notice went on to observe that as the law had not been altered, this went to show how "in general, changed circumstances made a more liberal interpretation of the law possible." *Nutid* observed this with satisfaction, adding "other times, other customs" (*andra tider, andra seder*).[97] Another article hailed the liberal and modern (*frisinnad och modern*) interpretation of the Helsinki court in allowing Lundell to act as advocate. This "showed that it was open to the non-dismissible demands of the time in the matter of authorizing women to cultivate in practice in public life the competence they had acquired through their professional education."[98]

Lundell partly won, partly lost her first court case in the Helsinki town court, which handed down its verdict on July 8, 1910. One defendant was acquitted altogether, but doctors Lövegren and Sibelius were fined for breach of duty and malpractice for incarcerating Strömberg unlawfully in a mental institute. However, Lundell herself was fined by the court for slandering Dr. Sivén and Prof. Sibelius "out of ignorance."[99] After this, Lundell also did minor legal work in both criminal and private law while establishing her name and clientele.[100]

Nor did Lundell shun work in the provinces. In 1910, she was in Vaasa representing the widow of district judge Swahn in her case against Swahn's former deputy Forss. The matter involved the plaintiff's missing final financial accounts for acting as her husband's surrogate judge. The local newspaper observed that this was the first time (June 6, 1910) a female advocate appeared at the town court of Vaasa.[101]

When discussing Lundell's role, the newspapers occasionally called her advocate (*asianajaja*; *advokat*),[102] although her title *hovioikeuden auskultantti/hovrättsauskultant* (then merely a title of graduated lawyers) was usually used after she obtained it in 1909.[103] She also seems to have used this title herself.[104] Sometimes the media erroneously identified her as having been trained at the bench (*varatuomari*), although this would have required her to take the judge's oath and practice as judge.[105] However, this was expressly denied first by the Turku Court of Appeal in 1909 and then confirmed by the Judicial Division of the Senate in 1910.[106]

Some newspapers, like the conservative and religious *Herättäjä* (*Awakener*) in its short notice about the Turku Court of Appeal denying Lundell the right to take the judge's oath, observed that "women do not yet have what it takes to become judges" (*sillä ei naisesta ole wielä tuomariksi*).[107] In an ironic piece in *Tammerfors Nyheter*, a writer under a pseudonym discussed whether the conservatism of the courts was justifiable or not (*berättigad eller oberättigad*) in denying women such as Lundell the right to take the judge's oath. He started to talk about women who had already obtained "dispensations from their sex" and worked as teachers and doctors—even those many women who "more or less graced the plenary hall of our legislative meetings." He then moved on to discuss women as judges and priests—"hitherto, pulpits in proper churches and judges' seats [*domaresäte*] had not been adorned by an officiating woman's sweet smile or imposing splendor." He welcomed women to the pulpit and the possibility of "poor abandoned male spinsters" marrying into wealthy parishes by marrying female vicars.[108]

As for female judges, the author was more doubtful. He claimed to dislike the decision of the Turku Court of Appeal, confirmed by the Senate, to deny Lundell the right to take the judge's oath, "as Miss Lundell is said to be a competent and clear-minded lawyer."[109] However, the author thought that there was a principle at stake (of women being granted the right to become judges), and that the "Messrs. lawyers were unwilling to create a possibly fatal precedent."[110] Again, on a more comic, but patronizing note, the author, "not being an entirely splendidly handsome man," would be afraid of litigating against "a seductive Adonis" in the courtroom "if the judge happened to be a woman of the usual type."[111] So, while the author welcomed women to the pulpits and pastoral work, he advised them to continue judging their fellow human beings over the rim of a coffee cup. Namely, in the judges' seat, one was to "keep, oh so strictly, to the evidence."[112] Obviously, this pen-named writer was expressing doubts about women's capacity for objectivity. Taking a partisan role as advocate perhaps suited the not-so-objective women better.

Others, like the Swedish-speaking worker's newspaper *Arbetet* (Labour), commented about the refusal of the Senate to grant Lundell the right to take the judge's oath that she had "as Miss Strömberg's advocate proved herself to be a better lawyer than many who wear trousers."[113] Socialists had generally positive attitudes toward equality between sexes. In its declaration in 1903, the Social Democratic Party wanted to abolish all restrictions "in private law or in law in general" that placed women in a weaker position than men. The Social Democratic Party, which had had its representatives in the new parliament since 1907, as well as the political left in general, was skeptical about lawyers and the entire bourgeois legal system. Together with the agrarian population, they were opposed to forbidding lay advocacy and establishing a monopoly of advocates. In fact, the 1898 statute was finally repealed in 1917 on the initiative of a socialist MP immediately after the declaration of independence.[114]

When the Finnish socialists established their own government for some months after the coup d'état in January 1918, they gave women the same opportunity to hold government and municipal offices. The "Red" court system that functioned during the civil war was also staffed by laymen as judges. Even some female judges are known from the "Red Courts" of 1918, although their percentage was minuscule among all "red" judges.[115] This was the first time women had acted as judges in Finland since Queen Ulrika Eleonora had formally acted as the superior judge in the country during her short reign (1719–1720). Only through the Act of Women's Competence for Government Office in 1925 and the decree of 1927 supplementing it did women gain equal access to almost all offices—up to and including judge. However, this outcome required considerable political pressure from female MPs and the women's movement.[116]

Meanwhile, Lundell, undeterred by not being allowed to take the judge's oath, petitioned the Economic Division of the Senate, i.e., the Finnish government, for a dispensation to act as an advocate. This the Senate granted on October 21, 1910, and the news was reported in the papers accordingly.[117] However, Lundell's joy was short lived as the Judicial Division of the Senate had not been consulted and they refused to consider the dispensation valid. She filed a new petition at the Judicial Division of the Senate, which initially denied the dispensation in April 1911, but then, happily, the judges changed their minds.[118]

In 1911, after the final dispensation from the Senate had been obtained, Lundell went into business with her former school fellow Hjalmar Erlund from Turku and established the bilingual firm Lundell & Erlund: Advocate and Business Office (*Asianajo- ja liiketoimisto*; *Advokat & affärskontor*), advertising that they did all kinds of legal, patent, and conveyance work. The firm opened after Pentecost in the center of Helsinki (Mikonkatu 2). Both partners had their own offices, a shared waiting room and female clerk, and a partly separate clientele.[119]

Lundell seems to have built up her business and reputation through her feminist activities. Lundell & Erlund regularly advertised in women's journals, such as *Naisten ääni* (Voice of Women), *Nutid*, and the socialist *Työläisnainen* (Female Worker).[120] *Naisten ääni* and *Koti ja yhteiskunta* wrote feature stories on Lundell's office with its American furniture, green-and-white curtains, and waiting female clients.[121] In 1913, however, the partnership of Lundell & Erlund came to an end, and Lundell's office was renamed Agnes Lundell's Advocate's Office (*Agnes Lundell'in Asianajotoimisto*).[122] During her career as advocate, Lundell did all kinds of legal work, as was customary in that period. Nevertheless, she established a particular reputation for taking on female clients and advocating their cause with spirit and, as some claimed, ruthlessness.[123] Lundell was a committed feminist activist who gave many lectures on legal issues at various women's meetings. In addition, she was involved in politics within the Swedish People's Party (*Svenska Folkpartiet*).[124] For Sweden, Anna Pettersson—the first female advocate in Sweden and proprietor of The Female Law Office (*Kvinnliga juridiska byrån*)—was publicly accused by some men of "disloyal means of attracting a female clientele."[125] Such sentiments may also have been shared by some of Lundell's male colleagues.[126] Obviously, her activity in the feminist movement, her advocacy of the condition of women in general, and her professional activities went hand in hand. Not least, she became a wealthy woman in the course of her career.

Conclusion

When women entered Finnish offices as clerks and cashiers, it was not surprising that they also entered the legal world, performing similar tasks in the judiciary and advocates' offices. In the Finnish system, whether a woman could be accepted as an advocate depended largely on the liberalism or complacency of the individual judge and opposing party. If neither the judge nor opposing party (or his advocate) challenged the woman's ability to represent another in court, she could successfully do so.

Based on newspaper material, Åkesson, an employee of an advocate's office in Viborg, had done this since 1886. We also find information in the newspapers that in Helsinki, Signe Fischer (née Silén), the female cashier in an advocate's office, had acted as an advocate in an employment-related case. As Helena Westermarck perceptively wrote: "where the liberal spirit of the new era rushes forth, previously barred doors are opened, but when a conservative draft blows, they are closed again. It is completely arbitrary; it depends on weather and winds, so to say."[127] In 1910, even other (male) liberals commented on the "consuming guerrilla war" (*utslitande guerrillakrig*), which women had to resort to every step of the way in order to obtain access to professions and civil offices that "no laws can prevent them from ultimately gaining."[128] However, the matter cannot be reduced to a purely conservative/liberal dichotomy, as the lines of battle were more fluid—as in the question of suffrage for Finnish women.[129]

Denmark had experienced a parallel struggle for women's right to act as advocates in the 1880s after Nanna Berg (1864–1908), who had earned her law degree in 1887, attempted to litigate a case in court. She had power of attorney from a male advocate that authorized her to plead even in the Supreme Court, but judicial officials refused to accept this. The case was heard in all three instances, but Berg's sex proved an obstacle in all courts. In 1888, the Supreme Court ruled against Berg, albeit after voting. Only in 1906 did Danish women obtain the right to become advocates themselves or be validly empowered by advocates by power of attorney.[130] In Sweden, by contrast, there seem not to have been institutional hindrances to women practicing advocacy in the early 1900s, although women advocates were rare there as well.

Anna Åkesson was ousted from the Finnish courts because of her sex. However, the fact that her court cases coincided with a campaign to keep laymen out of the courts indicates a conservative and protectionist attitude in the country against traditional lay advocacy, even though it was justified by the demands of the modernization of court procedure. The traditional (male) lawyer's hegemony was threatened within the administrative system because of the growth of other specialized professional groups. Conservatives also feared that advocacy would be a step for women toward becoming judges—something they were supposedly unsuited for as a result of their emotional and subjective nature. There were double reasons to keep Åkesson, a lay woman, out of the courtrooms.

After Åkesson's defeat, no other woman seems to have attempted to advocate until Lundell. As she had earned a law degree, she could only be excluded because of her sex. However, since Lundell acted publicly as an advocate first in a scandalous case, and after that in various courts and instances, the Judicial Division finally had to give in and grant her the official right to pursue advocacy. However, she could not be appointed to higher governmental or municipal offices, which was the problem the more numerous female doctors also faced.

Men and unmarried women were officially put on an equal footing as advocates with the reform of the Chapter of Procedure, passed in parliament on the same day as the Finnish declaration of independence, December 6, 1917. "All honest persons of good repute who were not under guardianship" could thereafter act as advocates. No czar could henceforth prevent the reform.[131] Still, until the Marriage Law of 1929 came into force the following year in 1930, the legal restrictions on becoming advocates regarding married women were upheld.[132]

Although Finnish women were hailed by some foreigners "as the most advanced women in Europe"[133] after they gained suffrage, in practice their entry into the legal profession was an uphill struggle. Despite their relatively early access to universities, there was delay and resistance to granting women the right to enter the professions and judicial offices. The legal profession was the slowest of all because of its aristocratic connections and its highly protectionist policy.[134] In this chapter, I have attempted to explain why. The male monopoly of law in Finland was finally broken by new legislation by parliament only in the 1920s after decades of pressure from the women's movement.

Notes

1 I would like cordially to thank the editors of this book and my colleague Anu Lahtinen for their generous comments and suggestions on a previous version of this chapter. Rod McConchie did once more a brilliant job of improving my English. All translations from the original Finnish and Swedish are mine unless otherwise indicated. This article was written while I was a fellow at the Helsinki Collegium for Advanced Studies.

2 Rättegångs Balk 15:2, *Sveriges Rikes Lag, Gillad och Antagen på Riksdagen Åhr 1734* (Stockholm: Institutet för rättshistorisk forsking, 1984), 219: "*The, som för andra måge tala och svara, skola vara oberychtade, ärlige, redelige och förståndige män. Ej bör någor almänneliga ther til brukas, som af Rätten, ther saken drifves, ej godkänd är, och lof ther til fått.*" In 1873, these declarations were only updated orthographically, Hans Kejserliga Majestäts Nådiga Förordning angående ändring i 2 och 3 §§ 15 kap. R. B., no 7, 24.2.1873.

3 Mary Jane Mossman, *The First Women Lawyers: A Comparative Study of Gender, Law and the Legal Professions* (Oxford and Portland, Oregon: Hart Publishing, 2006), 114–118; see also 41, 50, 89–98.

4 Mossman, *First Women Lawyers*, ix–xi: reprinting *The Illustrated London News*, November 13, 1897.

5 Louis Frank, *La Femme-Avocat: Exposé historique et critique de la question* (Paris: V. Giard et E. Briére, 1898). On Louis Frank, see, e.g., Françoise De Bueger-Van Lierde, "Louis Frank, pionnier du mouvement féministe belge," *Revue belge d'histoire contemporaine* 4, no. 3–4 (1973): 377–392; Mossman, *First Women Lawyers*, 239–268.

6 For various European countries, see, e.g., James C. Albisetti, "Portia Ante Portas: Women and the Legal Profession in Europe, ca. 1870–1925," *Journal of Social History* 33, no. 4 (2000): 825–857; Julie Fette, "Pride and Prejudice in the Professions: Women Doctors and Lawyers in Third Republic France," *Journal of Women's History* 19, no. 3 (2007): 60–86. For the United States and Canada, e.g., Constance B. Backhouse, "'To Open the Way for Others of my Sex': Clara Brett Martin's Career as Canada's First Woman Lawyer," *Canadian Journal of Women & Law* 1 (1985–86): 1–41; Jane M. Friedman, *America's First Woman*

Lawyer: The Biography of Myra Bradwell (Buffalo, New York: Prometheus Books, 1993); Mossman, *First Women Lawyers*, 23–112.

7 For Denmark, see Inger Dübeck, "'Lærde damer', kvindelige akademikere og kvindelige jurister," in *Jura og kvinder: Festskrift i anledning af 100-året for kvinders adgang til juridisk embedseksamen*, ed. Inger Dübeck, Jytte Lindgård and Ruth Nielsen (Copenhagen: Juristforbundets forlag, 1975), 11–30. For Norway, see Thordis Støren, *Justitias døtre: De første kvinnelige jurister i Norge* (Oslo: Universitetsforlaget, 1984); Thordis Støren, *Justitias gode tjenere: De første kvinnelige advokater* (Oslo: Dreyers Forlag, 1987). For Sweden, see Gunilla Strömholm, "Elsa Eschelsson: Sveriges första kvinnliga jurist," in *Ad studium et ad laborem incitavit Elsa Eschelsson*, ed. Elsa Eschelssons and Nils Jareborg (Uppsala: Iustus Förlag, 1997), 9–125; "Eschelsson, Elsa," in *Svenska kvinnor, föregångare—nyskapare*, ed. Carin Österberg, Inga Lewenhaupt and Anna Greta Wahlberg (Lund: Bokförlaget Signum, 1990), 115–116.

8 E.g., Pirkko K. Koskinen, "Laki kirjoittamattoman lain kumoamisesta eli vaiheita naisen tiellä tuomarin virkaan: erään tutkimuksen hahmottelua," in *Karjalaisen osakunnan juristikerho 1934–1982*, ed. Harri Hietala, Seppo Sairanen and Taru Turunen (Helsinki: Karjalaisen osakunnan juristikerho, 1982), 49–60; Anneli Winter-Mäkinen, *Naisjuristien 1. vuosisata: Poimintoja naisjuristien historiasta* (Helsinki: Lakimiesliiton kustannus, 1995), esp. 25–56; Harriet Silius, *Den kringgärdade kvinnligheten: Att vara kvinnlig jurist i Finland* (Åbo: Åbo Academy Press, 1992), 95–97; Harriet Silius, "Women Jurists in Finland at the Turn of the Century: Breakthrough or Intermezzo?" in *Women in the World's Legal Professions*, ed. Ulrike Schulz and Gisela Shaw (Oxford and Portland, Oregon: Hart Publishing, 2003), esp. 388–389. See also Heikki Pihlajamäki, *Kansan ja esivallan välissä: Suomalaisen asianajajakunnan historia* (Helsinki: Edita, 2009), esp. 120–125.

9 Ellen Kleman, "Vår kvinnliga advokatfirma," *Hertha* 8 (1919): 146–148; Strömholm, "Elsa Eschelsson," 72. There is no entry on Pettersson in the book on pioneering women in Sweden, although she is mentioned in Elsa Andén's "Andén, Elsa," in *Svenska kvinnor, föregångare—nyskapare*, 20–21.

10 Protokoll förda hos Finlands ridderskap och adel vid landtdagen år 1897, II, 7.5.1897, 878, 888.

11 The Finnish Diet as a meeting of the four Estates, nobility, clergy, burghers, and peasants, became a modern parliament in 1906. The first parliamentary election took place in 1907.

12 Jukka Kekkonen, *Merkantilismista liberalismiin: Oikeushistoriallinen tutkimus elinkeinovapauden syntytaustasta vuosina 1855–1879* (Helsinki: Suomalainen Lakimiesyhdistys, 1987).

13 The University of Helsinki was founded as the Royal Academy of Turku in 1640, and after the annexation of Finland to Russia it became the Imperial Academy of Turku. After the great fire of Turku in 1827, the university was moved to Helsinki, the new capital, and it was renamed the Imperial Alexander's University in Finland.

14 Matti Klinge, Rainer Knapas, John Strömberg, and Anto Leikola, *Helsingfors Universitet 1640–1990*, vol. 2 (Helsingfors: Otava, 1989), 333–350; Esa Konttinen, *Perinteisestä moderniin: Professioiden yhteiskunnallinen synty Suomessa* (Tampere: Vastapaino, 1991), 114–116.

15 Konttinen, *Perinteisestä moderniin*, 105–121; Jari Stenvall, *Herrasmiestaidosta asiantuntijatietoon: Virkamiehistön asiantuntemuksen kehitys valtion keskushallinnossa* (Helsinki: Hallintohistoriakomitea, 1995), 50–64.

16 Pihlajamäki, *Kansan ja esivallan välissä*, 97–115.

17 Konttinen, *Perinteisestä moderniin*, 222–227; Pihlajamäki, *Kansan ja esivallan välissä*, 132–139.

18 *Nainen ja naisen työ Suomessa* (Helsinki: J. C. Frenckell & Poika, 1898), 39, 50; Riitta Jallinoja, *Suomalaisen naisasialiikkeen taistelukaudet* (Helsinki: WSOY, 1983), 79–90; Anne Ollila, *Jalo velvollisuus: Virkanaisena 1800-luvun lopun Suomessa* (Helsinki: SKS, 1998), 43–44, 75–76.
19 Alec Tweedie, *Through Finland in Carts* (London: Adam and Charles Black, 1897), 10, 161–163. On Tweedie, see Elizabeth Baigent, "Tweedie, Ethel Brilliana (1862–1940)," *Oxford Dictionary of National Biography* (Oxford University Press, 2004), online ed., May 2009, accessed March 15, 2014, http://www.oxforddnb.com/view/article/45559.
20 Angel Ganivet, *Cartas finlandesas & Hombres del norte* (Madrid: Espasa-Calpe, S. A., 1940), 62: "*una es gimnasta, otra profesora de lenguas, otra escribiente de notario, otra profesora de masaje, otra cajera de un Banco, . . .*"
21 Hallsten, "Pääkohtia," 19–20; von Alfthan, *Sju årtionden*, 67–75; Hagner and Förstі, *Suffragettien sisaret*, 52–57, 66–71.
22 E.g., *Hemmet och Samhället* 3 (1893): 2; *Nutid* 2 (1898): 25.
23 E.g., von Alfthan, *Sju årtionden*, 183–201.
24 On *Suomen Naisyhdistys*, see Ilmi Hallsten, "Pääkohtia Suomen Naisyhdistyksen 50-vuotisesta toiminnasta," in *Puoli vuosisataa naisasiatyötä: Suomen Naisyhdistyksen 50-vuotisjuhlajulkaisu 1884–1934* (Helsinki: Otava, 1934), 15–45; Jallinoja, *Suomalaisen naisasialiikkeen*, 32–79, 99–104; Aura Korppi-Tommola, *Tahdolla ja tunteella tasa-arvoa: Naisjärjestöjen Keskusliitto 1911–2001* (Helsinki: Naisjärjestöjen Keskusliitto, 2001), 16–22, 27–34. On Unionen–Unioni, see Märta von Alfthan, *Sju årtionden med Unioni Naisasialiitto Suomessa r.y.– Unionen Kvinnosaksförbund i Finland r.f.* (Helsingfors: Unioni–Unionen, 1965), esp. 22–34, 78–88, 93–94; Minna Hagner and Teija Försti, *Suffragettien sisaret* (Helsinki: Unioni Naisasialiitto, 2006), 20–57; Ollila, *Jalo velvollisuus*, 44–45, 75–76.
25 Ganivet, *Cartas finlandesas*, 51–52.
26 Castrén & Snellman was originally established in 1888, Dittmar & Indrenius in 1899 (originally Granfelt & Indrenius), and Borenius & Kemppinen in 1911 (originally Palmén & Holma). E.g., Eero Relas, "Castrén & Snellman 100 vuotta kesäkuun 1 päivänä 1988," in *Castrén & Snellman 100 vuotta 1888–1988: Castrén & Snellman 100 år* (Helsinki: Castrén & Snellman, 1988), 9–34; Kullervo Kemppinen, "Tarinaa toimistomme vaiheista," in *Asianajotoimisto Borenius & Kemppinen 90 vuotta*, ed. Heidi Arvanne-Potrykus (Helsinki: Borenius & Kemppinen, 2001), 7–34; *Dittmar & Indrenius 110. Asianajotoimisto suomalaisen liike-elämän kumppanina* (Helsinki: Dittmar & Indrenius, 2009), 16–141.
27 Relas, "Castrén & Snellman," 3. See also Kemppinen, "Tarinaa," 24.
28 *Hufvudstadsbladet* (December 28, 1910): 1; *Hufvudstadsbladet* (August 30, 1910): 3.
29 *Aamulehti* (October 16, 1908): 4.
30 Mossman, *First Women Lawyers*, 132.
31 *Dittmar & Indrenius 110*, 16, 19.
32 Ibid. 37–39.
33 A. W. Westerlund ed., *Finlands jurister: Biografiska anteckningar* (Åbo: Åbo Tryckeri och Tidnings Aktiebolags Förlag, 1909), 227.
34 E.g., *Tammerfors Nyheter* (September 13, 1909): 2.
35 Mossman, *First Women Lawyers*, 132.
36 For example, in 1903 a "competent typist" who could take care of correspondence in Swedish, Finnish, and German and who was a competent shorthand writer with office experience advertised in *Hufvudstadsbladet* (January 1, 1903): 2. See also *Hufvudstadsbladet* (June 12, 1903): 1.
37 For example, *Hufvudstadsbladet* (April 30, 1908): 4; *Åbo Underrättelser* (March 27, 1910): 13.

38 *Dittmar & Indrenius 110*, 52.
39 Kvinnornas allmänna rösträttsmöte, mottagna adresser och telegram, November 7, 1904, accessed March 15, 2014, http://www.histdoc.net/varia/unioni4.html.
40 Photograph taken by Bernhard Åström, currently in Folkkultursarkivet and published in Arne Toftegaard Pedersen, *Urbana odysséer: Helsingfors, staden och 1910-talets finlandssvenska prosa* (Helsingfors: Svenska litteratursällskapet i Finland, 2007), 260. On Holmström, see also Yrjö Raevuori, *Suomen asianajotoiminnan vaiheita* (Helsinki: WSOY, 1968), 36, 40.
41 Marjaliisa Hentilä, "Mitä maksaa? Kaupan työn kehitys naisten matalapalkka-alaksi," in *"Työllä ei oo kukkaan rikastunna": Naisten töitä ja toimeentulokeinoja 1800—ja 1900-luvulla*, ed. Marjatta Rahikainen and Tarja Räisänen (Helsinki: SKS, 2001), 170–171.
42 *Hufvudstadsbladet* (October 31, 1909): 16.
43 Anna Åkesson, "Till tings," *Nutid* 17, no. 10 (1911): 317–321.
44 *Hufvudstadsbladet* (December 10, 1895): 2; *Borgå Nya Tidning* (December 11, 1895): 3; *Tammerfors* (December 12, 1895): 2.
45 *Wasa Tidning* (June 16, 1886): 3.
46 *Nya Pressen* (April 18, 1893): 2; *Wasa Tidning* (April 20, 1893): 2.
47 "Finsk Kvinnoförenings årsberättelse för 1893," in *Annual report of the Finnish Women's Society (Suomen Naisyhdistys —Finska Kvinnoföreningen)* (Helsingfors: Finska Kvinnoföreningen, 1897), 3: "*Kvinnor hafva för första gången inlemnat till senaten handlingar rörande revisionsmål.*"
48 Atle Wilskman, *Släktbok 1* (Helsingfors: Svenska litteratursällskapet i Finland, 1912–1916), 904–905.
49 *Flickskolan i Wiborg 1788–1937: Några anteckningar om nordens äldsta offentliga flickskola*, ed. Ingrid Borenius (Viborg: Flickskolan i Wiborg, 1937), 71, 75.
50 Ollila, *Jalo velvollisuus*, 44.
51 Ganivet, *Cartas finlandesas*, 62: "*La escribiente es hija de un magistrado; la lingüista, hija de un conde; la hija de un doctor o de un diputado está al frente de un despacho de vinos.*"
52 Tweedie, *Through Finland in Carts*, 163. See also Anka Ryall, "Europe's Northern Periphery and the Future of Women in the Travel Narratives of Ethel Tweedie," *NORA—Nordic Journal of Feminist and Gender Research* 17, no. 4 (2009): 279–281.
53 *Nutid* 2 (1896): 38: poem "Förr och Nu" (Then and Now) by the poet Hedvig von Schantz (1865–1942): "*Uti skolor, uti banker,/ På kontor, byråer sjukhus/ Se vi nu den unga kvinnan/ omsorgsfullt sitt arbet'sköta./ Själf kan hon sitt bröd förtjäna,/ ligger ej till last för släkten.*"
54 E.g., Enrolment records of the University of Helsinki 1853–1899, accessed March 15, 2014, http://www.helsinki.fi/ylioppilasmatrikkeli/1853–1899/henkilo.php?id=18613.
55 E.g., *Hufvudstadsbladet* (August 4, 1885): 1; *Fredrikshamns Tidning* (April 6, 1892): 2; *Fredrikshamns Tidning* (August 15, 1896): 3; *Hufvudstadsbladet* (February 6, 1894): 2; *Hufvudstadsbladet* (January 25, 1895): 2; *Fredrikshamns Tidning* (April 24, 1901): 3.
56 Wilskman, *Släktbok*, 904–905.
57 Karl Ferdinand Forsström, *Mietteitä 1) lainkäyntikielestämme ja 2) lainkäyntilainsäädäntömme parantamistoimista* (Mikkeli: Aleks. Kasurisen kirjapaino, 1896), 76.
58 Elli Hällström, "Naisylioppilaat 'De kvinnliga' 1893–1895," in *Muistikuvia III: Suomalaisia kulttuurimuistelmia*, ed. Eino E. Suolahti (Helsinki: Otava, 1956), 338.
59 *Hufvudstadsbladet* (November 16, 1896): 3.
60 Forsström, *Mietteitä*, 77–78.

61 Helena Westermark, "Kvinnorna och lagtolkningen," *Nutid* (December 1, 1896): 273–274.
62 E.g., *Hufvudstadsbladet* (November 13, 1896): 2; *Vasabladet* (December 10, 1896): 3; *Tammerfors Nyheter* (February 11, 1897): 3.
63 Kort redogörelse för Kejserliga Senatens Justitie-Departements utslag och domar för år 1897, *Tidskrift, utgifven af Juridiska Föreningen i Finland* [hereafter *JFT*], 34 (1898), Appendix.
64 E.g., *Östra Finland* (December 2, 1897): 2.
65 *Hufvudstadsbladet* (November 4, 1897): 3.
66 E.g., *Nutid* (January 1, 1897): 24; *Nutid* (February 1, 1897): 49.
67 "Dispensation for her sex," *Nutid* (December 1, 1897): 280–281.
68 Pihlajamäki, *Kansan ja esivallan välissä*, 136–137.
69 Ibid., 137.
70 E.g., Suomen pappissäädyn pöytäkirjat valtiopäiviltä v. 1897, III, Keskustelu 25.5.1897, esp. 1764–73; Borgareståndets protokoll vid landtdagen i Helsingfors år 1897, I, 30.1.1897, 23–25; Protokoll förda hos Finlands ridderskap och adel vid landtdagen år 1897, III, 31.5.1897, 1675–77; Suomen talonpoikaissäädyn keskustelupöytäkirjat 1897 vuoden valtiopäivillä, II, 4.5.1897, 835–836, 29.5.1897, 1575–77; Finsk Kvinnoförenings årsberättelse för år 1897, 14.
71 Pihlajamäki, *Kansan ja esivallan välissä*, 137–138.
72 Keisarillisen Majesteetin Armollinen asetus oikeudenkäymiskaaren 15 luvun 2 §:n muuttamiseksi toisin kuuluvaksi 23.11.1898, *Suomen suuriruhtinaskunnan asetus-kokoelma* 52 (1898), 1–2; Raevuori, *Suomen asianajotoiminnan vaiheita*, 18.
73 E.g., *Hufvudstadsbladet* (October 29, 1909): 8.
74 *Hufvudstadsbladet* (November 4, 1897): 5.
75 Enrolment records of the University of Helsinki 1853–1899, accessed March 15, 2014, http://www.helsinki.fi/ylioppilasmatrikkeli/1853–1899/henkilo.php?id=18621.
76 Kort redogörelse för Kejserliga Senatens Justitie-Departements utslag och domar för år 1898, *JFT* 35 (1899), Appendix: 118a–119a.
77 Cf, Konttinen, *Perinteisestä moderniin*, 170–171.
78 Ibid., 204–216.
79 Rabbe Axel Wrede, *Finlands gällande civilprocessrätt, I* (Helsingfors: G. W. Edlund, 1905), 199: "*Detta framgår af uttrycket 'man' i det åberopade lagrummet. På senare tid torde några domstolar hafva tillåtit kvinnor att uppträda såsom fullmäktige. Men att en sådan praxis ej är allmän synes af ett rättsfall—.*"
80 On Wrede's conservatism, see Tore Modéen, "Wrede, Rabbe Axel," in *Suomen kansallisbiografia* 10 (Helsinki: SKS, 2007), 699.
81 E.g., Aino Ottelin, *Konkordiaförbundet* (Söderström & C:o Förlagsaktiebolag: Helsingfors, 1924), 23, 32; *Östra Finland* (March 11, 1895): 3; *Nya Pressen* (March 11, 1895): 3; Kvinnornas allmänna rösträttsmöte, mottagna adresser och telegram, November 7, 1904, accessed March 15, 2014, http://www.histdoc.net/varia/uniooni4.html.
82 Von Alfthan, *Sju årtionden*, 136.
83 Enrolment records of the University of Helsinki 1892–1901, accessed March 15, 2014, http://www.helsinki.fi/keskusarkisto/matrikkelit/matrikkelit_1892_1901.htm.
84 Klinge et al., *Helsingfors Universitet 1640–1990*, vol. 2, 777.
85 Ibid., 648, 775.
86 E.g., *Wuoksi* (September 24, 1892): 2.
87 E.g., Suomen Naisyhdistyksen vuosikertomus v. 1905 [Annual report of the FWS, 1905], 8; Ottelin, *Konkordiaförbundet*, 79; Winter-Mäkinen, *Naisjuristien 1. vuosisata*, 25–26.

88 Agnes Lundell to Emmy Stenbäck (later Hultman), Nokkala, June 14, 1907, Library of Åbo Academy, manuscript department: family Hultman collection, 34 (Vån. II2: B: 4).
89 J. D., "En föregångskvinna: Advokaten Agnes Lundell fyllde den 13 Juli 50 år," *Astra* 10, no. 13–14 (1928): 309; Winter-Mäkinen, *Naisjuristien 1. vuosisata*, 27–29.
90 Irma Sulkunen, "Suomi naisten äänioikeuden edelläkävijänä," in *Naiset eduskunnassa: Suomen eduskunta 100 vuotta* 4, ed. Irma Sulkunen, Maria Lähteenmäki, and Aura Korppi-Tommola (Helsinki: Edita, 2006), 10–11, 14–21.
91 Discussion in Parliament on May 29, 1907, Parliamentary Session [Valtiopäivät] of 1907, Records [Pöytäkirjat] 1, 29.5.1907, 106–125; Parliamentary Session of 1907, Appendices III, Law proposals and petitions sent to the Legal Affairs Committee [Lakivaliokuntaan lähetetyt eduskuntaesitys- ja anomusehdotukset] nos. 11–12, 57–70; Raevuori, *Suomen asianajotoiminnan vaiheita*, 20.
92 Second Parliamentary Session of 1909, Appendices I–V, III, Law proposals and petitions sent to the Legal Affairs Committee, nos. 26–27 (Proposal no. 1 and petition 46), 115–119; Second Parliamentary Session of 1909, Appendices I–V, III Law proposals and petitions sent to the Legal Affairs Committee, nos. 15–16 (Proposal no. 11 and petition 184), 35–39.
93 J. D., "En föregångskvinna," 309.
94 E.g., *Nya Pressen* (September 27, 1909): 5; *Hufvudstadsbladet* (October 29, 1909): 8.
95 E.g., *Måndagen* (November 1, 1909): 3; *Måndagen* (November 8, 1909): 3; *Måndagen* (November, 1909): 3; *Måndagen* (November 22, 1909): 3; *Aamulehti* (January 23, 1910): 7–8; *Nya Pressen* (October 29, 1909): 6; *Nya Pressen* (December 3, 1909): 5; *Nya Pressen* (January 20, 1910): 4; *Nya Pressen* (May 27, 1910): 6.
96 E.g., *Nordisk damtidning* (*Oihonna*) 1910: 1.
97 *Nutid* (November 11, 1909): 440–441.
98 J[ohannes] G[ummerus], "Kvinnornas anmarch," *Framtid* 17 (1910): 5.
99 E.g., *Uusi Aura* (June 12, 1910): 7; *Uusi Aura* (August 18, 1910): 6; *Naisten ääni* 8, no. 27 (1913): 368.
100 E.g., *Suomalainen Kansa* (November 3, 1910): 2; *Työmies* (December 1, 1910): 7.
101 *Österbottningen* (May 10, 1910): 2; *Österbottningen* (August 30, 1910): 2.
102 E.g., *Suomalainen Kansa* (February 15, 1910): 4; *Suomalainen Kansa* (November 3, 1910): 2; *Österbottningen* (May 10, 1910): 2.
103 E.g., *Uusimaa* (April 25, 1910): 3.
104 *Hufvudstadsbladet* (May 7, 1910): 5.
105 *Naisten ääni* 12 (1911): 141.
106 Kort redogörelse för Kejserliga Senatens Justitie-Departements utslag och domar för år 1910, *JFT* 47 (1911), Appendix: 191a.
107 *Herättäjä* (April 8, 1910): 3.
108 *Tammerfors Nyheter* (October 3, 1910): 2.
109 Ibid., 2–3.
110 Ibid., 3.
111 Ibid., 3.
112 Ibid., 3.
113 "[T]y hon visade som fröken Strömbergs rättegångsbiträde att hon är bättre jurist än mången som går i byxor," *Arbetet* (October 7, 1910): 1.
114 As shown, e.g., by the program of the Socialists in Forssa in 1903, accessed May 3, 2016, http://fi.wikisource.org/wiki/Forssan_ohjelma; and by the discussion in Parliament in 1907 when the first representatives of the people could discuss the matter, Parliamentary Session of 1907, Records 1, 29.5.1907, 106–125. See also Pihlajamäki, *Kansan ja esivallan välissä*, 121, 137–139.

115 Jukka Siro, *Tuomiovalta kansalle: Vallankumousoikeudet sisällissodassa vuonna 1918* (Helsinki: Suomalainen Lakimiesyhdistys, 2010), 119–120.
116 E.g., Koskinen, "Laki kirjoittamattoman lain kumoamisesta," 49–60; Mandi Hannula, "Naiset ja virat," in *Puoli vuosisataa naisasiatyötä: Suomalaisen Naisyhdistyksen 50-vuotisjuhlajulkaisu 1884–1934* (Helsinki: Suomalainen Naisyhdistys, 1934), 101–106.
117 E.g., Winter-Mäkinen, *Naisjuristien 1. vuosisata*, 31; *Uusmaalainen* (October 24, 1910): 2.
118 J. D., "En föregångskvinna," 308–309; Winter-Mäkinen, *Naisjuristien 1. vuosisata*, 31.
119 *Naisten ääni* 12 (1911): 141–142.
120 E.g., *Naisten ääni* 17 (1911): 1; *Nutid* 7 (1911): 238; *Työläisnainen* 48–49 (1912): 1.
121 *Naisten ääni* 12 (1911): 141–142; *Koti ja yhteiskunta* 12 (1911): 121.
122 *Naisten ääni* 27 (1913): 1.
123 E.g., Winter-Mäkinen, *Naisjuristien 1. vuosisata*, 31–33; Pihlajamäki, *Kansan ja esivallan välissä*, 124–125.
124 *Hufvudstadsbladet* (May 7, 1910): 5.
125 Kleman, "Vår kvinnliga advokatfirma," 148.
126 *Naisten ääni* (1915), juhlajulkaisu 9.12.1915: unpag.
127 Westermark, "Kvinnorna," 274.
128 G[ummerus], "Kvinnornas anmarch," 6: "*—inga lagar dock förmå hindra dem att slutligen erövra.*"
129 Sulkunen, "Suomi," 74–77.
130 Dübeck, "Lærde damer," 25–29.
131 Laki Oikeudenkäymiskaaren 15 luvun 2, 3 ja 9 §:n muuttamisesta 31.12.1917, *Suomen asetuskokoelma* 119/1917, 8; Raevuori, *Suomen asianajotoiminnan vaiheita*, 20–23.
132 33 §, 36 §, Avioliittolaki, 13.6.1926, *Suomen asetuskokoelma* 234/1929, 745–746.
133 Ethel Brilliana Tweedie, *Women the World Over: A Sketch Both Light and Gay, Perchance Both Dull and Stupid* (London: Hutchinson and Co, 1914), quoted in: Ryall, "Europe's Northern Periphery," 280.
134 E.g., Robert Hermanson, *Anteckningar enligt Professor R. F. Hermansons föreläsningar öfver inhemsk förvaltningsrätt med tillstånd av föreläsaren utgifna av Hj. Nyqvist* (Helsingfors: Victor Pettersson & C:os tryckeri-aktiebolag, 1898), 142; Konttinen, *Perinteisestä moderniin*, 207–215; Hagner and Försti, *Suffragettien sisaret*, 115–121.

Part III

Transnational and International Intersections

13 Tracking Feminist Interventions in International Law Issues at the League of Nations

From the Nationality of Married Women to Legal Equality in the Family, 1919–1970

Catherine Jacques

Introduction

Feminism did not develop in isolation at either the national or the international level. On the contrary, at both levels, its action stems from the common oppression of women, whatever their nationality. Through numerous international congresses since the later nineteenth century, feminism has fostered contacts and exchanges between women's organizations of each country, triggering transnational bonds and interpersonal exchanges. By organizing itself around a representative or umbrella system within a top organization made of national delegates, international feminism not only increased its visibility, but also gained the means to become a valid negotiator, listened to by the League of Nations, the International Labor Organization (ILO), the International Labor Council (ILC), and the United Nations (UN).

By the end of the nineteenth century, two international organizations stood out from a strict feminist point of view: the International Council of Women (ICW, 1888) and the International Woman Suffrage Alliance (IWSA), which split from the former in Berlin in 1904. Historically, the ICW, the IWSA, and some years later, the Women's International League for Peace and Freedom (WILPF, 1915) were considered the three most important women's organizations due to the number of members, the length of time they had been in existence, and their lobbying of international bodies.[1] If their views on particular issues did not always converge, they nevertheless represented a "moderate" feminism. The 1920s saw the debut of international associations that opted for a more radical form of feminism, certainly in terms of rights equality. However, if the creation of the League strengthened international perspectives for feminism, the project of a common labor policy orchestrated by the ILO and the ILC divided them.[2] This policy notably triggered the creation of the Open Door Council (1926, afterwards, the

Open Door International for the Economic Emancipation of the Woman Worker [ODI], close to Equal Rights International), which objected to the increasingly stronger alignment of the social policy of many European countries with that of the ILO. From this time on, a clear split appeared among feminist ranks between what can be called a moderate wing, which put forward a "maternal" feminism, and a more radical form of feminism, which supported a strict legal equality between men and women.

One of the major requests from international feminism was the reform of the *Code civil*, which was prevalent in many European Countries. As historian Karen Offen mentioned, "Importantly for the future of Europe, the French Civil Code, with its punitive marriage rules, turned out to be anything but a local affair; it became nearly 'universal.'. . . The Napoleonic Code took root not only in Belgium, the Netherlands, a number of German princely states west of the Rhine, in some Italian states, in Spain and Portugal, and in Romania, but also in Egypt, the eventual Gulf States, and in the Latin American republics."[3] But in the United Kingdom, common law prevailed.[4] The patriarchal foundation of these civil codes permeated family law and actually legalized the subordination of married women (mostly Art. 213 but also Art. 212 to 226 in the French Code). Considered by many to be the focal point of the subjugation of women, the legal structure of the family through marriage, which was considered the foundation of social organization in most countries, consequently lay at the heart of all debates for sex equality. Indeed, to some, attacking family law appeared "revolutionary."[5]

Concerning women, two issues dominated the years after the end of the First World War: political equality and the nationality of married women. While the political implications of this latter issue were obvious (because civic rights and citizenship rights were directly linked to nationality), this also had implications for family law, because according to the *Code civil* (Art. 19),[6] a woman marrying a foreigner automatically forfeited her nationality to take on the nationality of her husband.

The feminists in countries that followed the *Code civil* and those managed by common law therefore found themselves in a common fight. Indeed, in 1914, the British Nationality and Status of Aliens Act stated that "the wife of a British subject shall be deemed to be a British subject, and the wife of an alien, shall be deemed to be an alien."[7] After the World Wars, this rule continued to provoke concrete and seemingly insoluble problems for wives.[8] Such problems could only be resolved by international agreements: international feminists used the nationality issue as a Trojan horse to insist on far-reaching changes in the legal status of married women.

This chapter presents the objectives, successes, and failures of international feminism in this arena and discusses its strategies as well as the internal divisions that arose to hamper its actions. From a discussion regarding the nationality of married women, feminists progressively broadened the debate to encompass the global legal status of women, which invoked the concept of complete legal equality between the sexes. This shift did not happen without difficulty, even within the feminist organizations. This chapter follows a chronological framework and shows that feminists, who initially addressed the issue of the nationality of married women, actually targeted a complete restitution of the civil capacity of these women. This whole process happened in the context of discussions on the status of women and the project of the codification of international law within the League and the ILO, which, still unresolved, were again called to the attention of the United Nations after 1945. If these issues are of a rare complexity, it is because they touched both the "private" and "public" spheres that had serious implications at both the national and international levels, as they threatened men's vested interests in retaining dominance. Studying these issues sheds light on the extraordinary capacity and tenacity of the feminist movement and the cooperation of its leaders across national boundaries in organizing strategies that eventually paid off with the attainment of international mandates for complete legal equality between men and women.

Explained here are the targets, successes, and failures of international feminism in this endeavor as well as the strategies utilized and the internal divisions that often hindered them. This research draws on a handful of studies dealing with the issue of the nationality of married women in various countries: included among them are the works of Jean-Yves Le Naour[9] and Patrick Weil of France,[10] Denis Scuto of Luxemburg,[11] Candice Lewis Bredbenner for the United States,[12] and Page Baldwin for the British Empire.[13] In addition to these, it looks at pioneering works on feminist international lobbies by historians such as Carol Miller and Karen Offen, as well as the research of Leila Rupp about sociability in the international feminist movement and the recent publication by Ellen Carol Dubois on "Internationalizing Married Women's Nationality: The Hague Campaign of 1930."[14] In contrast to previous scholarship, this chapter will examine the action of continental European feminists, such as the French attorneys Maria Vérone and Marie-Hélène Lefaucheux, the Danish activist Bodil Begtrup, and the Belgian attorneys Georgette Ciselet, alongside their American equivalents, such as feminist Alice Paul. Continental feminists were primarily concerned with the reform of civil codes and did not always agree with the Americans on definitions and priorities. In this great battle for equality, the internal infighting and dissidence provides many lessons for comprehending the complexity of the struggle for women's rights. This struggle was shaped not only by geography and legal and political cultures, but also by the personal experience of its main actors. My approach, partially tackled in some of my previously published research, is here broadened and deepened, both chronologically and with respect to the theme itself.[15]

This chapter also strives to go beyond an analysis limited strictly to the national or international dimensions and instead attempts to demonstrate their interconnectedness. Women's rights moved forward thanks to persistent lobbying at both the international and national levels. And most of all,

I wish to underscore how much these successes were due to a mere handful of women and their convictions, personal experiences, and affinities.

The primary sources used here are primarily from the archives of the ICW and the Open Door International (ODI), managed by the Archive Center for Women's History (CARHIF) in Brussels. These sources will need to be complemented by research in the archives of the other international feminist organizations and at the League of Nations library in Geneva as well as at the United Nations. Papers left by influential feminists, such as the French Maria Vérone, Marie-Hélène Lefaucheux, Sophie Vinaver-Grinberg,[16] and Marguerite Thibert,[17] the Danish Bodil Begtrup, and the Belgian Georgette Ciselet and the Swiss Emilie Gourd (who wrote for *Le Mouvement féministe*), to cite just a few, will undoubtedly provide additional useful details. At this stage, this chapter must therefore be read as an invitation for additional research.

The Nationality of Married Women: A Complex and Multifaceted Challenge

By favoring the nationality of the husband over that of the wife, the hegemonic French *Code civil* (Art. 12 and Art. 19), in a clear regression compared to the French legislation of the *ancien régime*,[18] imposed the thoroughly patriarchal vision of Napoleon I, symbolized by marital authority of the husband as a means of securing the "unity" of the family. The inferiority of the married woman was padlocked in place by the code: once married, a woman was not considered a full individual, was unable to act legally, and was a subordinate member of a family. Her legal incapacity legitimized her denial of her political rights.

The loss of a wife's own nationality not only implied the subordination of the wife to her husband, but could also lead to tragic consequences such as the loss of access to public sector jobs (reserved for nationals). During World War I, women from allied countries, having become Austrian or German through marriage, were treated as enemies in their own countries and were sometimes expelled or jailed. The patriotic undercurrent that prevailed after 1914 further heightened the allegiance of a wife to her nationality of birth. Gaining dual nationality for a couple appeared, therefore, to be a crucial battle for feminists; by confirming the legal individuality of the woman, a dent could be made in the civil code, allowing the question of women's subrogation in the family to rise to the surface. Indeed, far from solving all issues, such a step could lead to others. This step was heavily criticized by adversaries to the code's reform. What happened to a married woman if her husband became naturalized, even if she did not submit a request for citizenship? What happened to couples suddenly faced with changes in nationalities due to changes in borders after a war? How was the dissolution of a marriage to be dealt with? Which national legislation should apply? More importantly, what happened to the nationality of children who were supposed to take the nationality of their father? What should be done if the country of one of the spouses did not recognize the right to divorce? These multiple questions made the issue of a married woman's nationality a rather complex one because of its links with private and public law. But it was through this issue and because of its complexity that after 1919, feminists renewed their attacks against women's subordination in the law.

This was a tactical choice: after World War I, the problems associated with the nationality question for married women had become acute in many countries, and, thus, the context for action was favorable. Following Soviet Russia in 1918, Belgium was among the first to solve this complex issue in 1922 by leaving to the married woman the choice to keep her nationality of birth based on a single declaration. France made up its mind only in 1927,[19] and the Grand Duchy of Luxembourg finally acted in 1934. However, the issue was known everywhere and even found completely unexpected allies, such as in France where there was a strong natalist lobby (this nationalist movement would promote a policy to stimulate large families in response to a declining birth rate in France). The natalist lobby in France had been active since 1896, but after the war, many of its leaders were called into government service.[20] Lamenting that tens of thousands of French women had lost their nationality by marriage, the lobby requested that women could recover it to "keep young French people for France."[21]

The feminists active at the League of Nations seemed convinced that a comprehensive and universal legal code could be enacted through the framework of the League itself. Indeed, the initial project for the codification of international law, undertaken by the League in the late 1920s, appeared to them as offering a formidable opportunity, one that could either result in establishing equal rights for women and men or else forever freezing married women in a legally and politically inferior status.[22]

The 1930 Conference for the Codification of International Law in The Hague

On March 13, 1930, the first conference of the League of Nations for the codification of international law opened in The Hague. The ultimate (but utopian) objective of the League was to design a legal code that would apply to, or set guidelines for, every country in the world. The nationality question was one of three points on the agenda, as were "territorial waters and the responsibility of States for damage done in their territory to the person or property of foreigners."[23]

The first concern of the two largest international women's organizations, the ICW and the IAWSEC (formerly IWSA), was to raise public awareness of the necessity of guaranteeing to women equal rights in terms of nationality.[24] Initially, these organizations distributed a brochure written under the direction of Scottish feminist and barrister Chrystal Macmillan[25] for the International Federation of University Women (IFUW) on the occasion of its Fifth Congress in Geneva in mid-August 1929. It was particularly important to find allies within the official delegations sent by the governments to the Codification conference at The Hague; the two organizations leaned on their national affiliates to obtain from their governments the nomination to these national delegations of "competent and qualified women" favorable to feminist views.[26] In some countries, this first step had direct effects: in Belgium, the Minister for Foreign Affairs, the Liberal Paul Hymans, nominated among its delegates the young attorney Marcelle Renson, a convinced feminist and active member of the IFUW, the Groupement belge de la porte ouverte (GBPO), the ODI, and the IAWSEC. This nomination was greeted enthusiastically by both Belgian and foreign feminists.[27] Similarly Marie-Elisabeth Lüders was appointed as a government delegate for Germany.[28] Lüders earned a doctorate in economics and was granted an honorary law degree. An important feminist, she was a member of the German women's movement (Bund Deutscher Frauenvereine [BDF] and the Deutsche Akademikerinnenbund) and held seats in the Weimar National Assembly and later the Reichstag.

The second concern was to ensure the presence and visibility of feminists at the international codification conference. On March 14, 1930, the day after the opening of the International Codification Conference at The Hague, the ICW and IAWSEC arranged their own conference in parallel with the official sessions, calling it the Joint Demonstration on the Nationality of Married Women. This event brought together prominent personalities, including lawyers such as the Ciselet, a friend of Marcelle Renson, Macmillan, and Vérone, as well as the Englishwomen Ellen Wilkinson[29] and Winifred Cullis,[30] the American Maud Wood Park,[31] and others.[32] At that moment, the target was, *grosso modo*, to obtain "that the right of the woman to keep her nationality or to change it . . . should not be lost or restricted, either due to her sex, [or] to her marriage and that the nationality of a married woman cannot be changed without her consent [. . .], except under the same conditions affecting the nationality of the man."[33]

Despite these efforts to intervene, the outcome of the conference at The Hague was deeply disappointing to the feminists: the resulting The Hague Convention on Nationality maintained that the nationality of the married woman must be contingent on her husband's nationality (Articles 8 to 11). The only minor concession was a recommendation ("wish VI") that Marcelle Renson managed to insert in an appendix, which encouraged the member states to introduce into their legislation the principle of equality between the sexes in terms of nationality or, as the case may be, to guarantee that the nationality of a woman could not be changed without her consent. "I think," wrote Chrystal Macmillan to the members of the Commission on the Nationality of Married Women in the IAWSEC,[34] "we may congratulate ourselves that, if we did not succeed in having our policy included in the Convention, we made the conference realize that this is a live issue."[35]

But others, clearly more radical and grouped around Equal Rights International (ERI) and the Inter-American Commission of Women (IACW), thought that the resulting The Hague Convention on Nationality had thumbed its nose at the right for equality between the sexes and that feminists must prevent its ratification by the member states.[36] For these two organizations, the nationality of the married woman clearly represented a critical opening to a "World Code." That was the reason why their spokesperson, the veteran American suffragette and advocate for an Equal Rights Treaty, Alice Paul, thought it essential to make the League of Nations understand that women from the entire world were determined to oppose any codification that included sex discrimination.[37]

Within the League, the radical feminists found a heavyweight ally in Henni Forchhammer, a vice-president of the ICW who was also an official delegate of Denmark to the League. On October 3, 1930 she spoke to the General Assembly of the League, "not as a Danish delegate but in my personal capacity as a woman," to express the dissatisfaction of feminists: "The women's organizations [. . .] which during many years have demanded full equality between the sexes in this respect, are not satisfied with the nationality clauses of The Hague Convention, which are based on this principle of equality." After Forchhammer's speech, the assembly adopted the resolution of the Cuban delegate, Dr. Orestes Ferrarara, who had been influenced by the feminist leaders from the IACW, to request that the articles linked to the nationality of the married woman be submitted to a new examination. Consideration of the broader question of codification would be deferred to the next Assembly.[38]

The International Committee for Action on the Nationality of Married Women

After this first heated exchange, the ICW and the IAWSEC took back the initiative from the radicals and formed a targeted committee, the International Committee for Action on the Nationality of Married Women, chaired by Chrystal Macmillan and responsible for exercising pressure on the League to follow up the recommendation adopted during the last Assembly.[39] Alongside Macmillan we find Maria Vérone (France) for the ICW, Margery Corbett Ashby (England) for the IAWSEC, Madeleine A. Doty (United States) and Dorothy Evans (England) for the WILPF, and Doris Stevens (United States) for IACW. In this next phase of lobbying, American radicals Alice Paul and Margaret Whittemore, representing the ERI and IACW, worked concurrently to exercise influence. They pressured the Council of the League, which would meet from January 19 to 24, 1931, to adopt two resolutions: one questioning The Hague Convention and the other decreeing the establishment of a female consultative committee. When the Council opened, this objective seemed out of sight, as out of its fourteen members, only three were in favor. Undaunted, on January 22, 1931, Margaret Whittemore lobbied each member and received the backing of Persia and Japan, which was still insufficient for unanimity. The feminist front was faced with an urgent situation. All feminist organizations of the countries represented in Geneva contacted the delegates of their governments asking for their support of two resolutions, which were put forward by José Matos, the delegate of Guatemala. On January 24, the last day of the session, the Council adopted these resolutions unanimously. The efforts of the feminists were suddenly crowned with success: The Hague Convention on the issue of the nationality of the married woman would be re-examined, and a Women's Consultative Committee on Nationality, ultimately made up of delegates chosen from eight feminist organizations, would be formed to provide an expert opinion to the League.[40]

The creation of this Women's Consultative Committee was greeted with great enthusiasm because it meant, for the feminist movement, the first official recognition of women's input by the League of Nations.[41] Until then, the charter of the League recognized only the representatives of the member states as active members, and since no framework was foreseen for cooperation with NGOs,[42] contacts necessarily took place through informal means. However, we must not overestimate the influence of this committee, which was purely consultative. It was never part of the administration of the League, and its role was limited to providing reports to the secretary general, which would be included in an appendix of his report to the Assembly.[43]

Even so, the Women's Consultative Committee had enormous symbolic significance: the League had officially recognized the feminist lobby and was speaking directly to it. Therefore, the Consultative Committee became the privileged channel to transmit feminist perspectives on the issues in question. For this very reason, it rapidly became a site for power struggles, which in the future would make it impossible to paper over the ideological, strategic, and tactical tensions between the leaders of the different international feminist organizations. These differences would lead to the paralysis of feminist lobbying so that the gains anticipated in the wake of the committee's creation were compromised.

Maria Vérone, representing the ICW, was designated to chair the preparatory committee of the Women's Consultative Committee, but it took nearly six months for the different organizations invited by the League to come to agreement.[44] The letters exchanged between several of the principals reveal the mistrust that reigned among these organizations, each of which jealously affirmed its priorities. Meanwhile, the existing network of women's international organizations known as the Liaison Committee for the Women's International Organizations (1931), which was designed to optimize and channel women's lobbying efforts at the League, did not appreciate the advent of this new Committee.[45] This competition among feminist organizations and networks created real confusion, which was far from beneficial. In the end, eight of the nine organizations approached by the League were represented on the Women's Consultative Committee:[46] the ICW, IAWSEC, the WILPF, the IACW, the All-Asian Women's Conference, the World Union of Women for International Concord (l'Union mondiale des femmes pour la concorde internationale), ERI, and the IFUW.[47] Only the World Young Women's Christian Association (World YWCA) declined to participate.

After lengthy talks, the Women's Consultative Committee sent its first report to the secretary general of the League on July 16, 1931. This report reminded the League of the feminist opposition to The Hague Convention on Nationality because it created discrimination between men and women. This report supported the egalitarian proposition of the Chilean delegate and asked the League's Assembly to submit a new convention for ratification by the governments, based on the principle of equality of the sexes.[48] In the report, the feminists' fear of seeing women's inferiority sanctioned through international codification was palpable. Indeed, the struggle for the nationality of the married woman had come to stand for much more. On the one hand, there was the affirmation of sexual equality: "[T]he inclusion in The Hague Convention of articles giving an inferior position to women, is a matter of the utmost gravity because of the psychological effect of the adoption of such a Convention upon the status of women all over the world."[49] On the other hand, there was the prevention of an international agreement that acknowledges "the theory of women's subordination" and hence would refuse to "consider [. . .] woman as a citizen."[50] As this convention on nationality was understood as the first step toward an international code, it must absolutely "sanction without ambiguity the equality between man and woman."[51] The stakes thus transcended the particular issue of the nationality of the married woman to appeal to the "principle of justice on which alone an enduring system of law can be built."

On September 26, 1931, the General Assembly of the League approved the accompanying resolution; all the reports[52] were then distributed to each government for consideration at the next assembly.[53] In other words, the issue of the nationality of the married woman would be re-examined. But by 1932, the unified feminist front would be shattered, and tensions within the Women's Consultative Committee were such that it sent two reports to the Secretary General, Sir Eric Drummond;[54] the first was signed by the ICW, the IAWSEC, the IFUW, and World Union of Women for International Concord[55] and the second by the four other organizations. Their differences revolved around one point.

The Consultative Committee was nearly unanimous in its request regarding sex equality in nationality laws, but the radicals (ERI, IACW, WILPF, All-Asian Women's Conference) refused to compromise on their interpretation of the term "equality" as meaning identical laws for men and women in all fields. In reality, this position was defended primarily by Alice Paul, whose aim was to have the League adopt the Equal Rights Treaty, written by her some years before and already presented to the Conference of the American States.[56]

It was this attempt to expand the application of equality between the sexes that divided the Consultative Committee. For ERI and the IACW, represented by Alice Paul, the question of the nationality of married woman should be thought of as just one part of a much more fundamental issue. Therefore, the struggle over the nationality of married women became a pivot point in a global fight for equality: it opened the door for an international struggle for equal rights more generally. These two ostensibly separate topics had become inextricably intertwined.[57]

The partisans of a "maternalist feminism," revolving around the ICW and the IAWSEC, continued to favor specific legal protection for women at work—and, therefore, a differentiated treatment of the sexes in fields linked to employment; the others, represented by the ERI, the IACW, and the ODI, denounced such sex-specific protection as the nexus of discrimination between the sexes.[58] If the radical understanding of the term "equality" should prevail, it would apply to all fields, and would eliminate maternity protection for working women. This would create, *ipso facto*, an unbridgeable division between feminists, and neither the ICW nor the IAWSEC wanted to be dragged down this path. Their leaders greatly distrusted the supporters of Alice Paul's position. The Swiss suffragist Emilie Gourd, who represented the IAWSEC in Geneva, supervised Alice Paul as she sent two reports to the secretary general of the League "to be absolutely sure that there would be no last minute maneuvers." Gourd lamented privately to Louise van Eeghen: "It is awful to work in such a way, without mutual trust."[59] The work of consolidating the positions of multiple organizations (e.g., ICW, IAWSEC, IFUW and l'Union des femmes pour la Concorde) was achieved by Czech mediator Františka Plamínková (member of the ICW, ODI, and IAWSEC).[60] While these groups developed unanimity around the principle of equality in nationality law, a second group (composed of the ERI, IACW, WILPF, and the All-Asian Women's Conference) held out for legal equality across the board in all fields. In this sense, they adopted the position of Alice Paul who advocated that the League adopt an equal rights treaty.[61] Thus the feminists clashed on the question of enlarging the scope of sex equality. The European feminists, who advocated a social and maternalist feminism, rallied around the ICW and IAWSEC. The ERI allied with the American leadership within the IACW. Members of the ODI were divided between the two camps.[62] The rupture within the Advisory Committee worsened to the point that Plamínková (on behalf of the IAWSEC) demanded its dissolution in July 1932. She was opposed by the ICW, which opted for a tactic of "presence" cognizant of the need to defend women's interests within the League and sometimes against the position promoted by other women's associations.[63]

Despite its previous resolutions, on October 12, 1932, the Assembly of the League voted to ignore the feminist protest and encourage its member states to ratify The Hague Convention on Nationality "as is," while also asking the same states to amend their own national legislation by taking into account the desiderata of women's organizations. The Assembly resolutely held to the terms of the Hague document; for the feminists, this defeat was hard to swallow, but it did reconcile the majority of the organizations in the Consultative Committee together—at least for the time being.[64]

In January 1933, the council of the League decided to reconsider the Assembly's resolution of October 12, 1932.[65] Subsequent to this, on June 10 and 11, 1933, the Women's Consultative Committee (now representing only five organizations, ICW, ERI, IACW, WILPF, and the All-Asian Women's Conference), decided to renew its demand to halt the ratification of The Hague Nationality Convention and to step up its campaign "for an international agreement on equality."[66] But by May 1931, the IAWSEC and the IFUW left the committee of experts. They opposed the October resolution and believed that the fight must continue within individual national governments. They thus demonstrated their disapproval of Committee strategy and again demanded its dissolution.[67] By contrast, Vérone, in the name of the ICW, insisted that the IAWSEC's strategy was dangerous and disadvantageous. The committee had official recognition by the League, and scuttling the committee meant that the "Americans and their friends" would triumph, "while we 'dissidents,' if we stay united, could have a beneficial [*heureuse*] influence at the League."[68] The increased emphasis on this second point signaled a shift in attitude of the feminist lobby; it had become more committed to changing the overall legal status of women than to guaranteeing the nationality of the married woman. This shift actually cemented the victory of Alice Paul's faction, because for her, the topic of married women's nationality was only one point in the global struggle for equality between men and women. Paul further advocated that the feminist movement should actually negotiate with the League of Nations to obtain a treaty that would grant absolute equal rights between men and women in law.

From the Nationality of the Married Woman to the Status of Woman

Through obstinate lobbying work, orchestrated by Alice Paul's group, which was joined cautiously by the ICW, the Consultative Committee managed to see to the introduction of a resolution in 1933 by the Chilean delegate.[69] This resolution was adopted by the League Assembly in September 1934. It stipulated that the League of Nations should study not only the nationality of the married woman but also the status of women as a whole. This particular resolution was based on the Montevideo Convention on the Nationality of Woman (the Equal Nationality Treaty), which had been signed by nineteen South American republics in December 1933[70] and had been coupled with the Equal Rights Treaty, signed by Cuba, Ecuador, Paraguay, and Uruguay.[71] Playing on the confusion that reigned between these two treaties, feminists from the Inter-American Commission of Women exercised pressure on the League in order to have the same principles as "the needed wedge and the standard—for a full-fledged inquiry into the legal status of women by the League of Nations."[72]

The ICW, which had rallied behind only part of the proposal by Paul's group, still tried to control the work of the Consultative Committee and to limit Paul's impact, but it was clear that the issue of nationality was becoming intertwined with that of women's status in many people's minds. The League even seemed to accept this logic by considering that the nationality of the married woman could not be treated in isolation and that the whole legal status of women in society must be addressed. During 1934, the Americans of the IACW managed to convince ten Latin American states (Argentina, Bolivia, Cuba, the Dominican Republic, Haiti, Honduras, Mexico, Panama, Peru, and Uruguay) to call the attention of the League to their Equal Rights Treaty.[73] After many moves by Paul, in September 1935, the two questions would appear on the agenda of the first commission that treated legal questions at the sixteenth assembly of the League.[74]

The tenacious lobby irritated Princess Gabrielle Radziwill, feminist sympathizer and member of the League Secretariat who was responsible for relations with NGOs, who believed that demanding too much would result in no gains. Nevertheless, Radziwill solicited the intervention of the IAWSEC, and this resulted in the League Committee's rejection of the proposal to consider women's legal status as a whole. Ultimately, she counseled that only narrowly focused proposals were likely to be considered.[75] The broadening of the question actually made it more difficult for the feminist organizations to maintain a common platform.

Their differences came to the fore in January 1935 when the Assembly of the League finally authorized the diffusion of the new women's organizations' reports on the issue of the status of married women and nationality.[76] These reports revealed to all the divergences between the feminist associations. One of the divisions occurred on the question of protectionist labor policies favored by the ILO. The ODI (est. 1929) promoted gender equality in the workplace. An ODI report, submitted to the League during the summer of 1935, offered a brief in defense of absolute equality between men and women in terms of access to jobs, wages, and protection,[77] along with a violent denunciation of the protection of pregnant working women (including maternity leave) that had introduced differentiated protection based on gender among workers. Their attacks were directed at the Bern Convention (1906), the Convention of Washington (1919) on night work and maternity, and the Convention of Geneva (1921) on lead (*blanc de céruse*).[78] This incursion of the ODI put both the ICW and the IAWSEC in an awkward position, as they did not want to be led into the combustible territory of protection or non-protection of women at work. As the discussion now concerned not only women's nationality, but also their overall legal status, the Liaison Committee of Women's International Organizations (recognized by the League in 1931, but not a League-appointed entity like the Consultative Committee) re-appropriated the initiative. Nonetheless, the adoption of a common position in support of investigating the status of women was not arrived at smoothly. Finally, during the sixteenth assembly, the feminist associations grouped within the Liaison Committee (not in the Consultative Committee) obtained on a meeting on September 13 with Czech President Eduard Beneš, where they defended the idea that "an international agreement establishing universal recognition of the full equality of rights between the sexes, is the only remedy" to "trends emerging in several countries against women's wage labor, against women's rights."[79] They were, of course, referring to the campaigns to remove women from the labor force that had appeared, not only in fascist Italy and Nazi Germany, but in a number of other countries affected by the economic depression. This meeting was likely obtained thanks to the intervention of Radziwill and Plamínková, executive member of the ICW.[80] Initially, the Liaison Committee proposed to the League that they launch a large survey collecting evidence of "all moral and economic disadvantages created by the inequality of woman and of which the man suffers [. . .] as much as the woman as they live together from the cradle to the grave, the reciprocal influence of both sexes runs so deep that there is no free man aside a dependent woman."[81] Thanks to the interventions of women among the national delegations at the League, such as Henni Forchammer (Denmark), Aleksandra Kollontai (USSR), Johanne Reutz (Norway), Kerstin Hesselgren (Sweden), Germaine Malaterre-Sellier (France), Anna Westergaard (Denmark), and "the influence of many feminist organizations working behind the scene,"[82] the First Commission of the League decided in September 1935, after having refused to envisage the ratification of the Montevideo Treaty, to authorize a comprehensive survey on the political and civil status of woman. But it also recognized that "the question of the work conditions, both for men and women, falls [. . .] within the sphere of activities of the ILO."[83] The Commission nevertheless recommended launching a survey on "the legislation which includes discriminations, some of which leading to prejudice for the rights of women to work."[84] This last point, adopted at the initiative of the Belgian delegate Henri Rolin, was at the same time a victory and a failure for the ODI. On the one hand, the League recognized that equality in the right for work was, in the same way as a civil or political right, one of the constitutive elements for complete equality for women. But the League also sent the right for work equality question back to the ILO, which was not in favor of absolute equal rights but instead favored a protectionist and differentiated labor legislation.[85]

In reality, Rolin's intention was much more subtle and complex, as he had also submitted "a draft of resolution freezing the examination of the status of woman until the day when the League could take up the topic of the general protection of human and citizen rights."[86] He feared to see "too many states where fascism prides itself on this so-called equality given to women to boast about their own liberalism while in reality all—men and women—are submitted to a regime that deprives them of any freedom. I think that we must fight all together for men's and citizens' rights, and that, once these rights are obtained, they will be for all men and women."[87] In the menacing political context of the 1930s, Rolin wanted to bind the issue of sexual equality to the maintenance of democracy. He urged the "feminist organizations to become more interested in obtaining the freedom essential to human dignity for all individuals, men and women."[88] In other words, if we consider the equality of men and women as a fundamental human right, by defending it we also defend the values of the western democracies; however, on the contrary, if one accepts the idea of complementarity between the sexes, the democratic dimension disappears, as this pseudo-equality could then be written in reactionary, totalitarian, or fascist political systems. This argument linking strict equality of rights of men and women as a component of human rights at the base of the democratic system was developed in many articles of Belgian feminist and co-founder of the ODI, Louise De Creane-Van Duuren.[89]

As concerns the issue of the nationality of the married woman, the League of Nations reminded its members that although the Montevideo Convention was available for the adhesion of all its members, the League recommended the ratification of The Hague Convention on Nationality (1930). This position amounted to a defeat for international feminism, but more specifically for the ambitious project of Alice Paul.[90] Nevertheless, Paul had succeeded in convincing influential members of the League that the status of women in society was no longer a national issue and could only be resolved through international action.[91] This was a huge achievement.

The Survey on the Political and Civil Status of Women

After the Eighteenth General Assembly in September 1937, the League designated a committee of experts to examine thirty-eight national reports (out of which thirty-four were from European countries), to which the reports from the women's and feminist organizations were added. At the same time, it sanctioned "a resolution to establish a committee of experts of both sexes to prepare a comprehensive study on the issues of women's political and civil status."[92] The economic aspects were left to the ILO.[93]

This expert committee was made up of four women, among them Swedish Senator Kerstin Hesselgren (reporting member, one of the vice-presidents of the ICW and its liaison officer with the League), the French Suzanne Bastid-Basdevant, professor of international law and an ICW sympathizer,[94] and lawyer Dorothy Kenyon, an American who would lead the IAWSEC from 1946 until 1952, following Margery Corbett Ashby.[95] Of the three men, one was the British Professor Harold Cook Gutteridge[96] (committee chair), who had an international reputation as comparative lawyer.[97] This committee worked in collaboration with delegates from the feminist international organizations,[98] from whom they first anticipated the completed summaries about the existing legislation. They were also informed by the various national institutes of comparative law. They learned from "concrete examples presented in an objective way and illustrating the lack of coherence between written law and its application, either because the jurisprudence, or the customs modify its interpretation."[99] In this vast inquiry about the legal status of woman, the reports gathered by the international feminist and women's organizations became resources, in parallel with those furnished by the institutes of comparative law.[100]

The tensions between Alice Paul and the Europeans continued: the ICW, chaired by Belgian Marthe Boël, took the side of the IAWSEC initiative within the Liaison Committee and supported Belgian lawyer Frenande Beatens to compile all the legal data provided by the various national councils in a synthesis destined for the League's Committee of experts.[101] Until the end of 1939, the expert committee would continue to ask for additional information.[102] Despite feminist requests, the survey confined itself, for practical reasons, to Europe, North and South America, and a part of the Commonwealth: the president refused to extend it to "countries under Muslim or Hindu law" and to "backward societies."[103] In June 1939, in a call "[f]rom the Women's Consultative Committee on Nationality to the League of Nations Committee of Experts on the Status of Women," feminists worried about the rapid degradation of the situation of woman "in almost every part of the world," and they called for a clear statement from the League—if it did not want to see "the subordination of women spread "like a rot" through the nations of the League or witness their oppression from "reaction and barbarism."[104] Feminist emancipation was put forward as a guarantee of the good functioning of democratic states. However, the outbreak of war brutally interrupted these projects and confirmed the feminists' fears.

If one were to draw up a balance sheet on these years of the interwar period, one would see few actual results compared to the protracted efforts of the international feminists. And yet, there were results—a major shift in mind-set, which can be summarized in the words of Dorothy E. Evans (ERI): "Through the League discussions, equality for men and women is coming to be recognised as a foremost principle of civilisation."[105]

After 1945: "The Long Walk" of Married Women Toward Equality

Even during the war, reports continued to flow into the League from feminist groups on the issue of married women's equality. After World War II and the collapse of the League of Nations, feminists vested their hopes in the new United Nations Organization. This reinvigorated the equal rights project, which, in the course of the founding of the UN (February 25, 1945, San Francisco) and even more through its Universal Declaration of Human Rights (December 10, 1948), proclaimed equality between men and women as one of the fundamental human rights. From then on, the struggle for the respect of human rights not only superseded, but also encompassed the struggle for revisions in the legal status of woman. Indeed, equal rights appeared as the high road to democracy. This universal concept was shared by feminists when they defended the rights of women as human beings ("women's rights are human rights") and when they associated their struggle with the defense of western democracy. However, to some, their attitude would seem paradoxical when they demanded equal rights but also legitimized the intervention of women in the public and political sphere in the name of their maternal qualities. Discussion around the creation and retention of a commission specifically dedicated to the status of women within the UN seemingly embodied this tension.[106]

The United Nations Commission on the Status of Women

Created in 1946 at the initiative of Minerva Bernardino (vice-president of the ICW from 1947 to 1957 and vice-chairman and chairman of the Inter-American Commission of Women from 1944 to 1949), the UN Commission on the Status of Women (CSW) specifically addressed discrimination against women. Danish feminist Bodil Begtrup served as chair, and Minerva Bernadino acted as vice-president. Other ICW leaders assisted, among them Marie-Hélène Lefaucheux (President of French CNFF in 1954; ICW Vice-President from 1954–1957 and then ICW President, 1957–1963), delegate of the French government. They left their mark by transforming what was originally intended as a sub-commission into a full-bodied commission, achieving this despite the opposition of Eleanor Roosevelt, president of the Commission for Human Rights, who thought that women's rights were already included in human rights. Feminist and women's organizations became privileged partners, and from 1946 on, the CSW exercised some pressure on the UN General Assembly to carry on the work done regarding the legal status of women begun at the League of Nations.[107]

Creating and maintaining this Commission divided feminists: some saw it as useless and even against the philosophy of human rights, which at the time was still conceptualized as "men's" rights. Radicals thought that this commission was toxic "because its existence would permit the maintenance of the old way of thinking of 'sexes,' instead of adopting the new way of thinking of 'human beings.'"[108] The new conceptualization of human rights for all human beings was articulated by the UN Human Rights Commission and appeared in the UN's Charter. Doubling it with a special commission dedicated to women, according to Open Door International, "most of us would look like acceptance of the idea that the rights of women are different and less extensive than human rights."[109] We always come back to the underlying understanding of the concept of equality. The ODI and the ERI always remained opposed to legislation that protected the work of women and maternity uniquely. They preferred unequivocal texts and continued to track down any that made reference to only one gender.[110]

But faced with the striking absence of women in key positions at the UN, not to mention the overt antifeminism displayed by some representatives of the Human Rights Commission, in addition to the limited enthusiasm shown by the member states to change their legislation to favor sex equality, the majority of international feminist organizations ended up supporting the existence of the CSW.[111] They were convinced that the declaration of principles embedded in the Charter of the UN and in the Declaration of Human Rights would remain unheeded "unless public opinion in each country insists on their implementation."[112] They also admitted that "one organism seems still necessary to care for a technical and practical implementation in order to make sure that criticism can be formulated"[113] and any resulting reports transmitted to the ECOSOC or to the UN General Assembly; only thus would the new international conventions see the light. While perhaps transitory, in a world where male privilege still reigned supreme, this Commission provided "a way to activate the implementation of the principles of the Declaration of Human Rights, and more specifically the status of women."[114]

Yet the most important question remained tactical. The "boomerang strategy" had proved to be effective: it consisted of getting international conventions to guarantee the equality of the sexes by exercising pressure on the national representatives at the UN and then utilizing these texts to lobby for change at the national level.[115] By the end of World War II, the women's and feminist organizations seemed to be acting in concert. Coördination, however, was strained by the Cold War and by the increasingly important place given by the UN to NGOs, which prompted competition among the women's groups.[116] By the end of the 1940s, the ICW, the IAWSEC, and the newly founded (in 1945) Women's International Democratic Federation (WIDF) enjoyed a consultative status of B-category in the Social and Economic Council (ECOSOC), which allowed them to observe the sessions of the CSW, to consult its documents, and to enjoy the right to speak—with the approval of the Commission.

The CSW would dictate the agenda of preparatory works for the different international conventions that were intended to transform the principles of equality mentioned in the Charter of the UN and in the Declaration of Human Rights. In its report of May 1946, the CSW set its priorities: to first address the question of political and civil rights for women and only then rights related to their social and economic status and access to education. The Commission also proposed a way to proceed which remains applicable to this day: to launch massive surveys via national governments, to supplement these findings via the NGOs and special experts, and to provide a summary that can be used as a basis for elaborating proposals to submit to the ECOSOC.[117] The stamp of the leading European women—Begtrup, Bernadino, and Lefaucheux—was evident: these women would impose the conclusions reached by the feminists through the surveys on the status of women that had been collected by the end of the 1930s.

Survey on the Legal Status of Women in Public Law

As early as 1947, another survey was undertaken to examine the status of women in public law, including political rights, tax law, access to the civil service, education, employment, and married women's nationality. In May 1950, the CSW supplemented it with an analysis of the status of women in private law, which mainly dealt with married women's rights in family law in the terms of contracts and the management of wealth.[118] In the spring of 1952, the UN's Convention on the Political Rights of Women, which included voting rights and eligibility as well as access to all jobs in the public service, was submitted for ratification by the member states. On January 29, 1957, the UN General Assembly finally approved the Convention on the Nationality of Married Women, which stipulated that neither marriage nor its dissolution, nor the change of nationality of the husband during marriage, could *ipso facto* change the nationality of his wife. Thus did more than half a century of feminist labor finally arrive at a happy ending, giving birth to Article 15 of the Universal Declaration of Human Rights: "Everyone has the right to a nationality. No one shall be arbitrarily deprived of his nationality nor denied the right to change his nationality." This Convention addressed a highly sensitive issue that remains controversial.

In the democratic country of Belgium, for example, leaders did not sign the Convention on Nationality (1957) until July 1980.[119] The question of nationality emerged with renewed urgency after the Second World War during debates on the expansion of women's suffrage. A foreign woman who became Belgian by marriage was excluded from eligibility for the House and Senate (a right granted to women since 1921). This exclusion, not contained in any formal text, derived from the law of 1922, which equated Belgian nationality obtained through marriage to that of ordinary naturalization. This decision was confirmed in 1949.[120]

The Council of State limited the rights of women who became Belgian by marriage to local elections and excluded them from legislative elections.[121] This controversial decision was closely linked to a delicate situation after the war: the return of Belgian men from Germany accompanied by wives or concubines was frequently labeled as "matrimonial collaboration" and a denial of patriotism.[122] The purpose was to prevent the "new Belgians" from exercising the same political rights as native-born Belgians (*les femmes belges de souche*).[123] By contrast, a marriage of a Belgian with a German or an Austrian on Belgian territory during the war was nullified and the women were expelled. After the expulsion of their mother, the "enemy children" (Belgian from their father) were placed in homes governed by the Ministry of Justice, situated on the Avenue de la Chasse in Brussels. The law of December 31, 1951 brought further modifications governing the duration to acquire Belgian nationality, and the nationality of women remained tied to that of their husbands.[124] Problems continue to plague marriages between Belgians and immigrants, sometimes resulting in the loss of nationality. These current imbroglios are seemingly born from the historic linkage of rights to gender, justifying the decades of feminist struggle to establish equality under international law!

The Long Road to Obtaining Legal Rights for Wives in Family Law

Not long after the discussions that led to the Convention on Women's Political Rights (1952) and the Convention on the Nationality of the Married Woman (1957), most European women (with the notable exception of Swiss women) acquired equality in political rights and more egalitarian measures in terms of nationality (even if the question remained sensitive in the case of armed conflicts or regarding the nationality of children born of parents with different nationalities). But in the majority of Western, Central, and Southern European states, "the disadvantaged legal status of women in marriage remained high on the list of problems."[125]

Even though Article 16 of the Declaration of Human Rights (1948) stated that men and women of marriageable age "have the right to marry and found a family. They are entitled to equal rights as to marriage, during marriage and at its dissolution," few countries had acted to guarantee the legal capacity of married women, with the prominent exceptions of the Scandinavian and Anglo-Saxon countries. In many states, a married woman could neither work nor manage her own wages independently; she still had no control over her own assets and could not inherit without the agreement of her husband. Often, she could not even wield parental authority over her own children and was obliged to follow her husband wherever he deemed necessary.[126]

The complexity of this situation certainly explains the resistance to reform and the difficulty of arriving at an international agreement before the end of the 1960s. In the early 1950s, members of the CSW "agreed that they should bring out a resolution dealing with the subject of the equality of husband and wife in all the relationships of marriage;" indeed, its "final resolution (E/CN 6/L.96) declared that the commission believes that the authority, prerogatives and responsibilities of marriage should be shared by husband and wife."[127] As early as 1952, however, the Belgian feminist Fernande Baetens warned the board of the ICW that work would necessarily slow down because the question of women's civil rights implicated the family, and "we are far from being united in our views, necessary for speedy coordination."[128]

It took the feminist members of the Commission, such as Belgian attorney and Senator Georgette Ciselet, considerable time to make concrete progress in this area. They did manage to obtain resolutions from the ECOSOC. On July 23, 1953, this body recommended to member states to take all necessary measures to ensure the equality of rights and obligations between husband and wife and to ensure for the wife her full legal capacity (Resolution 504 D [XVI]). A second resolution, dated July 12, 1954, encouraged states to review their legislation on matrimonial regimes and adapt them to the principle of equality of rights between spouses (Resolution 547.I [XVIII]), and a third targeted the right of women to take a job without the authorization of their husbands. In the following year, on August 3, 1955, two new resolutions supplemented these, recommending the free choice of place of residence for women, single or married (Resolutions 587 D III [XX]) and the equality of rights and obligations of parents toward their children (Resolutions 587 D II [XX]), and were advocated in the speech of the ICW made before the CSW on February 8, 1955.[129]

Paralleling this, other UN agencies were also examining the rights of married women. In 1959, UNESCO mandated the International Institute of Differing Civilizations (INCIDI): this Institute was founded in Brussels in 1894, with the former name Institut Colonial International, to prepare a report about "the status of woman in Muslim legislation and in the ones of Western countries" (*le statut de la femme dans la legislation musulmane et dans celles des pays occidentaux*) that called on the expertise of the ICW. The main points, as before, were marital power and parental authority, the free choice of place of residence, the right for married women to get a job, the management of the wives' estate and the common estate, the right to sue and to be sued, and the limitation of marital authority.[130]

International pressure played a role in breaking the gridlock on these questions in some countries. For example, in Belgium in 1957, Ciselet, during discussions in the Belgian Senate about a proposal to abolish marital power, underscored the necessity of respecting international obligations and pointed to the disastrous image of Belgium, which appeared as a "backward country" compared to the United Kingdom, the countries of the Soviet bloc, Scandinavia, and the Netherlands since the law of June 14, 1956.[131]

The inequalities in laws concerning married women were still well-entrenched in many countries despite the repeated interventions of the ICW and the other NGOs that held consultative status in the CSW, as well as the organization of academic circles, such as the one in Bucharest in 1961 regarding women and the family and the one regarding the multiplication of reports in the 1960s.[132] International conventions were inadequate, with the exception of the Convention on Consent to Marriage, Minimum Age for Marriage, and Registrations of Marriages (1962).[133] This lack of progress resulted, in large measure, from the legal intricacies as well as "from the habits and customs to which each country holds to as much as the family framework, the expression of the personality of its citizens."[134]

By the mid-1960s, the discussions concerning a proposed Declaration on the Elimination of Discrimination Against Women provided opportunities for international feminist organizations to remind audiences that discrimination still existed in marriage law and to insist upon solutions.[135] The authors of this new draft convention, conceived as a synthesis of international texts on equality between men and women, intended to make a declaration of principle, affirming that the rights of women form an indivisible entity, which needs to be approached as a whole. Its adoption by the General Assembly on November 7, 1967 brought an end to decades of feminist struggle in favor of an Equal Rights Treaty, so dear to Alice Paul.

Article 5 reaffirmed that women must enjoy the same rights as men in terms of acquiring, changing, and conserving nationality, and Article 6 asked that all appropriate measures be taken, in particular the following: "legislative measures to ensure for married woman, the equality of rights with men in the field of civil rights" and "the principle of equality in the conditions of the husband and the wife."[136] It took another twenty years for this declaration, which breathed new dynamism into national feminist organizations, to become the Convention on the Elimination of All Forms of Discrimination against Women (CEDAW) in 1979, in which Article 9 dealt with nationality and Article 16 with all other questions relative to marriage.[137]

Conclusion

Equality within the family has taken much longer to achieve than political equality. Inequality within a marriage seems, in the majority of the world's societies, to be seen as a guarantee of family order, which in turn is supposed to guarantee social order. The principle of "unity of the family," which lay at the foundation of the French Civil Code of 1804, remained for a very long time the principal argument against the duality of nationality within the lives of the married couple. From this point of view, the creation of the Commission on the Status of Women, together with Article 6 of the Universal Declaration of Human Rights, which underlines that men and women "have equal rights in marriage," represents an indisputable success from a feminist perspective. Women conversant with the law and formally trained in the law played a major role in bringing the campaign for women's rights to fruition.

Notes

1 See principally: Leila Rupp, *Worlds of Women: The Making of an International Women's Movement* (Princeton, NJ: Princeton University Press, 1997); Karen Offen, *European Feminisms 1700–1950: A Political History* (Stanford, CA: Stanford University Press, 2000).

2 See chapter 16 in this volume: Susan Zimmermann, "Night Work for White Women and Bonded Labour for 'Native' Women? Contentious Traditions and the Globalization of Gender-Specific Labour Protection and Legal Equality Politics, 1926 to 1939."

3 Karen Offen, "National or International? How and Why the Napoleonic Code Drove Married Women's Legal Rights onto the Agenda of the International Council of Women and the League of Nations: An Overview," in *Family Law in Early Women's Rights Debates. Western Europe and the United States in the 19th and Early 20th Centuries*, ed. Stephan Meder and Christoph-Eric Mecke (Cologne: Böhlau, 2013), 44.

4 See Page Baldwin, "Subject to Empire: Married Women and the British Nationality and Status of Aliens Act," *Journal of British Studies* 10, no. 1 (October 2001): 522–556.

5 Ute Gerhard, "Women's Movements and Law. Legal, Historical and Sociological Aspects of Research in International Comparison," in *Family Law in Early Women's Rights Debates*, 36.

6 *Code Napoléon*, Art. 19. "Une femme française qui épousera un étranger, suivra la condition de son mari si elle devient veuve, elle recouvre la qualité de française pourvu qu'elle réside en France, ou qu'elle y rentre avec l'autorisation du Gouvernement, et en déclarant qu'elle veut s'y fixer" and Art. 12: "L'étrangère qui aura épousé un français suivra la condition de son mari," in *Code Napoléon expliqué par article d'après la doctrine et la jurisprudence suivi d'une table analytique et alphabétique à l'usage des Avocats, des Officiers ministériels, des Elèves en droit des Grands séminaires, etc.*, vol. 1, ed. J.-B.-C. Picot (Paris: J.-H. Michou, Gernat, 1868), 17, 24, http://gallica.bnf.fr/ark:/12148/bpt6k61437746/f26.image

7 See: Baldwin, "Subject to Empire," 528.

8 Catherine Jacques, "Les féministes et le changement social en Belgique (1918–1968). Programmes, stratégies et réseaux," PhD diss., Free University of Brussels and University of Angers, 2007, vol. 1, 172–173.

9 Jean-Yves Le Naour, "Le territoire national de la femme mariée (1914–1927)," in *Le genre des territoires. Féminin, masculin, neutre*, ed. Christine Bard (Angers: Presse de l'université d'Angers, 2004), 144–145.

10 Patrick Weil, *Qu'est-ce qu'un Français? Histoire de la nationalité française depuis la révolution* (Paris: Grasset, 2002).

11 Denis Scuto, *La nationalité luxembourgeoise 19–20è siècle. Histoire d'une alliage européen* (Brussels: Université Libre de Bruxelles, Histoire, 2012).

12 Candice Lewis Bredbenner, *A Nationality of Her Own: Women, Marriage, and the Law of Citizenship* (Berkeley and London: University of California Press, 1998). One chapter is dedicated to the initiatives of the American feminists at the League.

13 Baldwin, "Subject to Empire," 522–556.

14 See principally Leila Rupp, *Worlds of Women*; Offen, *European Feminisms*; Carol Miller, "Geneva—The Key to Equality: Inter-war Feminists and the League of Nations," *Women's History Review* 3 (1994): 219–245; Ellen Carol Dubois, "Internationalizing Married Women's Nationality: The Hague Campaign of 1930," in *Globalizing Feminisms, 1789–1945*, ed. Karen Offen (London: Routledge, 2010), 204–216.

15 Catherine Jacques, "Des lobbys féministes à la SDN: l'exemple des débats sur la nationalité de la femme mariée (1830–1935)," in *Femmes et relations internationales au 20ème*, ed. Jean-Marc Delaunay and Ives Dénèchere (Paris: Presses Sorbonne Nouvelle, 2006), 267–277; Ibid., "Mouvements féministes et dynamiques transnationales et internationales. Le cas belge (1918–1960)," in *Au-De là et en Deçà de l'Etat. Le genre entre dynamique transnationale et multi-niveaux*, ed. Bérengère Marques-Pereira, Petra Meier and David Paternottre (Louvain-la-Neuve: Academia/Bruylant coll. Science politique, 2009), 49–61; Ibid., "Construire un réseau international: l'exemple du Conseil international des femmes," in *Le Siècle des féminismes*, ed. Eliane Gubin, Catherine Jacques, Florence Rochefort, Brigitte Studer, Françoise Thebaud, and Michelle Zancarini-Fournel (Paris: Éd. de l'Atelier, 2004), 127–141; Ibid., "Les féministes belges: de la scène nationale à l'action internationale (1918–1970)," in *Femmes sans frontières. Stratégies transnationales féminines face à la mondialisation, XVIIIe–XXIe siècle*, ed. Marie-Pierre Arrizabalaga, Diana Burgos-Vigna and Mercedes Yusta (Bern: Peter Lang, 2011), 231–248.

16 "Mrs. Sophie Grinberg-Vinaver Former U.N. Aide, Dies in Paris," *The New York Times*, May 27, 1964, http://www.nytimes.com/1964/05/27/mrs-sophie-grinbergvinaver-former-u-n-aide-dies-in-paris.html?_r=0; Doctor of Laws from The University of Paris, after the Second World War, she joined the United Nations Secretariat and served as Secretary of the Commission on the Status of Women before becoming its chief from 1958 to 1962. She was also executive director of the ICW in New York.

17 Françoise Thébaud is preparing a book on Thibert's career at the ILO.

18 Weil, *Qu'est-ce qu'un Français?*, 212 and following.
19 Le Naour, "Le territoire national de la femme mariée," 144–145.
20 See notably for France, Françoise Thébaud, "Le mouvement nataliste dans la France de l'entre-deux-guerres: L'Alliance Nationale pour l'accroissement de la population française," *Revue d'histoire moderne et contemporaine* 32, no. 2 (1985): 276–346; and for Belgium: Eliane Gubin and Valérie Piette, "Mères au travail, mères au foyer: les controverses de l'entre-deux-guerres," in *Mères et nourrissons. De la bienfaisance à la protection médico-sociale (1830–1945)*, ed. Godelieve Masuy-Stroobant and Perrine C. Humblet (Brussels: Labor Press, 2004), 43–64; Karen Offen, "Body Politics: Women, Work, and the Politics of Motherhood in France, 1920–1950," in *Maternity and Gender Policies: Women and the Rise of the European Welfare States, 1880s–1950s*, ed. Gisela Bock and Pat Thane (London: Routledge, 1991), 138–159.
21 Weil, *Qu'est-ce qu'un Français?*, 220.
22 Jacques, "Des lobbys féministes à la SDN," 267–277.
23 *Société des Nations, Journal officiel*, suppl-spécial, 53 (1927): 9.
24 IWSA had amended its name to the International Alliance of Women for Social and Economic Change (IAWSEC, also IAW for short) in 1926.
25 Chrystal Macmillan (1882–1937), born in Edinburgh, became a leading national and international feminist and later barrister (after 1924). From 1913 to 1920 she served as a secretary of the International Alliance of Women for Suffrage (IWSA) and in 1923 co-founded the Open Door Council. See Sybil Oldfield, "Macmillan (Jessie) Chrystal (1872–1937)," *Oxford Dictionary of National Biography* (Oxford University Press, 2004), http://dx.doi.org/10.1093/ref:odnb/38526.
26 Call made by the ICW and the IWSA for the organization of the Joint Demonstration on the Nationality of Married Women of The Hague (December 3, 1929): Carhif: L. De Craene, 45.
27 Letter from Katrine Bompas to Elise Soyer, December 8, 1929; Letter from Emilie Gourd to Elise Soyer, March 29, 1930; and Letter from the National Women Party to Elise Soyer, March 15, 1930, Mundaenum: Féminisme, CNFB 01. Marcelle Renson was a well-known woman: she had already played the role of *éminence grise* for the Socialist Minister of Emile Vandervelde, author in 1922 of the draft law allowing women to join the bar.
28 Marie-Elisabeth Lüders, "Staatsangehörigkeit der Ehefau auf der Kodifikationskonferenz im Haag. Aufgaben und Möglichkeiten," *Die Frau* (1929/30): 449–454; Marion Röwekamp, "Gerechtigkeit für Frauen im Sozialstaat? Weibliche Staatsangehörigkeit im Kaiserreich und der Weimarer Republik," in *Gerechtigkeit im Sozialstaat. Analysen und Vorschläge*, ed. Ulrike Haerendel (Baden-Baden: Nomos, 2012), 71–87, here 83–84. Other countries, such as the Netherlands, the United States, Czechoslovakia, England, and Cuba also appointed women as delegates.
29 Ellen Wilkinson (1891–1947), English female syndicalist and politician. Influenced by Sylvia Pankhurst, she concentrated on the aims of women's labor and thus was nicknamed 'Red Ellen': Paula Bartley, *Ellen Wilkinson: from Red Suffragist to Government Minister* (Pluto Press, 2014).
30 Winifred Cullis (1875–1956), professor emerita in psychology of the University of London, a founding member of the British Federation of University Women and the International Organization of University Women. See R. E. M. Bowden, "Cullis, Winifred Clara (1875–1956)," rev. Ruth E. M. Bowden, *Oxford Dictionary of National Biography* (Oxford University Press, 2004), doi:10.1093/ref:odnb/32661.
31 Maud Park, ép. Wood (1871–1955), American suffragist, first president of the League of Women Voters. Her papers are in the Schlesinger Library on the History of Women in America, Harvard University.

32 *Report of the Joint Demonstration and Joint Conference* (March 14, 1930), published by IWC and IAWSEC, London, 4–5 (French version) and 2–3 (English version); 9–10: Carhif: L. De Craene, 45. On Vérone see Sara L. Kimble, "Popular Legal Journalism in the Writings of Maria Vérone," *Proceedings of the Western Society for French History* 39 (2011): 224–235.

33 Georgette Ciselet, "Une manifestation internationale à propos de la nationalité de la femme mariée," *L'Affranchissement de la femme. Bulletin trimestriel du Groupement belge pour l'affranchissement de la femme* (April–May 1930): 22.

34 Chrystal Macmillan was president of this commission.

35 Letter from Chrystal Macmillan to the members of the Commission on the Nationality of the Married Woman of the IAWSEC, July 30, 1930: Carhif: ICW, 213.

36 The Inter-American Commission of Women was created in 1928 during the 6th International Conference of the American States, held in Havana. It was presided over by Doris Stevens who, right from the beginning, had concentrated her efforts on obtaining a report on the status of women in Latin America and an Equal Rights Treaty. Offen, *European Feminisms*, 357.

37 Letter by the Inter-American Commission of Women, Geneva, October 3, 1930, 3.: Carhif: ICW, 213; Letter by Alice Paul to Louise van Eeghen, October 28, 1930: Carhif: ICW, 213.

38 Ibid.

39 Letter from Chrystal Macmillan and Lily van der Schalk Schuster in the name of the Joint Demonstration on the Nationality of Married Women, December 12, 1930 and letter by Chrystal Macmillan, December 22, 1930: Carhif: ICW, 213.

40 Magdeleine Boy, *Les associations internationales féministes* (Lyon: Imprimerie Paquet, 1936), 144–145.

41 "Nationalité de la femme," *Egalité. Revue Trimestrielle publié par le Groupement belge pour l'affranchissement de la femme* 12 (December 1931): 28.

42 Article 24 of the Charter of the League of Nations planned cooperation with international offices, and there was an international section of these offices dealing with NGOs. Furthermore, the creation of an International Women's Office failed due to financial and tactical reasons.

43 Speech of Mr. Buero at the opening of the comittee of organizations interested in the question of women's nationality, July 1931: Carhif: ICW, 2134.

44 About the multiple and diverse procrastinations, which illustrate notably the existing mistrust between the international organizations of women, see the correspondence included in the N°213 du Fonds CIF au Carhif.

45 In 1925, the ICW expressed the wish during its fifth assembly in Washington to create an organization that would exercise pressure to have women nominated in the Commission of the League. This would be done in 1925 with the creation of the Comité général permanent des Organisations féminines internationales. The Liaison Committee for the Women's International Organisations, created in 1931, worked together with the first committee, but its program was broader. These two merged in 1934 under the name of Comité de Liaison des Organisations féminines internationales, of which one subcommittee concentrated more specifically on the status of women. The ICW was also part of another grouping of international organizations: le Comité d'entente des grandes associations internationales founded in 1925. See: Rupp, *Worlds of Women*, 37–44; Eliane Gubin and Leen Van Molle eds., *Des femmes qui changent le monde. Histoire du Conseil international des femmes 1888–1988* (Bruxelles: Racine, 2005), 32–36.

46 The Young Women's Christian Association declined the invitation: Letter from the League to Lady Aberdeen, February 13, 1931, Carhif: ICW: 213.

47 Boy, *Les associations internationales féminines*, 145.
48 "La nationalité de la femme. Extrait d'un rapport présenté par le Secrétaire Général à Assemblée de la SDN," *Egalité* 11 (September 1931): 10–14.
49 Ibid., 12
50 Ibid., 11.
51 Ibid., 13.
52 Extract from a report by the secretary-general to the assembly of the League of Nations on the question of the nationality of women (document A. 19.1931.V.), publ. League of Nations, Annemasse (5p.).
53 "Nationalité de la femme," *Egalité* 12 (December 1931): 28.
54 Letter from Eugénie Meller to the secretary general of The League of Nations, August 15, 1932. Carhif: ICW, 213.
55 "Observations sur la nationalité de la femme et la convention de la Haye, Genève août 1932," in *Bulletin, CIF*, 11a, no. 2 (October 1932): 1–2: "Observations sur la nationalité de la femme et la convention de La Haye. Présenté par les organisations féminines internationales soussignées, membres du comité consultatif féminin sur la nationalité, créé par le conseil de la société des nations dans sa session de janvier 1932, Genève août 1932" (5 p.), typoscript: Carhif, ICW, 219.
56 Dorothy E. Evans, "Women's Consultative Committee. Report for the year 1936–1937. With a brief summary of its previous activities and the political results thereof," (typescript), 3. Carhif: ICW, 219 (no definitive classement).
57 Jacques, "Des lobbys féministes à la SDN," 270–271.
58 Eliane Gubin, "Pour le droit au travail: entre protection et égalité," 163–178; see Susan Zimmermann's chapter in this volume.
59 Letter from Emilie Gourd to Louise Van Eeghen, August 27, 1932, Carhif: ICW, 213.
60 Letter from F. Plaminkova to Lady Aberdeen, August 29,1932: Carhif: ICW 213.
61 Dorothy Evans, Women's consultative committee. Report for the year 1936–1937 (typoscript), p. 3: Carhif: ICW 219.
62 Gubin, "Pour le droit au travail. . .," 163–178; Circular letter IAWSEC to affiliated societies, September 12, 1932: Carhif: ICW 213.
63 Letter from Plamínková to Lady Aberdeen, July 29, 1932: Carhif: ICW 213.
64 Boy, *Les associations*, 146; Letter from the Consultative Committee to the President of the first Commission of the Assembly, October 10, 1932; Communication of the main women's international organizations, October 12, 1932; Letter to the member of the Consultative Committee, October 20, 1932: Carhif: ICW, 213.
65 Letter by the League of Nations, February 8, 1933: Carhif: ICW, 213.
66 Resolution of June 1933, of the Consultative Committee of the Women's Organization of Nationality (3p.): Carhif: ICW, 213.
67 Letter from Renée Girod to Louise van Eeghen, May 22, 1933: Carhif: ICW 213.
68 Letter from Maria Vérone to Louise van Eeghen, August 31, 1933: Carhif: ICW 213.
69 Letter from Marta Vergara (Santiago de Chile) to Alice Paul, June 30, 1933: Carhif: ICW, no. 213.); Letter by J. Avenol, general secretary of the League to Miss Dorothy Evans, secretary of the Consultative Committee, August 10, 1933: Carhif: ICW, 213. Letter by Louise van Eeghen to Alice Paul, August 13,1934 and Letter by ICW to the Minister of Foreign Affairs of Chile, July 5, 1934: Carhif: ICW, 213.
70 Request sent to delegations about the issue of the nationality of married women, September 1934: Carhif: ICW, 214.
71 Boy, *Les associations*, 147. This convention was also called the Montevideo Treaty.

72 Offen, *European Feminisms*, 358; Rupp, *Worlds of Women*, 219.
73 Rupp, Ibid., 219. "Statut de la femme," communicated to the Assembly, to the Council, and to the members of the League no. officiel, A 8, 1935 V, Geneva, May 15, 1935. (This document sums up the proposals on this issue after the one of September 26, 1934.).
74 Letter from Radziwill to Corbett Ashby, October 22, 1934: Carhif: ICW, 214.
75 Letter from Radziwill to Corbette Ashby, October 22, 1934: Carhif : ICW 214.
76 "Women's Consultative Committee. Report for the year 1936–1937. With a brief summary of its previous activities and the political results thereof" (typoscript), 4: Carhif: ICW, 219 (no definitive classement).
77 Talk of "Open Door International" for the economic emancipation of the female worker. "Status of Woman"—proposal submitted to the League of Nations, in: "Extrait du document: Société des nations," n°officiel: A.19, 1935, V.: Carhif: Louise De Craene, 45.
78 Proposal of "Open Door International" for the economic emancipation of women workers. Compare: "Sur le statut de la femme remis à la SDN," in: Ibid., 45.
79 Paper presented by the liaison committee by the spokesperson of the IWSA to M. Benès, September 13, 1935, in: Carhif: ICW, 222.
80 Rupp, *Worlds of Women*, 40.
81 Text: Carhif: ICW, 222.
82 *The International Women's News* (November 15, 1935).
83 "La société des nations et les femmes," *Egalité* 27 (1935): 24.
84 Ibid.
85 Ibid.
86 "Les droits de la femme. Le point de vue de M. Henry Rolin," *Le Peuple* (April 28, 1935).
87 Marcelle Leroy, "Un interview de Henri Rolin. A propos du traité des droits égaux," *Femmes dans l'action mondiale* (November/December 1935): press cutting, Carhif: GBPO, 50.
88 "Les droits de la femme."
89 Catherine Jacques, *Les féministes belges et les luttes pour l'égalité politique et économique 1918–1968* (Brussels: Royale des Sciences, Academie des Lettres et des Beaux-Arts de Belgique, 2013), 56–66.
90 Rupp, *Worlds of Women*, 219.
91 Miller, "Geneva—the Key to Equality," 238.
92 Offen, *European Feminisms*, 358–359.
93 Maria Vérone, "Succès à la SDN. Enquête sur la situation de la femme," *Le droit des femmes. Revue mensuelle* 33 (September/October 1937): 105–106.
94 Jacqueline Lucienne Lafon, "Suzanne Bastid-Basdevant," in *Women in Law: A Bio-Bibliographical Sourcebook*, ed. Rebecca Mae Salokar and Mary L. Volcansek (Westport, CO: Greenwood, 1996), 34–37.
95 Kate Weigand and Daniel Horowitz, "Dorothy Kenyon: Feminist Organizing 1919–1963," *Journal of Women's History* 14, no. 2 (2002): 126–131.
96 Charles John Hamson and Kurt Lipstein, "H. C. Gutteridge at Cambridge," in *International and Comparative Law Quarterly* 3, no. 3 (1954): 377–384.
97 Status of Women at Geneva. Meeting of the Committee of Experts (1938): Carhif: ICW, 2457; Francisca de Haan, "Un bref aperçu des droits des femmes de 1945 à 2009," http://unchronicle.un.org/fr/article/un-bref-aper-u-des-droits-des-femmes-de-1945–2009/.
98 Letter from the Secretary of the ICW to the presidents and secretaries of the councils of affiliated women, February 1939: Carhif, ICW, 2450.
99 Letter from the ICW to the chairwomen and secretaries of the National Councils, May 10, 1938: Carhif, ICW, 2449.

100 Meeting minutes of the eighth public session of the Committee in charge of the Survey on the legal status of women, League of Nations, January 7, 1939: Carhif: ICW, 2457.
101 Letter from Marthe Boël to Louise van Eeghen, September 21, 1937: Carhif: ICW 2455.; Letter from the Secretary of ICW to all presidents and secretaries of the national councils, February 1939: Carhif: ICW 2450.
102 Letter from the secretary of the ICW to the presidents and secretaries of the councils of the affiliated women, February 1939: Carhif: ICW, 2450.
103 Meeting minutes of the eighth public session of the Committee in charge of the Survey on the legal status of women, League of Nations, January 7, 1939: Carhif: ICW, 2457.
104 "An appeal from the Women's Consultative Committee to the League of Nations Committee of experts on Status of Women," July 1939: Carhif: ICW, 2457.
105 Report for the years 1936–1937 of the Women's Consultative Committee: Carhif: ICW, 2455.
106 Jacques, *Les féministes belges*, 72–74.
107 Offen, *European Feminisms*, 376.
108 Report of the 6th Congress of the ODI gathered in Brussels from July 5–9, 1948: Carhif: ICW, 2483: "Parce que son existence permettrait de maintenir l'ancienne façon de penser 'selon les sexes', au lieu d'adopter la nouvelle manière de penser à 'l'être humain.' "
109 Ibid.: "Équivaudrait pour la plupart d'entre nous à accepter l'idée que les droits des femmes sont différents et moins étendus que les droits humains."
110 Ibid.
111 As attested in different archival sources: Carhif: ICW, 2483.
112 Cited by Offen, *European Feminisms*, 379.
113 Meeting minutes of the Board of ICW on the Commission on the Status of Women (1948): Carhif: ICW, 2483: "Un organisme semble encore nécessaire pour veiller à son application technique et pratique car il faut que des critiques puissent être formulées."
114 Ibid.: "Un moyen d'activer la mise en application des principes de la Déclaration des droits de l'homme, en ce qui concerne le statut des femmes."
115 Jacques, "Mouvements féministes et dynamiques," 49–61.
116 Jacques, "Le CIF face aux enjeux géopolitiques," 39–55.
117 Report of United Nations Sub-Commission on the Status of Women presented to the United Nations Commission on Human Rights, May 14, 1946, United Headquarters, New York City, reprinted with permission of the editors, from Equal Rights, Official Organ of the National Woman's Party, Washington DC: Carhif: ICW, 2483.
118 See archives on this subject: answers of NGOs (1947–1952): Carhif: ICW, 2491, 2191, 2483, 2486.
119 Bernard Dutoit and Christine Sattiva-Spring, *La Nationalité de la femme mariée*, vol. 1 : Europe suppl. 1973–1989 (Geneva: Librairie Droz, 1990), 57.
120 Réponse au questionnaire de l'ECOSOC relatif à la condition juridique et au traitement de la femme établie par le CNFB [1948]: Carhif, F. GBPO 60g.
121 "Les femmes d'origine étrangère devenues belges par mariage ne voteront pas," in *La Dernière Heure*, 29/1/1949; "L'électorat des femmes étrangères belges par mariage," in *La Libre Belgique* (January 30, 1949).
122 Pieter Lagrou, *Mémoires patriotiques et occupation Nazi. Résistants, requis et déportés en Europe occidentale 1945–1965* (Bruxelles: Complexe, 2003), 157–158.
123 "La femme d'origine étrangère devenue belge par mariage pourra voter si elle réside depuis dix ans en Belgique ou à la colonie," *La Dernière Heure* (January 21, 1949).

124 "L'acquisition de la nationalité belge," *Bulletin du CNFB* (1952): 24.
125 Offen, *European Feminisms*, 379.
126 Germaine Cyfer-Diderich, *La situation actuelle des femmes diplômées des Universités. Un rapport 1956–1965* (London: FIFDU, 1966), 7–8.
127 Report of ICW's liaison officer at the seventh session of the Status of Women Commission. United Nations Headquarters, 1953: Carhif: ICW, 2486.
128 P. V. of the Board meeting ICW, January, Paris 1952: Carhif: ICW, 2486.
129 Resolution 547, I (XVIII) of the Economic and Social Council of the UN, 805th plenary session, July 12, 1954: Carhif: Ernst-Henrion, 8; Marlise Ernst-Henrion, "Les Nations Unies et la condition de la femme," *Journal des tribunaux*, 1968, reprinted in *La condition de la femme dans la famille et dans la société. Recueil de réflexions*, ed. Marlise Ernst-Henrion (s. l.: Zenner-Henrion, 1989), 66–67. Observation on some points on the draft agenda. Speech presented by the ICW during the 9th session of the UN Commission on the Status of Women, February 8, 1955 (E/CN.6/NGO/26): Mundaneum, CNFB, 012.
130 Brief analysis of our comparative survey, ICW 1958, and various correspondence: Carhif: ICW, 2165.
131 *Annales parlementaires*, Sénat belge, session 1957–1958, November 13, 1957.
132 See: Carhif, ICW, 2179, 2166, 2483, 2533.
133 Theanolte Bähnisch (ICW representative), Report on the 18th session of the UN Commission on the Status of Women. Tehran, March 1–20, 1965, Paris, 8.
134 ICW, *Report on the triennial Council meeting*, Athens (Greece), March 28–April 8, 1951, s.l., s. d., 37.
135 Draft Declaration on the Elimination of Discrimination Against Women. Memorandum by the secretary-general, 18th session of the Commission on the Status of Women, December 29, 1964: Carhif: ODI 632; ICW, 2510.
136 Declaration on the elimination of discrimination against Women, November 7, 1967: Carhif, ICW, 2168.
137 "The Convention on the Nationality of Married Women—adopted in 1957—is integrated under Article 9 providing for the nationality of women, irrespective of their marital status. The Convention, thereby, draws attention to the fact that often women's legal status has been linked to marriage, making them dependent on their husband's nationality rather than individuals in their own right." *Introduction of the Convention on the Elimination of All Forms of Discrimination against Women:* Website UN Women- United Nations Entity for Gender Equality and the Empowerment of Women, http://www.un.org/womenwatch/daw/cedaw/text/econvention.htm.

14 "Who Belongs" or the Question of Women's Citizenship in Switzerland Since 1798

Regina Wecker

In 2014, twenty-four percent of the inhabitants actually living in Switzerland were foreigners without Swiss citizenship.[1] This rather high percentage of non-citizens is due to migration because of the attractiveness of the Swiss labor market and living conditions, as well as the Swiss Law on Naturalization, which requires a minimum of twelve years of residence but does not automatically convey a right to naturalization. Since 1990, the percentage of non-citizens has continuously increased. The fear that this increased level of immigration might continue, especially given that Switzerland joined the bilateral Agreement on the Free Movement of Persons with the EU in 2000, has led to some rather heated political discussions and the acceptance of a popular initiative which intends to limit immigration.[2] Parallel to the discussion on immigration and the rights and status of immigrants, the discussion on citizenship and naturalization has intensified.

Generally speaking, the concept of a citizen has a dual dimension: the civil rights and duties (including the political rights) of a person and the status of nationality as a native or naturalized member of a state or nation. However, the concept of *Bürgerrecht*, which is most often used as the German language equivalent of citizenship in Switzerland, includes a third dimension: the municipal part of citizenship; that is, membership in or affiliation with a municipality, on which Swiss citizenship is based.[3] This third dimension lies at the core of Swiss citizenship, and it is one of its problems at the same time, as will be shown later. In the current political debates on nationalization, law, and citizenship, the status of a citizen is assumed to be permanent and fixed. In particular, cultural uniformity and equality are often considered the basis of citizenship; conformity to cultural norms and integration are asked of those who wish to become citizens.

Any challenge to these principles is alleged to threaten the identity of the nation. The history of citizenship in Switzerland from 1798 to the present day shows not only how much naturalization laws have changed, but also how inconsistent the meaning of citizenship has been. This holds true for men and women, but more accurately reflects women's inferior legal position:[4] women were called "citizens" (*Bürgerinnen*) but nonetheless denied the political rights that had been part of men's citizenship since 1848, even though the constitution spoke of "universal suffrage" and the "equality of all citizens." Swiss citizenship was "permanent" according to the letter of the law,[5] but women could lose it. Additionally, women's municipal citizenship, allegedly transferred from generation to generation and considered to be the basis of Swiss citizenship, was transferred by the spear side only, meaning a woman could not transfer her national or municipal citizenship to her husband or her children. By contrast, a man automatically "naturalized" his foreign spouse at marriage and transferred his citizenship to his children. Only an unmarried mother transferred her citizenship to her children.[6]

My contribution will, on the one hand, deal with the consequences of those discriminatory legal provisions and customary rights for women's everyday life; it will also address the influence these factors had on their family situation, marriage, and their opportunities and expectations in life. In addition, I shall analyze the meaning of women's "incomplete" and "dependent" citizenship in terms of the consequences for both citizenship and the inclusion of women in the nation. The longtime denial of political rights and citizenship to women was not unique to Switzerland, but the duration of this exclusion was considerably longer than in the rest of Europe. Therefore, I shall enquire as to the reason why this exclusion lasted for such a long time and how the connections, amalgamations, intersections, and disjunctions of the different dimensions of citizenship developed over time.

Swiss Citizenship Today

Swiss citizenship is a complicated matter because it consists of three parts: municipal, cantonal, and federal citizenship, and because there are large differences in the form of organization, responsibilities, and the process of naturalization among the 2000 municipalities and twenty-six cantons of Switzerland. Every Swiss citizen is, first of all, a citizen of a Swiss municipality.[7] The municipal citizenship, which he or she usually inherits from his or her father or, if the parents are not married, from the mother, is part of a person's identity. It is stated in the Swiss passport where, in other countries, the place of birth is indicated. At the beginning and, to a more limited extent, continuing until the middle of the nineteenth century, political or economic privileges such as the right to run for office or to own property and social security provisions were contingent on municipal and cantonal citizenship. But this is no longer the case.[8] Only a few municipalities still convey minor privileges.[9] Very often today, people do not even have a personal connection with "their municipality of origin," as it is transmitted from generation to generation without them ever having lived there.[10]

In the majority of the cantons there are two municipal organizations: the municipal corporation, the *Bürgergemeinde*, and the political municipality,[11] *Einwohnergemeinde*. The political municipality or the organization of Swiss residents is responsible for all political decisions in the municipality, such as local taxes, buildings, primary schooling, etc. Here, decisions are taken by all Swiss citizens living in the municipality at a meeting or by their elected representatives.[12] The second is the municipal corporation (*Bürgergemeinde*), which includes all persons who are citizens of the corporation—whether living there or not—usually by inheriting the respective citizenship. The *Bürgergemeinde* often holds property in the village and provides social and cultural services. For Swiss citizens' municipal citizenship, "the place of origin" has lost much of the legal importance it used to have, but decisions on naturalizations are usually made either by the corporative municipality (*Bürgergemeinde*), or by the political municipality (*Einwohnergemeinde*). In both cases, the new citizen becomes a citizen of the corporative municipality.[13]

The system of the two forms of municipalities was essentially shaped the way it now exists after the founding of the Federal Republic of Switzerland in 1848,[14] when political rights were no longer reserved to members of the corporate municipalities but granted to all male residents. The political organizations incorporated the rights (and duties) of the corporal municipalities step by step,[15] but the *Bürgergemeinde* kept the right to confer citizenship.

Before 1988 a woman used to acquire her husband's municipal citizenship at marriage and lost her original municipal citizenship, which means that her citizenship used to be a "contingent belonging."[16] Since the change in the marriage law in 1988, a woman could keep her former municipal citizenship at marriage but got her husband's in addition to it, while children got their father's municipal citizenship. This has once again changed quite recently: since 2013, marriage no longer has any influence on the municipal citizenship of a woman. She keeps her inherited citizenship.[17] Thanks to those recent changes, the municipal citizenship rights of men and women have become equal, with respect to the law.[18] But as I will show later, equality is a difficult concept to apply, especially when tradition, living conditions, gender-based notions, and power relations preserve substantive differences between men and women.

Municipal citizenship, without which the acquisition of Swiss citizenship is not possible, is important in the case of naturalization. Federal and cantonal authorities are responsible for compliance with the constitutional and legal prerequisites of naturalization, but the municipality or the canton can deny naturalization. The law requires twelve years of residence, integration into the Swiss way of life, familiarity with Swiss customs and institutions, compliance with Swiss law, and knowledge of at least one of the official languages of the country.[19]

With respect to naturalization, applicants depend on the goodwill and benevolence of their neighbors, especially in smaller municipalities. In general, it is easier for citizens of the "old" EU countries to become Swiss than, for example, Turkish citizens or members of the Balkan countries, because those EU citizens are considered to be better integrated, having a Christian background and being more familiar with customs and institutions, and because those who make the decision consider their way of life and religious orientation more easily compatible with that of new citizens.[20] There is no general right to naturalization and the municipality or in some cases the canton has the final say. The Federal Court decided only in 2004 that a refusal of naturalization had to be substantiated.[21] Only the so-called "facilitated naturalization," that is, the naturalization of the foreign spouses of Swiss nationals (after three years of marriage and five years of residence) remains the sole responsibility of the Federation, leaving solely a right of appeal to the respective municipality and canton.

Citizenship from the "Helvetic Republic" (1798–1803) to the Mid-Nineteenth Century

The history of the modern Swiss state begins in 1798. The old Swiss Confederation had remained neutral during the war against revolutionary France but was occupied in 1798 by French troops, who were welcomed by some as liberators from patrician rule but fought and detested by others as foreign invaders. Between 1798 and 1803, the so-called "Helvetic Republic" was installed as a centralized Swiss state. It was then that a joint constitution was drafted which abolished differences between the cantons and proclaimed equality and universal political rights for Swiss citizens regardless of their former status. There were, however, two exceptions from this "universality": Jewish inhabitants were not accepted as citizens, and women's citizenship did not convey any political rights. While Jewish citizenship had been discussed upon the request of the Federal Council (the parliament) and was rejected after three days of controversial debates in August 1798, there is no information that women's exclusion from political rights was even mentioned.[22] Thus, for women, the salutation of "Liberty and Equality" (formed after the French "Liberty, Equality, and Fraternity") remained—as in France—a mere formula.[23] There was, however, some progress with respect to citizenship: loss of citizenship because of interdenominational marriages, or poverty, common in the *ancien régime*, was banned. As municipalities seem to have disregarded this ban, and continued to collect fees, petitions were filed asking for freedom of marriage for citizens of different municipalities and for foreigners.[24] But those petitions were never discussed in the Federal Council.[25] A new civil law, which might have forced municipalities to accept the change, was not completed. Swiss women received their husband's municipal citizenship and kept it after his death and after a divorce,[26] but bi-national marriages did not seem to have had an influence on nationality. Besides, at that time, naturalization of foreigners required a residence of a twenty-year duration.[27]

After the short intermezzo of the "Helvetic Republic" (1798–1803) and following the Congress of Vienna in 1815, the old regime was restored, people lost their political rights, and citizenship was once again solely a matter of the sovereign cantons. Cantons and municipalities handled those rights differently and naturalization was often a question of the respective religious affiliations: Catholics were more easily accepted in Catholic cantons and Protestants in cantons where their denomination prevailed.

Naturalization was again not only a matter concerning foreign nationals; here the complex form of two different municipal organizations, the political municipality of all Swiss residents and the municipality as place of origin (*Bürgergemeinde*), were important. If they were citizens of a municipality other than their place of residence, Swiss nationals had to apply for the citizenship of that municipality and pay a considerable sum if they wanted to have the same economic and residential rights as the locals. Some liberal cantons tried to change this in the 1830s, but were not backed by the municipalities, which wanted the respective revenues.

On the other hand, the authorities of the municipality of origin had to express their consent to a marriage, especially if one of their citizens married a woman who was a citizen of a different municipality. The authorities of the municipality could interdict "poor" marriages and a marriage "with a bride from outside." They did so if they feared that the couple would not be able to support a family. Those decisions show an intersection of cantonal matrimonial laws, municipal citizenship rights, the common understanding that marriage had to be based on property, and the fact that women's citizenship could be called a "secondary citizenship"[28] since it was conveyed by their husbands upon marriage.[29]

The conflict was often enough not only between the husband's community and the future couple but also between the authorities of the different municipalities and cantons, as one can see in the following case: when the Bernese municipality of Lützelflüh prohibited the marriage between Barbara Tschudin from Läufelfingen in the Canton of Basel-Country and their citizen Johannes Pfister, a farm hand, who was citizen of Lützelflüh but had lived for years in the Canton of Basel-Country, the authorities of the Canton of Basel-Country intervened in favor of the couple. They were, however, told by the Bernese cantonal authorities that their law[30] backed their decision and that the municipalities were interested in preventing "frivolous and unhappy marriages" ("*leichtsinnige und unglückliche Ehen*"). Therefore, Barbara and Johannes could not marry.[31]

Since the middle of the nineteenth century, children would get the father's citizenship after marriage; only illegitimate children would get their mother's. Prohibitions to marry—such as in the case of Barbara and Johannes—aimed at reducing the number of "poor marriages" and children. Besides, by prohibiting a marriage—especially if the future wife was already pregnant—"the problem" remained that of the mother's municipality, for municipalities were obliged to care for their poor. This could cause severe problems for a couple. An illegitimate child—especially if it was not the first one—could well be a reason for imprisonment or a "foreign"[32] mother's expulsion from a municipality if a couple lived in the father's municipality, or the expulsion of the father if they lived in the mother's municipality. This procedure by the municipal authorities could severely damage the reputation and economic opportunities of an unmarried mother, as illegitimacy was a social stigma for mother and child. They would thereupon have severe problems in establishing an existence elsewhere. The anger of the government of the Canton of Basel-Country in the case of Barbara and Johannes had two causes: firstly, they would have to deal with the problem in case their citizen Barbara Tschudin should have children "out of wedlock," and secondly, the fact that at that time, the laws of Basel-Country did not permit them to prevent "poor marriages." They saw this as a problem, because most of the neighboring cantons had that possibility. They were therefore eager to add a respective provision to their poor law, which they finally did in 1859.[33] As it was always the right of the man's municipality to grant or deny a marriage license, this legal device increasingly caused suffering and sorrow when mobility rates rose as a result of industrialization. But it was a powerful obstacle intended to hinder women from entering into a relationship with "foreign" men and vice versa.

Marriage licenses were common not only in Swiss municipalities but also in southern Germany around the middle of the nineteenth century.[34] Marriages of bi-national couples were not actually handled differently, but they were even more complicated because of the different national laws and the distance to the place of residence, as research on marriage and illegitimacy in the Canton of Zurich shows.[35] The case of a German "bridegroom," a tanner from Wurttemberg, and the "bride," a servant from Wetzikon in the Canton of Zurich, may serve to illustrate this. The "bridegroom's" German municipality, Reutlingen, denied them a marriage license unless the "bride" provided an exorbitant sum, quite prohibitive in fact, given her financial situation. Thus, the municipality hindered such a marriage and avoided any responsibility for the children of such a union. The same had happened in Zurich in 1810 in a reverse case, when the marriage of a "bride" from Baden (Germany) and a "bridegroom" from Höngg in the Canton of Zurich was prevented because he could not raise the sum required for the naturalization of his "foreign" bride. Höngg even prohibited any contact between them until the sum was procured.[36]

Often enough, such a verdict heralded the end of a relationship. But in case it was continued, it ended more often than not with those concerned either being thrown into prison or "exiled"—that is, they were separated and sent back to their respective municipalities. Living together and sexual contact between an unmarried couple was illegal and liable to prosecution according to the order of the marriage court (*Ehegerichtsordnung*).

If the marriage license was granted, the bride then lost her former citizen's rights and was now considered a citizen of her husband's municipality. An 1808 decision of the *Tagsatzung*, the Diet of the Old Swiss Confederacy, was taken as legal basis for this. Though her loss of citizenship was not mentioned in that decision, federal authorities argued that it was the logical consequence.[37] In situations of need (sickness, old age, death of the husband), the wife had to rely on her husband's municipality for support, no matter where she lived. The municipality, however, was not obliged to support her at her place of residence but could request her to "return" to "her" municipality, a place she might not even know.

The link between marriage and citizenship was therefore a most welcome opportunity to control citizenship as well as the status of a citizen, the social order as well as the physical belonging and access to the privileges of a municipality. And it was proven again and again that women's ties, be it to the nation or the municipality, were weak ties, and that their citizenship amounted to only a contingent belonging.

The Federal Constitution of 1848 and Citizenship

The history of the Swiss federal state or Swiss Confederation began in 1848 when, after a successful revolution and a short military conflict between the cantons, the federal state was founded.[38] The new constitution guaranteed Swiss citizens a range of civic liberties: the right to reside wherever one wanted, equality before the law, and universal male suffrage. Although according to the letter of the law, Swiss citizenship conveyed political rights "on every citizen;" this did not hold true for women. For them, political rights were not an integral part of citizenship. In the 1830s, women's political equality had been discussed—hesitantly but without concrete results—and the issue was only taken up again in the 1860s when women in the Canton of Zurich sought political participation and those in the Canton of Basel-Country asked for access to better schooling and property rights during the revision of the cantonal constitutions—but without success.[39] The new federal constitution did not explicitly exclude women from political rights; they were, once again, simply not mentioned. Thus "equality," the most important device of the new constitution and, at the same time, a mythical and important element of social bonding in Switzerland, did not include women. They were citizens but they were not equal, and thus not visibly included in the invention and construction of Swiss national identity. While before 1848 political rights were not automatically conferred on all male citizens and political rights differed quite considerably among the various cantons, after 1848, the division now followed the sex line.

The rules of naturalization differed according to sex. The new constitution declared Swiss citizenship as unalienable. But women continued to lose their municipal and cantonal citizenship if they married a man from another municipality and/or canton, and even their national citizenship if they married a foreigner; for example, a woman became Italian or German, according to her husband's nationality. The law in most cantons declared that a woman had to accept her husband's municipal and national citizenship. This could cause a severe problem insofar as if after the death of her husband or in case of sickness she could no longer support herself or their children and became dependent on social welfare, she could be sent back to "her home country." The fact that a woman forfeited her citizenship by marriage and became a foreigner was still not sanctioned by law. It continued to be strictly a customary practice, a practice by which an important principle of the modern Swiss state was violated: the principle that there is no involuntary loss of nationality.

On the other hand, a Swiss man conveyed his citizenship—municipal, cantonal, as well as national—by marriage to his wife. The problems created by this legal situation on the national level were not different from those on the municipal level mentioned above, but due to the fact that mobility had increased, cases and difficulties snowballed.

In a period when national states were increasingly demarcating their territories and establishing borders, and took on a growing importance surrounding the construct of "national identity," women's relationship to the state became somewhat fragile. By the sheer possibility that they might lose their nationality, persons of the female gender became "temporary" citizens.

The procedure of naturalization was left to the cantons and municipalities and, especially after the unsuccessful revolution of 1848 in Germany and Austria, liberal cantons granted asylum to many refugees, along with their wives and children, and provided shelter by granting them municipal citizenship and, consequently, Swiss nationality. Although this caused considerable internal trouble between liberal and conservative cantons and diplomatic conflicts with the German states, the Swiss Confederation had no say in the matter.[40]

From the Revision of the Federal Constitution in 1874 to 1917

The revision of the Federal Constitution in 1874 changed the situation governing the conferral of rights. The constitution granted the federal authorities the right to determine conditions for the naturalization procedure: the approval of the federal authorities; two years of residence; and, as a result of the diplomatic conflicts of 1848, the guarantee that the applicants' naturalization would not prove detrimental to the Swiss state.[41] The revised constitution established a right to marriage and abolished the right of the municipalities to interfere. Municipal authorities deeply regretted this change.

Men conferred their citizenship on their wives.[42] The fact that a Swiss woman could not only *not* confer her citizenship on her husband but continued to lose her municipal citizenship upon her marriage to a citizen of a different municipality, and her Swiss nationality upon her marriage to a foreigner, did not cause any political discussions. The Swiss Civil Code (ZGB) of 1907, the first national codification of private law, simply stated that the wife obtained her husband's citizenship and thus resumed the *Tagsatzung* decision of 1808 and transferred it into a modern legal codex.[43] There was still no legal device stating that she would lose her former citizenship, neither with respect to her municipal citizenship nor her nationality, though this was continuously practiced until 1952.[44]

Between 1850 and 1910, the percentage of foreign residents in Switzerland had risen from three percent to 14.7 percent. In border cities such as Basel and Geneva, almost forty percent of the inhabitants were foreign nationals.[45] Industrialization and the growing opportunities on the Swiss labor market had encouraged immigration, mostly from Germany, France, and Italy. Switzerland was changing from a country of emigration to a country of immigration in the 1890s. As a result, bi-national marriages increased and so did naturalization or women's loss of citizenship by marriage. The municipalities now supported foreign workers when they needed assistance due to labor shortage, sickness, or old age, but officials tried to get the expenditure back from their native country. In the case of Italian nationals, there was no reasonable chance of reimbursement; the Basel Social Services decided in 1905 to no longer support Italians and forced them to leave the country. The reason was a mixture of suspicion against Italians, who had worked in road construction in Basel and were often out of work because of the seasonal character of that employment, and a feeling of the Italian "national character" being "dangerous," characterized by "seeking conflicts" and "being untidy and demanding."[46] In addition, people generally suspected them of having obtained financial support by fraud.

This interference of the construction of a national identity and of municipal structures, combined with the general suspicion against women who had married a foreigner, had severe consequences for women who had become Italian by marriage.[47] Forced repatriation was a cruel fate for workers who had left Italy maybe decades earlier. For a woman such as Elise Panozzo, née Schmidt, a widow, it was a country she did not know nor had any connection to; as she said in 1908, "Italy is a place where I have never been, do not know anybody and where I cannot understand the language."[48]

The survival of municipal citizenship is a particular feature of the Swiss political system and the Swiss system of social security; the loss of the ancestral national citizenship due to marriage is not.[49] Germany, Great Britain, and the United States had similar legal provisions. A comparison between the European and the U.S. system[50] is helpful, as in an immigrant society such as the United States the impact of citizenship and naturalization on the forming and construction of the populace becomes especially visible.[51] In the United States, citizenship was automatically obtained by birth (*jus soli*). A female American citizen lost her citizenship upon her marriage to a non-citizen until the 1920s, when citizenship status became increasingly conceptualized as being independent of marriage except in the case of Asian immigrants, who were considered "non-eligible" for American citizenship. Women who married men of Asian descent lost their American citizenship in case of an extended absence from the States. They also lost their right to a facilitated re-naturalization because of the provisions prohibiting immigration from Asia and the fact that re-naturalization was only possible after a return to the country. Racist immigration laws remained a barrier, even though after the proclamation of the "Equal Nationality Bill"[52] in

1934 marriage lost its influence on citizenship and foreign male and female spouses henceforth faced equal conditions with respect to naturalization.[53]

The high percentage of foreign nationals in Switzerland was not only due to immigration, but also to a reluctance to go after citizenship status, which was a pretty expensive undertaking. At the end of the nineteenth and the beginning of the twentieth centuries, this was seen as a problem because—as a statistician[54] put it—it had created a large group of people with no direct "ties and connections" to a state. They had, in his opinion, lost any connection to their home country and had not developed close bonds to the place they lived in and—very important in Switzerland—they had no political rights. Politicians and municipal authorities of towns and municipalities such as Basel, Zurich, and Geneva, locations with a high proportion of foreign nationals, tried to make naturalization more attractive by reducing fees and encouraging those who had lived there for some time or were even born there to apply for citizenship. This shows that in the question of citizenship, multilingual Switzerland was not divided along the language border.[55] Although the French-speaking part, *la Romandie*, the Romandy, is now often considered to be more liberal and sensitive regarding gender equality and the political rights of foreigners,[56] this did not generally apply to citizenship and naturalization law for the nineteenth and the first half of the twentieth century. Around 1900, economic factors and the number of foreign residents was more important than the difference between German and French-speaking cantons and aroused discussions in the parliaments in French-speaking Geneva as well as in German-speaking Basel and Zurich. This led politicians of those cities (or cantons) to campaign for more liberal naturalization laws on the federal level. However, their proposal to introduce *ius soli*—a facilitated naturalization of those born in Switzerland—was rejected by a vast majority of the cantons. Among those cantons were the French-speaking, while German-speaking cantons (Basel-City, Zurich, St. Galle, Thurgau) and the Italian-speaking Ticino would have agreed to these concepts. A compromise was finally accepted in 1903 when the new Federal Law on Citizenship entitled the cantons to enact laws allowing children born in Switzerland to become Swiss, if the mother [sic] was Swiss before her marriage with a foreigner or if the parents had lived in Switzerland at least five years before the birth of the child. This would even be applicable without the consent of the federal authorities.[57] However, none of the cantons took advantage of this possibility later on because the political climate changed quickly.

Around 1900, naturalization was seen as a perfect means of integration. The invitation to naturalize always aimed at winning male inhabitants as new citizens, although immigration was by no means confined to men. Many of the numerous servants in towns close to the borders came from adjacent Germany.[58] When Basel offered inhabitants living there for twenty-five plus years the opportunity to naturalize gratuitously in 1902, they explicitly did not send this invitation to women, because—as the *Bürgerrat*, the parliament of the *Bürgergemeinde* argued—women would not strengthen the municipality because they were not enfranchised and they did not constitute a potential military danger as they would not be called to arms by their native country.[59]

At the same time that politicians tried to reduce the percentage of foreign nationals by naturalization, a new concept arose, that of *Überfremdung*—literally alienation, a typically Swiss word, best translated by an analogue such as "domination by foreign influence" or simply "too many foreigners." The problem for those who adhered to that concept was not that the large percentage of foreigners was a problem because they were deprived of social and political rights, but that they were a danger to the *Schweizer Eigenart*, the "Swiss character" or nature. Naturalization was not seen as a means to integration but was to follow integration, and a complete acceptance of Swiss habits and culture was to be the very prerequisite of naturalization.[60] Although the definition of *Schweizer Eigenart* remained completely vague, it became part of the Law on Naturalization from the 1920s onwards.[61]

With the beginning of World War I, the percentage of foreign nationals dropped quite rapidly. Men were called "to arms" and their wives and children followed them, among them a considerable number of Swiss-born women who had become German, French, or Italian by marriage. Swiss women, who had lost their nationality by marriage but nevertheless tried to stay in Switzerland and be supported by their families, were probably ostracized in more than one way: as a woman who had married a foreigner and as a foreign national, as a member of "her" country who did not go "home," and as a wife who did not follow her husband. In general the number of naturalizations, which was not possible without becoming citizen of a community and a canton, increased during the war. Men who tried to naturalize themselves in order to escape military service were often not accepted. The government of the Canton of Basel-City suspended naturalization at the beginning of the war and when they re-started the process again the government explicitly prohibited naturalization of men who had received a draft notice, even if they had lived in Basel with their family for a long time, and taking the large number of foreigners in the canton and of bi-national marriages into consideration, formerly Swiss women must have often been affected. Independent naturalizations of women—that is, not as wives or daughters—were rare, though the number rose at the beginning of the war when women tried to stay in Switzerland. They were very often backed by their employers, who did not want to lose their servants or workers.[62]

The need to address the loss of nationality through marriage was realized by the Schweizerischer Verband für Frauenstimmrecht (SVF, Swiss Association for the Women's Vote)[63] in 1915 when the fate of formerly Swiss women, who had lived abroad outside the home country of their husbands, was brought to their attention. While their husbands—if they were considered enemy aliens—were detained in internment camps, their wives and children were not allowed to return to Switzerland but were "deported" to their so called "home countries." But the member-sections of the SVF were afraid of tackling that question, because it had nothing to do with the vote and the Association only decided in 1917 to deal with questions outside the scope of the vote.[64] They then proposed a kind of special protection for formerly Swiss nationals and shortly later dual nationality—proposals that drew no response from Swiss political authorities.[65]

1917–1945: Fear of Überfremdung*—Despite the Reduction of Foreign Residents*

Although the percentage of foreign nationals had dropped, naturalization laws were paradoxically tightened and, in 1920, the minimum time of residence before application was raised from two years to six years.[66] This clearly shows that from that time forward naturalization was understood to be the final consequence of a process of integration and assimilation.[67]

The Swiss Association for the Women's Vote had begun to take up the issue of a married woman's nationality and the question concerning the loss of Swiss citizenship by marriage with an "alien" again shortly after World War I. On the level of international women's organizations, their proposal for dual nationality was rejected: the International Alliance of Women (IAWSEC) favored independent nationality for women, irrespective of marriage. Repeated contacts of the SVF with officials of the Swiss Political Department were fruitless even though they could cite as a model the Swedish law, which specified dual nationality, without causing any problem.[68]

They decided to profit from the efforts made on an international level by IAWSEC to implement an independent citizenship for women. The Bund Schweizerischer Frauenverbände (BSF, National Council of Swiss Women), the umbrella organization of the Swiss women's movement and ICW affiliate, joined them and when the issue appeared on the agenda for The Hague Conference on Codification (1930), they again asked for an audience with a member of the Federal Council to present their demands and suggested sending a female lawyer to the conference.[69] At a meeting with Giuseppe Motta, Minister of Foreign Affairs, whom they had already contacted in 1923, they were, however, told to present their demands in writing: they officially proposed "Frl. Dr. Speiser-Basel" as delegate.[70] Antoinette Quinche, Ruth Speiser (BSF), Nelly Schreiber-Favre (SVF), and Annie Leuch-Reineck (president of SVF) met for a second official meeting with the Head of Department of Justice, Heinrich Häberlin, and the male delegates appointed for the conference. Annie Leuch reported that their suggestion to send a female lawyer to the conference was met by a complete lack of understanding ("*mit absolutem Unverständnis*").[71] Their proposal still was to grant dual nationality, arguing that no change of law was necessary since a married woman's loss of her original citizenship was not indicated in any legislation but was only customary and common practice.

In the 1930s, a national debate on naturalization was initiated, though this proved to be a highly controversial affair. On the one hand, it was characterized by distancing Switzerland from Germany by a definition of the Swiss state (and society) as not relying on any concepts of race.[72] But on the other hand, authoritarian forms of government were admired, the eugenic fear of a populace degenerating due to foreign influence pervaded the discussion, and any increase of the Jewish population was anxiously noted.[73]

In the process of changing the naturalization law of the Canton of Basel-City, the director of the psychiatric clinic, John E. Staehelin, requested that "mental health" be made a more decisive issue in accepting or denying citizenship. In the 1938 revision of the law, this was put into practice. It became an argument against naturalization if a person or a person's relatives had had any previous contact with a psychiatric clinic. This reference to the family's case history embodied the eugenic background of the new provision.[74] Physical and mental health was generally made a prerequisite for naturalization, and even if not sanctioned by law, it was common practice in Switzerland. In Geneva, the cantonal parliament turned a respective paragraph down in 1924 but finally accepted it in 1934.[75]

It was then that a debate on women's citizenship became part of a more general debate on naturalization, Swiss identity, and foreign influence. One of the most important discussants of the debate on citizenship was Max Ruth, a lawyer and high-ranking official of the Federal Department of Justice and Police (EJPD). Although he declared his point of view to be "private," his publications had semi-official character.[76] One of his main positions was that Switzerland—although he considered the country as "*übervölkert*" (over-populated)—had to try and bind those inhabitants who were foreigners "on paper only" to Switzerland. This seemed important to him with respect to the welfare of the country and its "*Wehrhaftigkeit*" (defensive potential). To him, the existing laws on naturalization were too complicated, and "a perverted nationalism"[77] hindered even those who had been born in the country and were completely "assimilated" to become Swiss. This had to be changed—according to his opinion—by accepting a modified *jus soli* and forcing the municipalities to accept as Swiss citizens those born in the country—and, in particular, the descendants of a (formerly) Swiss mother.

On the other hand, and despite his positive notion of (formerly) Swiss mothers, Ruth vividly opposed any change in women's citizenship status. The women's movement in Switzerland again called attention to the severe problems caused by a loss of Swiss citizenship. Not only did women lose the possibility of social security even if they stayed in Switzerland; if they were civil servants they could lose their jobs, or if they lived abroad they could lose diplomatic protection.

Max Ruth condemned the idea of maintaining Swiss citizenship after marriage or of dual nationality as completely destroying family bonds. The disadvantages for women were, in his eyes, not severe enough and women could "re-nationalize" if the marriage failed or if the husband died. After all, he said, "Marriage is destiny and fatherland is destiny—there is no remedy for it." The one and only "remedy" was "to abstain from marrying a foreigner."[78] A strange conclusion, because women's citizenship was not their "destiny;" it could be changed without them agreeing to it. If anything was "destiny" in that interpretation, it was certainly their sex. In the 1930s the relationship between the discussion about nationality and the deteriorating economic and political situation became obvious. The fear arose that dual nationality would not only allow a woman, married to a foreigner, to keep her employment, but that it also might give her husband a legitimate claim to stay and seek work in Switzerland.[79] On the one hand, denial of dual nationality became a means of "protecting" the Swiss labor market, and on the other hand, it was a safeguard against immigration, especially by Jewish immigrants. In 1935, Heinrich Rothmund, chief of the Federal Department of Justice and Police (EJPD), mentioned what the loss of nationality might mean when he hinted at the "danger" that (Jewish) women might enter into marriage with German Jews even more carelessly if they could keep their Swiss nationality. He said that the EJPD was "not very interested" (*haben wir wenig Interesse*) in marriages of Swiss women with German Jews, as their husband's German families would do anything "to establish themselves" (*sich zu etablieren*) in Switzerland.[80]

The naturalization of foreign women by marriage had also been discussed since the 1930s. Ruth feared that "bad elements" might have infiltrated Switzerland in this way.[81] In the 1940s, psychiatrist Staehelin, director of the Basel clinic *Friedmatt*, stated that the percentage of patients in his psychiatric clinic who had been naturalized since 1900 by far exceeded the percentage of patients from old and established families. In his opinion, this was the result of the fact that the canton dealt carelessly with applications for citizenship. And what particularly aroused his anger was that the canton had no say in the process of naturalization of women by marriage to a Swiss citizen.[82] He requested that the process as such be subjected to specific control. However, his endeavor was not successful this time and the provisions in question were not changed.

On an international level, the commitment of the women's organizations to dual citizenship was ultimately futile. Here, the different dimensions of citizenship rights (e.g., nationality and political rights) met. When The Hague Convention on Nationality failed to guarantee that women would receive the same national rights enjoyed by their male counterparts, American feminists pressed for a national solution. They were successful—the Equal Nationality Bill was signed by President Roosevelt and ratified by the Senate in 1934.[83] The fact that the Nineteenth Amendment to the U.S. Constitution granted women's suffrage in 1920 proved vital to this outcome—as voters women had become a political force to be reckoned with, even though the number of female members in the American Congress was still small.[84]

The British Nationality and Status of Aliens Act of 1914 had instigated a system similar to that of Switzerland. This meant that if a British woman married an "alien," she automatically lost her British citizenship. But in 1948, British women did have the vote, and the government passed the Nationality Act, giving women the same rights as men upon marriage to someone from another country. These precedents were carefully noted by Swiss feminists.

Swiss women did not yet have political rights; in vain they had tried to change this shortly after World War I by launching several cantonal initiatives. Although political rights were no guarantee for independent citizenship—as the German case showed[85]—without political rights, it was even more difficult to bring about change, especially in Switzerland, where any change of law could be put to a plebiscite and where any amendment of the constitution required a plebiscite.

Re-naturalization was, even in the 1930s, not as simple as Ruth had argued. Case studies show that the municipalities continued to prevent women from taking up their former Swiss citizenship after a divorce or the death of their husband, out of fear that the municipality might have to support them financially. Amazingly, sometimes even eugenic arguments were used against them, arguments that had otherwise been used against foreigners.[86]

The "destiny" of women's citizenship once again became a significant issue with dangerous consequences during the time of the Nazi regime in Germany.[87] Swiss women who were married to German Jews, or to Jews in countries invaded by the German army who had lost their citizenship rights because of the German Race Law, were, if they were Jewish themselves, not allowed to return to Switzerland in order to reestablish their former Swiss citizenship: in fact, Switzerland prevented any Jews from crossing the border. The "J" in their passport identified them. Violation of this prohibition to return could result in deportation and death. The fate of Margrit Barth may serve as an example: she had married a Dutch Jew in Amsterdam in 1938. Her application for a visa to return to Switzerland after the German occupation of the Netherlands in 1940 was denied. She then tried to illegally pass the Swiss borders near Geneva but was refused entry into the country. She was finally deported to Auschwitz.[88] It was not until December 1942 that the Federal Government decreed not to repel former Swiss citizens at the borders, but only in 1944 were formerly Swiss women given express permission to enter the country.[89] This was too late for many victims of the Holocaust, quite apart from the fact that it proved extremely difficult to get to the Swiss border at all.

Contrary to this "benevolence," there were two crucial modifications to, and tightenings of, the law. Many foreign women had married Swiss citizens in order to be allowed to stay in Switzerland. Communists or socialists were willing to enter into a so-called "*Bürgerrechtsehen* or *Scheinehen*," fictitious marriages. Before 1940, such a marriage could be annulled but women would remain Swiss. In 1940, a government decree made it possible not only to annul a fictitious marriage, by which a woman had obtained Swiss nationality, but to de-nationalize the woman.[90] The women's movement objected, but during the war, the Swiss government could issue emergency decrees, by the so-called *Vollmachtenregime*, without parliamentary consent or the risk of a referendum. In 1941, another government edict decreed the loss of citizenship for a woman at marriage with a foreigner. By the edict, what had been practiced for more than a century became the (written) law of the land for the first time.[91]

Toward Legal Equality: 1950–1989

Change in the laws regarding women's citizenship came about in the 1950s. The reason for this revision of the law on naturalization was not the status of women but the endeavor to hamper naturalization. Although women still did not have the vote,[92] the National Council of Swiss Women was able to nominate five female lawyers, among them Antoinette Quinche, the first lawyer in the Canton of Vaud and until 1951 the Vice President of the SVF, as well as connected to the International Federation for Women in Legal Careers,[93] as members for the government's advisory expert commission. The women's movement succeeded in publishing reports on the fate of women who had been deprived of their nationality in newspapers and to interest a wider public in the question of women's nationality.[94] It was this campaign in the press that laid the foundation for a change in public opinion, and in the opinion of the members of the commission, because it gave a face to the problem of the loss of nationality. It was the face of "German" women who had been prevented from returning to Switzerland during or shortly after the war, as well as those who had married Polish refugees who were former internees of Swiss labor-camps, women who had never lived outside Switzerland themselves, and—as one of them put it—"[did] not know how to explain to her son why he is not Swiss like his classmates."[95]

This change in opinion, which led to the alteration of the draft legislation and finally of the law was, however, not only the result of the pressure brought to bear by the women's movement and of broader European developments concerning marriage and citizenship. The only reason that had allowed some Swiss women to keep their nationality despite marriage to a foreigner had been that the husband's country would not automatically confer his nationality on his wife and she was threatened with statelessness. In the fifties most countries no longer changed or conferred citizenship by marriage, and the authorities had to allow more women to keep their nationality.

The bill passed both chambers in 1952 only after a fierce debate, but it was not put to a referendum. What Max Ruth had feared as the "end of family bonds" entered into force on January 1, 1953: women could keep their Swiss nationality upon request and women who had lost their nationality could demand repatriation.[96] Their children could be included in the request, only if they lived in Switzerland.[97] Most of the delegates of the women's organizations would have preferred an independent nationality, regardless of marriage, but they accepted what can be called an important step toward the integration of women and the temporary end of a long and engaged struggle by the SVF. Decisive for this outcome in the chambers was the support of younger members of the National Council or the Council of States like Peter von Roten,[98] and the dedicated presence and support of the newly elected Minister of the Department of Justice, Markus Feldmann.[99] Feldmann even convinced conservative catholic backbenchers to accept the law when he told them that the Schweizerische Katholische Frauenbund (SKF, Swiss Catholic Women's Organization), a conservative catholic women's movement, which had hesitated so long to take a stand, was now in favor of the law.[100] At the same time, the revised law on naturalization doubled the minimum time of residence before an application was possible by raising it to twelve years. This can be called an opening toward the inside accompanied by a closure toward the outside. Women still could not confer their citizenship on their husbands or children.

Swiss women who married a citizen of a different municipality continued, however, to lose municipal citizenship. For some left-wing Geneva politicians, this seemed to bring about a new kind of inequality. To place women who married citizens of a different municipality on equal footing with women who married foreigners, the 1955 Geneva Law on Citizenship introduced an article giving female citizens of a Geneva municipality the opportunity to keep their citizenship after marriage with citizens of a different municipality. This first step toward equality was nullified by the EJPD as not being congruent with federal law.

In 1959, the first vote on women's suffrage on the federal level failed decisively (thirty-three percent to sixty-six percent), but the cantons of Vaud, Neuchâtel, and Geneva had introduced the vote on the cantonal level in or shortly after 1959.[101] At least since that time, the French-speaking cantons could be called forerunners of equal rights for women. In 1961, they resumed the endeavor for equal municipal rights for women, which was accepted on the cantonal level in 1964.[102] Only in 1988 was this enacted for all cantons.[103]

In 1971, the male constituency finally granted political rights to all women on the federal level. Step-by-step the legal system was changed. A milestone on the way to equality was the 1981 constitutional amendment granting equality between men and women,[104] followed by the Law on Equality in 1995. Consequently, naturalization laws had to be changed; the fact that men could still convey their Swiss citizenship to their wives at marriage but women could not was no longer compatible with the notion of equality. Thus, the law[105] was changed; "facilitated naturalization," that is, the naturalization of the foreign spouses of Swiss nationals—after three years of marriage and five years of residence—was introduced for men and women alike. The proposition that it would have been fairer to transfer the previous legal situation of the privileged gender, men, to women was denied. The municipalities, however, which had remained strongholds of inequality, began to change municipal citizenship. Before 1988 a woman used to get her husband's municipal citizenship at marriage and lost her original citizenship. Since the change of marriage law in 1988, she could keep her former municipal citizenship at marriage but received her husband's in addition to it, while children received their father's municipal citizenship. This stipulation was changed quite recently: since 2013, marriage no longer has any influence on the municipal citizenship of a woman. She keeps her inherited citizenship.[106]

Recent Changes and the Challenge of Equality

Equality is a complicated concept, especially when living conditions and gender-based concepts are not equal. It has become obvious that, in a marriage, foreign women are more easily put under pressure by their husbands to stay in a difficult relationship in order not to lose the right to naturalization in the case of an early breakdown of marriage than vice versa. For example, if a husband should die earlier within the specified three-year period, it proved to be more difficult for a woman than for a man—especially if she did not take up gainful employment—to show that she was well integrated and "deserve[d]" to stay without having been naturalized.[107]

Equality between men and women obtained by the 2013 Law on Citizenship can still prove ambivalent, although the consequences are not as grave: a woman will keep her municipal citizenship (as well as her name) at marriage, the couple can decide the family name and citizenship of their (future) children, and can—if they are citizens of different municipalities—choose either his or her municipality as a "place of origin." But as family name and municipal citizenship are linked, it will likely be the name and citizenship of the husband in far more than fifty percent of the marriages. It is not only the fact that a wife sticks to tradition by choosing her husband's last name, as some newspaper comments state,[108] but that Swiss men generally do not accept that "their" children do not carry their name. A woman who decides to use her name may then have no "connection" with the "place of origin" of her children. Before equal citizenship rights were established, name and citizenship were not linked and, as I have mentioned, a woman received the municipal citizenship of her husband in addition to her own, and thus kept the connection to her children's place of origin and their name by adding her husband's name to hers.

To end discrimination equality must be applied. The pressure to achieve homogeneity forces a suppression of existing differences and adoption of some standards of privileged groups. The dilemma that arises for women through the demand to obtain equal rights is one of the most challenging aspects of politics for women.[109] In her work on the Sears case and on the French women's movement, Joan Scott has analyzed this "paradox of gender" as a structural trait of women's history.[110] The inclusion and participation of women requires the rejection of claims to homogeneity.[111]

The history of Swiss citizenship rights shows that the concepts of "national identity" as well as the homogeneity of law and of the populace are "invented traditions."[112] The aim and function of this concept is a demarcation and construction of borders; a loss of citizenship or prevention of naturalization goes far beyond the spectrum of those who apply for citizenship: it is of preventive and constructive character. The constructs of "national identity" and "equality" and the idea of the homogeneity of Swiss citizens and citizenship can and do impact social and political reality, but only if one ignores the problematic character of women's citizenship and denies the relevance of their right to naturalization.

The integration of their history shows not only how often women's citizenship rights have been changed in the course of time, but also that different concepts for men and women coexisted at the same time—examples that prove that citizenship has never been the "natural" concept some pretend it to be, but was dictated by the demands of respective political power structures.

The modern state defined nationality and established legal regulations for the process of nationalization. That a wife had to adopt her husband's nationality was introduced and codified in several countries in the late eighteenth and the early nineteenth centuries. Switzerland practiced the "marriage rule" but codified it only in 1940 and abolished it in 1952; with respect to nationality, under the pressure of the decisions taken by other countries, the inequality of municipal citizenship lasted until 1988 or even 2013. Why did this discrimination continue in Switzerland while other countries abolished discriminatory regulations? One reason is that Switzerland was deeply embedded in a Republican tradition with strong corporative elements focusing on the family and small municipalities with active (male) citizens. Women were considered a subordinate part of their family. The liberal 1848 Constitution preserved those corporative elements, as the municipal organization of citizenship clearly shows.[113] The male-headed municipalities tried whenever possible to prevent change and not to give up any authority.

The second reason is the late enfranchisement of women, who until 1971 had only an indirect method of intervening in political processes concerning their nationality. Any attempt to change this through an interpretation of the constitution or by a plebiscite failed. Here, the elements of citizenship discrimination and the corporate organization of Swiss politics meet and coincide: the argument that women were represented by their husbands and that the vote would make mischief in a family was used even as late as 1971. And some cantons and municipalities resisted even after the Federal decision: even after 1971, several municipalities of the Canton of the Grisons did not allow women to vote on the municipal level, and in 1991 the Canton of Appenzell had to be forced by the Federal Court to enfranchise women with respect to cantonal decisions.[114] In Switzerland, the battle for married women's independent nationality was not won easily. The battle for equality continues.

Notes

1 The number of inhabitants had risen from 7,255,700 in 2001 to 8,236,600 inhabitants in 2014, when 1,947,023 were foreign nationals. Reference date December 2014: Cf, https://www.bfm.admin.ch/bfm/de/home/publiservice/statistik/auslaenderstatistik/archiv/2014.html; http://www.bfs.admin.ch/bfs/portal/de/index/themen/01/01/new/nip_detail.html?gnpID=2015–049.

2 The so-called Volksinitiative "Gegen Masseneinwanderung" (popular initiative "against mass immigration") was accepted on Febrary 9, 2014 by a majority of 50.34 percent. Its political consequences are so far not clear at all.

3 Schweizerische Bundesverfassung (BV) (Swiss Federal Constitution) 1999 Art. 37, 1: "Schweizerbürgerin oder Schweizerbürger ist, wer das Bürgerrecht einer Gemeinde und das Bürgerrecht des Kantons besitzt." (Swiss citizen is who is a citizen of a municipality and a canton).

4 On the history of citizenship, including women's citizenship, cf.: Brigitte Studer, Gérard Arlettaz, and Regula Argast eds., *Das Schweizer Bürgerrecht. Erwerb, Verlust, Entzug von 1848 bis zur Gegenwart* (Zurich: Verlag Neue Zürcher Zeitung, 2008); Regina Wecker, " 'Ehe ist Schicksal, Vaterland ist auch Schicksal und dagegen ist kein Kraut gewachsen.' Gemeindebürgerrecht und Staatsangehörigkeitsrecht von Frauen in der Schweiz 1798–1998," *L'homme* 10, no. 1 (1999): 13–37; Regula Argast, *Staatsbürgerschaft und Nation. Ausschließung und Integration in der Schweiz 1848–1933* (Göttingen: Vandenhoeck & Ruprecht, 2007). For a commented bibliography, cf. Regina Wecker, "Die Politik mit dem Bürgerrecht," *traverse. Zeitschrift für Geschichte* 1 (2013): 141–155.

5 Schweizerische Bundesverfassung (BV) (Swiss Federal Constitution) 1848 Art. 43. "Kein Kanton darf einen Bürger des Bürgerrechtes verlustig erklären." (No Canton may deprive a citizen of his citizenship.) Schweizerische Bundesverfassung (BV) 1874 Art. 44. "Kein Kanton darf einen Kantonsbürger aus seinem Gebiete verbannen (verweisen) oder ihn des Bürgerrechtes verlustig erklären." (No Canton may ban a citizen from its territory and deprive a citizen of his citizenship).

6 Until the middle of the nineteenth century, in some Catholic cantons illegitimate children could take their father's name and citizenship; in Protestant cantons they took their mother's. After 1860 the *Maternitätsprinzip* (principle of maternity) became standard for illegitimate children. Cf. "Illegitimität," *Historisches Lexikon der Schweiz (HLS)*, http://www.hls-dhs-dss.ch/textes/d/D16112.php.

7 The *Bürgergemeinde* (municipality of "descent," as well: *Bürgergemeinde, Ortsbürgergemeinde, Tagwen.* In French: *bourgeoisie, commune bourgeoise*, Italian: *patriziat*, Romansch: *vischnanca burgaisa*), includes all individuals who are citizens of the *Bürgergemeinde*, usually by having inherited the *Bürgerrecht* (citizenship) or by naturalization, regardless of where they were born or where they currently live.

8 For social security rights, cf. Thierry Christ, "Fürsorge," *Historisches Lexikon der Schweiz (HLS)*, http://www.hls-dhs-dss.ch/textes/d/D25809.php. For political rights, cf. Tomas Poledna, "Stimm- und Wahlrecht," *Historisches Lexikon der Schweiz (HLS)*, http://www.hls-dhs-dss.ch/textes/d/D26453.php.

9 E.g., Diepoldsau, a municipality in the Canton of St. Gall, offers a free Christmas tree from the municipal forest; Eptingen, a municipality in the Canton of Basel-Country, offers free mineral water from a municipal source to members of the municipality living there.

10 Until 1988, a woman lost her municipal citizenship by marriage and obtained her husband's. When this was changed by the new marriage law, a considerable number of women applied for their original citizenship, displaying a certain emotional attachment to their municipality of origin.

11 *Gemeinden* or *Einwohnergemeinden* (German: *Gemeinden*/French: *commune*/Italian: *comuni*/Romansh: *vischnancas*, residential municipalities in contrast to *Bürgergemeinden*, cf. Note 8*)* are the smallest government division in Switzerland. At the beginning of 2015, there existed 2,352. The number of municipalities is decreasing to save administrative costs.

12 In four cantons (Neuchâtel, Jura, Vaud, Fribourg), foreigners are entitled to vote on the municipal level. In the canton of Geneva, they can vote and decide on a subject. Two cantons (Grisons, Appenzell AR) enabled the municipalities to decide whether or not they grant citizenship rights to foreigners. Foreigners may not cast ballots on federal matters.

13 In the cantons of Nidwalden, Schwyz, Appenzell IR, Neuchâtel, Geneva, and Vaud there are no *Bürgergemeinden*, the political municipalities fulfill their responsibilities. Citizenship of the *Bürgergemeinde* and the *Bürgerort* (place of origin) is still inherited.

14 This was foreshadowed in the Helvetic Republic (see below) when for the first time, two politically separate but geographically similar organizations were created.

15 Not until the Federal Constitution of 1874 were all male citizens granted equal political rights on the local (municipal and cantonal) level and were political voting and electoral rights removed entirely from the *Bürgergemeinde*. For a short English summary of the history of corporal municipalities, cf. http://en.wikipedia.org/wiki/Bürgergemeinde.

16 Brigitte Studer, "Citizenship as Contingent National Belonging. Married Women and Foreigners in Twentieth-Century Switzerland," *Gender & History* 13, no. 3 (2001): 622–654.

17 Schweizerisches Zivilgesetzbuch (ZGB) Art. 161.

18 Ziff. I des BG vom 30. September 2011 (Name und Bürgerrecht), in Kraft seit 1. January 2013 (AS 2012 2569; Bundesblatt, 2009 7573–7581). no I, 1 FL of September 30, 2011 (Name and citizenship), in force since January 1, 2013.

19 The Law on Naturalization was recently revised. The Federal Government had proposed to reduce the required time of residence from 12 to 8 years and accentuate language competence and integration into the community. The National Council (*Nationalrat*, the larger house of the Federal Assembly) decided to require 10 years of residence. The Council of States (*Ständerat*, the smaller house of the Federal Assembly) backed this proposal. The revised law will likely come into force in 2017.

20 Jens Hainmüller and Dominik Hangartner, *Does Direct Democracy Hurt Immigrant Minorities? Evidence from Naturalization Decisions in Switzerland*. January 2013, http://ssrn.com/abstract=2022064.

21 Decison of the Swiss Federal Court of May 12, 2004, *Bundesgericht (BGE 130 I 140) Urteil vom 12. Mai 2004*. http://relevancy.bger.ch/php/clir/http/index.php?lang=de&zoom=&type=show_document&highlight_docid=atf%3A%2F%2F130-I-140%3Ade.

22 *Amtliche Sammlung der Acten aus der Zeit der Helvetischen Republik (Official Publication of the Records of Time of the Helvetic Republic, ASHR) (1798–1803)*, 16 vols. (Bern/Fribourg: Stämpfli 1886–1966). Decision concerning Jewish citizenship: ASHR XI, 209–211.

23 Jews obtained citizenship in France in 1791 during the Revolution.

24 Cf. Anne-Lise Head-König, "Mariage et citoyenneté des femmes. L'influence de la Helvétique et la Révolution sur la conception du mariage en Suisse," in *Dossier Helvetik—Dossier Helvetique. Sozioökonomische Strukturen–Frauengeschichte/Geschlechtergeschichte*, ed. Christian Simon, vol. 2 (Basel: Hebing & Lichtenhahn, 1997), 151–166 (155, 156).

25 Head-König, "Mariage," 156.

26 Head-König, Ibid., 157. Head-König considers this a deterioration of the situation of the widow, because she might have had closer connection to her municipality of origin. Head-König, "Mariage," 159.

27 The period of the "Helvetic Republic" seems to have been too short to bring about profound changes with respect to municipal citizenship or nationality.

28 Beatrice Ziegler, "Frauenstimmrechtskampf in der Schweiz—zum Verhältnis von Frauen und Staat," *Schweizerische Zeitschrift für Geschichte (SZG)* 46, no. 3 (1996): 297–305 (300).

29 Studies of the situation prevalent in many cantons show this quite clearly: Eva Sutter, *"Ein Act des Leichtsinns und der Sünde." Illegitimität im Kanton Zürich: Recht, Moral und Lebensrealität (1800–1860)* (Zurich: Chronos, 1995), 192–193; Verena Schmid, *". . . von allem entblösst." Armut, Armenwesen und staatliche Reformpolitk in Schaffhausen (1800–1850)* (Zurich: Chronos, 1993); Annamarie Ryter, *Als Weibsbild bevogtet. Zum Alltag von Frauen im 19. Jahrhundert. Geschlechtsvormundschaft und Ehebeschränkungen im Kanton Basel-Landschaft* (Liestal: Verlag des Kantons Basel-Landschaft, 1994).

30 Gesetz über das Armenwesen 1847 (Poor Law, 1847), in Gesetze des Kantons Basel-Landschaft (Laws of the Canton of Basel-Country), vol. 8, 22ff.

31 Staatsarchiv Basel-Landschaft, Justiz B.I. Nr. 2180 and 240; Annamarie Ryter, *Als Weibsbild bevogtet*, 81.

32 "Foreign" here means that she was not a citizen of the municipality she lived in. The legal basis for imprisonment or expulsion were orders of the so-called marriage courts, ("Ehegerichtsordnungen," e.g. Cantons of Basel-Country and Basel-City) or matrimonial laws ("Matrimonialgesetze" in Zurich). When some of the cantons codified civil law in the middle of the nineteenth century they partly transferred the provisions. These provisions were abolished by the Amendment of the Federal Constitution in 1874.

33 Gesetz über das Armenwesen (Poor Law) vom 8. November 1859, § 16 und 17, in: Gesetze des Kantons Basel-Landschaft, vol. 8, 22ff. (Laws of the Canton of Basel-Country); Ryter, "Als Weibsbild bevogtet," 83.

34 Wolfgang Kaschuba and Carola Lipp, *Dörfliches Überleben. Zur Geschichte materieller und sozialer Reproduktion ländlicher Gesellschaften im 19. und frühen 20. Jahrhundert* (Tübingen: Tübinger Verein für Volkskunde, 1982), 312–320.

35 Sutter, *Ein Act*, 192f.

36 Staatsarchiv Zürich (State Archive of the Canton of Zurich) YY 3.8 and YY 3.9 Ehegerichtsprotokoll 1810, 1811; Sutter, *Ein Act*, 206–207, and footnote 15, 344.

37 Zaccaria Giacometti and Fritz Fleiner, *Schweizerisches Bundesstaatsrecht* (Zürich: Poligraphischer Verlag, 1949), 202.

38 The development of a federal state had been prepared and foreshadowed by several liberal movements in those industrialized cantons that had already introduced universal male suffrage in the 1830s, while other cantons stuck to the old, aristocratic privileges. The differences of political opinion between the liberal, mostly Protestant cantons and the conservative, mostly Catholic cantons remained insurmountable even after the Swiss Civil War and the founding of the Swiss Confederation. It led to different institutions and naturalization procedures.

39 For Zurich, cf. Elisabeth Joris, "Mündigkeit und Geschlecht: Die Liberalen und das 'Recht der Weiber,'" in *Im Zeichen der Revolution. Der Weg zum Schweizerischen Bundesstaat 1798–1848*, ed. Thomas Hildbrand and Albert Tanner (Zurich: Chronos, 1997), 88. For Basel-Country, cf.: Petition von 30 Sissacherinnen an den Verfassungsrat des Kantons Baselland vom 29. August 1862 (Petition by 30 women from Sissach to the Constituency of the Canton of Basel-Country),

in *Alles was RECHT ist! Baselbieterinnen auf dem Weg zu Gleichberechtigung und Gleichstellung*, ed. Pascale Meyer and Sabine Kubli (Liestal: Museum im alten Zeughaus, 1992), 17.

40 Martin Leuenberger, *Frei und gleich und fremd. Flüchtlinge im Baselbiet zwischen 1830 und 1880* (Liestal: Verlag des Kantons Basel-Landschaft, 1996).

41 Schweizerische Bundesverfassung (BV) (Federal Constitution of Switzerland), 1874 Art. 44, 2.

42 BV Art. 54, 1.

43 Kapitel 5. Wirkungen der Ehe im Allgemeinen (Chapter 5. General impact of marriage) Art. 161, "Die Ehefrau erhält den Namen und das Bürgerrecht des Ehemannes." (The wife obtains the name and the citizenship of her husband.)

44 Nicole Schwalbach, "Ausbürgerung zur Zeit des Zweiten Weltkriegs," in *Bürgerrecht*, 267–294; Studer, "Citizenship," 291.

45 Heiner Ritzmann-Blickenstorfer, ed. *Historische Statistik der Schweiz* (Zurich: Chronos, 1996), 138.

46 Jahresversammlung der Basler Armenpflege 1905 (Annual Meeting of the Poor Law Administration of the Canton of Basel-City), cited in Anna Katharina Schmid, "Die verwaltete Armut. Die Allgemeine Armenpflege in Basel 1898–1911," diploma (Master's) thesis, University of Basel, 1984, 118.

47 Schmid, "Verwaltete Armut," 116–117.

48 Schmid, Ibid., 122.

49 Legally, Swiss municipalities of origin (*Bürgergemeinden*) remained responsible for "their" poor, wherever they lived, up to the 1970s, when this responsibility was transferred to the residential municipality. This important change allowed welfare recipients to stay in their place of residence. But there are signs of problems in the municipal organization of welfare even in this new system: in small municipalities, one or two welfare cases may far exceed a municipal budget. To avoid a deficit in the municipality's finances, a member of the municipal council recently requested that owners of houses not rent flats to welfare recipients. Cf, http://www.aargauerzeitung.ch/aargau/kanton-aargau/keine-wohnungen-an-sozialfaelle-auch-glarners-gemeinde-macht-das-so-128239240.

50 For the history and interpretation of the meaning of American citizenship, cf. James H. Kettner, *The Development of American Citizenship 1606–1870* (Chapel Hill: University of Michigan, 1978), and Linda K. Kerber, "The Meaning of Citizenship," *Journal of American History* 84, no. 3 (1997): 833–854. Concerning the "citizenship" of women, Linda K. Kerber, "The Paradox of Women's Citizenship in the Early Republic, The Case of Martin v. Commonwealth, 1805," *American Historical Review* 97 (April 1992): 349–378; and Nancy F. Cott, "Marriage and Women's Citizenship in the United States, 1830–1934," *American Historical Review* 103, no. 5 (December 1998): 1440–1474.

51 Cott, "Marriage," 1443.

52 Cott, Ibid., 1471.

53 Cott, Ibid., 1469.

54 Hermann Kinkelin, *Die Bevölkerung des Kantons Basel-Stadt am 1. Dezember 1880. Im Auftrage des H. Regierungsrates* (Basel: Birkhäuser, 1884).

55 The four national languages of Switzerland are German, French, Italian, and Romansh. Sixty-five percent of the population of Switzerland live in the German and 24.4 percent in the French-speaking part, while 8.4 percent live in the Italian and 0.6 percent in the Romansh-speaking part. In 17 cantons, German is the only official language (Aargau, Appenzell Inner Rhodes [IR], Appenzell Outer Rhodes [AR], Basel-City, Basel-Country, Glarus, Lucerne, Nidwalden, Obwalden, Schaffhausen, Schwyz, Solothurn, St. Galle, Thurgau, Uri, Zug, Zurich).

In the cantons of Berne, Fribourg, and Valais, French is co-official; in the trilingual canton of Grison, more than half of the population speaks German, while the rest speaks Romansh or Italian. The French-speaking cantons, the so-called *Romandie* (Romandy), are Geneva, Vaud, Neuchâtel, and Jura. The cantons of Valais and Fribourg are divided but have a French-speaking majority.

56 The canton of Vaud was the first canton to enfranchise women in 1959; Geneva and Neuchâtel followed soon.

57 Argast, *Staatsbürgerschaft*, 181.

58 They had immigrated from Baden-Wurttemberg, or Alsace-Lorraine, which was German from 1871 until the end of World War I.

59 Regula Argast, "Das Basler Kantons- und Gemeindebürgerrecht," in *Bürgerrecht*, 197–228 (193).

60 Botschaft des Bundesrates vom 9. November 1920, Bundesblatt, V, 1920, 18.

61 Regina Wecker, "Eugenik—individueller Ausschluss und nationaler Konsens," in *Krisen und Stabilisierung. Die Schweiz in der Zwischenkriegszeit*, ed. Sebastian Guex, Brigitte Studer, Bernard Degen, Markus Kübler, Edzard Schade, Béatrice Ziegler (Zurich: Chronos 1998), 165–179.

62 Pierre-Yves Kocher, "Die Einbürgerungspraxis in Basel-Stadt 1910–1922," Licenciate thesis, University of Basel, 2001, 65–90.

63 Founded in 1909, the SVF was the first Federal organization to demand the vote. Schweizerischer Verband für Frauenrecht eds., *Der Kampf um gleiche Rechte. Le combat pour les droits égaux* (Basel: Schwabe Verlag, 2009).

64 Gosteli-Archiv zur Geschichte der schweizerischen Frauenbewegung, Worblaufen (Gosteli Archive for the History of the Swiss Women's Movement): Bund Schweizerische Frauenverbände (BSF), Bürgerrechtsgesetz. Zum Bürgerrecht der ausheiratenden Schweizerin 1915–1952 (Law on Citizenship, Married Women's Citizenship 1915–1952), Korrespondenz SVF 1951–1953, Bestand 103:925:350–06–06, 1. (Written by Annie Leuch-Reineck).

65 Gosteli Archiv, Zum Bürgerrechtsgesetz, 2. Cf. Ka Schuppisser, "Denn im Herzen bin ich eine 'Schweizerin' im wahrsten Sinne des Wortes." Wiedereinbürgerungsverfahren 1937–1947: Die ehemalige Schweizerin im Diskurs der nationalen Identität der Frau," Licenciate thesis, University of Bern, 1998, 66.

66 Studer et al., *Bürgerrecht*, 76. Georg Kreis and Patrick Kury, *Die Schweizerischen Einwanderungsnormen in Wandel der Zeiten* (Bern: Schweizerische UNESCO-Kommission, 1996), 30.

67 In 1928, a change of Art. 44 of the constitution, which might have allowed the child of a "former" Swiss mother to acquire Swiss citizenship if it was born and lived in Switzerland, was accepted by a majority of the voters, but the law was not enacted. Studer et al., *Bürgerrecht*, 144.

68 Gosteli Archiv, Zum Bürgerrechtsgesetz, 2.

69 Gosteli Archiv, Ibid., 3; Schuppisser, "Im Herzen," 66.

70 Ruth Speiser (1893–1976), first female Doctor of Juridical Science of the University of Basel, notary at the Civil Court of Basel.

71 Gosteli-Archiv, Zum Bürgerrecht, 3; Schuppisser, "Im Herzen," 66.

72 Botschaft des Bundesrates über die Organisation und die Aufgaben der schweizerischen Kulturwahrung und Kulturwerbung, in: Bundesblatt, II, 1938, 999.

73 Patrick Kury, *"Man akzeptierte uns nicht, man tolerierte uns!" Ostjudenmigration nach Basel 1890–1930* (Basel: Helbing & Lichtenhahn, 1998).

74 Gabriela Imboden, " 'Die geistesschwache Tante.' Einbürgerung und Eugenik in der Stadt Basel," *Itinera* 21 (1999): 264–271.

75 Anina Gidkov, "Das Genfer Kantons- und Gemeindebürgerrecht," in *Bürgerrecht*, 245–253. The paragraph was only abolished in the 1980s.

76 Max Ruth, "Das Schweizerbürgerrecht," *Zeitschrift für Schweizerisches Recht* 1 (1938): 1a–156a. Ruth states that the publication represented his private views

only but his conclusions can also be found in official writings, such as the publications of the Swiss Federal Statistical Office.

77 Ruth, "Schweizerbürgerrecht," 76a.

78 Ruth, "Schweizerbürgerrecht," 134a.

79 The argument that women would not perform military service was not part of that debate; after all, men did not lose their political rights if they were not capable of army service.

80 Silke Redolfi, "Die verlorenen Töchter–der Verlust des Schweizer Bürgerrechts bei der Heirat eines Ausländers," in *Der Kampf um gleiche Rechte*, ed. Schweizerischer Verband für Frauenrechte (Basel: Schwabe Verlag, 2009), 177.

81 Ruth speaks of "*Nieten*" (slouches), "Schweizerbürgerrecht," 86a.

82 John E. Staehelin, "Psychiatrische Erfahrungen mit Einbürgerungen im Kanton Basel-Stadt," *Schweizerische medizinische Wochenschrift* 71, no. 43 (1941): 329–341; Wecker, "Eugenik," 175–176.

83 Candice Lewis Bredbenner, *A Nationality of Her Own: Women, Marriage and the Law of Citizenship* (Berkeley and London: University of California Press, 1998), 230ff.

84 In 1933–34, 8 women were members of the Congress. Jennifer E. Manning and Ida A. Brudnick, *Women in the United States Congress, 1917–2013* (Washington, DC: Congressional Research Service, 2013), 93, accessed November 3, 2014, http://fas.org/sgp/crs/misc/RL30261.pdf. For American women's influence on the American delegation's decision at The Hague not to sign the treaty, cf. Ellen Carol Dubois, "Internationalizing Married Women's Nationality: The Hague Campaign of 1930," in *Globalizing Feminisms 1789–1945*, ed. Karen Offen (London and New York: Routledge, 2010), 204–216.

85 German women were enfranchised in 1918, but until 1957, they lost their nationality when they married a foreigner, see Marion Röwekamp, "Gerechtigkeit für Frauen im Sozialstaat? Weibliche Staatsangehörigkeit im Kaiserreich und der Weimarer Republik," in *Gerechtigkeit im Sozialstaat. Analysen und Vorschläge*, ed. Ulrike Haerendel (Baden-Baden: Nomos Verlag, 2012), 71–87.

86 Imboden, "Die geistesschwache Tante," 264–271; Regina Wecker, "'Liederlich.' Eugenik, Sexualität und Geschlecht," *Itinera* 21 (1999): 272–280.

87 Silke Redolfi, Nicole Schwalbach, and Regina Wecker, "Staatsbürgerrecht: Transnationale Aspekte einer nationalen Institution," in *Gender in Trans-it. Transkulturelle und transnationale Perspektiven. Beiträge der 12. Schweizerischen Tagung für Geschlechtergeschichte*, ed. Martina Ineichen, Anna K. Liesch, Anja Rathmann-Lutz and Simon Wenger (Zurich: Chronos, 2009), 117–124.

88 "*Privatarchiv Erich Frischhof*" (Private Archive E. F.) in Archiv für Zeitgeschichte der ETH Zurich, cited in Silke Redolfi, "Liebe über die Grenze. Der Verlust der Schweizer Staatsangehörigkeit durch die Heirat mit einem Ausländer und die Folgen für die Frauen," in *Grenzüberschreitungen: der alemannische Raum—Einheit trotz der Grenzen?*, ed. Wolfgang Homburger (Ostfildern: Thorbecke Verlag, 2012), 73–84, 83. More cases in Schuppisser, "Im Herzen."

89 Studer, "Citizenship," 642.

90 Bundesratsbeschluss (BRB) über Änderung der Vorschriften über Erwerb und Verlust des Schweizer Bürgerrechts vom 20, December 1940, in AS Neue Folge 56, 1940, 2027–2030; Schwalbach, "Ausbürgerung," 271ff. Of the 51 cases, Schwalbach had examined 15 that concerned the Romandy, mainly in the Geneva area.

91 Bundesblatt der Schweizerischen Eidgenossenschaft 2 (1941), 325–326; Schwalbach, "Ausbürgerung," 271–272.

92 Beatrix Mesmer, *Staatsbürgerinnen ohne Stimmrecht* (Zurich: Chronos, 2007).

93 Fédération international des femmes des carrières juridiques (FIFCJ).

94 Redolfi, "Liebe," 83.

95 Redolfi, "Die verlorenen Töchter," 178–183.

96 "Bundesgesetz über Erwerb und Verlust des Schweizerbürgerrechts," September 29, 1952, Art 9. (Federal Law on Acquisition and Loss of Swiss Citizenship). That it was granted on demand only is another clear sign that citizenship was considered something for which a woman had to make an effort.

97 Art. 20.

98 Peter von Roten, member of the National Coucil for the Catholic Conservative Party of the Canton of Valais, married to the lawyer and famous Swiss feminist Iris von Roten.

99 Feldmann, member of the Party of Farmers, Traders and Independents (BGB/PAI), now the Swiss People's Party (SVP), was also later engaged in the campaign for the vote.

100 Redolfi, "Die verlorenen Töchter," 183.

101 The first German-speaking canton, Basel-City, succeeded in 1966. Most other cantons and municipalities followed after 1971; the last canton, Appenzell IR, was forced by the decision of the Federal Court in 1991 to enfranchise women on the cantonal level while they had obtained the vote on the federal level twenty years before. For dates of all municipal, cantonal, and federal plebiscites, see Lotti Ruckstuhl, *Frauen sprengen Fesseln. Hindernislauf zum Frauenstimmrecht in der Schweiz* (Interfeminas Verlag: Bonstetten, 1986).

102 "Elle [the female citizen of a Geneva-municipality] conserve toutefois, à l'égard de la République et Canton de Genève, les droits inhérents à cette nationalité genevoise." "Gidkov Genfer Kantons- und Gemeindebürgerecht," in *Bürgerrecht*, 259.

103 See below.

104 "Schweizerische Bundesverfassung (BV)" (Swiss Federal Constitution) Art 4.2.

105 The change affected several legal provisions, most importantly: the Marriage Law of the Civil Code (ZGB) ("Eherecht," chapter "Die Wirkungen der Eheschließung im Allgemeinen"), and the Law on Citizenship ("Bundesgesetz über das Schweizer Bürgerrecht").

106 *Schweizerisches Zivilgesetzbuch (ZGB)* Art. 161.

107 Wecker, "Ehe ist Schicksal," 35–36.

108 "Noch behalten Frauen ihren Namen," *20 Minuten Online* (December 23, 2013), http://www.20min.ch/schweiz/news/story/28754638. "Ehepaare zeigen sich traditionell," *NZZ Online* (January 4, 2014), http://www.nzz.ch/aktuell/schweiz/ehepaare-zeigen-sich-traditionell-1.18214480.

109 Cf. i.e., Ute Gerhard ed., *Differenz und Gleichheit* (Frankfurt a. M: U. Helmer, 1990); Nancy Leys Stepan, "Race, Gender Science and Citizenship," *Gender & History* 10, no. 1 (1998): 27; Ute Gerhard, *Debating Women's Equality: Toward a Feminist Theory of Law from a European Perspective* (New Brunswick, NJ: Rutgers University Press, 2001); Andrea Maihofer, "Gleichberechtigung in der Differenz oder Gleichheit und Differenz: zur Kritik des herrschenden Gleichheitsverständnisses," in *Differenz und Gleichheit in Theorie und Praxis des Rechts*, ed. Susanne Altermatt (Basel: Schweizerischer feministischer Juristinnenkongresses, 1995), 17–31.

110 Joan W. Scott, *Only Paradoxes to Offer. French Feminism and the Rights of Men* (Cambridge: Harvard University Press, 1997); Joan W. Scott, "The Sears Case," in *Gender and the Politics of History* (New York: Columbia University Press, 1999), 167–177.

111 Iris Marion Young, "Das politische Gemeinwesen und die Gruppendifferenz. Eine Kritik am Ideal des universalen Staatsbürgerstatus in Gemeinwesen," in *Jenseits der Geschlechtermoral*, ed. Herta Nagl-Docekal and Herlinde Pauer-Studer (Frankfurt/Main: Fischer, 1993), 267–304.

112 On the "invention of traditions," cf. Eric Hobsbawn and Terence Ranger eds., *The Invention of Tradition* (Cambridge: University Press, 1983); Anthony Giddens, "Leben in einer posttraditionalen Gesellschaft," in *Reflexive Modernisierung. Eine Kontroverse*, ed. Ulrich Beck, Anthony Giddens and Scott Lash (Frankfurt: Suhrkamp, 1996), 113–193 (169–170).

113 Studer, "Citizenship," 625.

114 Regina Wecker, "Staatsbürgerrechte, Mutterschaft und Grundrechte," *Schweizerische Zeitschrift für Geschichte* 46, no. 3 (1996): 383–410; Regina Wecker, *Frauen in der Schweiz. Von den Problemen einer Mehrheit* (Zug: Klett, 1983), 15–18.

15 Legal Position of Women in Portugal

The Case of the Standing Committee on Legislation of the National Council of Portuguese Women (CNMP), 1914–1947

Anne Cova

This chapter addresses the legal position of women in Portugal by examining the legislative reform projects of the National Council of Portuguese Women (CNMP, Conselho Nacional das Mulheres Portuguesas), a feminist federation established in Lisbon on 27 April 1914, thirteen years after its French counterpart, the Conseil National des Femmes Françaises (CNFF), which had come into being in Paris on 18 April 1901.[1] The CNMP's activities reached a peak during the 1920s, before the 1926 military coup. At that time it had approximately 1,500 members distributed among twenty affiliated associations. It published a journal, of which 158 issues appeared between its launch in November 1914 and its closure in May 1947, when the organization was abolished by the Salazar dictatorship.[2] The main characteristic of the CNMP was the fact that it was the longest surviving of all Portuguese women's organizations in the twentieth century.

The CNMP affiliated with the International Council of Women (ICW), which had been founded in Washington in 1888 to foster a collective women's identity across national boundaries and "to stimulate the sentiment of internationalism among women throughout the world."[3] Eliane Gubin and Leen Van Molle have remarked that the ICW was "the only association which advocates a universal and particularly wide program."[4] The aim of the CNMP was similarly broad and, like the ICW and its other national affiliates, included an examination of the juridical situation of women.

In fact, legal questions figured importantly in the context of the women's rights movement in Portugal. Some of the prominent figures of the CNMP were female lawyers who encouraged the focus on juridical aspects of the issues that were under discussion. The CNMP even approached the right to vote not only as a political goal but also as a means for women to obtain other rights, particularly legal rights. The Portuguese feminists were aware of the necessity to promulgate laws that would improve the daily lives of women but also of the need to verify that the laws were properly applied. Concretely, the council's leaders acted by sending delegations, petitions, and protests to the government. In order to mobilize the maximum number of supporters, in its statutes the CNMP followed the ICW, in that it was an apolitical and neutral association that allowed it to have a critical opinion regarding all the laws discussed.

Following the model established by the ICW, during its thirty-three year existence the CNMP created thirty standing committees to address a wide range of issues.[5] Its most active period was during the 1920s (1922, 1923, 1927, and 1929), when it had thirteen standing committees working at the same time. Some standing committees, such as hygiene, peace, education, and propaganda, existed for more than twenty years, while others, such as art, social assistance, charity, emigration, finance, press, legislation, morality, and suffrage, lasted for more than ten. With the exception of the propaganda committee and the charity committee, which were created in 1917, the rest of these standing committees would be founded during the 1920s. The standing committee on legislation, which was later called the juridical committee, was particularly important because it focused on the analysis of women's legal status in Portuguese law. In relation to its duration and significance compared to other standing committees of the CNMP, the data shows that the legislation committee operated for eleven years (1922–1928 and 1932–1935), 35.5 percent of the entire activity of CNMP standing committees, while the juridical standing committee was active during nine years (1938–1946), representing 29 percent.[6] Thus, we can say that the concern of the CNMP with the question of Portuguese law absorbed around one-third of its energy.

As was the case elsewhere in Europe, many articles of the Portuguese Civil Code (1867) had been heavily influenced by the Napoleonic Code and were criticized by the feminists.[7] The CNMP's aim was both to propose new laws and, as mentioned above, to ensure that those promulgated were applied; feminists were aware that the main problem with Portuguese legislation was the gap between the law and its application. The CNMP was claiming women's rights as women, arguing they deserved them because they fulfilled their duties, namely as mothers.[8]

The CNMP's strategy was reformist, seeking to influence legislation through its close links with some deputies in the Portuguese Parliament and stimulating the public debates on all laws affecting women. The most active of CNMP members on legal issues were Elina Guimarães (1904–1991) and Aurora Teixeira de Castro e Gouveia (1891–1931), both university-trained lawyers who chaired the legislation and juridical standing committees.[9] Other women also played major roles; for example, Laura Côrte Real, who was president of the CNMP standing committee on legislation in 1927 and also served on the ICW's international standing committee on laws and the legal position of women; and Maria Clara Correia Alves (1869–1948), who wrote many articles on civil rights in the CNMP's journal, *Alma Feminina*.

The CNMP went through three phases during its lifetime: 1914–1935, under the presidency of Adelaide Cabete (1867–1935), which was highlighted by the organization of the first two Portuguese feminist congresses in 1924 and 1928. The second period, led by Sara Beirão (1884–1974), extended from 1936 to 1941. During the third period, the forties, there were two presidents: Isabel Cohen Von Bonhorst (1942–1945) and Maria Lamas (1945–1947).[10] One-third of the CNMP's life was spent under a republic (the first twelve years of its existence), with the remaining almost two-thirds (twenty-one years exactly) under a military dictatorship (1926–1933), followed by the dictatorial New State regime that was founded in 1933. In this chapter, the period under study begins at the foundation of the CNMP, continues until its end, and concentrates on the long presidency of Adelaide Cabete, who remained at the head of the council from its creation until her death in 1935.

By analyzing the genesis and the claims of the CNMP in the area of law and placing them in a comparative perspective, this chapter aims to contribute to the history of transnational feminisms and to a comparative women's history of the twentieth century.[11]

From the Proclamation of the First Republic in 1910 to the Foundation of the CNMP in 1914

The proclamation of the First Republic on 5 October 1910 brought important changes to Portuguese women. This new regime, replacing the centuries-old monarchy, lasted until the military coup of 28 May 1926. Influenced by the Third French Republic, which had enacted a law to definitively separate the church from the state in 1905, the new Portuguese Republic promulgated similar secularizing legislation in 1911.

The CNMP did not yet exist at the time of the proclamation of the Republic, but some of the women who were then members of the Portuguese Women's Republican League (LRMP, Liga Republicana das Mulheres Portuguesas), founded in 1908, and of the Republican Party that brought about the regime change, would become its founders. Even before that, though, on 3 November 1910, the republic enacted a secular divorce law that gave women the same rights as men to sue for divorce.[12]

Another set of important republican laws affecting Portuguese women were the "family laws" (*leis da família*) of 25 December 1910, which in certain cases even authorized paternity suits. Here the impact of debates in France, where feminists of the CNFF were calling for the abrogation of Article 340 of the Civil Code, which forbade paternity suits, had an impact in Portugal. The French feminist journal *Le Journal des femmes* was constantly asking for the repeal of Article 340: "The abrogation of Article 340 of the Civil Code was one of the most requested claim by the feminists."[13] It was one of their main requests since the beginning of the movement at the end of the nineteenth century, and they finally managed to obtain this right, subject to severe restrictions, with the promulgation of the law of 16 November 1912. Even so, the French feminists were not happy with this new law and criticized the criteria imposed to prove paternity suits. In

Portuguese law, following the Napoleonic Code, paternity suits were likewise forbidden unless in exceptional cases, and the new 1910 family laws changed and extended the possibilities for filing paternity suits. But the Portuguese feminists complained about Article 130 of the Civil Code of 1867, which forbade paternity suits for illegitimate children. They also deplored the fact that Article 137 of the Civil Code gave ultimate authority over the education of children to fathers.[14] Another new Portuguese law enacted in 1910 ended married women's obligation to obey their husbands (which had been enshrined in Article 1185 of the earlier Civil Code) and created new employment opportunities for women.

From that point on the CNMP kept a close eye on legislative matters. By 1918, women were authorized to practice law, although the CNMP leaders noted ironically that even so, female lawyers could only be employed as "assistants" since "women with law degrees were prevented from being notaries or registrars, even though they could serve as the assistant who substitutes for the notary and registrar in all their duties."[15] The CNMP leaders regarded the promulgation of this law on 17 July 1918 as a "feminist victory," but they still believed it necessary for "other laws to follow that would complete, ratify and modify all of the faults that had been overlooked in this one."[16]

Generally speaking, feminists within the CNMP congratulated themselves on this legislation and of their role in pushing it through; however, they were not completely satisfied and constantly pointed out its weaknesses, such as its failure to address the situation where a wife needed her husband's permission to draw her salary, as well as the continued disenfranchisement of women.

Well before 1918, however, women's suffrage had become a topic of conversation in Portugal. On 28 May 1911, Carolina Beatriz Ângelo (1877–1911) a female doctor and militant advocate of women's suffrage who, with Ana de Castro Osório (1872–1935), founded the Association of Feminist Propaganda (APF, Associação de Propaganda Feminista) in 1911, exercised her right as a widowed mother to vote as the head of her family.[17] The politicians closed this loophole on 3 July 1913 with the introduction of a law that restricted the franchise to literate men. Not surprisingly, relations between the republican and the feminist organizations were complicated by the republican men's refusal to grant women the right to vote, even though their innovative family legislation had given women some new rights.[18] This led directly to the founding of the CNMP.

Two outside factors affected the formation of the CNMP in 1914: the influence of its French counterpart (the CNFF), which created links between leading women, and the catalyzing force of the ICW congresses.[19] In a country where there were not so many associations as late as 1928, Elina Guimarães deplored this lack of "associative spirit" and pointed out the difficulties in convincing women to join a feminist association.[20]

Guimarães was influenced by her father in her struggle to defend women's legal rights. Born in Lisbon, she obtained her law degree in 1926 from

Lisbon University and became a lawyer, and in 1928 she married a colleague who was also a lawyer. Her role in the CNMP began early in her life: she was only twenty-one when the president of the CNMP, Adelaide Cabete, invited her to join the council in 1925. She occupied various leading posts within the CNMP: she was general secretary in 1927, vice president of the board in 1928–1929 and again in 1931, and vice president of the general assembly in 1946. Her knowledge of the law allowed her to play an active role in the standing committee on legislation from 1926–1928 and 1932–1934, as well as in the juridical standing committee from 1938–1946. She also took an active part in the suffrage standing committee from 1928–1929 and 1931, and she was on the propaganda committee from 1943 to 1944. At the age of twenty-three she opened the 1928 Congress with a speech on the protection of the women workers and on the position of working women in marriage. When Adelaide Cabete unexpectedly left for Angola in 1929 with her adopted son Arnaldo Brazão (1890–1968), she asked Elina Guimarães to edit the council's publication, which she did from September 1929 to December 1930.[21]

The process of establishing the CNMP was relatively slow compared to the experience in other countries. By the end of the nineteenth century, seven national councils of women had already joined the ICW, including those from Canada (1893), Germany (1897), the UK (1898), Sweden (1898), Australia (1899), the Netherlands (1899), and Denmark (1899). The earliest European ICW affiliates were all from the north of the continent, while it was not until the twentieth century that most southern European countries formed their councils (Italy: 1903, Greece: 1908).[22] Even after 1914, when the CNMP organized, it took eight years longer to organize its standing committee on legislation, under the direction of Aurora de Castro e Gouveia.

In the case of the CNMP, the role played by the influential French feminist Ghénia Avril de Sainte-Croix (1855–1939) was fundamental in its creation.[23] Since its founding in 1901, Sainte-Croix served as secretary-general of the CNFF and had made contact with two future leaders of the CNMP, Adelaide Cabete and Maria Clara Correia Alves. It was Sainte-Croix who proposed the CNMP's affiliation to the ICW, which was accepted at the organization's congress in Rome in 1914. The CNMP regarded her as their "godmother" and in 1920 made her an honorary member of their organization. Subsequently, she represented the CNMP at a meeting of the executive and standing committees of the ICW held at The Hague in 1922 and at the ICW congress held in Vienna in 1930.[24] The CNMP leaders could not attend especially because of financial difficulties.

Following the model set forth by the ICW, the CNMP's statutes defined it as a "feminine institution that is not subordinated to any philosophical, political or religious group or faction," a principle that would eventually lead to its break with the women's organizations that were linked either to political parties or to the Catholic women's movement.[25] Like other national councils, the CNMP structure was hierarchical with an administrative council, a board office, a yearly general assembly, and a fiscal board, which during the entire period under consideration here involved around one hundred women. As well as serving as president of the CNMP from 1920 to 1929, Adelaide Cabete also directed the organization's publication, *Alma Feminina*. She wrote more than forty articles for the publication, mainly on women's health, tuberculosis, alcoholism, and prostitution. Maria Clara Correia Alves, elected vice president of the CNMP in 1921, also published extensively in *Alma Feminina* between 1914 and 1919 and published a book in French entitled *Féminisme: toujours et encore*, which illustrates her multilingualism as well as the deep connections with the French culture.[26] The French and the Portuguese feminists of the CNFF and the CNMP belonged to an urban elite who spoke various languages and traveled in order to reinforce the links between the councils.

One characteristic of the council's structure was that members of its board had all risen through the hierarchy. For example, Sara Beirão was vice president in 1931–1934 before going on to become CNMP president from 1936–1941; she again served as vice president from 1943 to 1945. Before serving as president, Isabel Cohen Von Bonhorst had been vice president from 1937–1941. These charismatic figures helped identify the council with its leaders, following the example of the ICW, where the Scottish Marchioness Ishbel of Aberdeen and Temair, better known as Lady Aberdeen, held the position of president for a total of forty-six years (1893–1899, 1904–1920, and 1922–1936).

During the First World War, national councils, including that of Portugal, gave priority to the so-called "Sacred Union" that had been proclaimed by the governments of invaded nations such as France. Portugal entered the conflict on 9 March 1916 with Germany's declaration of war. Among the associations federated in the CNMP, the most important ones founded during the war in order to support the soldiers were the Cruzada das Mulheres Portuguesas (CMP) established in Lisbon on 27 March 1916 and the Núcleo Feminino de Assistência Infantil da Junta Patriótica do Norte founded in Porto in August 1916.[27] Fully sharing in their compatriots' patriotic fervor, the feminists of the councils asked women to set aside their demands and serve their countries, hoping that after the war their devotion to their nations would be rewarded with the right to vote. However, in Portugal, as in France, their hopes were dashed.

The Apogee of the CNMP in the 1920s

According to the historian Leila Rupp, by 1925 ICW membership stood at thirty six million; however, given that the affiliated councils provided the figures (based on the membership of their affiliated organizations), these numbers must be treated with some caution.[28] Nevertheless, this extensive membership does indicate the success of the ICW in organizing women on a global scale.

The President of the National Council of Uruguayan Women, Paulina Luisi (1875–1950), was an honorary member of the CNMP and represented it at two congresses in 1920: the International Woman Suffrage Alliance (IWSA) congress in Geneva and the ICW congress in Kristiana (Oslo), which was presided by Lady Aberdeen.[29] At the Geneva conference Luisi reported that the matters that were of concern in Europe, such as the nationality of married women, had already been resolved in Uruguay, where women were not obliged to take their husband's nationality.[30] At that time, she indicated, any Portuguese woman who married a foreigner immediately lost her nationality, and the CNMP was constantly asking for the right for Portuguese women who married foreigners to keep their nationalities. Nevertheless, a married woman in Portugal was not obliged to take her husband's surname. As for paternity suits and the rights of illegitimate children to inherit, Paulina Luisi said this was guaranteed in her country.[31] In Oslo, she presented a favorable image of Portuguese legislation, particularly with respect to illegitimate children.[32]

During the 1920s, the tone of the CNMP's *Alma Feminina* was particularly optimistic, proclaiming, "The triumph of feminism in Portugal seems to us assured."[33] Adelaide Cabete traveled to Rome to represent the CNMP at the 1923 congress of the IWSA and in 1925 attended the ICW congress in Washington, DC (both trips were underwritten by the Portuguese government).[34] The speeches she delivered at these meetings exuded optimism; in Rome she claimed that "the civil laws governing Portuguese women are more advanced than elsewhere."[35] She exulted that Portuguese law was admired overseas, particularly its laws on divorce, the family, illegitimate children, and paternity suits. On this latter point, she bragged that the "Portuguese delegates and Italian women in the session in which paternity suits was discussed praised the broad and liberal principle of Portuguese law that imposes no time limit for the initiation of court action, against the advice of the other delegates who, basing their opinion on the American law, want the illegitimate child to have recourse to the courts for only a short time following their birth."[36] Adelaide Cabete concluded that in Portugal "all that remains to be legislated for is female suffrage, which will affirm its position in the vanguard of civilized nations."[37]

In February 1923, the Minister of Justice, Abranches Ferrão, who was also a professor of law, received a delegation of women from the CNMP that called for the introduction of a law that would provide for "equal property rights" between husband and wife. While the feminists within the CNMP believed the ideal outcome would be the absolute 50–50 division of property, they demonstrated their pragmatism by limiting their demands using the strategy of small steps in the hope of obtaining concessions.[38]

At that time, Laura Côrte Real was at the head of the standing committee on legislation. Born in Coimbra, Côrte Real had studied law and arts at the university there during the First World War. While in Lisbon in 1922 she was initiated into the freemasons, choosing as her symbolic name that of the renowned French feminist, scientist, and freemason Clémence Royer (1830–1902), who was also admired by Ghénia Avril de Sainte-Croix. In fact, all members of the CNMP board were freemasons.[39] In a country where Catholicism was very strong and where the dictatorship that would be established in 1926 would authorize the creation of powerful organizations controlled by the Catholic Church and associated with Catholic Action, freemasonry represented a major form of resistance to Catholic hegemony. Catholic Action not only maintained and developed its autonomous associations but was also part of the female Catholic elite that formed the fundamental nucleus of the official organizations.

Côrte Real had also served as the CNMP's Secretary of the Interior (1923), board spokeswoman (1925), and president of the standing committee on emigration (1927), and she also served on other standing committees, including education (1933, 1934), hygiene (1943), and juridical (1944).[40] Along with Elina Guimarães and Aurora de Castro e Gouveia, she helped to organize the first feminist congress in Portugal in 1924. It was she who had thanked Abranches Ferrão for the interview he gave to the daily newspaper *Diário de Notícias* on 11 February 1923, in which he publicly deplored "the situation in which in patrimonial matters the woman is still a ward of her husband" and spoke "of the more advanced civilized nations, such as France, Italy, Switzerland, Germany and Brazil."[41] Adelaide Cabete, president of the CNMP, considered Ferrão's comments to be a guarantee for advancing Portuguese women's rights. Aurora de Castro e Gouveia claimed there was nothing more just than to guarantee married women's earnings and their participation in the administration of marital property.[42] She later regretted that the Minister of Justice had not proposed this.[43] She believed that the best solution was "the absolute division of property, with women having control of their own," an approach that would be debated at the first CNMP congress in 1924.

Abranches Ferrão's bill was presented to the Portuguese Parliament on 25 July 1923. In his speech he outlined his evolutionary tactic, stating, "What I propose here is small. I am aware of the reluctance to engage in a profound reform of our family law, and this being so, I believe it is better to move forward in stages in such a way as to prepare public opinion, without great disruption, to accept all that is already contained in the laws and customs of many of the more advanced civilizations, both Latin and non-Latin."[44] The minister sent a copy of his proposal to the CNMP with a note saying its ultimate aim was to dignify women.

In 1924, to celebrate its tenth anniversary, the CNMP organized a six-day conference—its first feminist educational conference. The organizing committee of this conference was comprised mainly of teachers and freemasons, and it received support from the National Women's Councils of Belgium, France, and Sweden and from the ICW. Several leading politicians attended, including the then Portuguese President Manuel Teixeira Gomes; former President Bernardino Machado; Grandmaster of the Freemasons and honorary CNMP member Sebastião de Magalhães Lima; lawyer and Minister of Justice Abranches Ferrão; Deputy Barbosa Magalhães; and Francisco Xavier da Costa, who represented the Ministry of Education. The declared aims of this conference were "to study, discuss and advance feminist and related ideas."[45] A total of sixteen talks were delivered, covering such subjects as "law, hygiene, education, sociology, and criminology."[46] Arnaldo Brazão, the conference's general secretary (and adopted son of Adelaide Cabete, the president of the CNMP), declared that the war had "brought [about] feminism's victory. [. . .] In Europe, on this very day, only Portugal, France and Switzerland have not yet introduced female suffrage legislation."[47] He spoke of victory in the sense that women in several countries had won the right to vote during and after the Great War: Denmark in 1915, the United Kingdom and Germany in 1918, the Netherlands in 1919, the United States in 1920, and Sweden in 1921. Women in other countries like Finland (1906) and Norway (1913) obtained this right before the First World War, and others still had to wait many years for their enfranchisement: France (1944), Italy (1945), Belgium (1948), Greece (1952), Switzerland (1971), and Portugal (1974).

The truth was that World War I had not brought a feminist victory; rather, the postwar period was a time of regression and backlash, characterized by the omnipresent slogan, "a woman's place is at home." The question of female suffrage was not straightforward; even within the Portuguese women's movement there was a wide range of opinions on the matter. For example, during the debate following Aurora de Castro e Gouveia's paper to the 1924 conference, "The Political Demands of Portuguese Women," some participants proposed the idea that only women with university degrees should receive the right to vote. Aurora de Castro e Gouveia did not mention the right to vote for women when she filed a report for the ICW regarding the years 1920–1922; instead she concentrated on the CNMP's main objective, which was to provide "moral protection to women and children."[48] She did mention the civil rights Portuguese women had obtained in 1919, which included, thanks to Barbosa Magalhães, "the right of becoming Doctor of law, solicitor and serving in juries; they may now be elected as members of the Commercial Jury."[49] In 1928, Elina Guimarães approved the Decree no. 5646 of 10 May 1919 that allowed female lawyers to accept warrants without their husband's authorization, the Article 42 of the Decree no. 1 of 25 December 1910, and the more recent Article 10 of the regulation of literary property of 3 June 1927 that allowed women to publish their writings without their husbands' permission. Nevertheless, she noted that other working married women could not do anything without their husbands' authorization and criticized the Civil Code that treated married women as minors.[50]

As elsewhere in Europe, the Civil Code continued to be the target of feminist attack. Portuguese feminists described it as anachronistic and unjust and criticized many of its articles.[51] The Portuguese articles that were the particular targets of feminist ire were Articles 1117 and 1189, which concerned the administration of marital property, in which all of a woman's property belongs to the husband regardless of the nature of the marriage (as a result, married women were financially dependent on their husbands, a situation that endured until the publication of the 1966 Civil Code); and Article 1885, which stated that a married woman must obey her husband.[52]

Comparing the position of women in Portugal with that of women in other countries, the Portuguese feminists often invoked the French law of 13 July 1907, which allowed women to spend their own salaries and to purchase goods and property without their husbands' permission.[53] In vain, Aurora de Castro e Gouveia asked for a provision to be added that would deal with the earnings of a woman working outside the home.[54]

Strong from the success of the 1924 congress, in 1928 the CNMP organized another congress on feminism and education. This time, however, the political situation was very different, the republic having been replaced with a military dictatorship, and *Alma Feminina* was under censorship. The congress took place in Lisbon from 24–28 June 1928. A few months before the beginning of that event, there was a general assembly of the CNMP that took place on 8 January 1928, and Adelaide Cabete called on the participants to defend their feminist principles. Of the twelve speeches delivered at the congress (Adelaide Cabete, on the teaching of child care at infant school), a few are of particular interest because they introduced to the public some of the younger female lawyers in Portugal: Elina Guimarães, on dealing with the protection of women workers, and feminist demands by Aurora Teixeira de Castro.[55] The progressive nature of some of the themes—particularly those on co-education, the right to vote, and feminist demands in general—raised at the 1928 congress, while Portugal was governed by a military dictatorship, is noteworthy. The matter of co-education had mobilized the CNMP in 1927 when, through its Secretary General Elina Guimarães, it sent a delegation to the Ministry of Education calling for an end to the suppression of co-education in primary schools.[56] But the law, not co-education, was the principal interest of Guimarães, who was the only daughter of a man who had served as Portugal's prime minister during the First Republic. During her long life (she died in 1991 at the age of eighty-seven), Elina Guimarães wrote many articles denouncing the inequities of the Portuguese laws regarding women, and especially married women. These following articles were in particular disadvantaged by the Civil Code: Article 1186, which obliged a married woman to accompany her husband within the country; Article 1187, which imposed the need for a married woman to obtain her husband's permission before being able to accept any employment or engage in any commercial activity and which prohibited a woman author from publishing without her husband's consent; Article 1189, which allowed only the husband to administer matrimonial and familial property; and Articles 1191 and 1193, which prohibited a married woman from purchasing or selling property or from engaging in contracts without her husband's consent.[57] Unlike in France, where the birthrate crisis fed many of the fears during parliamentary debates on women's status, the problem in Portugal was, according to Elina Guimarães, more a question of quality than quantity of people.[58] She asked for more laws protecting maternity and for the establishment of *crèches* (daycares).

Aurora Teixeira de Castro was another important younger participant at this 1928 congress. Born in Oporto in 1891, she studied at the University of Coimbra, where she obtained her law degree in 1916. Like Elina Guimarães, she married a lawyer, but unlike her younger colleague, she opened a practice in Lisbon in 1917 and exercised her profession. She was a member of several feminist associations, including the APF and the CMP. As with the other CNMP leaders, she was also a freemason. She became active in the CNMP during the 1920s, when the council reached its zenith, and occupied several of its leading positions, including: Overseas Secretary from 1921–1922, Vice President of the board from 1926–1927, and head of the standing committee on legislation in 1922 and again from 1924–1925.[59] She also played an active role in the standing committees on emigration in 1922 and in the suffrage committee in 1927. She redoubled her feminist activity following her divorce in 1927 and remained active until her early death in 1931 at the age of forty. Her final article in *Alma Feminina*, which was published in 1929, was dedicated to Adelaide Cabete, president of the CNMP.[60]

During the 1920s the Portuguese council maintained its links with the ICW. When the ICW launched an inquiry among its councils on the legal situation of women in their countries, the CNMP was one of the seventeen councils to respond.[61] However, the emergence of the New State regime in 1933 made the international networking of the CNMP much more difficult.

Under the Salazarist Dictatorship (1933–1947)

The CNMP would receive no financial support from the New State regime headed by António de Oliveira Salazar (1889–1970); support would have allowed its delegates to participate in the 1936 ICW congress in Dubrovnik (28 September–9 October). Nevertheless, it was authorized to continue operating and was able to maintain contacts with its counterparts, especially in France. The presence of some French feminists, members of the CNFF—notably the lawyer Maria Vérone (1874–1938), an expert on legislation who shared the same interests of the lawyers of the CNMP, and Marguerite Pichon-Landry (1878–1972)—in the ICW's standing committee on laws and the legal position of women strengthened the links between the Portuguese and the French councils.[62]

On 5 May 1931, the Salazarist regime introduced a limited franchise for women.[63] While the government sought to organize elections (which were not held), women aged twenty-one and over who had completed secondary school or who had a university degree were granted the right to vote. The

New State was following the example set by other dictatorships, such as that of Primo de Rivera in Spain, which gave women who were heads of families a limited right to vote. However, not until forty years later, after the Revolution of the Carnations on 25 April 1974, would the franchise be extended to include all Portuguese women over the age of twenty-one.

With a law on the defense of the family, enacted on 12 October 1935, the New State sought to ensure the "constitution and the defense of the family in its function as the source of preservation and development of the race." In order to protect and preserve the family, the New State set various priorities, although not all of them were respected. For example, rhetoric valorizing the protection of motherhood was undermined by a 10 March 1937 law cutting maternity leave to one month (half the previous length) and granting employers discretion to refuse to pay a subsidy to a mother on leave if "the employee was not worthy of such a subsidy or did not need it."[64]

The CNMP managed to ensure that it was represented at the ICW's fiftieth anniversary congress in Edinburgh in 1938 by the presence of the secretary of the CNMP, Cândida de Sousa Madeira Pinto, who read a letter written by Sara Beirão in honor of Lady Aberdeen.[65]

The CNMP used a strategy that involved sending petitions and protests both to the government and to the National Assembly. Some of their protests called for the return of co-education in primary schools, for an end to restrictions on women's right to vote, and against the New State Constitution of 1933 that stipulated the equality of citizens before the law "except for women, where natural differences and the family welfare are at stake" (Article 5).[66] The Constitution of 1933 asserted that Portugal was a "Unitarian and corporatist Republic;" it was inspired by the ideas of the extreme right political movement Action Française. In 1940, the New State signed a Concordat with the Vatican; henceforth, civil divorce was prohibited to those who had married in the Church.

The CNMP objected to the toleration of prostitution by girls as young as sixteen. On 10 February 1940, the president, Sara Beirão, and its future presidents, Isabel Cohen von Bonhorst and Maria Lamas, submitted their protest to the National Assembly. Their objection highlighted the contraction between the Civil Code that fixed the age of majority at twenty-one, when individuals could "freely dispose of his/her person" (Article 311), and the legality of prostitution by minors.[67] Only in 1944 did the regime prohibit the police from licensing female prostitutes under the age of twenty-one.

Despite the constraints imposed by the regime, the CNMP grew considerably during the 1940s.[68] In July 1945, Maria Lamas was elected president, and a group of young anti Salazarist university students joined the association. Under this new leadership, the organization renewed its international contacts, and in order to expand the association's membership at the national level, the CNMP created committees of propaganda in various parts of the country. In 1946, Lamas launched the Five Members Campaign, which called on each existing member to enlist five more. However, this upsurge of activity was soon brought to a halt following the CNMP's international exhibit of books written by women at Lisbon's *Sociedade Nacional de Belas Artes* (Fine Arts Society). The tremendous impact of the international exhibition ended the "toleration" of the CNMP; the authorities decided to abolish the CNMP. Under the pretext that the group's objective was "completely vague" and that it competed with existing (since 1936) state organizations, such as the Mother's Charity for National Education (OMEN, Obra das Mães pela Educação Nacional) and the Female Portuguese Youth (MPF, Mocidade Portuguesa Feminina), "which had as their objective the protection of mothers and children," the government disbanded CNMP in January of 1947.[69] The charge of "competition" had been used earlier by the Fascist regime in Italy as a pretext for opposing the National Council of Italian Women (CNDI, Consiglio nazionale delle donne italiane) in order to promote its own organization, the Fasci Femminili (Fascist Women).

The close relationship that had developed between the CNMP and the peace movement during the first years of the Cold War served as additional pretext for ordering its closure. Maria Lamas refused to step down from her position as CNMP president, and was subsequently dismissed from her position as editor of the magazine *Modas e Bordados*, published by the national daily newspaper *O Século*.[70]

The real reason for the CNMP's abolition, however, can be found in the changed political climate that existed after the end of the war: the defeat of fascism in Europe had triggered the emergence of stronger opposition, both legal and clandestine, to the New State. Deceived by the new international situation in 1945, some partisans of the opposition believed the regime's fall was imminent, particularly when Salazar announced that there would be elections "as free as in free Britain."[71] A group of CNMP leaders spoke out publicly to support candidates from the democratic opposition, and Maria Lamas and several others—Elina Guimarães, Maria Isabel Aboim Inglês (1902–1963), and Maria Palmira Tito de Morais (1912–2003)—had joined the Democratic Unity Movement (MUD, Movimento de Unidade Democrática), a youth organization. MUD was an anti-dictatorship electoral front authorized by the dictatorship at the end of the Second World War because after the defeat of fascisms Salazar wanted to improve the image of the Portuguese regime abroad, but MUD was subsequently abolished. Needless to say, under such circumstances, advances in women's position in the law were not likely.

Conclusion

A historical investigation of the CNMP shows that, like its counterparts in other European countries, it was led by a charismatic, urban, educated elite of middle-class women who served as its presidents for many years. This feminist elite could be considered avant-garde in a country where in 1930 more than 80 percent of the population was still rural. Many of the prominent figures of the Portuguese council were connected with the Republican legislators, which facilitated their attempts to influence progressive legislation. As concerns the standing committee on legislation of the CNMP, the lawyer Elina Guimarães (who served three times as Vice President of the CNMP and for a time as Secretary-General) played a major role in denouncing the inequities of the laws for women, especially married women.

During the First Republic (1910–1926), the Portuguese council had encouraged and approved the legislative changes that occurred, which consisted mainly of giving women rights with new marriage and filiation laws and legalization of divorce (law of 3 November 1910). Following the separation between church and state in 1911, the divorce law would be in force for thirty years, until the Concordat of 1940. At that time the Portuguese legislation on paternity suits, family laws, and especially the law on divorce, seemed quite advanced compared with the laws in other countries. Even so, the president of the CNMP was aware of the gap existing between the laws and their application.

These Portuguese feminists were unsatisfied with the lack of concern on the part of the Republicans to enact female suffrage. It is well known that, in the early twentieth century, political parties from the left were afraid of the conservative vote of women and the conservatives were against the principle of female suffrage. This was true of France and Belgium, Spain as well as Switzerland. Portuguese women had to wait thirty years longer than the French, who were enfranchised in 1944, but only three years longer than the Swiss, for their enfranchisement in 1974. In retrospect, it seems strange that these republican regimes opposed according the right to vote to women.

During the Portuguese dictatorship, which lasted almost half a century (1926–1974), the legislation concerning women regressed: as mentioned above, divorce for religious marriages was forbidden with the Concordat of 1940, co-education was suppressed, and maternity leave was diminished by half the previous length. Censorship was established in 1926, and the 1933 constitution's assertion stated that the differences between men and women were a fact of "nature." Even in such an adverse political climate, however, the CNMP managed to remain active. It continued advocating for women's rights for more than three decades and under three different political regimes. Despite this, considerable efforts were made to internationalize the CNMP, which is demonstrated by the organization's contribution to various meetings of the ICW and by its participation in the standing committee of the ICW on laws and the legal position of women. This participation strengthened its already existing links with the French feminists of the CNFF.

By focusing on the legal position of women in Portugal and efforts to reform it, this contribution has sought to reveal and analyze the development of a network of leading women and to uncover the transnational cooperation that existed between them. By doing so, it thereby aims to contribute both to the writing of European women's legal history and to the history of transnational feminisms.[72]

Notes

1 This chapter is part of my current research project on the National Councils of Women in Southern Europe and Latin America (1900–1945), which is being carried out at the Institute of Social Sciences, University of Lisbon. For findings to date, see Anne Cova, "International Feminisms in Historical Comparative Perspective: France, Italy and Portugal, 1880s–1930s," *Women's History Review* 19, no. 4 (September 2010): 595–612; Ann Taylor Allen, Anne Cova and June Purvis, "Introduction: International Feminisms," *Women's History Review* 19, no. 4 (September 2010): 493–501; Anne Cova, "Feminisms and Associativism: The National Councils of Women in France and Portugal, a Comparative Historical Approach, 1888–1939," *Women's History Review* 22, no. 1 (February 2013): 19–30; and Anne Cova, "The National Councils of Women in France, Italy and Portugal. Comparisons and Entanglements 1888–1939," in *Gender History in a Transnational Perspective: Biographies, Networks, Gender Orders*, ed. Oliver Janz and Daniel Schönpflug (New York: Berghahn Books, 2014), 46–76. I would like to thank very much Karen Offen (especially) and Sara Kimble for their comments on this chapter.

2 The journal of the CNMP changed names and frequency over the years: *Boletim Oficial do Conselho Nacional das Mulheres Portuguesas* (1914–1916) was trimestrial, *Alma Feminina* (1917–1946) was published monthly until December 1919; bimonthly from January 1920 until April 1924; quarterly from May 1924 until December 1924; every three months from January 1925 to December 1926; bimonthly from January 1927 until August 1933; quarterly from September 1933 until December 1933; bimonthly from January 1934 until June 1935; quarterly from July 1935 to October 1935; bimonthly from November 1935 until December 1936; no publication in 1937; bimonthly between January 1938 until April 1938; no publication between May 1938 until December 1938; one issue in 1939; semiannually between 1940 until 1946, and *A Mulher* (1946–1947) was published twice.

3 "Notice sur le Conseil International des femmes fondé à Washington (États-Unis d'Amérique) le 31 mai 1888," *L'Action Féminine. Bulletin Officiel du Conseil national des femmes françaises* 6 (December 1, 1909): 90. On the ICW, see Leila J. Rupp, *Worlds of Women: the making of an international women's movement* (Princeton, NJ: Princeton University Press, 1997); Eliane Gubin and Leen Van Molle eds., *Women Changing the World: A History of the International Council of Women, 1888–1988* (Brussels: Éditions Racine, 2005).

4 Gubin and Van Molle, *Women Changing the World*, 13.

5 Célia Costa, "Contributo para a Monografia do Conselho Nacional das Mulheres Portuguesas: Uma Organização Feminista," MA thesis, Open University of Lisbon, 2007, 378.

6 Costa, "Contributo," 378.

7 Maria O'Neill, "O trabalho das mulheres e dos menores," *Alma Feminina* 3/4 (March/April 1921).

8 Aurora de Castro e Gouveia, "A emancipação da mulher," *Alma Feminina* 1/2 (January/February 1921).

9 "Dra Aurora Teixeira de Castro," *Alma Feminina* 6 (July, November and December 1927).

10 Maria Lamas, *As Mulheres do meu País* (Lisbon: Caminho, 2002, first edition, 1950). On Maria Lamas (1893–1983), see Maria Antónia Fiadeiro, *Maria Lamas. Biografia* (Lisbon: Quetzal, 2003).

11 Anne Cova ed., *Comparative Women's History: New Approaches* (Boulder and New York: Social Science Monographs/Columbia University Press, 2006).

12 The law of 3 November 1910, which legalized divorce in Portugal, included 70 articles in six chapters.
13 J. Vialla-Martin, "Possession d'état," *Le Journal des femmes* 162 (February 1906): 2. On paternity suits, see: Anne Cova, *Maternité et droits des femmes en France, XIXe–XXe siècles* (Paris: Anthropos-Economica, 1997); Rachel G. Fuchs, *Contested Paternity. Constructing Families in Modern France* (Baltimore: The Johns Hopkins University Press, 2008).
14 "Conferências feministas," *Alma Feminina* 1/2 (January/February 1921).
15 *Alma Feminina* 8 (August 1918).
16 Ibid.
17 On Ana de Castro Osório, see Anne Cova, "Ana de Castro Osório," in *Feminist Writings from Ancient Times to the Modern World: A Global Sourcebook and History*, ed. Tiffany K. Wayne, vol. 2 (Santa Barbara: Greenwood, 2011), 372–374.
18 Anne Cova and António Costa Pinto, "Women and Salazarism," in *Political and Historical Encyclopedia of Women*, ed. Christine Fauré (New York: Routledge, 2003), 397–405.
19 For more details regarding the foundation of the CNMP, see Cova, "Feminisms and Associativism," 19–30.
20 Elina Guimarães, "O espírito associativo," *Alma Feminina* 5 (September/October 1928).
21 *Alma Feminina* 5 (September/October 1929).
22 Gisela Bock and Anne Cova eds., *Writing Women's History in Southern Europe, 19th–20th Centuries. Écrire l'histoire des femmes en Europe du Sud, XIXe–XXe siècles* (Oeiras: Celta, 2003).
23 On Ghénia Avril de Sainte-Croix, see Karen Offen, "Madame Ghénia Avril de Sainte-Croix, the Josephine Butler of France," *Women's History Review* 17, no. 2 (April 2008): 239–255, and Karen Offen "'La plus grande féministe de France': Pourquoi a-t-on oublié l'inoubliable féministe internationaliste française, Ghénia Avril de Sainte-Croix," in *Les Féministes de la première vague*, ed. Christine Bard (Rennes: Presses Universitaires de Rennes, 2015), 181–194.
24 Conseil International des femmes, *Rapport de l'assemblée Quinquennale*, ed. Marchioness of Aberdeen and Temair (Vienna: International Council of Women, 1930).
25 *Conselho Nacional das Mulheres Portuguesas, Programa geral* (Lisbon: no date).
26 Maria Clara Correia Alves, *Féminisme (toujours et encore)* (Lisbon: Imprensa de Manuel Lucas Torres, no date).
27 Anne Cova, "As mulheres foram ativistas na Guerra, depois voltaram ao lar," *Público*, August 20, 2014.
28 Rupp, *Worlds of Women*, 15.
29 Conseil International des femmes, *Rapport de l'assemblée quinquennale, Kristiana, 1920*, ed. Marchioness of Aberdeen and Temair (Aberdeen: The Rosemount Press, 1920).
30 Maria Clara Correia Alves, "Congresso feminista de Genebra," *Alma Feminina* 9/10 (September/October 1920).
31 Aurora Teixeira de Castro, "As idades legais da mulher," *Alma Feminina* 3 (Terceiro trimestre de 1926).
32 A redacção, "Dra Paulina Luisi," *Alma Feminina* 5/6 (May/June 1921).
33 "Conselho nacional das mulheres portuguesas," *Alma Feminina* 1/2 (January/February 1922).
34 Conseil International des femmes, *Rapport de l'assemblée quinquennale*, ed. Marchioness of Aberdeen and Temair (Washington: International Council of Women, 1925).

35 "Congresso feminista de Roma," *Alma Feminina* 5/6 (May/June 1923).
36 Ibid.
37 Ibid.
38 Aurora de Castro e Gouveia, "Uma proposta de lei do senhor ministro da Justiça," *Alma Feminina* no. 11/12 (November/December 1923).
39 Fernando Marques da Costa, *A Maçonaria Feminina* (Lisbon: Vega, 1979).
40 João Esteves, "Laura de Castro Côrte Real," in *Dicionário no feminino (séculos XIX e XX)*, ed. Zília Osório de Castro and João Esteves (Lisbon: Livros Horizonte, 2005), 495.
41 Laura Côrte Real, "O feminismo em Portugal," *Alma Feminina* 3/4 (March/April 1923).
42 Aurora de Castro e Gouveia, "Garantia do salário da mulher casada," *Alma Feminina* 9/10 (September and October 1923). Aurora Teixeira de Castro Sá d'Albergaria, "Reivindicações feministas," *Alma Feminina* 3 (May and June 1928).
43 Castro e Gouveia, "Uma proposta."
44 "O feminismo em Portugal," *Alma Feminina*, 11/12 (November/December 1923).
45 Arnaldo Brazão, *O primeiro congresso feminista e da educação (relatório)* (Lisbon: Edições Spartacus, 1925), 20.
46 Ibid., 15.
47 Ibid., 4.
48 International Council of Women, *Combined First and Second Annual Report of the Seventh Quinquennial Period*, ed. Anna Backer (The Hague: ICW, 1922), 149.
49 Ibid., 149.
50 Elina Guimarães, "Da situação da mulher profissional no casamento," *Alma Feminina* 2 (March/April 1928).
51 Aurora de Castro e Gouveia, "Reivindicações feministas. Garantia do salário da mulher casada," *Alma Feminina* 5/6 (May/June 1921).
52 Aurora de Castro e Gouveia, "Garantia do salário da mulher casada," *Alma Feminina* 9/10 (September/October 1923).
53 Guimarães, "Da situação da mulher profissional;" Elina Guimarães, "O trabalho da mulher casada perante a lei," *Alma Feminina* 14 (November 1945).
54 Castro e Gouveia, "Reivindicações feministas."
55 Adelaide Cabete, *O Ensino da Puericultura na escola infantil. Tese apresentada no 2 Congresso feminista e de educação promovido pelo Conselho Nacional das Mulheres Portuguesas* (Lisbon: Tip. Da Cooperativa Militar, 1928).
56 Elina Guimarães, "Relatório do Secretariado," *Alma Feminina* 1 (January/February 1928).
57 Elina Guimarães, "A mulher portuguesa na legislação civil," *Análise Social* XXII (92–93), no. 3/4 (1986): 557–577.
58 Elina Guimarães, "Protecção à mulher trabalhadora," *Alma Feminina* 2 (March/April 1928).
59 "Conselho nacional das mulheres portuguesas," *Alma Feminina* 1/2 (January/February 1922).
60 Aurora de Castro e Gouveia, "Doutora Adelaide Cabete," *Alma Feminina* 5 (September/October 1929).
61 "Reports on meetings of International standing committees, London, April 29th & May 1st, 2nd & 3rd," *Bulletin International Council of Women* 7 (May 1929): 1.
62 Conseil International des femmes, *Rapport de l'assemblée quinquennale, Washingmon, D.C. 1925*, ed. Marchioness of Aberdeen and Temair (New York: V.E. Scott, 1925); Maria Vérone, "The Evolution of the Family throughout the World," *Bulletin: Monthly Publication of the International Council of Women*, 16, no. 3 (November 1937): 18–19.

63 "Notes and News," *Bulletin* 10, no.1 (September 1931): 2.
64 Cova and Costa Pinto, "Women and Salazarism," 398.
65 "Our Golden Jubilee Conference," *Bulletin* 22, no. 1 (October 1938); "Assembleia geral do Conselho Internacional das mulheres realizada em Edimbourg (Escócia), de 11 a 21 de Julho de 1938," *Alma Feminina* 3/4 (March/April 1938).
66 *Diário do Governo* 1, no. 43 (February 22, 1933): 228.
67 "Um apelo," *Alma Feminina* 5 (October 1940).
68 For what happened in the 1940s for the CNMP, see Cova and Costa Pinto, "Women and Salazarism," 397–405.
69 Anne Cova and António Costa Pinto, "Women under Salazar's Dictatorship," *Portuguese Journal of Social Science* 1, no. 2 (July 2002): 129–146.
70 ICW Archives in Brussels, Letter of Maria Lamas and Maria Manuela Campos to Marthe Boël (1877–1956), president of the ICW, July 18, 1947.
71 Cova and Costa Pinto, "Women under Salazar's Dictatorship," 129–146.
72 See the special issue of *Women's History Review*, entitled "International Feminisms," edited by Ann Taylor Allen, Anne Cova and June Purvis 19, no. 4 (September 2010).

16 Night Work for White Women and Bonded Labour for "Native" Women?

Contentious Traditions and the Globalization of Gender-Specific Labour Protection and Legal Equality Politics, 1926 to 1939[1]

Susan Zimmermann

Gender-specific labour legislation—advocated by some as special "protection" for and opposed by others as gender-specific "discrimination" against women—has been a contested issue since the late nineteenth century. By the early twentieth century it had gained ground, especially in many European countries and internationally. On-going conflict and division in national and international women's and labour movements and organisations in and beyond Europe notwithstanding,[2] European governments emerged as key actors promoting the internationalization of gender-specific labour protection as their representatives hammered out the International Convention Respecting the Prohibition of Night Work for Women in Industrial Employment, known as the Berne Convention of 1906.[3] An earlier international initiative, the International Labour Protection Conference held in Berlin in 1890, in which high ranking representatives of more than a dozen European countries participated, had similarly advocated gender-specific labour law, including a ban of women's underground work in mines and restrictions of women's night work and Sunday work.[4] After World War I, the newly established International Labour Organization (ILO) contributed decisively to the further internationalization of these types of legal provisions. In the beginning, the ILO was strongly dominated by both the major European powers, many of whom reigned over large overseas empires, and by those forces and traditions in the European labour movement and labour internationalism which were supportive of gender-specific labour legislation;[5] the United States of America and the Soviet Union joined the organisation only in 1934. Two among the six ILO Conventions adopted in 1919—the Maternity Protection Convention (C3, 1919) and the Night Work (Women) Convention (C4, 1919)—encompassed gender-specific international labour law; the White Lead (Painting) Convention (C13) was added in 1921, the Underground Work (Women) Convention (C45) in 1935. Other ILO instruments contained additional gender-specific regulations.[6] ILO Conventions were binding for any given territory only if the relevant authority ratified them, and the organisation allowed for additional softening of the stipulations contained in its instruments and partial or postponed application of these instruments insofar as less industrially developed or not fully self-governing territories were concerned; these limitations notwithstanding, the influence and "soft power" of the ILO in framing discourse and politics over labour issues internationally and within many countries and territories made itself increasingly felt.[7]

Influential female trade unionists and other women's activists and politicians supported the ILO's politics of gender-specific labour protection; yet already in the early years of the ILO, the conflict over gender-specific labour law, as had developed especially within both the industrial countries of Europe and to an extent internationally, was present.[8] Even so, the period between the later 1920s and World War II marked the beginning of a new phase in the history of the struggle over gender-specific labour legislation on two levels.

On the first level, under the pressure of women's international activism, the ILO, albeit hesitantly, began to reconsider its unconditional support for special labour protection for women. The landscape of women's international organising underwent important change in these years.[9] New organisations and coalitions made their appearance, focusing exclusively upon, or foregrounding, a politics of strictly defined gender equality. One particularly important coalition of international women's organisations whose work focused on influencing the League of Nations and the ILO was the Liaison Committee of Women's International Organisations. New organisations soon became important political actors alongside the older international women's organisations, which pursued a more variegated agenda and either voiced ambivalent and lukewarm positions with regard to, or advocated in a straightforward manner, gender-specific labour law. Within this context, the Open Door International (ODI), one of the new organisations, emerged as a key opponent of the gender-specific international labour law promoted by the ILO. This organisation in particular launched a proactive, systematic, and on-going attack against all aspects of these politics.[10] The ILO for its part mobilised its various supporters, not only among the big international non-socialist women's organisations but also among trade union and socialist women and their organisations.

From a long-term perspective, the transnational challenges to special labour protection then unfolding contributed to turning the tide in favour of a gender-neutral labour law, which would prevail in the later decades of the twentieth century. In other words, what had begun in Europe, in the decades before 1914, as a conflict over gender-specific labour protection versus women's equality in labour law gave rise in the long run to a tendency in labour law internationally to advocate the principle of legal equality between the sexes. By the 1930s the conflict over labour law came to form one element in a broader political dynamic triggered by the efforts of the international women's organisations to embed the overarching principle of "equal rights" or "equality of status" of men and women in international law. These politics addressed the League of Nations in the first place.[11] Feminist opponents of gender-specific labour law played an important role in bringing about these larger developments and aimed to capitalise on them; the ODI's journal *The Open Door* argued in 1935 that any substantial, general "equal rights treaty ought to involve the denunciation by Governments of international agreements which place prohibitions on women's work . . . as well as the repeal of all such legislation."[12]

On a second level, the international labour standards of the ILO played a key role in globalizing the politics of women-specific labour protection in an unequally developing world. The women-specific ILO standards referred to above played a key role in internationalizing women-specific labour legislation and imbued this policy with the authority of the politics of the community of empires and states. These standards, which originally emerged in response to the labour conditions in the industrial countries of the Northern Hemisphere, increasingly were ratified by various countries worldwide, and directly or indirectly influenced the labour legislation of even more countries as well as non-self-governing territories during the interwar period. In addition, in the period from the late 1920s to the outbreak of World War II, the ILO developed a set of protective labour regulations aimed at restricting and protecting the bonded, or particularly oppressive,[13] labour of non-white populations in the Southern Hemisphere, which in ILO discourse throughout the interwar period was addressed as "native" or "indigenous" labour, and from the 1940s as "non-metropolitan" labour. The Forced Labour Convention of 1930 (C29), the Recruiting of Indigenous Workers Convention (C50) of 1936, the Contracts of Employment (Indigenous Workers) Convention (C64), and the Penal Sanctions (Indigenous Workers) Convention (C65) of 1939 were at the core of this policy. While the Forced Labour Convention had carefully avoided any restriction of the scope of application in terms of territories or populations concerned, by 1936 the ILO had settled for defining its "special" standards for "native labour" as concerning the "labour . . . of the indigenous populations of colonial territories or of self-governing countries where the indigenous populations are not in enjoyment of citizen rights but are in a position of dependency or tutelage;" included also was the labour of persons "assimilated" to these conditions.[14]

As this set of "special" standards for "non-metropolitan" workers emerged, the contest between gender-specific labour protection and legal equality between the sexes entered this new arena of international labour policy. In this process the already complex intersection of gender and class that had characterised the battle on gender-specific labour regulation in the industrial context began to visibly interact with political attitudes regarding race and unequal global development. Thus, the effort to craft international labour standards came to encompass both the conflict on special labour protection (with its implicit focus on "industrial" countries of the Northern hemisphere), and the question of engendering protective labour legislation of a different type for "native" populations in the Southern Hemisphere.

Taken together, the internationalization and globalization of gendered labour law and the mounting challenge to women-specific labour protection furnished one important component of a long-term historical shift of great importance for the future of women's labour worldwide. I argue that in the long run, as policies foregrounding gender equality made inroads into international labour law[15] and labour law in many countries, they would become instrumental in facilitating women's increasing inclusion in the world of paid labour in such a way that in many cases women's work would suffer from an absence of both gender-specific and sex-neutral labour protection. This chapter aims to shed light on the historical origins of this development in the international struggle on gendered labour protection in the interwar period; it also seeks to enrich our theoretical and historical understanding of the political and historical puzzles that undergird this long-term development and manifested themselves on a variety of levels in the clash on gender-specific labour legislation that unfolded between 1926 and 1939.

Rather than providing a full history of this clash, I focus here on the struggle over the revision of the ILO's 1919 Night Work (Women) Convention, and on several issues and conflicts over gender-specific international regulations of "native" labour between 1930 and 1939. In discussing these dimensions of the political struggle on gender and labour policy, I build on two lines of reasoning which allow us to make sense of some of the puzzles enshrined therein. Initially, we need to conceive of the clash between legal equality and differential labour legislation as a negotiation between politics focusing on reducing gender and class disadvantages. Secondly, we need to think of an implicitly white labour in the Northern Hemisphere and the bonded labour of "native" women and men in the Southern Hemisphere as unequally related constitutive elements of worldwide capitalist expansion, which drew into commodified labour an ever broadening strata of the population in the North and the South in the world of labour characterised by a race gap.

International Labour Legislation and the Puzzles of Gender-Specific Labour Protection in the Global North and the Global South

In June 1929, the British women's organisation Open Door Council called an international conference in Berlin which drew up the "Constitution" of the future ODI as well as a "Manifesto and Woman Worker's Charter of Economic Rights."[16] One year later, members of the British women's organisation Six Point Group, with the support of Alice Paul from the U.S.-based National Woman's Party, initiated the founding of another new international organisation, the Equal Rights International (ERI). Six Point Group member Helen Archdale would become the president of the new organization, which defined as its first object "to obtain the adoption of the Equal Rights Treaty by the nations of the world."[17] Both of these organisations pursued a politics of strict legal equality between women and men. With the Scottish barrister Chrystal Macmillan as its founding president and prominent feminists such as Františka Plamínková from Czechoslovakia and Gertrud Baer from Germany as long-term members of its Board,[18] the ODI focused primarily on women's work and international labour law, whereas the ERI worked relentlessly for the overarching international Equal Rights Treaty.

Legal equality feminism—as I will label the politics pursued by both these organisations—staged its appearance in international labour policy in a dramatic and confrontational style.[19] The ODI in particular accused the ILO of the "International Mass Production of Restrictive Legislation"[20] as "internationally financed by the governments of the world."[21] The ODI attacked legal stipulations providing for special labour protection for women as "restrictions" and "exclusion of women" as a "tyranny" which "however benevolent the intention . . . protects men by maintaining many employments and processes as monopolies for the male worker."[22] Whereas in the fields of suffrage, property, and education, the women's movement had achieved a lot already, the ILO, because it successfully promoted the internationalization of gender-specific labour standards, was guilty of the proliferation of new "discriminations against women," namely "in industry;" the ILO thus was viewed by the ODI as "a real danger to women."[23]

Within the ILO, the officers responsible for dealing with women's issues reacted with a mixture of indignation, disinterest, and condescension, claiming, for example, that the "Open Door ladies" simply had no idea of the burden that heavy night work in factories put on women, and labeling the legal equality feminism domiciled especially in English-speaking countries a more "extremist" section of feminism.[24] In the meantime, both the ODI and the ERI repeatedly stressed that they quite appreciated measures aimed at the protection of workers in general. The 1929 foundational manifesto of the ODI had affirmed that the ILO did "good work" in terms of advocating gender-neutral labour regulations internationally.[25] The ERI for its part, addressing members of the Governing Body of the ILO and the 1936 Session of the International Labour Conference, declared: "For the prevention of exploitation, and the safeguarding of health of the workers, industrial legislation is eminently necessary. Without it the standard of the workers would, in some quarters, tend towards a condition of slavery and the public spirited employer would suffer by the unfair competition of less enlightened rivals."[26] These statements give rise to a number of questions: Did the ILO and other supporters of gender-specific labour protection of women simply misread the campaign for legal equality that the feminists were waging against gender-specific protective legislation as being based in anti-working class liberalism? And, in turn, did legal equality feminists simply ignore the fact that special labour protection restricted the otherwise limitless entrepreneurial disposition of the work force?

The establishment of the ODI and the ERI offered a response not only to the internationalization of gender-specific labour law by the ILO, but it also reflected conflict amongst women and their international organisations on the principle of legal equality in a number of policy fields. The issue of gender-specific labour protection had sparked a serious crisis within the International Alliance of Women (IAW)[27] a few years earlier. At the IAW Congress in 1926, held in Paris, the new generation of legal equality feminists had tried hard but in vain to get this organisation, which had been the champion of legal equality concerning suffrage for decades, to declare itself against special labour protection for women. After this defeat, the legal equality feminists felt that they were "left . . . without an International body equipped for dealing with the various attacks on women's right to work made by the International Labour Organisation."[28] An additional conflict over the question of the international regulation of married women's citizenship culminated around 1930, when the conference on the Codification of International Law held under the auspices of the League of Nations discussed the "nationality of married women." Legal equality feminism was clearly gaining ground internationally with the related conflicts triggering substantial change on the landscape of women's organised internationalism.[29]

Thus, the conflict over legal equality had at this point triggered a major upheaval in international gender politics, with the ODI's on-going assault on the ILO and conflict amongst international women's organisations on gendered international labour policy becoming a basic feature for many years to come. In short, by the 1930s gender-specific labour legislation internationally was under severe attack.

However, in the years between 1926 and 1930, the ILO managed, with the active support of major international women's organisations and without provoking a real outcry from the legal equality feminists, to introduce a major new gendered element into international labour protection. This was the complete prohibition of forced labour for "native" women, as opposed to "native" men. The ILO's Forced Labour Convention of 1930, which had been under preparation since 1927, contained a clause according to which the responsible authorities of any country or territory could still draw "native" men into forced labour for public purposes. In preparing these gender-specific regulations, the ILO had garnered the support of prominent international and a number of British women's organisations. These organisations formally posited their requests for such action even before the first meeting, in 1927, of the ILO's own Committee of Experts on Native Labour, the body which within the organisation was to devise authoritative guidelines for any future dealings with bonded labour. The Committee assembled high-ranking experts, most of them with experience in, or otherwise connected with, colonial administration and colonial policy of the "powers;" exclusively male in the beginning, in February 1930 Madame Marzorati, Member of the Institute of Colonial Women in Brussels was added.[30] When the Committee of Experts convened in July 1927, it discussed two memoranda submitted by women's organisations, and, in a move that must be considered rather extraordinary for the ILO at the time, these documents were subsequently reprinted as an appendix to the International Labour Office's conclusive report on forced labour laid before the twelfth Session of the International Labour Conference sitting between 30 May and 21 June 1929.[31] These two memoranda had been drafted after a meeting in London in March 1927 during which the responsible officer of the ILO and a representative of the Antislavery and Aborigines Protection Society addressed the assembled delegates of the women's societies. At this meeting, ILO representative Harold Grimshaw laid out the baselines of the ILO's policies on forced labour, which indeed would become the guiding principles of the Forced Labour Convention adopted in 1930. He "stated that the suggestions he would make were based on the assumption that forced labour was in some cases justifiable, an assumption the merits of which he declined to discuss."[32] Measures intended to "minimize the dangers of such labour" included the complete prohibition of forced labour for women, the definition of a maximum percentage of males who "might be taken from any locality" at one time, and restrictions of the amount of forced labour which could be demanded from one individual. Following this meeting, the representatives of the women's organisations appointed an ad hoc committee to devise a memorandum to be sent to the ILO's Committee of Experts on Native Labour.[33] In the end, two parallel memoranda were sent to Geneva. One was co-authored by the International Council of Women (ICW), the politically moderate international umbrella organisation of women, and representatives from other important international organisations, among them the IAW and the Women's International League for Peace and Freedom (WILPF). The second memorandum was signed by a number of prominent British women's organisations, among them the British branch of the WILPF. The two documents agreed that, in principle, forced labour for private purposes as well as for women and children should be immediately prohibited, and both made a case for the principal demand, which was to abolish forced labour altogether as soon as possible. The argumentative emphasis of the two documents, however, was markedly different. The representatives of the international organisations, which rallied behind the ICW, made a firm case for gendered differential labour protection and a policy of strengthening gendered family and social structures as translated into the context of forced labour and "native communities." Women, children, and the "unfit and aged . . . should in any case be exempt" from forced labour. Care should be taken not "to call for any service, which would involve a break-up of family life. . . . We venture to suggest that . . . the claims of tribal and family life should always dominate" and form a core principle of any future convention in relation to forced labour.[34] The tone of the second memorandum submitted "by a Council of British Women's Organisations" was entirely different. It avoided reference to family and tribal life and talked exclusively about work. The total quantity of forced labour, i.e., adult men who would be obliged to do forced labour, "should not be so great that it causes local distress for lack of adequate male labour, nor should the period of work conflict with the village requirements in the matter of labour;" moreover, forced labourers must not be provided with prostitutes.[35] The ICW statement did not point to free labour as an alternative to forced labour, whereas the British memorandum did.[36]

In 1927 during its first session, the ILO's expert committee did indeed embrace the major common demand of both memoranda and established, without any further discussion, the principle that forced labour for women and children was to be prohibited at once.[37] In 1929, when forced labour was discussed at the twelfth Session of the ILO's International Labour Conference, Betzy Kjelsberg, who as a delegate represented the Norwegian government but was also vice-president of the ICW, underlined the importance of the documents submitted in 1927 by the women's organisations.[38]

Conspicuously absent among the signatories of the two memoranda were three organisations that represented, within the British context, the legal equality position in a most uncompromising manner and which were or would be instrumental in internationalizing legal equality feminism in these years: the Six Point Group, the Open Door Council, and the St. Joan's Social and Political Alliance.[39] Whereas the ICW indirectly made itself heard at the meeting of the International Labour Conference through the voice of Betzy Kjelsberg, there was no spokesperson for legal equality feminism at either the 1929 or at the 1930 Sessions of the International Labour Conference when the provisions of the Forced Labour Convention were discussed and adopted. The ODI, which with regard to "general," i.e., industrial, labour legislation waged its highly publicised battle against the ILO's politics of international "inequality conventions" as early as 1929, did at no point raise its voice. It was not until the second half of the 1930s, when the ILO prepared other conventions on bonded labour, that internationally organised legal equality feminists did weigh in on the subject of gender-specific regulation of "native" labour. "Indigenous" women should have, so they then argued, the same right as "indigenous" men to enter into long-term contract labour as opposed to those gender-specific restrictions to independent contract-making which the ILO had initially contemplated.[40] This intervention must be seen in the context of the intensifying preoccupation of Western-based, non-socialist international women's organisations and their coalitions with the legal status of "native" women.[41] Yet while the question of judging the reality of women's work in industrial countries and the argument that the female workers themselves should be given a voice in this regard were important tropes in the Northern-oriented debates by women's organisations on gender-specific labour law in the interwar period, these same tropes were invisible in discussions of the legal regulation of the particularly oppressive labour of non-white women in the Southern Hemisphere.

These developments in relation to gender-specific regulations of forced labour give rise to a number of questions: Why did the internationally organised legal equality feminists sidestep reference to the Forced Labour Convention in their highly publicised assault on gender inequality in international labour protection? Was legal equality feminism disinterested in "native" woman workers at this point? Was it that they did not dare to suggest, under the banner of legal equality, that "native" women should still be included among those adult individuals whom colonial and other authorities in the South would have the right to recruit into forced labour in the future? If so, why, then, did legal equality feminists not demand—alternatively—that forced labour should be completely abolished for both "native" men and women at once? And why, in turn, would legal equality feminists still lobby in the later 1930s for the gender-neutral involvement of "native" women in other forms of extremely exploitative labour in the Southern Hemisphere?

In the following sections I try to make sense of the puzzles built into the international struggle on gender-specific labour protection with a focus on the relationship between these two dimensions of international labour policy: the universal labour standards that emerged out of a preoccupation with labour relations in industrial countries, and the "special" labour standards that referred to particularly oppressive labour relations in the Southern Hemisphere.

The Northern-Centric Battle over Gender-Specific Labour Protection

As the newly formed ODI launched its campaign against the ILO's gender-specific international instruments, which its leaders considered to be "discriminations against women . . . spreading like a malignant growth,"[42] the question of gender-specific restriction of women's work at night developed—along with women's work in mines and other issues—into one of the most significant bones of contention. By 1930–1931, the ILO was contemplating a modification of its 1919 Night Work (Women) Convention, according to which the restrictions of women's night work would no longer apply "to persons holding positions of supervision or management." The pre-history of the related activities reached back to an intervention of the government of the United Kingdom in 1928, with the British Women's Engineering Society involved in the background.[43] In parallel, the ODI in 1929 launched its frontal attack on the ILO against gender-specific labour legislation. The impact of this campaign on the leadership of the ILO was clearly discernible—at least internally. The Director, Albert Thomas, engaged in repeated discussions with influential representatives of those women's organisations, who "were . . . emphatic in their anxiety to help the [International Labour] Office and . . . convinced of the rapidity with which the 'Open Door' movement was spreading." As a result, Thomas came to consider, especially in relation to the Night Work (Women) Convention, "whether the time is not ripe for a re-examination of the position of women in industry" along the line mentioned above.[44] After a failed attempt in 1931, in 1934 the ILO revised the Convention—resulting in the adoption of the Night Work (Women) Convention (Revised) (C41)—to make the definition of "night" somewhat more flexible and to exempt women in management positions from the restrictions.

Restrictions of women's work at night had long formed one of the most contentious issues in the conflict on special labour protection. The arguments put forward both in favour and against special labour protection for women were many, and many women engaged in women's and labour activism spoke out against special labour protection as discriminatory. They also reiterated their concern about male self-interest, in relation to both the world of work and the domestic sphere, as informing the preference of others for special protection for women workers; participants in the debate time and again pointed to male and trade-unionist interest in monopolizing well-paid night work for men as well as to men's interest in controlling female sexuality and the family by keeping women at home during the night. In addition, as women's and gender historians have repeatedly demonstrated, special protection laws in many countries in reality were effectively designed to exempt low-paid female night work, for example in the food industries and the service sector, from any restrictions.[45]

Those who defended special labour protection for women against the critique and politics of legal equality feminism—such as the majority of the labour women present at the January 1930 meeting of the International Advisory Committee of Women of the Labour and Socialist International, amongst them the British Marion Phillips and the German Gertrud Hanna[46]—had clear reasons to do so, reasons that cannot be reduced to adherence to or silent acceptance of male privilege or hierarchically structured gendered difference. These reasons stand out when we analyse both the defence of and the attack on special labour protection for women simultaneously from a gender-only and a class-only perspective, as well as against the dominant political context, or the actors' perception of this context, in a given historical moment. Schematically simplified, such an analysis reveals the following. From a gender-only perspective, abolishing or reducing gender difference in labour protection would reduce or abolish gender disadvantage or discrimination as described in the arguments against special protection (summarised above).[47] Such a policy, in other words—to use a convenient short hand—would close or at least narrow the gender gap in labour protection. In a context in which gender-specific labour protection did already exist, this gap could only be closed or narrowed either by applying current woman-specific standards of labour protection to men, so as to match or to approximate those for women, or by abolishing or lowering the pre-existing standards for women. From a perspective that foregrounds legal equality between the sexes, both of these policies would contribute equally to closing or narrowing the gender gap. At the same time, from a class-only perspective, these same two strategies of narrowing or closing the gender gap embodied two distinctly opposing moves. Applying pre-existing women-specific standards of labour protection to men too so as to match or get closer to those for women would mean that a growing number of individuals belonging to the working class would enjoy more labour protection. Such a move would contribute to curbing class exploitation or class disadvantage in the world of work; it would, in other words, reduce the class gap. By contrast, narrowing the gender gap by abolishing or lowering pre-existing women-specific standards of labour protection would effectively widen the class gap in the world of work; in other words, it would open the door for more exploitative labour relations. From the perspective of a combined gender and class analysis which itself does not prioritise gender over class or class over gender, there were thus not only two but three principal positions in the controversies over gender-specific labour protection.

First, there were those who would defend pre-existing women-specific labour protection or aimed to introduce such legislation. They regarded as a class-gain any such move, whatever the implications from the perspective of widening the gender gap might be. They prioritised, in other words, the reduction of the class gap over anything that would happen in the course of application in terms of the differential treatment of women and men in labour protection. In doing so, some of the supporters of such a position conceived of women-specific labour protection as a first step toward more comprehensive labour protection and/or as a measure which could be more easily achieved (despite the resistance of employers and, in some cases, the state) than many other measures of labour protection. This was clearly the official position represented by the International Labour Office and many of its officers, including the women officers co-directing the organisation's women's work agenda during the 1920s and 1930s, Martha Mundt and later Marguerite Thibert. The axiomatic contours of this position were expounded by Albert Thomas, the Director of the International Labour Office, in response to the arguments put forward on 30 September 1930 by a women's deputation, introduced by Alice Paul and including among others Helen Archdale, the Australian Jessie Street, and the Romanian Marie Boskoff-Zoty; all of these women were leading representatives of the emerging ERI. These women strongly argued in favour of legal equality; they demanded alterations of the ILO's Night Work (Women) Convention and White Lead (Painting) Convention that would make them conform to the principle of legal equality between the sexes. Pointing to concrete historical examples, Thomas explained to the delegates that "the task of protecting workers had been begun along the line of least resistance and the protection of women had led in due course to the protection of workers in general."[48] Yet critics of this view nevertheless had a point when they claimed that (historically speaking) special protection had resulted from a partial coalition of patriarchal interest amongst employers, trade unions, and states, and that in reality women's labour—despite all specific protection—had always been organised in such a way as to serve employers' interests in obtaining cheap and highly exploitable labour. Supporters of gender-specific labour regulations for women would, of course, claim in turn that protecting women as such did not equal "discrimination" against or "restrictions" on women.

The second position in the battle on gendered labour protection prioritised the reduction of the gender gap over the reduction of the class gap insofar as it did not combine its struggle against gender-specific labour protection with a definite statement as to whether or not legal equality in labour law between women and men should be achieved by lowering pre-existing women-specific standards or, alternatively, by raising the standards of protection for male workers. This was, as I will demonstrate below, the position of the ODI and other groups of legal equality feminists. In historical contexts where employers and their interests enjoyed a strong political and economic position, policies based in this position were indeed likely, via reference to gender equality, to contribute to political dynamics that could easily result in the erosion of pre-existing labour standards.

A third position in the conflict on gender-specific labour protection would resist prioritizing the reduction of the gender gap over the class gap, or the class gap over the gender gap. Where women-specific labour protection existed already, representatives of this position would work to develop labour protection standards further so as to include male workers. They would also argue in favour of introducing more and better measures of labour protection for both sexes at the same time. In terms of *realpolitik*, i.e., in terms of how they would relate to plans or action aimed at raising or lowering pre-existing gender-specific protection standards, representatives of this position would oppose a policy of lowering such standards because to do so would mean the prioritization of narrowing the gender gap over the class gap; in this way they would tolerate the gender gap as it had been enshrined in pre-existing legislation in order not to risk a trade-off between narrowing the gender gap via broadening the class gap. In taking this position they concurred, if for different reasons, with representatives of the first position who would similarly defend pre-existing gender-specific labour protection.

Partisans of ODI, including future president Chrystal Macmillan, definitely did not position themselves in this third way in the battle over special labour protection in the Northern Hemisphere as something evil or beneficial for women in the interwar period. In fact, their self-positioning resembled the second principle position described above in that it consciously chose to prioritise gender equality in labour protection over any clear position on the class question. In a March 1929 letter to Marie Heinen of the Dutch National Bureau for Women's Labour, Macmillan underlined that this was indeed the approach informing the principled statements of the emerging organization. Macmillan wrote in her capacity as chairman of the International Committee of the British Open Door Council, which was organising the foundational meeting of the new international organisation in Berlin. Expanding on the principles according to which her organisation had been operating, she explained to Heinen: "After reading your International Leaflet I see that you take in some questions that we do not take in, for instance you declare yourselves in favour of legislation for the regulation of the work of women and men. While probably every one of our Members as an individual approves of this, we as an organisation have concentrated on the one point, namely, that whatever regulations may be made, these should apply equally to men and women."[49] Macmillan went on to explain that the "Object" of the future ODI (as had already been drafted) would not be discussed or negotiated during the upcoming Berlin conference. Rather, the conference would "call together those who support our object with a view to getting together an International Body to support it in its three aspects."[50] The relevant first two parts of the statement describing the principal objective of the ODI as adopted in June 1929 read: "To secure that a woman shall be free to work and protected as a worker on the same terms as a man, and that legislation and regulations dealing with conditions and hours, payment, entry and training shall be based upon the nature of the work and not upon the sex of the worker."[51] Upon its foundation in 1929, the ODI demanded the revision of the ILO's Night Work (Women) Convention so as to ensure that wherever night work was "forbidden it shall be forbidden both to men and women," and that any particular regulations "shall apply equally to men and women." At its Stockholm conference in 1931, the ODI adopted a resolution which called upon the International Labour Conference "to abrogate the present [ILO] Convention" and, using the language agreed upon earlier, declared that no alternative instrument would be acceptable "unless it provides that any prohibition or regulation of night work is based on the nature of the work and not on the sex of the worker."[52]

Despite its positive attitude, at least in principle, toward (gender-neutral) labour regulation or protection, the priorities of the ODI manifested themselves on many occasions. One example was the response of the organisation to the Advisory Opinion of the Permanent Court of International Justice, which, by 1932, had established (in response to a query submitted by the ILO) that the 1919 Night Work (Women) Convention was indeed phrased in such a way as to include women who worked in management positions.[53] In response to this finding, the ODI launched a campaign by which countries that had ratified the ILO's 1919 Night Work (Women) Convention were asked to repudiate the Convention "at the earliest possible moment" or else to "immediately . . . denounce the Convention, and amend their legislation;" this "is a duty we owe to the women concerned, and to all women who believe that International Labour Conventions should be so framed as to protect the workers from low wages, bad conditions, and exploitation, and not to deprive them of opportunities of earning a good living."[54]

The ODI put forward a similar demand regarding the ILO's parallel deliberations on a future instrument concerning the forty-hour week. Here it argued that such a restriction of individual working hours was likely to produce additional disadvantages and dangers for those in many factories "to whom special restrictions apply" because the switch to the forty-hour week was likely to induce a new shift system involving night work or more night work. The ODI therefore asked the ILO to adopt "as prerequisite to any action with respect to the forty hour week" a new policy regarding night work: "As soon as it is constitutionally possible," the Night Work (Women) Convention "should be superseded by a convention placing the same restrictions as to night work on men and women alike" with "any necessary continuous processes or other desired exceptions being scheduled as exemptions for men and women alike."[55]

An analysis of the simultaneous implications of this policy in terms of widening or narrowing the class as compared to the gender gap reveals that with these demands, the ODI—while declaring itself in favour of regulation or restriction of night work (i.e., in favour of controlling the class gap)—actually prioritised the narrowing of the gender gap over the narrowing or widening of the class gap. In demanding the unconditional repudiation of the Night Work (Women) Convention, i.e., the repudiation of all special protection enshrined therein, the ODI on the international level advocated a closure of the gender gap in such a way that this would combine with a definite measure of widening the class gap. This move was combined with an indefinite statement about national "amendments" that left an open question as to whether or not such amendments would narrow or widen the class gap on the national level, as compared to the *status quo ante* in international law. When talking about a future international instrument that should, as soon as "constitutionally possible," replace the old Night Work (Women) Convention, the ODI gave voice to a similar political vision and employed a similar argumentative strategy. Referring in an indefinite manner to "restrictions" on night work, "continuous processes" that might be defined as requiring night work, as well as "exceptions" from the prohibition of night work in future regulations, the ODI talked in the affirmative about some measure of control of the class gap, yet it left undefined the particular measures that might be taken to control the class gap. Taken together, the politics of the ODI thus were based in a strategy which combined the demand for a definite measure of widening the class gap—via repudiation of the old, gender-specific international convention—while not making any statement about the desired measure of narrowing the class gap via the introduction of new, gender-neutral restrictions (as compared to a situation of no restriction of night work at all or pre-existing gender-neutral restrictions) on national or international levels. This kept an option open according to which the demand to close the gender gap—which was at the core of the ODI's politics—would actually be accompanied by a widening of the class gap in labour protection either in the labour legislation of some countries or internationally.

While the ODI never discussed the problem in these terms, the organisation, in avoiding any definite statement about the politics of widening or narrowing the class gap, in fact built its policy on tolerance regarding a possible widening of the class gap in the course of narrowing the gender gap. It is for this reason (among others) that actors involved in the battle over gender-specific labour protection, who, as was the case with the ILO, under no circumstances were prepared to open the door to a potential widening of the class gap in labour protection nationally or internationally, were alarmed by the ODI campaign against the ILO's Night Work (Women) Convention. The political and economic circumstances of the Great Depression in the aftermath of the stock market crash of 1929 lent additional weight to the fear that putting into question pre-existing international standards of labour protection would play into the hands of employers' growing power and increased disposition over the workforce. On the other hand, equal rights feminists—and the personnel of the ILO—were increasingly alarmed that the same economic depression was fostering (in part successful) endeavours in a number of countries to add new restrictions, especially to married women's right to earn their own living, i.e., that gendered restrictions in the world of work were ominously on the rise.[56]

It was no wonder that the conflict between legal equality feminists and the ILO continued to escalate throughout the 1930s. The 1934 Session of the International Labour Conference adopted by a large majority the limited revision of the Night Work (Women) Convention mentioned above. In the conference committee British trade unionist Julia Varley had given voice to the third position in the conflict on gender-specific labour protection described above: opposing "any exemptions from the Convention," she declared herself both "in favour of protective legislation for women" and "the prohibition of night work for men as well as women."[57]

This first sign in 1934 of the growing flexibility of the ILO was accompanied, however, by the preparation, and followed in 1935 by the adoption of the Underground [Women] Convention, prohibiting women's underground work in mines, a step bitterly opposed by legal equality feminists.[58] And still: in the second half of the 1930s the legal equality principle, in both its labour-related and more general incarnations, finally made tentative inroads into the ILO's approach to international labour protection, with American women and states playing an important role in the process.[59] The only previous substantial formal commitment of the ILO to gender equality had been the principle "that men and women should receive equal remuneration for work of equal value;" this principle was enshrined in its 1919 Constitution.[60] The first Labour Conference of the American States, sponsored by the ILO and held in Santiago, Chile in 1936, reaffirmed the ILO's affirmation of gender-specific labour protection, particularly regarding the Night Work (Women) Convention and minimum standards for maternity protection. The resolution on minimum wages, however, explicitly invoked the principle of fixing wages "according to the nature of the work irrespective of the sex of the worker." This phrasing had long been at the core of legal equality feminism's demands in relation to labour regulation.[61] In 1937 the general

Session of the International Labour Conference adopted a resolution which broadened the ILO's approach to women's issues beyond the traditional focus on gender-specific labour law. The basic idea of the resolution was—as underlined by the government delegate of the United States and well-known social reformer Grace Abbott, who had submitted it—that "much protective legislation would be unnecessary if women enjoyed equal civil and political rights with men."[62] The resolution itself, while bitterly critiqued by the ODI as a new "attack on women's civil rights" and an example of "confused thinking," still urged the governments to put into law and administrative practice a number of "principles of the greatest importance," among them the principle that "in addition to full political and civil rights . . . women should have full opportunity to work." The resolution reaffirmed, but also rephrased, the equal pay principle demanding that women should "receive remuneration without discrimination because of sex."[63]

By 1939 the authoritative ILO study *The Law and Women's Work* similarly mirrored the cautious process of opening toward more equality-oriented labour laws within the ILO. It described women-specific labour protection as dating from a time "when there was . . . little support for labour legislation" and as later being superseded in large degree by more general regulations. The study stated: "The laws and regulations that have been designed to solve the difficulties arising out of the social conditions of a given period often change at a slower rate than the circumstances, so that part of the [women-specific labour] legislation ostensibly in force meets the conditions of yesterday rather than those of to-day."[64] While referring in the affirmative to generalizing protective labour law in which women-specific regulations would be no longer as relevant as in the past, this approach simultaneously justified specific measures of protection as cornerstones of the historical and unfinished pathway toward such generalization.

The same ILO study classified forced labour as "heavy" work, which for this reason was completely prohibited for women by the ILO Forced Labour Convention of 1930; it did not address gender-specific regulations of other forms of "native" labour.[65] Yet during the 1930s the ILO was increasingly confronted with the demands of legal equality feminism in the latter field of international labour policy. In the following section, I explore how the confrontation rooted historically in industrial labour policy with an implicit focus on the North—regarding the role of gender-specific labour regulation and forming part of the historical struggle on the overall progress of labour protection played out in the policies of constructing labour standards for oppressive labour with a focus on the Southern Hemisphere.

Making Sense of Gender-Specific Regulations for "Non-Metropolitan" Labour

The process which had led international and British women's organisations to address the ILO in 1927 with their two memoranda regarding forced labour had been set in motion in the course of political manoeuvres and public debate in England prior to the first meeting of the Committee of Experts on Native Labour, which was to deal with the issue on behalf of the ILO. Both memoranda were designed to support the ILO's emerging politics of prohibiting forced labour for private purposes as well as for women and children. That is, the memoranda were agreed that with regard to forced labour—for lack of more far-reaching measures—special labour protection for women was indeed desirable. At the same time there was—as we have seen in section one above, describing the contents of the memoranda—a clearly divergent emphasis on the labour issue proper in the British memorandum versus a focus on family and social reproduction in the memorandum signed by the ICW and its partner organizations. In this way, from the very beginning, the on-going transnational Northern-centric debate on special labour protection unmistakably translated into the dealings of women's organisations with ILO politics concerning labour relations and social reproduction in the Southern Hemisphere. The British women's organisations which signed the first memorandum avoided any reference to differentialist and socially conservative family values while joining forces with all those for whom gendered gradualism in prohibiting forced labour by international labour law seemed to be the right way, or at least the only viable way, to proceed at this given historical moment. Yet why were the partisans of strict legal equality feminism and its critique of gendered labour law so conspicuously absent in 1927 when various national and international women's organisations discussed the gendered abolition of forced labour? Why did the ODI not extend its vociferous campaign against gender-specific "restrictions" in labour law to the question of forced labour? After all, forced labour—including its gender-specific prohibition—became the key item on the agenda of the Sessions of the International Labour Conferences in 1929 and 1930, and the ODI, upon establishment during the 1929 Session of the International Labour Conference, immediately launched an uncompromising campaign against the ILO's pre-existing conventions and its plans to devise additional international instruments involving gender-specific regulations of labour. In December 1929, for example, the ODI, in relation to the work of women in mines—which the ILO similarly classified as "heavy" work,[66] which justified gender-specific restrictions—publicly declared that, while it did not wish to express itself "either for or against women working underground," recent proposals of the ILO for a convention that would "prohibit all paid underground work to adult women . . . must be combatted."[67] On the issue of forced labour there was no activism that would have been based in an analogous self-positioning as expressed by the ODI in relation to the underground work of women in mines, but rather there was a distinct reticence. I argue that this reticence resulted from a fundamental misalignment between the legal equality agenda as represented by the ODI and the problem of how to deal with forced labour in international labour law. One unresolvable problem involved the issue of independence and choice. The ODI, or at least its Chairman Chrystal Macmillan, stood unrelentingly for linking legal equality on the one hand with independence and choice as two further combined elements of women's individualization in the world of work.

In a parallel international struggle between the coalition of international women's organisations and the 1930 conference on the Codification of International Law sponsored by the League of Nations and sitting at The Hague, and amongst women's organisations themselves, on the question of married women's citizenship, the complex relation between legal equality and independence or choice would soon prove to be divisive amongst legal equality feminists themselves. In this conflict Chrystal Macmillan was probably the most prominent spokesperson for a political position that would see to it that legal equality and independent choice be always combined.[68] Regarding forced labour, however, such a combination was impossible because forced labour by definition was opposed to choice, in other words, choice as enshrined in the institution of the labour contract, which in turn was based in the principle that women and men should be legally free to decide about their engagement with the world of work. By the late 1930s the ODI indeed defined the "right of contract" as "a condition and the first advance from the lower condition of status; . . . the slave had status, and emerged from that status into the condition of contract, after which other civil rights accrued."[69] Such self-positioning ruled out the option to simply demand legal equality of men and women in relation to forced labour because such demand might be construed as justifying forced labour as legally permissible—a contradiction in terms to the principle of choice and freedom of contract for women and men.

The insistence on choice as a foundational element of the ODI's politics thus might have suggested in principle that the organisation would demand the immediate abolition of forced labour for both women and men. Yet such a course of action would have been irreconcilable with the ODI's principle of refraining from declaring itself in any definite manner in favour or against certain types of labour protection (i.e., beyond legal equality between the sexes in any such instrument). If we approach the question of forced labour from the point of view of the ODI's principle of prioritizing gender-neutrality in labour-policy over any definitive statement on the desirable forms and development of labour protection in general, then the organisation would have been likely to demand, in relation to any regulation of forced labour, gender equality alone; yet this would have opened the door to a policy of postponing the prohibition of women's forced labour to a time when all forced labour would be abolished. This, again, was not an option for legal equality feminists such as Macmillan because it would have contradicted the free choice principle.

The ODI consequently did not opt for any of these alternatives. The lack of a straightforward self-positioning of legal equality feminism on the issue of forced labour in the years between 1927 and 1930 was a response to the problem described above. Only avoidance of the issue of forced labour enabled the ODI to circumvent these irresolvable tensions. The first was to potentially compromise the principle of choice and to tolerate explicitly the possibility of the prolonged legality of forced labour for women, options which the organisation could not rule out if in the field of forced labour it demanded legal equality alone. The second was to compromise the exclusive focus on demanding legal equality between men and women in labour law, as would be the case if the organisation—based in its attitude advocating choice—demanded immediate abolition for both sexes so as to remain true to the principle of choice. The ODI was caught logically between a rock and a hard place.

The principle pursued by the ODI of avoiding combining the demand for gender equality in a given policy field with demands aimed at reducing other dimensions of inequality or oppression bore clear resemblances to the legal equality politics concerning suffrage as pursued by the IAW. The latter had always demanded that suffrage be granted to women on the same terms as men, and in this way the IAW sidestepped all demands to declare itself—despite its principle commitment to full democracy—in favour of or against either general or restricted suffrage.[70] If, in relation to the ILO's project for a Forced Labour Convention, legal equality feminism in 1927 or 1930 wished to remain true to this principle, it would not speak out in favour of immediate abolition of all forced labour for women and men. This is so even if we cannot rule out the possibility that other—coincidental—circumstances may have also contributed to the silence of the ODI on the problem of forced labour.

Weaving together these considerations, it appears that the reticence of legal equality feminists to speak out on the subject of forced labour, while the ILO's Forced Labour Convention was in the making, was due to the fact that the ODI did not wish to be identified with the political option of postponing or demanding the abolition of forced labour for women while silently accepting its prolongation for public purposes for men. One relevant public statement was published in the periodical of the ODI, *The Open Door*. It was a minor comment, hardly on the scale of the huge articles, manifestos, and campaigns launched by the ODI against any other "inequality" convention or policy pursued or proposed by the ILO; it referred to a zealous statement by Roland Venables Vernon, an advisor to the government of the British Empire (and Assistant Secretary at the Colonial Office) and reporter of the conference committee on forced labour at the 1930 Session of the International Labour Conference. Vernon had described forced labour as here to stay once the Forced Labour Convention would be ratified (i.e., forced labour for public purposes performed by adult males) as "virtually as completely protected . . . and in many respects . . . just as well off" as any other labour regulated by progressive labour law.[71] *The Open Door* reflected on this statement, and commented critically on the exclusion of women from forced labour laws that Vernon had characterised as providing "complete" protection. The ODI also focused on the implications of this exclusion for the future of women's work after the complete abolition of forced labour. The ODI claimed, "If this is so," that is, if forced labour as legalised by the ILO convention was "just as well off" as other labour, then:

> we wonder at the unanimity of Governments and the Conference in excluding women from Forced Labour. We would point out that if, and when, forced labour is regulated as strictly as is claimed by the advocates of the draft Convention, the effect will be to exclude women from paid work. Moreover, in the different countries as forced labour disappears, and is replaced by free labour, women will necessarily be less experienced and trained in certain work than the men who have been doing it for pay, though they will, of course, have been doing the essential work on the land and in the home left undone by the man, but *without pay*.[72]

The ODI framed its policy in such a way that it could not be mistakenly interpreted as a policy that would accept in principle the political option of postponing the abolition of forced labour for women. This was remarkable if read against the organisation's self-positioning in all fields of industrial labour protection. Through its politics of avoiding rather than clearly addressing the question of forced labour as put on the political agenda internationally by the ILO, legal equality feminism implicitly revealed its position that forced labour for women (on the same terms as men) was not a tolerable political option. Avoiding a clear statement in this regard was their only option to convey this message without compromising, qualifying, or contradicting the case for legal equality between the sexes and the principle of choice extended to women, and the priority of these two principles over other issues; the same silence, however, implicitly compromised the principle of choice so far as "native" men, forcibly drawn into the service of economic activities of the colonial state and other public authorities in the Southern Hemisphere, were concerned. In turn, the self-positioning of the ODI with regard to forced labour implicitly conveyed the message that capitalist expansion in the Global South indeed was or could be associated with a certain type of labour relations whose character was such that it justified its prohibition exclusively for women (and children). By contrast, in the implicitly Northern context—i.e., a context where forced labour was considered non-existent—the ODI, because it prioritised the reduction of the gender gap over the reduction of the class gap, would have objected at all times to the special protection of women—even in highly exploitative forms of involvement in labour in the service of profit.

The same would soon turn out to be true in relation to extremely exploitative forms of labour other than forced labour in the Southern Hemisphere. Following the footsteps of the ILO's emerging "native" labour policies, international women's organisations from the late 1920s broadened their perspective on international labour politics so as to include the labour of "native" or "indigenous" populations in the Southern hemisphere. The political action on forced labour marked only the beginning of the ILO's sustained engagement with bonded labour in the non-metropolitan world throughout the 1930s. The ILO from the outset aimed to come up with a whole set of regulations of "native" labour as put into the service of capitalist expansion and development in the Global South. This process, according to the ILO, had resulted in "an increasing pressure" on "native" labour; the organisation consequently aimed to regulate all of the resultant forms of recruited and bonded labour and to hasten their transformation into both free labour, which then would be protected by the ILO's "general" international labour standards, and independent peasant production for the market.[73] The Forced Labour Convention, for these reasons, was followed by the adoption of three further conventions in 1936 and 1939 on three dimensions of "native" labour: recruitment, terms of contract, and penal sanction.

At least for some of the women's organisations engaging with the ILO's preparations for the Forced Labour Convention, it had become obvious already in 1927 that to devise adequate gender politics in relation to this larger context of labour relations in the Global South would become far more complicated when the focus was on forms of bonded labour other than forced labour. An article in the journal of the Women's International League, the British section of the WILPF and one of the signatories of the second women's memorandum submitted to the ILO, made plain that once the issue at stake was no longer that woman were to be "entirely exempted from forced labour . . . the whole question of their position in contract labour, both as workers and companions of men workers need[ed] long and careful study and thought."[74] As the ILO prepared its related conventions in the 1930s, it soon became clear that in the eyes of the ODI and other international women's organisations, forced labour had been and was to remain the only type of bonded labour that was to be silently dismissed as a type of work through which women, on the same terms as men, should be involved in capitalist labour relations in the Global South. This became apparent, for instance, during one highly visible confrontation that unfolded from 1937 on as the ILO embarked on the preparation of what was to become the ILO Contracts of Employment (Indigenous Workers) and the Penal Sanction (Indigenous Workers) Conventions. The International Labour Office first aimed to proactively prepare the ground for gender-specific and indeed paternalistically framed restrictions of access to long-term contract labour. While stressing the importance of the "general principles of equal opportunity of employment," the Office still planned to consult the governments on the question of whether special international regulations were advisable "for conditions under which women . . . may conclude contracts;" the Office specified that this might include a provision according to which women would "not . . . be permitted to conclude contracts except when accompanying, and for employment with, their husbands or adult male relatives, or for employment as domestic servants."[75] The ODI, together with the St. Joan's Social and Political Alliance and one more organisation, immediately instigated protest. A communication addressing the ILO was drafted and signed initially by these organisations, with the large majority of the organisations represented on the Liaison Committee of Women's International Organisations added later.[76] The statement, which in this way expressed a position shared by a large group of non-socialist international women's organisations, focused on both women's independence and capitalist development as factors that demanded legal equality in order to prevent the oppression and disadvantage of "indigenous" women:

> We realize fully that the intention of the International Labour Conference is to safeguard and promote the well-being of indigenous workers under contract of employment. But we urge the Conference to realize that with the spread of industrial development women's employment is bound to grow, and that regulations of the kind proposed in the questionnaire will be greatly to the detriment of women in earning their own living. We recall to the conference that if indigenous women are permanently made dependent on their male relatives for economic subsistence such retrogressive tribal practices as forced marriages . . . will be perpetuated, since the women . . . will not even have the chance of buying herself free from marital contracts entered into on her behalf but against her will . . . we beg the International Labour Conference . . . to frame the regulations that they shall truly protect indigenous women workers from exploitation.[77]

The International Labour Conference took note of this letter.[78] In the conference committee, which reworked the draft questionnaire for plenary discussion during the 1938 Session of the International Labour Conference, there was intense discussion of the women-specific clause. The British workers' representative in particular opposed the "limiting" of "the contracting rights of women" and insisted, "that in the case of adults there should be no discrimination between the sexes."[79] In the end, and due to a number of overlapping interferences in which ideas of legal equality feminists played a role, the ILO asked a very different question from the governments. This question inquired about alternatives, i.e., it no longer suggested one concrete course of action—a procedural circumstance rather atypical within the ILO's technical course of action.[80] In the questionnaire as finalised, the ILO asked national governments to declare themselves as to whether a future international instrument "should not include any provisions restricting the right of indigenous women to conclude such contracts" or whether "alternatively" special provisions should be considered; in the latter case, the governments were asked to declare themselves—in relation to married women—with regard to a number of clearly specified "conditions," whereas in relation to "single women" they were once again asked to position themselves as to whether these women "should be permitted to conclude contracts . . . without any restrictions, or with restrictions."[81] Marguerite Thibert, head of the ILO's section concerned with women's work, explained not long thereafter that she was confident that the question thus revised would "completely satisfy the organizations concerned not to put obstacles to the possibilities of employing women."[82]

And still, during the year elapsing between the 1938 and the 1939 Sessions of the International Labour Conferences—the latter being designed to definitely adopt or reject the new international instruments on contract labour—the debate took on new momentum. The World Woman's Party, established in 1938 by Alice Paul (and merged in 1941 with the ERI),[83] defined the ILO as a key target against which to direct its legal equality politics, and now staged a highly publicised campaign against any potential restriction of married "indigenous" women's right to seek employment independently. The organisation also took the lead in demanding that the ILO "incorporate in its constitution" a much broader "provision requiring that all conventions concluded under the I.L.O. be founded upon the principle of equal rights for men and women."[84]

Confronted with this campaign, leading officers of the ILO responsible for "native" and women's labour at the International Labour Office took pains to explain the inclusion of the question on potential gender-specific regulations (as reframed by the 1938 Labour Conference) or the rejection thereof. These officers underlined first "that these proposals would only affect Native unskilled workers (labourers or coolies)" signing long-term contracts, with these documents regularly involving penal sanction for breach of contract.[85] Second, the potential gender-specific regulations "would be in effect a restriction of power to involve such women in long term written contracts rather than a restriction on feminine initiative;" if the stakeholders within the ILO, including the colonial governments, did not consider "that these proposals are necessary to protect Native women from exploitation they will not be adopted."[86] Third, "native" women might be in need of such special protection—"in their own interest and in that of the Native communities"—because they "know nothing of life outside their family and their Native villages."[87] In "many cases such women accept offered contracts with no realization of what they entail. Contracted women removed from their family and tribal setting often become social outcasts. In some regions power to involve such women in contracts has resulted in serious disorganization of native life and even in recruitment serving immoral ends."[88]

Yet these arguments did not convince many women's organisations. Groups and organisations directly linked to the World Woman's Party were not the only ones who shared the Party's opposition to what they collectively perceived as a gender-specific potential restriction in a future ILO instrument on contract labour. The president of the International Federation of Business and Professional Women, for instance, in a response sent to Alice Cheney of the ILO, shared as her "personal observations" her doubts as to whether male "native" workers were not "in some degree" as helpless as "native" woman workers.[89] She also doubted "whether one can restrict the power of contract without restricting the power of initiative," and she claimed that "while such restrictions do not seem to touch business and professional women directly I am more and more of the opinion that the entire group of women workers is affected in some degree by what happens to a smaller section of it."[90] The British branch of the ODI for its part declared itself against any "limitation on the right of [native] women to sign contracts of employment" in an international labour convention. In particular, the organisation disputed the reasonableness of any differentiation in this regard between different territories as had been suggested by the British government in its reply to the ILO's government questionnaire. The government had argued that for women belonging to "primitive indigenous communities," restrictions "to conclude written contracts" might be "frequently desirable and necessary," whereas applied to territories "where a far more advanced stage of development has been attained," any such limitation might work to the "disadvantage" of the women concerned.[91] The British Open Door Council argued, by contrast, that gender-specific limitations to contract-making "in every case" were "in the long run inimical to the women's true interest and . . . an important factor in delaying and even preventing an advanced stage of development;" such limitations, so the organisation argued in a related resolution, "will in every case result in the eventual segregation of the woman worker at the bottom of the labour market, and be a bar to her continued development as an independent and respected person within her own community."[92]

Taken together, these statements reveal that women's organisations dedicated to the legal equality cause accepted and indeed campaigned for the involvement of women on the same terms as men into extremely exploitative forms of bonded labour in the Global South. This referred to the labour performed by workers now termed " 'indigenous workers' . . . employed in tropical and sub-tropical territories by agricultural and industrial undertakings which are owned and managed by Europeans or . . . worked in accordance with European methods."[93] If promoting the involvement of "native" women into forced labour had not formed part of the agenda of internationally organised legal equality feminism in 1929 and 1930, European-dominated capitalist exploitation and development in the Global South was now explicitly accepted as a given or as something to be shaped in such a way that "indigenous" women would be in a position legally and economically to be involved on the same terms as "indigenous" men. Any gender-specific international legal restriction of the freedom of contract would be to the disadvantage of these women and/or would hinder the economic advancement of the territories in question. The ILO's paternalistic vision of engendering labour protection for "native" workers was to be replaced by the vision of individualizing "native" women via granting them direct access to work in "European"-type industrial and agricultural undertakings.

When in 1939 the International Labour Office laid before the Labour Conference the draft of what would become the Contracts of Employment (Indigenous Workers) Convention, the text did not include any special reference to women. The Office explained that it had omitted the women's clause because of far-reaching "diversity of opinion" in the government responses to the questionnaire. The "position in the various territories . . . is too varied to permit of the application of uniform principles in regard to this aspect of the regulation of the employment of women;" for this reason, so the Office concluded, "the matter must be left entirely to the countries and territories concerned."[94]

Conclusions: Gender Equality, Individualization, and the Commodification of Women's Work in Long-Term Global Perspective

In a global perspective, we can see the conflicts with regard to night work and bonded labour discussed in this study as two landmarks in a broader struggle over gender-specific versus gender-neutral international labour law in the interwar period. The related disputes between women's organised internationalism and the International Labour Organization from the late 1920s were instrumental in bringing about long-term change.

The doctrine of legal equality—or equal opportunity between the sexes in international labour law—gained ground in the 1930s amidst the struggle unfolding around policies of special "protection" for or—as legal equality feminism would have it—"discrimination" against women. The doctrine of legal equality feminism in this context involved a particular construction of the relationship between gender, class, and race. First, it prioritised gender equality in labour law with regard to both night work in industrial undertakings and long-term contract labour over any particular measure of labour protection; contract labour was a sector of work characterised by extremely harsh labour conditions involving exclusively or overwhelmingly "native" women and men. Legal equality feminism in this way promoted the increasing inclusion of women in very demanding labour relationships (night work and contract labour) without combining these politics with a class politics of demanding definitive minimum standards of labour protection for women and men in both night work and contract labour—in other words with a class politics aimed at definite measures of protection of labour. It has to be underlined, however, that legal equality feminists expected that gender equality in labour regulation would challenge gendered labour market segmentation and, more generally, help change the subaltern status of women on the labour market, and in this way contribute to the overall improvement of labour conditions.[95] Second, as legal equality feminism refrained from a class politics (as might have been added to the gender equality doctrine) of demanding definitive minimum standards of labour protection for both women and men, it also eschewed definite demands aimed at narrowing the race gap in global labour relations. In the context discussed here, this race gap was embodied by the fact that contract labour simultaneously constituted a highly radicalised sector of capitalist labour and a sector of labour which was far more exploitative than other labour relations involving many white workers; such a politics of narrowing the race gap in global labour relations would have involved, for example, demands aimed at the accelerated improvement of protective measures for, and/or the elimination of, those labour relations which were extremely exploitative and involved overwhelmingly or exclusively "native" labour.

In addition, the doctrine of legal equality advocated the individualised and contract-based involvement of women in capitalist labour relations, including within the framework of capitalist expansion in the Southern Hemisphere. Only in relation to forced labour did legal equality feminism silently tolerate gender inequality. This was so because it was impossible to translate smoothly the relationship as two mutually supportive principles of legal equality, on the one hand, and choice, independence, and individualization on the other, from the Northern-industrial context into the context of regulating forced labour. With a view to the Northern-industrial context, by contrast, the ODI was able at all times to hold on to the assumption that involvement into paid labour on the same terms as men would promote women's "independence." With a view to the Southern Hemisphere, internationally organised legal equality feminists conceived of contract labour as a first step on the road toward "free" and protected labour and thus as an acceptable type of labour occurring especially in the context of the "valorization" of non-self-governing territories in the South; "native" women should have the "right" to partake in this development on terms equal with their male counterparts.

On the principal vision regarding capitalist expansion in the Global South as increasingly built on contract-based "free" labour, legal equality feminists quite agreed with the ILO. Yet, in contrast to legal equality feminists, the International Labour Organization insisted on a politics of gender-specific labour law. These politics were based in both affirmation of or tolerance for a pre-existing paternalistic gender order and a class-based political strategy of bringing about and defending internationally any possible element of labour protection, including group-specific protection. If the ILO's politics on forced labour and the attempts of the International Labour Office to engender labour law for contract labour built, among other things, on the envisioned globalisation of elements of paternalistic gender order of European origin to the Southern Hemisphere, legal equality feminism aimed to globalise an individualistic doctrine of legal equality between the sexes—which was of similarly European and Northern origin—in the world of commodified labour.

At the same time, with regard to the gender politics of the ILO, the exemption of certain more privileged small groups of working women from the prohibition of night work, the abandonment of the idea to restrict "indigenous" women's access to contract labour, and other developments of the 1930s signalled a turnabout toward what the ILO at the time conceived of as the "conciliation" of the principle of equality between the sexes and special labour protection for women.[96] These developments were to form part of a larger shift in international legal gender order that was triggered in the 1930s. This shift would be of crucial relevance for the fates and fortunes of labour law in relation to gender well beyond 1945. The struggles of the 1930s marked the beginning of the internationalization of legal equality or "equality of status" politics with regard to nearly all spheres of life; they triggered the inclusion in a specific form of gender as a visible and all-encompassing normative category in international politics and international law. Soon thereafter, the vision of legal equality between the sexes and equal rights for individuals of both sexes would indeed be enshrined into the Charter of the United Nations. Corresponding politics based on both the idea of women's individualization in the world of work and of prioritizing legal gender equality over any potential benefit for women through differential legislation would gain further ground in international labour law in the decades to come.

As discussed in relation to the conflicts on night work and bonded labour in the 1930s, such gender-only politics, as long as they did not challenge but silently tolerated other inequalities and discriminations, could work so as to sustain the reification or deepening of other inequalities (for example, ones based on class or race) on local and global levels. In recent decades, special labour protection for women is visibly in retreat everywhere in the world, and it is largely replaced by forms of gender-equal labour law that offer few safeguards against large-scale and increasing exploitation of the labour of either sex within a highly racialised and unequal global division of labour. If the 1920s can be seen as the heyday of gender-specific international labour standards, the struggles of the 1930s discussed in this study marked the onset of a long-term trend by which politics of gender equality in labour law combined with increasing commodification and exploitation of female labour in globally divided racialised labour markets. The policy of legal gender equality which gained ground internationally in the 1930s contributed not just to globalising the principle of gender equality framed as a gender-only principle in international politics. It also advocated the vision that the involvement of women on the same terms as men in capitalist labour relations and in the various dynamics of expanding capitalist labour in the Southern Hemisphere was good for women under all circumstances, save when forced labour was involved.

Notes

1 Translations from the French are mine. The term "native labour" was in use in official documents produced by the International Labour Office, and in the institutional structure of the Office, throughout the interwar period. I am most

grateful to Karen Offen for her generous help in making this study more readable than it was in its original version.

2 Ulla Wikander, Alice Kessler-Harris, and Jane Lewis eds., *Protecting Women: Labor Legislation in Europe, the United States, and Australia, 1880–1920* (Urbana, Chicago: University of Illinois Press 1995); Karen Offen, *European Feminisms, 1700–1950. A Political History* (Stanford, CA: Stanford University Press 2000), 160–164, 229–235.

3 Madeleine Herren, *Internationale Sozialpolitik vor dem Ersten Weltkrieg. Die Anfänge europäischer Kooperation aus der Sicht Frankreichs* (Berlin: Duncker & Humblot 1993), esp. ch. D.3. The English text of the Convention was republished in *The American Journal of International Law* 4, no. 4 (1910): 328–337.

4 *Protokolle der Internationalen Arbeiterschutzkonferenz. Im amtlichen Auftrag* (Leipzig, 1890), accessed April 10, 2009, http://ia311333.us.archive.org/0/items/dieprotokolleder00confuoft/dieprotokolleder00confuoft.pdf.

5 The ILO in its constitution assigned special weight to those members defined as being "of . . . chief industrial importance." The constitution originally formed a part of the Paris Peace Treaties of 1919, The Versailles Treaty, Part XIII "Labour," Article 393, accessed August 1, 2012, http://avalon.law.yale.edu/imt/partxiii.asp. On internal structures, and the struggles around the preponderance of the North within the ILO, see Susan Zimmermann, "Special Circumstances in Geneva. The ILO and the World of Non-Metropolitan Labour in the Interwar Period," in *ILO Histories. Essays on the International Labour Organization and its Impact on the World During the Twentieth Century*, ed. Jasmien Van Daele, Magaly Rodriguez Garcia, Geert Van Goethem, and Marcel van der Linden (Berne etc.: Peter Lang, 2010), 221–250, esp. 241–246. On the importance especially of the German and related traditions of social policy in shaping the international labour policy of the ILO, see Sandrine Kott, "De l'assurance à la sécurité sociale (1919–1944). L'OIT comme acteur international," accessed Novermber 14, 2011, http://www.ilo.org/public/english/century/information_resources/download/kott.pdf. On the (growing) emphasis on gender-specific labour legislation in European labour internationalism, see Ulla Wikander, "Some 'Kept the Flag of Feminist Demands Waving.' Debates at International Congresses on Protecting Women Workers," in *Protecting Women*, 29–62, here 33–43.

6 All ILO Conventions and Recommendations are available on ILO, NORMLEX. Information System on International Labour Standards, http://www.ilo.org/dyn/normlex/en/f?p=NORMLEXPUB:12000:0::NO. All relevant quotations in this study are taken from this source. See also Carol Riegelman Lubin and Anne Winslow, *Social Justice for Women. The International Labor Organization and Women* (Durham, London: Duke University Press 1990), 25–34; Sandra Whithworth, *Feminism and International Relations. Towards a Political Economy of Gender in Interstate and Non-Governmental Institutions* (New York: St. Martin's Press 1995), ch.5.

7 On the differentiated application of ILO instruments in industrialized and less or differently industrialized territories as well as territories of diverse status, see Zimmermann, "Special Circumstances," 223–227. The literature discussing—in part controversially—the character and growing importance in shaping legal developments on the ground of international legislation is vast, though the ILO in this regard has not formed a focal point of attention.

8 Geert van Goethem, "An International Experiment of Women Workers: The International Federation of Working Women, 1919–1924," *Revue belge de philologie et d'histoire* 84, no. 4 (2006): 1025–1047, accessed November 27, 2011, http://www.persee.fr/web/revues/home/prescript/article/rbph_0035-0818_2006_num_84_4_5059; Dorothy Sue Cobble, "U.S. Labor Women's Internationalism in

the World War I Era," *Revue française d'études américaines* 122, no. 4 (2009): 44–58; and the literature quoted in fn. 5.

9 The organisational and political dimensions of this change, including the newly emerging international women's coalitions representing and being affected by this change, are discussed in detail in Susan Zimmermann, "Liaison Committees of International Women's Organizations and the Changing Landscape of Women's Internationalism, 1920s to 1945," in *Women and Social Movements, International. 1840 to Present*, ed. Kathryn Kish Sklar and Thomas Dublin (Alexandria: Alexander Street Press, 2012), http://wasi.alexanderstreet.com/help/view/liaison_committees_of_international_womens_organizations_and_the_changing_landscape_of_womens_internationalism_1920s_to_1945.

10 The journal of the ODI, *The Open Door. Organ of the Open Door International*, published between 1929 and 1939, provides insight into all aspects of this struggle. To my knowledge no comprehensive history of the ODI has as yet been written.

11 "Equality of status" was the term commonly in use by the middle of the 1930s to denote this larger initiative. Carol Miller, " 'Geneva—the Key to Equality:' Inter-war Feminists and the League of Nations," *Women's History Review* 3, no. 2 (1994): 218–245; Zimmermann, "Liaison Committees."

12 *The Open Door*, no. 14 (1935): 1.

13 In the following I use these two terms interchangeably when referring to forced, recruited, and long-term contract labour—even though the International Labour Office made sure that it be understood that the Recruiting of Indigenous Workers Convention of 1936 referred to recruitment into short-term contracts too, and thus to types of labour considered less problematic. A detailed analysis of the ILO's policies concerning bonded labour can be found in Susan Zimmermann, *Internationale Arbeitstandards, Frauenarbeit, und ungleiche Entwicklung. Die ILO, die Internationalistinnen, und der Aufstieg globaler Geschlechterpolitik in den 1920er und 1930er Jahren* (forthcoming with Löcker Verlag).

14 This is the wording of the explanation given by the International Labour Office. *International Labour Conference, Twentieth Session. The Regulation of Certain Special Systems of Recruiting Workers* (International Labour Office: Geneva 1936), 119–120. The legal definition is contained in the Recruiting of Indigenous Workers Convention.

15 For an overview of the long-term development of the ILO's related politics see Eileen Boris and Jill Jensen, "The ILO: Women's Networks and the Making of the Women Worker," in *Women and Social Movements, International*, ed. Kish Sklar and Dublin.

16 ODI, *Manifesto and Charter. Unanimously Adopted at Berlin*, June 16, 1929 (no place, publisher and date given).

17 ERI, *A Memorandum Showing the Connection Between the Status of Women and the Relations Between Countries Together with the Formation of the Equal Rights International to Obtain the Equal Rights Treaty* (London: ERI, no date given); Helen Archdale to Lily van der Schalk Schuster, 08/07/1930, Archdale to Van der Schalk Schuster, 04/12/1930, both Box 333, Folder "Van der Schalk Schuster," Records of the Equal Rights International Group 1926–1934 5ERI, Women's Library at London School of Economics LSE (formerly Fawcett Library, and then Women's Library) Archives, London (hereafter WL @ LSE).

18 After Macmillan's death in 1937, the Danish Anna Westergaard became the president of the ODI. ODI, *Report of the Conference held in Berlin June 15th and 16th, 1929* (no date and place given), 3; ODI, *Report of the Fifth Conference in Cambridge*, July 25th–29th, 1938 (London: Open Door International, 1938), 3.

19 Ellen Carol Dubois, "Internationalizing Married Women's Nationality: The Hague Campaign of 1930," in *Globalizing Feminisms, 1789–1945*, ed. Karen Offen (London: Routledge, 2010), 204–216, describes the new political style of these organisations and their representatives.

20 Notice of and Invitation to Conference in Berlin June 1929, Records of the Open Door International Group 5ODC, WL @ LSE.

21 ODI, *Manifesto and Charter 1929.*

22 Ibid.

23 Ibid.; Notice of and Invitation to Conference in Berlin June 1929, and Open Door Council, Third Annual Report 1928/1929, 10, both 5ODC, WL @ LSE.

24 On the lack of understanding of the meaning of night work in factories, see Martha Mundt to Van der Schalk Schuster, 31/10/1930, WN 12/42/1, International Labour Organization Historical Archives, Geneva (hereafter ILOA); the quote on "extremist" feminism is taken from the ILO Director's Report 1929 as quoted in *The Open Door* (1929) 1, 2. After the Director's Report 1930 had admitted to the ILO's initial overreaction, the ODI still blamed the ILO for its ongoing "tone of condescension" which it would have never allowed itself in relation to men's organisations and which was "equally unsuitable" in relation to women's organisations, *The Open Door* (1930): 1, 3. In later years, the ILO would accommodate the strained relationship with legal equality feminism in different ways and by using additional strategies.

25 ODI, *Manifesto and Charter 1929.*

26 ERI, The Equal Rights Treaty and unfettered liberty to earn a living, 18/02/1936, WN 9/01/3, ILOA.

27 Originally, the name of the organisation was International Woman Suffrage Alliance; it was renamed International Alliance of Women for Suffrage and Equal Citizenship in 1926, and later became, and has remained to the present day, the International Alliance of Women; I use the latter name and the related acronym throughout this study.

28 Open Door Council, First Annual Report 1926/1927, 7, 5ODC, WL @ LSE.

29 Zimmermann, "Liaison Committees."

30 Marzorzati's mandate was renewed (once again) in 1939. Zimmermann, "Special Circumstances," 237; *International Labour Office, Minute of the Eighty-Sixth Session of the Governing Body*, Geneva, February 2–4, 1939 (no place, publisher and date given), 64–65, 95.

31 *International Labour Conference. Twelfth Session. Forced Labour, Report and Draft Questionnaire* (International Labour Office: Geneva 1929), 313–317.

32 Quoted from the report on the meeting in Women's International League Monthly News Sheet, March 1927, Women's International League (British Section of the WILPF), Conference on Forced Labour, 1927, London, WN 1000/6/10, jacket 1, ILOA.

33 Ibid.

34 Lady Aberdeen et al. to Dear Sir [Albert Thomas], 14/05/1927, N 206/1/01/1, ILOA.

35 Woodman to Director [Albert Thomas], attachment, 01/06/1927, N 206/1/01/1, ILOA.

36 Ibid.; Lady Aberdeen et al. to Dear Sir [Albert Thomas], 14/05/1927, N 206/1/01/1, ILOA

37 In *Forced Labour, Report and Draft Questionnaire*, 262, 308–317, besides these documents, only one other memorandum submitted by civil society organisations was printed. Archival material suggests that the women's organisations' action might have been prompted by male figures in the orbit of the ILO in an endeavour to rally support behind the ILO's planned action against forced

labour. Woodman to Director, 1/06/1927; Lady Aberdeen et al. to Dear Sir [Albert Thomas], 14/05/1927; Grimshaw, no adressee, 13/11/1927, all contained in N 206/1/01/1, ILOA. See also *Informations Sociales*, no. 23 (1927): 76.

38 At the International Labour Conference in 1919, Kjelsberg had declared herself in favour of the "prohibition of all absolutely unnecessary night work" for both sexes, i.e., against the gender-specific prohibition of night work. *International Labour Conference, Twelfth Session, Geneva 1929*, vol. 1, parts 1 to 3, 74; Riegelman, Lubin and Winslow, *Social Justice for Women*, 30 (incl. Kjelsberg quote).

39 Lady Aberdeen et al. to Dear Sir [Albert Thomas], 14/05/1927; Woodman to Director, attachment, 01/06 1927, N 206/1/01/1, ILOA.

40 Letter as printed in *The Catholic Citizen*, June 15, 1938, Equality of Workers, WN 9/01, jacket 1, ILOA. See also below.

41 This development was closely intertwined with the international inquiry into the legal status of women sponsored by the League of Nations. The emergence of this new interest is documented in the protocols of the meetings of the Liaison Committee of Women's International Organisations from 1936 on; by 1937, one of the organisations represented on the Liaison Committee had submitted an extensive report on the status of "Women of Native Races" to the League of Nations. The protocols are contained in the Liaison Committee of Women's International Organisations Archives 1926–1977, International Institute of Social History, Amsterdam (hereafter IISH). The Report "Statement from St. Joan's Social and Political Alliance on the Status of the Women of Native Races, presented to the XVIII Assembly of the League of Nations (May 30) 1937" is available in the Pamphlet Collection of the WL.

42 ODI, *Manifesto and Charter 1929*.

43 *Anatomy of Prohibition*, accessed October 11, 2011, http://www.ilo.org/public/english/standards/relm/ilc/ilc89/pdf/rep-iii-1b-c2.pdf, 28–33; International Labour Office, *The Law and Women's Work. A Contribution to the Study of the Status of Women* (Geneva: ILO 1939), 177–178.

44 The Director 16/08/1929 (quote), and other documents, all contained in WN 1000/7/1, ILOA. For an overview of the ODI's campaign, see *The Open Door*.

45 The contributions in *Protecting Women*, ed. Wikander, Kessler-Harris, and Lewis, offer a rich discussion of the debates and positions of the many women involved.

46 The Committee by majority vote declared the politics of the ODI as being "against the interests of industrial women workers;" the disagreement had concerned the question as to whether the related resolution should refer to labour protection—other than maternity protection—in women-specific terms. *Women's Supplement to "International Information"* 7, no. 1 (1930): 4–6.

47 I do not discuss here or in what follows whether or not the legal equality-based arguments against gender-specific labour regulation as having "discriminatory" consequences for women stood or did not stand the overall historical or empirical test; neither do I engage those arguments of the pro-special labour protection camp which denied that gender difference in labour law could lead or had led to the discrimination of women and thus to a problematic gender gap to the disadvantage of women in the world of work. Rather, I focus on the gender, class, and race dimensions of both the labour standards themselves, and the politics seeking to bring about change with regard to such standards.

48 This is how the director's communication to the delegation was summarized by the ILO and shared in writing with members of the deputation so as to "avoid being misquoted," and it was how Thomas' statement at the meeting on September 30 was indeed reported in the equal rights press. Director of the International Labour Office to Director of the London Office, and attachment, D

600/1000/329/1, ILOA; Equal Rights XVI, October 25, 1930, no. 42. Meeting of the Equal Rights International 1930, WN 1000/18/1, ILOA. The names of Paul, Street, and Boskoff-Zoty (here: Boscoff Zoty) were given as representatives of the respective "Founder Members of Council" in a letter dated 09/11/1930, Box 331, Folder "Formation of International," 5ERI, WL @ LSE.

49 Macmillan to Heinen, 26/03/1929, Archive Nationaal Bureau voor Vrouwenarbeid (National Bureau for Women's Labor), inv. no. 469, Atria, Institute on Gender Equality and Women's History (formerly IIAV, and then Aletta) Archives, Amsterdam (hereafter Atria).

50 The exchange between Heinen and Macmillan, which also addressed other questions and was accompanied by the exchange of a number of documents, clarified that the Dutch organisation would not join the ODI. Macmillan to Heinen, 26/03/1929 and 25/04/1929, both contained in inv. no. 469, Atria.

51 ODI, *Manifesto and Charter 1929*.

52 ODI, *Report of the Conference held in Berlin 1929*, 60; ODI, *Report of the Second Conference*, held in Stockholm, August 17–21, 1931 (not date and place given), 20–21; ODI, Second Conference, Stockholm, August 1931, Resolutions Adopted, Box 333, Folder "ODI," 5ERI, WL @ LSE.

53 For this move and further details, see *Anatomy of Prohibition*, 31.

54 ODI to Dear Madam, 25/11/1932, and attachment, inv. no. 469, Atria.

55 Ibid.

56 ILO, *International Labour Conference, Twenty-Third Session, Geneva 1937, Record of Proceedings* (International Labour Office: Geneva 1937), 785; International Labour Office, *The Law and Women's Work*, IIX, 347–349; WN 10/01/2, jacket 1, ILOA. *The Open Door* regularly described and scandalized such political efforts and praised successful resistance to related measures.

57 International Labour Conference 18th Session 1934, Committee on the Night Work of Women, First Sitting, June 6, 1934, 4, and Second sitting, June 8, 1934, 1–2, both D 618/1201/1.

58 Women and the Right to Work in Mines, Supplement to *The Open Door*, December 1929, inv. no. 469, Atria; "The Equal Rights Treaty and unfettered liberty to earn a living," 18/02/1936, WN 9/01/3, ILOA; see also WN 101/2/101, ILOA.

59 Riegelman, Lubin and Winslow, *Social Justice for Women*, 48; Whitworth, *Feminism and International Relations*, 135–139; Zimmermann, *Internationale Arbeitstandards*.

60 The Versailles Treaty, Part XIII "Labour."

61 Members of the ILO, *Santiago (Chile) January 2–14, 1936, Record of Proceedings* (Geneva: International Labour Office, 1937), esp. pp. 156, 158, 283–287. For the demand that labour legislation should be "based on the nature of the work and not on the sex of the worker," see for example ODI, *Manifesto and Charter*.

62 ILO, *International Labour Conference 1937, Record of Proceedings*, 495.

63 Ibid., 497–500, 785; ODI, *The Modern Line of Attack on Women's Civil Rights. An Examination of Confused Thinking* [September 1937], inv. no. 469, Atria.

64 International Labour Office, *The Law and Women's Work*, esp. XI-XII, 172.

65 Ibid., 244, 251.

66 Ibid., 251.

67 Women and the Right to Work in Mines, Supplement to The Open Door, December 1929, and other published and unpublished documents, inv. no. 469, Atria.

68 Zimmermann, "Liaison Committees;" Leila Rupp, *Worlds of Women. The Making of an International Women's Movement* (Princeton, NJ: Princeton University Press, 1997), 146–147.

69 These statements of the ODI representative in a League of Nations' Committee for the Study of the Legal Status of Women hearing of international women's organisations in January 1939 was implicitly also related to the conflict on

contract labour discussed below. Minutes 21/03/1939, attachment (January 7, 1939), Box 2, Liaison Committee, IISH; *The Open Door*: no. 23 (1939): 23.

70 Susan Zimmermann, "A Struggle over Gender, Class, and the Vote. Unequal International Interaction and the Birth of the 'Female International' of Socialist Women," in *Gender History in a Transnational Perspective*, ed. Oliver Janz and Daniel Schönpflug (New York: Berghahn Books, 2014), 101–126.

71 Vernon as quoted in *The Open Door*: 4 (1930): 16. *The Open Door* reproduces Vernon's statement correctly. See ILO, *International Labour Conference, Fourteenth Session, Geneva 1930*, vol. 1, first and second parts (Geneva: International Labour Office, 1930), 269–272.

72 *The Open Door* 4 (1930): 15–16.

73 This is how the Deputy Director described this position in his welcome speech during the meeting of the ILO's Committee of Experts on Native Labour in 1927. Meeting of the Committee of Experts on Native Labour, July 1927, Stenographic Record, July 7, 1927, morning, ILOA N 206/2/1/5.

74 Women's International League Monthly News Sheet, February 1927, Women's International League (British Section of the WILPF), Conference on Forced Labour, 1927, London, WN 1000/6/10, jacket 1, ILOA.

75 *International Labour Conference, Twenty-Fourth Session Geneva 1938, Report II, Regulation of the Contracts of Employment of Indigenous Workers* (Geneva: International Labour Office, 1937), 119–120, 208.

76 The sources provide no way to unmistakably identify the organisations cooperating with the ODI on this issue. The Liaison Committee as an organisation did not support the statement; the Committee in its capacity as a cooperative body addressed other international bodies only if all individual organisations were in agreement on a certain issue or statement; in this case, representatives of ten member organisations signed the letter. Liaison Committee minutes and attached draft letter 23/03/1938, minutes 02/05/1938, minutes 07/06/1938, minutes 12/07/1944, attachment, all contained in Box 2, Liaison Committee, IISH; Letter as printed in *The Catholic Citizen*, June 15, 1938, Equality of Workers, WN 9/01, jacket 1, ILOA; ODI, *Report of the Fifth Conference in Cambridge 1938*, 21. For the Liaison Committee and its membership, see Zimmermann, "Liaison Committees."

77 Liaison Committee, Draft Letter to the Governing Body . . ., attached to minutes 23/03/1938, Box 2, Liaison Committee, IISH.

78 International Labour Conference, Provisional Record, Monday, June 26, 1939, WN 12/01/8, ILOA.

79 ILO, *International Labour Conference, Twenty-Fourth Session, Geneva 1938, Record of Proceedings* (Geneva: International Labour Office, 1938), 545–546.

80 In the initial stages of preparing an international instrument, the International Labour Office regularly translated its vision of what was to be included in a future instrument into the questions enlisted in its draft questionnaire for the governments; the questionnaire then would be discussed and finalized during the Session of the International Labour Conference in a given year, a step which was to be followed—based on (among other things) the government replies—by the discussion of a draft instrument and its possible adoption in the final form in the following year.

81 This is the final wording as adopted (without discussion) by the conference; this wording differed slightly but not in substance from the text as drafted by the conference committee. *International Labour Conference, Twenty-Fifth Session, Questionnaire II, Regulation of Contracts of Employment of Indigenous Workers* (Geneva: International Labour Office, 1938), 19–23, 55–56, 70; ILO, *International Labour Conference, Twenty-Fourth Session, Geneva 1938, Record of Proceedings* (Geneva: International Labour Office, 1938), 289.

82 Marguerite Thibert to Mademoiselle van Veen 2?/09/1938, attachment, WN 1000/5/01, ILOA.
83 Rupp, *Worlds of Women*, 142–143.
84 ILO Governing Body 89/3/456 (quote); see also C.R.P. no 24/1939, both contained in WN 12/01/8, ILOA.
85 The quote is taken from a note produced by the officer responsible for "native" labour in the International Labour Office. In terms of contents it was destined for public use (yet not to be identified with the author). Alice Cheyney to Frieda Miller, 19/11/1938, and attached Note I, WN 12/01/8, ILOA.
86 Cheyney to Anderson, 19/11/1938, and attached note addressed to the members of the Correspondence Committee on Women's Work in the U.S., WN 12/01/8, ILOA.
87 Cheyney to Miller, 19/11/1938, and attached Note I, WN 12/01/8, ILOA.
88 Cheyney to Anderson, 19/11/1938, and attached note addressed to the members of the Correspondence Committee on Women's Work in the U.S.; see also Anderson to Cheyney 08/12/1938, both contained in WN 12/01/8, ILOA.
89 Lena Madesin Philips to Alice Cheyney, 12/12/1938, WN 12/01/8, ILOA.
90 Ibid. The author of the letter made sure to underline that her concerns were not prompted by the activism of and around the World Woman's Party.
91 *International Labour Conference, Twenty-Fifth Session Geneva 1939, Report II, Regulation of the Contracts of Employment of Indigenous Workers* (Geneva: International Labour Office, 1938), 22.
92 Anne P. Jones to the Director, International Labour Office, 21/04/1939, WN 1000/7/0/3, ILOA.
93 This definition is from *Regulation of the Contracts of Employment of Indigenous Workers, Report 1938*, 5.
94 *Regulation of the Contracts of Employment of Indigenous Workers, Report 1939*, 61–63.
95 See for example *The Open Door* 2, no. 1 (1930): 4.
96 Statements on behalf of the ILO as quoted or referenced in *The Open Door* 2, no. 1 (1930) 4, 8.

Contributors

Anne Cova is a historian (EUI, 1994) and researcher at the Institute of Social Sciences of the University of Lisbon (ICS-UL). She has been Visiting Scholar at Stanford, Princeton, and California-Berkeley Universities. She is the author of *Au service de l'Eglise, de la famille et de la Patrie; Femmes catholiques et maternité sous la IIIe République* (2000); *Féminismes et néo-malthusianismes sous la IIIe République: "La liberté de la maternité"* (2011) and co-edited with Gisela Bock *Writing Women's History in Southern Europe, 19th-20th Centuries* (2003). She is editor of *Comparative Women's History: New Approaches* (2006) and co-editor with Bruno Dumons of *Destins de femmes. Religion, culture et société (France, XIXe-XXe siècles)* (2010).

Iwona Dadej is a historian at the Jagiellonian University in Cracow. She wrote her PhD thesis on a comparative history of the German and Polish academic female organizations in the interwar period at the Institute for East-European Studies of the Free University Berlin. She is also a fellow at the Science Center Berlin for Social Research and the German Historical Institute in Warsaw. She has authored articles in *Aspasia* (International Yearbook of Central, Eastern, and Southeastern European Women's and Gender History) and anthologies and Polish historical journals. Currently she is a fellow at the German Historical Institute in Warsaw.

Krassimira Daskalova is a professor of history at Sofia University. She has been a guest professor in various European universities and held fellowships all over the world, most recently at Stanford and Harvard universities. She served (2005–2010) as President of the International Federation for Research in Women's History. Since 2007 she has been editor of *Aspasia* (The International Yearbook of Central, Eastern and Southeastern European Women's and Gender History [Berghahn Books]). Her most recent books include as author *Women, Gender, and Modernization in Bulgaria, 1878–1944* (Sofia University Press 2012) and as co-editor *Women's Activism. Global Prespectives from the 1890s to the Present* (Routledge, 2012) and *Gendering Post-Socialist Transition. Studies of Changing Gender Perspectives* (LIT Verlag 2012), among others.

Evdoxios Doxiadis is a historian and Assistant Professor at Simon Fraser University. He has previously worked at the International Center for Hellenic and Mediterranean Studies. He was a Ted and Elaine Athanassiades Postdoctoral Fellow at Princeton University from 2007–2008. He received his PhD in history from the University of California at Berkeley in 2007. He has also been a frequent lecturer and visiting scholar at the Center for Modern Greek Studies at San Francisco State University. His recent book is *The Shackles of Modernity: Women, Property, and the Transition from the Ottoman Empire to the Modern Greek State 1750–1850* (2011).

Melissa Feinberg is a historian and Associate Professor at Rutgers University. She teaches and researches on European history, with particular interests in gender history, Eastern Europe, and the history of feminism. Her publications include *Elusive Equality: Gender, Citizenship and the Limits of Democracy in Czechoslovakia, 1918–1950* (2006) and articles in *Contemporary European History* and the *Journal of Women's History*.

Ute Gerhard studied law, history, and sociology and is a retired professor of sociology from Johann Wolfgang Goethe University in Frankfurt/Main. She was the first woman to receive tenure for women's and gender research in a German university. She was director of the Cornelia Goethe Center for Gender Studies at Frankfurt University and guest-professor at University of Wisconsin-Madison. Her research includes women's rights, social policy in a European comparison, the history of feminism, and feminist theory. She has published inter alia: *Debating Women's Equality. Towards a Feminist Theory of Law from a European Perspective* (2001); *Frauenbewegung und Feminismus. Eine Geschichte seit 1789* (2009); and a co-edition of classics of feminist theory (2010).

Catherine Jacques holds a PhD in history from the Free University of Brussels (ULB Belgium) and the University of Angers (France). She is Scientific associate at the Center for legal history and legal anthropology of the Free University of Brussels (ULB). Her publications include the history of the Belgian women's movement and the international feminist movement. Her most recent book discusses the impact of the Belgian feminists on women's economic and political rights in Belgium (19th-20th centuries) and was published by the Royal Academy of Belgium in 2013.

Sara L. Kimble is a historian and Assistant Professor at DePaul University in Chicago with a PhD from the University of Iowa. Her research concerns the history of feminism in France and the history of women's participation in the legal profession before 1945. Her publications include articles in *French Colonial History* and *French Historical Studies* on feminism in French North Africa during the interwar years, and the campaign for women's right to work as judges in early twentieth century France. She is currently finishing a book on *Women, Feminism, and the Law in Modern France: Justice Redressed*.

Mia Korpiola is Professor of Legal History at the University of Turku. In her research she is focusing on the history of marriage and family law, the history of ecclesiastical law, and the history of legal education. She also leads the research project Speeding Towards the Future: New Vehicles, Modernization and the Law in Finland, 1830–1950.

Anne Logan is a Senior Lecturer in Social History, School of Social Policy, Sociology and Social Research, University of Kent. She is the author of *Feminism and Criminal Justice: A Historical Perspective* (Palgrave, 2008) and she has also published articles on women magistrates in England and Wales and the position of women on trial juries between 1920 and 1972. She is currently writing a biography of the British educationalist and penal reformer, S. Margery Fry (1874–1958).

Gloria Nielfa is a historian and professor at the Universidad Complutense in Madrid. She is head of the research group "Gender relations in the contemporary world. An interdisciplinary perspective from history, geography and law." She has edited the anthology *Mujeres y hombres en la España franquista: sociedad, economía, política, cultura* at Editorial Complutense (2003), and *Mujeres en los Gobiernos locales. Alcaldesas y concejalas en la España contemporánea* (Biblioteca Nueva, 2015).

Karen Offen is a historian and independent scholar, affiliated as a Senior Scholar with the Clayman Institute for Gender Research at Stanford University. She has received numerous fellowships, awards, and prizes, including a John Simon Guggenheim Memorial Fellowship, and has just completed a five-year term on the executive board of the International Committee on the Historical Sciences. Her most recent books include as editor of *Globalizing Feminisms, 1789–1945* (2010). Her book *European Feminisms, 1700–1950: A Political History* (2000) has been published in French (2012) and Spanish (2016). Her career-spanning study of the debates on the woman question in France will be published in two volumes by Cambridge University Press.

Jana Osterkamp is a legal scholar, historian, and research fellow at the Collegium Carolinum, the Research Centre for the History of Bohemian Lands in Munich. After having received her PhD from the University of Frankfurt with a study on constitutionalism in interwar Czechoslovakia, she is currently working on the history of federalism and societal diversity in 19th Century Austria-Hungary. Since 2012 she holds an Emmy Noether Fellowship of the Deutsche Forschungsgemeinschaft and is head of a young research group on federalism. In 2014 she was awarded with a Feodor Lynen Fellow of the Alexander von Humboldt Foundation for a stay at the University Vienna.

Marion Röwekamp is a German historian and lawyer. She has been a Visiting Scholar at Columbia University and Kennedy Fellow at the Center for European Studies at Harvard University. She was Feodor Lynen Fellow of the Alexander von Humboldt Foundation at UNAM and the Colegio de México in Mexico City and is currently working at the Institute for Latin American Studies of the Freie University Berlin. She has authored *Juristinnen. Lexikon zu Leben und Werk* (2005), *Die ersten deutschen Juristinnen: Eine Geschichte ihrer Professionalisierung und Emanzipation 1900–1945* (2011), and *Marie Munk. Rechtsanwältin, Richterin, Rechtsreformerin* (2014) and co-edited *Eine Soldatenheimschwester an der Ostfront. Briefwechsel von Annette Schücking mit ihrer Familie (1941–1943)* (2015).

Eva Schandevyl is a historian at Vrije Universiteit Brussel who has published articles on intellectual history and leftist politics in *European Review of History* (2006) and *Revue Belge de Philologie et d'Histoire* (1999), on migration and Brussels in *National Identities* (2010) and *Migration and Activism in Europe Since 1945* (2008), and on the social and political history of justice administration in *Cahiers d'Histoire du Temps Présent* (2011) and *Historica* (2008). The focus of her current research lies in particular in gender and legal history. She recently edited the volume *Women in Law and Lawmaking in Nineteenth and Twentieth-Century Europe* (2014). She also co-edited *In haar recht. Vrouwe Justitia feministisch bekeken* (2009) and is the author of the book *Tussen revolutie en conformisme. Het engagement en de netwerken van linkse intellectuelen in België, 1918–1956* (2011).

Gordana Stojakovic's main research interests and experience is women's history and the history and the presence of the women's movement in Serbia and Yugoslavia. She received a PhD in gender studies from the University of Novi Sad—Association of Centre for Interdisciplinary and Multidisciplinary Studies and Research (2011). Her recent publications include: *Solidarnost ili lajkovanje: Dnevnik feministkinje o feminizmu i levici u Srbiji (1978–2007)* (Solidarity or Facebook like: Feminist Diary about Feminism and the Left Movements in Serbia [1978–2007]) (2011); "Women's World (1886–1914): Serbian Women's Laboratory as an Entrance into the Public Sphere" in *Serbian Women and the Public Sphere: 1850–1950*, special issue of Serbian Studies (2011); and *Rodna perspektiva u novinama Antifašističkog fronta žena (1945–1953)* (A Gender Perspective in the Newspaper of the Women's Antifascist Front [1945–1953]) (2012).

Regina Wecker is a historian and retired professor of women's and gender history at the university of Basel. She has taught at several German and Swiss universities. Her research focuses on women's legal history and citizenship rights of women in Switzerland. She was president of the Society of History of Switzerland (SGG) untill 2014, founding member of the Society for Gender Research in Switzerland (SGGF), member of the scientific committe of the journal *Traverse*, co-editor of *Basler Beiträge* *zur Geschichte*, and member of the International Federation for Research in Women's History. Wecker has published five monographs on women's history, co-edited seventeen books, and authored various articles. Her most recent monograph, *Eugenik und Sexualität* (2013), concerns eugenics in Switzerland.

Susan Zimmermann is a historian and University Professor at the Central European University in Budapest. Her research focuses on international labor policy, internationalism and global inequality, the history of women's movements, and comparative history of welfare and social policy. Zimmermann was a fellow of the Wissenschaftskolleg zu Berlin. Her most recent books include *Overstepping Borders. International Networks, Organizations and Movements and the Politics of Global Inequality, 17th to 21th Centuries* (2010) and *Divide, Provide and Rule. An Integrative History of Poverty Policy, Social Policy and Social Reform in Hungary under the Habsburg Monarchy* (2011); her chapter in Thomas Hippler and Milos Vec eds. *Paradoxes of Peace in Nineteenth Century Europe* (2015) discusses the ICW and inequality.

Index

Printed in the United States
By Bookmasters